THE WORLD OF *caffeine*

Frontispiece from Dufour's *Traitez Nouveux & curieux Du Café, Du The, et Du Chocolate*. This French engraving, frontispiece for Dufour's famous 1685 work on coffee, tea, and chocolate, depicts a fanciful gathering of a Turk, a Chinese, and an Aztec inside a tent, each raising a bowl or goblet filled with the steaming caffeinated beverage native to his homeland. On the floor to the left is the *ibrik*, or Turkish coffeepot, on the table at center the Chinese tea pot, and on the floor to the right the long-handled South American chocolate pot, together with the moliné, or stirring rod, used to beat up the coveted froth. Baker, writing in 1891, commented that this image demonstrates "how intimate the association of these beverages was regarded to be even two centuries ago." It is evident from the conjunction of subjects in the engraving that, long before anyone knew of the existence of caffeine, Europeans suspected that some unidentified factor united the exotic coffee, tea, and cacao plants, despite their dissimilar features and diverse provenances. (The Library Company of Philadelphia)

THE WORLD OF

caffeine

The Science and Culture of
the World's Most Popular Drug

BENNETT ALAN WEINBERG
BONNIE K. BEALER

ROUTLEDGE
New York and London

Published in 2001 by
Routledge
29 West 35th Street
New York, NY 10001

Published in Great Britain by
Routledge
11 New Fetter Lane
London EC4P 4EE

Routledge is an imprint of the Taylor & Francis Group

Printed in the United States of America on acid-free paper.
Design and typography: Jack Donner

10 9 8 7 6 5 4 3 2 1

Library of Congress Cataloging-in-Publication Data

Weinberg, Bennett Alan.
    The world of caffeine : the science and culture of the world's most popular drug /
    Bennett Alan Weinberg and Bonnie K. Bealer.
        p.   cm.
    Includes bibliographical references and index.
    ISBN 0-415-92722-6 (acid-free paper)
        1. Caffeine. I. Bealer, Bonnie K. II. Title.

QP801.C24 W45 2001
613.8'4—dc21   00-059243

Bennett Alan Weinberg
dedicates his efforts on this book to his parents,
Herbert Weinberg, M.D., and Martha Ring Weinberg,
who made so much possible for him.

Bonnie K. Bealer
dedicates her efforts to Ms. P.H.,
who knows who she is.

contents

acknowledgments

The authors acknowledge with thanks the research assistance of the staff of the Library Company of Philadelphia; the staffs of the Free Library of Philadelphia and the New York Public Library; the staff of the Philadelphia Museum of Art, Rights and Reproductions Department; Lynn Farington and John Pollack, librarians of the University of Pennsylvania Rare Book Collections; Charles Kline, director of the University of Pennsylvania Photo Archives; Charles Griefenstein, Historical Reference Librarian at Philadelphia's College of Physicians; Ted Lingle, then director of the Specialty Coffee Association of America; and Paul Barrow, photographer at the Biomedical Imaging Center of the University of Pennsylvania School of Medicine.

We also thank Thomas Meinl of Julius Meinl, A.G., for generously supplying photographs, posters, and especially for providing us a transparency of and permission to reproduce the painting *Kolschitzky's Café*, which hangs in the boardroom of Julius Meinl, A.G.

Three books deserve special mention as rich sources for our text: *Coffee and Coffeehouses*, by Richard Hattox; above all, *All about Coffee* and *All about Tea*, by William H. Ukers, merchant and scholar, whose masterworks have been drawn upon extensively for information and illustrations by nearly every book on coffee and tea written in the seventy years since their publication.

Our warmest thanks extend to Professor Roland R. Griffiths, Professor of Behavioral Biology and Neuroscience, Johns Hopkins University School of Medicine, who encouraged our work from the beginning, advised us throughout its early development, and performed a professional and meticulous review of the medical and scientific portions of our manuscript in its early stage for which we are very grateful.

And, of course, we thank our editor, Paula Manzanero, who saw merit in our book and applied her talents and experience to win acceptance for it at Routledge and who, together with our copy editor, Norma McLemore, and our proofreader, Roland Ottewell, contributed the insight and diligence that turned our sometimes rough manuscript into a finished text of which we are proud. For our cover, which is itself a work of art, we thank Jonathan Herder, art director for Routledge. For the book design and typography, we thank Jack Donner. And for putting the many pieces together and graciously accommodating our last-minute emendations, we thank Liana Fredley.

Finally, we warmly acknowledge the help of Antony Francis Patrick Vickery, our dear friend, who saved the book many times when the text seemed about to disappear beneath the rough seas of computer problems, patiently and generously devoting exigent efforts to keep our project afloat, providing advice on content and style, and extending moral and material support without which this book might never have been completed.

overview
Caffeine Encounters

> The Turks have a drink called Coffee (for they use no wine), so named of a berry as black as soot, and as bitter, (like that black drink which was in use amongst the Lacedaemonians, and perhaps the same), which they sip still off, and sup as warm as they can suffer; they spend much time in those Coffee-houses, which are somewhat like our Ale-houses or Taverns, and there they sit chatting and drinking to drive away the time, and to be merry together, because they find by experience that kind of drink so used helpeth digestion, and procureth alacrity.
>
> —Robert Burton, "Medicines," *Anatomy of Melancholy*, 2d ed., 1632

> Tea began as a medicine and grew into a beverage. In China, in the eighth century, it entered the realm of poetry as one of the polite amusements. The fifteenth century saw Japan ennoble it into a religion of aestheticism, teaism, a cult founded on the adoration of the beautiful among the sordid facts of everyday existence. It inculcates purity and harmony, the mystery of mutual charity, the romanticism of the social order. . . . It expresses conjointly with ethics and religion our whole point of view about man and nature.
>
> —Kakuzo Okakura, *The Book of Tea*, 1906

> Caffeine Chem. [ad F. caféine, f. café, coffee + ine] A vegetable alkaloid crystallizing in white silky needles, found in the leaves and seeds of the coffee and tea plants, the leaves of guarana, maté, etc.
>
> —*Oxford English Dictionary*, 1971

Caffeine, by any measure, is the world's most popular drug, easily surpassing nicotine and alcohol. Caffeine is the only addictive psychoactive substance that has overcome resistance and disapproval around the world to the extent that it is freely available almost everywhere, unregulated, sold without license, offered over the counter in tablet and capsule form, and even added to beverages intended for children. More than 85 percent of Americans use significant amounts of caffeine on a daily basis; yet despite that, and despite the fact that caffeine may be the most widely studied drug in history, very few of us know much about it.

This book is not about drug addiction, the preparation of gourmet beverages, botany, psychology, religion, social classes, international trade, or love, art, or beauty. But, in telling the story of the natural and cultural history of caffeine, it necessarily encompasses all of these topics and many aspects of the human condition. We fully consider the health effects of caffeine and also present an engaging tour of the fascinating cultural history of the drug that, through the agency of some of their favorite beverages, has captivated men and women, young and old, rich and poor, conventional and bohemian in virtually every society on earth.

Coffee, tea, and cola are the three most popular drinks in the world. They taste and smell different, but all contain significant amounts of caffeine. From the staggering demand for these drinks, it is easy to see that caffeine, the common denominator among them, must be a substance with almost universal appeal that may have stimulated people for many millennia. Some anthropologists speculate, without hard evidence, that most of the caffeine-yielding plants were discovered in Paleolithic times, as early as 700,000 B.C. Early Stone Age men, they say, probably chewed the seeds, roots, bark, and leaves of many plants and may have ground caffeine-bearing plant material to a paste before ingestion. The technique of infusing plant material with hot water, which uses higher temperatures to extract the caffeine, was discovered much later. Infusion brought to popularity the familiar caffeine-containing beverages, coffee, tea, and chocolate, and the more exotic ones, such as guarana, maté, yoco, cassina, and cola tea.

After the introduction of coffee and tea to the Continent in the seventeenth century, caffeine quickly achieved a pervasive cultural presence in Europe maintained to this day. In 1732 Bach composed the "Coffee Cantata," a pæan with lyrics by the Leipzig poet Picander, who celebrated the delights of coffee (then forbidden to women of child-bearing age because of a fear it produced sterility) in the life of a young bride. It included an aria that translates as, "Ah! How sweet coffee tastes! Lovelier than a thousand kisses, sweeter far than muscatel wine!" In answer to denunciations of tea, Samuel Johnson confessed in 1757 to drinking more than forty cups a day, admitting himself to be a "hardened and shameless tea drinker, who has for twenty years diluted his meals with only the infusion of this fascinating plant . . . who with tea amuses the evening, with tea solaces the midnight, and with tea welcomes the morning." Thomas De Quincey, the famous celebrant of opium, wrote, "Tea, though ridiculed by those who are naturally coarse in their nervous sensibilities, or are become so from wine-drinking, and are not susceptible of influence from so refined a stimulant, will always be the favored beverage of the intellectual."

By the twentieth century, the cultural life of caffeine, as transmitted through the consumption of coffee and tea, had become so interwoven with the social habits and artistic pursuits of the Western world that the coffee berry had become the biggest cash crop on earth, and tea had become the world's most popular drink.

Although the chemical substance caffeine remained unknown until the beginning of the nineteenth century, both coffee and tea were always recognized as drugs. They excited far more comment, interest, and concern about the physical and mental effects we now attribute to their caffeine content than about their enjoyment as comestibles. You may be surprised to learn that, at the time of their discovery and early use, both coffee and tea and, much later, cola elixirs, were regarded exclusively as medicines. For example, Robert Burton, quoted above, who had neither seen nor tasted the beverage, describes coffee, in the section of his *Anatomy of Melancholy* devoted to medicines, as an intoxicant, a euphoric, a social and physical stimulant, and a digestive aid. He explicitly compares it with both wine and opium. By doing so, he identifies coffee with the effects of the drug caffeine, which, two hundred years later, scientists were to isolate as its pharmacologically active constituent.

In England, health claims and warnings, often fanciful, were touted almost as soon as the first cup of coffee was served. In the early seventeenth century, William Harvey (1578–1657), the physician famous for describing the circulation of the blood, used coffee for its medical benefits. In 1657 an English advertisement for coffee read, "A very whoesom and Physical drink, having many excellent vertues, closes the Orifice of the Stomack, fortifies the heat within, helpeth Digestion, quickneth the Spirits, maketh the Heart lightsom, is good against Eye-sores, Coughs, or Colds, Rhumes, Consumptions, Head-ach, Dropsie, Gout, Scurvy, Kings Evil, and many others." In *Advice Against Plague*, published in 1665, Gideon Harvey (no relation to William), an English physician and medical writer, counseled, "Coffee is recommended against the contagion," that is, against the bubonic plague that was then in the process of killing a quarter of London's population. However, there were two sides to this debate: A translation of an Arabian medical text admonished English readers that coffee "causeth vertiginous headache, and maketh lean much, occasioneth waking . . . and sometimes breeds melancholy."

The health claims for tea are even older. The Chinese scholar Kuo P'o, in about A.D. 350, in annotating a Chinese dictionary, describes preparing a medicinal drink by boiling raw, green tea leaves in kettles. Because boiling kills bacteria, the putative health benefits and claims for longevity may have had some foundation. In England, during the years of Cromwell's Protectorate, the importation of tea was made acceptable only by its sale as a medicinal drink. A typical advertisement in a London newspaper at the time claimed, "That Excellent and by all Physitians approved China drink, called by the Chineans Tcha, by other Nations Tay alias Tea."

The scientific history of caffeine itself began in 1819 when, as Henry Watts reports in his *Dictionary of Chemistry* (1863), Friedlieb Ferdinand Runge first isolated the chemical from coffee.[1] In 1827, a scientist named Oudry discovered a chemical in tea he called "thein," which he assumed to be a different agent but that was later proved by another researcher, Jobat, to be identical with caffeine. Pure caffeine is a bitter, highly toxic white powder, readily soluble in boiling water. It is classified as a central nervous system stimulant and an analeptic, a drug that restores strength and vigor. After caffeine is ingested, it is quickly and completely absorbed into the bloodstream, which distributes it throughout the body. The concentration of caffeine in the blood reaches its peak thirty to sixty minutes after it is consumed, and, because it has a half-life from two and one-half hours to ten hours, most of the drug is removed within twelve hours. Other drugs can affect the way people react to caffeine: For example, smoking can increase the rate at which caffeine is metabolized by half, while alcohol reduces this rate, and oral contraceptives can decrease it by two-thirds.

In the twentieth century, medical studies have credibly linked caffeine to causing or aggravating PMS, lowering rates of suicide and cirrhosis, fostering more efficient use of glycogen and other energy sources such as body fat and blood sugars, improving performance of simple tasks, impairing short-term memory, potentiating analgesics, improving athletic performance, causing insomnia, alleviating migraine headaches, depressing appetite, relieving asthma, and so on. There remains considerable ambiguity about many of these putative effects. For example, some researchers have found that caffeine improves mood and performance only when people are aware that they have consumed it, which if true would mean that even the most widely acknowledged results of taking the drug are simply placebo effects!

However, if you have any doubt that caffeine is a drug, and a potent one, consider that a dose of only 1 gram, equivalent to about six strong cups of coffee, may produce insomnia, restlessness, ringing in the ears, confusion, tremors, irregular heartbeat, fever, photophobia, vomiting, and diarrhea. Severe intoxication may also cause nausea, convulsions, and gastrointestinal hemorrhage. The lethal dose for a two-hundred-pound adult is estimated at about 10 to 15 grams. Sudden withdrawal from caffeine-containing beverages frequently results in headaches, irritability, and difficulty concentrating.

The discovery of the enjoyment of coffee beans is credited by one legend to Kaldi, an Ethiopian goatherd said to have lived in the sixth or seventh century, who noticed that his goats became unusually frisky after grazing on the fruit of certain wild bushes. Some say that, in coffee's early days, Arabian peoples used the drink in a way still practiced in parts of Africa in the nineteenth century: They crushed or chewed the beans, fermented the juice, and made a wine they called "*qahwa,*" the name for which is probably the root of our word "coffee." The first written mention of coffee occurs in tenth-century Arabian manuscripts. Possibly as early as the eleventh century or as late as the fifthteenth century, the Arabs began to make the hot beverage, for which they used the same name as the wine.

In the seventeenth century, at the same time that coffee was introduced to Europe from Turkey, Dutch traders brought tea home from China. In 1657 Thomas Garraway, a London pub proprietor, claimed to be the first to sell tea to the general public. The word "tea" is derived from the Chinese Amoy dialect word "*t'e,*" pronounced "tay." In China, tea had been cultivated as a drink since, if Chinese legends are to be believed, the time of the Chinese emperor Shen Nung, to whom the discovery of tea, the invention of the plow, husbandry, and the exposition of the curative properties of plants are traditionally credited. An entry in his medical records dated 2737 B.C. (although certainly interpolated by a commentator much later) states that tea "quenches thirst" and also "lessens the desire for sleep." As illustrated in the quotation above from Kakuzo Okakura, tea, after its arrival in Japan around A.D. 600, became the center of an elaborate ritualized enjoyment that distilled much of the essence of Japanese culture. In Europe, even though it was very expensive, tea's use spread quickly throughout all levels of society and in certain circles displaced coffee as the favorite beverage.

John Evelyn, an English diarist and art connoisseur, writing in his *Memoirs*, in an entry dated 1637, describes the first recorded instance of coffee drinking in England: "There came in my time to the College, one Nathaniel Conopios, out of Greece. . . . He was the first I saw drink coffee; which custom came not into England until thirty years after."[2] Perhaps because of the bohemian daring that infests universities and the early example set by Conopios, the first coffeehouse in England opened in Oxford in 1650. It was followed in 1652 by the first London coffeehouse, in St. Michael's Alley, off Cornhill, under the proprietorship of an Armenian immigrant, Pasqua Rosée. The story of these English coffeehouses and a host of others over the next fifty years, at which not only coffee but tea and chocolate were commonly served, is a colorful chapter in literary, political, business, and social history. Often the occasion for lively discussion, visits to these early coffeehouses were recorded in the diaries of Samuel Pepys and many other contemporary sources. By the beginning of the eighteenth century, English café society had become so sophisticated that the noted social observer Sir Richard Steele was able to assign conversational specialties to the London houses: "I date all gallantry, pleasure and entertainment . . . under the article of White's; all poetry from Will's; all foreign and domestic news from St. James's, and all learned articles from the Grecian."[3]

Curiously, neither coffee nor tea was responsible for the first infusion of caffeine into European bloodstreams: Chocolate, hailing from South America and carried across the Atlantic by the Spaniards, beat them to the punch by over fifty years. It was received with considerable favor, and, from the mid-seventeenth century, was often served alongside more caffeine-rich drinks in such London coffeehouses as the Cocoa Tree, a favorite hangout of the literati in the early eighteenth century. Chocolate has a much smaller amount of caffeine than coffee, tea, or colas. However, it contains large amounts of the stimulant theobromine, a chemical with a pharmacological profile somewhat similar to that of caffeine. The presence of theobromine augments the effects of the caffeine and probably helps to account for chocolate's popularity, which rivals that of the beverages with significantly higher amounts of caffeine.

Caffeine-bearing beverages are so common in the late twentieth century that it is difficult for us to imagine the curiosity, wonder, excitement, fanfare, disapproval, intrigue, and even reverence that surrounded their early use in the East and attended their introduction to the West. Today the culture of caffeine is experiencing a renaissance in the dramatic increase of cafés and coffeehouses occurring in virtually every major American city; and there can be no doubt that the ancient Turkish tradition of meeting at cafés to discuss, gossip, mingle, and relax, carried forward by the English coffeehouse institution, has come to life around us. In the workplace, most Americans have developed a deep sympathy with T. S. Eliot's J. Alfred Prufrock, who said, "I have measured out my life in coffee spoons." The story of caffeine, as a controversial drug of work and play, is what we explore in the pages that follow.

prologue

The Discovery of Caffeine

Although caffeine-bearing plants may have been used for their pharmacological effects from before recorded history, it was not until the flowering of interest in plant chemistry in Europe in the beginning of the nineteenth century that caffeine itself was first isolated and named. The discovery was made by Friedlieb Ferdinand Runge, a young physician, in 1819 as a result of an encounter with the seventy-year-old Johann Wolfgang von Goethe, baron of the German empire, one of the greatest poets the world had seen, and the preeminent intellectual and cultural hero of the Europe of his day.

Runge was born in Billwärder, a small town near Hamburg, Germany, on February 8, 1794, a pastor's son and the third of what was to become a family of seven children. As a boy, Runge demonstrated the scientific curiosity and sharp powers of observation that presaged his creative career in analytical chemistry. While he was preparing a medicine from the juice of the deadly nightshade, or belladonna plant, a drop splashed accidentally into his eye, and he noticed that the pupil dilated and his vision blurred. Ten years later, just after Runge completed a medical degree at the University of Jena, his early observation brought him the audience with Goethe that would lead to the discovery of caffeine.

Although Goethe's reputation throughout his lifetime rested primarily on poetic genius, in his mature years he became an avid and accomplished amateur scientist, pursuing a broad range of empirical studies, including optics, pharmacy, chemistry, botany, biology, mineralogy, and meteorology. In his 1790 monograph on plant development and his essays on animal morphology, Goethe conceived of organic evolution and anticipated significant aspects of Darwin's theory.[1]

We know that caffeine and alcohol had enlivened his youthful transports, for, as Goethe approached his thirtieth birthday in 1779, he resolved to lead a purer life and later that year rejoiced in having cut his consumption of wine in half and significantly reduced his intake of coffee. Despite having frequented the Café Greco in Rome and Café Florian in Venice during his life-altering Italian sojourn, he evidently continued in the conviction that coffee contained a drug deleterious when taken in excess, for in his fortieth year he wrote to Charlotte von Stein, rejoining to her criticisms of his character by charging that she was again indulging in coffee, despite having forsworn this habit as part of their covenant to lead spiritual and exemplary lives.

In his soberer middle years Goethe outgrew the influences of cabalistic alchemy and mysticism. He became interested in an inquiry into the "secret *encheiresis*," or hidden handiwork and connections, of nature, the sort of investigations proper to the rapidly developing analytical sciences of his day.[2] During this period of his life, it is not surprising that Goethe's earlier somewhat inchoate reservations about coffee should have been supplanted by pointed curiosity about its pharmacological constituents and medical effects. Goethe must have questioned his prior misgivings about the beverage after learning that the medical faculties at the Universities of Jena and Wittenberg, where he had seated his intellectual court, harbored a venerable tradition promoting the pharmacological and medicinal value of both coffee and tea. As Fielding H. Garrison explains in his *History of Medicine* (1929), the followers of the leading Dutch physician Franciscus Sylvius (1614–72), such as his countryman Stephan Blankaart, "had recommended enormous quantities of the newly important novelties, tea and coffee, as panaceas for acidity and blood purifiers. The universities of Jena and Wittenberg espoused his [Sylvius's] doctrines."[3]

In his voluminous autobiographical writings and diaries, Goethe makes only a few passing references to his two brief encounters with Runge. In notes made in 1819, he comments on meeting, "a young *Chemicus*, by the name of Runge, who seems to me to be quite promising." Naturally, the meeting had much more significance for the young scientist. Fifty years later, Runge was still talking and writing about the interview with excitement and pride, and, in an article published in 1866, he related the story of his audience and how it led to the discovery of caffeine.

At the time of his encounter with Goethe, Runge was twenty-five and studying under the great chemist Johann Wolfgang Döbereiner (1780–1849), whose important theoretical work contributed to the development of the periodic table. As it happens, Döbereiner was greatly admired by Goethe, served as his chemical advisor, and was one of several scientists with whom Goethe maintained a close connection during his later years. Runge was pursuing research into plant chemistry, and Döbereiner brought his discoveries to Goethe's attention. Goethe, fascinated when Döbereiner told him of Runge's ability to dilate the eye of his cat at will with belladonna extract, asked that the gifted student visit him to demonstrate the feat.

Wearing a high hat and tails borrowed for the occasion, and carrying his pet under his arm, Runge attracted considerable notice from his fellow students (who had nicknamed him "*Gift*," or "Poison," because of his investigations into toxic chemicals) as he made his way through the Jena marketplace to keep his appointment. Runge relates that their amusement changed to awe when he told them whom he was hurrying to meet.

It was natural that they should have felt awe. By 1819 Goethe, Europe's first great literary celebrity, had long been one of the most famous and sought-after men on the Continent.[4] Goethe's celebrity grew until, as Auden tells us in his foreword to *Werther*, "during the last twenty years or so of Goethe's life, a visit to Weimar and an audience with the Great Man was an essential item on the itinerary of any cultivated young man making his Grand Tour of Europe."[5]

Imagine the youthful Runge, draped in his borrowed formal frock coat, ruddy-cheeked, clutching his cat firmly in his arms, as he proudly but nervously tells the story of his teenage accident. He performs the requested experiment by placing a few drops of belladonna extract in the cat's eye. Goethe is impressed by the dramatic results, and, as Runge stands to leave, the aging poet reaches over his desk, a small box of rare Arabian mocha coffee beans in his hand, admonishing his visitor to perform an analysis of the contents. At this moment Runge, in leaning forward to accept the precious gift, fails to notice as his cat bounds off toward the corner of the room.

Runge, excited by his gift, starts to leave without his pet.

"You are forgetting your *famulus*," Goethe tells him, humorously alluding to the magical animal companions that were supposed to have attended the alchemists of an earlier day.

Runge returned to his laboratory and within a few months had successfully extracted and purified caffeine.

"He was right," Runge wrote later, referring to Goethe's belief in the value of studying coffee. "For soon after I discovered in these beans the caffeine that has become so famous."

Exigent and orderly, but energetic and good-spirited, Runge, who never married, was devoted to scientific studies. His visit with Goethe led him to a brilliant career in purine chemistry. In 1819, in addition to isolating caffeine, he was the first to discover quinine, although virtually all sources erroneously award this honor to Pierre Joseph Pelletier (1788–1842) and Jean Bienaimé Caventou (1795–1877). After completing his studies at Jena, Runge returned to the University of Berlin, where he earned a doctorate in chemistry in 1822. He then took his own Grand Tour of Europe, a trip that lasted more than three years. After returning to Germany, he served for a few years as extraordinary professor of technical chemistry at the University of Breslau. Finding academia unreceptive to his practical interests, he ended his academic career in 1831, taking a job in a chemical factory where he investigated and developed synthetic dyes. In 1833 he was the first to make aniline blue, a discovery of major importance, as it was the earliest artificial organic coloring prepared from a product of coal tar. As a result of such investigations by Runge and his contemporaries, coal tar became the basis of several major industries by making possible the synthesis of dyes, drugs, explosives, flavorings, perfumes, preservatives, resins, and paints. Runge was also a pioneer in and, some would account, the inventor of paper chromatography, still a vital tool in chemical analysis for resolving a chemical mixture into its component compounds.

In 1850 E. E. Cochius, the business director of the company for which Runge worked, managed to acquire ownership of the company. For a long time he had considered his position and authority threatened by Runge's farsighted suggestions for the development of new coal-tar technologies. And so in 1852 he dismissed Runge, granting him a small pension and allowing him to continue living in the small company house that had been his home for years.

As a result of ill will arising from a dispute over the rights to a process Runge had developed for making artificial guano, Cochius' widow, who had inherited the chemical plant following her husband's suicide, fought a successful legal battle in 1856 to evict him from his house and reduce his pension. Moving to a nearby house owned by a friend, Runge spent the last ten years of his life "in the company of a few chosen companions . . . puttering a little, writing much for newspapers and magazines."[6]

Profile of Runge, bronze memorial medallion erected at his gravesite. A painting also exists of Runge drinking his synthetic wine, perhaps toasting his discovery of caffeine. In addition to pursuing his serious chemical investigations, Runge was a fine chef who loved to give dinner parties to exhibit his skills. He was also very interested in household tasks and applied his chemical knowledge to stain removal, canning meats and vegetables, and making wines from fruits. (Courtesy of *Goethe and Pharmacy*, G. Urdang, American Institute of the History of Pharmacy, Madison)

One of the most brilliant technical chemists of the nineteenth century, Runge died in poverty and relative obscurity in 1867. Two years after his death, the German Chemical Society collected donations to place a memorial at his grave. In 1873 they erected an obelisk with a bronze medallion showing a relief of Runge's profile.

Scientific discovery was rife in Germany at the inception of the nineteenth century, and Runge's analytical work was by no means pursued in isolation. Perhaps the most important precursor to his discovery of caffeine was the isolation of morphine by Frederich Wilhelm Adam Serturner, who, in 1803, at the age of twenty, had identified it as the active principle of opium (the so-called *principium somniferum*,[7] to which he later gave the name "morphine"). At the same time he formulated the concept of the alkaloid, a member of a class of organic compounds composed of carbon, hydrogen, nitrogen, and usually oxygen that are generally derived from plants. Many alkaloids present a double face, exhibiting both poisonous and curative properties. Caffeine and morphine are both alkaloids, and other alkaloids discovered around this same time include strychnine, quinine, nicotine, atropine, and cocaine. Serturner's work made it possible for doctors to prescribe a precise dose of the pure morphine alkaloid itself, instead of a weight of plant matter or extract, which carried a host of impurities and an uncertain amount of the therapeutic drug itself.

If Goethe had never met Runge, never presented him with that gift of mocha beans, would caffeine have lain undiscovered for untold years? It might tickle the romantic fancy to think so, but the facts are otherwise. At least four scientists, including Pierre-Jean Robiquet and the team of Pierre Pelletier and Caventou, are reliably credited with the independent discovery of caffeine within only a year or two of Runge's work. Serturner himself, without having heard of Runge's results, duplicated Runge's find in 1820. And when Jobat[8] discovered Oudry's *"thein"* in tea to be identical with caffeine, it was recognized that the stimulating and mood-altering effects of both coffee and tea were the result of their caffeine content. In 1843 caffeine was isolated from maté (a South American plant infused as an energizing beverage), and it was found in cola nuts in 1865. On July 22, 1869, the London *Daily News* reported "A piece of kaffeine, of the size of a breakfast plate, produced from 120 pounds of coffee." It would seem that the time for the discovery of caffeine had come.

Nevertheless, the fact remains that it was as a result of an encounter between a scientist and a poet that caffeine was first revealed to the world; a curiously symbolic origin when one considers the vast panorama of the drug's history, encompassing, as it does, so much of the disparate worlds of science and culture.

PART 1

caffeine in history

1

coffee

Arabian Origins

> The earliest employment of [coffee and tea] is veiled in as deep a mystery as that which surrounds the chocolate plant. . . . One can only say that . . . they have all been used from time immemorial, and that all three are welcome gifts from a rude state of civilization to the highest which exists today. By the savages and the Aztecs of America, by the roving tribes of Arabia, and by the dwellers in the farther East, the virtues of these three plants were recognized long before any one of them was introduced into Europe.
>
> —William Baker, *The Chocolate Plant and Its Products*, 1891

With every cup of coffee you drink, you partake of one of the great mysteries of cultural history. Despite the fact that the coffee bush grows wild in highlands throughout Africa, from Madagascar to Sierra Leone, from the Congo to the mountains of Ethiopia, and may also be indigenous to Arabia, there is no credible evidence coffee was known or used by anyone in the ancient Greek, Roman, Middle Eastern, or African worlds.[1] Although European and Arab historians repeat legendary African accounts or cite lost written references from as early as the sixth century, surviving documents can incontrovertibly establish coffee drinking or knowledge of the coffee tree no earlier than the middle of the fifteenth century in the Sufi monasteries of the Yemen in southern Arabia.[2]

The myth of Kaldi the Ethiopian goatherd and his dancing goats, the coffee origin story most frequently encountered in Western literature, embellishes the credible tradition that the Sufi encounter with coffee occurred in Ethiopia, which lies just across the narrow passage of the Red Sea from Arabia's western coast. Antoine Faustus Nairon, a Maronite who became a Roman professor of Oriental languages and author of one of the first printed treatises devoted to coffee, *De Saluberrimá Cahue seu Café nuncupata Discurscus* (1671), relates that Kaldi, noticing the energizing effects when his flock nibbled on the bright red berries of a certain glossy green bush with fragrant blossoms, chewed on the fruit himself. His exhilaration prompted him to bring the berries to an Islamic holy man in a nearby monastery. But the holy man disapproved of their use and threw them into the fire, from which an enticing aroma billowed. The roasted beans were quickly raked from the embers, ground up, and dissolved in hot water, yielding the world's first cup of coffee. Unfortunately for those who would otherwise have felt inclined to believe that Kaldi is a mythopoeic emblem of some actual person, this tale does not appear in any earlier Arab sources and must therefore be supposed to have originated in Nairon's caffeine-charged literary imagination and spread because of its appeal to the earliest European coffee bibbers.

Another origin story, attributed to Arabian tradition by the missionary Reverend Doctor J. Lewis Krapf, in his *Travels, Researches and Missionary Labors During Eighteen Years Residence in Eastern Africa* (1856), also ascribes to African animals an essential part in the early progress of coffee. The tale enigmatically relates that the civet cat carried the seeds of the wild coffee plant from central Africa to the remote Ethiopian mountains. There the plant was first cultivated, in Arusi and Ilta-Gallas, home of the Galla warriors. Finally, an Arab merchant brought the plant to Arabia, where it flourished and became known to the world.[3] The so-called cat to which Krapf refers is actually a cat-faced relative of the mongoose. By adducing its role in propagating coffee, Krapf's tale was undoubtedly referencing the civet cat's predilection for climbing coffee trees and pilfering and eating the best coffee cherries, as a result of which the undigested seeds are spread by means of its droppings. (For a modern update of this story, see the discussion of Kopi Luak, chapter 12.)

Both stories, of prancing goats and wandering cats, reflect the reasonable supposition that Ethiopians, the ancestors of today's Galla tribe, the legendary raiders of the remote Ethiopian massif, were the first to have recognized the energizing effect of the coffee plant. According to this theory, which takes its support from traditional tales and current practice, the Galla, in a remote, unchronicled past, gathered the ripe cherries from wild trees, ground them with stone mortars, and mixed the mashed seeds and pulp with animal fat, forming small balls that they carried for sustenance on war parties. The flesh of the fruit is rich in caffeine, sugar, and fat and is about 15 percent protein. With this preparation the Galla warriors devised a more compact solution to the problems of hunger and exhaustion than did the armies of World Wars I and II, who carried caffeine in the form of tablets, along with chocolate bars and dried foodstuffs.

James Bruce of Kinnarid, F.R.S. (1730–94), Scottish wine merchant, consul to Algiers and the first modern scientific explorer of Africa, left Cairo in 1768 via the Red Sea and traveled to Ethiopia. There he observed and recorded in his book, *Travels to Discover the Source of the Nile* (1790), the persistence of what are thought to have been these ancient Gallæn uses of coffee:

> The Gallæ is a wandering nation of Africa, who, in their incursions into Abyssinia, are obliged to traverse immense deserts, and being desirous of falling on the towns and villages of that country without warning, carry nothing to eat with them but the berries of the Coffee tree *roasted* and *pulverized*, which they mix with grease to a certain consistency that will permit of its being rolled into masses about the size of billiard balls and then put in leathern bags until required for use. One of these balls, they

claim will support them for a whole day, when on a marauding incursion or in active war, better than a loaf of bread or a meal of meat, because it cheers their spirits as well as feeds them.[4]

Other tribes of northeastern Africa are said to have cooked the berries as a porridge or drunk a wine fermented from the fruit and skin and mixed with cold water. But, despite such credible inferences about its African past, no direct evidence has ever been found revealing exactly where in Africa coffee grew or who among the natives might have used it as a stimulant or even known about it there earlier than the seventeenth century.

Yet even without the guidance of early records, we can judge from the plant's prevalence across Africa in recent centuries that coffee was growing wild or under cultivation throughout that continent and possibly other places during the building of the Pyramids, the waging of the Trojan War, the ascendancy of Periclean Athens, and the conquest of Persia by Alexander the Great, and that it continued to flower, still largely unknown, through the rise and fall of the Roman Empire and the early Middle Ages.

If this is so, then why was coffee's descent from the Ethiopian massif and entry into the wide world so long delayed? It is true that some of the central African regions in which coffee probably grew in the remote past remained impenetrable until the nineteenth century, and their inhabitants had little or no contact with men of other continents. But the Ethiopian region itself has been known to the Middle East and Europe alike for more than three thousand years. Abyssinia, roughly coextensive with Ethiopia today, long enjoyed extensive trading, cultural, political, and religious interactions with the more cosmopolitan empires that surrounded it. Abyssinia was a source of spices for Egypt from as early as 1500 B.C. and continues as a source today. The Athenians of Periclean Athens knew the Abyssinian tribes by name. Early Arabian settlers came from across the narrow Red Sea and founded colonies in Abyssinia's coastal regions. It is inescapable that this area, although far from being a political and social hub, was known to outsiders throughout history. The discovery of coffee, therefore, is one that ancient or medieval European or Middle Eastern traders, soldiers, evangelists, or travelers should have been expected to have made very early, here, if nowhere else. The fact remains that, for some unknown reason, they did not.[5]

Coffee as *Materia Medica*: The First Written References

There is evidence that the coffee plant and the coffee bean's action as a stimulant were known in Arabia by the time of the great Islamic physician and astronomer Abu Bakr Muhammad ibn Zakariya El Razi (852–932), called "Rhazes," whose work may offer the first written mention of them. The merit of this attribution depends on the meaning, in Rhazes' time, of the Arabic words "*bunn*" and "*buncham*." Across the sea in Abyssinia these words referred, respectively, to the coffee berry and the drink, and they still have these meanings there today. In his lost medical textbook, *Al-Haiwi* (*The Continent*), Rhazes describes the nature and effects of a plant named "*bunn*" and a beverage named "*buncham*," and what he says about the beverage's effects is at least consistent with a reference to coffee in terms of humoral theory: "*Bunchum* is hot and dry and very good for the stomach."[6]

However, the oldest *extant* document referring to *buncham* is the monumental classic discourse *The Canon of Medicine (Al-Ganum fit-Tebb)*, written by Avicenna (980–1037) at the turn of the eleventh century. The fifth and final part of his book is a pharmacopoeia, a manual for compounding and preparing medicines, listing more than 760 drugs,[7] which includes an entry for *buncham*. In the Latin translation made in the twelfth century, this entry reads in part, "*Bunchum quid est? Est res delatade Iamen. Quidam autem dixerunt, quod est ex radicibus anigailen* . . . [Bunchum, what is that? It comes from Yemen. Some say it derives from the roots of anigailen . . .]"[8] In explaining the medicinal properties and uses of *bunn* and *buncham*, Avicenna uses these words in apparently the same way as Rhazes (the unroasted beans are yellow):

> As to the choice thereof, that of a lemon color, light, and of a good smell, is the best; the white and the heavy is naught. It is hot and dry in the first degree, and, according to others, cold in the first degree. It fortifies the members, cleans the skin, and dries up the humidities that are under it, and gives an excellent smell to all the body.[9]

The name "Avicenna" is the Latinized form of the Arabic Ibn Sina, a shortened version of Abu Ali al-Husain Ibn Abdollah Ibn Sina. He was born in the province of Bokhara, and when only seventeen years old he cured his sultan of a long illness and was, in compensation, given access to the extensive royal library and a position at court.[10] Avicenna himself is credited with writing more than a hundred books. Some of his admirers claim, perhaps too expansively, that modern medical practice is a continuation of his system, which framed medicine as a body of knowledge that should be clearly separated from religious dogma and be based entirely on observation and analysis.[11]

Leonhard Rauwolf (d. 1596), a German physician, botanist, and traveler and the first European to write a description of coffee, which he saw prepared by the Turks in Aleppo in 1573, was familiar with these Islamic medical references:

> In this same water they take a fruit called *Bunn*, which in its bigness, shape and color is almost like unto a bayberry with two thin shells surrounded, as they inform me, are brought from the *Indies*; but as these in themselves are, and have within them, two yellowish grains in two distinct cells, being they agree in their virtue, figure, looks, and name with the *Buncham* of Avicenna and the *Bunca* of *Rasis ad Almans* exactly; therefore I take them to be the same.[12]

It was no accident that Rauwolf and other early European writers on coffee should have been acquainted with Avicenna's *Canon of Medicine*, which, following its translation into Latin in the twelfth century by Italian orientalist Gerard Cremonensis (1114–87), became the most respected book in Europe on the theory and practice of medicine. Few books in history have been as widely distributed or as important in the lives and fortunes of so many people around the world.[13] The *Canon* was required reading at the university of Leipzig until 1480 and that of Vienna until nearly 1600. At Montpellier, France, a major center of medical studies, where Dr. Daniel Duncan was to write *Wholesome Advise against the Abuse of Hot Liquors, Particularly of Coffee, Chocolate, Tea* (1706), it remained a principal basis of the curriculum until 1650.[14]

The fact that the *Canon* apparently mentions the coffee plant and the coffee beverage, describing them in the same humoral terms used by later physicians and ascribing to them several of the actions of the drug we now know is caffeine, makes the stunning silence about coffee in the Middle East and Europe, from Avicenna, in the year A.D. 1000, until the Arab scholars of the 1500s, the more puzzling. This accessible, apparently safe plant with stimulating and refreshing properties was destined to become an item of great interest in Islam, whose believers were not permitted to drink alcohol. It was equally well received in Christian Europe, where water was generally unsafe and where the drink served at breakfast, luncheon, and dinner was beer. Once people from each of these two cultures had had a good taste of coffee, history proves that the drink made its way like a juggernaut, mowing down entrenched customs and opposing interests in its path. Yet, after the time of Avicenna, coffee was apparently forgotten in the Islamic world for more than five hundred years.

One way to gain an appreciation of the mystery of coffee's late appearance is to note that, even if the Rhazian reference is deemed genuine, *coffee remained unknown to the Arabs until after Arab traders had become familiar with Chinese tea.* Arab knowledge of tea as an important commodity is demonstrated by an Arabian traveler's report in A.D. 879 that the primary sources of tax revenue in Canton were levies on tea and salt. Awareness of tea's use as a popular tonic is evinced in the words of Suleiman the Magnificent (1494–1566): "The people of China are accustomed to use as a beverage an infusion of a plant, which they call *sakh*. . . . It is considered very wholesome. This plant is sold in all the cities of the Empire."[15] Considering that tea was produced in a land half a world away, accessible only by long, daunting sea journeys or even more hazardous extended overland routes, the lack of Arab familiarity with coffee, which grew wild just across narrow passage of the Red Sea, becomes even harder to understand.

The Coffee Drinkers That Never Were:
Fabulous Ancient References to Coffee

Of course, if we were to find that the ancients *had* known about and used coffee, this lacuna would be filled in and the perplexity resolved.

Some imaginative chroniclers in modern times, uncomfortable with the possibility that their age should know of something so important that had been unknown to the ancient wise, have satisfied themselves that coffee was in fact mentioned in the earliest writings of the Greek and Hebrew cultures. These supposed ancient references, though exhibiting great variety, have one common element that mirrors the understanding of coffee at the time they were asserted: They present it primarily as a drug and measure its significance in terms of its curative or mood-altering powers.

Pietro della Valle, an Italian who from 1614 to 1626 toured Turkey, Egypt, Eritrea, Palestine, Persia, and India, advanced in his letters, published as *Viaggi in Turchia*,

Persia ed India descritti da lui medesimo in 54 lettere famigliari, the implausible theory that the drink nepenthe, prepared by Helen in the *Odyssey*, was nothing other than coffee mixed with wine. In the fourth book of the epic, in which Telemachus, Menelaus, and Helen are eating dinner, the company becomes suddenly depressed over the absence of Odysseus. Homer tells us:

> Then Jove's daughter Helen bethought her of another matter. She drugged the wine with an herb that banishes all care, sorrow, and ill humour. Whoever drinks wine thus drugged cannot shed a single tear all the rest of the day, not even though his father and mother both of them drop down dead, or he sees a brother or a son hewn in pieces before his very eyes. This drug, of such sovereign power and virtue, had been given Helen by Polydamna wife of Thon, woman of Egypt, where there grow all sorts of herbs, some good to put into the mixing bowl and others poisonous. Moreover, every one in the whole country is a skilled physician, for they are of the race of Pæeon. When Helen had put this drug in the bowl, . . . [she] told the servants to serve the wine round.[16]

These wondrous effects sound more like those of heroin mixed with cocaine than of coffee mixed with wine. The word "*nepenthes*," meaning "no pain" or "no care" in Greek, is used in the original text to modify the word "*pharmakos*," meaning "medicine" or "drug."[17] For at least the last several hundred years, "nepenthe" has been a generic term in medical literature for a sedative or the plant that supplies it; as such, it hardly fits the pharmacological profile of either caffeine or coffee. Nevertheless, the pioneering Enlightenment scholars Diderot and d'Alembert repeated Pietro della Valle's idea in their *Encyclopédie* (much of which was drafted in daily visits to one of Paris'searliest coffee houses). The fact that Homer tells us that the use of nepenthe was learned in Egypt, which can be construed to include parts of Ethiopia, together with the undoubted capacity of coffee to drive away gloom and its reputation for making it impossible to shed tears, may have helped to make this identification more appealing.

In the seventeenth and eighteenth centuries it became fashionable for European scholars to continue, as della Valle had begun, in theorizing about the knowledge the ancients had had of modern drugs. Not everyone, of course, was convinced. Dr. Simon André Tissot, a Swiss medical writer working in 1769, acknowledges the value of coffee as stimulant to the wit, but warns that we should neither underestimate its dangers nor exaggerate its value: for "we have to ask ourselves whether Homer, Thucydides, Plato, Lucretius, Virgil, Ovid, and Horace, whose works will be a joy for all time, ever drank coffee."[18] Many others, however, followed an imaginary trail of coffee beans leading back to ancient Greece. Sir Henry Blount (1602–82), a Puritan teetotaler frequently dubbed the "father of the English coffeehouse," traveled widely in the Levant, where he drank coffee with the Sultan Murat IV. On his return to England, he became one of the earliest boosters of the "Turkish renegade," as coffee was sometimes called. He brewed a controversy when he repeated a gratuitous claim that the exotic beverage he had enjoyed in the capitals of the Near East was in fact the same as a famous drink of the ancient Spartans:

They have another drink not good at meat, called *Cauphe*, made of a B*erry* as big as a small *Bean*, dried in a Furnace and beat to Pouder, of a Soot-colour, in taste a little bitterish, that they seeth and drink as hot as may be endured: It is good all hours of the day, but especially morning and evening, when to that purpose, they entertain themselves two or three hours in *Cauphe-houses*, which in all Turkey abound more than *Inns* and *Ale-houses* with us; it is thought to be the old black broth used so much by the *Lacedaemonians* [Spartans], and dryeth ill Humours in the stomach, and the Brain, never causeth Drunkenness or any other Surfeit, and is a harmless entertainment of good Fellowship; for thereupon Scaffolds half a yard high, and covered with Mats, they sit Cross-leg'd after the *Turkish* manner, many times two or three hundred together, talking, and likely with some poor musick passing up and down.[19]

Blount's howler was passed along by Robert Burton (1577–1640), an Elizabethan divine, George Sandys (1578–1644), an Anglo-American poet and traveler, and James Howell (1595–1666), the first official royal historian of England, and with this pedigree entered the arcana of coffee folklore. Putting the Sparta story aside, we should notice Blount's evocative account of the Turks in their preparatory customs and convivial consumption of the black brew. The social scene Blount sets is almost eerily similar to coffeehouse ambiance in most parts of the world today.

Perhaps even more far-fetched than the putative Spartan coffee were the efforts to discover coffee stories in the Old Testament. George Paschius, in his Latin treatise *New Discoveries Made Since the Time of the Ancients* (Leipzig, 1700), wrote that coffee was one of the gifts given David by Abigail to mollify his anger with Nabal (I Samuel 25:18), even though the "five measures of parched grain" mentioned were clearly wheat, not coffee beans. Swiss minister, publicist, and political writer Pierre Étienne Louis Dumont (1759–1829) fancied that other biblical references to coffee included its identification with the "red pottage" for which Esau sold his birthright (Genesis 25:30) and with the parched grain that Boaz ordered be given to Ruth.[20]

Because in the Middle Eastern world, no less than the European, caffeine-bearing drinks have invariably been regarded as drugs before they were accepted as beverages, it is not surprising that a number of early Islamic legends celebrate coffee's miraculous medicinal powers and provide coffee drinking with ancient and exalted origins. The seventeenth-century Arab writer Abu al-Tayyib al-Ghazzi relates how Solomon encountered a village afflicted with a plague for which the inhabitants had no cure. The angel Gabriel directed him to roast Yemeni coffee beans, from which he brewed a beverage that restored the sick to health. According to other Arab accounts, Gabriel remained busy behind the heavenly coffee bar until at least the seventh century; a popular story relates how Mohammed the Prophet, in this tradition supposed to have been stricken with narcolepsy, was relieved of his morbid somnolence when the angel served him a hot cup infused from potent Yemeni beans. Another related Islamic story, repeated by Sir Thomas Herbert, who visited Persia in 1626, held that coffee was "brought to earth by the Angel Gabriel in order to revive Mohammed's flagging energies. Mohammed himself was suppose to have declared that, when he had drunk this magic potion, he felt strong enough to unhorse forty men and to posses forty women."[21] Al-Ghazzi, whose tales place the first appearance of coffee in biblical times—and who was aware that his grandparents had never heard of the drink—explains that the ancient knowledge of coffee was subsequently lost until the rediscovery of coffee as a beverage in the sixteenth century.

In other Islamic folk accounts, which may have some factual basis, a man named "Sheik Omar" is given credit for being the first Arab to discover the bean and prepare coffee. D'Ohsson, a French historian, basing his claims on Arab sources, writes that Omar, a priest and physician, was exiled, with his followers, from Mocha into the surrounding wilderness of Ousab in 1258 for some moral failing. Facing starvation, and finding nothing to eat except wild coffee berries, the exiles boiled them and drank the resulting brew. Omar then gave the drink to his patients, some of whom had followed him to Ousab for treatment. These patients carried word of the magical curative properties of coffee back to Mocha, and, in consequence, Omar was invited to return. A monastery was built for him, and he was acknowledged as patron saint of the city, achieving this honor as father of the habit that soon became the economic lifeblood of the region. In another version of this tale, Omar was led by the spirit of his departed holy master to the port of Mocha, where he became a holy recluse, living beside a spring surrounded by bright green bushes. The berries from the bushes sustained him, and he used them to cure the townspeople of plague. Thus coffee and caffeine established his reputation as a great sage, healer, and holy man.[22]

Coffee to Coffeehouses: *Marqaha* and the Slippery Slope

'Abd Al-Qadir al-Jaziri (fl. 1558) wrote the earliest history of coffee that survives to this day. As unconvinced by the Omar stories as modern scholars are, he provided several alternative accounts of coffee's inception in Arabia, of which the first, and probably most reliable, is based on the lost work of the true originator of literature on coffee, Shihab Al-Din Ibn 'Abd al-Ghaffar (fl. 1530). According to Jaziri, 'Abd al-Ghaffar explained that at the beginning of the sixteenth century, while living in Egypt, he first heard of a drink called "*qahwa*" that was becoming popular in the Yemen and was being used by Sufis and others to help them stay awake during their prayers. After inquiring into the matter, 'Abd al-Ghaffar credited the introduction and promotion of coffee to "the efforts of the learned shaykh, imam, mufti, and Sufi Jamal al-Din Abu 'Abd Allah Muhammad ibn Sa'id, known as Dhabhani."[23]

The venerable Dhabhani (d. 1470)[24] had been compelled by unknown circumstances to leave Aden and go to Ethiopia, where, among the Arab settlers

he found the people using qahwa, though he knew nothing of its characteristics. After he had returned to Aden, he fell ill, and remembering [qahwa], he drank it and benefited by it. He found that among its properties was that it drove away fatigue and lethargy, and brought to the body a certain sprightliness and vigor. In consequence . . . he and other Sufis in Aden began to use the beverage made from it, as we have said. Then the whole people—the learned and the common—followed [his example] in drinking it, seeking help in study and other vocations and crafts, so that it continued to spread.

A generation after 'Abd al-Ghaffar, Jaziri conducted his own investigation, writing to a famous jurist in Zabid, a town in the Yemen, to inquire how coffee first came there. In reply, his correspondent quoted the account of his uncle, a man over ninety, who had told him:

> "I was at the town of Aden, and there came to us some poor Sufi, who was making and drinking coffee, and who made it as well for the learned jurist Muhammad Ba-Fadl al-Halrami, the highest jurist at the port of Aden, and for . . . Muhammad al-Dhabhani. These two drank it with a company of people, for whom their example was sufficient."

Jaziri concludes that it is possible that 'Abd al-Ghaffar was correct in stating that Dhabhani introduced coffee to Aden, but that it is also possible, as his correspondent claimed, that some other Sufi introduced it and Dhabhani was responsible only for its "emergence and spread." 'Abd Al-Ghaffar and Jaziri are in accord that it was as a stimulant, not a comestible, that coffee was used from the time of its earliest documented appearance in the world. More than this we may never discover. For the astonishing fact is that, although all the Arab historians are in accord that the story of coffee drinking as we know it apparently begins somewhere in or around the Yemen in a Sufi order in the middle of the fifteenth century, *additional details of its origin had already been mislaid or garbled within the lifetimes of people who could remember when coffee had been unknown.*

In any case, the spread of coffee from Sufi devotional use into secular consumption was a natural one. Though the members of the Sufi orders were ecstatic devotees, most were of the laity, and their nightlong sessions were attended by men from many trades and occupations. Before beginning the *dhikr*, or ritual remembrance of the glory of God, coffee was shared by Sufis in a ceremony described by Jaziri Avion: "They drank it every Monday and Friday eve, putting it in a large vessel made of red clay. Their leader ladled it out with a small dipper and gave it to them to drink, passing it to the right, while they recited one of their usual formulas, 'There is no God, but God, the Master, the Clear Reality.'"[25] When morning came, they returned to their homes and their work, bringing the memory of caffeine's energizing effects with them and sharing the knowledge of coffee drinking with their fellows. Thus, from the example of Sufi conclaves, the coffeehouse was born. As coffeehouses, or *kahwe khaneh*, proliferated, they served as forums for extending coffee use beyond the circle of Sufi devotions. By 1510 coffee had spread from the monastaries of the Yemen into general use in Islamic capitals such as Cairo and Mecca, and the consumption of caffeine had permeated every stratum of lay society.

Although destined for remarkable success in the Islamic world, coffee and coffeehouses met fierce opposition there from the beginning and continued to do so. Even though the leaders of some Sufi sects promoted the energizing effects of caffeine, many orthodox Muslim jurists believed that authority could be found in the Koran that coffee, because of these stimulating properties, should be banned along with other intoxicants, such as wine and hashish, and that, in any case, the new coffeehouses constituted a threat to social and political stability.[26] Considering that coffee was consumed chiefly for what we now know are caffeine's effects on human physiology, especially the *marqaha*, the euphoria or high that it produces, it is easy to understand the reasons such scruples arose.[27]

Perhaps no single episode illustrates the players and issues involved in these controversies better than the story of Kha'ir Beg, Mecca's chief of police, who, in accord with the indignation of the ultra-pious, instituted the first ban on coffee in the first year of his appointment by Kansuh al-Ghawri, the sultan of Cairo, 1511. Kha'ir Beg was a man in the timeless mold of the reactionary, prudish martinet, reminiscent of Pentheus in Eurypides' *Bacchæ*,[28] someone who was not only too uptight to have fun but was alarmed by evidence that other people were doing so. Like Pentheus, he was the butt of satirical humor and mockery, and nowhere more frequently than in the coffeehouses of the city.

Beg, as the enforcer of order, saw in the rough and ready coffeehouse, in which people of many persuasions met and engaged in heated social, political, and religious arguments, the seeds of vice and sedition, and, in the drink itself, a danger to health and well-being. To end this threat to public welfare and the dignity of his office, Beg convened an assembly of jurists from different schools of Islam. Over the heated objections of the mufti of Aden, who undertook a spirited defense of coffee, the unfavorable pronouncements of two well-known Persian physicians, called at Beg's behest, and the testimony of a number of coffee drinkers about its intoxicating and dangerous effects ultimately decided the issue as Beg had intended.[29] Beg sent a copy of the court's expeditious ruling to his superior, the sultan of Cairo, and summarily issued an edict banning coffee's sale. The coffeehouses in Mecca were ordered closed, and any coffee discovered there or in storage bins was to be confiscated and burned. Although the ban was vigorously enforced, many people sided with the mufti and against the ruling of Beg's court, while others perhaps cared more for coffee than for *sharia*, the tenants of the holy law, for coffee drinking continued surreptitiously.

To the rescue of caffeine users came the sultan of Cairo, Beg's royal master, who may well have been in the middle of a cup of coffee himself, one prepared by his *battaghis*, the coffee slaves of the seraglio, when the Meccan messenger delivered Beg's pronouncement. The sultan immediately ordered the edict softened. After all, coffee was legal in Cairo, where it was a major item of speculation and was, according to some reports, even used as tender in the marketplaces. Besides, the best physicians in the Arab world and the leading religious authorities, many of whom lived in Cairo at the time, approved of its use. So who was Kha'ir Beg to overturn the coffee service and spoil the party? When in the next year Kha'ir Beg was replaced by a successor who was not averse to coffee, its proponents were again able to enjoy the beverage in Mecca without fear. There is no record of whether the sultan of Cairo repented of his decision when, ten years later, in 1521, riotous brawling became a regular occurrence among caffeine-besotted coffeehouse tipplers and between them and the people they annoyed and kept awake with their late-night commotion.

In 1555, coffee and the coffeehouse were brought to Constantinople by Hakam and Shams, Syrian businessmen from Aleppo and Damascus, respectively, who made a fortune by being the first to cash in on what would become an unending Ottoman love affair with both the beverage and the institution.[30] In the middle of the sixteenth century, coffeehouses sprang up in every major city in Islam, so that, as the French nineteenth-century historian Mouradgea D'Ohsson reports in his seven-volume history of the Ottoman Empire, by 1570, in the reign of Selim II, there were more than six hundred of them in Constantinople, large and small, "the way we have taverns." By 1573, the German physician Rauwolf, quoted above as the first to mention coffee in Europe, reported that he found the entire population of Aleppo sitting in circles sipping it. Coffee was in such general use that he believed those who told him that it had been enjoyed there for hundreds of years.[31]

As a result of the efforts of Hakam and Shams and other entrepreneurs, Turks of all stations frequented growing numbers of coffeehouses in every major city, many small towns, and at inns on roads well trafficked by travelers. One contemporary observer in Constantinople noted "[t]he coffeehouses being thronged night and day, the poorer classes actually begging money in the streets for the sole object of purchasing coffee."[32] Coffee was sold in three types of establishments: stalls, shops, and houses. Coffee stalls were tiny booths offering take-out service, usually located in the business district. Typically, merchants would send runners to pick up their orders. Coffee shops, common in Egypt, Syria, and Turkey, were neighborhood fixtures, combining take-out and a small sitting area, frequently outdoors, for conversationalists. Coffeehouses were the top-of-the-line establishments, located in exclusive

Photograph of Café Eden, Smyrna, from an albumen photograph by Sebah and Joaillier (active 1888–c. 1900). The sign in the foreground reads "Jardin de L'Eden." This café is typical of top-of-the-line establishments located in the better neighborhoods of the larger cities throughout the Levant. (Photograph by Sebah and Joaillier, University of Pennsylvania Museum, Philadelphia, negative #s4–142210)

neighborhoods of larger cities and offering posh appointments, instrumentalists, singers, and dancers, often in gardenlike surroundings with fountains and tree-shaded tables. As these coffeehouses increased in popularity, they became more opulent. To these so-called schools of the wise flocked young men pursuing careers in law, ambitious civil servants, officers of the seraglio, scholars, and wealthy merchants and travelers from all parts of the known world. All three—shop, stall, and house—were and remain common in the Arab world, as they are in the West today.

But the debates over the propriety of coffee use did not end with Beg's tenure or the proliferation of the coffeehouse. Two interpretive principles continued to vie throughout these debates. On the one side was the doctrine of original permissibility, according to which everything created by Allah was presumed good and fit for human use unless it was specifically prohibited by the Koran. On the other was the mandate to defend the law by erecting a *seyag*, or "fence" around the Koran, that is, broadly construing prohibitions in order to preclude even a small chance of transgression.

The opponents of coffee drinking continued to assert their disapproval of the new habit and the disquieting social activity it seemed to engender. Cairo experienced a violent commotion in 1523, described by Walsh in his book *Coffee: Its History, Classification, and Description* (1894):

> In 1523 the chief priest in Cairo, Abdallah Ibrahim, who denounced its use in a sermon delivered in the mosque in Hassanaine, a violent commotion being produced among the populous. The opposing factions came to blows over its use. The governor, Sheikh Obelek [El-belet], a man wise in his generation and time, then assembled the mullahs, doctors, and others of the opponents of coffee-drinking at his residence, and after listening patiently to their tedious harangues against its use, treated them all to a cup of coffee each, first setting the example by drinking one himself. Then dismissing them, courteously withdrew from their presence without uttering a single word. By this prudent conduct the public peace was soon restored, and coffee was ever afterward allowed to be used in Cairo.[33]

A covenant was even introduced to the marriage contract in Cairo, stipulating that the husband must provide his wife with an adequate supply of coffee; failing to do so could be joined with other grounds as a basis for filing a suit of divorce.[34] This provision shows that, even though banned from the coffeehouses, women were permitted to enjoy coffee at home.

Around 1570, by which time the use of coffee seemed well entrenched, some imams and dervishes complained loudly against it again, claiming, as Alexander Dumas wrote in his *Dictionnaire de Cuisine*,[35] that the taste for the drink went so far in Constantinople that the mosques stood empty, while people flocked in increasing numbers to fill the coffeehouses. Once again the debate revived. In a curious reversal of the doctrine of original permissibility, some coffee opponents claimed that simply because coffee was *not* mentioned in the Koran, it must be regarded as forbidden. As a result coffee was again banned. However, coffee drinking continued in secret as a practice winked at by civil authorities, resulting in the proliferation of establishments reminiscent of American speakeasies of the 1920s.

Murat III, sultan of Constantinople, murdered his entire family in order to clear his way to the throne, but drew the line at allowing his subjects to debauch in the coffeehouses, and with good reason. It seems that his bloody accession was being loudly discussed there in unflattering terms, insidiously brewing sedition. In about 1580, declaring coffee "*mekreet,*" or "forbidden," he ordered these dens of revolution shuttered and tortured their former proprietors. The religious sanction for his ban rested on the discovery, by one orthodox sect of dervishes, that, when roasted, coffee became a kind of coal, and anything carbonized was forbidden by Mohammed for human consumption.[36] His prohibition of the coffeehouse drove the practice of coffee drinking into the home, a result which, considering his purpose of dispelling congeries of public critics, he may well have counted as a success.

During succeeding reigns, the habit again became a public one, and one that, after Murat's successor assured the faithful that roasted coffee was not coal and had no relation to it, even provided a major source of tax revenue for Constantinople. Yet in the early seventeenth century, under the nominal rule of Murat IV (1623–40), during a war in which revolution was particularly to be feared, coffee and coffeehouses became the subject of yet another ban in the city. In an arrangement reminiscent of the intrigues of the *Arabian Nights*, Murat IV's kingdom was governed in fact by his evil vizier, Mahomet Kolpili, an illiterate reactionary who saw the coffeehouses as dens of rebellion and vice. When the bastinado was unsuccessful in discouraging coffee drinking, Kolpili escalated to shuttering the coffeehouses. In 1633, noting that hardened coffee drinkers were continuing to sneak in by the posterns, he banned coffee altogether, along with tobacco and opium, for good measure, and, on the pretext of averting a fire hazard, razed the establishments where coffee had been served. As a final remedy, as part of an edict making the use of coffee, wine, or tobacco capital offenses, coffeehouse customers and proprietors were sewn up in bags and thrown in the Bosphorus, an experience calculated to discourage even the most abject caffeine addict.

Less draconian solutions to the coffeehouse threat to social stability were implemented in Persia, notably by the wife of Shah Abbas, who had observed with concern the large crowds assembling daily in the coffeehouses of Ispahan to discuss politics. She appointed *mollahs*, expounders of religious law, to attend the coffeehouses and entertain the customers with witty monologues on history, law, and poetry. So doing, they diverted the conversation from politics, and, as a result, disturbances were rare, and the security of the state was maintained. Other Persian rulers, deciding not to stanch the flow of seditious conversation, instead placed their spies in the coffeehouses to collect warnings of threats to the security of the regime.

The coffeehouses brought with them certain unsettling innovations in Islamic society. Even those who counted themselves among the friends of coffee drinking were not entirely comfortable with the secular public gatherings, previously unheard of in respectable society, that these places made inevitable and commonplace. The freedom to assemble in a public place for refreshment, entertainment, and conversation, which was otherwise rare in a society where everyone dined at home, created as much danger as opportunity. Before the coffeehouses opened, taverns had been the only recourse for people who wanted a night out, away from home and family, and these, in Islamic

Photograph of Palestinian or Syrian peasants playing backgammon while drinking coffee and sharing a hookah pipe at a recent version of the modest Arab coffee shops that have been traditional for several hundred years, from an albumen photograph, c. 1885–1901, by Bonfils, active 1864–1916. (Photograph by Bonfils, University of Pennsylvania Museum, Philadelphia, negative #s4–142209)

lands, where tavern keepers, like prostitutes, homosexuals, and street entertainers, were shunned by respectable people. Jaziri, when chronicling the early days of coffee in the Yemen, complained, for example, that the decorum and solemnity of the Sufi *dhikr* was, in the coffeehouse, displaced by the frivolity of joking and storytelling. Worse still was malicious gossip, which, when directed against blameless women, was deemed particularly odious.

From Jaziri we also learn that gaming, especially chess, backgammon, and draughts, was, in addition to idle talk, a regular feature of coffeehouse life. Card playing, reported by travelers, may have been a later introduction from Europe. However, contemporary Islamic writers, a strait-laced group to a man, disapproved of such frivolous activities, even when no money was being wagered. One of the mainstays of coffeehouse entertainment spoken of by Moslem writers was the storyteller, an inexpensive addition to the enjoyment of the patrons that was more acceptable than either gossip or gaming to the exacting moral monitors of the day.

Musical entertainments, in contrast with literary ones, though also commonplace in coffeehouses, were regarded with more disfavor. The "drums and fiddlers"[37] of

Mecca's coffeehouses were mentioned by Jaziri as one of their aspects offensive to Kha'ir Beg. Evidently sharing the belief of St. Augustine that music was a sensual enjoyment that threatened to divert attention from the contemplation of God, and as such was to be regarded as a subversive force among the faithful, the Islamic moralists of the day asserted that musical entertainments deepened the debauchery into which coffeehouse patrons habitually sunk. Secular music was considered dangerous in itself, but worse for the encouragement it gave to revelry. Especially damning was the early practice, taken over from the taverns, of featuring women singers. Even when they were kept from customers' eyes behind a screen, their voices alone were thought to offer improper sexual stimulation, which, it was often charged, led to sexual disportment with the patrons. Later accounts make it clear that these temptresses were finally banished, leaving the Islamic coffeehouses strictly to the men.

Even more corrupting than women, or so these Islamic thinkers believed, was the use of hard drugs by coffeehouse denizens. Jaziri deplores the mixing of hashish, opium, and possibly other narcotic preparations with what, in his judgment, was an otherwise pure drink. He says, "Many have been led to ruin by this temptation. They can be reckoned as beasts whom the demons have so tempted."[38] Another Islamic writer of the time, Kâtib Celebi, states, "Drug addicts in particular finding [coffee] a life giving thing, which increases their pleasure, were willing to die for a cup."[39]

As to the intoxicating effects of coffee itself, which we now understand are a consequence of its caffeine content, Islamic opinion was divided in bitter controversy from at least as early as 'Abd al-Ghaffar. Some moralists likened the *marqaha* to inebriation with alcohol, hashish, or opium. Other writers, including an unnamed predecessor of 'Abd al-Ghaffar, found this identification preposterous, both in degree and kind. This unresolvable dispute was of practical importance in a society in which many prominent men were coffee users and in which indulgence in any intoxicant was grounds for severe punishment. In the end, caffeine triumphed in the Islamic world, and coffee was accepted as the earthly approximation of the "purest wine, that will neither pain their heads nor take away their reason," which the Koran teaches the blessed will enjoy in the world to come.

From the standpoint of modern secular taste, it is difficult not to find sympathetic an environment which presented the first informal, public, literary, and intellectual forum in Islam. Many of the conventions that were established in those early coffeehouses remain hallmarks of our coffeehouses today. Poets and other writers came to read their works; the air was filled with the sounds of animated colloquies on the sciences and arts; and, as in Pepys' England and in so many other times and places, the coffeehouse became, in the absence of newspapers, a place where people gathered to learn and argue about the latest social and political events.

Because the coffeehouse is so important and coffee is so freely available today, we may be disposed to regard the Arab and Turkish attempts at prohibition as quaint and archaic. Such condescension would demonstrate an ignorance of similar efforts in later periods of history and a failure to recognize those in our own. The "caffeine temperance" movement has reasserted itself, with greater or lesser effectiveness, in almost every generation. France, Italy, and England have recurringly witnessed men who sought to enlist the power of law to enforce their own disapproval of caffeine. In the

Year of the First Coffeehouses	
City	Year
Mecca	<1500
Cairo	c. 1500
Constantinople	1555
Oxford	1650
London	1652
Cambridge	early 1660s
The Hague	1664
Amsterdam	mid-1660s
Marseilles	1671
Hamburg	1679
Vienna	1683
Paris	1689
Boston	1689
Leipzig	1694
New York	1696
Philadelphia	1700
Berlin	1721

United States in the early twentieth century, reformers such as Harvey Washington Wiley vigorously campaigned against the use of caffeine in soft drinks. Today such groups as Caffeine Prevention Plus, who use the Internet to promote their cause, and all sorts of meddlesome do-gooders would be happy to add caffeine to the list of highly regulated or banned substances. Americans, who live with the prohibition of marijuana, heroin, and certain pharmaceuticals in general use worldwide and who are witnessing serious efforts within our government to further control or ban cigarettes, should recognize elements of their own society when hearing the story of Kha'ir Beg.

Travelers' Tales: Visitors to the Yemen, Constantinople, Aleppo, and Cairo

There was nothing remarkable in the King's Gardens [in Yemen], except the great pains taken to furnish it with all the kinds of trees that are common in the country; amongst which there were the coffee trees, the finest that could be had. When the deputies represented to the King how much that was contrary to the custom of the Princes of Europe (who endeavor to stock their gardens chiefly with the rarest and most uncommon plants that can be found) the King returned them this answer: That he valued himself as much upon his good taste and generosity as any Prince in Europe; the coffee tree, he told them, was indeed common in his country, but it was not the less dear to him upon that account; the perpetual verdure of it pleased him extremely; and also the thoughts of its producing a fruit which was nowhere else to be met with; and when he made a present of that that came from his own Gardens, it was a great satisfaction to him to be able to say that he had planted the trees that produced it with his own hands.[40]

—Jean La Roque, *Voyage de L'Arabie Heureuse*, 1716

Europeans, as compared with the other peoples of the world, have historically demonstrated a strong inquisitiveness about the secrets of distant nations; they have been, in short, natural tourists. It is therefore no surprise that it was from returning travelers that knowledge of the habits of the Arabs and Turks was first brought to the capitals of Italy, France, England, Portugal, Holland, and Germany.[41]

These European travelers throughout the Islamic domains provide many vivid accounts of early coffeehouses.[42] However, as Carsten Niebuhr (1733–1815), a German biographer and traveler, comments in *Travels through Arabia and Other Countries in the East* (1792), many of the establishments they visited were situated in khans—combination inns, caravansaries, and warehouses—which served merchants and other travelers, and we should keep in mind that they may not have been typical of the coffeehouses catering to a residential population.

One of the earliest descriptions to reach Europe of the denizens of the coffeehouses of Constantinople was this dour assessment by Gianfrancesco Morosini, a Venetian traveler, in 1585:

> All these people are quite base, of low costume and very little industry, such that, for the most part, they spend their time sunk in idleness. Thus they continually sit about, and for entertainment they are in the habit of drinking in public in shops and in the streets—a black liquid, boiling [as hot] as they can stand it, which is extracted from a seed they call Caveè ... , and is said to have the property of keeping a man awake.

William Biddulph, an Elizabethan clergyman, shared Morosini's disdain, observing that coffeehouse habitués of Aleppo were occupied exclusively with "Idle and Alehouse talke."

Although many sipped coffee at tiny stalls or in spare public rooms, an atmosphere of luxury pervaded the grand coffeehouses, which were invariably located, according to the French coffee merchant Sylvestre Dufour, in the swankiest neighborhoods.[43] Pedro Teixeira (1575–1640), a Portuguese traveler and explorer, describes one such place in Baghdad, where coffee was served in a place "built to that end": "This house is near the river, over which it has many windows, and two galleries, making it a very pleasant resort."[44] The French traveler Jean de Thévenot (1633–67), in his *Relation d'un voyage fait au Levant*, a book that helped convince his countrymen to regard coffee as a comestible instead of merely as a drug, tells us that the cafés of Damascus are all "cool, refreshing and pleasant" retreats for the natives of a parched region, offering "fountains, nearby rivers, tree shaded spots, roses and other flowers."[45] Outdoor enjoyment included resting on mat-covered stone benches and enjoying the street scene.[46] He certainly found more to approve in coffeehouse conviviality than did Morosini or Bidduph:

> There are public coffeehouses, where the drink is prepared in very big pots for the numerous guests. At these places, guests mingle without distinction of rank or creed....

When someone is in a coffeehouse, and sees people whom he knows come in, if he is in the least ways civil, he will tell the proprietor not to take any money from them. All this is done by a single word, for when they are served with their coffee, he merely cries, "Giaba," that is to say, "Gratis!"[47]

Evidently little changed over the ensuing century, for D'Ohsson confirmed the picture of coffeehouse leisure, writing, "Young idlers spend whole hours in them, smoking, playing draughts or chess and discussing affairs of the day."

Alexander Russel, in *The Natural History of Aleppo* (1756), describes the coffee-house use of hashish and opium in waterpipes, and other writers, such as Edward Lane, an English Arabic scholar, in his *Account of the Manners and Customs of the Modern Egyptians* (1860), also testifies to these sordid indulgences. Niebuhr, blaming the stupefied languor of the coffee imbibers on intense tobacco use, comments:

In Egypt, Syria, and Arabia, the favorite of amusement of persons in any degree above the very lowest classes, is, to spend the evening in a public coffee-house, where they hear musicians, singers, and tale-tellers, who frequent those houses in order to earn a trifle by the exercise of their respective arts. In those places of public amusement, the Orientals maintain a profound silence, and often sit whole evenings without uttering a word. They prefer conversing with their pipe; and its narcotic fumes seem very fit to allay the ferment of their boiling blood. Without recurring to a physical reason, it would be hard to account for the general relish which these people have for tobacco; by smoking, they divert the spleen and languor which hang about them, and bring themselves in a slight degree, into the same state of spirits which the opium eaters obtain from that drug. Tobacco serves them instead of strong liquors, which they are forbidden to use.[48]

The Reverend R. Walsh was a senior member of the British diplomatic service stationed in Constantinople in the early nineteenth century. In his book *Narrative of a Journey from Constantinople to England* (1828), he describes a coffeehouse he visited while staying the night at an inn, typical of the sort of establishment that had been so often visited by earlier European travelers, on his way home:

I passed a very feverish sleepless night, which I attributed to either of two causes; one, the too free use of animal food and vinous liquors, after violent exercise. . . . Another, and perhaps the real cause, was that we slept on the platform of a miserable little coffee-house, attached to the kahn, which was full of people smoking all night. The Turks of this class are offensively rude and familiar; they stretch themselves out and lay across us, without scruple or apology; and within a few inches of my face, was the brazier of charcoal, with which they lighted their pipes and heated their coffee. After a night passed in a suffocating hole, lying on the bare boards, inhaling tobacco smoke and charcoal vapors, and annoyed every minute by the elbows and knees of rude Turks; it was not to be wondered at, that I rose sick and weak, and felt as if I was altogether unable to proceed on my journey."[49]

However, Walsh could not afford the luxury of a layover; and so, taking refreshment from an exhilarating breeze, he allowed himself to be helped onto his horse and made his way down the road.

Life among the Bedouins has always maintained a distinctive savor. W. B. Seabrook, in his book *Adventures in Arabia* (1927), gives a vivid account of coffee's place in a timeless nomadic culture where lunch consisted of dried dates, bread, and fermented camel's milk and the one cooked meal of each day was a whole carcass of a sheep or goat, served over rice and gravy:

> Coffee-making is the exclusive province of the men. Its paraphernalia for a sheik's household fills two great camel hampers. We had five pelican-beaked brass pots, of graduated sizes, up to the great grand-father of all the coffee pots, which held at least ten gallons; a heavy iron ladle, with a long handle inlaid with brass and silver, for roasting the beans; wooden mortar and pestle, elaborately carved, for pounding them; and a brass inlaid box containing the tiny cups without handles.[50]

Seabrook enjoyed the honor of sharing coffee with the Pasha Mitkhal, leader of the tribe, whom he describes as "a born aristocrat," about forty, with a slender build and a small pointed black beard and mustache, who "wore no gorgeous robes nor special insignia of rank." Except for a headcloth of finer texture and a muslin undergarment which he wore beneath his black camel hair cloak and his black headcoil of twisted horsehair, he dressed exactly as his warriors. Once Mitkhal was seated in his tent, Mansour, his black attendant, "approached with a long-spouted brass coffee pot in his left hand, and two tiny cups without handles in the palm of his right."[51]

On another occasion, Seabrook, observing a man accidentally overturn the large communal coffeepot, was surprised to hear the company exclaim, "*Khair Inshallah!*," which means, "A good omen!" Mitkhal later explained that this old custom may have originated with a desire to help the klutz save face, although Seabrook speculated that it traces to pre-Moslem pagan libations in the sand.[52]

A less favorable prognostication, however, attends the deliberate spilling of coffee. Among the Druse, Bedouin warriors of the Djebel, Seabrook took coffee with Ali bey, the ranking patriarch, in the company of his four sons and ten solemn Druse elders. Sitting cross-legged before the charcoal fire, Ali bey honored his guests by making the coffee himself and serving it in two small cups which were passed around and around the circle, telling a tale how an overturned coffee cup could amount to a sentence of death:

> If a Druse ever shows cowardice in battle, he is not reproached, but the next time the warriors sit in a circle and coffee is served, the host stands before him, pours exactly as for the others, but in handing him the cup, deliberately spills the coffee on the coward's robe. This is equivalent to a death sentence. In the next battle the man is forced not only to fight bravely but to offer himself to the bullets or swords of the enemy. No matter with how much courage he fights, he must not come out alive. If he fails, his whole family is disgraced.[53]

Evolving from the Sludge:
African and Arabian Preparations of Coffee

Even though, as we noted at the outset of our discussion, no one has any direct evidence that the Nubians or Abyssinians or tribes of central Africa made use of coffee in ancient times, coffee's prevalence as both a wild and cultivated plant and its use by modern natives, as observed by Europeans from the seventeenth century onward, suggest ways caffeine *may* have been ingested before recorded history. A credible tradition holds that in Africa, before the tenth century, a wine was fermented from the pulp of ripe coffee berries, and we have already seen that the Galla warriors rolled the fruit into larded balls, which they carried as rations. Some say that in the eleventh century, the practice of boiling raw, unripe coffee beans in their husks to make a drink was instituted in Ethiopia. Sir Richard Burton's vivid account of coffee use in the wilds of nineteenth-century Africa includes a description of boiling unripe berries before chewing them like tobacco and handing them out to guests when they visit.

In the early 1880s, Jean Arthur Rimbaud (1854–91), the French expatriate Symbolist ex-poet, laid plans to visit Africa to write a book for the Geographical Society, including maps and engravings, on "Harar and Gallaland."[54] As far as we know, he never got further than writing the title, complete with publisher and projected publication date: *THE GALLAS, by J.-ARTHER RIMBAUD, East-African Explorer, with Maps and Engravings, Supplemented with Photographs by the Author*; Available from H. Oudin, Publishers, 10, rue de Mézieres, Paris, 1891. Although he never wrote the book, Rimbaud traveled among the Galla, becoming, to his embarrassment, on several solitary expeditions, the first white man the tribal women had ever seen. While among the tribesmen, he partook of their foods, which included green coffee beans cooked in butter.[55] A testimonial to coffee's importance can be found in a letter in which he writes of his distaste at being forced to share coffee with the bandit Mohammed Abou-Beker, the powerful sultan of Zeila, who preyed on European travelers and traders and controlled the passage of all trading caravans as well as the slave trade. Rimbaud needed Abou-Beker's sanction to travel in that area, and this would not be forthcoming before participating in the ritual sharing of coffee, brought, at the clap of the sultan's hands by a servant "who comes running from the next straw hut to bring *el boun*, the coffee."[56]

We do not know all the details of the earliest Arab preparations. The best information is that, when Arab traders brought coffee back to their homeland from Africa for planting, they made two dissimilar caffeinated drinks from the coffee berry. The first was *"kisher,"* a tealike beverage steeped from the fruit's dried husks, which, according to every authority, tastes nothing like our coffee, but rather something like an aromatic or spiced tea. In the Yemen, *kisher*, brewed from the husks that had been roasted together with some of the silver skin, was regarded as a delicate drink and was the choice of the connoisseur. The second was *"bounya,"* its name deriving from *"bunn,"* the Ethiopian and early Arabic word for coffee beans, a thick brew of ground or crushed beans. It was probably drunk unfiltered, and, in a practice persisting for several hundred years, downed with its sediment, a drink that could fairly be called "sludge." Early *bounya* was made from raw, boiled beans. A Levantine refinement

Photograph of Arab peasants making coffee in Gaza, c. 1885–1901. The print is from an albumen photograph taken by Bonfils, who was active from 1864 to 1916. We can see all the stages of the process: the man seated on the left roasts the beans in a pan, the man seated on the right grinds them with a pestle, while the man seated in the center oversees the boiling pot and the remaining man stands with a tiny cup ready to drink the brew. (Photograph by Bonfils, University of Pennsylvania Museum, Philadelphia, negative #s4–142208)

introduced the technique of roasting the beans on stone trays, before boiling them in water, then straining and reboiling them with fresh water, in a process repeated several times, and the thick residue stored in large clay jars for later service in tiny cups. In another development, the beans were powdered with a mortar and pestle after roasting and then mixed with boiling water. In a practice that persisted for several hundred years, the resulting drink was swallowed complete with the grounds. Later in the sixteenth century Islamic coffee drinkers invented the *ibrik*, a small coffee boiler that made brewing easier and quicker. Cinnamon, cloves, sugar might be added while still boiling, and the "essence of amber" could be added after the coffee was doled out in small china cups.[57] A cover was affixed to the boiler a few years later, creating the prototype of the modern coffeepot.

Infusion was the latest arrival, its development dating only from the eighteenth century. Ground coffee was placed in a cloth bag, which was itself deposited in the pot, and upon which hot water was poured, steeping the grounds as we steep tea. However, boiling continued as the favorite way of preparing the drink for many years.

The Origin of the Word

In pursuing the origin of the uses of the coffee bean, we are led on a chase reminiscent of Scheherazade's tales in the *Arabian Nights*. We are quickly lost in a world where names of things and people and places are confounded and uncertain, and where the central subject of our speculation seems to simply have appeared, like a *jinn*, without revealing the secret of its provenance even to living witnesses of its advent.

The word "coffee" itself is the best example of this dubietous panorama of the fabulous and the real. The word enters English by way of the French "*café*," which, like the words "*caffè*" in Italian, "*koffie*" in Dutch, and "*Kaffee*" in German, derive from the Turkish "*kahveh*," which in turn derives from the Arabic word "*qahwa*." Of this much we may be sure. But once we inquire into the origin of the Arabic word, we are quickly lost in a labyrinth of tantalizing, mutually exclusive etymological conjectures.

One etymological theory with considerable academic support is that the word "*qahwa*" in Arabic comes from a root that means "making something repugnant, or lessening someone's desire for something."[58] "*Qahwa*," in the old poetry, was a venerable word for wine, as something that dulls the appetite for food. In later usage, it came to refer to other psychoactive beverages, such as khat, a strong stimulating drink infused from the leaves of the *kafta* plant, *Catha edulis*, which is still popular in the Yemen. This theory holds that the Sufis took the old word for wine and applied it to the new beverage, coffee. The notion seems particularly appealing when we consider that the Sufi mystics, who sought to empty their minds of circumstantial distractions by whirling furiously until entering an ecstatic state, and who were constrained, like all Muslims, from drinking wine, used wine and intoxication in their poetry as sensual emblems of divine afflatus;[59] they might have happily used the word for this forbidden wine to name the new, permitted brew, a drink that would in fact help to sustain their devotions. A variation of this theory is that, just as the word "*qahwa*" was used for wine because it diminished the desire for food, it was naturally used for coffee because it diminishes the desire for sleep.

At least one old Arab account says that what we call coffee today borrowed its name directly from the drink brewed from *kafta*, or khat, after the redoubtable al-Dhabhani recommended to friends that they substitute coffee for the *qahwa* made from *kafta*, when supplies of the latter were exhausted. According to this notion, coffee is a kind of poor man's khat, to which the Sufis resorted only when khat was unavailable. This preference may still obtain today in the Yemen, where the more profitable cultivation of khat, despite government efforts to discourage khat's use, is increasingly displacing the cultivation of coffee.[60]

Still another etymology, but one with slight lexicographical authority, traces the word "coffee" to "*quwwa*," or "*cahuha*," which means "power" or "strength," holding that the drink was named for what we now recognize as the envigorating effects of caffeine. A story advancing this etymology is that, toward the middle of the fifteenth century, a poor Arab traveling in Abyssinia stooped near a stand of trees. He cut down a tree covered with berries for firewood in order to prepare his dinner of rice. Once done eating, he noticed that the partially roasted berries were fragrant and that, when crushed, their aroma increased. By accident, he dropped some of them into his scanty water supply. He discovered that the foul water was purified. When he returned to Aden, he presented the beans to the mufti, who had been an opium addict for years. When the mufti tried the roasted berries, he at once recovered his health and vigor and dubbed the tree of their origin, "*cahuha.*"[61]

An evocative etymology provided for the word "coffee" links it to the region of Kaffa (now usually spelled "Kefa") in Ethiopia, which is today one of Africa's noted growing districts.[62] Some say that because the plant was first grown in that region, and was possibly first infused as a beverage there, the Arabs named it after that place. Others, with equally little authority, turn this story on its head and claim that the district was named for the bean.

But perhaps the best fabulous etymology combines two of these theories and throws in a prototypical Arabian fantasy of the divine, demonic, and the marvelous. It accepts that coffee was named for Kaffa and at the same time links the word "*qahwa,*" in the sense of "wanting no more," to the name of the district. The idea is based on several Islamic tales that derive the name "Kaffa" from the same Arabian root for "it is enough" as mentioned above:

> A priest . . . is said to have conceived the design of wandering from the East towards Western Africa in order to extend the religion of the prophet, and when he came into the regions where Kaffa lies, Allah is reported to have appeared to him and to have said, "It is far enough; go no further." Since that time, according to tradition, the country has been called Kaffa.[63]

There, of course, the priest promptly discovered a coffee tree laden with red berries, which berries he immediately boiled, naming the brew after the place to which Allah had led him.

2

tea

Asian Origins

If Christianity is wine, and Islam coffee, Buddhism is most certainly tea.
—Alan Watts, *The Way of Zen* (1957)

From ancient times, the Chinese have elaborated a pretense of tradition and descent that can best be described as a dream of antiquity in a time that never was. Affecting to trace her customs, philosophies, and pedigrees to a more venerable age than those of other nations, the Chinese culture has, in the mirror of mythological history, assumed the cloak of dignity that accords with precedence. Because tea has long been uniquely prominent in Chinese life, an effort to locate its origin in the remote past became inevitable.

Such an effort was realized in the legend of Shen Nung, mythical first emperor of China, a Promethean figure, honored as the inventor of the plow and of husbandry, expositor of the curative properties of plants, and, most important for our story, the discoverer of tea. According to the legend, Shen Nung sat down in the shade of a shrub to rest in the heat of the day. Following a logic of his own that would have appeared mysterious to an onlooker, he decided to cool off by building a fire and boiling some water to drink, a practice he had begun after noticing that those who drank boiled water fell sick less often than those who imbibed directly from the well. He fed his fire with branches from a tea bush, and a providential breeze knocked a few of the tiny leaves into his pot. When Shen Nung drank the resulting infusion, he became the first to enjoy the stimulant effect and delicate refreshment of tea.[1]

Shen Nung, true to his cognomen, "Divine Healer," details the medicinal uses of *ch'a*, or tea, in the *Pen ts'ao*, a book-length compilation of his medical records, dated, with daunting precision by much later scholars, at 2737 B.C. The entries in this book include unmistakable references to the diuretic, antibacterial, bronchodilating, stimulating, and mood-enhancing effects we now attribute to caffeine:

Good for tumours or abscesses that come about the head, or for ailments of the bladder. It [*ch'a*] dissipates heat caused by the phlegms, or inflammation of the chest. It
quenches thirst. It lessens the desire for sleep. It gladdens and cheers the heart.[2]

In fact, the earliest edition of the *Pen ts'ao* dates from the Neo-Han dynasty (A.D. 25
to 221), and even this book does not yet mention tea. The tea reference was interpolated after the seventh century, at which time the word "*ch'a*" first came into widespread use.

Another traditional account purporting to tell about the early use of tea by an
ancient emperor says that, as early as the twelfth century B.C., tribal leaders in and
around Szechuan included tea in their offerings to Emperor Wen, duke of Chou and
founder of the Chou dynasty (1122–256 B.C.). Wen was a legendary folk hero and purported author of the *Erh Ya*, the first Chinese dictionary. However, because the earliest extant source for this tea tribute is the *Treatise on the Kingdom of Huayang*, by
Chang Ju, a history of the era written in A.D. 347,[3] the story is not very helpful in establishing that tea was used in China before the first millennium B.C.

To Lao Tzu (600–517 B.C.), the founder of Taoism, is ascribed, by a Chinese text
of the first century B.C., the notion that tea is an indispensable constituent of the
elixir of life. The Taoist alchemists, his followers, who sought the secret of immortality, certainly believed this, dubbing tea "the froth of the liquid jade." (Unlike their
Western counterparts, who searched for both the secret of eternal life and the power
to turn base metal into gold, the Chinese alchemists confined their quest to improving health and extending life.) The custom of offering tea to guests, still honored in
China, supposedly began in an encounter that occurred toward the end of Lao Tzu's
life. An embittered and disillusioned man, the spiritual leader, having seen his teachings dishonored in his own land and foreseeing a national decline, drove westward
on a buffalo-cart, intending to leave China for the wild wastes of Ta Chin in central
Asia, an area that later became part of the eastern provinces of the Roman Empire.
The customs inspector at the Han Pass border gate turned out to be Yin Hsi, an elderly
sage who had waited his entire life in the previously unsatisfied expectation of encoun-
tering an avatar. Recognizing the holy fugitive and rising to the occasion, Yin Hsi
stopped Lao Tzu, served him tea, and, while they drank, persuaded him to commit his
teachings to the book that became the revered *Tao Te Ching*, or *The Book of Tao*.

Probably what was genuinely the earliest reference in Chinese literature adducing the capacity of tea, through what we now know is the agency of caffeine, to
improve mental operations is found in the *Shin Lun*, by Hua Tuo (d. 220 B.C.). In
this book, the famous physician and surgeon, credited with discovering anesthesia,
taught that drinking tea improved alertness and concentration, a clear reference to
what we today understand as caffeine's most prominent psychoactive effects: "To drink
k'u t'u [bitter *t'u*] constantly makes one think better."[4]

Awareness of caffeine's efficacy as a mood elevator was also evidenced in Liu Kun,
governor of Yan Chou and a leading general of the Qin dynasty (221–206 B.C.), who
wrote to his nephew, asking to be sent some "real tea" to alleviate his depression. In
59 B.C., in Szechuan, Wang Bao wrote the first book known to provide instructions
for buying and preparing tea.[5] The volume was a milestone in tea history, establish-

ing that, by its publication date, tea had become an important part of diet, while remaining in use as a drug.

One of the most entertaining stories about tea to emerge from Oriental religious folklore is a T'ang dynasty (618–906 A.D.) Chinese or Japanese story about the introduction of tea to China. This story teaches that tea's creation was a miracle worked by a particularly holy man, born of his self-disgust at his inability to forestall sleep during prayer. The legend tells of the monk Bodhidharma, famous for founding the school of Buddhism based on meditation, called "Ch'an," which later became Zen Buddhism, and for bringing this religion from India to China around A.D. 525. Supposedly, the emperor of China had furnished the monk with his own cave near the capital, Nanging, where he would be at leisure to practice the precursor of Zen meditation. There the Bodhidharma sat unmoving, year after year. From the example of his heroic endurance, it is easy to understand how his school of Buddhism evolved into *za-zen*, or "sitting meditation," for certainly *sitzfleisch* was among his outstanding capacities.[6] The tale is that, after meditating seated before a wall for nine years, he finally fell asleep. When he awoke and discovered his lapse, he disgustedly cut off his eyelids. They fell to the ground and took root, growing into tea bushes containing a stimulant that was to sustain meditations forever after.

The Origin of the Word and the Drink

Tea, despite these legends of its antiquity, is, in the long view of things, but a recent introduction to China. The Chinese probably learned of it from natives of northern India, or, according to another account, from aboriginal tribesmen living in Southeast Asia, who, we are told "boiled the green leaves of wild tea trees in ancient kettles over crude smoky campfires." Some Chinese histories report that tea was brought to China from India by Buddhist monks, as the Arab accounts tell us that coffee was introduced into Arabia from Abyssinia by Sufi monks, although, as with the Arab stories, we have no unequivocal proof these stories are true. Nevertheless it is clear that, though in the West we strongly associate tea with China in the way that we associate coffee with Arabia, each was regarded as an exotic drink when introduced into its respective "region of origin" within historical times. The details of tea's pre-Chinese history, like the details of coffee's pre-Arabian history, are unfortunately lost.

From the time tea arrived, however, the Chinese words for tea provide a kind of chronological map which reveals the contours of the plant's history there. The Chinese character "*ch'a*," the modern Mandarin word for tea, is, except for a single vertical stroke, identical with the character "*t'u.*" "*T'u*" is used in the *Shih Ching*, or *Book of Songs*, one of China's oldest classics (c. 550 B.C.), to designate a variety of plants, including sowthistle and thrush and probably tea as well. Typical phrases in which the word occurs: "The girls were like flowering *t'u*," "The *t'u* is as sweet as a dumpling."[7] Although the choice of renderings of "*t'u*" into English are somewhat arbitrary and fanciful, it is clear that the word referred to a drink of some sort at least as early as the sixth century B.C. From that time forward, one or another of the words for tea was included in every Chinese dictionary.

The "tea change" in terminology occurred during the Early Han dynasty (206 B.C. to A.D. 24), as recorded in the seventh-century work *The History of the Early Han*, by Yen Shih-ku, who notes that at that time the switch occurred from "*t'u*" to "*ch'a*" when the tea plant was being specified. This change was even read into the names of places. For example, "T'u Ling," the "Tea Hills" in the Hunan province, an important and ancient tea-producing region, was redubbed "Ch'a Ling" during the Han dynasty.

Another dictionary, the *Shuo Wên*, presented to the Han emperor in A.D. 121, defines "*ming*" as "the buds taken from the plant *t'u*," which strongly suggests that the Chinese were already aware that the bud is the best part for making the beverage and that carefully plucking it forces the plant to produce new flush.

The shift to "*ch'a*" is confirmed in the edition of the *Erh Ya* prepared by Kuo P'u, an A.D. fourth-century redactor who completely recast the lexicon, dividing it into nineteen parts. Despite the tradition attributing the *Erh Ya* to the Emperor Wen in the twelfth century B.C., it was written much later, probably around the third or fourth century B.C. Tea appears in P'u's edition seven hundred years later as "*chia*," defined as "bitter *t'u*," and the text explains, "The plant is small like the gardenia, sending forth its leaves even in the winter. A decoction is made from the leaves by boiling."[8] This drink was strictly a medicinal preparation, used to alleviate digestive and nervous complaints, uses strongly suggesting the pharmacological actions of caffeine, and it was also sometimes applied externally to palliate rheumatic pains. By A.D. 500, the *Kuang Ya*, yet another dictionary, defines *ch'a* as an enjoyable drink, and it was in this period that the use of tea as a comestible became predominant over its pharmacological applications.[9]

In a striking parallel with the evolution of the word "*qahwa*," the Arabic word for coffee, which, as we have seen, began as an old Arabic word for wine and a variety of stimulating infusions, the word "*cha*" originally designated a panoply of decoctions from herbs, flowers, fruits, or vegetables, some of which were intoxicating. This old generic sense survives in contemporary Mandarin, in which any cooling liquid comestible, from bean soup to beer, is called "*liang cha*," or "cooling tea." It was only in the time of the T'ang dynasty and the publication of Lu Yü's *Ch'a Ching* that *ch'a*'s meaning underwent the pattern of change linguists call "specialization," and the word "*cha*" came predominantly to designate *Camellia sinensis*, the plant that carried caffeine, and the beverage infused from its leaves.[10]

The English word "tea" and its cognates in many languages derive from the Chinese Min form, "*te*," which may itself be one of China's most important contributions to the story of the beverage worldwide. In a linguistic transformation opposite to that of the Chinese "*ch'a*," the English the word "tea" has undergone "generalization," and the word, which when it first entered our language designated a single species of plant and the brew made from it, now refers to virtually any infusion of leaves or herbs.

From the time of the Han dynasty tea as a drink grew steadily in popularity. During succeeding dynasties, it spread quickly in the south and more slowly in the north, until, by the Jin dynasty in A.D. fourth-century tea was acknowledged widely as a medicinal and was also generally used as a beverage. Records indicate that it was prescribed by a Buddhist priest to relieve a Jin emperor's headache. It was from this time, when demand had so increased that it could no longer be met by harvesting wild tea trees and stripping their branches, that the first cultivation of tea is dated.[11] In A.D. 476 Chinese trade records reveal that it had already been used as barter with the Turkic tribes.[12] In the Sui dynasty (A.D. 589–618) tea was introduced by Buddhist monks into Japan.

We have already noted three of the most interesting parallels between the apparently unconnected histories of coffee and tea: Each was first harvested as a wild leaf or berry and used only as a stimulant and a medicine; each was first cultivated and used as a beverage relatively recently; and each was brought into the regions that today are associated with its origin by religious devotees returning from a nearby country, who initially used it to stay awake during their meditations. Another parallel is the way the Chinese tried to keep tea cultivation to themselves, just as the Arabs tried to do with coffee. Finally, almost from its first appearance in China, tea leaves were used as a medium of exchange, as were coffee beans in Arabia, cola nuts in Africa, and cacao pods and maté leaves in the Americas. Bricks pressed from dried tea leaves served as currency among the peasantry of the interior, who preferred them to either coins or paper money, which diminished in value as one traveled farther from the imperial center.[13]

Tea's wild popularity in China dates only from the T'ang dynasty, a golden age in China's genuine history, when her power, influence, scope, attainments, and splendor were reminiscent of the late Roman Republic or the early Roman Empire; for as Rome had been hundreds of years earlier, the Chinese empire in its T'ang heyday was the most extensive, most populous, and richest dominion in the world. It was in this period that the Japanese, idolizing T'ang culture, adopted tea drinking as part of their efforts to emulate their neighbors. During the reign of T'ai-tsung (627–49), China extended her power over Afghanistan, Turkistan, and Tibet. Succeeding emperors brought Korea and Japan under China's rule, and additional consolidations were effected by Empress Wu (r. 690–705), one of China's rare women sovereigns. The T'ang government and the T'ang code of laws, resting on Confucian teachings, became models for neighboring countries. Towns grew in size and prosperity, foreign trade increased, bringing new cultural ideas and new technologies, and, in this cosmopolitan milieu, the arts flourished. A custom instituted in the seventh century under the reign of the T'ang ruler T'ai Tsung, of paying a tea tribute to the emperor, continued through the Ch'ing dynasty (1644–1911), the last imperial dynasty of China. During the T'ang dynasty, a time of luxuries and refinements, individual tea trees were celebrated for the quality of their leaf. For example, one called the "eggplant tree" grew in a gully and was watered by the seepage from a rock above. It was also during this dynasty that Chinese tea merchants commissioned Lu Yü to write a manual of tea connoisseurship, *The Classic of Tea* (*Ch'a Ching*).

The Classic of Tea: Teaching Tea Tippling

Sometimes one man and one book can have a critical effect on an entire culture. For example, the fact that despite the existence of a generally agreed-upon normative definition of tragedy, there is in the West no corresponding account of comedy, may be traced to the fact that the part of Aristotle's *Poetics* treating the tragic drama survived, while that treating the comic was lost. Similarly, that tea in the West has never become the central feature of culture that it is in the East may be a result of the fact that Lu Yü wrote his great book in Chinese rather than in English or French. In the year A.D. 780 the tea merchants of China hired this leading Taoist poet to produce a work extolling tea's virtues. The result of this public relations effort was a book dealing exhaustively and, for the most part, extremely soporifically, with every aspect of tea. After telling you more than you want to know about the cultivation, harvesting, curing, preparation, apparatus of consumption, and use of tea, Lu Yü closes with anecdotes and quotations from eminent historical figures "whose love of tea and proper conduct resulted in health, wealth, and prestige."[14] As explained in an old preface to his work, Lu Yü has long been acknowledged as the godfather of tea authorities: "Before Lu Yü, tea was rather an ordinary thing; but in a book of only three parts, he has taught us to manufacture tea, to lay out the equipage, and to brew it properly."[15] The earliest surviving edition of the *Ch'a Ching* dates from the Ming dynasty (1368–1644). Lu Yü also authored several lost works about tea, probably drawn in even more detail, such as a book distinguishing twenty sources for water in which to boil tea leaves.[16]

According to legend, Lu Yü was an orphan who was adopted by a Ch'an Buddhist monk of the Dragon Cloud Monastery. When he refused to take up the robe, his stepfather assigned to him the worst jobs around the monastery. Lu Yün ran away and joined a traveling circus as a clown, but the adulation of the crowd could not assuage his yearnings for wisdom and learning. He quit show business and immersed himself in the library of a wealthy patron. It was at this time that he is supposed to have begun writing the *Ch'a Ching*. To Lu Yü, tea drinking was emblematic of the harmony and mystical unity of the universe. "He invested the *Ch'a Ching* with the concept that dominated the religious thought of his age, whether Buddhist, Taoist, or Confucian: to see in the particular an expression of the universal."[17]

No aspect of tea, real, imaginary, or elaborate beyond reason, escaped Lu Yü's attention. Among his extensive expositions of tea varieties:

> Tea has a myriad of shapes. If I may speak vulgarly and rashly, tea may shrink and crinkle like a Mongol's boots, or it may look like the dewlap of a wild ox, some sharp, some curling as the eaves of a house. It can look like a mushroom in whirling flight just as clouds do when they float out from behind a mountain peak. Its leaves can swell and leap as if they were being lightly tossed on wind-disturbed water. Others will look like clay, soft and malleable, prepared for the hand of the potter and will be as clear and pure as if filtered through wood. Still others will twist and turn like the rivulets carved out by a violent rain in newly tilled fields.
>
> Those are the very finest of teas.[18]

Here is his reasoned catalogue of waters:

> On the question of what water to use, I would suggest that tea made from mountain streams is best, river water is all right, but well-water tea is quite inferior. . . .

Water from the slow-flowing streams, the stone-lined pools or milk-pure springs is the best of mountain water. Never take tea made from water that falls in cascades, gushes from springs, rushes in a torrent, or that eddies and surges as if nature were rinsing its mouth. Over usage of all such water to make tea will lead to illnesses of the throat. . . . If the evil genius of a stream makes the water bubble like a fresh spring, pour it out.[19]

Not only does he itemize types of tea and types of water, he even classifies stages of what we might regard as the undifferentiable chaos of boiling. The initial stage is when the water is just beginning to boil:

When the water is boiling, it must look like fishes eyes and give off but the hint of a sound. When at the edges it clatters like a bubbling spring and looks like pearls innumerable strung together, it has reached the second stage. When it leaps like breakers majestic and resounds like a swelling wave, it is at its peak. Any more and the water will be boiled out and should not be used.

The subsequent stage of boiling is described in even more elaborate and fanciful terms:

They should suggest eddying pools, twisting islets or floating duckweed at the time of the world's creation. They should be like scudding clouds in a clear blue sky and should occasionally overlap like scales on fish. They should be like copper *cash*, green with age, churned by the rapids of a river, or dispose themselves as chrysanthemum petals would, promiscuously cast on a goblet's stand.[20]

As a result of the success of this book, Lu Yü was lionized by the emperor Te Tsung and became enormously popular throughout China. Finally he withdrew into an hermetic life, completing the circular course begun in his monastic childhood, and died in A.D. 804. His story did not quite end there, however. Lu Yü was supposed on his death to have been transfigured into Chazu, the genie of tea, and his effigy is still honored by tea dealers throughout the Orient.

The Forms of Tea: From Bricks to Powder

To make tea into bricks or cakes, the leaves were pounded, shaped, and pressed into a mold, then hung above an open pit to dry over a hardwood or charcoal fire. When ready, the bricks were placed in baskets attached to either end of a pole for delivery to every part of the nation. In earlier times the cakes of pressed leaves were chewed, and later they were boiled with "onion, ginger, jujube fruit, orange peel, dogwood berries, or peppermint,"[21] or rice, spices, or milk.[22] After the T'ang dynasty the use of brick tea underwent a steady decline. However, throughout the eighteenth century, Chinese brick tea became the favorite of the Russians, who imported millions of tons.

In the Sung dynasty (960–1279), brick tea was largely replaced by a powdered tea that was mixed with hot water and whipped into a froth. Along with the new fashion of preparation came new names for tea varieties, such as "sparrow's tongue," "falcon's talon," and "gray eyebrows." The Sung emperor Hui Tsung (1101–24), who widely influenced China's culture, wrote a treatise championing powdered tea, which helped it attain preeminence. To see how seriously tea was then taken consider that a Sung poet in the Taoist tradition, possibly Li Chi Lai, declared that the three most venal sins were wasting fine tea through incompetent manipulation, false education of youth, and uninformed admiration of fine paintings.[23]

When China fell under the rule of the Mongols, tea as a cultural force fell into decline. Marco Polo (1254–1324), an avid and meticulous observer of Chinese life and customs, never discusses tea drinking and mentions tea only in connection with the annual tea tribute paid to the emperor. Nevertheless, it was during this era of relative desuetude that the Chinese tea ceremony was born. It existed at least from the Yuan dynasty (1280–1368), for it is described in a 1335 edition of the *Pai-chang Ch'ing Kuei*, a book of monastery regulations supposedly promulgated by Pai-Ch'ing (d. 814).[24]

The prominence of tea returned with the reassertion of native imperial power in the Ming dynasty (1368–1644). In the Ming dynasty tea was first prepared by steeping the cured leaf in a cup. Some wealthy tea drinkers placed a silver filigree disk in the cup to hold down the leaves. During this period, new methods of curing the leaf were developed, with the result that, when travelers from the West arrived, they encountered leaves fermented to varying extents, which they mistakenly thought were different species: black, green, and oolong. The "pathos of distance," to use Nietzsche's phrase, between the extravagant imperial family and their humble subjects is exemplified in the story of a certain rare tea, prepared only for the emperor, which grew on a distant mountain so inhospitable that it could be harvested only by provoking the rock-dwelling monkeys into angrily tearing off branches from the tea trees to hurl down upon their tormentors, who were then able to strip the leaves at their convenience.[25] The most celebrated tea of the Ming period was Fukien tea, grown in the hills of Wu I, which the Chinese believed could purify the blood and renew health. It was also during the Ming period that tea ascended to its full status as a ritual enjoyment and a spiritual refreshment that transcended the condition of ordinary comestibles, a standing that it retains to this day.

According to Okakura, the stages of tea development, as epitomized in the manner of tea preparation in each, correspond with the three great historical stages of Chinese civilization and culture:

> The Cake-tea which was boiled, the Powdered-tea which was whipped, the Leaf-tea which was steeped, mark the distinct emotional impulses of the T'ang, the Sung, and the Ming dynasties of China. If we are inclined to borrow the much abused terminology of art-classification, we might designate them respectively, the Classic, the Romantic, and the Naturalistic schools of Tea.[26]

Outside China, the peoples of the Orient had their own special ways of making use of the caffeine in the tea plant. In ancient Siam, steamed tea leaves were rolled into

Photograph of Tibetan men carrying brick tea from China, where they had obtained it by barter. They marked about six miles a day bearing three-hundred-pound loads of the commodity, regarded as a necessity in their homeland. (Photograph by E.H. Wilson, Photographic Archives of the Arnold Arboretum, copyrighted by the President and Fellows of Harvard College, Harvard University, Cambridge, Massachusetts)

balls and consumed with salted pig fat, oil, garlic, and dried fish. The Burmese prepared *letpet*, or "pickled tea salad," by boiling wild tea leaves, stuffing them into a
hollow bamboo shoot and burying them for several months, after which they were
excavated to serve as a delicacy at an important feast. Tibetans still make tea using
blocks of leaves that they crumble into boiling water. Like the early Turkish preparations of coffee, this tea is heavily reboiled. Like the Galla warriors of the Ethiopian
massif, who mix ground coffee beans with lard to sustain them in the harsh conditions
of high altitudes, the Tibetans, who also struggle with life in a difficult environment,
mix their tea with rancid yak butter, barley meal, and salt to make a nourishing breakfast treat or snack.[27]

Tea and the Tao: Yin, Yang, and the Importance of a Balanced Diet

Tea, in a more highly concentrated, less exhaustively processed form than in later centuries, was one of the important and most powerful ingredients known to ancient Chinese medicine. Long before its fashionable ascension as a comestible in the T'ang
dynasty, tea had joined the ranks of ginseng and certain mushrooms to which a considerable body of folklore had ascribed a marvelous range of benefits. The *Pen ts'ao
kang-mu* (1578), an herbal by Li Shih-chen (1518–93), generally thought to contain
material surviving from a much earlier period, illustrates the high esteem in which the
leaf was held in the traditional Chinese pharmacopoeia. As Jill Anderson says, speaking of tea in China in *An Introduction to Japanese Tea Ritual* (1991), Li attributed to
tea the power to

> promote digestion, dissolve fats, neutralize poisons in the digestive system, cure dysen-
> tery, fight lung disease, lower fevers, and treat epilepsy. Tea was also thought to be
> an effective astringent for cleaning sores and recommended for washing the eyes
> and mouth.[28]

We can only wonder if the recent discoveries that caffeine can increase the rate of lipolysis, or fat burning, has protective effects against the pulmonary complications of
smoking and congestive lung disease, kills bacteria, and may be useful for atopic dermatitis, are significantly or only coincidentally foreshadowed in a drug manual that
is at least five hundred years old.

The Tao, evocatively translated as "the Way," is an early Chinese word for the
mystical totality of Being, or Nature, of which all things were understood to be part.
It comprised two opposing principles, the yin and yang, or the feminine and masculine aspects, the interplay between which was held to generate or constitute the variety of the world's particulars. The practice of Taoism was intended to enable its
adherents to bring their minds and bodies into harmony with the all-encompassing
and everywhere present Tao. This attainment was to be achieved by appeals to the
gods or ancestral spirits, the proper alignment of houses and burial plots, and, most
important for our story, the consumption of a balanced diet, that is, a regimen
informed by a knowledge of the yin and yang properties of different foods. Thus,
like the humoral theory of Galen, the Taoist medical theory relied on restoring or pre-

serving the proper interplay of forces within the human organism. In senses analogous to the terminological practice of European humoral theory, foods or medicines were considered "cold" or "hot," depending on whether they contained more of the female principle or the male. What we know to be caffeine's pharmacological properties made tea central to Taoist treatments.

One traditional Taoist scheme applied in Lu Yü's time identifies six vapors or atmospheric influences descending from heaven, an imbalance among which will result in various infirmities. As in the humoral theory, this "atmospheric theory" associates a specific health problem with an excess of each of the vapors. In his notes to his translation of *The Classic of Tea*, Francis Carpenter lists these six health problems:

1. An excess of *yin* creates chills.
2. An excess of *yang* creates fever.
3. An excess of wind creates illness of the four limbs.
4. An excess of rain creates illness of the stomach.
5. An excess of darkness leads to delusions.
6. An excess of light creates illness in the heart.[29]

According to Carpenter, these vaporal elements combine in various ways to create the five flavors (salt, bitter, sour, acid, sweet); the five sounds or notes of the pentatonic scale (*kung, shang, chiao, chih, yü*); and the five colors (red, black, greenish-blue, white, and yellow). Any imbalance among them can cause trouble.

The Taoist nutritional theory was carried a step further by those adepts who believed that, through an intense study of the yin and yang of different foods and medicines, they could confect an elixir of life, the use of which would attain a subtler and more complete balance of these properties and a biological stability tantamount to immortality. Although the varying components of this potion included botanicals such as ginseng and mushrooms, and elements such as gold and mercury (lethal metals that were also a favored part of humoral treatments through at least the eighteenth century in the West), in every Taoist recipe tea, perhaps because the stimulating effects of caffeine conferred feelings of strength and power, invariably topped the list of ingredients in the brew.

The Chinese Tea Ceremony: A Confluence of Buddhist, Taoist, and Confucian Streams

Lao Tzu and his followers regarded tea as a natural agent that, properly used, could help beneficially transform the individual human organism and, as such, was a tool for the advancement of personal salvation. Confucius, who lived at about the same time as Lao Tzu, saw in the ceremonial use of tea a powerful reinforcement of the conventionalized relationships indispensable to an ethical society. Confucius ennobled the ancient Chinese *li*, or "ritual etiquette," into a moral imperative. He taught that, when conjoined with the requisite attitude of sincere respect, conduct guided by decorous ceremony such as ritual tea drinking cultivated the person and allowed him to live harmoniously with his fellows.

The success of Confucius' program demanded attention to the minute or, some might say, trivial aspects of everyday life. *Li* required that every detail of a gentleman's conduct, including "the way his meat was cut or his mat was placed," determined his character, his relation to others, and even his place in the balance of the cosmos. As time went on, this doctrine devolved into fussiness over the details of etiquette, and eventually came to signify little else. As Anderson says, morality, etiquette, and the methods of maintaining social order became blended indistinguishably: "A gentleman's social position and access to luxuries (such as tea) were considered morally justified because he observed etiquette appropriate to his social position."[30] The uses of tea came to exemplify this integration of manners and morals better than any other aspect of Chinese society.

The elaborate preparation of tea fit easily into this way of understanding things, as Lu Yü, over a thousand years after Confucius, was to make clear in his *Classic of Tea*. Typifying the Confucian response to Taoism, Lu Yü's work reflects the affirmation of both Confucian social decorousness and the Taoist cosmic harmonies that were to shape the tea ceremony in later centuries. Anderson says of *The Classic of Tea*, "The passages that emphasize the value of moderation in tea-drinking and lifestyle; close attention to detail, cleanliness, and form; and the careful consideration of the guest's comfort are particularly significant as each point evinces a Confucian regard for *li*."[31]

These were the early cultural precursors to the development of the tea ceremony. But its most immediate sources, as it has come to be practiced for more than a thousand years, were the rituals and beliefs of Ch'an Buddhism. Ch'an, one of the three streams into which the Indian Mahayana Buddhism diverged on entering China, and which was to become the progenitor of Zen Buddhism in Japan, taught that nirvana, Buddhahood, or salvation could be sought through the austere cultivation and emptying of the mind and could be attained in a sudden flash of insight, or Enlightenment. Not surprisingly, all those who proclaimed themselves spiritual descendants of Buddha claimed that their teachings were true to Gautama's Way. But the Ch'an Buddhists were, in this respect, the most authentic. For Buddha himself had rejected the rituals and substantive doctrines of Hinduism, because he rejected attachment to any ritual or any doctrine or indeed to any affection or assertion whatever. Buddha therefore taught no doctrine but instead guided his followers on the Way of salvation from suffering, advising that after the desires for sex, food, glory, money and other worldly lusts had been overcome, our last remaining pernicious attachments are to ideas, the belief that one thing is so and another thing not so. True to the original quest of the Buddha, the Ch'an monks initiated use of the *kung-an*, forerunner of the Zen *koan*, as a way of freeing the mind from what they understood to be the limitations of logic and the intellect. Following Hui-neng (E'no, 638–713), one of Ch'an's founders, who taught that enlightenment could occur at any time or place in ordinary life, Ch'an disciples rejected both scriptural authority and philosophical texts, turning away from orthodox ritual practices. The tea ceremony, in which a commonplace of life attains a kind of mystical, contemplative, and emblematic dimension, became the external embodiment of their religious quest.

The early Ch'an monks who drank tea did so from a single large bowl which they passed around in a circle, as the Sufi devotees were to do in sharing coffee hundreds of years later. This custom is mentioned in *Pai-chang Ch'ing Kuei*, a book of monastery regulations supposedly promulgated by Pai-Ch'ing (sometimes known as Huai-hai, Hyakujo Ekai, or Riku).[32] However, in the earliest recorded example of the Ch'an tea ceremony, the host would present each participant with his own bowl of powdered tea, add hot water, and whip it vigorously. As we will see in chapter 9, this led smoothly into *chado*, or the Way of Tea, and *chanoyu*, or the tea ceremony, in Japan.

The Chinese contributed importantly to the creation of the tea ceremony and incorporated within it symbols from several philosophical systems. However, when compared with what Anderson calls the "full-blown cognitive synthesis later to be realized in Japan,"[33] the Chinese experience can be seen to represent only an early stage of the *chado*'s development. Therefore, although it was in China that the integration of Confucian, Taoist, and Buddhist spirituality in the tea ceremony had its beginning, it was only in Japan, where indigenous Shinto and other influences came into play as well, that the tea ceremony developed into a central transformational device advancing the Buddhist quest for enlightenment.

Teahouses in China date from the thirteenth century, becoming, in the Ming dynasty, important centers of social life. Like coffeehouses in the Islamic world and Europe, they played a large part in the political life of the country—for example, the 1911 revolution was plotted in the back room of a Shanghai teahouse.[34] Again, it was only in Japan, however, after tea's conquest of that country in the seventeenth century, that the teahouse and tea garden, like the tea ceremony, reached their full development.

Europeans, the world's greatest explorers, returned with stories of the Islamic enthusiasm for coffee and coffeehouses within about a hundred years of their inception in the Middle East. However, no travelers returned to Europe from China as witnesses to the days of the Chinese encounter with tea, because none visited there in ancient times. By the time anyone from Europe knew about tea or tea drinking, both the commodity and practice had been familiar in China for at least two thousand years. Therefore, we have no travelers' tales to give us outsiders' impressions of the first ebullient days of tea in China.

Arab traders knew of tea by A.D. 900, but the first references to tea by Europeans (after Polo's) came more than six hundred years later, for it was first named in print in the West in 1559 in a book by a Venetian author celebrated for accounts of adventurous voyages in ancient and modern times. A short time later, in 1567, two Russian travelers brought glowing reports of the plant upon their return from China. It wasn't until the beginning of the seventeenth century, toward the end of the Ming dynasty, that a Dutch ship left Macao with a bale of tea leaves for delivery to Amsterdam, which became the first tea known to have reached the West.

3

cacao

American Origins

The use of the cacao bean is often erroneously thought to have originated with the Maya of Mesoamerica, much as coffee is erroneously thought to have originated with the Arabs and tea with the Chinese. But recent archeological discoveries reveal that the Olmecs (1500 to 400 B.C.), members of the earliest American high civilization, who lived in the fertile coastal Mexican lowlands centuries before the Maya arrived, harvested wild cacao pods that they made into a chocolate drink. They were almost certainly the first to cultivate the tree.

Little is known about the early Olmecs; even the name "Olmec" is applied to them only as a back-formation, as it was what their descendants called themselves, while their true name remains hidden in undeciphered hieroglyphs. The early Maya (1000 B.C. to A.D. 250) became the second people to cultivate cacao, which they began in the Yucatán peninsula. Their cacao plantations, which expanded throughout their dominions, made the Maya very wealthy. After the passing of the Mayan age, in the ninth century A.D., chocolate was drunk by the Toltecs, who flourished from the tenth to the twelfth centuries, and by the Aztecs, whose ascent began in the twelfth century. It was from Aztec hands that the Spanish conquistadors were first served chocolate at the outset of the sixteenth century.

Hemispherical bowl of light brown pottery, made during the Classic Maya period (A.D. 250–900) in Mexico. Originally there were three sunken oval panels with carved bas-reliefs, but one has been destroyed. These were separated by incised columns of glyphs. Each oval panel had a shorter column of glyphs. Of the two surviving reliefs, one shows a figure, probably the god of cacao, seated on a low dais. He points to a pottery jar. The striped oval objects in front of him represent cacao pods, and his curious headdress represents the branches of a cacao tree before harvesting. This is the oldest surviving vessel containing traces of a caffeinated beverage. Compare its date with that of the clay wine jar in the University of Pennsylvania Museum that was found in Iran, with wine residues from about 5500 B.C. Although wine making is more complex than coffee, tea, or chocolate making, Neolithic men made wine, whereas the first direct evidence of caffeine use came at least six thousand years later. (Dumbarton Oaks Research Library and Collections, Washington, D.C.)

Pre-Columbian History of Chocolate

The Maya were the first people of the New World to maintain historical records, although most of their records were lost when conquistadors and missionaries, eager to establish a foothold in the New World, eradicated all the traces of native religion and culture they could find. However, because of their remoteness and the surrounding inhospitable, heavily overgrown terrain, the ruins of some ancient Maya cities remained unknown until the nineteenth century, and, therefore, escaped the systematic destruction by the European invaders. These surviving Maya inscriptions on pots, jade, bones, stones, and palace walls begin to appear around 50 B.C., tracing the history of their royal line from that time until the Spanish conquest. The Maya may have also kept bark-paper books, in which they recorded inventories or recipes, but these would have long since perished in the humid heat of the tropics. The only surviving Classic Maya (A.D. 250–900) records of cacao use are decorated vessels found in the tombs of the powerful. The Maya used cacao beans as currency throughout their domains, and prices were fixed "by the bean," for example, eight to ten for a rabbit, a hundred for a slave, four for a squash. A 1545 Nahuatl document lists an exchange value of one bean for a large tomato, two hundred for a turkey cock, one hundred for a turkey hen, three for a turkey egg, and three for a fish wrapped in maize husks. Combining these price lists with the reports of Alonso de Molina, who published the first Nahuatl-Spanish dictionary in Mexico City in 1571, which reports that the daily wage of a porter in central Mexico was a hundred beans, we can gain some idea of the cost of living for the native population of the time and what an expensive luxury cacao must have been for the average Maya peasant. When the Maya were defeated by their rivals, the Aztecs, sacks of cacao beans were among the items of tribute exacted from them.[1]

In their onslaught, the Maya appropriated Teotihuacan, the New World's greatest pre-Columbian city of the age, which dominated the Valley of Mexico and much of Central America. The Maya warrior merchants assumed control of Teotihuacan's lucrative trade routes, which they maintained until the late seventh century when the Toltecs moved into the Valley of Mexico, gaining the ascendancy that they maintained from the tenth century until the middle of the twelfth. Toltec acolytes carried cacao branches and culminated their rites by sacrificing dogs the color of cacao paste. About 1150 the Toltec capital, Tula, was destroyed, and their power waned.

Stories of the savagery of the early Mesoamericans abound. The Maya who settled in Chichen Itzá, a Yucatán city that became the center of a mixed Maya and Mexican culture, before sacrificing a prisoner to their goddess of sustenance, hospitably served him a cup of thick, cold chocolate, hoping to bring about a literal change of heart. For, once the cup was empty, they believed that the heart, transformed into a cacao pod, would be ripe for cutting from his chest and burning as an offering. The Spanish explorers were impressed with the ceremony attending the growing and harvesting of cacao among the Aztecs, in which many of these primitive components still survived. According to their accounts, this ceremony included human sacrifice, masked dancing, and sexual abstinence relieved by erotic games on the day of the harvest.

The chief deity of the Aztec state religion was the ancient tribal god, Huitzilopochtli, now styled as a sun god and god of victory in war. He had an unquenchable appetite for human hearts. Like Frazier's goddesses of fertility, who demanded the sacrifice of the king each year to secure the rebirth of spring, Huitzilopochtli required daily human sacrifices to ensure the rising of the sun each morning. His requirement in this regard, not an inchoate obsession with death or cruelty, was the reason behind the thousands of such sacrifices that took place each year.

The Aztec religion offered the soldiers and aristocrats other powerful and often terrifying gods, prominent among whom was Tezcatlipoca, the "Smoking Mirror."[2] His chief rival was Quetzalcoatl, the "Feathered Serpent," patron of the priesthood and also worshiped by the common people. The everyday lives of these ordinary Aztecs, including their crops and crafts, were protected by this benign demigod, born to a virgin and a god. He was a kindly, bearded, fair-skinned deity who hailed from the golden land beyond the sunset, and whom they took to be the purveyor of practical knowledge and the ideal of self-sacrifice. Demonstrating striking parallels with Shen Nung, Quetzalcoatl ruled as the Aztec priest-king and taught his people the use of the calendar, how to plant maize, and the art of working gold and silver, and also brought caffeine to the world in the form of the seeds of the cacao tree, which he taught the people to grow and prepare. One account of Aztec beliefs states that Quetzalcoatl, growing old, or having been tricked by another deity into drinking a poison potion that robbed him of divine strength, worried that his unsightly decrepitude would frighten his subjects. He burned his palace and buried his treasures of gold, jade, blood-stones, and rare shells. He then sailed on a raft of snakes to his homeland, where he rules in perpetuity. He promised to return in the year "One Reed," which recurred every fifty-two years on the calendar he had taught the Aztec people to use.[3]

Just as the Muslims had found in coffee a substitute for wine, the Aztecs especially prized chocolate because it gave them a substitute for their traditional native drink, *octli*, the fermented juice of the agave. Although, unlike the Muslims, the Aztecs were not absolutely forbidden to use alcoholic beverages, drunkenness among them was strongly disapproved. The consumption of *octli* was restricted to those of sufficiently mature age, which sometimes meant those old enough to have grandchildren. Public intoxication was not a misdemeanor, as it is in Western societies today, but a capital offense, the most common punishment for which was execution. Not surprisingly, the Aztecs had a large cautionary temperance literature, including many horrific tales about the evils of inebriation. [4]

Because chocolate could serve as a safe alternative to *octli* and offered its own unique stimulating effects, it was highly esteemed by the Aztec aristocracy. They kept the drink largely to themselves, forbidding its use by commoners, including priests. However, because of caffeine's value in the rigors of a military adventure, the Aztec nobility granted an exception for soldiers on campaign and the *pochta*, the hereditary class of merchant-adventurers who fought their way across Mesoamerica to bring exotic trade goods, needed to exalt the king and court, from outlying regions to the capital.

Montezuma II Meets Cortés

Motecuhzoma Ilhuicamina, Montezuma I (1390–1464), seventh king of Mexico, expanded the Aztec empire until a loose confederation of nearly five hundred cities, including those of the Maya and Toltecs, paid tribute to his capital, Tenochtitlán. These conquered cities supplied food and raw materials for Tenochtitlán's growing population. They also provided luxury goods, including gold, feathers, gemstones, amber, jaguar skins, and, of course, cacao, as well as an ample provision of warm bodies for sacrifice to the martial gods of their conquerors. It was Montezuma I who promulgated the law that no one who had not participated in armed conflict, not even the king's son, could affect the trappings and enjoy the privileges of wearing cotton or feathers, smoking tobacco, eating delicacies, or drinking chocolate.[5]

In Montezuma I's time, the Aztecs were capable tenders of their indigenous crops and livestock, although wheat, barley, cattle, horses, and sheep were unknown. The land was communally cultivated and a portion of the yield paid as tax to the central government. In many ways, however, the Aztecs had not advanced beyond the Bronze Age. They had neither wheeled vehicles, nor any machines depending on rotary motion, and had not yet discovered the working of iron and steel. Such European com-monplaces as glass, gunpowder, and alphabetic writing were absent from their culture.

Hernán Cortés (1485–1547), the light-skinned, bearded Spanish conquistador, received one of the warmest welcomes in history when he disembarked in Mexico in

1519, a year that, it so happened, coincided with a recurrence of "One Reed" on the Aztec calendar, the anniversary of the time that Quetzalcoatl, the light-skinned, bearded patron deity of everyday life had promised to return from a realm beyond known lands. The Aztecs had waited expectantly for countless cycles, and the arrival of Cortés and his troops in Tenochtitlán seemed to be a fulfillment of Quetzalcoatl's promise, and Cortés, the merciless conquistador, and Quetzalcoatl, the kindly and beneficent god, became one and the same.

Motecuhzoma Xocoyotzin, Montezuma II (1466–1520), eleventh king of Mexico, grandson of Montezuma I, sat on the Aztec throne in the year Cortés arrived. If we are to believe his own accounts and those of the Spanish conquistadors, Montezuma II had a taste for luxury and the talent and resources to gratify it. His imperial banquets, examples of gastronomic artistry, were reminiscent of the feasts of the early Roman emperors, in that they began with rare birds and exotic fruits imported from the far reaches of his domain. Also as at Roman feasts, performers amused the assembled with singing and dancing. But the final course of the banquet was something that neither Cortés, nor any other European, Asian, or African, ancient or modern, had ever encountered: After ceremonially washing their hands, the respectful serving women would bring *cacahuatl*, a cold, thickly frothing, bitter beverage brewed from roasted cacao beans, seasoned with vanilla or spices, which they proffered in golden goblets to the king. Witnesses vary as to whether the guests and household were also so honored.[6]

According to early and probably exaggerated Spanish accounts, Montezuma downed fifty cups of chocolate daily, including many consumed each time he consorted with his concubines, for what the Spanish erroneously thought was the Aztec belief in chocolate's aphrodisiacal powers. Some Aztecs may have added a fermented corn mash to their chocolate, giving the drink an extra kick, although it is probable that only the nobility and warriors had an opportunity to partake of it. Although they knew nothing of caffeine's and theobromine's physical and mental stimulating powers, the Aztecs were convinced that chocolate imparted both strength and inspiration from Quetzalcoatl, and it was chiefly owing to its pharmacological powers that cacao was highly esteemed.

Fabulous stories, from diverse sources, proliferate surrounding Montezuma II's chocolate consumption. There are Montezuma II's own accounts of the splendor of his court. We also have *The True History of the Conquest of Mexico*, by Bernal Diaz del Castillo (1572), written in Guatemala by the eighty-year-old former comrade of Cortés who seemed to be committed to recording the literal truth, although its trustworthiness is compromised by the fact that his recollections were decades old. In addition, there survive many sycophantic, purple accounts penned by Cortés' admirers, often obviously exaggerated. For example, one writer tells us that more than two thousand pitchers of chocolate were consumed daily in the palace.[7] Others say that Montezuma, like some of the Roman emperors, sent runners to the mountains for snow, which he mixed with chocolate to create a sherbet. Legend even has it that cleaning up after Montezuma's chocolate bouts was a difficult but rewarding job. For as he emptied each golden goblet, he tossed it out the palace window into the lake below.

If we put aside these exaggerated chronicles, the importance of cacao at the time of the conquest remains evident in the *Codex Mendoza*, prepared by an Aztec artist for Antonia de Mendoza, the first Spanish viceroy of Mexico. One of the few surviving contemporary native documents, it celebrates cacao's prominence, illustrating large sacks of beans among precious commodities that included cotton, honey, feathers, and gold, paid by the surrounding tribes to the Aztecs in tribute.[8]

It is nearly certain that cacao seeds were the first caffeinated botanicals to reach Europe in historical times, arriving with Columbus, who, on his return from his fourth trip to the New World in 1502, presented the pods to King Ferdinand of Spain. However, the record contains no indication that the virtues of the plant were known to the Spanish even in the New World until 1528,[9] when Cortés watched the preparation and shared in the consumption of the fortifying drink, *cacahuatl*, at the court of Montezuma II. As Cortés encountered it, chocolate was a bitter brew of crushed, roasted cacao beans, steeped in water, and thickened with corn flour, to which vanilla, spices, and honey were sometimes added. There is no evidentiary basis for the frequent claim that Cortés brought the beans to Spain for the enjoyment of the royal family. However, although he never presented the beans to his sovereign, Cortés was the first to bring news of their use. In an excited letter to King Charles V of Spain, Cortés called chocolate the "drink of the gods," and in so doing ultimately provided the scientific names for both the species, *Theobroma cacao*, and for caffeine's pharmacological cousin, theobromine, responsible for some of chocolate's stimulating powers. Both terms are compounded from Latin roots of the same meanings. During the middle of the sixteenth century, after some unknown Spaniards crossed the Atlantic with the secrets of chocolate making, the Spanish aristocracy immediately adopted the fashion of their Aztec counterparts, and the initiation of caffeine and theobromine into the culture of Europe began. Cortés, who during his previous visits had destroyed his image as a benevolent deity by executing Montezuma and his heir and conquering and looting the Aztec empire, returned to the New World, to establish cacao plantations for Charles V in Haiti, Trinidad, and Fernando Po.

The Origins of the Words "Cacao" and "Chocolate"

"Cacao" and "chocolate" and their cognates are today among the most widely used non-Indo-European words in the world. Surprisingly, no one is certain exactly how or even if the roots of these words are related.

"Cacao" derives from *"kakawa,"* which is thought to have originated as a word in what linguists have recently decided was the Olmec language, a member the Mixe-Zoquean family of languages, the source of many important loan words in later Mesoamerican languages. Although no texts from the period survive, scholars have inferentially assigned *"kakawa"* to the Olmec vocabulary of around 1000 B.C.[10] Sometime between 400 B.C. and A.D. 100, the Maya, the Olmecs' Izapan successors, presumably borrowing from this Olmec word, also began using *"kakawa"* to designate the domesticated cacao plant and the beans harvested from it. ("Cocoa" is simply a corrupt form of "cacao.")

In Guatemala, the original Mayan homeland, in the village of Rio Azul, a well-preserved pottery jar dating from before A.D. 500 and containing cacao residues, found in 1984, bears the Mayan glyphs for *"ka-ka-w(a)."* This is the earliest known inscription of the root of the word "cacao."[11] The first glyph, "ka," represents a comb or feather; the second glyph, also pronounced "ka," represents a fish fin; and the third, "w(a)," is simply the sign for a final "w." This late-fifth-century jar, discovered in a opulent Classic Maya tomb replete with chocolate-drinking paraphernalia, has a stir-rup handle and a screw-on lock-top lid. Its stucco surface is brightly painted to resemble a jaguar, with a half-dozen hieroglyphs, including two that designate cacao.[12] When this jar was submitted to the laboratories of the Hershey Company of Pennsylvania, traces of both caffeine and theobromine were identified within the lid. This Mayan jar contains the oldest caffeinated comestible residues ever discovered.

The importance of cacao to the Indians at the time of the conquest is betrayed in the rich variety of words they used to differentiate its vegetable sources. The Spanish naturalist and physician to Phillip II, Francisco Hernandez (1530–87), was sent to Mexico to discover and catalogue plants with medicinal value. In his work on the plants of the Americas, he lists more than three thousand species and gives their native names. Hernandez mentions four cultivated varieties of the tree:[13] *cuauhcacahuatl*, "wood cacao"; *mecacahuatl*, "maguey cacao"; *xochicacahuatl*, "flower cacao"; and *tlalcacahuatl*, "earth cacao."

As noted above, the English word "chocolate," which designates various preparations of cacao, has an etymologically uncertain relationship to "cacao." It derives from the Spanish usage *"chocolatl,"* which first appeared in the New World sometime after 1650. But no one seems to know how or why the Aztec word for chocolate, *"cacahuatl,"* formed by combining the Mayan *"kakawa"* with the word *"atl,"* meaning water, was replaced by *"chocolatl."* Many reputable reference books derive *"chocolatl"* from a supposed Nahuatl word for the drink that was unrelated to *"kakawa,"* but recent scholarship proves this word does not actually appear in the pre-Columbian sources of the language. Others blame the coinage on Spanish squeamishness over using a word reminiscent of a cant term for excrement, especially as the root "caca" in Latin and the Romance languages is frequently found in combinations that form other words relating to defecation. All we know for certain is that, from wherever it came, *"chocolatl"* quickly spread, replacing the Aztec word for the drink, and became the source of the word for chocolate in most languages today.

Native Methods of Preparing Chocolate

The earliest depiction of chocolate making appears on an eighth-century Late Classic Maya vase, now in the Princeton Art Museum. The vase shows a woman pouring chocolate from a smaller jar into a larger one, a transfer intended to bring up the foam, probably considered the most desirable part of the drink in those days as it certainly was in later Aztec times. Not much is known for certain about the Late Classic Maya recipes, but it appears that they confected a wide variety of both hot and cold drinks and "gruels, porridges, powders, and probably solid substances,"[14] to which were added spices and other flavors. The only spice the Maya added to chocolate that we can identify today with certainty is the chili pepper.

Modern scholarship suggests that the Aztec chocolate drink, which was usually taken cold, was made from beans that had been dried in the sun and fermented in their pods. The beans were then crushed, roasted in clay pots, and ground into paste in a

Late Classic Maya vase (A.D. 672–830), of gray buff clay, about ten inches high and seven inches in diameter, showing a woman pouring chocolate from one vessel to another in a palace setting. This is the earliest depiction of the froth-making process that characterized native preparations of cacao. (The Art Museum, Princeton University, Museum Purchase, gift of the Hans A. Widenmann, class of 1918, and Dorothy Widenmann Foundation)

concave stone called a "metate." It is believed that vanilla and various spices and herbs were added and that maize flour was sometimes used to palliate the bitter taste. The resulting paste was shaped into small wafers or cakes which were left outside to cool and harden in the shade. When ready for use, the finished cakes were crumbled, mixed with hot water, and stirred rapidly with tortoiseshell spoons. Here is one of the earliest surviving European accounts of native methods of making chocolate from cacao beans, published in 1556 by a man identified only as having recently returned to Venice from an American expedition in the company of Cortés, in which he praises the fortifying power of the drink:

These seeds which are called almonds or cacao are ground and made into powder, and other small seeds are ground, and this powder is put into certain basins . . .
and they put water on it and mix it with a spoon. And after having mixed it very well,
they change it from one basin to another, so that a foam is raised which they put in a
vessel made for the purpose. And when they wish to drink it, they mix it with certain
small spoons of gold or silver or wood, and drink it, and drinking it one must open
one's mouth, because being foam one must give it room to subside, and go down bit
by bit. This drink is the healthiest thing, and the greatest sustenance of anything you
could drink in the world, because he who drinks a cup of this liquid, no matter how
far he walks, can go a whole day without eating anything else.[15]

Thomas Gage, in *New Survey of the West Indies* (1648), an important source of
information about the Mayas in their post-Columbian twilight, describes the typical
Indian methods of preparing and consuming the drink as he encountered them a
century later:

The manner of drinking it is diverse. . . . But the most ordinary way is to warme
the water very hot, and then to poure out half the cup full that you mean to drink; and
to put into it a tablet [hardened spoonful of chocolate paste] or two, or as much as will
thicken reasonably the water, and then grinde it well with the Molinet, and when it
is well ground and risen to a scumme, to fill the cup with hot water, and so drink it
by sups (having sweetened it with sugar) and to eat it with a little conserve or maple
bred, steeped into the chocolatte.[16]

Gage assumes that the use of the moliné, or stirring rod with which the liquid was
beaten to a frothy consistency, and the use of sugar were native practices. However, in
light of information from other sources, we must assume that both practices had, by
the middle of the seventeenth century, been widely adopted in America in imitation
of early Spanish innovators. Compounding his error about the moliné, Gage adds to
the etymological confusion over the origin of the word "chocolate" by providing his
own factitious but widely quoted onomatopoetic account that word was born when
the "choco choco choco" sound of the whipping moliné was combined with the
Nahuatl word for water.

Despite the new popularity of hot chocolate among the Maya, the old Maya
custom of consuming chocolate thick and cold seems to have survived until Gage's
time, at least at religious or civic festivals. As he observed:

There is another way yet to drink chocolatte, which is cold, which the Indians at
feasts to refresh themselves, and it is made after this manner: The chocolatte (which
is made with none, or very few, ingredients) being dissolved in cold water with the
Molinet, they take off the scumme or crassy part, which riseth in great quantity,
especially when the cacao is older and putrefied. The scumme they lay aside in a
little dish by itself, and then put sugar into that part from whence was taken the
scumme, and then powre it from on high into the scumme, and so drink it cold.[17]

PART 2

europe wakes
up to caffeine

monks and men-at-arms

Europe's First Caffeine Connections

> The main benefit of this cacao is a beverage which they make called Chocolate, which is a crazy thing valued in that country. It disgusts those who are not used to it . . . [but] is a valued drink which the Indians offer to the lords who come or pass through their land. And the Spanish men—and even more the Spanish women—are addicted to the black chocolate.
>
> —José de Acosta, S.J., commenting on chocolate use in Mexico, *Natural and Moral History*, 1590

In 1502, on his fourth voyage across the Atlantic, Columbus overshot Jamaica and anchored at Guanaja, one of what are today called the Bay Islands, thirty miles off the Honduran coast. While stopping among the Maya villagers, he became the first European on record to have encountered cacao beans. On August 15, Columbus was among the members of a scouting party dispatched from the Spanish ships that encountered two 150-foot canoes propelled by slaves tied to their stations by their necks. One of these great boats, which resembled Venetian gondolas, was captured without incident. It turned out to be filled with trading goods, including cotton clothing, stone axes, and copper bells from the Yucatán Peninsula and carried women and children under a shelter of palm leaves. A description of the meeting was recorded in a 1503 Spanish account, written in Jamaica by Columbus' son, Ferdinand, and finally published, in a corrupt Italian edition, seventy years later, in Venice:

> For their provisions they had such roots and grains as are eaten in Hispaniola . . . , and many of those almonds which in New Spain [Mexico] are used for money. They seemed to hold these almonds at a great price; for when they were brought on board ship together with their goods, I observed that when any of these almonds fell, they all stooped to pick it up, as if an eye had fallen.[1]

What he called "almonds" were actually cacao beans. Columbus' party was impressed

This late-seventeenth-century French engraving features the artist's conception of an Aztec in feathered regalia, armed with bow and arrow and feathered club, and illustrates a pot for making chocolate, the moliné used for stirring the froth, and the two-handled goblet from which the chocolate was enjoyed. (The Library Company of Philadelphia)

by the high value placed on the beans by the natives; but because they had no translator, they failed to discover cacao's use in making chocolate. Nevertheless, Columbus brought back some of the pods for King Ferdinand of Spain, and these were the first caffeinated botanicals known to have reached Europe.

As we have seen, although Cortés delighted to find in cacao an agent that could stimulate and fortify his soldiers and recommended cultivation of the plant to the young Charles V of Spain, the stories attributing to Cortés the actual delivery of beans to Spain or the preparation of chocolate in Spain have no historical basis. The inventory of Cortés' American booty, supplied to the king to document the payment of the crown's share, never mentions cacao. Nor was cacao among the novelties exhibited to the king in 1528 by the returning Cortés, including Europe's first bouncing rubber ball, a menagerie complete with jaguars and armadillos, and miscellaneous noblemen and human oddities from the New World.

No one knows, or is likely ever to know, which of the myriad commercial, military, or religious Spanish enterprises first brought the beverage to the court. However, chocolate's earliest documented appearance in Spain came in 1544, when a delegation of Dominican friars transported a group of Maya dignitaries to meet Prince Philip (later Philip II), son of Charles V. The visiting Americans carried rich gifts for Philip, among them vessels filled with chocolate. In 1585, the first recorded commercial shipment of cacao beans reached Seville.

Chocolate Consumes the Spanish Court

Charles V, His Most Catholic Majesty, is credited with achieving the happy admixture of chocolate and sugar, a confection that yielded a drink not only palatable but delicious to Europeans. Cane sugar, imported from the Orient at great cost, had already become available in Europe by the time cacao arrived, and the king blended the two to make a fabulously expensive drink that became a rage at the Spanish court. The cacao paste was also often mixed with vanilla and sometimes with rose water or cinnamon, nutmeg, almonds, pistachios, or even musk, cloves, allspice, or aniseed. Chocolate was enjoyed cold and thick at first, just as it had been by the Aztecs, but within a few years an unknown Spaniard thought up the idea of serving it hot, and a whole new tradition, restoring a more ancient preference of the Maya in this respect, began. Chocolate was thereafter served from a pot, similar to the coffeepot but with the addition of the moliné, a stick for stirring and mixing. The cups into which the chocolate was poured were taller and slimmer than those for coffee or tea, and from their shapes it is possible to determine which of these beverages is being consumed in paintings of the period.

Chocolate, which relies for its analeptic effect on a combination of small amounts of caffeine and larger amounts of the much weaker methylxanthine theobromine, is not as electrifying as coffee in the way these drinks are commonly prepared today. However, the early European chocolateers, like their Aztec and Maya predecessors, cooked their chocolate strong and thick. This chocolate was undoubtedly a powerful stimulant, as well as a nutritious and filling drink; we know that its flavor was strong enough to hide a variety of poisons and that it became the medium of choice throughout Europe for dispatching inconvenient persons until at least the time of the French Revolution. The crumbly coarse paste from which it was prepared contained carbohydrates and a large proportion of easily digested fats, protein, and minerals, making it an excellent concentrated high-energy food. This was the special reason that chocolate was so readily taken up by the Catholics of the time and became popular as a clerical resort during fasting. It was only later that chocolate became fashionable among the aristocracy, for whom it served, as many paintings of the period show, as a drink to accompany the start of a leisurely morning.

During most of the sixteenth century, chocolate and the stimulating effects of its caffeine remained a cherished Spanish secret. The Spanish monks enjoyed a de facto monopoly in cacao, and they busied themselves perfecting methods of roasting the beans, brought from Mexico and plantations established in the West Indies and on the African coast. They would grind and shape the hot cacao paste into rods or wafers, leaving them to dry at room temperature, and sell them to aristocratic patrons. Wherever the story of caffeine takes us, we usually find those who have taken religious vows nearby. The Jesuits widely cultivated maté in Paraguay; and the Spanish monks, who took to drinking hot chocolate regularly, became some of their own best customers and were among its most ardent promoters. Also to the Spanish clergy—in this instance, nuns serving in Mexican cloisters—seems to belong the honor of having been the first Europeans to make hard chocolate, a skill they probably learned from native American examples. These nuns are said to have made a great deal of money selling it in confections for the European aristocracy. Most Spaniards who could afford to indulge were caught up in the fad for the new drink, at a time when few other European nationals had even had an opportunity to try it or any other caffeinated product. During this period, Dutch and English raiders who captured Spanish galleons would jettison cacao beans shipped from the growing numbers of Spanish plantations in South America, for they were unaware of the crop's value as a luxury trade item.

But caffeine secrets are hard to keep, and it was inevitable that the Spanish secret of chocolate, like the Chinese secret of tea and the Islamic secret of coffee, would soon be revealed. For one thing, by the early seventeenth century, Spain had become the center of European fashion and society, and travelers from all over the Continent assembled in Madrid to learn the latest trends. For another, the Spanish monks taught the habit of drinking hot chocolate to their visiting brothers from abroad, who took it home with them. There, among the brothers and laity, it was touted as good tasting and productive of many health benefits and was warmly received.

Cacao Goes to Italy, France, Holland, England, Austria, Switzerland, and Returns Across the Atlantic

Italy was the second European nation where chocolate became popular. In 1606 Antonio Carletti returned from a visit to Spain with the latest recipe for the drink, and his countrymen quickly became avid users. By 1662 its popularity was so great that its use had become a religious issue. The Roman cardinal Brancaccio was called upon to decide whether chocolate offered so much nourishment and sensual satisfaction that its consumption during Lent was unlawful. As Pope Clement VIII had done in 1600 when ruling on coffee, Brancaccio came down on the side of chocolate, stating, "*Liquidum non frangit jejunum*," which means, "Liquids do not break the fast."[2] This ruling confirmed a use of chocolate that had already made it a popular commodity throughout the Catholic world, for it was highly regarded for sustaining the devoted with nourishment and energy during their fasts.[3]

France, the third nation to take up the chocolate craze, was introduced to the drink by Spanish Jews who settled near Bayonne in the sixteenth century;[4] however, the use of chocolate remained confined to that city, until enjoying a second, royal introduction in 1615. In that year, when each was fourteen, Anne of Austria (actually a Spanish princess) married Louis XIII, bringing in her dowry lavish gifts of cacao cakes, of the sort that would be crumbled and mixed with hot water and sugar for drinking. Thus the French court was initiated to a new luxury. Although the aristocrats embraced Anne's gift slowly, by the time of Anne's regency, after Louis' death in 1643, the most coveted invitation in Paris became "to the chocolate of her Royal Highness."[5] Cardinal de Richelieu, her husband's tutor, credited chocolate with instilling his remarkable energy, which he applied to duties of state and by virtue of which he had secured for his sovereign the absolute power that would soon descend to the king's son, Louis XIV. (Supposedly Richelieu learned to drink chocolate from his brother Alphonse de Richelieu [1634–80], one of its earliest French adopters, who used the drink as a remedy for his ailing spleen.)[6] We do not know if the Sun King recognized this debt to the cacao bean; but it was under his rule and after his marriage to the Spanish princess Maria Theresa in 1660 that chocolate became abidingly popular among the upper classes. It remained in France, as in Spain, an expensive indulgence accessible only to the aristocracy.

Holland was modern Europe's first republic, and, accordingly, in that country there emerged a pattern of chocolate usage different from that which prevailed in the monarchies. Once the use of the beans was understood, Dutch merchants imported them in great quantities, and the drink of the gods was available to the middle classes. After Holland won her freedom from Spain in the beginning of the seventeenth century, the Dutch began to compete with the Spanish on the lucrative sea routes. Amsterdam quickly became the most important cacao port outside of Spain. Still, today, about 20 percent of the world's cacao beans pass through Amsterdam, and Holland is the world's largest exporter of cacao powder, cacao butter, and chocolate.

From Amsterdam, chocolate went to Germany and Scandinavia and crossed the Alps to enter northern Italy, where the Italian chocolate masters created recipes that became popular all over the Continent. Austria imported her chocolate directly from Spain, and only in Austria did chocolate become what could be called a national drink. It may have achieved such general popularity because King Charles VI, unlike other monarchs of his day, kept tariffs on the product low. Chocolate producers in Vienna, who prepared a dozen varieties of chocolate as medicines and beverages, formed a powerful trade organization to establish their interests. An oil painting by Jean-Etienne Liotarda, a Swiss painter working in Austria, called *La Belle Chocolatière* (1743), which depicts a chambermaid bearing the artist's breakfast drink, is the first known example of chocolate featured in the European visual arts outside of Spain.

It has been claimed, on little or no evidence, that chocolate had been introduced to England in 1520, in the reign of Henry VIII,[7] but that the drink made no progress there for more than a hundred years. The first printed mention of cacao in English occurs in *Decades W. Indies* (London, 1555) by Richard Eden (1521–76) almost half a century before either coffee or tea had been named in print: "In the steade [of money] the halfe shelles of almonds, whiche kinde of Barbarous money they [the Mexicans] caule cocoa or cacanguate." Another early English reference occurs in 1594 in the works of Thomas Blundevil(le) (1561–1602), who specialized in writing about equestrianism: "Fruit, which the inhabitants cal[l] in their tongue, cacaco, it is like to an Almond . . . of it they make a certaine drinke which they love marvellous well."[8]

We know from these references and others that the English were becoming increasingly familiar with chocolate over the next fifty years. In 1648, Thomas Gage, the Dominican who had traveled throughout the New World, told his countrymen, in *New Survey of the West Indies*, with the air of imparting a traveler's oddity, that, among the natives, "All rich or poor, loved to drink plain chocolate without sugar or other ingredients," presupposing that his readers expected chocolate to be mixed with these things.[9]

In 1655, during Cromwell's Protectorate, England acquired some flourishing cacao plantations, which were to become her main sources for the bean, when she wrested Jamaica from Spanish control. In London, in 1657, an expatriate Parisian shopkeeper, proprietor of the city's first chocolate house, advertised in the *Public Adviser*, "In Bishopgate Street, in Queen's Head Alley, at a Frenchman's house, is an excellent West India drink called chocolate, to be sold, where you may have it ready at any time, and also unmade at reasonable rates."[10]

In contrast with Spain and France, where both coffee and cacao were initially trappings of the aristocracy, in England, as in Holland, both were sold to the public in shops almost from the start, to consume there or take out, although at ten to fifteen shillings a pound, these earliest "reasonable rates" were so high that only the prosperous could afford to partake frequently.

Thus, within only five years after London's first coffeehouse brewed its first cup of coffee in the mid-1660s, competition had arisen from another caffeinated beverage. From about 1675 to 1725 chocolate drinking in coffeehouses was very common, but by 1750 the practice had dwindled to an oddity. Samuel Pepys, who is often associated with the early coffeehouse life of the city, first tried chocolate in 1662 and adopted it, not coffee, as his "morning draft." The oldest surviving English chocolate pot, specially designed to serve hot chocolate, was made by silversmith George Garthorne in 1685. The chocolate pot was similar in design to the coffeepot, but featured a hole in its hinged finial through which the Spanish moliné, then called a "mill," was inserted.

Two upscale chocolate houses, White's and the Cocoa Tree, were established in the 1690s. Schivelbusch, in *Tastes of Paradise*, says that these chocolate houses had a culture of their own, readily distinguishable from the coffeehouses, which he describes as bourgeois and puritanical. The chocolate houses or chocolate parlors, in contrast, were "meeting places for an odd mixture of aristocracy and demimonde, what Marx would later refer to as the *bohème*; in any case, they were thoroughly antipuritanical, perhaps even bordello-like places."[11]

The English experimented with methods of preparing chocolate, concocting a caudle, or warm spiced gruel, mixed with egg yolk and wine, of the sort then commonly served to invalids or women lying in, surely one of the least appealing ways ever devised for consuming methylxanthines. By about 1730, they had improved the drink by introducing milk in place of or mixed with water.

In England, as elsewhere, tariffs played a major part in determining which of the caffeinated beverages was most used at different times. The alternating vogues, first for coffee, then for tea, and in the rise and fall of chocolate consumption, can be charted from the rising and falling import duties from the seventeenth through the nineteenth centuries. It was not until the mid-nineteenth century, when the English duty dropped to a penny a pound, that chocolate attained the general use it enjoys there to this day.

From Liquid to Solid: Eating Chocolate Comes of Age

The biggest breakthrough in cacao-processing technology came in 1828, when a Dutch chemist, Coenraad J. Van Houten, patented a press that removed most of the bitter fat, which accounts for more than half the weight, from the ground, roasted beans. He also developed the process of alkalization, still called the "Dutch process," to neutralize acids and make the resulting powder more soluble in water. Through the use of Van Houten's invention, two distinct products were produced: a hard cacao cake and cacao butter. The cake was ground into a soluble powder, from which most of the bitterness of the original cacao had been removed along with the fat, and which became very popular as a flavoring. Previously, bakers had been unable to concoct appealing chocolate-flavored pastries because of cacao's bitterness and graininess. The famous Viennese Sacher Torte, first served in 1832, could not have been prepared before Van Houten.[12] Cocoa butter, the other product of the Van Houten process, was the basis of chocolate for eating so familiar to us today. One of the first to produce it was Fry and Sons, of Bristol, who made chocolate bars in 1847. During this time, *Lancet*, the leading British medical journal, published its analysis of fifty brands of commercial cacao, finding that 90 percent were adulterated with starch fillers or, horrible to contemplate, brick dust and toxic red lead pigment. Cadbury's stood out as selling a pure product. The most important remaining innovations in chocolate technology were accomplished in Switzerland, when Henri Nestlé invented condensed milk and joined forces with Daniel Peter in 1875 to create the world's first milk chocolate. Also in Switzerland at this time, Rudolph Lindt devised "conching," a process by which granite rollers were applied to cacao paste in shell-shaped containers to improve its fineness and homogeneity.

These refinements in processing engendered a complex and sometimes confusing lexicon of terms. The plant (*Theobroma cacao*) and unprocessed parts of it are called "cacao." "Chocolate" is a dried paste pressed from the bitter powder of the ground, roasted beans, called "cacao beans" or "cocoa beans," or the drink made by crumbling this paste and stirring it into hot water. "Cacao powder" or "cocoa powder" is chocolate with most of its bitter fat removed by further pressing, sometimes processed to increase its solubility. "Chocolate liquor" (so called because it starts as a liquid), and "chocolate matter" or "baking chocolate," a thick, dark paste, are by-products of pressing. "Eating chocolate" is cacao powder mixed with sugar and with "cacao butter" or "cocoa butter," a light-colored fat that is another by-product of pressing. "Milk chocolate" is eating chocolate with dried milk added.

Consumption has increased more than tenfold since the turn of the twentieth century, commercial cacao cultivation having spread around the world in a belt within twenty degrees of the equator and the varieties of chocolate-flavored confections having proliferated wildly. However, unlike coffee and tea, which, after reaching Europe, were embraced equally by peoples of every continent, the love of chocolate is still developing in Africa and never took hold in the Far East. Even today, it takes a thousand Japanese to eat as many chocolate bars as a typical Englishman in a year.

Considering their American provenance, cacao beans came surprisingly late and by a surprisingly circuitous route to North America, where they were first sold by a Boston apothecary in 1712, having been imported, oddly enough, from England, to which they had earlier been shipped from the West Indies. For many years, only pharmacists sold cacao in the New World colonies, and they used it as an ingredient in their compounded medicines, or "confections." As with coffee and tea in their early days in Europe, chocolate in the colonies was consumed for its medicinal value and did not immediately achieve its English currency as a tasty and stimulating treat. It was only in 1755 that imports to North America directly from the West Indies were initiated. In 1765, John Hannon, an Irish immigrant, turned an old mill into the first cacao factory in North America.[13] Nearly one hundred and fifty years had passed since cacao's arrival in Europe before cacao came home to the northern part of the hemisphere from which it originated. Once it had done so, it became extremely popular. Milton Snavely Hershey, a veteran sugar candy and caramel maker, bought the German chocolate-manufacturing machinery that he saw exhibited at the 1893 Chicago Exposition and sold his first chocolate bar in 1894. In the ensuing half-century, "Hershey bar" became almost a generic name for any chocolate candy bar. In the venerable tradition of using caffeinated seeds and nuts as the basis of high-energy foods, the United States issued chocolates as rations to American soldiers during World War II.

5

the caffeine trade supplants the spice trade
Tea and Coffee Come to the West

After Marco Polo returned to tell tales of his travels in Cathay (1275–94), Venice, increasingly a center of trade and a crossroads for traffic from the East, grew eager to learn more of strange peoples and their strange goods. However, vividly detailed and inclusive as it was, Marco Polo's book does not mention tea, save in connection with the imperial tax that was levied on its use, reporting that, in 1285, a Chinese minister of finance promulgated an arbitrary increase. Polo failed to say more about tea because, from the standpoint of a visitor to the Mongol court of the Khan, tea was an inconsequential predilection of the subject native Chinese population.

Tea was described, however, in later Venetian travelers' accounts. After Polo, it was first named in print in the West in 1559 as "*Chai Catai*," or the "tea of China," in the posthumous publication *Navigatione et Viaggi*, or *Voyages and Travels*, by Giambattista Ramusio (1485–1557), a Venetian author celebrated for accounts of voyages in ancient and modern times. While abroad, Ramusio heard about tea from Hajji Mahommed (or Chaggi Memet), a Persian caravan merchant. After this early notice in Venice, tea was not mentioned again in any known Italian book until 1588, when a 1565 letter of the Florentine Father Almeida was published by the famous author Giovanni Maffei as part of his voluminous collection of traveler's papers, *Four Books of Selected Letters from India* (Florence).

Early Portuguese Explorers Encounter Tea

At the same time that the Venetian travelers were making their way back and forth overland to the East in furtherance of the ancient spice trade, the Portuguese explorers, excited by the example of Columbus, were searching for new ways to get to new places. In 1497 Vasco da Gama discovered a sea route to the Indies by way of the Cape of Good Hope. In consequence, the Portuguese were able to expand their explorations eastward, relying on superior armaments to displace the Arab seamen who until then

Chinois auec son pot de Thé

Engraving from Dufour's 1685 treatise on coffee, tea, and chocolate. This French engraving features a contemporary European impression of a Chinese man with his pot of tea and the porcelain cup and saucer in which the tea was served. (The Library Company of Philadelphia)

had controlled the exotic trade from India and beyond. They founded a settlement at Malacca on the Malay peninsula. Sailing from Malacca in 1516, the Portuguese became the first Europeans to reach China by sea, where they found favorable opportunities for trade. To make the most of these rich markets, a fleet was soon dispatched to the commercial ports, and an ambassador was sent to Peking. By 1540 the Portuguese had even reached Japan. Finally, as a result of diplomatic persuasions, in

1557 the Chinese allowed them to settle and erect a trading post at Macao, near the estuary of the Canton River (now called the Pearl River).

The Portuguese traders and the Portuguese Jesuit priests, who like Jesuits of every nation busied themselves with the affairs of caffeine, wrote frequently and favorably to compatriots in Europe about tea. Strangely enough, there is no record of their sending tea shipments from the East for the enjoyment of their countrymen. In 1556, Father Gasper Da Cruz, a missionary, became the first to preach Catholicism in China; when he returned home in 1560, he wrote and published the first mention of tea in Portuguese, "a drink called *ch'a*, which is somewhat bitter, red, and medicinall."[1] Another Portuguese cleric, Father Alvaro Semedo, in 1633 wrote an early account of the tea plant and the preparation of the beverage in his book about China, *Relatione della Grande Monarchia della Cina* (1643). He mentions the custom, initiated at the Han Pass by Yin Hsi, of offering tea to guests, and explains that when it is offered for the third time, it is time for the guest to move along.

The adventurous Portuguese, though they charted new sea routes for trade around the world, and whose people were the first to enjoy the new influx of spices, silks, and other amenities, failed to participate in the early movement of caffeinated commodities to Europe. Oddly, they were soon to play a seminal role in the tea enthusiasm of England, through the agency of the Portuguese infanta Catherine of Braganza. Her story, as the bringer of many exotic luxuries to her somewhat unsophisticated adopted homeland, when she became the wife of King Charles II, we tell in a later chapter.

For a few decades, the Portuguese faced no competition on the sea routes from the other European powers. England dreamed the impossible dream of sailing across the Atlantic to find a northern sea route to correspond with Magellan's southern one, while the Swedes and Danes fancied they could discover a similar northern sea route eastward to China. The Germans, weighted down by domestic political conflicts, never even set sail.

However, by closing their trading settlements to rival nations, the Portuguese virtually compelled the English, Dutch, Swedes, Danes, and others to seek out genuine trade opportunities for themselves. In addition to providing stimulus to the Dutch enterprise occasioned by example and exclusion, the Portuguese helped to bring word of tea to their Dutch competitors through the accounts of Jan Hugo van Linschoten (1563–1611), a Dutch navigator and intrepid traveler, who sailed with the Portuguese fleet. In his *Linschoten's Travels* (1595), which was translated into English and published in London in 1598, this redoubtable man penned some of the earliest European descriptions of tea and tea drinking, as he met with them in Japan:

> Their manner of eating and drinking is: everie man hath a table alone, without table-clothes or napkins, and eateth with two pieces of wood like the men Chino: they drinke wine of Rice, wherewith they drink themselves drunke, and after their meat they use a certain drinke, which is a pot with hote water, which they drinke as hot as ever they may indure, whether it be Winter or Summer. . . . the aforesaid warme water is made with the powder of a certaine hearbe called *Chaa*, which is much esteemed, and is well accounted among them.[2]

Here we find some of the trappings Europeans still associate with Japan, including saki and chopsticks. As a result of this information and the interest it engendered in Lin Schoten's countrymen, the introduction of tea to Europe became the work of the Dutch, the great trading rivals of the Portuguese. In the beginning of the seventeenth century, a Dutch ship, sailing from Macao to the port of Amsterdam, brought the first bale of green tea leaves to the Continent. In 1641, the Dutch captured Malacca from the Portuguese and signed a ten-year truce at The Hague ratifying their conquest. The Dutch became the only Europeans allowed to trade in Japan until 1853.

Early Ports of Arrival for Coffee and Tea: Venice, Marseilles, Amsterdam

Before the international trade in coffee began, private persons had brought small quantities of coffee beans into Europe. In 1596, Charles de l'Écluse (*Lat.* Carolus Clusius) (1524–1609), a French-Dutch physician and botanist, received from an Italian correspondent what were probably the first beans to cross the Alps.[3] Within the next decade, Pieter van dan Broeck brought the first beans from Mocha to Holland. But Siegmund Wurffbain (1613–61), a German merchant-traveler, became the first to sell Mocha beans there commercially in 1640. Regular imports to Holland from the Yemen began only in 1663. It is reported that Pasqua Rosée, known to have opened the first coffeehouse in London in 1652, sold coffee publicly in Holland in 1664. Shortly thereafter, the first Dutch coffeehouse was opened in The Hague, and others soon appeared in Amsterdam and Haarlem. The first commercial shipment of Java coffee from the Dutch East Indian plantations, amounting to less than a thousand pounds, did not arrive in Amsterdam until 1711.

The Dutch East India Company, chartered in 1602, investigated the possibility of importing coffee to Holland from the port of Aden in the Yemen as early as 1614, but failed to do so. Venice and Marseilles, from vantages convenient to the Mediterranean, were the first ports to receive commercially imported coffee from Arabia. The first major cargo of coffee beans was shipped into Venice in 1624, most likely having entered the stream of commerce as part of the spice trade from Constantinople, which included silks, perfumes, dyes, and other exotic items. Around 1650 several Marseilles merchants began bringing coffee home from the Levant. Within a few years, a syndicate of pharmacists and merchants instituted commercial imports from Egypt and were soon followed in this business by their counterparts in Lyon. Coffee use became common in those parts of France. In 1671 a coffeehouse opened in Marseilles near the city market, the success of which prompted many imitators, while private use continued to increase.

The sea lanes charted by the Portuguese were quickly overrun with Dutch fleets, and Portugal and Holland began contesting for supremacy in the sea lanes to the East. By 1700, it was clear that the Dutch were the new masters of this burgeoning ocean-going trade around the world. But the story of caffeine in Europe could not expand further, until this explosion of sea trade in the seventeenth and the early eighteenth centuries was combined with international cultivation to make coffee, tea, and cacao available at a popular price.

Engraving from Dufour's 1685 book. This two-paneled engraving shows the coffee plant and roasted beans and early Middle Eastern coffee appurtenances. (Department of Special Collections, University of Pennsylvania)

As Dutch tea imports grew, far exceeding the value of the coffee imports of their French predecessors, Holland became Europe's first major caffeine connection. In around 1640 in The Hague, the use of tea began to spread as a fashionable and costly luxury, and the beverage was introduced to Germany from Holland by around 1650 and was regularly traded there, appearing on the price lists of apothecaries by 1657. Tea came to Paris in 1648, where it enjoyed a brief fad, as coffee was to do twenty years later. As Thomas Macaulay was the first to notice in print, "tea went through a phase of extreme fissionability there while it was still hardly known in Britain."[4] Gui Patin (1602–72), a Paris physician and writer, called it *"nouveauté impertinenté du siècle,"* or "impertinent novelty of the century," in a letter in which he denounced the recent treatise by Dr. Philibert Morisset, *Ergo Thea Chinesium, Menti Confert* (Paris, 1648), or *Does Chinese Tea Increase Mentality?*, that, having praised tea as a panacea, was so ridiculed by other medical men that no other doctors in Paris took up the defense of tea for many years.[5] Despite the admonitions of most physicians, the public entertained a growing appetite for the drink. According to Father Alexander de Rhodes, in 1653 the tea drinkers of Paris were paying high prices for Dutch tea of poor quality:

> The Dutch bring tea from China to Paris and sell it at thirty francs a pound, though they have paid but eight and ten sous in that country, and it is old and spoiled into the bargain. People must regard it as a precious medicament; it not only does positively cure nervous headache, but it is a sovereign remedy for gravel and gout.[6]

Cardinal Jules Mazaran (*Lat.* Giulio Mazzarino) (1602–61), a French-Italian cleric and statesman, used tea to relieve his gout. By 1685 tea had become popular among the French literati. Jean Racine (1639–99) grew enamored of tea in his old age, using it as his breakfast drink. As usual in matters pertaining to caffeine, the clergy were leading participants in the literary celebration of the drink. In 1709, the bishop of Avranches, Pierre Daniel Huet (1630–1721), published *Poemata*, which included the Latin elegy "*Thea, elegia,*" a fifty-eight-stanza encomium of tea. After explaining that tea was planted by Phoebus Apollo in his "eastern gardens," and watered by "Aurora's dew," he plays on the meaning of the Greek word "*thea,*" or "goddess," and lists the divine gifts that were presented to the young plant. These gifts presaged the marvelous mood-elevating, health-instilling, revitalizing, and intellectually and artistically stimulating powers of the new beverage:

> Comus brought joyfulness, Mars gave high spirits,
> And thou, Coronide, doest make the draught healthful.
> Hebe, thou bearest a delay to wrinkles and old age.
> Mercurius has bestowed the brilliance of his active mind.
> The muses have contributed lively song.[7]

Despite this early flurry of interest in Paris, the predilection for tea abated and, as noted by Pierre Pomet (1658–99), "chief druggist" to Louis XIV and author of *Histoire generale des drogues* (which appeared in English translation as *A Compleat History of DRUGGS*), was succeeded within fifty years by a taste for coffee and chocolate.

It has never revived since. Tea remained available at great expense from apothecaries, as shown in Pomet's 1694 price list, which offered Chinese tea at seventy francs a pound and Japanese tea at one hundred and fifty to two hundred francs a pound.

Though the British East India Company had been chartered in 1600, none of the British merchantmen brought back samples of tea (or coffee either) in the early years. On June 27, 1615, R. Wickam, the company's agent in Hirado, Japan, made one of the earliest known mentions of tea by an Englishman, in a letter to a man named Eaton who was the agent in Macao. The reference is part of a list of desiderata that presupposes his correspondent's familiarity with the leaf: "Mr. Eaton I pray you buy for me a pot of the best sort of chaw in Meaco, 2 Fairebowes and Arrowes, some half a dozen Meaco guilt boxes square for to put into bark and whatsoever they cost you I will be alsoe willinge acoumptable unto for them."[8] It was not until 1664 that there is any record in the British East India Company's books respecting a purchase of tea, and that of a shipment of only two pounds and two ounces of "good thea" for a promotional presentation to King Charles II, so that he would not feel "wholly neglected by the Company."

From this time forward, the Dutch faced a rival in the English, as their competing East India Companies each promoted the sale of its tea and coffee imports throughout Europe. The Dutch took the major step of introducing the coffee plant to Java in 1688, and as a result that island became one of the world's leading fine coffee producers, giving rise to the epithet "Java" as an enduring nickname for coffee. However, despite Dutch commercial successes, their largely craft-based society failed to grow into a modern industrial economy that could successfully compete in the long run with the one that was to develop in England.

Between 1652 and 1674, there were three largely indecisive wars between the Dutch and English that grew out of their trading rivalry. After 1700, the brief, celebrated Dutch leadership in international trade, science, technology, and the arts increasingly fell into decline, and their fourth and final conflict, fought from 1780 to 1784, ended disastrously for Dutch sea and colonial power. On December 31, 1795, the Dutch East India Company was dissolved, and the triumph of the British East India Company was complete.

Coffee, as well as tea, was both promoted and denounced by Dutch physicians of the time, while the popularity of both drinks continued to increase among all classes. In 1724, the Dutchman Dominie Francois Valentyn wrote of coffee that "its use has become so common in our country that unless the maids and seamstresses have their coffee every morning, the thread will not go through the eye of the needle." He goes on to blame the English for what he regarded as the deleterious invention of the coffee break, which he calls "elevenses," after the hour of morning in which it was taken. In the years 1734–85, Dutch imports of tea quadrupled, to finally exceed 3.5 million pounds yearly, and tea became Holland's most valuable import.

Caffeine Gets the Pope's Blessing: Acceptance in Italy

According to one story, the encounter between Pope Clement VIII (1535–1605) and caffeine was a fateful one, in which the future of caffeine and perhaps of the pope's infallible authority (because, despite many decrees by sultans and kings, none banning a caffeinated beverage had lasted long) in much of Europe may well have hung in the balance.

Trade in coffee in Italy before the turn of the seventeenth century was confined to the avant-garde, such as the students, faculty, and visitors at the University of Padua. Whether as a result of the petitions of fearful wine merchants or in consequence of the appeals of reactionary priests, Pope Clement VIII, in the year 1600, was prevailed upon to pass judgment on the new indulgence, a sample of which was brought to him by a Venetian merchant. Agreeing on this point with their Islamic counterparts, conservative Catholic clerical opponents of coffee argued that its use constituted a breach of religious law. They asserted that the devil, who had forbidden sacramental wine to the infidel, had also, for his further spiritual discomfiture, introduced him to coffee, with all its attendant evils. The black brew, they argued, could have no place in a Christian life, and they begged the pope to ban its use. Whether out of a sense of fairness or impelled by curiosity, the pope decided to try the aromatic potation before rendering his decree. Its flavor and effect were so delightful that he declared that it would be a shameful waste to leave its enjoyment to the heathen. He therefore "baptized" the drink as suitable for Christian use, and in so doing spared Europe the recurring religious quarrels over coffee that persisted within Islam for decades if not centuries.

This bar of heaven having been breached, coffee joined chocolate as an item sold by Italian street peddlers, who also offered other liquid refreshments such as lemonade and liquor. There is an unconfirmed story of an Italian coffeehouse opening in 1645, but the first reliable date is 1683, when a coffeehouse opened in Venice.

Early Coffee Stalls and Houses: Ottoman Customs Invade the West

In 1669 Mohammed IV, the Turkish sultan, absolute ruler of the Ottoman Empire, sent Suleiman Aga as personal ambassador to the court of Louis XIV. Their meeting did not go well. Arriving in Versailles, Suleiman was presented to the Sun King, who sat decked in a diamond-studded robe costing millions of francs, commissioned for and worn only on this occasion to overawe his foreign guest. But the rube was not razzed. Suleiman, draped in a plain wool outer garment, approached and stood, unbowing, before the king, stolidly extending a missive that he declared had been sent by the sultan himself and addressed to "my brother in the West." When Louis, unmoving, allowed his minister to take the letter and said that he would consider it at a more convenient time, Suleiman in astonishment begged to know why his royal host would delay attending to the personal word of the absolute ruler of all Islam. Louis, in answer, and true to the spirit of his motto, "*l'état, c'est moi*," coldly responded that he was a law unto himself and bent only to his own inclination, at which Suleiman, with appropriate courtesies, withdrew and was escorted to a royal carriage that conveyed him to Paris, where he was to remain for almost a year.

Knowledge of coffee and even coffee itself came to France a hundred years before Suleiman. The earliest written reference to coffee to arrive there was in a 1596 letter to Charles de l'Écluse by Onoio Belli (*Lat.* Bellus), an Italian botanist and author.[9]

Engraving from Dufour's 1685 treatise on coffee, tea, and chocolate. This French engraving illustrates a Turk drinking coffee from a handleless cup with an *ibrik*, or Turkish pot for boiling coffee, standing in the corner. (The Library Company of Philadelphia)

Bellus referred to the "seeds used by the Egyptians to make a liquid they call *cave*" and instructed his correspondent to roast the beans he was sending "over the fire and then crush them in a wooden mortar."[10] In 1644 the physician Pierre de la Roque, on his return to Marseilles from Constantinople, became the first to bring the beans together with the utensils for their preparation into the country. By serving coffee to his guests, and turning them on to caffeine, he achieved some notoriety among the medical community. Around this time news about coffee reached Paris, but samples of the beans that were sent there went unrecognized and were confused with mulberry. Pierre's son, Jean La Roque (1661–1745), famous for his *Voyage de L'Arabie Heureuse* (1716), an account of his visit to the court of the king of Yemen, records that Jean de Thévenot became one of the first Frenchmen to prepare coffee, when he served it privately in 1657. And Louis XIV is said to have first tasted coffee in 1664.[11] Yet, despite all of these precursors, it was Suleiman whose lavish Oriental flair first fired the imaginations of Paris about coffee and the lands of its provenance.

Suleiman, who had made such an austere appearance at court, surprised Paris society by taking a palatial house in the most exclusive district. Exaggerated stories spread that he maintained an artificial climate, perfumed with the rosy scent that presumably filled Eastern capitals, and that the interiors were alive with Persian fountains. Inevitably, the women of the aristocracy, drawn by curiosity and wonder, and perhaps impelled as well by the boredom endemic to their class, filed through his front gate in answer to his invitations. Ushered into rooms that were dimly lit and without chairs, the walls covered with glazed tiles and the floors with intricate dark-toned rugs, they were bidden to recline on cushions and were presented with damask serviettes and tiny porcelain cups by young Nubian slaves. Here they became among the first in the nation to be served the magical bitter drink that would soon become known throughout France as "café."

Isaac Disraeli paints a rich picture of taking coffee with the Ottoman ambassador in Paris in 1669:

> On bended knee, the black slaves of the Ambassador, arrayed in the most gorgeous costumes, served the choicest Mocha coffee in tiny cups of egg-shell porcelain, but, strong and fragrant, poured out in saucers of gold and silver, placed on embroidered silk doylies fringed with gold bullion, to the grand dames, who fluttered their fans with many grimaces, bending their piquant faces—be-rouged, be-powdered, and be-patched—over the new and steaming beverage.[12]

The women had come seeking intelligence; instead, coffee induced them to supply it. Suleiman spoke fluently of his homeland but confined his remarks to such innocuous matters as stories of coffee's discovery by the Sufi monks and the manner of coffee's cultivation and preparation, describing for them the plantations of southwestern Arabia, planted around with tamarisk bushes and carob trees to protect them from locusts.

Meanwhile the well-born ladies, the wives and sisters of the leading military and political men in Louis XIV's realm, felt their tongues loosening with the expansive effects of a heavy dose of caffeine on nearly naive human sensoriums; for the Turkish coffee Suleiman served, "as strong as death," boiled and reboiled and swilled down together with its grounds, was some of the strongest ever made. Inevitably, they began to talk, to titter, to chatter, to gossip, their words animated by the stimulant power of caffeine. Thus it was that by the same drug, caffeine, which a few decades earlier in the vehicle of chocolate had enabled Cardinal Richelieu to create the conditions for Louis XIV's absolute power, that any prospect of securing an alliance with Mohammed IV was now undone.

For it was in this way, by plying the women with strong drink, that the devoted Suleiman, though exiled from the Bourbon court, discovered its inner plottings and strategies and concluded that the Sun King dealt with the Turks only to create apprehension in his old enemy, King Leopold I of Austria, and that Louis could not be relied on by the sultan to send troops to assist, for example, in the next siege of Vienna, which, as it turned out, was less than fifteen years away. Perhaps this was the first time in history when the relations between two great monarchs were in large part conditioned, mediated, and even decided by the power of caffeine.

Although coffee was introduced to the French aristocracy and the common man alike in the time of Louis XIV, because of its limited popularity at Versailles, coffee's further progress into good society was slow. In any case, so long as Parisians could procure coffee only from Marseilles, only the wealthiest could undertake to provision themselves by sending for a supply. The trappings of Turkish customs, including turbans and imitation Oriental robes, endured a brief enthusiasm among the upper classes. But Turkomania became an object of ridicule, and, accordingly, it and the consumption of coffee soon waned. Molière, in his comedy *Le Bourgeois Gentilhomme*, produced when Suleiman Aga was still in Paris, mocked the aristocratic cult that indulged in the sacrament of coffee drinking. Perhaps because of the Gallic aversion to foreign intrusions, the French aristocrats, after indulging a momentary dalliance, turned their backs on coffee, at least for the decade, with disdain. The time for caffeine's wide enjoyment was not to come in France until Louis XV. In order to flatter his mistress, Madame du Barry, who had herself painted as a Turkish sultana being served coffee, Louis spent lavishly to give the drink vogue. He was to commission at least two solid gold coffeepots and direct Lenormand, his gardener at Versailles, to plant about ten hothouse coffee trees, from which six pounds of beans would be harvested annually, for preparation and service to his special friends by the king's own hands.[13]

During much of the centuries-long struggle between the Ottoman and Hapsburg Empires, the Armenians, as Christian subjects of the Turks, traveled and traded up and down the Danube, freely crossing the shifting border between the contesting powers. It is therefore no surprise to learn that an Armenian, one Pascal, whether he came to Paris on his own or in attendance to Suleiman Aga, should have become, in 1672, the first to sell coffee to ordinary Parisians. Until then, few people had had the opportunity to drink it. As Heinrich Edward Jacobs says, "It was consumed only occasionally in the houses of distinguished persons, whose family economy was self-contained."[14]

Pascal the pitchman, spotting an opportunity, aimed at the bourgeois market when he erected one of the 140 booths that filled nine streets with commercial exhibits and offerings in the gala annual fair in St. Germain, just across the Seine and outside the walls of Paris proper. His *maison de caova* was designed as a replica of a Constantinople coffeehouse, and its exotic Turkish trappings, when all things Turkish were in vogue among the élite, drew curious members of the public with its mystery and with the novel sweet, roasted scent of fresh coffee. Carrying trays of *le petit noir*, as it was called, black slave boys darted among members of the street crowd who, either from shyness or inability to find an open space, hung back from approaching the stall itself. Pascal recognized that to make headway with the public, coffee would have to be as cheap as wine; and by importing directly from the Levant and cutting out the Marseilles middlemen, he was able to sell the rare drink for only three sous a cup.

Flush with his success at the fair, the enterprising Pascal decided to open what he intended would be a permanent coffeehouse at Quais de l'École near the Pont Neuf. When business proved slow, he instituted the practice of sending his waiters, carrying coffeepots heated by lamps, from door to door and through the streets, crying "Café! Café!" Despite this aggressive retailing strategy, he soon went broke, packed up, and moved to London. Once there, he may well have headed straight for St. Michael's Alley in Cornhill, where London's first coffeehouse had been opened twenty years before by another Armenian immigrant, who, confusingly enough for us, was also named Pascal.

From Then to Now: Café Procope and Other Regency Cafés

> Great is the vogue of coffee in Paris. In the houses where it is supplied, the proprietors know how to prepare it in such a way that it gives wit to those who drink it. At any rate, when they depart, all of them believe themselves to be at least four times as brainy as when they entered the doors.
> —Charles-Louis de Secondat, baron de La Brede et de Montesquieu (1689–1755),
> personal letter, 1722

> Pistols for two; coffee for one.
> —Wry commonplace about the orders given before dueling,
> Paris, *La belle Epoque*

The world's first café, a French adaptation of the Islamic coffeehouse, was opened in 1689 in Paris by François Procope. Procope, a Florentine expatriate, started his food service career as a *limonadier*, or lemonade seller, who attracted a large following after adding coffee to his list of soft drinks. Undeterred by Pascal's recent failure, Procope decided to target a better class of customers than had the Armenian by situating his establishment directly opposite the Comédie Française, in what is now called the rue de l'Ancienne Comédie. His strategy worked. As the London coffeehouses were doing across the Channel, it attracted actors and musicians and a notable literary coterie. Over the two centuries of its operation as a café, the Procope served as a haunt for such writers as Voltaire, a maniacal coffee addict, Rousseau, Benjamin Franklin, Beaumarchais, Diderot, d'Alembert, Fontanelle, La Fontaine, Balzac, and Victor Hugo. Like Johnson's famous armchair in Button's coffeehouse, Voltaire's marble table and his favorite chair remained among the café's treasures for many years. Voltaire's favorite brew was a mixture of chocolate and coffee, which gave him effective doses of both caffeine and theobromine. He is quoted as having remarked of Linant, a pretentious and untalented versifier, "He regards himself as a person of importance because he goes every day to the Procope."

Like its English counterparts, the Café Procope became a center for political discussions. Robespierre, Marat, and Danton convened there to debate the dangerous issues of the day, and were supposed to have charted the course that led to the revolution of 1789 from the café. Napoleon Bonaparte, while still a young officer, also frequented the Café Procope, and was so poor that the proprietor prevailed on him to leave his hat as security for his coffee bill. The Café Procope was an astonishing success, and from its advent coffee became established in Paris. By one accounting, during the reign (1715–74) of Louis XV there are supposed to have been six hundred

Café House, Cairo, by Jean-Léon Gérome (1824–1904). An example of nineteenth-century French Orientalism, this oil painting shows the coffeehouse as a setting for casting bullets and is reminiscent of the tradition of the French café as the scene of real and imagined revolutionary intrigue. (Metropolitan Museum of Art, bequest of Henry H. Cook, 1905)

cafés in Paris, eight hundred by 1800, and more than three thousand by 1850. According to another more modest reckoning, there were 380 by 1720. Whatever the exact numbers, it is clear that, from the beginning of the eighteenth century, cafés proliferated as rapidly in Paris as the coffeehouses had in London in the last half of the seventeenth century.

Another itinerant Parisian coffee seller, Lefévre, also opened a café near the Palais Royal around 1690. It was sold in 1718 and renamed the Café de la Régence, in honor of the régent of Orléans. Well located to attract an upscale crowd, the café attracted the nobility, who assembled there after withdrawing from paying homage to the French court. The café drew many of the Procope's customers, and the list of literary and other patrons reads like a Who's Who of French literature and society over the next two centuries. Robespierre, Napoleon, Voltaire, Alfred de Musset, Victor Hugo, Theophile Gautier, J. J. Rousseau, the duke of Richelieu, and Fontanelle are still remembered in connection with their visits there. In his *Memoirs*, Diderot records how his wife gave him nine sous every day to pay for coffee at the Régence, where he sat and worked on his famous *Encyclopédie*. The historian Jules Michelet (1798–1874), writing many years later, gives a vivid account of the ways in which coffee and the café changed and enlivened Parisian life:

> Paris became one vast café. Conversation in France was at its zenith.... For this sparkling outburst there is no doubt that honor should be ascribed in part to the auspicious revolution of the times, to the great event which created new customs, and even modified human temperament—the advent of coffee.
>
> This sudden cheer, this laughter of the old world, these overwhelming flashes of wit, of which the sparkling verse of Voltaire, the *Persian Letters*, give us a faint idea![15]

Like the coffeehouses of London, the Parisian cafés attracted a heterogeneous collection of patrons. Charles Woinez announced in his leaflet periodical *The Café, Literary, Artistic, and Commercial* in 1858, "The Salon stood for privilege, the Café stands for equality." A similar observation was made in an early-eighteenth-century broadside:

> The coffeehouses are visited by respectable persons of both sexes: we see among the many various types: men-about-town, coquettish women, abbés, country bump-kins, *nouvellistes* [purveyors of news], the parties to a law-suit, drinkers, gamesters, par-asites, adventurers in the field of love or industry, young men of letters—in a word, an unending series of persons.[16]

Despite this pervasive heterogeneity, many Paris cafés catered to special clienteles. Café Procope's chief rival in regard of attracting poets was the Café Parnasse.[17] The Café Bourette also attracted the literati, the Café Anglais was favored by actors and the after-theater crowd, the Café Alexandre was patronized by musical performers and composers, the Café des Art drew opera singers and their entourage, and the Café Boucheries was a place where directors came to hire actors for new productions. But the arts and letters did not have an exclusive hold on the institution. The Café Cuisiner was the favorite of coffee connoisseurs and featured a variety of exotic blends. The Café Defoy was known for sherbet as well as coffee. The Café des Armes d'Espagne was an army officers' hangout. The Café des Aveugles, which featured musical enter-tainment by blind instrumentalists, was a den of prostitution.

Toward the end of the nineteenth century, after the Procope and the other cafés had lost their literary reputations, Paul Verlaine, the leader of the Symbolist poets, made the Procope his favorite haunt and thereby partly restored, for a time, its for-mer glory. The Procope is still in business today as a restaurant.

Austria: Kolschitzky's Bean Bags Hit Vienna

The epochal conflict between the Ottoman and Hapsburg Empires well merits the Yiddish epithet "*fershlepte kraynk*," which means "long drawn-out difficulty," for the military, political, and economic rivalry between them began in the fifteenth century and did not abate until almost the end of the nineteenth. As is true for any longtime enemies, each influenced the other, in this case by means of example and trade and through the agency of writers, travelers, merchants, and diplomats. The network of rivalries within Christian Europe, especially the contest between the Protestant Bourbons and the Catholic Hapsburgs and the vagaries of Louis XIV, who one year was more jealous of the Austrians and the next was more fearful of the Turks, created problems for the West, opportunities for the East, and confusion for everyone.[18]

The ratification of one of the many peace treaties concluded by the Viennese and the Turks was the occasion for the introduction of coffee to the city. Kara Mahmud Pasha was a Turkish ambassador who, with an entourage of three hundred, arrived in 1665 to open an embassy in the court of Emperor Leopold I. He spared no effort to impress the local citizens. Kara arrived in Oriental splendor to which the Europeans were unaccustomed, and among his exotic household were camels, Arabian stallions, two coffee brewers, Mehmed and Ibrahim, and a supply of coffee beans. We know that the brewers were kept busy during their several months' stay, because the city archives record many complaints about the unusually high wood consumption of the Turks, who kept a fire always burning in order to assure a fresh supply of the drink.[19] To some extent the habit caught on with the natives. After the ambassador and his retinue departed in 1666, city records report private trade in coffee and that an Oriental trading company, which operated from 1667 until the invasion of 1683, was a primary source for the beans.

The traditional account of coffee's first appearance in Vienna is considerably different. This folk history dates coffee's arrival to the 1683 Turkish attempt on the city, a gigantic undertaking, in support of which General Kara Mustafa had led an army of more than three hundred thousand Turkish troops up the Danube from the heartland of the distant eastern empire. The beleaguered city was ringed with twenty-five thousand Turkish tents. Kara settled in for a prolonged siege, during which he sent raiding parties into the surrounding countryside, from the Alps to the Bavarian border. Meanwhile, the Islamic equivalent of the Army Corps of Engineers began tunneling under Vienna's walls, preparing an entrance for the Janissaries, the empire's elite troops, to storm. As the situation worsened, the isolated Viennese sent a scout through the Muslim lines to deliver a message to their allies, who had massed just upriver, that the counterattack could be delayed no longer. These Christian troops, led by King John III Sobieski of Poland and Duke Charles of Lorraine, arrived just as the city's troops poured out of the gate, catching the invaders by surprise and forcing the Islamic general to abandon his camp and hastily withdraw up the Danube. The defeated Turkish armies, in their retreat, took with them over eighty-five thousand slaves captured on these raids, including fourteen thousand nubile girls who would almost certainly be tapped for initiation into the suffocating luxury, enforced helplessness, and fatal intriguing of the Turkish harem. Because of his failure to take Vienna, Mustafa was met on the way home by assassins and suffered strangulation by the gold cord, a death reserved for the sultan's most intimate enemies.

The Viennese enjoy recalling the glories of their history, and many earnestly commemorate the siege of 1683. As part of this remembrance, Austrian schoolchildren are taught the proverbial story of Georg Kolschitzky, a Pole, who happened to be in

Kolschitzky's Café, oil painting by Franz Schams. This painting hangs in the main boardroom of Julius Meinl, A.G., an international company that began almost a hundred and fifty years ago as a Viennese coffee-roasting firm. The company's founder erected a factory on the spot where Kolschitzky found the abandoned Turkish bean bags. (Photograph courtesy of Julius Meinl, A.G., Vienna, Austria)

town when the assault began, and who is honored for his heroic part in defending the city. Kolschitzky was an adventurer who had traveled widely in the Ottoman domains, serving for a time as a dragoman, or interpreter, in the capitals of the East. Happily, because of his intimate knowledge of the Turkish language and customs, he was able to volunteer service to Vienna as a surveillance agent. On August 13, 1683, Kolschitzky and his servant Milhailovich, each in Oriental disguise, wandered around and through the Turkish encampment northwest of the city. The information they collected about the size and disposition of the enemy forces proved invaluable, or so the story goes. Others say that he was the scout who carried a letter through the enemy lines telling the duke of Lorraine when to attack.

The legend adds that, after the crisis had passed, the city fathers of Vienna asked Kolschitzky to name his reward. He disingenuously asked only for the bags of camel fodder that had been abandoned by the retreating Turks, along with their guns, armor, tents, and other appurtenances of war, and was granted his wish. The "camel fodder," as he, and he alone in Vienna, well knew, was actually five hundred pounds of green coffee beans, the virtues of which and the methods of roasting, grinding, and boiling he had learned in his travels to the East. Using this supply, he opened the first coffeehouse in Vienna, known as the "Blue Bottle," but found a limited market. Then he struck upon the idea of using sugar and milk to attenuate the bitter, thick brew. After this innovation, coffee attained the great popularity in Vienna that it has maintained to this day.

The truth about the first coffeehouse in Vienna was more mundane. Vienna's archives reveal that Kolschitzky was forced to petition the town council for years, reminding them of his valuable wartime services, before being granted a permit to do business in what was then, as now, a tightly controlled and regulation-ridden city. He had run afoul of the trade restrictions of the day, often grounded in the protection of the rights of various guilds to practice their crafts or trades to the exclusion of all outsiders.

Despite the color and charm of the story of Kolschitzky, it is now thought that at least two coffeehouses had been open for business in Vienna, possibly before the siege of 1683 and almost certainly before Kolschitzky's petition had been granted. Two Armenians, Johannes Diodato and Isaak de Luca, are believed to have been the first to sell coffee from permanent premises.[20] Diodato, whose father was a Turkish convert to Roman Catholicism who had settled in Vienna's thriving Armenian community, obtained the rights to sell Turkish goods in Vienna and enjoyed fabulous commercial success with many commodities. On January 17, 1685, Diodato obtained the first permit in Vienna to open a coffeehouse, although he probably had operated it earlier without benefit of the legal protection from competition that the license afforded. He finally secured a royal monopoly from Leopold I on the sale of coffee in the city for twenty years. Unfortunately for Diodato, his extensive commercial intercourse with the Turks, which was the basis for his success, also brought him under suspicion, and he was forced to flee to Venice in 1693, turning over the operation of his coffeehouse to his wife.

In 1697 de Luca secured the right to do business in Vienna and married the daughter of a wealthy citizen. Fortunately for him the city fathers were then asserting themselves against the abundance of restrictive royal concessions. Later in the same year, together with two other Armenians, Andreas Pain and Philip Rudolf Kemberg, de Luca acquired a license from the city which gave him, in derogation of Diodato's royal license, the exclusive right to trade in coffee, chocolate, tea, and sherbet. Diodato's wife was in no position to argue on behalf of her absent husband, because the royal grant to him had been inalienable.[21] De Luca immediately opened a coffeehouse to take advantage of his new privileges. By the time Diodato returned to Vienna in 1701, he must have been astonished to see the growth of the coffee business. Perhaps promoted effectively by the example of the new Turkish embassy staff, who consumed several tons of coffee a year, coffee had come into almost universal use, and the number of coffeehouses exploded accordingly. In 1714, eleven coffee makers joined to found a trade association, and the coffee trade in Vienna had come of age. As coffee grew in popularity, a bitter contention arose between the coffee-boilers guild and the distillers guild. In 1750 Maria Theresa finally settled the quarrel by forcing the coffee-boilers to sell alcohol as well as coffee and the tavern keepers to sell coffee as well as alcohol, a measure which unified the two guilds.

A modern café in Vienna. (Photograph courtesy of Julius Meinl, A.G., Vienna, Austria)

On the advice of Greiner, one of her ministers, she later imposed a tax on alcohol so heavy that it helped coffee to increase in popularity.

Between the end of the nineteenth century and the early twentieth century, from before the First World War to the start of the Second, Vienna became notable for its cafés and café society. People of every sort, from professional men and civil service workers and artists and students, to unemployed laborers and penniless émigrés, would pass hours in the cafés. One of the funniest stories to emerge from this Viennese coffeehouse milieu is about Leon Trotsky:

> There was a little-known Russian émigré, Trotsky by name, who during World War I was in the habit of playing chess in Vienna's Café Central every evening. A typical Russian refugee, who talked too much but seemed utterly harmless, indeed, a pathetic figure in the eyes of the Viennese. One day in 1917 an official of the Austrian Foreign Ministry rushed into the minister's room, panting and excited, and told his chief, "Your excellency . . . Your excellency . . . Revolution has broken out in Russia!" The minister, less excitable and less credulous than his official, rejected such a wild claim and retorted calmly, "Go away. . . . Russia is not a land where revolutions break out. Besides, who on earth would make a revolution in Russia? Perhaps Herr Trotsky from the Café Central?"[22]

Pre–World War II Viennese fancy grocer on Karntnerstrasse, specializing in coffee and tea, prepared for take-out or bagged for home brewing. (Photograph courtesy of Julius Meinl, A.G., Vienna, Austria)

Europeans Improve and Serve Turkish Coffee, Chinese Tea, and Indian Chocolate

A Turkish adage admonishes that coffee should be sweet; but Turkish coffee, as originally prepared, was bitter indeed. Despite this fact, when Vesling visited Cairo in the early seventeenth century, he found two thousand to three thousand coffeehouses, and noted that "some did begin to put sugar in their coffee to correct the bitterness of it, and others made sugar-plums of the berries." Boiled or brewed coffee, as prepared by the Egyptians, Arabs, and Turks, was unpleasant to most European tastes. By 1670, while Viennese traditionalists sat cross-legged and sipped poisonously potent coffee in tiny cups, Eastern style, the first "coffee machines" were being invented in England and France and the Westernization of coffee consumption was under way. These were the first of an abundant variety of devices that culminated in the microprocessor-driven machines of today.

At this time, books instructing the public in coffee preparation began to proliferate. Nicholas de Blegny (1652–1722), a French surgeon who practiced without benefit of a medical diploma, wrote *Le Bon Usage du Thé, du Caffe et du Chocolate pour la preservation & pour la guerison des Maladies* (Lyons, 1687), or *The Proper Use of Tea, Coffee, and Chocolate for the preservation of health and overcoming Diseases*, what may be the first European work on the preparation of all three beverages that did more than simply parrot travelers' accounts. Jacob Spon and Philippe Sylvestre Dufour also provided their readers with good instructions. In 1685 the first serious coffee recipe book was published in Vienna. By the year 1700, books and pamphlets, generally authored by interested parties, such as coffee dealers or coffee-promoting doctors, became common in England and Holland as well.

The single greatest technological revolution in the preparation of coffee was invented by a diligent and creative German housewife in the twentieth century. In 1908, Frau Melitta Bentz, with no more exalted purpose than preparing good coffee to please her husband and her Kaffeeklatsch friends, invented what the world has come to know as "filter drip coffee." Previously, one or another variations in boiling ground beans had been used exclusively. The result was usually bitter and sometimes laden with the coarse grounds, although even before Bentz's invention, the use of a cloth bag to screen the boiling grounds had become common. At first she tried linen towels, which did not work well, but then she tried blotting paper placed in a brass pot with a perforated bottom. Pouring water into the brass container, she succeeded in making the world's first filtered coffee.

Bentz soon replaced the blotter paper with a strong porous paper, the sort we are familiar with today, and engaged a tinsmith to produce aluminum pots, more than a thousand of which were sold at the Leipzig Trade Fair. Encouraged by this early success, Bentz's husband created and assumed the management of a company in 1912, which he named after his wife, to produce the coffeepots and filters. Despite improvements and variations, the basic Melitta method of making coffee, which is simple, dependable, convenient, and produces a rich, clear brew, is still in use today in more than 85 percent of German households and in almost every country around the world.[23]

The fashions of preparing, serving, and drinking tea also evolved. The Europeans imitated the Chinese, who made tea in unglazed red or brown, plain or decorated stoneware pots, the use of which they believed made for the best brew. These stoneware pots arrived with the first Dutch shipments of tea and were subsequently widely copied by European craftsmen.

The Portuguese and Spanish began to return from the Orient with porcelain as early as the sixteenth century, but, because of porcelain's expense, its use outside their homelands remained limited.[24] This changed when the Dutch began to import large quantities of Chinese and Japanese porcelain, making it cheaper and spreading its use by reexporting it throughout the Continent. It was so cheap in its countries of origin that the Dutch captains loaded their holds with tons of porcelain to ballast their ships, making the previously rare commodity increasingly common. As early as 1615, published accounts make certain that Chinese porcelain was in everyday use in most Dutch homes. As ordinary as these imports had become, some still saw in them the hallmark of exotic splendor. In 1641, the Dutch physician Nikolas Dirx, "Dr. Tulpius," wrote of the delicate, handleless porcelain cups and opulent tea services that were now being used in his country: "the Chinese prize them as highly as we do diamonds, precious stones and pearls." Later, so much porcelain was brought into England by that country's East India Company that it can fairly be said that never, before or since, had ordinary people, poor by our standards, drank or dined with such luxurious appurtenances.

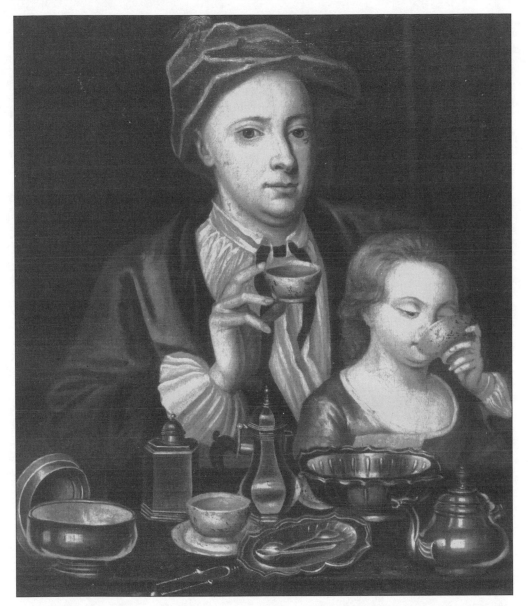

Man and Child Drinking Tea, artist unknown, c. 1725. This painting is sometimes called *Tea Party in the Time of George I.* The silver equipage includes a silver container and cover, a hexagonal tea canister, a hot water jug or milk jug, slop bowl, teapot, and sugar tongs. The cups and saucers are Chinese export porcelain, which was in good supply in the colonies as well as throughout Europe. (Colonial Williamsburg Foundation)

Porcelain was coveted because of its beauty and impermeability, which made it easy to wash. During the seventeenth century, almost all the porcelain brought to Europe was the Ming blue-and-white variety. The Dutch began copying the Ming ceramics and, by the middle of the century, the famous blue-and-white Delft potteries produced credible imitations of the Eastern originals in the chinoiserie style that was later to become popular in Europe.

From the end of the seventeenth century, both coffee and tea services began to assume their modern forms. The first English silver teapot, with a nearly conical shape, was made in 1670. Between 1650 and 1700, the broad flat Chinese bowls were more and more frequently placed on saucers. However, the practice of pouring the coffee from the bowl into the saucer persisted even after handles had been devised for the bowls. This upside-down way of drinking remained customary until the end of the eighteenth century, when drinking from the saucer became socially frowned upon.

It was also in the eighteenth century that the Germans became adept at designing and producing fine porcelain teapots. By the century's close, the full development and importance of the modern equipage in Germany is evident in the words of Caspar David Friedrich (1774–1840), the Romantic German painter of spiritual, desolate, and brooding landscapes, in a letter to his family, dated January 28, 1818: "Coffee drum, coffee grinder, coffee siphon, coffee sack, coffee pot, coffee cup have become necessaries; everything, everything has become necessary."[25] By the Biedermeier period (c. 1815–48) in Germany and Austria coffee and tea machines and the accompanying porcelain equipage became widely recognized status symbols. Paintings from the period illustrate that the social rank of a family might be accurately estimated from the deliberate display of the items necessary to take morning coffee or tea.

the late adopters
Germany, Russia, and Sweden Join In

> Everybody is using coffee. If possible, this must be prevented. My people must drink beer.
>
> —Frederick the Great, from a proclamation against coffee, September 13, 1777

Beethoven (1770–1827) avidly drank coffee, a habit which he pursued with meticulous, almost numerological, particularity:

> For breakfast he partook of coffee, which for the most part he had prepared himself in a glass machine. Coffee appears to have been his most indispensable form of nourishment, which he consumed to the same excessive degree as was known to be the case with Orientals. Sixty beans would go into one cup of coffee, often counted out exactly, particularly if guests were present.[1]

However, in Beethoven's day, because royal edicts interfered with and sometimes prohibited the consumption of coffee and tea, these caffeinated beverages were not widely accepted in Germany and Sweden as they had long been throughout most of Europe.

Germany Joins In: Beyond Beer Soup for Breakfast

Caffeine was accepted more slowly in Germany and the rest of central Europe (except Vienna) than it had been in Western Europe.[2] This meant that England and France began to take the caffeine cure about eighty years before their central European neighbors, who continued, during this time, drinking alcohol heavily as before. At a time when the English, for example, had already started to "dry out," Germans were largely innocent of temperate alternatives to beer. Once the Germans, Hungarians, and other East Europeans became caffeine converts, coffee and coffeehouses became indispensable fixtures of the society and tea and chocolate came into general use across the breadth of the old Hapsburg Empire.

Beer was Germany's old love, and one to which, despite an intense dalliance with wine after the establishment of trade with ancient Rome, its countrymen returned, as not only their favorite intoxicant but also as the primary source of nutrition for the peasantry. Although it may turn many stomachs today, beer for breakfast was standard fare among the common people from the close of the Middle Ages onward to well into the eighteenth century.

After the use of beer had returned to Germany, German beer was shipped from Hamburg to Holland, Sweden, Denmark, and Russia. In a war between Hamburg and Denmark, two-thirds of the expenditures for provisions went to buy beer. It was recorded in account books of the Hanseatic League that German sailors drank an average of three gallons of beer a day. In 1400, a census of trades in Hamburg listed more than twelve hundred people, nearly half of whom were employed in brewing or cooping.[3]

Beer is nothing if not fattening, and it would seem that its heavy consumption contributed to the fact that, as far as we can tell, toward the end of the Middle Ages a large number of northern Europe's population developed beer bellies. Fat people begin to predominate in northern European art as *zaftig* became the prevalent body type in northwestern and northeastern Europe. From 1400 to 1700 a kind of cult of obesity developed, which equated corpulence with health, talent, and position. In reaction to this celebration of blubber, Jacob Balde (1604–68), Alsatian Jesuit, Latin poet, and famous preacher, founded the Congregatio Macilentorum, or the "Society of the Lean," a group that faced a challenge for, in Heinrich Jacob's words, "in 1638 a slim and upright German figure had become a rarity among the well-to-do; one and all of them were pot-bellied."[4]

At the height of beer's popularity, in the fifteenth through the seventeenth centuries, it was brewed and consumed primarily at home and only exceptionally in public houses. Many Germans of all classes were two-fisted drinkers during and after the Thirty Years' War (1618–48). Pickling their brains in booze, whether beer, brandy, or wine, was the almost universal recourse for those who were suffering under the depredations and dislocations of a ruinous internecine war and its aftermath.[5]

The German resistance to adopting new habits was reinforced in relation to coffee in the seventeenth century by a travelogue, *Vermehrte newe Beschreibung der Muscowitisch und Persischen Reyse* (1656), written by Adam Olearius (Oelschlaeger) (1599–1671), an Orientalist who served as astronomer, surveyor, and interpreter for his traveling party. Olearius' book was primarily a factual account of a diplomatic mission (1635–39), undertaken by the author with Paul Fleming (1609–40), a German poet, at the prompting of the duke of Holstein. The mission's purpose was to establish a trading company to do business with Persia, cutting out the Dutch and English middlemen. The book also included accounts of local customs and stories encountered along the way, and, in an entry dated 1637, Olearius provides this description of Persian coffee drinking and of the appearance of unroasted beans: "They drink with their tobacco a certain black water, which they call *cahwa*, made of fruit brought out of Egypt, and which is in colour like ordinary wheat, and in taste like Turkish wheat, and is of the bigness of a little bean."[6]

One of the tales his book tells is the legend about a king of Persia who had become so addicted to coffee that he turned away from women:

> However if you partake to excess of such kahave water, it completely extinguishes all pleasures of the flesh. They write of a king, Sultan Mahmud Kasnin, who reigned in Persia before Tamerlane [Timur], and who became such an habitual drinker of kahave water that he forgot his spouse and developed a repugnance of intercourse which displeased his queen greatly. For on one occasion as she sat in the window and espied how a stallion was being held down prior to castration, it is said that she inquired what was happening. And upon being told with all due frankness that the intention was to tame the lust of the horse that it would no longer mount another or service a mare, she expressed the view that such steps were unnecessary, all that had to be done was to give him the shameful kahave water, and he would soon be like the king.[7]

This lurid story helped dissuade generations of Germans from becoming coffee drinkers and was used by beer and wine merchants and other enemies of coffee to support their arguments. Olearius' travelogue was translated into French by Wicquefort and published in Paris in 1666, and the tale's repetition bolstered the faction in Marseilles that preached opposition to the black potion.

Nevertheless, coffee drinking made limited inroads in Germany in the seventeenth century. As in other countries, private persons had early isolated encounters with the bean. In 1631, for example, a German merchant from Merseburg was sent a parcel of coffee from a Dutch business associate. Unfortunately, his wife decided to improve the recipe that accompanied it by substituting chicken broth for water, and the resulting drink did little to spread the use of the beverage.[8] Coffee was also promoted by printed pamphlets and street-criers. The drink was first sold publicly in temporary stalls, like that of Pascal the Armenian in Paris. In fact, the early spread of coffee drinking in Germany probably owes more to the influence of foreigners than to the example of the upper classes. In the early eighteenth century, Hamburg and Leipzig were the only German cities regularly visited by people from abroad, and it is no accident that the first German coffeehouse was founded by a Dutchman to serve the tastes of English merchants and sailors in Hamburg, and that the coffee used there was also an English import. Called the "English Coffee House," it was opened in Hamburg by Dr. Cornelius Buntekuh in 1679, a man known throughout Europe for promoting the health and longevity benefits of drinking enormous amounts of tea daily. The first German advertisement for the sale of the caffeinated beverages appeared in the Frankfurt *Journal* of 1686: "Notice is hereby given to all and sundry, that all kinds of chocolate, coffee and tea, as well as raw coffee may be purchased at the premises of Matthia Guaitta, Italian in the Narnberger Hof."[9] Other coffeehouses were soon opened in other cities, in Regensburg in 1689, Leipzig in 1694, and Berlin in 1721. By about 1725 the coffeehouses in Germany had brought caffeine into broad use by the middle class, finally overcoming such stringent opposition as the threat by the bishop of Paderborn to levy high fines on coffee and place coffee drinkers in the stocks.

Frederick the Great's Campaign against Coffee

The wine dealers in France and Italy had resisted the incursion of coffee, and coffee met with similar opposition from ale-house keepers in Germany. The greatest obstacle to coffee use in Germany came not from interested merchants, however, but proceeded directly from the intercession of Frederick the Great (1712–86), who, in the course of a lifelong campaign against the bean, promulgated bans, taxes, and even a special police squad to keep his subjects safe from coffee's threat to their health and pocketbooks.

In 1766, Frederick imposed a state monopoly on coffee imports. He decided that, although coffee was a suitable drink for the aristocracy, it served as a ruinous luxury for the common people. Following a strange theory of international commerce that is still current, he believed that, as a result of the German purchase of coffee beans from abroad, money would "flow out" of the country and deepen the economic distress. He also accepted the verdict of German physicians that coffee was bad for the health, especially the medical warnings that coffee caused effeminacy in men and sterility in women. He used his monopoly and authority to levy taxes in an attempt to restrict its use to the upper classes, causing much discontent among the populace.

Over the ensuing decades, Frederick continued and even expanded his war on coffee. He himself had been brought up on the old beer soup and reasoned that if beer soup was good enough for the monarch, it was good enough for his subjects. In a royal attempt to turn back the culinary clock, he issued the following proclamation on September 13, 1777:

> It is disgusting to notice the increase in the quantity of coffee used by my subjects, and the amount of money that goes out of the country in consequence. Everybody is using coffee. If possible, this must be prevented. My people must drink beer. His Majesty was brought up on beer, and so were his ancestors, and his officers. Many battles have been fought and won by soldiers nourished on beer; and the King does not believe that coffee-drinking soldiers can be depended upon to endure hardship or to beat his enemies in case of the occurrence of another war.[10]

His efforts were partially successful for a short period, and beer soup enjoyed a brief revival. However, as it had everywhere else, coffee's progress ultimately proved ineluctable. By 1781, Frederick attempted to contain the evil by creating a royal monopoly on roasting, the *Déclaration du Roi concernant la vente du café brûlé*. He granted special roasting licenses to the nobility, the clergy, and government officials, but even they had to buy the green beans from him. The license fees and the profits from the sales of beans made Frederick a fortune.

The average German was forced into seeking various unpleasant substitutes for coffee, including beverages brewed from wheat, barley, corn, dried figs, and chicory. (Many Germans resorted to similar replacements, with equally unsatisfactory results, during World War II.) The pursuit of real coffee created a thriving black market, which Frederick fought to suppress. A French minister whom he had charged with the enforcement of his edict created a special squad of agents, popularly called "coffee

smellers" or "coffee sniffers," to go among the people and sniff out violators by following the undisguisable aroma of roasting coffee. The spies, mostly wounded or
retired soldiers from the last war, were given a quarter of all the fines they were responsible for collecting. Needless to say, the people considered them insufferable intruders.

From this period dates Bach's famous "Coffee Cantata" (1732), a one-act comic
operetta in which the excesses of both sides of the argument are satirized. Bach had
read and been impressed by a frightful poem by Picander, a Leipzig poet, published as
part of his *Parisian Fables* in 1727. The poem pretended to satirize the health debates in
France and Louis XV's grant of a state monopoly for coffee as a means of restricting
its use to the court, but was obviously aimed closer to home, at Frederick's restrictions:

> "Alas!" Cried the women, "take rather our bread.
> Can't live without coffee! We'll all soon be dead!"[11]

The French king is supposed to have relented only after his subjects began dying in
droves, and the nation was saved. After Bach read this poem, he commissioned Picander to write a libretto for a cantata on the subject of the "coffee mania among women."
The resulting libretto tells the story of a father, Schlendrian, or "Slow Poke," who
attempts to dissuade his daughter, Lieschen, from using the dangerous drink. He
enjoys a brief success when he threatens to interfere with her marriage plans. But when
her mother and grandmother both start imbibing, his cause is lost. Lieschen's over-
weening craving for coffee is expressed in the famous line, "Ah! How sweet coffee
tastes! Lovelier than a thousand kisses, sweeter far than muscatel wine!"

Coffee use in Germany declined during Frederick's campaign to control it and
nearly vanished from Hamburg, its first German home. In Leipzig, however, it had
taken firmer root. Known at this time as "little Paris," it was a city which, until about
1750, set the cultural pace for the entire country. Richer and more powerful than
Berlin or its closest rival, Dresden, Leipzig was not only a center of international trade
but soon succeeded Frankfort-on-Main as the national center of book printing, so both
merchants and the literati came there in great numbers. Leipzig became celebrated
for its gardens and its coffeehouses, which developed distinct followings as the London
coffeehouses had done generations before. The Kaffebaum was a favorite of university
students. Ricter's was a center for foreigners, travelers, and merchants, and people who
were concerned with mounting the famous city fairs. It was a hangout as well for the
intellectuals, such as the scholarly satirist Zachariae. As it had done in England, the
coffeehouse culture began to jostle and awaken the literary taste, and a new German
classical literary style sprouted from the arid Gottsched rococo period, marked by
"spiritlessness" and "turgidity."[12]

In Berlin, too, coffee caught on, and there, as across Germany, *Kaffeekrazchen*,
mostly for women, became increasingly popular from the end of the eighteenth
through the nineteenth centuries. Outdoor cafés and tents from which coffee and
other refreshments were served also began to appear.

Tea, like coffee, arrived in Germany in the seventeenth century. It was at first available only from apothecaries, and appears on their price lists by 1657. At this time, it
was also served in salons for the enjoyment of the upper classes. Its use spread slowly,

Coffee House (*Kaffeehaus*), lithograph by German Expressionist artist Georg Grosz, 1917. The satirical scene depicts a Berlin café, epitomizing the brooding, sinister atmosphere dominating post–World War I Germany. (Berlinische Galerie, Landesmuseum Fur Moderne Kunst, Photographie und Architektur)

except in coastal areas such as Ostfriesland where it was enthusiastically embraced; unlike coffee, tea never achieved great popularity nationwide.

Although chocolate arrived in Germany from Holland well after coffee and did not enjoy any aristocratic status from precedence, it nevertheless, at least during the eighteenth century, became associated with elegance and leisure. Schivelbusch asserts the theory that chocolate was a habit of the aristocratic and conservative ancien régime, while coffee was the choice of the rising middle class and the age of enterprise:

> Goethe, who used art as a means to lift himself out of his middle class background into the aristocracy, and who as a member of a courtly society maintained a sense of aristocratic calm even in the midst of immense productivity, made a cult of chocolate, and avoided coffee. Balzac, who, despite his sentimental allegiance to the monarchy, lived and labored for the literary marketplace and for it alone, became one of the most excessive coffee-drinkers in history. Here we see two fundamentally different working styles and means of stimulation—fundamentally different psychologies and physiologies.[13]

This dichotomy seems more clever than correct, although Balzac certainly preferred coffee to tea, which he described as "an insipid and depressing beverage," or to chocolate, for that matter. But Goethe too had enjoyed coffee—even, in his later judgment, excessively. Leipzig, which he visited at sixteen, though it had suffered the heavy indemnities imposed by the Prussians and was already in decline, was the first sizable city he ever saw, and, as a teenager, he wrote of its coffeehouses in *Memories of Youth*. Like many other Germans of his day, he also frequented the cafés of Italy during his Grand Tour, especially the Café Florian of Venice and the Café Greco of Rome. Because of this tourist traffic, the Café Florian, named for its first proprietor, who founded it in 1720, became one of the most celebrated on the Continent, the haunt of the Venetian aristocracy and a fast international set, as well as of artists and writers, whose ranks included Goldoni, Casanova, Rousseau, Byron, Alfred de Musset, and George Sand. The Café Greco, named for its Greek founder, Nicola della Maddelena, opened for business sometime before 1750. Its patrons included many famous Germans such as Schopenhauer, Mendelssohn, Liszt, Wagner, as well as Stendhal, Thackeray, Gogol, Mark Twain, Bizet, and Arturo Toscanini.[14]

So, although it is true that, in his mature years, Goethe had reservations about coffee's excessive use and berated his mistress for her lapse in their vow to abstain, it would be misleading to say that he "avoided coffee" altogether. And, as it turns out, Goethe was a kind of culinary pioneer, for, in the last decade of his life, at a time when "chocolate," to most of his countrymen, meant a beverage, he discovered the solid confection while vacationing at an Austrian resort and made a present of a boxful of geological samples mixed with chocolate candies to Ulrike von Levetzow, a nineteen-year-old girl, attaching this couplet:

> Enjoy this whenever it suits your mood,
> Not as a drink but as a much-loved food![15]

the world of caffeine

Russia: Rallying Round the Samovar

The Russian love for tea was relatively late in coming. In 1567, Ivan Petroff and Boornash Yalysheff, two Russian travelers returning from China, brought home glowing reports of the tea plant but no samples. In 1618, a Chinese embassy carried some chests filled with tea on an overland journey lasting eighteen months as a gift to the Moscow court of Czar Alexis. This was the first tea to arrive in Russia, and the Russians were not very interested.

Vassily Starkoff, the Russian ambassador to the court of Mogul Kahn Altyn, tried tea in 1638 but did not care for it. He declined the offer of a gift of a sizable supply for Czar Michael Romanoff, founder of the Romanoff dynasty, expressing the judgment that it would prove of no value to his master.[16] As a result of his demurrer, Russia's introduction to tea was delayed by half a century. After signing the Nerchinsk treaty with China in 1689, she began regularly to import brick tea by way of an overland caravan route through Manchuria and Mongolia, ending in the border town of Usk Kayakhta (Kiahta), which, by agreement, was to remain the sole site of commerce

Russian family from rural Siberia drinking tea around a copper samovar, an appurtenance indicating genteel status. The photograph was discovered in 1898 by the expedition of Harrison and Hiller. The reigning czar, Nicholas II, banned the manufacture and sale of vodka and encouraged use of the temperance beverage tea. "*Khlebosolstvo*—literally translated 'bread and salt' but in practice the Russian word for 'hospitality'—centered on the great samovar which every household owned. This uniquely Russian device for keeping tea water always at the boil ensured visitors a welcome all day long. It consisted of a charcoal-burning base, a central chimney surrounded by an urn of water, and a top rack for holding a pot in which the infusion steeped." (Quotation from Hale, *The Horizon Cookbook: An Illustrated History of Eating and Drinking Through the Ages*.) (University of Pennsylvania Museum, Philadelphia, negative #s4–142239)

The Soldier Drinks, an oil painting by Russian artist Marc Chagall, 1911–12, in which the samovar shares equal prominence with the titular subject of the painting. Perhaps the soldier is tipping his cap to his favorite things: his lover, his hometown, and, of course, his tea. (Solomon R. Guggenheim Museum)

between the parties.[17] Russian caravans of several hundred camels, bearing furs for exchange, took a year to complete the round trip. Each camel returned bearing four chests, totaling about six hundred pounds of tea, traveling at the rate of only twenty-five miles a day. By 1700, more than six hundred camel loads of tea reached Russia every year, arriving at an exorbitant cost.

Czarina Elizabeth Petrovna (1709–61) established a regular imperial shipment in 1735 with the intention of increasing the supply of tea and bringing the price down. It was also during her reign that the samovar, a metal container with a pipe up the center to keep the water heated by the fire below, became a fixture in nearly every Russian household.[18] The Russians became habitual imbibers of very strong tea, which they palliated by sipping it through a lump of sugar clenched between their teeth. By the time of the death of Catherine the Great (1729–96), the six hundred camel loads had risen to six thousand, bringing the total importation to more than three million pounds and the price within reach of the average person. Caravan transport reached its height around 1860 and continued until after 1880, when the first leg of the Trans-Siberian Railway was opened. The final camel caravan transplanting tea from Peking to Russia arrived in 1900. After the completion of the rail line, what had been a six-teen-month journey could be completed in seven weeks. Subsequently, tea transport was made by train through the port of Vladivostok.[19] Russia also began importing tea through the port of Odessa from the Levant in the middle of the nineteenth century, a source that increased in significance after the 1890s. At the same time, the Russians also began importing teas from London. So-called Russian caravan tea, sold by various companies today, still tries to evoke the allure and mystery of these lost days but has no legitimate claim to the epithet, nor any resemblance to the high-quality brick teas of the original.

Today Russia is the largest tea-consuming nation in Europe. Her tea, usually drunk with lemon and sugar, is brewed very strong, and boiling water is often added to the cup to dilute it. The Russians supplement their traditional single large after-noon meal with cups of tea served throughout the day. The samovar promotes the custom because it keeps water near the boil, the perfect temperature for brewing tea.

Sweden Gives In to Coffee

Caffeinated beverages were little used in any Scandinavian country before the turn of the eighteenth century. However, to judge from the royal edict promulgated against coffee and tea in Sweden in 1746, which inveighed against "the misuse and excesses of tea and coffee drinking," their enjoyment had become general within less than fifty years. A heavy tax was levied on the users of the temperance drinks, and the fail-ure of coffee and tea drinkers to confess themselves and pay the tax resulted in a heavy fine and "confiscation of cups and dishes," seizure of the paraphernalia supporting the use of these psychoactive intoxicants.

Later that year any use of coffee was made illegal in Sweden. As alcohol prohibi-tion in the United States was to do in the 1920s, the Swedish coffee prohibition engen-dered a flourishing bootlegging trade. Penalties against coffee drinking were made even stricter in 1766, but the flow of beans into Sweden continued.

King Gustav III (1746–92), determined to prove that coffee was a poison, ordered a convicted murderer to drink coffee every day until he died. In an attempt to do things scientifically, he ordered another murderer to drink tea daily, as a control, and appointed two doctors to oversee the experiment and report on which prisoner died first. Unfortunately, both doctors died and Gustav III was murdered before either prisoner succumbed. The two prisoners enjoyed, or at least endured, a long life until the tea drinker finally succumbed first at the age of eighty-three.

The outcome of this royal experiment had little effect on social policy. After switching from prohibition to a program of high taxation, Sweden's regent again attempted to reimpose a coffee ban in 1794. This effort was renewed, without success, again and again until the early 1820s, after which Sweden's government finally acceded to the will of her people. Ever since, Sweden's per capita coffee consumption, and, correspondingly, her per capita caffeine consumption, has been among the highest in the world.

judgments of history
Medical Men Debate Caffeine

> We advise tea for the whole nation and for every nation. We advise men and women to drink tea daily; hour by hour if possible; beginning with ten cups a day, and increasing the dose to the utmost quantity that the stomach can contain and the kidneys eliminate.
>
> —Dr. Cornelius Buntekuh, Medizinischen Elementarlehre, Dutch physician in the pay of the Dutch East India Company, c. 1680

Caffeine itself was not known until Goethe exhorted Runge to determine the chemical constituents of coffee beans and was not isolated from tea or cacao until some years later. However, the content of the spirited, often vituperative medical debates attending the introduction of coffee, tea, and chocolate proves that the medical men of the seventeenth and eighteenth centuries saw in these drinks a common, if unidentified, agency and that many of what we would today call the pharmacologic and psychoactive properties of caffeine were well recognized long before the drug itself was known. As a result, coffee, tea, and chocolate were frequently addressed together as medicinal products in early European texts. A famous example, widely translated in Europe, was Sylvestre Dufour's *Traitez Nouveaux & curieux Du Café, Du Thé et Du Chocolate, Ouvrage également necessaire aux Medecins, & tous ceux qui aiment leur santé* (1685), which means *New and Curious Qualities of Coffee, Tea and Chocolate, a Work Equally Necessary for Doctors, & for All Who Value Their Health*. As the title illustrates, at the time of Dufour's book, all three caffeinated drinks were still considered drugs, and their distribution in most countries was limited to apothecaries and physicians.[1] As all three caffeinated drinks became available to the lay public and became popular throughout most of the Western world, their ubiquity only served to fuel the ongoing medical controversies over the hazards of casual or indiscriminate consumption and stir new inquiries into their effects on the human body.

Some skilled in the medical lore of the seventeenth century devoted their time and talents to praising the caffeinated drinks for their ability to quicken the circulation,

Printer's ornamental engraving from Dufour's *Traitez Nouveux & curieux Du Café, Du The et Du Chocolate*. This engraving, appearing at the top of each chapter in Dufour's famous 1685 work, is one of many contemporary depictions of men of three exotic nations and the caffeinated beverages indigenous to their homelands: The Turk with his coffee, the Chinese with his cup of tea, and the Aztec with a goblet of chocolate. (The Library Company of Philadelphia)

dispel inebriation and promote sobriety, increase alertness and creativity, cure gout, scurvy, and dropsy, relieve headaches and kidney stones, improve appetite and digestion, purify the blood, stimulate the wit, and prolong life. Others applied themselves to blaming these drinks for desiccating body and brain and inducing headaches, emaciation, impotence, and premature death. However, medical debates have rarely been conducted in isolation, free from the influences of political, economic, social, or religious forces, and the historical controversies over the merits of caffeinated beverages have been no exception. Important commercial interests were at stake in these disputes. At the same time that the Dutch East India Company tea merchants were underwriting Buntekuh, the physician who was perhaps Europe's biggest promoter of caffeine, the French wine merchants were sponsoring his counterparts in their anti-caffeine campaign.

The Muslims not only gave to Europe the secret of drinking coffee and the institution of the coffeehouse; their sophisticated culture and science provided the basis for the medical controversies attending coffee's introduction and proliferation in Europe as well. Medieval medical learning in the Muslim world was founded on the ancient humoral theory of Hippocrates as elaborated by Galen, and by the time coffee, tea, and chocolate arrived in and spread throughout Europe in the seventeenth century, medical thinking in the Western world, under the influence of Islamic learning, was defined by the humoral theory as well. Galen, a Greek physician who lived in Rome in the second century, posited four personal types: the melancholic, choleric, phlegmatic, and the sanguine, each corresponding with the predominance of one of the four humoral fluids and its associated properties. Food, drinks, and medicines were all considered by humoral theorists to possess one or more of these properties in one degree or another. Where a given property is present in the first degree, we have a food. Where present in the second degree, we have a food or a medicine. Where present in the third degree, we have a medicine only. Where present in the fourth degree, we have a poison.

The Humoral Scheme

Humor	Temperament	Properties*
Black Bile	Melancholic	Dry-Cold
Yellow Bile	Bilious	Dry-Hot
Phlegm	Phlegmatic	Moist-Cold
Blood	Sanguine	Moist-Hot

*Present in the first, second, third, or fourth degrees

A Sobering View of Caffeine

Medical men, who worried over the actions of caffeinated drinks as drugs, and laymen, who accepted them as fortifying comestibles, agreed that the beverages, whether used as medicaments or refreshments, were effective antidotes to drunkenness and could induce and promote sobriety. Walter Rumsey (1584–1660), a Welsh judge who had been a student of both Francis Bacon and William Harvey, observed in a book chapter entitled "Experiments of Cophee" that the drink had the "power to cure drunkards." Remnants of this theory survive today in the prevalent but erroneous belief that a cup of strong coffee can make you sober.[2]

Nevertheless, people who drink coffee or tea throughout the day are more likely to be sober and efficient than those who drink beer. From Rumsey's time onward, the energizing and sobering effects of the caffeinated beverages were emphatically contrasted with the laziness and impairment attending consumption of other available drinks—almost all of which were alcoholic because the drinking water was generally unsafe. Because of the pervasiveness of alcoholic drinks in the lives of medieval and early modern Europeans, the institution of chronic sobriety constituted a radical change of life. Beer, for example, in addition to being consumed, as it is today, at celebrations and holidays, of which there were many, or simply as a recreational intoxicant, was also a primary a source of nourishment, second in importance in the average diet only to bread, and its consumption was nothing less than unremitting. Johann Breschneider (*Lat.* Johann Placotomus, 1514–76), German physician and educator, wrote of beer in 1551, "Some subsist more upon this drink than they do on food. . . . People of both sexes and every age, the hale and the infirm alike require it."[3]

Schivelbusch asserts that a typical English family in the seventeenth century averaged three quarts of beer per person, including children, every day, and that brewing beer was part of a housewife's usual duties. One of the reasons consumption was so high was that breakfast generally consisted of beer soup. If you are interested in trying a bowl, here is a recipe that survived in rural Germany at the end of the eighteenth century:

> Heat the beer in a saucepan; in a separate small pot beat a couple of eggs. Add a
> chunk of butter to the hot beer. Stir in some cold beer to cool it, then pour over the

eggs. Add a bit of salt, and finally mix all the ingredients together, whisking it well to keep it from curdling. Finally, cut up a roll, white bread, or other good bread, and pour the soup over it. You may also sweeten to taste with sugar.[4]

When each day began with a dish like this and when there were frequent drinking contests, in the course of which competitors fell one by one into an unconscious stupor, until a lone victor, like Socrates in the *Symposium*, rose and went home in singular awareness of his heady triumph, a nearly unmitigated state of alcoholic impairment was endemic.

Eventually a new attitude toward alcohol, arising with and perhaps in part as a consequence of the beginnings of modern industrial society, began to predominate in Europe, an attitude that had less patience for drinking bouts or alcoholism as a way of life. Considered in the context of pandemic inebriation that plagued Europe before caffeine's arrival, some of the more effusive claims made on behalf of the health benefits of the temperance beverages seem more reasonable; after all, simply curtailing alcohol consumption would have made millions feel better and work better from morning to evening.

Old ways die hard, and the ascent of the three new temperance beverages and the decline of traditional alcoholic drinks sometimes occasioned complaint. Elizabeth Charlotte (1652–1722), often called Liselotte von der Pfalz, a German princess who, after her marriage to the duke of Orléans, was required to relocate to Paris, wrote frequently in her correspondence to criticize the new drinks available at the court of Versailles:

> Tea makes me think of hay and dung, coffee of soot and lupine-seed, and chocolate is too sweet for me—it gives me a stomachache—I can't stand any of them. How much I would prefer a good *Kalteschale* [a cold soup made with wine and fruit] or a good beer soup, that wouldn't give me a stomachache.[5]

To judge from her letters, all three, coffee, tea, and chocolate, could still be credibly referred to at the beginning of the eighteenth century as "dainties" and "foreign spices." But the future belonged to the temperance beverages. Even in North America, the popularity of coffee was apparent by 1670, only six years after the British took over Dutch New Amsterdam, by which time coffee had replaced beer as New York's favorite breakfast drink.

Carolus Linnæus, the great eighteenth-century Swedish botanist who brought the first viable tea plants to Europe, seemed to foresee the change from the alcoholic to the workaholic that caffeine heralded: "On this account [coffee] might be considered useful by those who set a higher worth upon saving *their time than on maintaining their lives and health*, and who are compelled to work into the night." His comment demonstrates a lucid understanding of what we now consider the primary benefit of caffeine: imparting energy, increasing alertness, and forestalling sleep, and its primary application, in helping us to work when it is required we do so. He seems equally sensible of the personal danger that the use of stimulants, or overwork, may entail.

Jules Michelet (1798–1874), French historian, philosopher, and poet, writing of Europe in the seventeenth century and envisioning coffee as the elixir of mental clarity that saved Europe from the diabolical ruination of alcohol, vividly contrasts the old excesses of alcohol with the new sobriety of coffee:[6]

> Henceforth is the tavern dethroned, the monstrous tavern is dethroned which even half a century earlier had sent youths wallowing twixt casks and wenches, is dethroned. Fewer liquor-drenched songs on the night air, fewer noblemen sprawled in the gutter. . . . Coffee, the sober drink, the mighty nourishment of the brain, which unlike other spirits, heightens purity and lucidity; coffee, which clears the clouds of the imagination and their gloomy weight; which illumines the reality of things suddenly with the flash of truth.

German and Dutch Doctors Dispute about Coffee and Tea

As we have observed, the first European to make written mention of the coffee plant and beverage was a physician. Leonhard Rauwolf (d. 1596), a distinguished German doctor, famous in his time for both medicine and botany, is remembered chiefly for the book *Travels in the Orient* (1582), in which he tells the story of a two-and-a-half-year trip to the East. Rauwolf had embarked from Marseilles in 1573 and traveled as far as Persia before returning home to Augsburg in 1576. In the chapter depicting the sights and habits of the ancient city Aleppo, there occurs the passage in which the use of *chaube*, as he calls coffee, is inaugurated to Western letters:

> If you have a mind to eat something or to drink other liquors, there is commonly an open shop near it, where you sit down upon the ground or carpets and drink together. Among the rest they have a very good drink, by them called *Chaube* that is almost as black as ink, and very good in illness, chiefly that of the stomach; of this they drink in the morning early in open places before everybody, without any fear or regard, out of *China* cups, as hot as they can; they put it often to their lips but drink but little at a time, and let it go round as they sit.
>
> In this same water they take a fruit called *Bunnu* which . . . have within them, two yellowish grains in two distinct cells, and besides, being they agree in their virtue, figure, looks, and name with the *Bunchum* of *Avicenna*, and *Bunca* of *Rasis ad Almans* [Rhazes] exactly; therefore I will take them to be the same, until I am better informed by the learned. This liquor is very common among them, wherefore there are a great many of them that sell it, and others that sell the berries, everywhere in their *Batzars*.[7]

In Dr. Edward Pocoke's translation (Oxford, 1659) of Rauwolf's *The Nature of the Drink Kauhi, or Coffee, and the Berry of which It Is Made, Described by an Arabian Physician*, we find a good account of what was understood about the bean and its medical value in terms of contemporary humoral theory:

> *Bun* is a plant in the *Yaman* [Yemen], which is prepared in *Adar*, and groweth up and is gathered in Ab. It is about a cubit high, on a stalk about the thickness of one's thumb. It flowers white, leaving a berry like a small nut, but that sometimes is broad

like a bean; and when it is peeled, parteth in two. The best of it is that which is weighty and yellow; the worst, that which is black. It is hot in the first degree, dry in the second: it is usually reported to be cold and dry but it is not so; for it is bitter and whatsoever is bitter is hot. It may be that the scorce is hot, and the *Bun* it selfe either of equall temperature, or cold in the first degree.

That which makes for its coldnesse is its stiptickness. In summer it is by experience found to conduce to drying of rheumes, and flegmatcick coughes and distillations, and the opening of obstructions, and the provocation of urin. It is now known by the name of Kohwah. When it is dried and thoroughly boyled, it allayes the ebullition of the blood, is good against the small poxe and measles; the bloudy pimples; yet caught vertiginous headheach, and maketh lean much, occasioneth waking, and the Emrods, and asswageth lust, and sometimes breeds melancholly.

He that would drink it for liveliness sake, and to discusse slothfulnesse, and the other properties that we have mentioned, let him use much sweat meates with it, and oyle of pistaccioes, and butter. Some drink it with milk, but it is an error, and such as may bring in danger of the leprosy.[8]

The humoral terminology has not changed since Avicenna. And the uncertainty remains, as to a point that seems fairly fundamental, over whether coffee is, in terms of this theory, hot or cold in the first degree, although its dryness seems beyond dispute. The humoral hypothesis was rendered meaningless before it was discarded entirely. Medical experts after Rauwolf, in continuing their attempt to apply humoral analytical categories to coffee, eventually adopted the truistic formula that coffee somehow contained all the properties manifest in the fourfold scheme. In consequence, no possible experience with coffee could disprove the cogency of the humoral categories. Of course, this simply meant that nothing substantive was any longer being asserted, and, where nothing meaningful is being said, there can be nothing false either. Such looseness made it possible to attribute the widest range of benefits to coffee; for example, it could at once be said to dispel the gloom of the melancholy, mollify the choleric, and enliven the phlegmatic. Likewise, all manner of ills could be laid at its door.

Many new medical and ecclesiastical panegyrics on tea, coffee, and chocolate appeared, praising the drinks as panaceas. The first and fiercest opponent of their salutary view was Dr. Simon Pauli (1603–80), a German physician, who published *Commentarius de Abusu Tabaci et Herbae Thee, etc.* (Rostock, 1635), a medical tract with many dire admonitions about the detrimental effects of tea, coffee, chocolate, and, for good measure, tobacco. Both on account of his authority as physician to the king of Denmark and, later, through the translation of his work into English by one Dr. James as *A Treatise on Tobacco, Tea, Coffee, and Chocolate* (London, 1746), Pauli's enmity toward the three caffeinated beverages enjoyed a widespread and enduring influence.

Pauli judged all the drinks to be equally injurious:

Hence we may reasonably infer, that as *Chocolate* agrees with *Coffee* and *Tea*, . . . so all these three exactly agree with each other, in producing Effeminacy and Impotence. . . . I therefore hope, that for the future, the Europeans will be wise, and reject *Coffee,*

Chocolate, and *Tea*; since they are all either equally bad, or equally good: Nay, I hope to see People of all Ranks and Conditions, have as great an Aversion to them as the *Mahometans* and *Turks*, or rather their Emperors have to Tobacco, the Lovers of which as well as those who are idle, prodigal, barren, impotent, or effeminate, they will not suffer to live within their Territories.[9]

His book begins by proclaiming that the Chinese "are guilty of fulsome Exaggeration" when they assert that tea prolongs life, although he grants to tea a few genuine virtues in which we can see recognition of the effects of caffeine. "The first of which, according to *Rhodius*, is, that it alleviates Pains of the Head, and represses Vapors: The second, that it corroborates the Stomach: And, the third, that it expels the Stone and Gravel from the Kidneys."[10] In any case, there was no reason to risk tea's hazards in the hope of gaining such benefits. Pauli believed that betony, a traditional European medicinal herb, bestowed them and more and without the attending risks.[11]

Pauli rehearses a long list of health problems consequent to the use of tea and asserts that chocolate is at least as bad and that coffee is worse. But, according to Pauli, drinking tea had special problems for Westerners, because as a result of the rigors of transportation and the change in climate, tea loses the virtues that "it may be admitted that it does posses in the Orient," becoming dangerous indeed, so that, having deteriorated, "It hastens the death of those that drink it, especially if they have passed the age of forty years."[12] In the face of this menace, Pauli saw himself as a hero carrying forward a venerable tradition of public health education:

> As *Hippocrates* spared no Pains to remove and root out the *Athenian* Plague, so I have used the utmost of my Endeavours to destroy the raging epidemical Madness of importing *Tea* into *Europe* from *China*.[13]

The Netherlands was the only major European nation in which there never arose a movement advocating caffeine temperance, or coffee and tea prohibition. The Dutch scientists and medical men, unlike many of their French and German counterparts, were more than tolerant of the new arrivals, and their enthusiastic or even fanatical promotion of the use of coffee, tea, and chocolate might well be called "caffeinomania." For example, Jean Baptista van Helmont (1577–1644), a Flemish chemist, physiologist, and physician, taught his students that tea had the cleansing effects of leeches or laxatives and should be used in their place. Nikolas Dirx (1593–1674), another famous Dutch doctor, was also one of the earliest European physicians to promote the benefits of tea. In *Observationes Medicae* (Amsterdam, 1641), writing under the name "Dr. Tulpius," he called attention to what are today some of the well-recognized effects of caffeine:

> Nothing is comparable to this plant. Those who use it are for that reason, alone, exempt from all maladies and reach an extreme old age. Not only does it procure great vigor for their bodies, but it preserves them from gravel and gallstones, headaches, colds, ophthalmia, catarrh, asthma, sluggishness of the stomach and intestinal troubles. It has the additional merit of preventing sleep and facilitating vigils, which makes it a great help to persons desiring to spend their nights writing or meditating.[14]

Franz De le Boë (1614–72), or Franciscus Sylvius, a fellow Dutch physician, who helped establish modern chemistry as a science and championed Harvey's theory of the circulation of the blood, influenced Dutch doctors such as Stephan Blankaart and many German physicians as well to recommend copious quantities of the "newly important novelties, tea and coffee, as panaceas for acidity and blood purifiers."[15] As a result of his efforts, several of the great German universities, including Jena and Wittenberg, promulgated these doctrines.

However, of all the physicians who wrote in praise of the medicinal value of coffee and tea at the close of the seventeenth century, yet another Dutchman, Dr. Cornelius Decker (1648–85), of Alkmaar, otherwise known as Dr. Cornelius Buntekuh (or Bontekoe), was their most distinguished and fervent advocate and a fitting adversary of Simon Pauli. An entrepreneur as well as a flamboyant medical theoretician, he is said to have opened the first coffeehouse in Hamburg in 1679.

Buntekuh did more than anyone else to promote the general use of both coffee and tea in Europe. In a book published in 1679, Buntekuh advised drinking a minimum of ten cups of tea daily, and recommended building up to fifty, one hundred, or two hundred cups, amounts he frequently consumed himself.[16] Based on a record that the company paid him a handsome honorarium in gratitude for the boost his advocacy gave to tea sales, it is said that Buntekuh may have initially been hired by the Dutch East India Company to write in praise and defense of tea. This was perhaps the first grant of money in the West by a commercially interested party to a physician or scientist friendly to the use of a caffeinated beverage to write in its favor, an endowment reminiscent of Lu Yü's commission from the Chinese tea merchants nearly a thousand years earlier. Of course, the provision of money by merchants to support publishable research friendly to caffeine continues to this day.

Frederick William (r. 1640–88) inherited his throne following the destruction of the Thirty Years' War, when towns stood abandoned, Berlin was devastated, and productive industry was suspended. Because the ruler admired the Dutch people for their stalwart character, determination, and diligence, Frederick induced thousands to immigrate to help repopulate his desolate kingdom. He also mounted a campaign to lure foreign intellectuals to Germany, to help in working a miraculous revival for the nation. Partly in consequence of this effort, he became a man ahead of his time in respect to coffee and tea, when Dr. Buntekuh, then regarded as an eminent physician, became one of many to accept Frederick's invitation to relocate from Holland to Germany. As a result of Buntekuh's blandishments, Frederick started drinking coffee himself and imported his personal supply of beans from Buntekuh's homeland.[17]

Buntekuh's scientific goal, to improve the dietary habits of Europe, was greatly advanced by his new place in Frederick's court. Because his father was an innkeeper under the sign of the "Bunte Kuh," or the "brindled cow," his neighbors dubbed him with the cognomen he later signed to his scientific monographs. After studying philosophy, with special attention to Descartes, Buntekuh moved to Amsterdam and then to Hamburg. Frederick William enticed him to come to Germany by seeing that he was offered an appointment at the University of Frankfurt-on-the-Oder. In his *Medizinischen Elementarlehre* and other books Buntekuh wrote extensively about the analeptic effects of coffee and tea, clearly reflecting his recognition of the pharmacological properties that we now attribute to caffeine.

Buntekuh taught his students that Harvey's was the greatest scientific discovery in several hundred years.[18] Like many other contemporary physicians, Buntekuh thought that any substance that enlivened or accelerated the circulation of the blood was bound to be beneficial. Because coffee and tea evidently promoted and stimulated this circulation, they boosted the vitality of the Cartesian living machine. As we shall see, Harvey himself was also one of the great seventeenth-century caffeine enthusiasts.

In the historical saga of caffeine, Buntekuh is also remembered for having published the earliest European depiction of the cacao tree. His engraving accurately shows how the tree bears its pods directly from the main branches, one of the plant's more unusual properties. It also shows how a larger tree may be planted nearby, as is often done, to shade the young cacao plant.

Buntekuh's death at thirty-eight did not add credibility to his treatise *Traktat van het Excellentie Cruyt Thee* (1679), on the extension of human life by the use of tea, coffee, and chocolate, for he certainly was a man who took his own medicine. However, we must add for completeness' sake that he died not of ill health but by accident, falling down a darkened staircase while carrying books for the Great Elector, as Frederick was called in recognition of his miraculous revival of the nation. A doubt remains, however, if the chronic use of toxic doses of caffeine might not have created tremors, excitement, or even delirium that caused him to lose his footing. At the very least, we might assume that he was critically sleep deprived at the time of his fall.

Because of Buntekuh's presence, coffee was brewed at the Berlin Court in the 1670s, although its circulation was limited to an aristocratic coterie. But despite this brief flirtation with it and the other caffeinated drinks, Germany was not yet ready for caffeine, and, after Buntekuh's death, caffeine was not to become widely popular there for several decades.

Medical Disputes in Marseilles and the Rest of France

At least once, toward the end of the seventeenth century, the provinces overtook Paris in a matter of fashion. For while the popularity of coffee remained limited in that city by royal indifference and the lack of any regular commercial supply until 1692, in Marseilles, a port of entry, coffee had become readily available and prevalent more than twenty years before.

Around 1650, several Marseilles merchants, after spending time in the Near East, began bringing coffee home with them in small amounts. Within a few years, merchants and pharmacists formed a syndicate to institute commercial imports of coffee from Egypt, and their example was soon followed by their counterparts in Lyon. These imports allowed coffee use to become common in the countryside surrounding both towns. In 1671 a coffeehouse opened in Marseilles, the success of which prompted the creation of many others, all of which, we are told in contemporary accounts, were heavily patronized. At the same time, household coffee use became more common, so that, as Jean La Roque reports in *Voyage de L'Arabie Heureuse* (Paris, 1716), "In fine, the use of the beverage increased so amazingly that, as was inevitable, the physicians became alarmed, thinking it would not agree with the inhabitants of a country hot and extremely dry."[19]

These concerns and the corresponding disputes over the salubrity of coffee were essentially those voiced in Mecca, Cairo, and Constantinople more than a hundred years before, and they were, as we have seen, also based on the humoral theory propounded by Avicenna and other Islamic physicians. Overall the French public leaned heavily in favor of the caffeinated beverages, while the French physicians leaned heavily against them. La Roque describes a late-seventeenth-century face-off between the caffeine users and the doctors during which "the lovers of coffee used the physicians very ill when they met together, and the physicians on their side threatened the coffee drinkers with all sorts of diseases."[20]

One difference between these controversies in France and the Islamic disputes was the part played by the French vintners, who were not disposed to share their customers with coffee merchants and who therefore subsidized caffeine's opponents in this war of letters. In 1679 Castillon and Fouqué, two physicians of the Faculty of Aix, rented the town hall and sent a freshman medical student, named "Colomb," to argue a brief against coffee before the city magistrate and an audience of local physicians and laymen. In his thesis, entitled "Whether the Use of Coffee Is Harmful to the Inhabitants of Marseilles," Colomb acknowledged that coffee was used in many nations, where it had often entirely displaced wine, while arguing that, nevertheless, it was in every way inferior to that more familiar beverage. With characteristic Gallic xenophobia, he then damned coffee as an unwholesome foreign introduction, brought to the attention of men by goats and camels. As to its health effects, he asserted that coffee had been accepted by European physicians on the strength of self-serving Arab testimonials disseminated to develop new markets for their produce. Coffee, he continued, had no value as a cure for distempers and was in humoral terms hot, not cold as its proponents claimed, and that, because it consumed the blood, it caused impotence, emaciation, and palsy. Colomb concluded:

> Some assure us that coffee is a cooling drink and for this reason they recommend us to drink it very hot. . . . The burned particles, which it contains in large quantities, have so violent an energy that, when they enter the blood, they attract the lymph and dry the kidneys. Furthermore, they are dangerous to the brain for, after having dried up the cerebro-spinal fluid and the convolutions, they open the pores of the body, with the result that the somniferous animal forces are overcome. In this way the ashes contained in coffee produce such obstinate wakefulness that the nervous juices are dried up; . . . the upshot being general exhaustion, paralysis, and impotence. Through the acidification of the blood, which has already assumed the condition of a river-bed at midsummer, all the parts of the body are deprived of their juices, and the whole frame becomes excessively lean.[21]

His references to "juices" designate the body's fluids, the balance of which, according to humoral theory, determined a person's health. Once again, it is easy to see the actions attributable to caffeine among the effects Colomb describes, including what was then often called "desiccation," or increased urination, and its power to overcome "somniferous animal forces" and induce "obstinate wakefulness."

Colomb's diatribe did not dissuade many caffeine users, for coffee had already insinuated itself into popular affections and was not to be easily displaced. In France, where doctors of medicine were lampooned in contemporary plays as pretentious pseudo-savants, their anticoffee blandishments won little regard from the public. Therefore, despite the reformatory admonitions of physicians such as Castillon and Fouqué, coffeehouses continued to increase in popularity, as did coffee drinking in the home, and the merchants imported green coffee from the East in ever increasing quantities to satisfy the demand.

Though Colomb's exhortations and the admonitions of the physicians of Aix failed to impress the public at large, they did help to prejudice the views of the medical community for some time. Partly as a result of Colomb's arguments, most French doctors toward the end of the seventeenth century advised against the use of coffee as a comestible, maintaining that it was a potent and potentially dangerous drug that should be taken by prescription only. Lurid stories about coffee poisoning abounded. When Jean Baptiste Colbert (1619–83), financier and statesman, died, it was whispered that his stomach had been corroded by coffee. According to another letter penned by Elizabeth Charlotte, duchess of Orléans, an autopsy revealed that the princess of Hanau-Birkenfeld had hundreds of stomach ulcers, each filled with coffee grounds, and it was concluded that she had died of coffee drinking.

Not every Gallic scientist was so easily persuaded of the evils of caffeine. Philippe Sylvestre Dufour (1622–87), an archaeologist, joined with Charles Spon (1609–84), a Lyon physician, scholar, and Latin poet, and Cassaigne, another local physician, to perform a chemical analysis of coffee. Based on this collaborative effort, Dufour wrote his famous work mentioned at the opening of this chapter, which was reissued in many editions and translations, but which is now only to be found in rare book rooms, *Traitez Nouveaux & curieux Du Café, Du Thé et Du Chocolate* (1685).[22] This was the first book to attempt to derive the pharmacologic effects of coffee from its chemical constituents. Among its other benefits, Dufour asserted that coffee counteracted drunkenness and nausea and relieved menstrual disorders. He repeated other long-standing claims for the drink, including that it relieved kidney stones, gout, and scurvy, and also stated that it strengthened the heart and lungs and relieved migraine headaches. He noted with surprise that some people can sleep at bedtime even immediately after drinking coffee. His overall judgment was a favorable one: "Coffee banishes languor and anxiety, gives to those who drink it, a pleasing sensation of their own well-being and diffuses through their whole frame, a vivifying and delightful warmth."[23] (Dufour also wrote an earlier book about the preparation of the caffeinated beverages, *The Manner of Making Coffee, Tea, and Chocolate as It Is Used by Most Parts of Europe, Asia, Africa, and America, with Their Virtues* [Lyon, 1671; London, 1685].)

Dr. Louis Lemery (1677–1743) published *Traité des Aliments* (Paris, 1702; translated by John Taylor and printed in London as *A Treatise of Foods*, 1704), in which he summarized what he saw as the beneficial and harmful effects of coffee. Among the good effects were: strengthening the stomach, speeding digestion, abating headaches, alleviating hangovers, stimulating the production of urine and flatulence and the onset of menses, and stimulating the memory and imagination. The bad effects included emaciation and loss of sexual appetite.[24] In the English edition, while ascribing to chocolate most of the same pharmacological effects as coffee, he also credited it with allaying "the sharp Humours that fall upon the Lungs," a clear reference to caffeine's antiasthmatic properties, and with promoting "venery" as opposed to diminishing the erotic impulse.

Toward the close of the seventeenth century, Daniel Duncan (1649–1735), a Scottish physician on the faculty of Montpellier, wrote a polemic addressing all three known caffeinated beverages and throwing in brandy and distilled spirits for good measure. His book, published in France in 1703, attained considerable circulation in

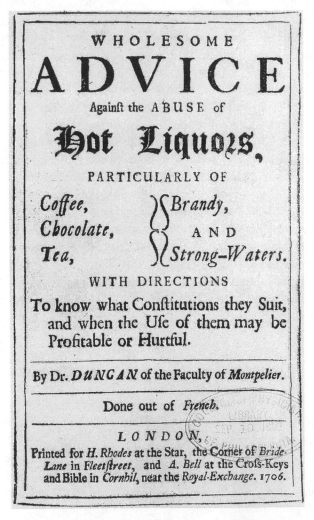

Title page: *Wholesome Advise against the Abuse of Hot Liquors, Particularly of Coffee, Chocolate, Tea, Brandy and Strong-Waters, with directions, To know what Constitutions they Suit, and when the Use of them may be Profitable or Hurtful*, by Dr. Duncan of the Faculty of Montpelier, London, Printed for H. Rhodes at the Star, 1706. This book, by a Scottish physician who took a position on the medical faculty in France, warned against the dangers of excessive coffee, tea, and chocolate consumption. (Philadelphia College of Physicians)

that country and was translated into English under the title *Wholesome Advise against the Abuse of Hot Liquors, Particularly of Coffee, Chocolate, Tea, Brandy, and Strong-Waters.* This 1706 London edition published by H. Rhodes was widely referenced as an authority throughout the eighteenth century. Dr. Duncan saw himself as a man of moderation and reason, one who fairly considered all sides of every question and eschewed extremes of all sorts. On the first page of his book he states, in what was an apparently unknowing recapitulation of a compelling neo-Platonic Augustinian theodicy, that any being, however base, is better than nothing. "There's nothing absolutely good, but God. . . . Among Creatures there's nothing absolutely Bad, for [that] they are the workmanship of that infinitely good being, communicates to each of them some degree of that goodness."[25] After four or five pages more in this vein, he continues:

> That's the design of this Treatise, and to make a particular Essay upon this Gen-eral Maxim, by describing the Good and Bad Use of Hot Things, and especially of Coffee, Tea, Chocolate, and Brandy, of which abundance of Good has been said by some, and abundance of Ill by others.[26]

A garrulous moralist, Duncan saw in the pleasures of coffee, tea, and chocolate a dangerous snare. "Voluptuousness," he explains, "creates in us an Aversion to good Things, because they are not pleasant; and an inclination to bad Things, because they please us." He adds, "Both these things happen in the use of Coffee, Chocolate, and Tea." Coffee's bitterness is so pronounced that coffee at last becomes "agreeable . . . not so much by Custom, as by the mixture of Sugar . . . and since it became pleas-ant, it's become pernicious by the abuse of it." Calling them all "liquors," Duncan pro-nounces a single verdict on all three caffeinated beverages, suggesting how strongly their common nature as vehicles of a drug was suspected and providing a vivid impres-sion of how completely caffeine had conquered France by the turn of the eighteenth century:

> The use or abuse of those Liquors has become almost universal. Towns, villages, and all sorts of people are in a manner over-flow'd by them. So that not to know them is reckoned barbarous. They are in all Societies, and to be found everywhere. For-merly none but Persons of Qualities or Estate had them, but now they are common to high and low, rich and poor, so that if they were poison, all mankind would be poison'd; and if they be good medicines, all men may reap advantage by them when they come to know the true use of them.

Duncan finally issues the balanced judgment he promised to deliver at the begin-ning of his book: that coffee, chocolate, and tea have good and bad effects, depend-ing on who is using them and how much he is using, but that none of them is either a deadly toxin or a panacea. However, he also observes, too much of any caffeinated beverage is harmful to anyone, and even a small amount can be harmful to some people. Duncan concludes, as had so many before him, that many of coffee's delete-rious effects resulted from its diuretic actions, or "desiccative influence."[27] Although admitting that coffee could be beneficial for those "whose blood circulates sluggishly, who are of a damp and cold nature," he asserted that the French did not suffer from this problem and so joined other French physicians in their opposition to its indiscriminate use in his adopted country.

The Early English Health Debates

Meanwhile, in England, despite republication of Duncan's cautionary book there, caffeine continued to grow in popularity. And, although England had not been among the first Western nations to become alert to coffee, none took to the drink quite so avidly; in consequence, from 1680 to 1730, Londoners consumed more coffee than the inhabitants of any other city in the world.

What Goes Around Comes Around: Harvey Puts Caffeine into Circulation

The caffeine in coffee stimulated and sustained the investigations of the early members of the Royal Society, and in this way helped Robert Boyle create the science of chemistry and make possible caffeine's discovery. Another remarkable tale of caffeine and the history of science depicts a man fifty years Boyle's senior, William Harvey (1578–1657), physician and professor of anatomy, the greatest medical researcher and theoretician of his century, and a true pioneer of caffeine use in England.

Harvey, who discovered and demonstrated the circulation of the blood and is acknowledged, with Vesalius, as one of the two primary founders of modern scientific medicine, was also one of the first Europeans who is known to have taken caffeine regularly. He drank coffee for more than fifty years before coffeehouses came to London, at a time when he was forced to import his own supply of beans, the habit and the trade connections both having been acquired during his student days in Padua.

Harvey was born in Folkestone, Kent, the oldest of nine scions of a wealthy international trader. Five of his six brothers, following in their father's footsteps, became "Turkey merchants," as Englishmen called those who traded with the Eastern nations. Harvey's singular academic bent was recognized early, and when he was ten years old he was enrolled in Kings School, where he was rigorously drilled in the Latin and Greek that was to give him access to the intellectual inheritance of the Classical world. At sixteen, he matriculated at Caius College at Cambridge, a school popular, then as now, among students interested in becoming physicians. (It had been named for Dr. John Caius, who had shared an apartment with Vesalius when both were students in Padua.) Harvey received his B.A. in 1597 and two years later embarked to study medicine in Italy. In 1602 he was granted his doctoral diploma from Padua. Thereafter, he returned to London, where, over the years, his upscale medical practice included James I, Charles I, and Lord Chancellor Bacon. Here he engaged in the methodical and creative investigations that led to the formulation of his history-making theory of the circulation of the blood.

The University of Padua, when Padua was under Venetian rule, aspired to become for the academic world what Venice already was for the community of trade: the foremost international center, where the best of everything would be gathered together for exchange by and enrichment of all. By the time of Harvey's tenure, it had succeeded, becoming one of the most exciting intellectual centers in Europe and winning special distinction in medical studies. While attending the University of Padua, Harvey encountered three things that were to change his life and the history of medicine forever. It was at Padua that Harvey learned the biological and medical texts of the ancients, including, of course, the highly revered works of Aristotle and Galen. It was also in Padua that Harvey fell under the influence of Fabricius, a man who instilled in him a recognition of the essential place of observation and experimentation in the study of biological systems. Finally, it was at Padua that Harvey first heard of coffee and developed a lifelong passion for the psychoactive and medicinal powers of caffeine.

Because the great trading city of Venice was nearby, it was natural that members of the faculty of the University of Padua should be among the leaders in writing books about scientific field trips abroad. Therefore it is no surprise that the second book published in Europe to mention coffee was written by Prospero Alpini (1553–1617), an eminent physician and professor of botany at Padua, after his return from a trip to the Orient. In this book, *The Plants of Egypt* (Venice, 1592), the author tells of the nature and popularity of the Islamic coffeehouse and lists some of the medicinal benefits coffee drinking confers. Whether Harvey encountered coffee in the works of Alpini, or whether it was, as some say, first served to him by Arab fellow students, we may never know. One thing is sure, however: When, after three years, Harvey returned to England, he brought with him the seeds of ideas that would change scientific thinking and other seeds as well, ones that, when properly prepared, would stimulate and augment the energy and clarity of thought, seeds that he was to use and recommend to others for this purpose for the rest of his life, and the enjoyment of which he was to attempt to perpetuate among his colleagues after his death. [28]

Like Shakespeare, who died a week before Harvey's first Lumleia Lecture before the College of Physicians in 1616, Harvey managed to attain immortal fame while leaving behind few discoverable traces of his personal life. We know he was married and childless and that his wife died ten years before he did. What little else is known of the man apart from the record of his work must be gleaned from the biographical sketch included in John Aubrey's collection *Brief Lives*, the value of which may be compromised by the fact that Aubrey and Harvey did not become friends until Aubrey was twenty-five and Harvey was seventy-three. We find in Aubrey's sketch the image of a man whom we can easily envision talking up his friends at intellectual coffee klatches.

Nuland offers his impression of the Harvey whom Aubrey depicts: "the image of an olive-complexioned, dark-eyed man of quite slight stature, filled with nervous energy of the high-output kind. But though his physical movements may have been fitful, his brain was full of purpose."[29]

Surely this representation is consistent with a man who employs caffeine to keep his motor running in high gear. There may be more truth than fiction in an anecdote alleging that Harvey had discovered the secret of the circulation of the blood because his own heavy coffee drinking so stimulated his own system that he noticed his blood racing around his body.[30] In any event, among Aubrey's brief remarks is the following picture of Harvey as a man whom late coffee drinking might well have kept awake nights:

He was hott-headed, and his thoughts working would many time keepe him from
sleepinge; he told me that then his way was to rise out of his Bed and walke about his
Chamber in his Shirt till he was pretty coole, i.e. till he had began to have a horror
[chill], and then returne to bed, and sleepe very comfortably.

Aubrey testifies that Harvey and one of his brothers were inveterate coffee
drinkers before the custom became popular in England.[31] Indeed, as Harvey was
seventy-three when the first coffeehouse opened for business in London, he must have
done most if not all of his coffee drinking privately, from the stock that he had had
specially imported from Italy.

He died in 1657, exclaiming to his solicitor and friend, if some undocumented
accounts are to be believed, "This little fruit is the source of happiness and wit!"
while running his thumbnail along the groove of a coffee bean. It was really caffeine
that was the object of his praise and celebration. In his will he leaves his coffeepot
and fifty-eight pounds of coffee beans, his entire stock, to his brothers in the Royal
College of Physicians, directing that they celebrate the date of his death each month
by drinking coffee until the supply he had provided became exhausted. The disbelief and controversy surrounding his theory, as expounded to the Royal College of
Physicians (known then as the London College of Physicians), ultimately resolved
into resounding acclaim, and the circulation of the blood was accepted into the
arcana of great scientific discoveries. We leave the story of Harvey with the image
in our minds of the members of the Royal College of Physicians toasting Harvey
with the hot, stimulating brew and entertaining a few more ideas and pursuing a few
more experiments than they might, without caffeine's benefits, have otherwise
undertaken.

John Ovington's *Essay* and Other Rave Reviews of Tea

The English love of tea, which began in the seventeenth century, was recorded by
a host of writers whose books can be read in rare book libraries today. Dr. William
Chamberlayne (1619–89), an English physician and poet, in his *Treatise of Tea*, praises
the drink for its ability to sustain mental efforts into the night:

> When I have been compell'd to sit up all Night about some extraordinary Busi-
> ness, I needed to do no more than to take some of this Tea, when I perceiv'd my self
> beginning to sleep, and I could easily watch all Night without winking; and in the
> Morning I was as fresh as if I had slept my ordinary time; this I could do once a week
> without any trouble.[32]

In his elegantly styled *Essay upon the Nature and Qualities of Tea* (1699), John
Ovington (fl. 1689–98), an English traveler and churchman, who, as the frontispiece
declares, served as "Chaplain to His Majesty," begins his book with a discussion of "the
various Kinds of this foreign Leaf, and the Season wherein it should be gather'd, of
the Method of making choice of the best, and the Means whereby it is preserv'd."
His fifth and final chapter, "The several Virtues for which it is fam'd," encompassing

half the volume, exposits tea's medicinal effects. He claims that "Gout and Stone," common disorders in Europe, are virtually unknown in China because of their constant use of tea. The remedial effects appear, he continues, "especially if it be drunk in such a Quantity, and at such convenient Times, when the Stomach is rather empty than over-charge'd."[33]

Ovington's claims for the medical benefits of tea went beyond the treatment of gout and kidney stones. Unknowingly referencing one of caffeine's most characteristic effects, he wrote enthusiastically about tea's ability to induce urination, "fortify the Tone of the Bowels," and also noted tea's ability to aid digestion, "to strengthen a faint Appetite, and correct the nauseous Humours that offend the Stomach." He considered these effects tokens of many additional benefits attendant upon the resulting purification of the body, especially for "weak and feeble Constitutions."

Ovington reserves his highest praise for those mentally stimulating powers of tea we now know are caused by caffeine. He believed that not only could tea act as an antidote to alcohol, which "inflames the Blood, and disorders the Phantisms of the Brain," but that it could actually promote imaginative and lively thoughts: "It nimbly, ascends into the Brain, . . . it actuates and quickens the drowsy Thoughts, adds a kind of new Soul to the Fancy, and gives fresh Vigor and Force to the wearied Invention."

Thus it is with Ovington, in the penultimate year of the seventeenth century, that the notion of caffeine as a stimulant broadens. Previously, the caffeinated beverages had been credited with the power to sustain physical strength, as in the conquistador's boasted that those who drank chocolate could march for a day without food, and the power to prolong wakefulness, as in the Sufi observation that coffee sustained their nocturnal devotions or the Taoist observation that tea sustained their prolonged meditations. To these stimulating powers Ovington adds the idea that tea can provoke "invention" or "fancy," or, as we should say, "creativity," and that it is therefore the natural liquor of the "sons of the Muse." As to the identity of the "ingenious Persons" who, Ovington says, had personal benefit from tea's power to stimulate creativity, we can only speculate, save for the certainty that he meant to include Edmund Waller (1606–87), whose poem, "Of Tea, commended by Her Majesty," addressed to Catherine of Braganza (1638–1705), he presents in full. This poem praises tea as "the Muse's friend," which "does our Fancy aid." This idea is well envisioned in Ruffio's painting *Coffee Comes to the Aid of the Muse*.

Although Ovington, like others before him, commends the ability of tea to forestall sleep and induce wakefulness, he regards this ability not so much as a result of the stimulation of the body, but as a consequence of tea's power to fire the imagination by "animating the Faculties":

> So that a few Cups of this excellent Liquor will soon rowze the cloudy Vapors that be night the Brain, and drive away all Mists from the Eyes. 'Tis a kind of another Phoebus to the Soul, both for inspiring and inlightening it; and in spight of all the Darkness of the Night, and all the Heaviness of the Mind, 'twill brighten and animate the Thoughts, and expel those Mists of Humors that dull and darken Meditation.[34]

Coffee Comes to the Aid of the Muse, a drawing from a painting by Ruffio. This drawing reminds us of the line from Waller, "Tea, the Muse's friend," and the expressions of many famous artists and scientists to the effect that the caffeinated beverages were important if not indispensable to their creative exertions. (W. H. Ukers, *All about Coffee*)

His concluding cautionary remarks are surprisingly moderate and modern:

> And yet after all, though these rare and excellent Qualities have long been observable in Tea, yet must we not imagine that they always meet with the same Effect indifferently in all Persons, or that they universally prevail. For either the Height of a Distemper, or the long Continuance of it; either the Constitution of the Person, or some certain occult Indisposition may avert the Efficacy, and obstruct or delay the desir'd Success. It may either be drunk without Advice, or at unseasonable Times; either the Water, or the Tea, may be bad; and if the Physick itself be sickly, we cannot easily expect much Health by it.[35]

Mixed Notices for Coffee, Tea, and Chocolate

From the middle of the seventeenth century to the middle of the eighteenth century, a variety of extreme opinions about the three temperance beverages competed in England. Most English physicians, who, unlike their French counterparts of the time, were respected in their native land, advanced the view that coffee and tea had indispensable medicinal value.[36] We get a quick look into the medical opinions of both countries about tea, coffee, and chocolate from *A Compleat History of DRUGGS*, a compendious French *materia medica*, translated into English in 1712:

Of Tea

The Tea is so much in vogue with the Eastern People, that there are very few who do not drink it; and the French some Years ago had it in universal Esteem; but since Coffee and Chocolate have been introduced into that Country, there is nothing near the quantity used as before. . . .

. . . The Leaf is more used for Pleasure in the Liquor we call Tea, than for any medicinal Purpose; but it has a great many good Qualities, for it lightens and refreshes the Spirits, suppresses Vapours, prevents and drives away Drowsiness, strengthens the Brain and Heart, hastens Digestion, provokes Urine, cleanses or purifies the Blood, and is proper against the Scurvy. . . .

We have six kinds of Tea used in England. . . . The Bohea, however is esteemed softening and nourishing, and good in all inward Decays; the Green is diuretick, and carries an agreeable Roughness with it into the Stomach, which gently astringes the Fibres, and gives them such a Tensity as is necessary for a good Digestion: Improper or excessive Use may make this, or any thing else that has any Virtues at all, do Mischief; but there are very few Instances of that; and with Moderation it certainly is one of the best, pleasantest, and safest Herbs ever introduced into Food or Medicine, and in the frequent Use of which, People generally enjoy a confirm'd Health: the Green, indeed, if drank too freely, is prejudicial to such as have weak Lungs; such People, therefore, ought to drink the Bohea with Milk in it.[37]

Of Coffee

Caffe, Coffe, Coffi, Buna, Bon, Ban, or Elkaire . . . Coffee is used for little or nothing I know of, but to make a Liquor with Water and Sugar, which is more or less esteem'd, by different Nations. . . .

It is an excellent drying Quality, comforts the Brain and dries up Crudities in the Stomach: Some Author says, it cures Consumptions, Rickets, and Swooning Fits; it helps Digestion, eases Pains of the Head, rarefies the Blood, supresses Vapours, gives Life and Gaiety to the Spirits, hinders Sleepiness after Vituals, provokes Urine and the Courses, and contracts the Bowels; it is an excellent Dryer, fit for most Bodies, and most Constitutions, but that of young Girls, subject to the Green-Sickness; and likewise is prevalent in such as are apt to have running Humours, sores, or King's Evil upon them: It prevents Abortion, and confirms the Tone of the parts drunk after eating; but with this Observation, that this Liquor be always made fresh; for if it stands but two or three Hours, it will be pall'd and grow naught.[38]

Of the Cacao, or Chocolate-Nut

This Fruit is cooling, as may easily be discern'd by their cold nitrous Taste. They open Obstructions, restore in deep Consumptions, stimulate to venery causing Procreation and Conception, facilitate Delivery, preserve Health, help Digestion, make People inclinable to feed, ease Coughs of the Lungs, Gripings of the Bowels, and Fluxes thereof, cause a sweet Breath, and assist in a Difficulty of making Urine. The chief Use of them is in Chocolate, which is so well known there needs no longer discourse about it.[39]

Thomas Gage (1597–1656), an English missionary, traveler, and travel writer, who lived for a while in South America and wrote a book about the West Indies (referenced in chapter 3), recommends that his European readers take chocolate cold for health reasons, writing that this is the way the Indians do and "thus certainly it doth no hurt." Gage believed that something about living in America weakened the stomach, stating that "stomachs are more apt to faint than here." His account of his own consumption of chocolate has an addict's characteristically insistent enthusiasm:

For myself I must say, I used it twelve years constantly, drinking one cup in the morning, another yet before dinner, between nine or ten of the clock; another within an hour or two after dinner, and another between four and five in the afternoon; and when I was proposed to set up late to study, I would take another cup about seven or eight at night, which would keep me waking till about midnight. And if by chance I did neglect any of these accustomed houres, I presently found my stomach fainty. And with this custome, I lived twelve years in those parts healthy, without any obstructions, or oppilations, not knowing what either ague or fever was.[40]

We note that he specifies two among what today are recognized as the major effects of caffeine usage: forestalling sleep and a physical dependence that can cause an upset stomach if a dose is skipped.

Other observations about of tea's pharmacological effects are found in an anonymous slim volume, published in London in 1722, *Essay on the Nature, Use, and Abuse of Tea: In a letter to a lady: with an account of its mechanical operation.* The author states that tea is to be regarded primarily as a drug, one that has medicinal value when prescribed properly by a physician. The book compares tea's destructive effects with opium's and warns:

Among many other Novelties in our Diet, there is one which seems particularly to be the Cause of the *Hypochondriack Disorders* [pains and discomforts beneath the breast bone and melancholy]; and is generally known by the Name of *Thea* or *Tea*. It is a Drug, which has of late Years very much insinuated itself, as well into our Diet, as Regales and Entertainments, tho' its Operation is not less destructive to the Animal Oeconomy, than *Opium*, or some other Drugs, which we have at present learn'd to avoid with more Caution. That this Drug is useful in Physick, is what I can by no means deny: But as a Medicine, makes it very hurtful as a Diet. And it may be said of all Bodies whatever, which are useful as Medicines, that they are Poisons as a Diet.[41]

It is reported in Hawesworth's *Voyages* that Commodore John Byron (1723–86), a British admiral, found cacao growing abundantly on King George's Island in the South Seas. Henry Phillips, in *The Companion for the Orchard: An Historical and Botanical Account of Fruits Known in Great Britain* (1831), reports that Byron's claims for cacao's pharmacological benefits were expansive:[42]

> The oil of the cacao-nut is the hottest of any known, and is used to recover cold, weak, and paralytic limbs. The Mexicans are said to eat the nuts raw, to assuage pains in the bowels.[43]

Medical Debates: The Mid-Eighteenth through the End of the Nineteenth Century

With the emergence of modern medical theory and practice in the eighteenth century, two-thousand-year-old humoral theory, having already suffered punishing blows by Vesalius and Harvey in the sixteenth and early seventeenth centuries, came to a lingering and belated end. During this transitional period there appeared a parade of curious, now mostly outmoded ideas about what caffeine does, and how it does what it does, in the human body.

Dr. Simon André Tissot

Fifty years after the death of Cornelius Buntekuh and fifty years before Runge discovered caffeine, elements of humoral theory were still prominent in European medicine. Dr. Simon André Tissot (1728–97), a Swiss-French physician and medical writer, writing at a time by which coffee had come into general use even in Germany, accepted coffee's place in the *materia medica* but expressed serious objections to its widespread consumption as part of an everyday diet. In his book *Von der Gesundheit der Geleharten*, or *The Health of Scholars* (Leipzig, 1769), Tissot argued that Buntekuh, in promoting coffee and tea, had "corrupted the whole of northern Europe."[44] He asserted that accelerating the circulation of the blood, as coffee would admittedly do, had no value in curing illness and, in fact, will do positive harm:

> It is a foolish belief of many sick persons that their ailments are due to an excessive thickness of the blood. Owing to this fallacy, they drink the harmful beverage coffee. The coffee-pots and tea-pots that I find upon their tables remind me of Pandora's box, out of which all evils came. . . .
> The repeated stimulation of the fibers of the stomach weakens them in the end; . . . the nerves are stimulated, and become unduly sensitive; the energies are dissipated.[45]

In this passage Tissot expresses his views about the consequences of coffee's "desiccative" effects. Both coffee's defenders and detractors agreed that the beverage had an important relationship to the humoral fluid, phlegm, or mucus, which it dried up, whether to good or bad effect, depending on the interpretation of the writer. It was to this effect that Benjamin Moseley, an English physician and medical writer, referred when he wrote, "coffee, which through its warmth and effectiveness, thins the mucous moistures, and improves the circulation of the blood."[46] It was likewise of these desiccative effects that Denis Diderot (1713–1784), in his *Encyclopédie*, was speaking when he praised coffee's effect on "heavy-bodied, stout, and strongly phlegm-congested persons," while advising that it proved deleterious to the "thin and bilious."[47] In a chastening response to those who affected to find coffee indispensable, Tissot pointed out that the great ancient writers, from Homer onward, wrote their great books without its benefit.

Benjamin Moseley, M.D., for the Defense

Benjamin Moseley, M.D. (1742–1819), in *A Treatise Concerning the Properties and Effects of Coffee* (London, 1785), presents a comprehensive study of what was known about the origins and health effects of coffee in his time, including a particularly interesting critique of prior medical writers such as Simon Pauli. Moseley sees himself as going beyond mere anecdote and basing his conclusions on observation and analysis. Like Thucydides, he did not have a similarly high opinion of the methods of his predecessors:

> Among the furious enemies . . . of Coffee was SIMON PAULLI of Rostock, afterwards physician to the King of Denmark . . . PAULLI founded his prejudice against coffee, as he had his prejudices against Tea, Chocolate, and Sugar—not on experience, but on anecdotes, that had been picked up by hasty travellers, which had no other foundation than absurd report and conjecture . . . its supposed effects, on Sultan MAHOMET CASNIN, a King of Persia; who it is said, from an excessive fondness of Coffee, had sotted away the vigour of his constitution. But chemistry and experience have brought the subject into light, and Paulli's baseless fabric has vanished.

Moseley continues by lampooning the arbitrary and contradictory humoral classifications into which coffee's effects had been traditionally assigned by various medical writers, demonstrating the shift away from the ancient order in medicine that was starting to occur:

> Many have been the dogmas concerning Coffee: some Authors allege that it is dry, and therefore good for the gross and phlegmatic, but hurtful to lean people; some contend that it is cold, and therefore good for sanguine, bilious, and hot constitutions; others that it is hot, and therefore bad for the sanguine and bilious, but good for cold constitutions. Some assure us that it acts only as a sedative; others that it acts only as a stimulant.[48]

Moseley offers one of the last efforts to present a scientific analysis of coffee's active constituents before the discovery of caffeine by Runge less than thirty-five years later. "The chemical analysis of Coffee, evinces that it posses a great portion of mildly bitter and light astringent gummois and resinous extract; a considerable quantity of oil; a fixed salt; and a volatile salt.—These are its medicinal constituent principles." Although his chemical analysis is fanciful, Moseley rightly recognized the importance of good roasting technique, freshness, and proper storage for preparing a desirable beverage:

> The roasting of the berry to the proper degree, requires great nicety. . . . If it is under-done, its virtues will not be imparted; and in use, it will load and oppress the stomach:—If it is over-done, it will yield a flat, burnt, and bitter taste; its virtues will be destroyed; and in use, it will heat the body, and act as an astringent.
>
> The closer it is confined at the time of roasting, and till used, the better will its volatile pungency, flavour, and [medicinal] virtues be preserved.[49]

Moseley continues the tradition of exaggeration that had already become well established among both proponents and opponents of the caffeinated beverages, attributing a remarkable variety of medicinal benefits to coffee. However, in his judgment, the uses of coffee as a medicine fall into two broad categories. The first is alleviating "disorders of the head," including headaches, of which he says, "There are but few people who are not informed of its utility." The second includes its actions as a stimulant and cleansing agent or purgative, its "detergent properties . . . used in all obstructions of the viscera; it assists the secretions; powerfully promotes the menses, and mitigates the pains attendant on the sparing discharge of that evacuation." These opinions, obviously reflecting experience with some of caffeine's physiological effects, are exposited at length in his book.

Expressing a theory that has been confirmed in the twentieth century, Moseley spells out some of the therapeutic benefits of the caffeine in coffee for respiratory problems, a benefit which had been known, apparently, at least as early as the first decade of the eighteenth century:[50]

> A dish of strong Coffee without milk or sugar, taken frequently in the paroxysm of an asthma, abates the fit; and I have often known it to remove the fit entirely. Sir JOHN FLOYER [(1639–1734), physician and medical writer], who had been afflicted with the asthma from the seventeenth year of his age until he was upwards of fourscore, found no remedy in all his elaborate researches, until the latter part of his life, when he obtained it by Coffee.

In Moseley's time, opium, that "inestimable medicine," which had the ability to "relieve corporal pain by tranquility, and mental affliction by sleep . . . and whose excellence no human praise can reach," was among the most powerful agents in the pharmacopoeia, and its active constituent agents and derivatives, such as morphine and heroin, remain among the most powerful drugs available today. Sovereign against pain, opium, especially when taken to excess, had a variety of side effects that limited its safety. In Moseley's opinion, among coffee's valuable qualities was its unique ability to counteract or reduce opium's detrimental side effects; they are, he writes, "only remediable by Coffee." Moseley thought that coffee was the specific antidote to opium's hypnotic effects that had been sought after in vain from "the time of King MITHRADATES down to the days of Doctor JONES." He also believed that the "heaviness, giddiness, sickness, and nervous affections, which attack the patient in the morning, who has taken an opiate at night, are agreeably removed by a cup or two of strong Coffee." In his extensive discussion of this ability, it is evident that Moseley is referring to pharmacological actions that we today ascribe to caffeine:

> The general opinion is erroneous, though of long standing, that the Turks used Coffee, exclusive of culinary purposes, only against the sleepy effects of Opium. The Turks, as well as the Persians and Indians, take Opium as a cordial, to invigorate them for the temporary enjoyment of amorous pleasures; and to enable them to support fatigue and to stimulate their nerves to the exertions of courage and enterprize. But when the desired effects of this cordial are over, langour, lassitude, and ejection of spirits succeed.—It is for these indispositions, that Coffee is so medicinally necessary to the Turks, and that they use it as their only remedy.[51]

Moseley sums up his study with reasonable reflections that have a surprisingly modern sound. Although acknowledging that coffee and tea may be harmful to some people in some conditions of health, he finds, overall, that their use is both pleasant and potentially of great benefit to the public at large, whose new access to these drinks, afforded by the drop in duties, he celebrates as offering an antidote to the "chronical infirmaties" attending the rise of modern urban life. Sounding almost like a twentieth-century environmentalist, Moseley advances coffee as a kind of green remedy for the ills of urban life:

> Let us reflect on the state of atmosphere [air quality]; the food, and modes of life of the inhabitants so injurious to youth and beauty, filling the large towns and cities with chronical infirmaties; and I think it will be evident what advantages will result from the general use of Coffee in England, as an article of diet from the comforts of which the poor are not excluded, and to what purposes it may often be employed, as a safe and powerful medicine.[52]

Hahnemann: The Hazards of Upsetting the Body's Balance

Samuel Christian Hahnemann (1755–1843), the man for whom Philadelphia's Hahnemann Hospital was named and the creator of the school of homeopathic medicine (a theory of drug treatment that reached the acme of its influence in the United States in the 1890s but persisted especially in and around Philadelphia, remained in vogue as a quack therapy among the British and European royalty and aristocracy, and is undergoing a revival today),[53] recognized that caffeine delivered temporary energizing effects but asserted that, like other intoxicating, stimulating, or psychoactive drugs, its value to the user was more than offset by its harm. Hahnemann based his conjectures about caffeine on a general theory of homeostasis, a notion, harkening back to humoral theory, that good health consists of the proper regulation or balance of the bodily systems. According to this notion, anything that interfered with this balance, even if the interference initially produced apparently beneficial effects, would ultimately prove deleterious to the organism. Hahnemann acknowledged that caffeine could increase endurance, strength, and mental acuity. His disapproval of its use was based on his recognition of its power to do these things; for Hahnemann argued that, though caffeine allows you to burn energy more quickly now, you will suffer a corresponding letdown later, initiating a debilitating cycle that is ultimately less productive than staying on an even keel by abstaining from caffeine altogether. As he states, coffee engenders an "artificially heightened sense of being.... Presence of mind, alertness, and empathy are all elevated more than in a healthy natural condition."[54] These apparently benign effects, he says, disturb the natural cadence of the biological system, which depends on the alternating rhythms of wakefulness and sleepiness.

In 1803, Hahnemann wrote in *Der Kaffee in seinen Wirkungen*:

> In the first moments or first quarter hour of waking, especially when waking occurs earlier than usual, probably everyone who does not live in an entirely primitive state of nature experiences an unpleasant sensation of less than fully roused consciousness, gloominess, a sluggishness and stiffness in the limbs; quick movements are difficult, and thinking is hard. But lo and behold, coffee dispels this natural but unpleasant feeling, this discomfort of mind and body, almost immediately.... [The] unpleasant fatigue of mind and body with the natural approach of sleep, quickly vanishes with this medicinal drink; sleepiness vanishes, and an artificial sprightliness, a wakefulness wrested from Nature takes its place.[55]

John Cole, Esq.: The Dangers of Tea and Coffee

In 1833 John Cole published a much-cited study in the English medical journal *Lancet*, in which he presented some of the harms that could befall excessive users of tea and coffee.[56] Cole never mentions caffeine and may not have been acquainted with Runge's isolation of the chemical a decade earlier; for the word "caffeine" had been first used in English only three years before, by Lindley, in his *Natural History of Botany* (1830): "Coffee is ... supposed to owe its characters to a peculiar chemical principle called Caffein."[57]

In any case, Cole probably did not attribute the pharmacological actions of coffee to caffeine, and it was even less likely that he attributed the actions of tea to the drug, because "theine," isolated only six years before as tea's active agent, had probably not yet been identified as caffeine. Citing the "almost universal use of tea and coffee as articles of diet" as proof that their effects are generally agreeable, Cole nevertheless asserts that there are many exceptions. It was these exceptions that prompted him to study the harmful effects of tea, as Cole, like many before him, thought that a discussion of tea's effects would suffice for coffee as well.

Cole must have been serving some strong infusions of caffeine, to judge from the following statement, in which he distinguishes the effects of highly caffeinated coffee and black tea from those of green tea, which is low in caffeine:

> When black tea, or coffee, has been taken, considerable excitement often ushers in this succession of phenomena; the face becomes flushed, the eyes sparkle with an unusual brilliance, all the earlier effects of intoxication from alcohol are observable;

the pulse being full and throbbing, and considerably quickened. If green tea have been taken, the previous excitement is less, or perhaps not at all perceptible. The skin soon becomes pale, the eyes are sunken, the pulse feeble, quick, and fluttering, or slow and weak.

Cole next discusses the symptoms that indicate the harmful effects of tea, the use of which, in some frail persons, he thinks results in an identifiable disease:

> To the coldness and benumbed feeling of the back of the head, there is added formication of the scalp, violent pain in the head, dimness of the sight, unsteadiness in walking, vertigo, and these are accompanied by a feeble fluttering pulse. . . .
> I may add here, that the mind does not escape, but partakes of the disorders of the body, as is seen by the temper becoming peevish and irritable, so as to render the sufferer a torment to himself, and all those about him.

The following are among the nine case studies which Cole proceeds to review, diagnosing tea as the culprit in all of them: "Pain at Stomach . . . rejection of Food"; disturbance in "The Functions of the Heart"; "Syncope," or fainting; "sudden attacks of Insensibility"; "Headache"; and, finally, "Convulsions." Cole concludes with what may be the first attempt to link cardiovascular pathology with chronic caffeine use:

> If it be true, as it has been held, that the continued disturbance of the function of an organ will induce change of structure, what are we to expect from the use of tea twice a day, when it deranges the function of the heart for three or four hours after each time of its being taken? If the answer be, that it may be expected to induce some structural disease, there arises this other question,—May not the greater prevalence of cardiac disease of late years have been considerably influenced by the increased consumption of coffee and tea?[58]

Les Cafêomanes: Honoré de Balzac and the Pleasures and Pains of Caffeine

> Coffee is an affair of fifteen or twenty days; just the right amount of time to write an opera.
> —Gioacchino Antonio Rossini (1792–1868) to Balzac

Honoré de Balzac (1799–1850), one of the greatest and most prolific storytellers in history, was unquestionably a drug addict. His drug of choice was caffeine. Because he was unacquainted with the chemical itself, Balzac, like many other caffeine enthusiasts before him, equated the effects of caffeine with those of its primary vehicle, coffee.

While still at boarding school, Balzac indebted himself to a corrupt concierge, who smuggled in the forbidden beans, still expensive colonial produce, to secure his first supply. His mother was furious over his self-indulgence, perhaps sensing that it was the beginning a lifelong love-hate relationship with the stimulant and a nearly forty-year slide into dissipated health. In his adult life, Balzac slept in the early evening and, rising at midnight, wrote his novels through the night, the next morning, and into the early afternoon. It was coffee, compulsively and systematically consumed in incrementally increasing doses, that made these lucubrations possible. Like any true drug addict, he believed the output of his creative energies depended upon coffee's chemical arousal.

In the tradition of Ovington's claim that caffeine comes to the aid of the muse, Balzac, in his book *Traité des Excitants Modernes* (1839), or *On Modern Stimulants*, provides us with a compelling account of the use of caffeine as an analeptic to keep you awake so you can work, and as an aid to the imagination, which stimulates the flow of ideas and images. In this passage, Balzac conceives of coffee exclusively as a drug, speaking of increasing the "dose" to maintain its pharmacological effects and noting its toxic effects on the stomach and the unstable behavior that attends its sustained use. It would be impossible to improve on the words of one of history's greatest prose stylists when he describes his encounter with caffeine:

> Coffee is a great power in my life; I have observed its effects on an epic scale. . . . Many people claim coffee inspires them, but, as everybody knows, coffee only makes boring people even more boring.
>
> Coffee sets the blood in motion and stimulates the muscles; it accelerates the digestive process, chases away sleep, and gives us the capacity to engage a little longer in the exercise of our intellects.
>
> Coffee . . . reaches the brain by barely perceptible radiations that escape complete analysis: that aside, we may surmise that our primary nervous flux conducts an electricity emitted by coffee when we drink it. Coffee's power changes over time. "Coffee," Rossini told me, "is an affair of fifteen or twenty days; just the right amount of time to write an opera." This is true, but the length of time during which one can enjoy the benefits of coffee can be extended.
>
> For a while—for a week or two at most—you can obtain the right amount of stimulation with one, then two cups of coffee brewed from beans that have been crushed with gradually increasing force and infused with hot water. For another week, by decreasing the amount of water used, by pulverizing the coffee even more finely, and by infusing the grounds with cold water, you can continue to obtain the same cerebral power.
>
> When you have produced the finest grind with the least water possible, you double the dose by drinking two cups at a time; particularly vigorous constitutions can tolerate three cups. In this manner, one can continue working for several days.
>
> Finally, I have discovered a horrible, rather brutal method that I recommend only to men of excessive vigor. It is a question of using finely pulverized, dense coffee, cold and anhydrous [dry], consumed on an empty stomach. This coffee falls into your stomach, a sack whose velvety interior is lined with tapestries of suckers and papillae. The coffee finds nothing else in the sack, and so it attacks these delicate and voluptuous linings; . . . it brutalizes these beautiful stomach linings . . . sparks shoot all the way up to the brain. From that moment on, everything becomes agitated. Ideas quick-march into motion like battalions of a grand army to its legendary fighting ground, and the battle rages. Memories charge in, bright flags on high; the cavalry

of metaphor deploys with a magnificent gallop, the artillery of logic rushes up with clattering wagons and cartridges; on imagination's orders, sharpshooters sight and fire; forms and shapes and characters rear up; the paper is spread with ink—for the nightly labor begins and ends with torrents of this black water.

I recommended this way of drinking coffee to a friend of mine, who absolutely wanted to finish a job promised for the next day: he thought he'd been poisoned and took to his bed. . . .

The state coffee puts one in when it is drunk on an empty stomach under these magisterial conditions, produces a kind of animation that looks like anger: one's voice rises, one's gestures suggest unhealthy impatience; one wants everything to proceed with the speed of ideas; one becomes brusque, ill-tempered, about nothing. One assumes that everyone is equally lucid. A man of spirit must therefore avoid going out in public. I discovered this singular state through a series of accidents that made me lose, without any effort, the ecstasy that I had been feeling. Some friends witnessed me arguing about everything, haranguing with monumental bad faith. The following day I recognized my wrongdoing, and we searched the cause . . . and we found the problem soon enough: coffee wanted its victim.[59]

In this passage coffee is treated in terms that are commonplace among users of heroin and cocaine, but more unusual among users of caffeine. Especially noteworthy is Balzac's account of ratcheting up doses so as to maintain the effect despite a growing tolerance. For Balzac, this process culminates in eating dry coffee powder. In a manner reminiscent of alcoholics, he speaks of socially unacceptable conduct induced by caffeine intoxication that became so embarrassing it kept him indoors whenever he drank coffee heavily thereafter.

The road of drug addiction often ends in premature death. This was the French novelist's fate, according to Dr. Nacquart, Balzac's physician, who had known him since 1815, the year he began to use the toxic substance: "An old heart complaint, frequently aggravated by working through the night and by the use or rather the abuse of coffee, to which he had recourse in order to counteract man's natural propensity to sleep, had just taken a new and fatal turn."[60]

France in the 1890s: *Treatise Du Caféisme Chronique*

> *Il rend la mémoire et l'imagination* . . .
>
> —Written of coffee, Octave Guelliot,
> *Treatise Du Caféisme Chronique*, quoting Lemery

It is sometimes difficult to keep in mind, when reading passages of early medical texts about the ability of coffee and tea to maintain wakefulness, that the authors had never heard of caffeine and had no direct evidence that the same unknown agency was at work in both beverages. The change in practice, from referring to "coffee" to using the word "caffeine" and acknowledging its existence, occurred sometime around the middle of the nineteenth century. We know that it was still far from complete when Octave Guelliot (b. 1854) published his monograph *Du Caféisme Chronique*, or *On Chronic Coffeeism*, in Rheims in the 1890s. From the title of his essay, it is obvious that, at this time, the excessive use of coffee constituted an identifiable syndrome, and it is so regarded in this paper; but, though caffeine had been described more than seventy years earlier, it was still possible to write a fifty-page medical treatise dealing primarily with coffee and incidentally with tea as drugs without mentioning the word "caffeine" even once. *Du Caféisme* is a strange amalgam of Victorian science and a recapitulation of Pauli's seventeenth-century hall of horrors. With respect to understanding the history of caffeine, it provides an excellent example of science in transition.

How persistent were the Paulian charges against the relatively innocent caffeinated drinks! In somewhat more modern medical terminology than Pauli's, Guelliot blames them for causing sleeplessness, sleep-walking, dyspepsia, tremors, melancholy, pneumonia, loss of appetite, pains in the legs, loss of libido, red tongues, remarkably brilliant eyes, and dozens of other pathological conditions.

In Guelliot's treatise, we encounter a list of other substance abuse problems that Guelliot compares with *caféisme*: *théisme, alcholisme, absinthisme, cocainisme,* and *morphinisme*. It is then that we remember that the root of the word "caffeine," which today designates a chemical compound found in coffee, tea, maté, guarana, cola nuts, and other plants, is the French word "*café*," which simply means "coffee." And during the nineteenth century the words "thein," and even "matein" and "guaranine," were still in use to refer to the identical drug as it occurred in tea, maté, or guarana. Guelliot ascribes to opium intoxication symptoms that he says are very similar to those of *caféisme*, including loss of appetite and wasting away and chills.

In the notes to his treatise, Guelliot gives us an amusing, literate review of the histories of coffee and tea, especially of their progress in Europe. He tells us that Bernard Le Bovier de Fontanelle (1657–1757) and Voltaire were both inveterate coffee addicts. In response to the common admonitions of his day that coffee was a poison and its use would shorten life, Fontanelle, who was to live to a hundred, remarked late in his life, "*Si le café est un poison, c'est un poison lent*" (If coffee is a poison, it is a slow poison).

This monograph, written at a time when doctors recognized the existence of caffeine and theine and many understood their common identity, and yet in which caffeine was still often overlooked in discussions of the syndromes of chronic, excessive use of coffee or tea, represents the end of an era. Within a few years following its publication, we encounter the rigorously scientific, double-blind studies of caffeine's physical and mental effects by the Hollingworths at Columbia, after which the recognition of caffeine as the most important active agency in coffee and tea was finally complete.

postscript

Why Did Caffeine Come
When It Came?

To people alive today it may seem incredible that the classical and medieval worlds did not have any stimulant drug, and, even more incredible that they seem to have managed happily without one.[1] Since the seventeenth century, however, Europeans have relied on caffeine to help them keep to their work schedules by waking them up when they are sleepy and keeping them going when they are tired, and they have done so to such an extent that it is difficult to imagine what modern life would be like without it.

It may be that some of the advantages of using caffeinated drinks became apparent only once society could no longer mark appointments by the sun and stars. During medieval times, schedules were lax, holidays many, and disorganization pervasive. Throughout this period in the West there was not a single accurate clock on the entire Continent.[2] The exactness of timepieces was so limited that a single-handed clock face, indicating the quarter hours, sufficiently answered to their precision. This remained true until the uniformity of pendulum motion was discovered by Galileo in 1583, during his sophomore year at the University of Padua. Over the next hundred years, it came into general use in Europe as the basis for the first accurate clockwork mechanism. By around 1660 the minute hand, representing a fifteenfold increase in accuracy, became common in England.[3] Larger-scale industrial and economic endeavors became possible only once the measurement of small units of time had become standardized and routine, allowing for coordinated efforts across time and space. This improvement in precision occurred in the same decades when caffeine use became general in Venice, Paris, Amsterdam, London, and across the Continent.[4] Its date corresponds well with the opening of the first coffeehouses in London and the beginning of the vigorous coffeehouse culture as a center of the trades, the sciences, and the literary arts.[5] Once this chronometric standardization occurred, the use of an analeptic became a virtual necessity to regulate the biological organism, allowing people to meet the demands of invariant scheduling. The only suitable analeptic, one easily available, well tolerated, safe, and effective, is caffeine. There is a sense, therefore, in which the combination of the clock and caffeine may have been essential to the development of modern civilization, and it may not be going too far to assert that the modern world, at least as we know it today, could neither have been envisioned nor built without this combination to make it possible.[6]

It also may be that another advantage of the caffeinated drinks, that they did not contain alcohol, could only be appreciated by peoples who, having been troubled by intemperate drinking, were no longer able to afford the resulting impairments. During medieval times, most heavy work was done by people who had been drinking alcohol since breakfast and who continued to drink it throughout the working day. In a besotted Europe, the caffeinated beverages were heralded as the great agents of sobriety, which could free men from the intoxication and distress of alcoholic drinks. It is a challenge to the twentieth-century imagination to conceive how medieval man designed and built the great cathedrals during a period when beer for breakfast was standard fare. The tour guides conducting visitors through European or English cathedrals frequently point out a site near the ceiling where some hapless person, often the architect or chief engineer, slipped off a scaffold to his death. Considering how much alcohol was being consumed, it is easy to envision how this mischance could have been so often repeated.

Brian Harrison, writing of the temperance movement in Victorian England, ably sums up both aspects of the relation of modern work to caffeine:

> The effects of industrialization on drinking habits are complex . . . in some ways it made sobriety more feasible. The change in methods of production at last created a class with a direct interest in curbing drunkenness. Traditionally, work-rhythms had fluctuated both within the day and within the week: idleness on "Saint Monday" and even Tuesday was followed by frantic exertion and long hours at the end of the week. . . . Early industrialists needed to create a smooth working rhythm and to induce their employees to enter and leave their factories at specified times. Investment in complex and costly machinery placed the employee's precise and continuous labor at a higher premium than the spasmodic exertion of his crude physical energy. Once this need had arisen, customary drinking patterns had to change.[7]

Caffeine, therefore, in the vehicles of coffee and tea, fostered the productivity gains that a newly competitive environment demanded, and did so in two important ways. First, caffeine helped large numbers of people to coordinate their work schedules by giving them the energy to start work at a given time and continue it as long as necessary and, in some cases, even increased the accuracy of their work. This meant that people could work longer hours and accomplish, proportionately, even more than they had before. Second, the caffeinated beverages, by displacing the heavy consumption of alcohol, markedly reduced one of the endemic impairments of medieval industry. Sober workers always produce more and better work than drunken ones.

In the sixteenth century, an an additional factor made the drinks in which caffeine was served desirable and perhaps indispensable, even apart from their value in conveying a stimulant.[8] Beginning at this time, a mini–ice age gradually overtook

Europe, bringing with it famine, hard winters, and cold summers. The Swiss scholar H. J. Zumbühl searched drawings, paintings, and photographs in museums and private collections throughout the Continent, amassing more than three hundred visual representations of the Lower Grindelwald glacier between 1640 and 1900. When Zumbühl systematically dated the pictures and made suitable adjustments for each artist's viewpoint, he was amazed to note these images proved the ice had been in overall advance since the start of that period, and in overall retreat since about 1850. Detailed histories of the Mont Blanc region of the Alps confirm the advance of the glacier, which apparently began around 1550.

Extensive seventeenth-century French accounts of the "impetuosity of a great horrible glacier" were confirmed in the early 1970s by climatologist and cultural historian E. Le Roy Ladurie. Some of the stories that survive tell a chilling tale of how, in 1690, poor peasants from Chamonix paid the travel expenses for the bishop of Geneva, in the hopes he would exorcise the juggernaut of ice from their farmlands and meadows. His prayers were apparently answered when the ice withdrew. Unfortunately, it resumed an inexorable return a few years later.[9]

The chill deepened over the decades. Famine claimed many lives in Finland, Estonia, Norway, and Scotland in the winter of 1695, the coldest winter of a cold decade. In 1771, famine struck again, after a long sequence of snowy summers in central Europe, and the beginning of a rapid spurt forward by the Swiss glaciers.[10] Possible causes of the mini–ice age include the earth shifting on her axis, increasing sunspots that reduced the amount of solar heat, or exploding volcanic activity that spewed light-filtering dust into the atmosphere. Whatever brought on the chill, this long freeze may have prompted Europeans to resort to the caffeinated drinks for their value in staving of hunger and keeping warm and may well have been the initial impetus for the adoption of the caffeinated beverages and the spread of caffeine as the most popular drug on earth.

PART 3
the culture of caffeine

Introduction

Coffee and tea have given rise to a great duality: two major, largely divergent streams in the cultural history of caffeine. Coffee has become associated with all things masculine and with the the artist, the nonconformist or political dissident, the bohemian, even the hobo, as well as the outdoorsman. Its use is often considered a vice, its consumption linked with frenetic physical and mental activity, intense conversation, and with other indulgences that threaten health and mental balance, such as tobacco, alcohol, and late nights of hard partying or excessive work. Tea, in contrast, is associated with the feminine and with the drawing room, quiet social interaction, spirituality, and tranquillity and is regarded as the drink of the elite, the meditative, the temperate, and the elderly. These differences between coffee and tea are easily seen by comparing the ancient, worldwide, socially inclusive, and rough and ready institution of the coffeehouse with the decorous traditions of the Japanese tea ceremony and the English afternoon tea. An acknowledgment of these differences must underlie the fact that, although coffee has been the subject of many bans by sultans, kings, chiefs of police, and religious leaders and opposed by many temperance movements, tea has rarely, if ever, appeared on anyone's list as a substance that ought to be put beyond the pale of law or morality.

The more it is pondered, the more paradoxical this duality within the culture of caffeine appears. After all, both coffee and tea are aromatic infusions of vegetable matter, served hot or cold in similar quantities; both are often mixed with cream or sugar; both are universally available in virtually any grocery or restaurant in civilized society; and both contain the identical psychoactive alkaloid stimulant, caffeine. It is true that coffee is generally brewed to a caffeine strength over twice that of a typical cup of tea, yet, because more than one cup of each beverage is commonly consumed, there is no doubt that you can get a full dose of caffeine from either one.

So the question remains: Why has the duality between the culture of coffee and the culture of tea become so universally and so sharply delineated? For example, why did tea become the center of a proper, conventionalized, intimate social gathering in both England and Japan, while coffee failed to do so anywhere? And again, why did coffee become the stimulant of gossip, business, and political and intellectual banter in medieval Turkey, in London in the seventeenth century, and in dozens of American cities at the end of the twentieth century, while tea failed to do so anywhere?

Coffee Aspect	Tea Aspect
Male	Female
Boisterous	Decorous
Bohemian	Conventional
Obvious	Subtle
Sordid	Beautiful
Discord	Harmony
Common	Refined
Indulgence	Temperance

Coffee Aspect	Tea Aspect
Vice	Virtue
Excess	Moderation
Passion, Earthiness	Spirituality, Mysticism
Down-to-Earth	Elevated
Mornings, Late Nights	Afternoons
American	English
Occidental	Oriental
Casual	Formal, Ceremonial
Demimonde	Society
Full-blooded	Effete
Vivacious, Extroverted	Shy, Introverted
Loquacious	Reticent
Aggressive	Lordotic
Yang	Yin
Hardheaded	Romantic
Promiscuous	Pure
Work	Contemplation
Individualism	Conformity
Excitement	Tranquillity
Tension	Relaxation
Kinetic Energy	Potential Energy
Spontaneity	Deliberation
Topology	Geometry
Heidegger	Carnap
Beethoven	Mozart
Outlaw	Good Citizen
The Frontier	The Drawing Room
Libertarian	Statist
Balzac	Proust

We cannot answer this question definitively, but can only observe that these disparate traditions are visible early in the history and development of caffeine culture as realized in the spreading consumption of coffee and tea. The duality is consistent enough that divergent examples, such as the Bedouin coffee ceremonies and Arab concentrated tea swilling emerge as exceptions to a rule.[1] Cola beverages and other carbonated soft drinks containing caffeine do not have a long enough history to be as elaborately differentiated as coffee and tea: They do have distinctive associations, however, such as youth, high-energy, America, pop culture, and "good, clean fun."

Among all the nations, the two that best exemplify both this unlogical duality and the avid and widespread influence of coffee and tea on art, literature, architecture, politics, commerce, manners, and society are Japan and England. In Japan, the ancient discipline and enjoyment of teaism is a perfect embodiment of the tea aspect of caffeine; while the coffeehouse in twentieth-century Japan, a place of fast-paced conversational, social, and business interactions, is an instance of the coffee aspect. In England, the boisterous male mélange of the early coffeehouses ideally exemplifies the coffee aspect, while the refined, feminized afternoon tea, arriving two centuries later, manifests the tea aspect. And finally, in both Japan and England, the old and the new abide together, so that coffee and tea are used in both traditional and contemporary ways. Thus, a presentation of the culture of caffeine in Japan and England offers a uniquely comprehensive view of caffeine's dual and powerful agencies.

islands of caffeine (1)
Japan: The Tradition of Tea, the Novelty of Coffee

> The taste of *ch'an* [Zen] and the taste of *ch'a* [tea] are the same.
> —Old Buddhist saying

Tea was brought to Japan from China by Buddhist monks more than a thousand years ago. As a result of the Japanese adaptation and codification of the Zen tea ceremony about six hundred years later, the preparation, service, and imbibing of tea became a mirror of a national aesthetic, moral, social, and metaphysical ideal. In the Japanese tea ceremony, taking tea was said to be an earthly finger that "pointed to the moon" of enlightenment, the awakening to which all Buddhists aspired. In modern Japan, with its Western scientific, educational, industrial, and commercial models, the frenzied ethos of the rat race has created a largely urban Japanese market for a new drink to fuel their work and play. As a consequence, while tea use and tea ceremonies abide, coffee has achieved a powerful and growing presence there. In Japan today, the coffeehouse plays the important part it played in Arab countries in the sixteenth and seventeenth centuries, serving as a place in which people can meet and mingle with others outside of their families or circle of close friends. Because Japanese living quarters are so small, people flee from their confinement to enjoy the pleasant social respite of the coffeehouse, and this resort is even more important to them than to the average American or European.

Of course, old Japan and new Japan exist together, intertwined and inseparable, two aspects of a nation that is in many cultural aspects different from anything European. Yet in the Japanese love of both tea and coffee, we find a twin affection familiar to the West. Tea and coffee, emblematic of the traditional and the new, are enjoyed side by side, there as here.

The Origin of Tea in Japan

In the seventh century, Japanese monks discovered tea in China and introduced it to their homeland, where it was used by Zen practitioners in their communal ceremonies and as a curative drug. In the early ninth century in Hei-an-kyo, the national capital, during a long civil war, tea enjoyed a brief early vogue as a comestible. It was not until four hundred years later, however, that, the publication of a book made tea a nearly universal fixture of Japanese society.

At the end of the twelfth century,[1] Yeisai (1141–1215), or Senko-Soshi, the leader of a Zen sect, planted tea seeds he had brought from China in a friend's monastary and several other favorable spots around the country. Relying on what he had learned of tea in China and his own experience with its cultivation, Yeisai wrote *Kitcha-Yojoki*, or *The Book of Tea Sanitation*, the first Japanese book on tea. Yeisai's work, which praised the plant as a powerful pharmaceutical, a "divine remedy and a supreme gift of heaven,"[2] marked a watershed in the history of caffeine use in Japan. Before this book appeared, tea drinking had been confined to monks and aristocrats; after its publication, the practice spread to every stratum of society.

The great influence of Yeisai's book came about in the following way. The shogun of the time, Minamoto Sanetomo (r. 1203–19), whom gluttony had severely sickened, called on Yeisai to pray for his recovery. But Yeisai did more than that. He sent to the temple for some of his homegrown tea crop and prepared and served the healing brew to Sanetomo. When the military leader promptly regained his health, he asked to learn more about the wonderful remedy. To satisfy Sanetomo's curiosity, Yeisai copied his book by hand and presented it to the ruler. After reading it, Sanetomo became a tea enthusiast himself, and, from his example, the use of tea as a medicinal tonic rapidly spread from his court into general use across the nation.

Caffeine and Ceremony in the East: The Religion and Art of *Chanoyu*

> "As to the Buddha, he never makes an equivocal statement.
> Whatever he asserts is absolute truth."
> "What then is the Buddha's statement?" asked Hofuku.
> "Have a cup of tea, my brother monk."
>
> —An exchange between two Zen masters,
> Chokei (853–932), also called Ch'ang-ch'ing Hui-ling,
> and Hofuku (d. 928), also called Pao-fu Ts'ung-chan,
> adapted from Suzuki's translation of a passage
> from the *Dentoroku*, or *Transmission of the Lamp*[3]

Although Yeisai must have observed tea ceremonies during his visit to China, it was Dai-ō the National Teacher (1236–1303), also a Zen monk, who in 1267 introduced the tea ceremony he had encountered in China's Zen monastaries to the Zen monastaries of Japan. Following Dai-ō's lead, succeeding generations of Zen monks continued to practice this ceremony within their own religious communities. Finally, in the fifteenth century, the monk Shukō (1422–1502) employed his artistic talents to adapt the ceremony to Japanese tastes and in so doing originated the first form of *chanoyu*, the distinctively Japanese tea ceremony that is still practiced today. The tea ceremony itself can be illuminated for western readers by comparing it with the dialectal method of Socrates. Through the grammar of this ceremony, the superficialities and illusions of everyday life and practical pursuits were to be broken down and transcended. The ultimate goal for any practitioner of the shared mundanities of the Zen tea ceremony was *satori*, the insight into the ultimate reality.[4] Shukō taught *chanoyu* to Ashikaga Yoshimasa (1435–90), shogun and patron of the arts, who helped to establish it as a national tradition. As a result, during Ashikaga's reign, the practice of the tea ceremony escaped the confines of the monasteries and was discovered by the lay population, especially by the warrior class, the samurai.[5]

Sen-no-Rikyu (1522–91), a tea merchant by trade, was in some ways the most important, and, by reputation, the best, in a long line of tea masters in Japan. It was Rikyu who systematically expounded the principles of *chanoyu* and designed the features of the modern tea ceremony and teahouse, and who became the progenitor of the three major tea schools flourishing in Japan today. In a country where the profession of tea master has been highly regarded for centuries, Rikyu remains the master of them all. It was largely as a result of Rikyu's efforts that, from his time forward, tea became a symbol of the national culture.

In Rikyu's day, three groups shared leadership of the nation: the emperor and aristocrats, the warlords, and the merchants. The emperor on his imperial throne had become little more than a ceremonial prop, in this respect comparable in status to Hirohito during World War II or Queen Elizabeth today. The once-feared shogun, who carried what had degenerated into an hereditary title, had suffered the same fate. The actual leaders of the country were a new breed of military dictators who arose from the ranks of the feudal warlords and conspired with the wealthy merchants to increase and solidify their control of the nation.

Although the warlords wielded military power and the merchants amassed large fortunes, the social heirarchy, in which aristocrats and priests enjoyed the highest status, remained anachronistic. It was nearly impossible for anyone outside of their closed circles to attain the respect and honor, the desire for which, shared even by the wise, has been called by Aristotle "the last infirmity of the noble mind." In the throes of this infirmity, the warlords and merchants tried to establish their legitimacy by patronizing art and culture. They joined in promoting Zen Buddhism and the Ming Chinese culture in opposition to the native styles cultivated by the aristocracy. Encouraged by these military rulers, monk-artists shuttled between China and Japan, established flourishing ateliers, and, for the first time, through these studios, commoners enjoyed the possibility of advancement based on talent and achievement. The tea ceremony became a central device for laying siege to the aristocratic social edifice. In this era of *gekokuje*, that is, a topsy-turvy world in which the formerly humble ruled the formerly great, the incongruous sight of an illiterate peasant samurai pausing to indulge in the refinement of the tea ritual became increasingly common.

The last Ashikaga shogun was succeeded by Oda Nubunaga (1534–82), strongest of the feudal lords who fought for ascendancy after the shogun's death. Nubunaga had nearly succeeded in unifying the country when he died in a fire that started while he was brewing tea. After his death, Toyotomi Hideyoshi (1536–98), a peasant who had risen to the rank of Nubunaga's first lieutenant and who is sometimes called, on account of his military and political acumen, "the Napoleon of Japan," took over his power and completed the work of unifying the country that Nubunaga had begun. Mindful of his low birth and eager to assure the respect of the increasingly important merchant class,

Hideyoshi, like Nobunaga before him, was a generous patron of *chanoyu*. In order to effect a tranquil transition of power and in recognition of Rikyu's fame as a tea master, Hideyoshi reconfirmed Rikyu's position as curator of the palace tea ceremony and equipage. As fate would have it, this favor was the beginning of Rikyu's undoing.

Hideyoshi was an avid tea lover and was among the growing number of samurai, or professional soldiers, who, somewhat incongrously, liked to "seclude themselves in the tearoom and meditatively sipping a cup of tea, breathe the air of quietism and transcendentalism."[6] Hideyoshi went further, however, in his vanity, nourishing the conceit that he was a great tea master himself. During each of Hideyoshi's military engagements, his attendants would erect a portable teahouse on the battlefield. Hideyoshi would then calmly practice the tea ceremony in view of both his own troops and his enemies, inspiring confidence in the first and fear in the second. Hideyoshi, rembering his humble origins, resented that Rikyu, although nominally his servant, was the more honored because of his family's wealthy merchant connections and his own celebrated status as the leading tea master. Because the dictator imagined himself Rikyu's competitor in the practice of *chanoyu*, a strange rivalry gradually developed between them.

Over the years, Hideyoshi's envy blossomed into paranoia, a transformation nourished by Rikyu's deep involvement in the complex social and political intrigues of the day, perilous pursuits for a man with no real power of his own. Finally, giving in to a grudge over a real or imagined conspiracy against him or, some say, out of envy over a statue erected in Rikyu's honor, Hideyoshi determined to execute his friend, though, in the spirit of good fellowship, he granted him the honorable option of suicide, a privilege ordinarily reserved for his samurai brothers.

The story of Rikyu's death bears an unsettling similarity to the story of the death of Socrates as told in the *Phaedrus*. Each was honored for his simplicity, austerity, honesty, integrity, and wisdom, and each, having come into conflict with a despotic civil authority and condemned unjustly for subverting the state, was directed to commit suicide, and each, forgoing the opportunity of fleeing to escape his end, did so peacefully, surrounded by disciples. Just before plunging the dagger into his heart, Rikyu addressed it in brief lines imbued with the mind-bending antinomy so dear to the practitioners of Zen:

> Welcome to you,
> O sword of eternity!
> Through Buddha
> And through Daruma alike
> You have cleft your way.[7]

Rikyu helped to shape and define every aspect of teaism, the teahouse, the tea garden, and the tea ceremony. Among his important innovations was replacing the character "*kin*," or "reverence," in the famous traditional hortatory mnemonic *Kin Kei Sei Jaku*, or "reverence, respect, purity, and tranquillity," with "*wa*," or "harmony." This change signaled a shift from an emphasis on service to one's superiors to the more Confucian ideal of harmony and mutual obligation. In Rikyu's *chanoyu* "harmony" referenced the harmony between the participants and the implements of tea preparation; "respect" referenced the respect shown by the participants to each other and the implements; "cleanliness," a Shinto inheritance, referenced the symbolic hand-washing and mouth rinsing practiced before entering the teahouse; and "tranquillity," which is imbued throughout every aspect of the tea ceremony, referenced the deliberate and attentive exercise of each of its components. Rikyu is also credited with the introduction to the laity of passing the commensural bowl of tea, which Chinese Zen monks had centuries before shared among themselves in their ceremonies and which, before his time, was practiced in Japan only among the priesthood. Some people advance the notion that the rituals of the Roman Catholic Mass may have influenced the development of *chanoyu*, because the tea ceremony became important in lay Japanese life shortly after the Jesuit and Franciscan missionaries began proselytizing. According to this view, the increased use of the commensural bowl, for example, is the result of Christian influence.

In a parallel development, tea competitions, which had been widely popular in China during the Sung dynasty (960–1289), became the rage in Japan between the fourteenth and seventeenth centuries. In their new home, these contests were blended with a prior native tradition of *monoawase*, social competitions involving rival presentations of "poems, flowers, insects, herbs, shellfish"[8] and other items. To play the new tea game, guests assembled in a tea pavilion, where they were offered four kinds of tea and challenged to determine by taste and scent which were *honcha*, grown at Toganoo or Uji, and which were *hicha*, tea grown elsewhere.[9] These tea competitions, although not direct ancestors of the Japanese tea ceremony, presaged many of the elements of what was soon to become the defining rituals of *chanoyu*.

Caffeine and Culture: Teaism, Teahouse, Tea Gardens, and the Manners, Art, and Architecture of Japan

The sense of an infinitely expanded present is nowhere stronger than in cha-no-yu, the art of tea. Strictly, the term means something like, "Tea with hot water," and through this one art Zen has exercised an incalculable influence on Japanese life, since the *chajin*, or "man of tea," is an arbiter of taste in the many subsidiary arts which cha-no-yu involves—architecture, gardening, ceramics, metalwork, lacquer, and the arrangement of flowers (*ikebana*).

—Alan Watts, *The Way of Zen* (1957)[10]

In the Chinese tea ceremony, which arose from the intermingling of Buddhist and Taoist traditions, the mundane was ennobled by the otherworldly loftiness of aesthetic ideals, and the quest for salvation was brought down to earth by contemplation of the commonplace. Its practitioners had discovered an austere beauty and a code of conduct conducive to peace and joy and, ultimately, *satori*, or enlightenment. In Japan, the spirit and practice of *chanoyu* maintained this spiritual identity, and, in consequence of the ceremony's popularity, Japanese art, architecture, and social mores were imbued with the flavor of Zen.

Zen traditions shone through *chanoyu* in the secular spirituality of the tea ceremony itself, which entirely lacked the liturgical character of a service in a church, synagogue, or mosque. However, politics, business, and money were not discussed at the ceremony. Sometimes a friendly exchange about a philosophical topic was acceptable, but the preferred subjects of conversation were nature and art. Discretion was the guiding principle for the participants. As the host brought the tea utensils, offered the guests sweets, and whipped each serving of powdered tea within its cup, ideal conversation consisted of praising the beauty and inquiring after the provenance of the serving implements.

In Japanese tradition, following a Way leads to *makoto*, or ultimate truth. There is a Way of Flowers, a Way of Painting, a Way of Poetry, and many others. However, of all the innumerable Ways, it is the Way of Tea that has affected Japanese culture the most deeply. Over the centuries in Japan, architects, painters, gardeners, and craftsmen have worked under the stylistic guidance of the tea masters in creating the houses, gardens, and utensils of the tea ceremony. As a result of this tutelage, Japanese artists and artisans could not help but impart the flavor of Zen tastes to the surroundings and objects of everyday use, including such ordinary items as kitchen implements, teapots, cups, and floor mats, fabric design, and bottles and jars.

A type of pottery originally devised for the tea ceremony as codified by Rikyu became the source of some of Japan's most revered art objects. It received its name after Hideyoshi, who, as we have seen, was a great patron of tea-related culture, rewarded an artisan with a gold seal engraved with the word "*raku*," or "felicity." Because Rikyu's ceremony was characterized by "*wabi*," which means "simplicity" or "tranquillity," this *raku* ware was made in a simple style: Wide, straight-side bowls placed on a narrow base, originally with a dark brown glaze. *Raku* wares were molded by hand, not modeled on a wheel, so that each piece is more elaborately differentiated than is typical for ceramic work. As time went on, the choice of glazes expanded to include light orange-red, straw color, green, and cream. The glazed ware was placed in a hot kiln for about one hour then removed and cooled rapidly, as opposed to the usual process of warming the pottery slowly in a cold kiln. This rapid cooling and, an additional special process unique to the production of *raku* ware, reduction firing, multiplied dramatic, random surface variations in the glaze.

In Hideyoshi's day, the tea master Hon'ami Koetsu (1558–1637) established a colony of Nichiren Buddhist artists and craftsman northwest of Kyoto dedicated to expressing the philosophy of teaism. It had a major influence on the development of Japanese art and style. Koetsu himself, a man of many parts, connoisseur of swords, landscape gardener, as well as artisan of lacquerwork and pottery, calligrapher, and poet, is sometimes called "the Leonardo of Japan." He created what is often regarded as the finest *raku* Japanese tea bowl ever made, today esteemed a national treasure. In the words of art critic Joan Stanley-Baker in *Japanese Art*, "Its taut, straight lines taper slightly towards the bottom, the reddish body is covered entirely in a blackish matt slip with opaque white glaze over the upper half, leaving the darker glaze for the bottom: the effect produced by firing is that of gently falling snow. The vigour and grandeur of Mount Fuji are suggested. . . . The impression is of monumentality." Today this bowl is part of the Sakai Tadamasa Collection in Tokyo.

From Koetsu's artist's colony arose a major school of decorative painting, dedicated to expressing the philosophy of teaism. It later became known as the Korin school, after Ogata Korin (1658–1716), a relative of Koetsu and descendant of the Ashikaga family, who was one of its most illustrious practitioners. Korin is especially esteemed for his screen paintings and lacquerwork executed in an abstract, asymmetrical style and based on the close observation of nature.

No stylistic traditions better illustrate the minimalist motto "Less is more" than the Zen temples and the tea gardens that surround them. In *kare-sansui*, or "dry landscape" gardens, a few stones and sand are all that remain to conjure the sense of the traditional ornaments of ponds, waterfalls, and flowering plants. Zen monks were primarily interested in the balance of form and were therefore, like the Chinese Sung painters, sparing in their use of color. Therefore, unlike English gardens, tea gardens are not primarily designed around masses of color. Despite their simplicity, celebrated sand gardens, each with its own aesthetic character, present changing faces to visitors coming at different times, as they are meant to be experienced successively in rain, sun, moonlight, and covered in snow, and are designed to present themselves differently with alterations in light and shadow.

The most famous sand gardens are in Kyoto, the finest example of which may be Ryonan-ji's garden, comprising five groups of rocks laid out on a rectangular plot of raked sand, surrounded by a low stone wall and trees. In Alan Watts' words:

> It suggests a wild beach, or perhaps a seascape with rocky islands, but its unbelievable simplicity evokes a serenity and clarity of feeling so powerful that it can be caught even from a photograph. The major art which contributes to such gardens is *bonseki*, which may well be called the "growing" of rocks.[11]

Among the simplest of these sand gardens is the tea garden, the *roji*, or "dewy path," the functional garden path that leads to the teahouse. As with much else in the tea ceremony, Rikyu's designs set the standard for future excellence. A *roji* comprises the *soto roji*, the outer part near the garden entrance, and the *uchi roji*, or the inner part, near the teahouse. The intention of the Zen designers is not to create the illusion of a landscape, but to pursue a more abstract ambition: to evoke its general atmosphere in a confined space.

The teahouse, the *cha-shitsu*, is a small, one-room hut with a thatched roof, set apart from the main dwelling, featuring a charcoal pit covered with straw mats and paper walls supported by wooden rods. On one side is a tiny alcove, or *tokonoma*, in which is hung a single painted or calligraphed scroll below which is placed a rock, bouquet of flowers, or other simple decorative object. Much care is devoted by the tea master to choosing the object to place in the *tokonoma*, as the contents of this niche are intended to set the mood for the ceremony to follow.

Although the Zen masters lavish great care and hard work on designing, building, and maintaining these houses and gardens, as with everything pertaining to Zen, they are ambivalent about acknowledging their individual intellectual and artistic contributions. Their goal is to execute designs with such a light touch that they appear to have been merely helped, rather than governed, by human agency. With this in mind the Zen architect or gardener attempts to follow the "intentionless intention" of the natural forms themselves, achieving his results in a way that could be called "accidentally on purpose."

Teaism Today and the Traditions of Japan
Restoring the Traditions: The Okakuran Campaign

Kakuzo Okakura (1862–1913), curator of Chinese and Japanese art at the Boston Museum of Fine Arts, undertook a lifelong mission to preserve, purify, and introduce the West to Japanese art, ethics, and social customs. He brought to this work an integrated, original vision of entire artistic movements in China and Japan, and it is said that under his direction "the study of Oriental art attained its first maturity."[12] The Boston Museum's collections became world-famous, attracting a small community of Japanese artisans who settled in the area to perform restorations. Today Okakura is most famous for his *Book of Tea* (1906), a turn-of-the-century apology to the West for Japanese tea tradition as exemplified in the cult or philosophy of teaism. Written in English, it was read by hundreds of thousands of Americans as their introduction to Japanese culture. In adducing the pervasive importance of tea, Okakura mentions a locution that has entered general use:

> In our common parlance we speak of the man "with no tea" in him, when he is insusceptible to the serio-comic interests of the personal drama. Again we stigmatize the untamed aesthete who, regardless of the mundane tragedy, runs riot in the springtide of emancipated emotions, as one "with too much tea" in him.[13]

There is no question about the identity of Okakura's favorite among the leading beverages:

> There is a subtle charm in the taste of tea which makes it irresistible and capable of idealization. . . . It has not the arrogance of wine, the self-consciousness of coffee, nor the simpering innocence of cocoa.[14]

Okakura explains the great influence the tea masters have had on the customs and conduct of Japanese life. Preparing and serving delicate dishes, as well as dressing and decorating in muted colors, have encouraged what he believes is the nation's natural aspiration for simplicity and humility. Okakura states that despite the Western disdain for most Eastern customs, the West has fallen under the spell of *chado* and *chanoyu*. The English ceremony of afternoon tea is no more than a Western imitation of the great tea ceremony of Japan:

> Strangely enough, humanity has so far met in the tea-cup. It is the only Asiatic ceremonial which commands universal esteem. The white man has scoffed at our religion and our morals, but has accepted the brown beverage without hesitation. The afternoon tea is now an important function in Western society. In the delicate clatter of trays and saucers, in the soft rustle of feminine hospitality, in the common catechism about cream and sugar, we know that the Worship of Tea is established beyond question. The philosophic resignation of the guest to the fate awaiting him in the dubious decoction proclaims that in this single instance the Oriental spirit reigns supreme.[15]

Japanese women performing the traditional tea ceremony, from a 1905 photograph by Jessie Tarbox Beals (1870–1942). (University of Pennsylvania Museum, Philadelphia, negative #s4–142240)

The example he gives is of the English essayist Charles Lamb, an ardent tea lover, who seemed to evince the authentic spirit of teaism. For Lamb "the greatest pleasure ... was to do a good action by stealth, and to have it found out by accident." As Okakura explains, "For Teaism is the art of concealing beauty that you may discover it, of suggesting what you dare not reveal."[16]

Nevertheless, like the first boil of tea in Lu Yü's recipe, Okakura's passionate prose should be taken with a grain of salt. In his view teaism is, in effect, coextensive with human wisdom, irrespective of whether the wise men who authored the wisdom in question were thinking of, were inspired by, or had even ever heard of tea:

> It is the noble secret of laughing at yourself, calmly yet thoroughly, and is thus humor itself,—the smile of philosophy. All genuine humorists may in this sense be called tea-philosophers,—Thackeray, for instance, and, of course, Shakespeare.[17]

A Contrarian View: Urasenke, or the Church That Caffeine Built

The ideals of religious and cultural movements are often poorly realized in the institutions and activities that advance under their banners. For example, Christ's ideals of poverty, self-denial, and the primacy of the spirit were not well represented in the opulence, self-indulgence, and depravity of Renaissance papal courts. What of the traditional ideals of *chanoyu*? To what extent are they faithfully represented in the current practice of teaism and the tea ceremony in Japan? And to what extent does the use of the drug caffeine play a part in the tea ceremony experience?

The green tea that today is served everywhere and endlessly in Japanese restaurants is, by Western standards, brewed for a very short time and extremely weak, almost hard to distinguish from water, and must be very low in caffeine. In contrast, the whipped brew served at formal tea ceremonies is strong and bitter, a completely different drink. *Ma-cha* literally means "powdered tea," and it is this tea which is whipped into a bright green froth in the tea ceremony. There are two types of *ma-cha*: *usu-cha*, or thin tea, and *koi-cha*, or thick tea. The tea most often referred to in speaking of the tea ceremony is *usu-cha*. The use of *koi-cha* is reserved for very special ceremonies among intimate friends. In these ceremonies only one cup is used and tea is drunk by turns without washing the cup.

Ma-cha is the cured tips of the just-budding tea plant. Japanese laboratory analysis reveals that these tips contain about 4.6 percent caffeine by weight (compared with only 2 percent for other green teas), more caffeine than any other part of the tea plant, and indeed, more caffeine by weight than any other vegetable source. This caffeine-rich tea is sometimes used by Japanese students to help them stay up late for study, the way coffee is by used by their American counterparts.

Small, hard candies made entirely of sugar accompany the tea and are freely consumed during the ceremony. Thus, in addition to a large caffeine wallop, the participants' blood-sugar levels increase quickly. Some participants claim that the combination of caffeine, sugar, and the enforced discipline of remaining almost perfectly still and composed during the ceremony account for what one called "the huge 'rush' often attributed to 'mystical' aspects of the tea ceremony." Because the minds of the participants are free from distraction and imbued with tranquillity and harmony, we can only assume that they would have a more acute awareness of the effects of any drug circulating in their systems. If this evaluation is even partially accurate, caffeine has certainly played more than an incidental part in the flowering of the tea ceremony and the traditions of teaism.

As to the spiritual elevation of the Urasenke school and the Urasenke tea masters, some observers are skeptical. Rikyu, the shrewd intriguer and grand master of tea, worked to increase the wealth and political influence of the Kyoto-based Urasenke tea masters. Urasenke is still the leading school of the tea ceremony and commands a major worldly presence that in Japan today, like that of the Catholic Church in many lands, is immense. Despite such comparisons of Urasenke worldly power and pomp with that of the Catholic Church, *chanoyu* is usually regarded as entirely secular. Some people see the contemporary tea ceremony as a pastime or hobby of the idle rich. Studying and practicing the tea ceremony is very expensive, in part because of the exorbitant cost of tea ceremony lessons. Also costly are the tools required, including the bowls, implements, and other equiment, not to mention the necessity of buying or renting a traditional teahouse, typically something only the very wealthy can afford to do. Add to these costs the leisure necessary to devote to the study of teaism, and it is easy to understand why average Japanese cannot afford to indulge. Many, perhaps most, Japanese have never attended a tea ceremony. Certainly only a small percentage of Japanese actively pursue serious study of the ceremony, mostly women with inherited wealth or the wives of wealthy businessmen. Many other women study some tea ceremony lore in high school or in special schools for prospective brides, but few continue through advanced studies.

As a conventional accomplishment of young ladies, *chanoyu* has unquestionably become associated with sentimental absurdities of brocaded girls lined up like dolls, straining to attain what they fancy are the most elevated feelings about porcelain and flower blossoms. In fairness, however, one must acknowledge that such costume displays are by no means the only examples of *chanoyu* today. The Soshu Sen school of *chanoyu*, for example, is an austere Zen tradition that requires no fancy or expensive surroundings or equipment, only a bowl, tea, and hot water.[18]

Westerners may have difficulty understanding how Urasenke, a tea school, has attracted millions of tuition-paying students each year, and maintains economic and cultural control of a dozen of the nation's traditional crafts, including architecture, gardening, ceramics, metalwork, lacquerwork, and the arrangement of flowers. It wields such authority in modern Japan that it has been called "the Vatican of Japanese culture." When tea is to be offered to the imported Buddhist or autochthonous Shinto gods, visiting royalty, or heads of state, the hereditary Urasenke grand tea master is tapped to officiate.

In the early 1990s, with what justice we cannot say, Urasenke became the center of a scandal after being accused of sanctioning the pollution of village water sources in order to protect its leaders' interest in a luxury golf course development. This, together with a number of other factors, has eroded the reputation of the school and the standing of the values it represents, at least in some quarters. Some modern Japanese reject the tea ceremony utterly, judging it to be nothing more profound or spiritual than an elitist, self-indulgent intellectual exercise in aesthetic appreciation through affected but harmless chatter, accompanied by the ingestion a psychoactive drug.

Contemporary Caffeine: The Society and Commerce of Coffee Come to Japan

Dutch merchants, who record drinking coffee in Japan in 1724, were the first people known to have consumed it there. The Japanese themselves were remarkably cool to the new drink. Their affection for coffee only began to develop more than a century later. In 1888 two establishments called "*Kahisakan*," or "coffee-tea houses," were opened in Tokyo, advertising that they combined the atmosphere of an exotic European café with the familiar Chinese tearoom.[19] Other coffeehouses followed, each offering its own special Eastern interpretation of the Middle Eastern and European tradition. More coffeehouses appeared in the 1920s, founded by Japanese who had lived abroad, often in France, and who had returned with the idea of re-creating the atmosphere of the Parisian cafés. By the 1930s, the brew had percolated through Japanese culture to the extent that certain shops known as "pure tearooms" began selling only coffee. In the tense and dangerous days before the outbreak of World War II, the Japanese government closed these coffeehouses, perhaps because of their potential role as "seminaries of sedition."[20]

Following the war, the coffeeshop, or small short-order restaurant, similar in nature to those that are so common in Western nations and invariably serving coffee, tea, and caffeinated soft drinks, began to proliferate. In the 1950s and 1960s, these establishments often served as meeting spots for businessmen as well as social gathering places for young people. In the 1970s and 1980s, the prewar coffeehouse or café reemerged in more than a dozen different styles. Some are classified according to the style of recorded music they feature—jazz, chamber music, folk songs, and so on. Others are known as *"bijin,"* or "beautiful girl," coffee shops because they treat their patrons to waitresses chosen for their good looks. Still others, especially to be found in larger cities such as Tokyo, set up to attract foreign tourists, function as meeting spots for Japanese who are interested in forming a liaison with a person of different nationality. Some simply prepare and serve coffee as their main attraction, sometimes accompanied by small sandwiches or curried rice and sometimes only by a small cup of green tea.

Contemporary Japan has a growing coffee, or *koh-hi*, culture unique to itself, featuring such un-Western preparations as hot or cold canned coffee, available from countless vending machines for a dollar a can, and even jellied coffee. Coffeeshops and cafés charge as much as $5 a cup for a non-refillable serving. An American traveler recently counted more than twenty-five coffeehouses in a six-block stretch of downtown Tokyo. The hundreds of cafés that line the streets have assumed a place in Japanese society similar to that occupied by coffeehouses in early Arabia. With cramped conditions in offices and homes, the coffeeshops have become a kind of second home for many Japanese, a place to meet for business, a romantic rendezvous, a casual chat with friends, or just to take a break from a busy day. Some natives and visitors chalk up the high price for a cup to getting a little peace and a place to rest. In a crowded, bustling city where space is the most valuable commodity, one can rent a little space for a few minutes while drinking a cup of coffee.

The giant among Japanese coffeehouse chains is Doutor, which, starting around 1980, took command of the market by offering good coffee much cheaper than their competitors. Today they charge only about ¥180, or about $1.80, for a non-refillable cup, less than half of what you would pay at many other places. Doutor operates nearly five hundred shops nationwide and for a time opened about five new ones every month. In 1995 the company began to encounter competition with America's Seattle-based coffeehouse chain Starbucks, which had decided to make Japan its first overseas target, beginning with Tokyo. Yuji Tsunoda, president of Starbucks Coffee Japan, speaks of Starbucks as a "new lifestyle concept" for Japan and about the "Starbucks experience." Although such puffing sounds like a public relation man's dream, we must acknowledge that references to a new style of living and an atmosphere filled with new experiences was and is genuinely to be associated with coffeehouse culture everywhere.

The brick-and-mortar coffeehouses are apparently carrying on the Middle East-ern and European traditions of creating centers of recreational socializing with strangers or friends. Coffeehouse environments range from student hangouts in Tokyo playing new wave jazz, and cafés that provide comic books, magazines, and books for their customers, to those reminiscent of teahouses, featuring traditional lute music and scroll paintings. Rolnick, in *The Complete Book of Coffee* (1982), comments on their large numbers and exotic variety:

> Today, it is said that there are 16,000 *kohi* shops in Tokyo alone, while 100,000 is reckoned for the country. Some are miniature concert halls, where symphonies, opera, jazz and rock music are relayed over sophisticated stereophonic systems. Others have romantic music, poetry readings, or the most opulent decor. Places like Lily of the Valley or Picasso, Hygiene, Ten Commandments (the latter looking as if it were straight out of a Cecil B. DeMille epic) and Magicland, have everything from mon-strous five-storey-high stained-glass murals and Finnish wood, to something resem-bling a High Anglican church.[21]

As she is in many technological areas, Japan is in the forefront in the rush into cyberspace. A cursory search of the Internet turns up dozens of so-called cybercafés, with such names as Electronic Café International, KISS, Café Des Pres, and Cyber-net Café. Following the Japanese lead, other Asian countries, such as Hong Kong, Sin-gapore, Malaysia, South Korea, and Taiwan, now boast cybercafés in great numbers.

Japan has been the launching pad for the Asian coffeehouse. Taiwan, under Japanese influence, now boasts many coffeehouses with geishalike companionship for the patrons. Korea also has a number of coffeehouses, often featuring classical music, after the Japanese model, in the Myongdong district. And in Hong Kong, coffee drinkers sit at outdoor cafés on benches in the springtime, in a manner reminiscent of Rome, Paris, and even harkening back to the first Islamic coffee drinkers in Mecca, Cairo, and Constantinople.

David Landau, editor of *Coffee Talk Magazine*, who describes himself as a "Japanophile," says that, even though we associate the Japanese with green tea, they have regularly used coffee for years, and many consider it a fixture of life just as Amer-icans do. In fact, ten years ago, Landau judges, the Japanese were making better cof-fee than Americans. Today, however, with our now maturing and widespread love of specialty coffees, Americans could teach them a great deal. According to Landau, these higher-grade coffees are available in upscale restaurants but are not yet in general use:

> So far, the new wave of North American quality coffee has not made popular inroads. [However] If you go to a chic Italian restaurant in the Akasaka or Roppongi district of Tokyo, you will undoubtedly find an espresso that holds its own with the best of Milano or of Seattle.[22]

It's expensive, though. A non-refillable cup will cost $2 or more. In any case, outside of fancy restaurants, which are out of reach for average Japanese, fine coffee is still hard to find.

   The All-Japan Coffee Association, the primary coffee trade group, estimates the total value of the Japanese coffee market at about ¥1 trillion ($10 billion) per year. The association contends that the traditional markets for instant and regular brewed coffee are saturated, but it is optimistic about the growth of specialty coffees. Although Japanese coffee customs are evolving, the average Japanese apartment, perhaps in part because space is tight, doesn't have a coffeemaker of any sort. Japanese typically make instant coffee at home for themselves and serve the same to their guests. A person looking for coffee brewed from exotic beans or fancy drinks such as a "double-tall café latte" in Japan must go to a *kissaten*, or coffeeshop.

10

islands of caffeine (2)
England: Caffeine and Empire

> "Look here, steward, if this is coffee, I want tea; but if this is tea, then I wish for coffee."
> —Cartoon in *Punch* at the end of the nineteenth century

Caffeine Comes to England: From Rumor to Reality

The first written mention of coffee in English occurs in the context of the first written mention of tea, in a 1598 translation of *Linschoten's Travels*, in a chapter entitled "Of the Island Japan." Bernard Ten Broeke Paludanus (1550–1633), a professor of philosophy at the University of Leyden and world traveler, translated and annotated the Latin text (Holland, 1595) of the Dutch adventurer Hans Hugo Van Linschoten (1563–1611). Highlighting his interpolation with a distinctive typeface, Paludanus inserts the following remarks, comparing Turkish coffee drinking with Oriental tea drinking, into Linschoten's discussion of Japanese tea:

> The Turks holde almost the same manner of drinking of their *Chaona*, which they make of certaine fruit, which is like unto the Bakelaer [laurel berry], and by the Egyptians called *Bon* or *Ban*: they take of this fruite one pound and a half, and roast them a little in the fire and then sieth in twenty poundes of water, till the half be consumed away: this drinke they take every morning fasting in their chambers, out of an earthen pot, being verie hote, as we doe here drinke *aquacomposita* [*brandewijn*] in the morning: and they say that it strengtheneth and maketh them warme, breaketh wind, and openeth any stopping.[1]

Paludanus links the two beverages in this passage with respect to the similarity of their physiological effects, and, in the chapter in which the passage is found, introduces both drinks to English readers, suggesting that the English, from the very start, though unaware of caffeine, were informed that coffee and tea, which they regarded as drugs, were united by a common agency.

...clokes when we meane to goe abroad unto the towne or countrie, they put them off when they goe forth, putting on great wyde breeches, and coming home they put them off again, and cast their clokes upon their shoulders: and as among other nations it is a good sight to see men with white and yealow hayre and white teeth, with them it is esteemed the filthiest thing in the world, and seeke by all meanes they may to make their hayre and teeth blacke, for that the white causeth their grief, and the blacke maketh them glad. The like custome is among the women, for as they goe abroad they have their daughters & maydes before them, and their men servants come behind, which in *Spaigne* is cleane contrarie, and when they are great with childe, they tye their girdles so hard about them, that men would thinke they should burst, and when they are not with Childe, they weare their girdles so slacke, that you would thinke they would fall from their bodies, saying that by experience they do finde, if they should not doe so, they should have evill lucke with their fruit, and presently as soone as they are delivered of their children, in steed of cherishing both the mother and the child with some comfortable meat, they presently wash the cylde in cold water, and for a time give the mother very little to eate, and that of no great substance. Their manner of eating and drinking is: Everie man hath a table alone, without table-clothes or napkins, and eateth with two peeces of wood, like the men of *China*: they drinke wine of Rice, wherewith they drink themselues drunke, and after their meat they use a certaine drinke, which is a pot with hote water, which they drinke as hote as ever they may indure, whether it be Winter or Summer.

Annotat. D. Pall.

The *Turkes* holde almost the same maner of drinking of their *Chaona*, which they make of certaine fruit, which is like unto the *Bakelaer*, and by the *Egyptians* called *Bon* or *Ban*: they take of this fruite one pound and a half, and roast them a little in the fire, and then sieth them in twentie poundes of water, till the half be consumed away: this drinke they take euerie morning fasting in their chambers, out of an earthen pot, being verie hote, as we doe here drinke *aquacomposita* in the morning: and they say that it strengtheneth and maketh them warme, breaketh wind, and openeth any stopping.

The manner of dressing their meat is altogether contrarie unto other nations: the aforesaid warme water is made with the powder of a certaine hearbe called Chaa, which is much esteemed, and is well accounted of The 1. Booke.

among them, and al such as are of any countenance or habilitie have the said water kept for them in a secret place, and the gentlemen make it themselves, and when they will entertaine any of their friends, they give him some of that warme water to drinke: for the pots wherein they sieth it, and wherein the hearbe is kept, with the earthen cups which they drinke it in, they esteeme as much of them, as we doe of Diamants, Rubies and other precious stones, and they are not esteemed for their newnes, but for their oldnes, and for that they were made by a good workman: and to know and keepe such by themselues, they take great and speciall care, as also of such as are the valewers of them, and are skilfull in them, as with us the goldsmith priseth and valueth silver and gold, and the Jewellers all kindes of precious stones: so if their pots & cuppes be of an old & excellent workmans making, they are worth 4 or 5 thousand ducats or more the peece. The King of *Bungo* did giue for such a pot, having three feet, 14 thousand ducats, and a Iapan being a Christian in the town of *Sacay*, gaue for such a pot 1400 ducats, and yet it had 3 peeces upon it. They doe likewise esteeme much of any picture or table, wherein is painted a blacke tree, or a blacke bird, and when they knowe it is made of wood, and by an ancient & cuning maister, they giue whatsoever you will aske for it. It happeneth some times that such a picture is sold for 3 or 4 thousand ducats and more. They also esteeme much of a good rapier, made by an old and cunning maister, such a one many times costeth 3 or 4 thousand Crowns the peece. These things doe they keepe and esteeme for their Iewels, as we esteeme our Iewels & precious stones. And when we aske them why they esteeme them so much, they aske us againe, why we esteeme so well of our precious stones & iewels, whereby there is not any profite to be had, and serue to no other use, then only for a shewe, & that their things serue to some end.

Their Iustice and gouernment is as followeth: Their kings are called Iacatay, and are absolutely Lords of the land, notwithstanding they keepe for themselues as much as is necessary for them and their estate, and the rest of their land they deuyde among others, which are called Cunixus, which are like our Earles and Dukes: these are appointed by the king, and he causeth them to gouerne & rule the land as it pleaseth him: they are bound to serue the king as well in peace, as in warres, at their owne cost & charges, according to their estate, and the auncient lawes of Iapan. These Cunixus haue others under them called Toms, which are like our

Lords

The first mention of tea and coffee in print in English. This page is from a 1598 edition of *Linschoten's Travels,* in a chapter entitled "Of the Island Japan," translated from Latin by Bernard Ten Broeke Paludanus. Coffee appears as *"Chaona"* in the second line of the text notation by Paludanus. Note that this interpolated text on coffee appears in a Roman typeface inserted into the Gothic typeface of the original text. Tea appears as *Chaa* in the first column, two lines from the bottom. (W. H. Ukers, *All about Tea*)

Only ten years later, the English read a vivid description of the Middle Eastern coffeehouse. William Biddulph, in his *Travels of Certayne Englishmen in Africa, Asia, etc. . . . Begunne in 1600 and by some of them finished—this yeere 1608* (London, 1609), describes the use of coffee and Turkish coffeehouses at a time when England knew only the tavern:

> Their most common drinke is *Coffa*, which is a blacke kinde of drinke, made of a kind of Pulse like Pease, called *Coaua*. . . . It is accounted a great curtesie amongst them to give unto their friends when they come to visit them, a Fin-ion or Scudella of *Coffa*, which is more holesome than toothsome [more healthy than it is good tasting], for it causeth good concoction, and driveth away drowsinesse.
>
> Some of them will also drink Bersh or Opium, which maketh them forget themselves, and talk idely of Castles in the Ayre, as though they saw Visions and heard Revelations. Their *Coffa* houses are more common than Ale-houses in England; but they use not so much to sit in the houses, as on benches on both sides the streets, neere unto a *Coffa* house, every man with his Fin-ionful; which being smoking hot, they use to put it to their Noses & Eares, and then sup it off by leasure, being full of idle and Ale-house talke whiles they are amongst themselves drinking it; if there be any news, it is talked of there.[2]

No catalogue of early references can permit us to determine precisely when coffee, tea, and chocolate first significantly entered the English awareness. However, some indirect evidence can shed light on the question. Shakespeare (1564–1616), who uses more tropes of language and a greater range of vocabulary than any other writer and whose work features treatments of virtually every aspect of daily life, including, of course, food, drink, and the habits and delicacies of the table, both in England and the exotic city-states of Italy and ancient Greece and Rome, makes no mention of coffee, tea, or chocolate. Because of the comprehensive nature of the Shakespearean universe of discourse, the absence of these references helps fix the time after his death as the earliest boundary for their general presence in England even by reputation.

Less than ten years after Shakespeare died, Francis Bacon (1561–1626), lord chancellor of England and one of the fathers of empiricism, whom some suppose to have been the true author of the Bard's works, makes two references to coffee, which he almost certainly never saw, much less tasted, unless it was from the hands of his physician, Dr. William Harvey. The first Baconian reference occurs in the *Historia Vitae et Mortis* (1623): "The Turkes use a kind of herb which they call *caphe*." By 1624, when Bacon wrote *Sylva Sylvarum* (1627), he must have read a few more of the early travelers' accounts of Middle Eastern coffee use, phrases from which recur in his discussion of a variety of Oriental drugs:

> They have in Turkey a drink called *coffa* made of a berry of the same name, as black as soot, and of a strong scent, but not aromatical; . . . and they take it, and sit at it in their coffa-houses, which are like our taverns. This drink comforteth the brain and heart, and helpeth digestion. Certainly this berry coffa, the root and leaf betel, the leaf tobacco, and the tear of poppy (opium) of which the Turks are great takers (supposing it expelleth all fear), do all condense the spirits, and make them

strong and aleger. But it seemeth they were taken after several manners; for coffa and opium are taken down, tobacco but in smoke, and betel is but champed in the mouth with a little lime.[3]

Notice that Bacon classifies "coffa" with opium, tobacco, and betel, as a fortifying and analeptic drug, not a beverage, and distinguishes these drugs as drugs only according to how they are taken, whether eaten, smoked, or chewed.

Other early references by Englishmen include remarks made in the 1626 correspondence of the twenty-year-old aristocrat Sir Thomas Herbert, who traveled in the company of Sir Dodmore Cotton, ambassador to the Persian shah. Herbert alludes to caffeine's effects when he reports to his friends that Persian coffee "is said to be healthy, dispelling melancholy, drying tears, allaying anger, and producing cheerfulness."[4] Robert Burton, quoted in an epigraph to our introduction, added a reference to coffee in the 1632 edition of *Anatomy of Melancholy*, in the chapter called "Medicines." Burton apparently heard about coffee sometime after the publication of the first edition in 1621, in which he does not mention the drink.

The English physicians of the day enjoyed at least a limited respect from their countrymen,[5] and their approval of the caffeinated drinks helped caffeine to make quick progress in their homeland. The influence of these medical men is apparent in the first printed advertisement in England for a caffeinated beverage, appearing on May 19, 1657, in the *Public Adviser*, which lists the maladies it was believed to cure:

> In *Bartholomew* Lane on the backside of the Old Exchange, the drink called *Coffee*, which is a very wholsom and Physical drink, having many excellent vertues . . . , fortifies the heat within, helpeth Digestion, quickneth the Spirits, maketh the heart lightsome, is good against eye-sores, Coughs, or Colds, Rhumes, Consumptions, Head-ach, Dropsie, Gout, Scurvy, Kings Evil, and many others is to be sold both in the morning and at three of the clock in the afternoon.[6]

The Great Instauration: The Oxford Coffee Club and the Birth of the Royal Society

In the sixteenth and seventeenth centuries, as now, university students were frequently travelers, aficionados of the exotic, and members of the avant-garde. It was such a student from abroad, Nathaniel Conopios, a Cretan, who was first documented to have prepared and served coffee in England. Before coming to England, Conopios was educated in the Greek Orthodox Church and served as *primore* to the patriarch of Constantinople. When his employer was murdered by strangulation, Conopios, to avoid meeting the same end, escaped to England. He presented his credentials to Archbishop Laud, who sponsored his entry to Balliol College, Oxford.

The eclectic scholar and Oxonian diarist John Evelyn, F.R.S., provides an eyewitness account of Conopios drinking coffee, the earliest dated record of this practice in England, in a retrospective entry for May 1637. He states:

There came in my Time to the College one *Nathaniel* Conopios, out of Greece sent into England ... and was the first that I ever saw drink Caffé, not heard of then in England, nor till many years after made a common entertainment all over the nation, as since that the Chineze *Thea;* Sack & Tobacco being till these came in, the Universal liquor & Drougs.[7]

Anthony à Wood (1632–95), an historian of Oxford life, confirms Evelyn's account, commenting that although Conopios was soon expelled from the university by "Parliamentry Visitors," his brief tenure initiated the use of coffee there:

It was observed that while he continued in Balliol College he made the drink for his own use called Coffey, and usually drank it every morning, being the first, as the antients of that House have informed me, that was ever drank in Oxon.[8]

The story of the first coffeehouse in the Western world is known through the chronicles of the same Anthony Wood, published as *Athenae Oxonienses: An Exact History of all the Writers and Bishops who have had their Education in the most ancient and famous University of Oxford from the Fifteenth Year of King Henry the Seventh Dom. 1500 to the end of the Year 1690* (London, 1692), which was written with considerable research assistance from the biographer John Aubrey. Wood was a "suspicious, lonely, intolerant" man, more at home with old books than with his fellows, and, as he admitted of himself, he was "a Person who delights to converse more with the Dead, than with the Living."[9] Because there were no existing records, he depended on personal interviews to provide the information he needed for his history. To collect much of this oral intelligence, the reclusive, cantankerous Wood relied on the affable Aubrey. Though Wood was much disliked by his contemporaries, today we owe him thanks for recording some of the most authoritative early accounts of coffeehouse life in England. Wood relates that in 1650 a Lebanese Jew arrived in Oxford in the service of a Turk, bringing with him both a supply of coffee beans and the knowledge of their use:

In this year a Jew by the name of Jacob opened a coffeehouse ... *at the Angel in the parish of St Peter in the East* ... [in this establishment, coffee was] ... *by some who delighted in noveltie, drank.*[10]

A few years later, Jacob took his business to London, opening a coffeehouse in Holborn. Confusingly enough, he may have turned over the Angel to a man named "Jacobson," a recent Jewish convert to Monophysite Christianity. Speaking of this latter "outlander," Wood reports in an entry dated 1654:

Cirques Jacobson, a Jew and a Jacobite, born in the vicinity of Lebanon, sold coffee in a house at Oxford between Edmund Hall and Queen's College Corner ... at or neare the Angel within the East Gate of Oxon.

In another reference, Wood speaks of Jacobson as selling both coffee and chocolate, a bill of fare that was to become common in London over the next decade. Establishing what must be the world's record for café longevity, the original coffee room of Jacob's Angel remained in use as a restaurant for more than three hundred years.

Within a decade, coffeehouses multiplied and became the rage at Oxford. Their success elicited opposition from some, who, like Wood, thought them inimical to rather than productive of serious intellectual activity. In 1661, Wood declared, the conversations of the University men of his day, instead of talk about academic matters, consisted of "nothing but news, and the affairs of Christendome is discoursed off and that also generally at coffeehouses." A few years later, he blamed this cultural deterioration on the rise of the coffeehouse:

> Why doth solid and serious learning decline, and few or none follow it now in the university? *Answer:* Because of coffeehouses, where they spend all their time; and in entertainments . . . in common chambers whole afternoons and thence to the coffeehouse.[11]

The Oxford University administrators apparently agreed with Wood and attempted, without much success, to curtail or eliminate the coffeehouse dissipation. In 1677, an order of the vice chancellor barred coffee vendors from opening after evening prayers on Sundays and also from selling the drink as a carry-out "to prevent people to drink it in their houses." A few years after, the mayor tried to completely shut down the coffeehouses on Sunday. Despite these reactionary efforts, in Oxford, as elsewhere, coffee's popularity continued to grow.

The ancient rivalry between Oxford and Cambridge seems, in respect of coffee usage, to have been settled in Oxford's favor, for the first coffeehouse in Cambridge is not reported until the early 1660s. We read about it in a letter by Roger North in which he refers to the student days of Dr. John North (1645–83), an older relation who went on to become a master of Trinity College. While John North was an undergraduate, this coffeehouse, owned by a man named Kirk, became a favorite haunt for academics. It was also the publication site of *The Trade of News*, the first newsletter to appear as an alternative to the "publick Gazette.[12]

As a result of Kirk's success, several new coffeehouses opened in Cambridge within a few years. Their popularity as student hangouts was noticed in the Cambridge University Statutes, which, on November 9, 1664, ordered, "all in *pupillari statu* that shall go to coffeehouses without their tutors leave shall be punished according to the statute for the haunters of taverns and ale-houses." However, despite these reformatory efforts, the coffeehouse was destined to become as popular at Cambridge as it had already become at Oxford. In 1710, by which time the institution had clearly become well accepted, von Uffenbach, a young German visitor to Cambridge, speaks of a coffeehouse that was a favorite of the senior faculty, and of an atmosphere marked more by collegiate congeniality than by dissipation, a place where after 3 o'clock in the afternoon, "you meet the chief Professors and doctors who read the papers over a cup of coffee and a pipe of tobacco, and converse on all subjects."[13]

In 1655 a group of Oxford students and young Fellows persuaded Arthur Tillyard, a local apothecary, whom Wood refers to as an "Apothecary and Great

Royalist," to prepare and sell "coffey publickly in his House against All Soules College." This Oxford Coffee Club, an informal confraternity of scientists and students, was the beginning of the Royal Society, which quickly became and remains today one of the leading scientific societies in the world. Its academic members had something in common with Timothy Leary, the Harvard professor who experimented with LSD, in that they were dabbling in the use of a new and powerful drug unlike anything their countrymen had ever seen. Surviving recorded accounts confirm that the heavily reboiled sediment-ridden coffee of the day was not enjoyed for its taste, but was consumed exclusively for its pharmacological benefits.

Although he admired many of its members, the dour Wood was contemptuous of the Oxford Coffee Club itself, perhaps because he had little interest in the scientific topics that furnished the subjects for its discussions. He evidently believed, in this case at least, that the whole was less than the sum of its illustrious parts, because he derisively records in his history that a club was built, "at Tillyards, where many pretended wits would meet and deride all others." The first participants included Hans Sloane, founder of the British Museum, Sir Edmund Halley, the great astronomer, and Sir Isaac Newton, originator of the calculus, celestial mechanics, and the postulates of classical physics. The members' avid curiosity prompted hands-on scientific investigation: Sloane, Halley, and Newton are said to have dissected a dolphin on a table in the coffeehouse before an amazed audience.

The Oxford Coffee Club quickly absorbed the membership of a competing science club, which had been set up concurrently by an Oxford tutor, Peter Sthael of Strasbourg. Christopher Wren (1632–1723), in Evelyn's words, "the prodigious young scholar," who had not yet become an architect but who was already reputed a philosopher, inventor, mathematician, and the man in whom many of the intellectual ideals of his age were embodied, was among those who were initiated into the Oxford Coffee Club at the time of this acquisition. As Wood explains:

> After he [Sthael] had taken in another class of six, he translated himself to the house of Arthur Tillyard, an apothecary, the next door to that of John Cross (saving one, which is a tavern), where he continued teaching till 1662.

Perhaps energized by their peppy potations, the Oxford Coffee Club members soon took their coffee tippling to London. They may have joined forces with existing London groups that, from about 1645, had held weekly meetings to discuss science, or "what hath been called the New Philosophy of Experimental Philosophy." These were probably the societies referred to by the chemist Sir Robert Boyle when he spoke of the "Invisible College." In any case, it is known that the Oxonians convened in London sometime before 1662, for in that year they were granted a charter by Charles II as the Royal Society of London for the Improvement of Natural Knowledge. They soon settled into headquarters at Gresham College, taking their favorite drink at the Grecian coffeehouse, in Devereux Court, near Temple Bar. Wren, having come to London with the club, was soon appointed professor of astronomy at Gresham College.[14]

Early Coffeehouses: Penny Universities or Seminaries of Sedition?

Pasqua Rosée established the first coffeehouse in London in 1652, and his original handbill promoting coffee's pharmacological benefits survives in the British Museum (See Appendix A). Pasqua's story is told in a handwritten note by William Oldys (1696–1761), a celebrated English antiquary, bibliographer, and herald:

> Mr. Edwards, a Turkey merchant, brought from Smyrna to London one Pasqua Rosee, a Ragusan youth, who prepared this drink for him every morning. But the novelty thereof drawing too much company to him, he allowed his said servant, with another of his son-in-law, to sell it publicly, and they set up the first coffeehouse in London, in St. Michael's alley, in Cornhill. The sign was Pasqua Rosee's own head.[15]

Such coffeehouse signs soon became mailing addresses for their regular customers. For example, a writer and friend of Rosée's addressed verses "to Pasqua Rosee, at the Sign of his own Head and half his Body in St. Michael's Alley, next the first Coffee-Tent in London." From a curious book, *The Character of the Coffee-House by an Eye and Ear Witness* (London, 1665), we learn that these signs, often mock-Oriental in style, had by the date of its publication become a common sight over the doorways of public houses throughout the city. Bryant Lillywhite, in his meticulously documented compendium, *London Coffee Houses* (London, 1963), records more than fifty houses using the Sign of the Turk's Head. A desire to evoke the splendor of Suleiman the Magnificent (r. 1520–86), the fourth emperor of the Turks, inspired the use of this emblem by coffeehouse keepers both on signs and the tokens they commonly issued because of a shortage in the supply of small coins.

The partnership between Rosée, the immigrant servant, and Bowman, the coachman of Edwards' son-in-law, prospered and was quickly imitated. In 1656, a barber and tavern keeper, James Farr, sometimes given as Ffarr, Farre, or Far, converted his pub into London's second coffeehouse. According to Aubrey, this was the Rainbow on Fleet Street. It was so successful that it aroused the jealousy of Farr's taproom competitors. On December 21, 1657, they filed the "Wardmote Inquest presentment" under the section of Disorders and Annoys:

> Item, we pr'sent James Ffarr, barber, for makinge and selling of a drink called coffee, whereby in makeing the same, he annoyeth his neighbours by evil smells and for keeping of ffire for the most part night and day, whereby his chimney and chambr. hath been sett on ffire, to the great danger and affrightment of his neighbours.[16]

Despite this opposition, the Rainbow carried on, surviving even the Great Fire of 1666 (which destroyed the buildings in St. Michael's alley), and, when it was razed in 1859, another Rainbow was built and still stands on the same spot today. The original Rainbow was a favorite of Sir Henry Blount, often called "the father of the English coffeehouse," a great champion of coffee as a temperance drink, of whom Aubrey writes:

Since he was [unreadable] years olde he dranke nothing but water or Coffee. . . .

I remember twenty yeares since he inveighed much against sending youths to the Universities—*quaere* if his sons were there—because they learnt there to be debaucht. . . . Drunkeness he much exclaimed against, but wenching he allowed. When Coffee first came in he was a great upholder of it, and hath ever since been a constant frequenter of Coffee houses, especially Mr. Farre at the Rainbowe, by Inner Temple Gate, and lately John's coffeehouse, at Fuller's rents.[17]

Though Aubrey praises the Rainbow as an asylum of sobriety, this early London coffeehouse was also the scene of political turbulence. On May 8, 1666, Samuel Speed (d. 1681), a stationer, bookseller, and writer headquartered at the Rainbow, was arrested on charges of publishing and selling treasonable books.[18] Although the Rainbow continued doing business without interruption by the king's Proclamation of 1675, discussed below, "Farr's Coffee-house the Rainbow near the Temple" and Blount appear in a list of suspicious houses and persons published in 1679.[19]

A good idea of how coffee was being enjoyed in these Restoration coffeehouses can be gotten from this London recipe from 1662:

> To make the drink that is now much used called coffee
> The coffee-berries are to be bought at any Druggist, about three shillings the pound; Take what quantity you please, and over a charcoal fire, in an old pudding-pan or frying-pan, keep them always stirring until they be quite black, and when you crack one with your teeth that it is black within as it is without; yet if you exceed, then do you waste the Oyl, which only makes the drink; and if less, then will it not deliver its Oyl, which makes the drink; and if you should continue fire till it be white, it will then make no coffee, but only give you its salt. The Berry prepared as above, beaten and forced through a Lawn Sive, is then fit for use.
> Take clean water, and boil one third of it away what quantity soever it be, and it is fit for use. Take one quart of this prepared Water, put in it one ounce of your prepared coffee, and boil it gently one-quarter of an hour, and it is fit for your use; drink one-quarter of a pint as hot as you can sip it.[20]

In the beginning, these coffeehouses served only coffee, but soon chocolate, tea, and sherbet were added to the bill of fare. Although some coffeehouses served ale and beer as early as 1669, the position of the coffeehouses as bastions of temperance was not seriously eroded until at least twenty years later. Elford the younger, around 1689, said that "Drams and cordial waters were to be had only at coffeehouses newly set up." During this time, private consumption of the caffeinated beverages was beginning to take hold, as evidenced in a 1664 advertisement for the Grecian coffeehouse, which announced the sale of chocolate and tea and also offered free lessons in how to prepare them.

One of the new coffeehouses was Miles', in New Palace Yard, Westminster, at the Sign of the Turk's Head. In 1659, the famous Coffee Club of the Rota convened there. The Rota was one of the first clubs in England, "a free and open Society of

Watercolor drawing of a London coffeehouse by unknown artist who lived during the early eighteenth century. W. H. Ukers, in *All about Coffee*, describes it as follows: "This little body color drawing by an unknown English artist of the reign of Queen Ann was given by Mr. R.Y. Ames to the British Museum. It is a document of considerable interest for students of social history. It is a naive and obviously faithful representation of the interior of a London coffee house, with its clients seated at tables, smoking and drinking coffee, which is poured out from a black pot by a boy waiter, while other coffee pots are kept hot before a blazing fire. It is possible that these pots were also used for tea at this period. An elegant lady in a fontange head dress presides at a bar under a tester on the left, and is handing out a glass, the contents of which may be guessed from a framed notice on the wall: 'Heare is right Irish Usquebae.' Of the newspapers which lie on the tables no word but 'April' is legible. Pictures, perhaps for sale, adorn the wall: A connoisseur is examining one of them by the light of a candle. The prevailing colors are scarlet, pale blue, grey, and white, against a background of the various browns of wall, tables, and floor. The probable date, judging by the costume, is about 1705. The drawing resembles in several respects a small engraving of a coffee house which appeared in 1710, but is not the original of that engraving, and represents the fashions of a slightly earlier period. The date 'A.S.' (for Anno Salutis) 1668 which appears to the left is obviously a later and spurious addition." (Photograph courtesy of British Museum)

ingenious gentlemen" who were happy to be free from the tyranny of Cromwell. Aubrey, Andrew Marvell, and possibly even John Milton were members of this group, which Pepys called simply "the Coffee club," and which became proverbial for its literary censures in the phrase "damn beyond the fury of the Rota." Its founder, the political writer, James Harrington (1611–77), held meetings nightly.[21] The Rota is also famous as the forum for of the first ballot box in England, a novelty that created even more excitement among its members than coffee did.[22]

For all the hubbub, the club burned itself out quickly. Pepys describes what was to be its final meeting, in 1660: "After a small debate upon the question whether learned or unlearned subjects are best, the club broke up very poorly, and I do not think they will meet any more."

After the Great Fire of 1666, many new and larger coffeehouses sprang up all over the city. Ironically, because of their reputation as refuges for sobriety, they attracted increasing numbers of disreputable fugitives from the taverns, who sought to remediate their reputations by changing their venue. As a result, many of the distinctive features of the original coffeehouses began to become effaced. Of this pejoration we shall speak more later. However, any novel social practice or institution, should it meet with quick acceptance by many, will incite disapproval from some. The history of coffee drinking and coffeehouses is no exception.

In 1674, perhaps after spending too many lonely nights at home while their husbands regaled at the coffeehouses, which, according to the custom of the English, were forbidden to women, the wives of London, echoing the Persian Mahmud Kasnin's sultana's complaint, published *The Women's Petition against Coffee, representing to public consideration the grand inconveniences accruing to their sex from the excessive use of the drying and enfeebling Liquor*, a broadside which asserted that coffee made men

> as unfruitful as the deserts where that unhappy berry is said to be bought; that since its coming the offspring of our mighty forefathers are on the way to disappear as if they were monkeys and swine.

In another passage they describe the plight of what we might call the "coffeehouse widow": "on a domestic message [errand] a husband would stop by the way to drink a couple of cups of coffee" and be gone for hours. Echoes of their complaints are evident in King Charles II's proclamation banning coffeehouses the following year.

Later the same year of the women's petition, the husbands responded with *The Men's Answer to the Women's Petition Against Coffee, vindicating . . . their liquor, from the undeserved aspersion lately cast upon them, in their scandalous pamphlet*, in which they defended their conduct and the drink they had come to fancy. Another broadside in the same vein, also appearing that year, and the first to feature illustrations, was *A Brief Description of the Excellent Vertues of that Sober and Wholesome Drink Called Coffee, and the Incomparable Effects in Preventing and Curing Most Diseases Incident To Humane Bodies*, which sold "at the sign of the coffee mill and tobacco-roll in Cloath-fair near West-Smithfield, who selleth the best Arabian coffee powder and chocolate in cake or roll, after the Spanish fashion."

Meanwhile, injured parties other than desolate wives were complaining against coffee's increased popularity. One leaflet asserted that the coffeehouse seduced men into an idle life of dissipated conversation with people they hardly knew. Such promising, worthy gentlemen and merchants, once trustworthy, were lured by their coffeehouse friends into a habit that took them away from their occupations "for six or even eight hours."[23] And, expressing even a greater alarm, a political economist, writing on behalf of established trade interests that were being injured by the popularity of coffee, asserted:

The growth of coffee-houses has greatly hindered the sale of oats, malt, wheat, and other home products. Our farmers are being ruined because they cannot sell their grain; and with them the landowners, because they can no longer collect their rents.[24]

To read these bills of particulars, one might think that a general economic catastrophe had befallen the nation. All on account of the little bean and the houses in which it was brewed and served.

By 1700, there was an abundance of coffeehouses in London, many of which catered to a special professional, social, mercantile, or artistic clientele. Every writer on the subject entertains a different opinion as to how many there were, but no one seems to really know. The estimates have declined over the years. As a reference point, consider that, at the end of the seventeenth century, Gregory King (1648–1712), an English herald, genealogist, and engraver, calculated that the entire population of Britain was 5.5 million based on the hearth-tax returns between 1662 and 1682,[25] a figure with which modern demographers concur.[26] London, at the turn of the eighteenth century, had reached about 500,000 (almost twenty times the size of Bristol, the next-largest city of the day) and, even more rapidly than the other English seaport cities, was expanding as a center for business and politics. The rapid growth of the coffeehouse business is suggested by the French writer Sylvestre Dufour, who in 1683 relates claims by returning visitors that there were more than three thousand coffeehouses in London, a remarkable, even preposterous figure that has been widely repeated in such respected works as *The Story of Civilization*, by Will and Ariel Durant. Another testimonial comes from John Ray (1627–1705), a London botanist, who computed in 1688 that coffeehouses were nearly as general in London as in Cairo.[27] Timbs, in his classic *Clubs and Club Life in London* (1872), quotes an early edition of the *National Review* to the effect that "Before 1715, the number of Coffee-houses in London was reckoned at two thousand. Every profession, trade, class, party, had its favorite Coffee-house." However, Stella Margetson, in her incisive and entertaining book *Leisure and Pleasure in the Eighteenth Century* (1970), writing of the age of Addison, provides a considerably smaller estimate, stating that there were "more than 500 coffeehouses in London alone at this time."

Extrapolating from Dufour's figure for London coffeehouses, we should expect almost fifty thousand in New York City today; extrapolating even Margetson's more modest estimate, we should expect seventy-five hundred. For comparison, consider that, by actual count in the spring of 1994, Phillips/Norwalk, a real estate consulting firm, found only fifty-five coffeehouses in New York City and estimated that this number had doubled to more than a hundred by the start of 1995. It has probably at least doubled again since. The Specialty Coffee Association reported that in 1989 there were about two hundred coffeehouses in the entire country, about five thousand by the start of 1995, and correctly predicted over ten thousand by the new millennium.

Thus, taking even the most conservative estimates, London around 1700 had one coffeehouse for every thousand people, or nearly forty times the proportion of coffeehouses than New York today, in what are the early stages of the contemporary coffeehouse revival. These exotic flowers of the East were not to thrive for long, for by 1815, however many there may once have been, there were fewer than twelve coffeehouses left in the entire city. In only one hundred and fifty years, the coffeehouse had come and gone in London. But as consequence of its vogue, coffee, tea, and, to a lesser extent, chocolate had become commonplace dietary items that were welcomed as fortifying temperance drinks, even as far as the conservative English countryside.

Caffeine and the Crown: Charles II Bans Coffee and Catherine of Braganza Takes Tea

Kings and sultans have a long history of involvement with caffeine. Many have made attempts to ban its use by their subjects, while some—often the same ones—have enjoyed preparing and serving it to their intimates or have made a considerable amount of money from taxing its sale. A good example of inconsistency in state policies with respect to coffee and tea is an English king's disapproval of the tumultuous atmosphere of the early coffeehouses, while his queen played a starring role in introducing the fashion of tea to England.

The promiscuous mingling of political opinions, the trademark of the new coffeehouses, engendered fear and suspicion, bolstering opposition to coffee and the establishments in which it was served. This opposition culminated in a proclamation by Charles II, made on December 23, and issued on December 29, 1675, banning coffeehouses from London after January 10, 1676:

BY THE KING:
A PROCLAMATION FOR THE SUPRESSION OF
COFFEE HOUSES

Charles R.

Whereas, it is most apparent that the multitude of Coffee Houses of late years set up and kept within this kingdom, . . . the great resort of Idle and disaffected persons . . . , have produced very evil and dangerous effects; as well for that many tradesmen and others, do herein mispend much of their time, which might and probably would be employed in and about there Lawful Calling and Affairs; but also, for that in such houses . . . diverse false, malicious and scandalous reports are devised and spread abroad to the defamation of his Majesty's Government and to the Disturbance of the Peace and Quiet of the Realm; his Majesty hath thought it fit and necessary, that the said Coffee Houses be (for the future) Put down, and supressed, and doth . . . strictly charge and command all manner of persons, That they or any of them do not presume from and after the Tenth Day of January next ensuing, to keep any Public Coffee House, or to utter or sell by retail, in his or her or their house or houses (to be spent or consumed within the same) any Coffee, Chocolate, Sherbett, or Tea, as they will answer the contrary at their utmost perils . . . (all licenses to be revoked).

Given at our Court at Whitehall, this third and twentieth day of December, 1675, in the seven-and-twentieth year of our reign.

GOD SAVE THE KING

Some of the reasons for the ban that are enunciated in the edict, such as their danger as fire hazards, may, because of the need to maintain a continuous open flame, have been genuine concerns less than ten years after the Great Fire of 1666. Other reasons, especially the apparent desire to protect adults from their own folly, sound strangely similar to the feigned aims of modern socialist politicians. But the king's primary motivation was a fear that coffeehouses could act as breeding grounds for political and social unrest, and Charles II may well have been haunted by sentiments encapsulated in a couplet from a 1685 comedy:

> In a coffeehouse just now among the rabble,
> I bluntly asked, which is the treason table?

Moseley, who recounted the stories of coffeehouse persecutions in the Islamic world, saw this concern as the king's primary motive. "However strange it may appear at this time, Coffee had similar difficulties to encounter soon after its introduction into England; . . . it having been found an encourager of social meetings, Coffee-houses were shut up by proclamation, as seminaries of sedition."[28]

Charles II was no stranger to proclamations designed to promote the welfare of his subjects. In Isaac Disraeli's *Curiosities of Literature* (London, 1848), is described how, in 1660, the king promulgated a lengthy proclamation for the strict observance of Lent "for the good it produces in the employment of *fishermen*."[29] In other proclamations he inveighed against "the excess of gilding of coaches and chariots," and, to help avert the increasing congestion of the city, against new construction, which posed, he thought, many of the same threats to fire safety, health, and public order as coffeehouses. But the king's true motive may have been his own protection, a point stridently voiced by those who thought the coffeehouse ban had been designed to restrain the "licentious talking of state and government" and according to which "speakers and hearers were made alike punishable."[30, 31]

Charles II's ruling was even shorter-lived than had been the edict of Kha'ir Beg more than 150 years before, if it can be said to have had a life at all. A loud protest arose from coffeehouse owners and coffee drinkers, who even by this early date constituted a considerable economic and social constituency in the kingdom. In consequence, Charles II backed down from his order and revoked it within eleven days, on January 8, 1676, citing the king's "princely consideration and royal compassion" as the basis for the recission, although he omitted to explain why his empathy had not been operative a week and a half before.

Coming from his pen, the prohibition of coffeehouses had been, in any case, a particularly incongruous edict. Among others, Sir William Coventry had, from the first, spoken out against the measure, stating that it was well known that many of the king's early supporters had rallied in the coffeehouses during the Commonwealth, forums where they spoke more freely "than they dared to do in any other," and it was justly remarked that he might never have come to the throne but for the revolutionary fervor of the gatherings that occurred there. Perhaps the king had never been in earnest in promulgating the brief ban, for, as Coventry also remarks, he was one of England's foremost beneficiaries of coffeehouse operations. Evelyn observes that his financial dissipation forced Charles II to rely upon the personal dissipation of his subjects for revenue, in that the king found the taxes on tobacco, alcoholic drinks, and coffee, chocolate, and tea indispensable to his support, and we know that the last three were served almost exclusively in the institutions his edict would have abolished.[32]

One of the earliest links between tea and the London coffeehouse occurs in connection with Garraway's in Exchange Alley, one of the first coffeehouses in the city. In 1660 Thomas Garraway, or "Garway," issued the first broadside advertisement of tea in England, an excellent original copy of which survives in the British Museum: "An Exact Description of the Growth, Quality and Vertues of the Leaf TEA." Writing of the "regalia for high treatments and entertainments, presents being made thereof to princes and grandees," Garroway sought to capitalize on the beverage's prestige.[33] Tea was consumed in his coffeehouse and others alongside coffee and chocolate but had not yet attained the popularity of its fellow temperance drinks.

It was not until after the marriage of Charles II to Catherine of Braganza in 1662 that tea became an English pastime, preoccupation, and emblem of national life, displacing the ales, wines, and spirits that in England, no less than on the Continent, "habitually heated or stupefied" the brains of both ladies and gentlemen, "morning, noon, and night."[34] The infanta of Portugal, twenty-two at the time of her wedding, brought with her the richest dowry in Europe, almost double what any king had ever received before. Lisbon had replaced Venice as the European mart for silks, fine cottons, indigo, myrrh, spices, such as ginger, pepper, cinnamon, and cloves, and Oriental gems and pearls, and the Portuguese aristocrats, the most sophisticated on the Continent, had become accustomed to such exotic luxuries. Although tea had not been among the prizes with which the Portuguese traders had returned in their heyday, by the time of this marriage it had nevertheless become known and popular there among the upper classes.

Among the array of treasures included in Catherine's dowry were a large chest filled with tea, and the title to the colony of Bombay. In consequence of the first gift, green tea, served without milk and sipped from handleless Chinese bowls of blue-and-white porcelain, instantly became a fad at court. It was prepared by pouring hot water directly onto the leaves. In consequence of the second, the British East India Company acquired a natural harbor that offered access to all the riches of India, a resource it had long coveted and had unsuccessfully attempted to persuade Cromwell to purchase. With this gift, Portugal's access to the Eastern trade, which her explorers had been the first to chart, was functionally ended, and the Dutch finally became what they had proclaimed themselves to be, the "Lords of the Southern Seas." This Dutch supremacy did not sit well with Charles II. He instigated a series of wars between the Dutch and English, in pursuit of which the English king created in his East India Company a kind of shadow government, with the authority to make war and coin money.

Catherine's seminal role in bringing tea to England is celebrated in the famous poem by Edmund Waller (1606–87), written for the queen's twenty-third birthday in 1663, "On Tea commended by Her Majesty," in which he pays a tribute not only to Catherine and tea, and to the first for introducing the second, but offers an unknowing tribute to caffeine as "the Muse's friend."[35]

Catherine also brought sugar into general use in England, where honey had been the most common sweetener. Sugar, used as ballast in her ship when she sailed from Portugal, became increasingly available as the Eastern markets now opened to the

English. Along with tea, sugar was destined to become a major source of profit for the British East India Company.

With tea's growing popularity outside the court, new methods of preparing it appeared. In the *Book of Receipts* (London, 1669), Sir Kenelm Digby (1603–65), an English naval commander and eccentric intellectual, wrote that Philip Couplet (1623–92), a Flemish Jesuit missionary, returned in 1659 from a journey to China and provided Waller with a recipe for tea calling for a couple of raw egg yolks. According to Digby, the priest, who promulgated the knowledge of tea throughout London in the 1660s, had advised that this brew was perfect for those occasions on which you "come home very hungry after attending business abroad, and do not feel like eating a competent meal."[36] Supposedly the eggs helped the tea to settle the stomach and the tea helped the eggs to diffuse throughout the bloodstream.

In fashion, Catherine's court was ever at the vanguard. Soon all of London found reason to acquire tea services, fabricated of porcelain, silver, or pewter, depending on the purchaser's resources. In the coffeehouses tea had been brewed and stored in kegs like beer and served exclusively to men without ceremony. After Catherine's arrival and tea's entry into the life of the aristocracy, the expensive tea leaves were stored by variety in compartmentalized caddies made of wood, tortoiseshell, brass, or silver, which featured a lock to secure them from pilferage by servants. Other appurtenances included thimble-sized china cups and a crystal bowl for blending varieties of tea.

This passion for tea and porcelain took on a life of its own in England and grew even greater after Charles II died and Catherine returned to her homeland. It grew greater still when William and Mary took the throne; Mary brought from Holland an enthusiasm for both that reinforced what Catherine had begun. By the time Anne (r. 1702–14), Mary's sister, succeeded her as queen, the practice of taking tea was a necessary element of a fashionable life. Anne held court at a circular tea table adorned with a silver tea service, and, in imitation of her, women all over England began buying similar tables at which they too could sip Chinese tea from small porcelain bowls. Aristocratic ladies paid calls upon one another, embarking on little adventures that were enlivened by gossip to become more interesting than merely formal ceremonial occasions: "a sip of Tea, then for a draught or two of Scandal to digest it, . . . till the half hour's past and [callers] have disburthen'd themselves of their Secrets, and take Coach for some other place to collect new matter for Defamation."[37] Samuel Johnson, a celebrated tea maniac, who comments elsewhere that sugar tongs were among the "common decencies" of the tea service, describes his encounter with and triumph over the rigors of this social event:

> The lady [who] asked me for no other purpose but to make a zany of me, and set me gabbling to a parcel of people I knew nothing of. So I had my revenge of her; for I swallowed five and twenty cups of her tea, and did not treat her to as many words.

The standing social ritual of taking afternoon tea at about 5 o'clock, often including invited guests, did not begin until the 1840s.

It was during Anne's reign that beer was finally superseded as breakfast fare, in England at least, by tea and toast. In 1710 the *Tatler* reports that in place of a breakfast of "three rumps of beef, . . . tea and bread and butter . . . have prevailed of late years."[38]

The Honeymoon, a print by British artist John Collett, c. 1760. The tea table and its furnishings are carefully depicted, complete with a fashionable tea urn, symbolically topped with a pair of love-birds, as the newlyweds enjoy their morning tea. (Colonial Williamsburg Foundation)

The Great Conversation: The Coffeehouses and the Writers of England

Tavern and court represented and promoted the excessively exclusionary proclivities of the early Restoration. But, by the early eighteenth century, a time that might be called the age of converging sensibilities, leaders in taste were progressively withdrawing from the extremes of both vulgarity and courtliness pursued by the previous generation. The common became more refined, by the dissemination of letters and the ideal of gentlemanly conduct and restraint; and the elite became more ordinary, as they mixed increasingly in the culture of their common countrymen. The coffeehouse, where every sort of person might assemble, and where use of the newly popular drug caffeine stimulated conversation, was ideally suited to foster the inclusionary predilections of the day. It is not extravagant to claim that it was in these gathering spots that the art of conversation became the basis of a new literary style and that a new ideal of general education in letters was born.

The writers who frequented the coffeehouses entered a forum in which those from different social classes had occasion to mingle and exchange opinions, and their enthusiasm for the rough energy and extemporaneous disclosure typical of caffeine-animated coffeehouse conversation engendered new conventions in English prose. Before the coffeehouse, English expository and narrative prose was predominantly laconical and monolectical; that is, most of what was said was said briefly and in one voice.[39] With the rise of the coffeehouse, expansive prose dialogue enjoyed a remarkable vogue. Diverse writers, from hack pamphleteers to sophisticated essayists, churned out the prose dialogues that became by their better efforts highly esteemed. Many writers of the time celebrated the formal beauty of the dialogue, in which the interplay of opposing elements is artfully represented. Philip Stubbs (1665–1738), F.R.A.S., for example, a divine and author of the Platonic-style *Dialogue on Beauty* (1731), argued that harmony was the essence of beauty and spoke for many of his generation when he asserted that the dialogue, which is founded on harmony, "enlivens Philosophy with the Charms of Poetry." [40]

The engaging style of the prose dialogue, new in English, a literary image of living conversation[41] and an expository technique that aimed at persuading instead of mandating, was only one aspect of a broader cultural upheaval. Changes in beliefs about the social good, resulting in part from an ebullient, unprecedented, and vigorous mixing of classes and peoples, were under way in England. The encounters among strangers, newly possible in the coffeehouses, and the drug that provoked and animated their exchanges helped initiate the development of new ideals of humanism and popular education. The critic Harold Routh comments about the way in which the coffeehouse discussions began to advance these ideals:

> Conversation has a strange effect upon nascent ideas. He who has trained his mind by an exchange of thoughts in conversation, becomes more subtle and pliable than when he has nourished his spirit exclusively by reading. He speaks in more pithy sentences, because the ear cannot, so easily as the eye, follow long periods. . . . Thus the middle classes began to complete their education. Coffee houses provided them with a place for the interchange of ideas and for the formation of public opinion. They were (although those who frequented them were not fully conscious of the fact) brotherhoods for the diffusion of a new humanism—and only at these foci could an author come into contact with the thought of his generation.[42]

This part played by the coffeehouse is also acknowledged by Dobrée, who portrays it as the matrix out of which a new literature and a movement to disseminate learning arose:

> each coffeehouse would seem to have provided the ephemeral literature of the day, whether haunted by parsons, men of letters, city clerks, chairmen, footmen, or wool-traders. . . . There would be some items which although as topical as could be, and thus popular, would also, by the chance that they were written by men of genius, induct the unsuspecting into the house of literature.[43]

As the prose dialogue became a favorite literary form, the new manner of down-to-earth, middle-class directness also became fashionable. As this happened, poetry lost all trace of its seventeenth-century courtliness, often becoming, as in Pope's works, philosophically and morally didactic, and so more practical, engaging, and less remote. Prose for the first time replaced poetry as the common medium of drama; in place of blank verse or couplets, theatergoers now heard prose exchanges judged to represent genuine conversation more faithfully than metered language could.

The simpler, freer style had many sources. Among them were the scientific writings of the members of the Royal Society. Another were the publications of Sir Roger L'Estrange (1616–1704), a journalist and pamphleteer who in his magazine, *The Observator* (1681–87), frequently couched his political attacks in a dialogue of questions and answers. His prose has been well described as "colloquial, forceful, and conversational."[44]

If innumerable works exemplify the literary movement that used conversation as the model for the forms of entertainment and instruction, Swift's book *A complete Collection of polite and ingenuous Conversation* (London, 1738), written under the pseudonym Simon Wagstaff, Esq., is the movement's epitome. In this book Swift satirizes the "stupidity, coarseness, and attempted wit of the conversation of fashionable people."[45] In three dialogues, characters such as Lord Sparkish, Miss Notable, Lady Smart, Tom Neverout, and others provide an animated, good-natured sampling of truisms, catch phrases, repartees, and other conversational commonplaces that "to adorn every kind of discourse that an assembly of English ladies and gentlemen, met together for their mutual entertainment, can possibly want."

The English coffeehouse as a place in which men of every degree intermingled socially, in familiarity, was not to last long. While they endured, these coffeehouses offered democratic resorts in which, for a penny, a man could sit in comfort drinking coffee, and smoke, read, or converse in a manner marked by what Francis Maximillian Mission (1650–1722), a French traveler, called "the universal liberty of speech among the English."[46] By the 1760s and 1770s, however, the coffeehouses and chocolate houses yielded precedence to fashionable new clubs that showcased the aristocracy and had less and less to do with literature. One exception was a long-unnamed coffeehouse club, later called "The Literary Club," founded in 1764, that maintained the old traditions and provided the ideal forum for eliciting Samuel Johnson's conversational skill, which, in the words of Macaulay, "was nowhere so brilliant and striking as when he was surrounded by a few friends whose abilities and knowledge enabled them, as he once expressed it, to send back every ball that he threw."[47] Like the Rota, which had convened at a different Turk's Head coffeehouse more than a century before, this club, at the Turk's Head on Gerrard Street

> gradually became a formidable power in the commonwealth of letters. The verdicts pronounced by this conclave on new books were speedily known over all London, and were sufficient to sell off a whole edition in a day, or to condemn the sheets to the service of the trunk-maker and the pastry-cook.

The nine original members, one for each of the Muses, were, in addition to Johnson, Sir Joshua Reynolds, Edmund Burke, Sir John Hawkins, Oliver Goldsmith, Dr. Nugent, Mr. Beauclerk, Mr. Langton, and Mr. Chamier. It was expanded to thirty-five, so reports Johnson's follower James Boswell, a young Scottish lawyer of good family, described by Macaulay as "a bore, weak, vain, pushing, curious, garrulous," whose conversation made clear to all "that he could not reason, that he had no wit, no humor, no eloquence." One of several sources of friction between Johnson and Boswell was their disparate drinking habits.[48] Johnson stuck to tea, explaining that, though he had consumed alcoholic drinks at the university "without being the worse for it," he had found himself inclined to excess and sworn off their use so as to keep his mind clear, while Boswell was "a wine-bibber, and indeed little better than a habitual sot." In 1791 Boswell wrote an account of the club's history. Some say that the pursuit of the literary profession in England became fashionable only with this club's advent.[49]

This immense mixing and broadening of tastes, so concordant with the culture of the coffeehouse and its mix of popular and academic, was nowhere better exemplified than in the great success of Daniel Defoe and the various collaborative publications of Addison and Steele. Of his goals, Addison said, "I shall be ambitious to have it said of me that I brought philosophy out of the closets and libraries, schools and colleges, to dwell in clubs and assemblies, at tea-tables and coffeehouses."

This was the time the first true newspapers appeared, successors to odd journals such as Dunton's *Athenian Mercury* (1691–97), in which questions about scientific, theological, literary, and social matters were asked and answered. Defoe, a coffeehouse habitué and admirer of Dunton's publication, launched the *Review* (1704–13), a newspaper that he published three times a week. Written almost entirely by Defoe himself, it featured opinion pieces about political matters and initiated the tradition of editorial journalism. In speaking of his methods of courting readers, Defoe expounds the ideal of popularizing culture that animated Addison and Steele and many other leaders of coffeehouse conversations. By his style, Defoe explains that, in addressing a wide audience, he attempted to "*wheedle them in* (if it be allowed that expression) to the knowledge of the world; who, rather than take more pains, would be content with their ignorance, and search into nothing." Because some of these early news publications featured verse, they even served as their readers' introduction to poetry:[50]

> It was possibly in this way that a mass of new readers, intent in the first instance upon the actual, the practical, the useful, came to regard verse as a natural medium, would read at first, perhaps, Defoe's "True Born Englishman," . . . and finally to better things . . . even Pope's "Windsor Forest."[51]

Joseph Addison (1672–1719) and Sir Richard Steele (1672–1729) were two towering figures of early London journalism and coffeehouse literary life, perhaps best remembered for the daily *Spectator*, which they edited together. This publication was read by almost every literate person in London, especially the women, and was frequently read aloud to the illiterate. In contrast with Pope, their contemporary and rival, who addressed the elite, these famous collaborators spoke to a middle-class audience of businessmen and professionals, the mixed company who frequented

Watercolor drawing of the Lion's Head sign for Button's Coffee House, London. It was designed by Hogarth and erected by Addison in 1713. (W. H. Ukers, *All about Coffee*)

the coffeehouses of London at the turn of the eighteenth century. The two had met at the Charterhouse public school where for a while at least, according to Pope's malicious pen, they had been homosexually involved. Steele grew up to be a profligate debtor, although he settled down somewhat after his marriage in 1707, while Addison became a man of income and influence at court.

Addison held his own intellectual court at Button's Coffee House (founded by his longtime retainer Button) on Russell Street, Covent Garden, where the favored among his followers gathered to enjoy his discourse, which, reportedly, combined "merriment with decency and humour with politeness," and in conversations with such luminaries as Dryden and Pope, "reconciled wit and virtue after a long and disastrous separation."[52] Button's boasted a mailbox with a lionine figurehead, designed by Hogarth in imitation of the lion of Venice, that was set up by Addison to receive mail sent to his publication the *Guardian*. Meanwhile, the *Spectator*, which had been born on a Button's coffeehouse table, was in demand in other coffeehouses throughout the city. Around 1720, the popularity of Button's coffeehouse declined, following Addison's death and Steele's retirement to Wales.

Many other coffeehouses, in which some of the more memorable conversations in late-seventeenth- and early-eighteenth-century London undoubtedly transpired, figured in the traditions of London letters. Will's Coffee-House, named for its proprietor, William Unwin, was frequented by poets and men of letters, such as Wycherley, Addison, Pope, and Congreve. In the first issue of Steele's periodical *Tatler*, April 12, 1709, Steele states that the publication would feature "all accounts of Gallantry, Pleasure, and entertainment . . . under the article of White's Chocolate House, all poetry from Will's, all foreign and domestic news from St. James', and all learned articles from the Grecian." Will's is especially remembered for the literary disputes, which Dryden (1631–1700) presided over. Johnson wrote, in his *Lives of the English Poets*, that Dryden had assigned to himself an "armed chair, which in the winter had a settled and prescriptive place by the fire, was in the summer placed in the balcony. . . . From there he expressed his views on men and books, surrounded by an admiring crowd who said "ay" to all his remarks." Will's was the leading competitor of Button's among the literati.

The Bedford Coffee-House, at Covent Garden, was described by its proprietors as "the emporium of wit, the seat of criticism and the standard of taste." When Button's fell out of favor, the Bedford became the new hangout for actors and writers. Some of its famous frequenters were: Garrick, Samuel Foote, Richard Sheridan, Hogarth, Fielding, and William Collins. In January 1754, the premiere issue of the *Connoisseur*, edited by Coleman and Thornton, stated, "This coffee-house is every night crowded with men of parts. Almost everyone you meet is a polite scholar and a wit."

Lloyd's Coffee-House, in Lombard Street, was founded by Edward Lloyd around 1688. There the captains and merchants of England's burgeoning sea trade met and cut deals with underwriters and insurance brokers to protect their investments from the hazards of expeditions that could last many months and take them through many uncertainties of weather and welcome. This was the beginning of two institutions, the Royal Exchange Lloyd's, which, at least prior to its recent financial boondoggle, was the largest insurance company in the world, and Lloyd's Register of Shipping.

Thomas Garraway's Coffee-House, on Exchange Alley in Cornhill, which served as an auction house, is mentioned by Addison, Pope, and Swift. Jonathan's Coffee-House, also in Exchange Alley, referred to in the *Tatler* and *Spectator*, was a center of trading in company shares. Shares in the South Sea Company, formed in 1711 by the earl of Oxford to advance trade with Spanish America, were, together with its ill-fated imitators, hotly traded there. The speculation spread, and confidence men took advantage of the public's eagerness to share in the wealth expected from the New World by selling them stock in impossible ventures that quickly went bankrupt. Although the South Sea Company's investors initially saw their holdings multiply tenfold, the enterprise soon failed and left them with nothing.

The Grecian Coffee-House in Devereux Court, Essex Street, Strand, was first presided over by Constantine, a Greek immigrant. It was attended by Addison and Steele, who dated his learned articles in the *Tatler* from there, as well as by Goldsmith and many members of the Royal Society. There Ralph Thoresby (1658–1725), an antiquarian and topographer from Leeds, witnessed "Dr. Douglas dissecting a dolphin lately caught in the Thames," evidently a favorite stunt of the members of the group, which had performed the same procedure while meeting at Tillyard's.

Certain coffeehouses seemed to hold special attraction for men in particular professions or "callings." Child's Coffee-House, a favorite of the *Spectator* crowd, was popular with the clergy and the members of the Royal Society as well. Old Slaughter's Coffee-House on St. Martin's Lane was opened by Thomas Slaughter in 1692. It is remembered for the painters who assembled there, including Hogarth and Gainsborough. Tom's Coffee-House, named for Thomas West, its proprietor, was located on Russell Street, Covent Garden, the theater district. After the curtain fell, the cream of the audience and performers would collect there, including Johnson, Goldsmith, and Garrick. It became a private club in 1768.

Don Saltero's Coffee-House was founded in 1690 by John Salter, a former servant of Sir Hans Sloane, on Cheyne Walk in Chelsea. Salter, described by Steele in 1709 as "a Sage of thin and meagre Countinance," decorated his establishment with strange curios and memorabilia, which Steele called "extraordinary absurdities." Salter, who had been nicknamed "Don Saltero," or "Old Salt," by an English admiral, was, to put it mildly, a colorful character. While tending his famous house, he performed the services of a barber, including therapeutic bleeding, shaving, and pulling teeth, free of charge, played the violin, and wrote poetry. From his time as valet to Sloane (1660–1753), an Irish physician, scientist, traveler, and collector, Salter developed a passion for accumulating curiosities, including "Tiger's tusks, the skeleton of a guinea pig, the Pope's candle, a fly-cap monkey, Mary Queen of Scots pincushion, and pair of Nun's stockings." Although Steele thought little of these oddities, they attracted large crowds. When Salter died in 1728, he took with him the coffeehouse's distinctive atmosphere, but the business survived until at least the middle of the nineteenth century, at the time when Thomas Carlyle (1795–1881) moved to the same street.

White's Chocolate House, founded in 1697 by Francis White on St. James's Street, was converted about thirty-five years later into a stylish club whose members were "the most fashionable exquisites of the town and court." Even in its early coffeehouse days, it charged high prices and was frequented by the upper classes. According to Escott, it was the "one specimen of the class to which it belongs, of a place at which, beneath almost the same roof, and always bearing the same name, whether as coffeehouse or club, the same class of persons has congregated during more than two hundred years." It still exists today, and patrons look out a bay window dating from the time of George Bryan "Beau Brummell"—1755. At White's and other clubs, such as Boodle's and Brooks', also on St. James's Street, admission was by subscription only, and extravagant gambling continued all night. These became the resorts of the aristocrats, military officers, and important government officials.

Among the intellectual and artistic vanguard, Augustan civility was losing favor to self-imposed Romantic rustication. Coffeehouse conversation, with its sophisticated urban and urbane banter, held little attraction for William Wordsworth (1770–1850) and his confederates, who affected to celebrate the natural, rural, and commonplace. Of course, though the Romantics deserted the coffeehouses and "the smoke, the mud, and the cries of London,"[53] which Johnson had so loved, and went hiking around the countryside in search of pastoral inspiration, they did not leave their coffee or tea behind. In his voluminous notebook diaries, Coleridge troubles to record the following recipe for making coffee, in an entry dated December 1802:

One half of the white of an egg—a cup of tepid water after the egg has been beat up—Water enough to make the Coffee moist whatever it be

—Then put in the ground *Coffee*, (*one heaped Coffee* Cup to *six* cups of boiling water to be after put in) mix up the Coffee with the beat up egg & tepid water

then put it into the Coffee Boiler, & add boiling water in the proportion of 6 to 1—put it on a quick fire—& let it boil up, two or three times. Then throw it into the China or Silver Coffee pot thro' a Strainer

After boil & decant the Coffee grains & use the Decantia instead of hot water the next time.[54]

As these instructions show, at least until the early nineteenth century the Turkish taste for boiled and reboiled coffee, a brew that must have been strong enough to rattle a person's bones, was still current in England. As for the egg, it seems to have repeatedly made its way into English coffee and tea cups, as witness Waller's Chinese recipe for tea.[55]

Tea also figured into the lives of the Romantic poets. Coleridge was familiar with at least several varieties of tea, and he took time to complain in verse of the increase in their cost.[56] He valued "lean mutton and good Tea" at dinnertime. Tea was not entirely indispensable at breakfast—whiskey could be made a serviceable replacement. The egg seemed de rigueur:

Arrived at Letir Finlay, IX oclock
all in bed—they got up—scarce any fire in; however made me a dish of Tea & I went to *bed*.—Two blankets & a little fern & yet many Fleas!—Slept however till 10 next morning
no more Tea in the House—3 Eggs beat up, 2 glasses of Whisky, sugar, & 2/3rds of a Pint of boiling water I found an excellent Substitute.[57]

Lord Byron, a fellow Romantic poet, in his later years became a tea enthusiast, writing that he "Must have recourse to the black Bohea," and calling green tea "the Chinese nymph of tears."

Teatime in England

Peter Kalm (1715–79), a Swedish traveler, commented that in England, unlike in his homeland, a breakfast consisting of tea and toast was enjoyed by everyone who could afford it. Toast was an English invention that continued to surprise foreigners into the early nineteenth century; one theory is that the English devised toast in order to help counteract the cold, damp climate. Chocolate was sometimes substituted for tea at breakfast, but coffee only rarely. In London, when the men left for the day, the women often had their servants bring tea or chocolate to their bedrooms. Meanwhile, in the countryside, the traditional breakfast of bread and cheese, still served with beer or cider, remained common until about 1800. Tea's ascendancy was promoted by the powerful East India Company, which persuaded the government to lower the high duties on tea, a move that greatly helped to bring the beverage within the reach of the average Englishman.

The Tea Party, cartoon drawing by Thomas Rowlandson (1756–1827), in which the afternoon gathering is lampooned as an excuse for romantic disportment and the affectation of a blackamoor attendant. (Photo courtesy of Frick Art Reference Library)

From Coffeehouse to Clubhouse, Tea Garden, Tea Shop, and Tavern

By 1750, the traditional London coffeehouse was dead. No longer was it the favored men's forum for transacting business, reading newspapers, exchanging ideas about art, science, and manners, and sharing the day's gossip.[58] In the hopes of increasing their profits, coffeehouse keepers increasingly promoted sales of alcoholic drinks, taking one of the first steps in the decline of the coffeehouse as a bastion of learned conversation and affable good manners. Already by the time of Hogarth (1697–1764), the coffeehouses were less centers of intellectual exchange than dens of the demimonde, where pimps not poets commanded the floor. An illustration of this transformation is found in Hogarth's painting *Morning* (1738), depicting Tom King's Coffee-House, which by then had become a bordello managed by King's widow, Moll, before later becoming a fashionable club.[59] Daniel Defoe, after visiting Shrewsbury in 1724, wrote:

> I found there the most coffeehouses around the Town Hall that ever I saw in any town, but when you come into them they are but ale houses, only they think that the name coffeehouse gives a better air.[60]

These vanished coffeehouses, in their rough splendor, were frequently transformed into clubhouses, taverns, or, as tea increased in popularity, tea gardens and teahouses catering to women and serving all three caffeinated beverages accompanied by crumpets and desserts. The tea gardens and teahouses entertained a large new patronage of caffeine, for England had been the only country in the West to deny women access to the coffeehouse.

Naturally, there was considerable overlap between the age of coffee and the age of tea and among the people who frequented the coffeehouses and those who frequented the teahouses. Addison and Steele, who, as we have seen, were noted hangers-out at several literary London coffeehouses, were also partial to the new fashion of a "dish of tea." Apparently attempting to capitalize on its popularity, they wrote in the *Spectator* (1711) that "I would therefore in a particular manner recommend these my speculations to all well-regulated families that set apart an hour every morning for tea, bread and butter; and would earnestly advise them for their good to order this paper to be punctually served up and to be looked upon as a part of the tea-equipage."[61]

A few of the clubs are worth mentioning for our story. The most famous was a Whig club, the Kit-Cat Club, founded in the early eighteenth century by Steele, Addison, Congreve, and their associates. They convened in the house of Christopher Cat, or Kat, in Shire Lane. Cat, a pastry chef, was noted for his mutton pies, an English favorite. These pies, nicknamed "Kit-cats," became eponymous for the club.

An early Tory club, which came into existence in 1711, while the coffeehouse still reigned supreme, was the Brothers' Club, founded, on the suggestion of Swift, by Henry St. John, first Viscount Bolingbroke (1678–1751), a philosophical writer influenced by Locke. After the accession of George I, Bolingbroke had fled to France, where he remained until 1725, when he returned to practice political journalism alongside Swift and Pope, whose "Essay on Man" he is supposed to have influenced. The declared purpose of the Brothers' Club was "to advance conversation and friendship" and support and encourage the work of men of letters.

The Cocoa-tree Club, on St. James's Street, was converted from the early chocolate house of the same name. It first served as a den of Tory and then of Jacobite political discussion. As revealed in Horace Walpole's correspondence, the Cocoa-tree Club had become a fashionable gambling house by the 1740s, where, as in increasing numbers of similar establishments, young aristocrats would exchange thousands of pounds nightly on a single throw of the dice or turn of a card.

Dr. Samuel Johnson is an excellent symbol of this transitional era, for, although he founded several coffeehouse circles, he was one of the earliest great English proponents of tea drinking. Jonas Hanway (1712–86), an English merchant, reformer, philanthropist, and traveler, crossed pens with Dr. Johnson in the matter of whether tea was injurious or wholesome. In Hanway's book, especially entitled *Journal of an Eight Days Journey from Portsmouth to Kingston-upon-Thames, to which is added an Essay on Tea, considered as Pernicious to Health, obstructing Industry and Impoverishing the Nation* (London, 1756), he earnestly condemned tea on the grounds that it weakened the nerves, rotted the teeth, ruined women's looks, diminished the stature of men, and caused other infirmities and, further, that the time wasted brewing and drinking it, according to his calculations, cost the nation £166,666 a year, an enormous amount of money in the eighteenth century.[62] He had particular distaste for expensive frivolity, into which category he put both tea and the equipment required. It is no surprise that Hanway's opinions did not sit well with Johnson, who, according to his biographer, Sir John Hawkins (1719–89), was "a lover of tea to an excess hardly credible." Hawkins states, "Whenever it appeared, he was almost raving, and called for the ingredients which he employed to make the liquor palatable. This in a man whose appearance of bodily strength has been compared to Polyphemus."[63]

In articles published in *The Literary Magazine* in 1756 and 1757,[64] Johnson turned his caustic wit against the man who had dared impugn his favored beverage. Apparently following the prescription of Dr. Buntekuh, Johnson became famous for drinking thirty to forty cups of tea daily. He calls himself

> a hardened and shameless tea-drinker, who has for many years diluted his meals with only the infusion of this fascinating plant; whose kettle has scarcely time to cool; who with tea amuses the evening, with tea solaces the midnight, and with tea welcomes the morning.

With increasing numbers of fashionable people and social climbers of the era, Johnson also enjoyed taking tea in what became known as the "tea gardens." Gardens, which were really city parks, had been popular recreational centers for Londoners at least since the dedication of New Spring Gardens in 1661 under the reign of Charles II. Their higher destiny, however, was not realized until 1732, when New Spring Gardens was renamed Vauxhall Gardens and was made over into London's first tea garden. Vauxhall Gardens featured outdoor walks lit by thousands of lamps, bandstands, performers, dancing, fireworks, and food and drink, including, of course, coffee, tea, and chocolate. The success of Vauxhall Gardens was followed in 1742 by the opening of Ranelagh Gardens in Chelsea, which, though much smaller, featured a small lake, an Oriental-style house, and a Venetian-style villa. It also boasted a large circular room called the "Rotunda," with an ornate colonnade and enormous fireplace which was used to keep things lively on cool evenings. Still a third famous tea garden was Marylebone, frequented by Horace Walpole (1717–97) and George Frideric Handel (1685–1759).

These gardens rapidly overtook the established coffeehouses in popularity, perhaps in large part because, unlike the coffeehouse, they were open to women as well as men. They became great favorites of the women, and their patronage attracted the men. Perhaps also because of the preeminence of their female clientele, these gardens became more and more identified with "the elegant Regale," or tea accompanied by bread and butter, which was sometimes included in the steep price of admission. Whether on their account, or as a result of a confluence of forces, including decreased duties, tea became the national beverage of England contemporaneously with the fashionableness of these gardens.

At the same time as the tea gardens were flourishing, the institution of the tea shop was also on the rise as a women's favorite. In 1717, Thomas Twining converted

Tom's Coffee-House into a tea shop, which he called the Golden Lion. By the middle of the eighteenth century, such tea shops were separated by a widening social gulf from the increasingly disreputable coffeehouses. Later, these teahouses were to become among the fashionable sites for afternoon tea.

Heroines of Caffeine: Mary Tuke Founds a Tea Dynasty, and Anna of Bedford Starts a Tea Tradition

At least two Englishwomen did far more to promote the cause of tea than merely drinking it. The first was Mary Tuke, an early tea importer, and the second was Anna, wife of the seventh duke of Bedford, credited with creating the hallowed custom of afternoon tea.

In 1725, under the reign of George I, when Robert Walpole was prime minister and nearly fifty years before the advent of the industrial revolution in England, a thirty-year-old unmarried woman of York, her parents long dead, decided to go into business as a tea merchant. In those days, permission to trade in York depended on being a freeman of the city and member of the York Merchant Adventurers' Company. The first qualification posed no difficulty for Tuke, whose father had been a freeman, and who thereby inherited the same status. She entered her name in the Roll of the Freemen of the City of York in 1725, "Maria Tewk, Spinster, Fil. Willelmi Tuke." However, a woman who was neither the widow nor daughter of a member of the company was deemed ineligible for membership, and so she could not obtain a license to trade.

Undeterred by fears of consequences, she opened her business, ignoring threats and indictments from the company and fines for "Merchandising and following Trade without being free of this Fellowship." Fortunately, imprisonment for failure to pay fines required a special act of Parliament, the passage of which would have incurred a bigger expense than the company was willing to spend on a renegade like Tuke. In any case, Mary Tuke prevailed. After seven years of conflict, the Merchant Adventurers' Company imposed, and she agree to pay, a modest fine, after which she was permitted to pursue her business without further obstruction.

R. O. Mennell, one of Tuke's distant descendants, in a charming little book published in 1926, proudly recounts the significance of his ancestor's actions:[65]

> This particular instance of a woman challenging and defeating a powerful monopoly was of historic significance, as showing how the old restrictions were thrown off as a result of the determined courage of a few strong minded individuals. Thus Mary Tuke not merely founded a firm which, handed down through seven generations of the same family, still flourishes, but by her pertinacity helped to mould the character of the eighteenth century.[66]

In 1746, while the French were attempting to drive the English from India, Mary's fourteen-year-old nephew, William Tuke, began an apprenticeship to her that was to last for six years. When he was only twenty, she died and left the business and property to him. After a rough start, he became extremely successful and controlled the thriving business for sixty-two years.

Tea adulteration, which had become a concern since the first shipments arrived from China, remained significant. Among the Tuke firm's archives is a copy of an interesting contemporary act, 4 Geo. II cap. 14, by which it was decreed that fines would be levied on any dealer who "shall dye, fabricate or manufacture any Sloe leaves, Liquorice leaves, or the leaves of tea that have been used, or the leaves of any other tree, shrub or plant, in imitation of tea, or shall mix, colour, stain or dye such leaves or tea with terra japonica, sugar, molasses, clay, logwood, or with any other ingredients or materials whatsoever."[67] As evidence shows that the practice was increasing rather than abating, this edict may have served more as an advertisement of various methods of adulteration than as a deterrent against them. As a defense against this practice, John Horniman began selling measured amounts of tea in sealed paper packets. His company was later acquired by the two teenage Tetley brothers, and the use of tea bags became a general practice.[68]

Among the English, the ceremony and institution of afternoon tea has had the unifying force of the old Latin Mass in the Catholic Church. After all, like the members of the one true church, the English have long fancied themselves members of the one truly civilized society on earth, a claim that was bolstered by the fact that wherever in the world he was or whatever he was doing, every Englishman of any station throughout the empire reputedly observed the afternoon break for tea. This custom is still followed in situations Americans might find surprising. For example, international cricket matches in England, which of themselves demand almost supernal patience, are made still more spiritually challenging when interrupted at four o'clock for afternoon tea.

Tea has a habit of becoming identified with the best features of a civilization that sees itself as a refined and accomplished culture. Not only has it become so identified in England, but the traditions of China and, as we have seen, especially of Japan, elevate tea to the status of an emblem for their society and civilization. Afternoon tea, the introduction of which is credited to Anna of Bedford (1788–1861), epitomizes the meaning of tea in English life. Like the tea ceremony of Japan, the English afternoon tea did not spring full-grown into the world, but has a long and sometimes uncertain history.

Almost from its earliest use in English, the word "tea" referred not only to the plant and the beverage but also to an occasion such as a reception where tea was served. The use of the word to refer to a light evening meal or supper, with tea as the accompanying beverage, first occurs in the eighteenth century. For example, John Wesley (1703–91), founder of Methodism, reported in 1780 that he encountered all the important persons of society "at breakfast and at tea," which suggests that tea was an acknowledged repast at that time. High tea, or "meat tea," which is sometimes confused by Americans with afternoon tea, is a full meal and came into existence sometime later, but exactly when is unknown.

At the time of Anna, the duchess of Bedford, the English ate large breakfasts, generally served with tea, snacked informally for lunch, and waited until eight in the

The Tea, by American Impressionist Mary Cassatt, 1880. One of Cassatt's most popular paintings, it shows two young women enjoying the decorous ritual of afternoon tea. (M. Theresa B. Hopkins Fund. Courtesy Museum of Fine Arts, Boston. Reproduced with permission. © 2000 Museum of Fine Arts, Boston. All Rights Reserved)

evening to have their dinner, after which they also drank tea. Anna was one of the many people who experience a profound afternoon slump. To relieve what she called the "sinking feeling," she is reputed to have directed her servants to bring her a tray of tea, bread and butter, and cake around four o'clock. This little repast picked her up so effectively that she busied herself spreading the new custom among her aristocratic friends and acquaintances.

By the 1880s, Anna's invention had become a daily event, for which ladies, following an afternoon carriage ride, changed their costume and donned long tea gowns in expectation of the elegant ritual of refreshment. Meanwhile, the tea service, like its Japanese ceremonial counterpart, continued to evolve in sophistication, elaboration, and delicacy, including bread and butter plates and cake stands. By the turn of the twentieth century, wealthy Englishwomen and their escorts were able to take their tea at fancy establishments, the most famous of which was Rumpelmeyer's. When the rage became international, establishments named "Rumpelmeyer's," in imitation of the original, were opened in Paris and elsewhere. Another Rumpelmeyer's, in the St. Moritz on Central Park West, New York, still stands and was ambitiously redecorated in deco style in 1996.

Caffeine in Victorian and Contemporary England

It is difficult today to grasp how unsafe were most beverages available even in highly developed countries before the twentieth century. Because of the pure water shortage, even alcoholic drinks were regarded primarily as thirst quenchers. Despite increased investments in water companies after 1805, outbreaks of water-borne diseases created several scandals over succeeding years. In the 1820s it became difficult for Londoners to find any drinking water, which created a new profession: water carrier. London hospitals served their patients only alcoholic drinks, and they were prudent to do so. In the 1840s it was an open secret that the poorer quarters of London were supplied with water that was clearly unfit for human use. In the 1850s private water supplies remained scarce and the city had few public pumps. At this time, even in upper-class households, water supply from the mains was intermittent, and only when the wooden pipes were replaced with iron ones would the shortages be alleviated.

Other sources of liquid refreshment were just as bad. Milk was dangerous even when fresh, and it was of poor quality or even adulterated, especially in the anonymously produced supplies reaching the city. In addition, this bad milk was very expensive, and around 1850 was double the price of beer. Carbonated soda water was not sold in England until after 1790, and no Parisian-style *limonadiers* wandered the streets to slake the thirst of passersby. London residents were wise to rely on intoxicants, for which the water had been pumped from deep wells, or on the temperance drinks, coffee, tea, and chocolate, for which the water had been boiled. Adulteration of foodstuffs was still an unpleasant and nearly unavoidable fact of life, as it had been in Mary Tuke's day. In a poem called "London Adulterations" published in 1825, the anonymous author laments these depredations:[69]

> Here tradesmen, 'tis plain, at no roguery stops.
> They adulterate everything they've in their shop;
> You must buy what they sell, and they sell what they please,
> And they would, if they could, sell the moon for green cheese.
>
> Now it is well known imitation's the rage:
> Everything's imitated in this fair old age;
> There's tea, coffee, beer, butter, gin, milk, in brief,
> No doubt they'll soon imitate mutton and beef.
>
> The grocer sells ash leaves and sloe leaves for tea,
> Tinged with Dutch pink and vertigris, just like bohea [tea],
> What sloe poison means Sloman[70] now has found out;
> We shall all to a T be poisoned, no doubt.
>
> Some grocers for pepper sell trash called PD[71];
> Burnt horse beans for coffee—how can such things be?
>
> . . . .

The milkman, although he is honest, he vows,
Milks his pump night and morn quite as oft as his cows;
Claps plenty of chalk in your score—what a bilk—
And, egad, claps you plenty of chalk in your milk.[72]

However, the cost of the nonalcoholic drinks, still high, was falling, and by the end of the first quarter of the nineteenth century these drinks became more available for home consumption. By the 1880s tea had declined in price so far that it had become a necessary fixture in working-class homes. Unfortunately, how much of this "tea" was actually *Camellia sinensis* is doubtful. The demand for tea created a large market in ersatz tea, actually compounded of blackthorn leaves and other substitutes, colored to make them resemble true tea. As Daniel Pool states, "The government estimated that for every seven pounds of authentic East India tea being sold under the monopoly, there were four phony pounds being sold to unsuspecting buyers." By the 1840s, the plight of tea drinkers was further exacerbated by the operations of eight London factories, "busily recycling used tea leaves, often dyeing them and then mixing them with new tea for resale."[73] Perhaps eighty thousand pounds of tea were recycled annually in this way.

The reductions on duties on coffee enacted in 1808 and the subsequent renaissance in the London coffeehouses boosted coffee sales rapidly through the 1850s. In 1815 there were no more than a dozen coffeehouses in London. In 1821 William Lovett (1800–1887), an English writer and cartographer, found "comparatively few" and was forced to eat in a tavern. Further reductions in duties in 1825 helped to change this picture dramatically. By 1830, coffee had finally become cheap enough to compete with beer. As a result, coffeehouses began to open in greater numbers and reinstituted the custom of providing newspapers for the enjoyment of their patrons.

Chocolate was still a minor player in the story of English beverages. Van Houten's invention of the modern process for making cacao was made only in 1828, and in 1830 John Cleave, a London merchant, was able to advertise chocolate as a "new beverage" called "theobroma." The word "cocoa" was not generally in use until after 1840.

Despite all these developments, alcoholic drinks remained the cheapest and, because of the prevalence of the adulteration of milk and the temperance drinks, arguably the safest refreshments available. In 1830, a pint of coffee cost about three pence, at least twice the cost of gin or ale. In 1840, coffee cost about one and a half shillings a cup, tea about two shillings a cup, and chocolate about four shillings a cup. In comparison, at this same time, a decent pint of porter, a dark brown bitter beer, was only two and a half shillings. By later Victorian times, coffee and tea had been fully integrated into the roster of necessaries kept and used in every working-class household. In "How Five and Twenty Shillings Were Expended in a Week," a poem published in an 1876 Birmingham broadside, a housewife accounts for her weekly expenditures for coffee, tea, alcohol, and the occasional luxury of soda pop:

It's of a tradesman and his wife,
I heard the other day,
Who did kick up a glorious row,
They live across the way.
The husband proved himself a fool,
When his money was all spent,
He called upon his wife, my life,
To know which way it went.

> *So she reckoned up and showed him,*
> *And she showed him all complete,*
> *How five and twenty shillings was*
> *Expended in a week.*

. . . .

There is two and threepence house rent,
Now attend to me, she said:
There is four shillings goes for meat,
And three and ninepence bread;
To wash your nasty dirty shirt
There is sixpence-halfpenny soap,
There's one and eightpence coals, old boy,
And tenpence wood and coke.

There's fourpence for milk and cream,
And one and twopence malt,
Three halfpence goes for vinegar
And twopence halfpenny salt;

. . .

A shilling potatoes, herbs and greens,
Tenpence butter now you see,
Sixpence coffee, eightpence sugar,
And one and fourpence tea.

. . .

There's eightpence for tobacco,
And seven-farthings swipes,
There is threepence halfpenny snuff,
And two pence halfpenny tripes;
A penny you owed for strings
Over at the cobbler's shop.
And you know last Sunday morning
You had a bottle of ginger pop.

. . .

And while every night to a public house
You go to drink and sing,
I go to the wine vaults over the way
To have a drop of gin.[74]

   As the saga of caffeine in England continues today, coffee remains popular, and soft drinks have become an important part of the new mix, but tea continues to be England's most important source of the drug. Consider that in America, the country of coffee bibbers, about half of all caffeine comes from coffee; in England, more than three-quarters of the caffeine consumed comes from tea. England and her cousins, Ireland, Australia, and New Zealand, constitute four of the twelve top tea-consuming countries in the world per capita, and they are the only Western nations to make the list.[75] England makes, sells, serves, and consumes, imports, and exports tremendous quantities every year.

   Like the queen and Buckingham Palace, the afternoon tea, although it has declined in importance among the natives since World War II, has become a major tourist profit center. Establishments such as the Ritz hotel and Fortnum and Masons department store serve afternoon tea in a sometimes hectic environment that would have seemed like a nightmare to its originators. Nevertheless, the aristocratic patina of the afternoon tea, an inheritance from generations of English ladies, from Queen Catherine, through Anne of Bedford, and one reminiscent of the upper-class connections of the Urasenke tea masters, remains to this day. An attempt to capture and trade off this patina is evident in four-star hotels throughout the world that serve afternoon tea daily in a quiet, decorous setting, presented by a discreet serving staff and accompanied by the finest tea service that the establishment can afford. There, twentieth-century ladies and sometimes gentlemen meet to inhale a breath of the atmosphere of elegance and tranquillity that have been associated with tea over the centuries.

11

the endless simmer
America and the Twentieth Century
Do Caffeine

ZING! What a feeling
—Line from Coca-Cola jingle, 1960s

Captain John Smith, who founded the colony of Virginia at Jamestown in 1607, brought the earliest firsthand knowledge of coffee to North America and is sometimes credited with having been the first to bring the beans as well. Smith was familiar with coffee from having traveled through Turkey. Neither the passengers of the Mayflower in 1620 nor the first Dutch settlers of Manhattan in 1624 are recorded to have included any tea or coffee in their cargo. It is impossible to be sure if the Dutch introduced either into their colony of New Amsterdam or whether that distinction belongs to the British, who succeeded them in 1664 and renamed the settlement "New York." In any case, by the time of the earliest printed reference to coffee drinking in America, which occurs in New York in 1668, the drink, brewed from roasted beans, sweetened with sugar, and spiced with cinnamon, was already in common use. Around this time coffee seems to have displaced beer as the favorite breakfast beverage, and chocolate is recorded to have arrived in small private shipments, primarily as a pharmaceutical. In 1683 William Penn, who probably introduced both coffee and tea into Philadelphia, recorded in his *Accounts* that he purchased coffee in New York for his year-old Pennsylvania settlement and complained of the price per pound of eighteen shillings nine pence. At this price, the beans required to make a cup of coffee would have cost more than a dinner at an "ordinary," or informal eatery, of the time. In light of this expense, it is not surprising that, during these first days in the colonies, beer and ale remained the usual drinks at meals other than breakfast, and both tea and coffee were pricey luxuries, with tea the more common of the two, especially in domestic use.

Boston has an early and distinguished place in the American annals of caffeine. Even before any American coffeehouse had opened its doors, Dorothy Jones was granted the first known license to sell coffee in America, in Boston in 1670, though

Colonial American tea tray with cartouch of ladies reading coffee grounds, illustrating the common practice of using grounds for divination, one similar to the practice of reading tea leaves that is more familiar today. (Colonial Williamsburg Foundation)

no one knows if she was a purveyor of "coffee powder," the name for the ground roasted beans, or of the drink itself. It was also in Boston that the London Coffee House, the first coffeehouse in America, opened for business. It constitutes the earliest example in America of the now popular bookshop café, for it is reliably reported that "Benj. Harris sold books there in 1689," the first year of its operation. Of course, the tradition of selling books in coffeehouses dates back to at least 1657 in London, and after their invention in the eighteenth century, newspapers were printed and sold from the coffeehouses in both England and the New World.

In 1696 the King's Arms, the first coffeehouse in New York, was opened near Trinity Church by John Hutchins. Its yellow brick and wood structure, with rooftop seating and a splendid view of the city and bay, is supposed to have been standing in Holland when it was purchased, dismantled, and its parts transported to America, where it was reassembled.

The first coffeehouse in Philadelphia was opened by Samuel Carpenter around 1700 on the east side of Front Street, above Walnut Street. Because it remained the only such establishment in the city for some years, it was referred to in the old days simply as "Ye Coffee House." The Coffee House was apparently used as a post office, to judge from this 1734 excerpt from Benjamin Franklin's *Pennsylvania Gazette:*

All persons who are indebted to Henry Flower, late postmaster of Pennsylvania, for Postage of Letters or otherwise, are desir'd to pay the same to him at the old Coffee House in Philadelphia. [1]

Benjamin Franklin (1706–90), always alert to new business opportunities, sold coffee, running an advertisement claiming, "Very good coffee sold by the Printer." Around 1750 William Bradford, another Philadelphia printer, opened his own London Coffee House, at the southwest corner of Second and Market Streets. It became a thriving center for merchants, mariners, and travelers, and was used as a market for horses, food, and slaves, the last of which were displayed on a platform in the street in front of the coffeehouse.

American coffeehouses, which continued the British coffeehouse traditions as "penny universities" and enhanced their feared and celebrated status as "seminaries of sedition," soon opened in every colony. At first they were simply taverns serving ale, port, and Jamaican rum, as well as coffee. But soon these coffeehouses featured in American official civic life in ways that had been unknown even in England: Their "assembly rooms" became the sites of court trials and council meetings. The Green Dragon, a coffeehouse tavern and inn, established in 1697, which Daniel Webster called the "headquarters of the Revolution," was frequented in the next century by Paul Revere, John Adams, James Otis, and other illustrious rebels, and remained open in Boston's business center for 135 years. Throughout this time, the Green Dragon remained a center of activity, hosting from the first, "Red-coated British soldiers, colonial governors, bewigged crown officers, earls and dukes, citizens of high estate, plotting revolutionists of lesser degree, conspirators in the Boston Tea Party, patriots and generals of the Revolution."[2] The Grand Lodge of Masons, under the leadership of the first grand master of Boston's first Masonic group, convened there as well.

It was in the Green Dragon that Revere and his co-conspirators are supposed to have met to plan the Boston Tea Party. The story of the Stamp Act of 1765, a British tea tax that turned Americans into some of the world's most avid coffee drinkers, is well known. Tariffs and taxes frequently determined which of the caffeinated beverages, if any, were within reach of the average person, and had often been designed to do so. The opposition to the British tax prompted the Boston Tea Party of 1773, in which the British East India Company's cargoes of tea were jettisoned into the harbor. From this moment in history, coffee became the favored caffeinated drink of Americans, indispensable at the breakfast table and the workplace ever after. The Bunch of Grapes, another of the earliest Boston coffeehouses, was the site of the first public reading of the Declaration of Independence.

New York's Merchants Coffee House, at the intersection of Wall and Water streets, hosted the Sons of Liberty on April 18, 1774, who, following the example of their Boston compatriots, met there to plan their own blockage of British tea imports. The next month, leaders of the revolution gathered there to draft their call for the First Continental Congress. Neither was this coffeehouse forgotten in the aftermath of war and victory. For in 1789, New York City's mayor and the state's governor threw a lavish party there in honor of the election of George Washington.

The Exchange Coffee House, Boston. This was the largest and most costly coffeehouse ever built. Erected in 1808, of stone, marble, and brick, it stood seven stories and cost $500,000. It was modeled after Lloyd's of London, and was, like Lloyd's, a center for patrons from the shipping business. (W. H. Ukers, *All about Coffee*)

With the opening of the Exchange coffeehouse on Exchange Street in Boston in 1808, the institution reached a kind of acme. The Exchange was modeled after Lloyd's of London and, like Lloyd's, served as a center for ship brokers and mariners. Designed by Charles Bulfinch, the most celebrated American architect of the day, it stood seven stories high and was constructed of stone, marble, and brick, at a cost of half a million dollars. In 1817 the Exchange hosted a banquet for James Monroe, attended by John Adams and many other dignitaries. Probably the largest and most expensive coffeehouse ever seen in the world, before or since, the Exchange burned down in 1818.

The early days of American coffeehouses were times of heavy alcohol drinking both in England and the colonies. The English "gin epidemic," against which the College of Physicians had warned in 1726, asserting that it was a "growing evil which was, too often, a cause of weak, feeble, and distempered children," continued unabated on both sides of the Atlantic. The revolution and the decades after marked a high level of alcohol use that exceeded any achieved in the twentieth century. In 1785, this widespread drunkenness prompted Benjamin Rush (1735–1814), a famous physician and reformer, to found an anti-alcohol movement, that, like many other such movements since, began by advocating temperance and later advocated abstinence. Rush was as fervent an advocate of the temperance beverages as he was an opponent of the alcoholic ones. His followers, who purchased tens of thousands of copies of his temperance booklets, helped to advance the cause of coffee, tea, and chocolate drinking in the new nation. Yet despite his efforts, around 1800 Americans still annually consumed about three times as much alcohol per person as they were to consume in the 1990s.

Amercia, Land of the Free—Refill

By the second half of the nineteenth century, America was consuming more coffee than any country in the world, and the drink had, in the minds of many of its inhabitants, come to be more identified with their pioneering, robust, democratic country than the stuffy, effete, class-stratified society of Europe. Coffee's status in America is attested by Mark Twain (1835–1910) in his travelogue *A Tramp Abroad*, in which he celebrates coffee, which he has obviously come to regard as quintessentially American, and recounts experiences with it abroad that many American travelers may find familiar today:

> In Europe, coffee is an unknown beverage. You can get what the European hotel keeper thinks is coffee, but it resembles the real thing as hypocrisy resembles holiness. It is a feeble, characterless, uninspiring sort of stuff, and almost as undrinkable as if it had been made in an American hotel. . . . After a few months' acquaintance with European "coffee," one's mind weakens, and his faith with it, and he begins to wonder if the rich beverage of home, with its clotted layer of yellow cream on top of it, is not a mere dream after all, and a thing which never existed.

In an 1892 entry in his *Autobiography*, Twain presents a somewhat more attractive picture of Italian tea drinking, which he observed while passing through Florence on the way to Germany:

> Late in the afternoon friends come out from the city and drink tea in the open air, and tell what is happening in the world; and when the great sun sinks down upon Florence and the daily miracle begins, they hold their breaths and look. It is not a time for talk.[3]

As the emergent capital of industry and the marketplace and the symbol of revolution and the mixing of peoples, America was the country best fitted to assume leadership in the twentieth-century saga of caffeine. However, if you ask a European visitor what, in his opinion, is the most noteworthy feature of American cafés, he is most likely, instead of mentioning complex ideological or social factors or the characteristic taste complexity of the American roast, to say, "They refill your cup without charge, even without asking!" American readers may wonder why this ordinary courtesy should be regarded as so important. But if you consider that many European coffee lovers and coffeehouse habitués spend hours nursing small cups that cost them twice as much as Americans pay, and that if they want another they must pay the full price again, you can see how, in the course of a life of café hopping, these refills could add up to a small fortune.

Perhaps the endless refill is symbolic of America's special affection for coffee and of its general culture of largesse and informality as well. Coffee certainly plays the dominant part in the story of caffeine in the United States. Ever since their defiance of British tea taxes inspired the colonials to exchange the leaf for the bean as a patriotic duty, Americans cultivated a taste for coffee to the extent that they became by far the largest single national coffee importers on earth, and today they account for more than half of world coffee imports. It is overwhelmingly the source of most of the caffeine consumed here.

The coffeehouse tradition of troubadour and balladeer, which began in the Middle East in the early sixteenth century, continued in the English coffeehouses of the Restoration (when these establishments became "the usual meeting-places of the roving cavaliers, who seldom visited home but to sleep"),[4] and was impressively revived in twentieth-century America, first by the nonconformist Beat Generation of the 1950s and then by the folk and flower child social rebels of the 1960s. The Beat Generation movement began in San Francisco's North Beach, Los Angeles' Venice West, and New York's Greenwich Village. Its members affected an exhausted sophistication and demoralized bohemian irony that put them in the company of a certain tradition of coffeehouse denizens. The apolitical Beat Generation take on café culture is represented by Beat poets Lawrence Ferlinghetti and Allen Ginsberg, who read their works at coffeehouses such as the Coexistence Bagel Shop in San Francisco and emphasized personal fulfillment through self-expression, nonconformity, free love, and the use of drugs and alcohol. Their more socially minded but more drug-dependent hippie successors are represented by folk singers such as Bob Dylan, who began performing professionally in the coffeehouses of Greenwich Village, where he sang Woody Guthrie's Depression-era songs and others of his own composition to a young audience that had ridden into adulthood on an unprecedented wave of prosperity that had not yet crested. Dylan's works, and those of his fellow singer-composers, such as Joan Baez and Phil Ochs, helped shape the music of a generation and embodied the social values of the civil rights and anti–Vietnam War movements.

What are we to make of the coffeehouse renaissance of the 1990s? Certainly it is no flash in the pan. New York real estate prices have seemed high for generations, but they have recently been driven still higher by the competition for space among a new generation of coffeehouse and café proprietors. Many of the new establishments are the progeny of the chain behemoths, such as Starbucks, Timothy's, and Brothers Gourmet Coffee, each of which boasts many new outlets in Manhattan. Others, like Coopers Coffee and New World Coffee, are the offspring of smaller ventures hoping to expand to compete with their bigger rivals. Bookstores and department stores are increasingly including cafés under their roofs. Some traditional proprietors are benefiting from the upswing. For decades Chock Full o' Nuts was the ultimate coffee-shop chain, providing cheap but good cups of coffee and fast sandwiches to busy city workers. After ten years of relying on institutional sales, and sales of coffee beans and spices, it is again turning to the development of coffeehouses and cafés.

Bubbling Caffeine: The Hard Soft Drinks

The caffeinated drinks, coffee and tea, wherever they were first encountered, were invariably regarded as medicines before they came into use as comestibles. Coca-Cola, the first of the caffeinated soft drinks, also began as a patent medicine, and was first sold in the form of a tonic syrup at pharmacies. Before the turn of the century, however, Coca-Cola had become a popular soft drink that encountered public relations problems, first over its still unverified cocaine content and then because of its caffeine. In the decades since, the Coca-Cola Company has distanced itself from any association in the public's mind with drugs. Cocaine, if it was ever present in more than a negligible quantity, was eliminated. The caffeine content was cut in half. However, caffeine remains to this day the only pharmacologically active ingredient present in beverages that are dispensed from vending machines, soda fountains, and convenience stores.

Coca-Cola and the Wiley Campaign: Wiley as the Kha'ir Beg of the Twentieth Century

Dr. Harvey Washington Wiley (1844–1930), who at the height of his career enjoyed great national celebrity and power, waged a war against Coca-Cola in the early twentieth century that almost wrecked the company. Like Kha'ir Beg in early-sixteenth-century Mecca, Wiley was a governmental official charged with protecting the public welfare. As the first director of the U.S. Bureau of Chemistry, the forerunner of the Food and Drug Administration (FDA), Wiley found nothing amusing about the blithe and celebratory indulgence in caffeinated soft drinks that was sweeping the country. Kha'ir Beg had been concerned about social subversion; Wiley was worried about food adulteration and the health of the nation's children. Each had a large measure of reason on his side.

Wiley saw an essential difference between coffee and tea as caffeinated beverages and Coca-Cola and its imitators. Adults were by far the primary consumers of coffee and tea, and everyone was keenly aware that these drinks contained caffeine. Children, however, were the greatest consumers of Coca-Cola, and most people did not associate the drug with the drink, an association strongly discouraged and underplayed by the company's brilliant advertising and public relations efforts.[5] The epochal conflict between Wiley and the Coca-Cola Company, one of the nation's most powerful corporations, epitomizes the issues and players that have featured in the centuries-long struggle between caffeine's purveyors and detractors. In 1902, after twenty years of leading the U.S. Bureau of Chemistry in a fight against the adulteration of food, Wiley achieved national prominence when he created a "poison squad," a group of twelve young healthy adult volunteers who would test the safety of additives. He campaigned against the nostrums of the patent medicine industry and became a fervent advocate of the frequently proposed and invariably defeated efforts to enact pure food and drug legislation. In 1906 public sympathies began to change, and the Pure Food and Drugs Act, known then as "Dr. Wiley's Law," was finally passed. Wiley wasted no time investigating Coca-Cola as a vehicle of caffeine. Headlines appeared in 1907 reading, "Dr. Wiley Will Take Up Soda Fountain 'Dope.'" John Candler, who was running Coca-Cola at that time along with his brother Asa, was outraged. Candler could not understand Wiley's animus, asserting, "There can be no more objection to the consumption of caffeine in the form of Coca-Cola than there is to the importation of tea and coffee and their use."[6] The company had no sooner overcome the scandalous rumors about cocaine, which had finally been decisively dispelled, than this new problem over caffeine had arisen. It was to prove more difficult to resolve.

Candler and Wiley had similar backgrounds, including fundamentalist upbring-
ings and training in medicine and chemistry, but they took opposite positions on this
central issue. Wiley had no quarrel with caffeine as it occurred naturally in coffee or
tea. His lifelong campaign was against adulterants, in acknowledgment of which his
followers called him "a preacher of purity," while his detractors dubbed him "a chemical fundamentalist." It was from this perspective of concern about adulterants or additives that Wiley saw the caffeine question. He regarded the introduction of the drug
into soft drinks as pernicious and deceptive and potentially harmful, especially to the
children. Wiley's positions, which he maintained for the rest of his life, are well represented in his speech in favor of coffee, "The Advantages of Coffee as America's
National Beverage," and the magazine articles from the same period which he used to
batter the Coca-Cola Company.

Wiley was caught in a bind. He had tried to initiate seizures of Coca-Cola, but the
federal government refused to cooperate, arguing that caffeine had not been proved
harmful and that, furthermore, should it be so proved, coffee and tea would have to
be banned as well as Coca-Cola. However, Wiley insisted that if parents really understood that their children were using a drug every time they drank a Coke, there would
be more sympathy on his side.

The conflict was finally joined in a federal suit, called, in the legal fashion of
such things, *The United States vs. Forty Barrels and Twenty Kegs of Coca-Cola*, which
opened in court on March 13, 1911, the second case do so under the new drug laws.[7]
The witnesses included religious fundamentalists who argued that the use of Coca-

*Any powerful drug, such as caffein is acknowledged to be, should not be offered indis-
criminately to the public in other than its natural condition, and certainly not without
the knowledge of the consumer*

Cartoon of Wiley admonishing an innocent public about the evil goblins lurking unseen in a glass
of Coca-Cola. (*Good Housekeeping*, 1912)

Cola led to wild parties and sexual indiscretions by coeds and induced boys to masturbatory wakefulness. But most of the testimony was scientific in nature. Coca-Cola presented an array of expert witnesses with impressive credentials. Unfortunately, by today's standards, the experiments on which their testimony relied were compromised by inadequate protocols. That is, their conclusions tended to support the prior opinions of the investigators regardless of the data actually gathered.

The one exception was the work of Harry Hollingworth, a young psychology professor at Columbia University, and his wife and research assistant, Leta, who designed and performed the first comprehensive double-blind experiments on the effect of caffeine on human health. These studies are still being cited in journal articles today. For example, a 1989 study published in the *American Journal of Medicine* referenced the Hollingworths' 150-page 1912 study,[8] to the effect that "a total day's caffeine dose of 710 mg was necessary to lessen subjective sleep quality." Their careful work demonstrated that caffeine in modest doses improved motor performance and did not disturb sleep. In sum, their work failed to support Wiley's concerns; although in fairness it must be added that in large part it also failed to address them in any significant way.

Coverage of the trial was frequently sensationalistic, with one headline reading, "EIGHT COCA-COLAS CONTAIN ENOUGH CAFFEINE TO KILL."[9] Wiley himself never testified, leading us to speculate that his group of young food tasters had not experienced any harmful consequences from their exposure to the drink. The case was finally decided on technical grounds that have little to do with caffeine and make little sense. The District Court judge Sanford, who later was appointed to the U.S. Supreme Court, directed a jury verdict in favor of Coca-Cola, ruling that their drink was not mislabeled, because it did contain minute amounts of both cocaine and cola, and that, furthermore, because caffeine had been part of the original formula or recipe for the beverage, it could not be legally regarded as an additive. Generous in victory, Coca-Cola voluntarily agreed never to feature any child under twelve in their advertisements, a forbearance they relaxed only in 1986.

Wiley did not give up. He used the publicity from the case to try to push through provisions adding caffeine to the federal list of habit-forming and harmful substances that must be named on product labels. Still shy of promoting the presence of caffeine in their products, Coca-Cola successfully fought the amendments.

Meanwhile the government successfully appealed the District Court's ruling to the Supreme Court. It was now determined that caffeine was an added ingredient after all, and the case was remanded to Judge Sanford for retrial on the issue of caffeine's safety. This time the case was settled out of court, and Coca-Cola agreed to cut the amount of caffeine in its soft drink by half. In return there was an unwritten accord that the Bureau of Chemistry, by then operating under new leadership, would, from then on, leave Coca-Cola in peace.

Coca-Cola has not relied on that ancient truce to protect its interests from those meddlers, newborn in every generation, who would use the law to control what ostensibly free adult citizens are allowed to eat or drink. In the 1970s, largely as a response to reformational grumblings stirred up by concern over an unsubstantiated link between caffeine and pancreatic cancer, Coca-Cola and other purveyors of dietary caffeine set up and funded the International Life Sciences Institute (ILSI) and its public relations arm, the International Food Information Council (IFIC), both based in Washington, D.C., to help forestall any efforts to regulate or ban caffeine. The heart of these groups was their Caffeine Committee. In the last twenty years ILSI has sponsored and IFIC has publicized dozens of reputable research projects and international conferences of scientists to evaluate the role of caffeine in human health. Naturally, the Caffeine Committee is careful to search out and support those researchers who see caffeine as a relatively harmless compound and to avoid supporting those who would like to see it removed from the market. Nevertheless, the ILSI studies are good scientific efforts, and their results have made important contributions to the inadequate understanding of caffeine's pharmacological effects.

Cola as Cultural Icon

"Caffeine is caffeine," the logician might observe, bringing to bear the powerful insight of sovereign reason. Yet with respect to caffeine, coffee and tea, its major natural sources, differ in at least one important way from caffeinated colas and other caffeinated soft drinks, to which caffeine has been added: Coffee and tea are primarily the drinks of adults, while soft drinks, as Wiley admonished, are as commonly or more commonly consumed by children, even small children.

It is strange to say, but the twentieth century, the time of unmatched enlightenment in education and medical science, has witnessed the first widespread acceptance of the general and unmonitored use of a psychoactive stimulant drug by the juvenile population. In fact, except for khat, widely used by adolescent Yemenis, we know of no other mood-altering drug whose use anywhere by the young is or has been not only legal, but approved and fostered by adults.

Coca-Cola, the forerunner of all commercially caffeinated soft drinks, was, during its first years, an elixir sold in pharmacies. After the turn of the century, the Coca-Cola Company had to make a choice as to whether to continue promoting the drink as a tonic, which might suggest it was a strong stimulant with a limited application, or to advertise it as a simple beverage, suitable for everyone, including children. Some Coca-Cola leaders had reservations about the latter strategy, partly because they were concerned over the potential danger to children. However, the simple beverage theory won, even though it meant sacrificing any claim, in the words of executive correspondence, for "excellency or special merit," and Coca-Cola faced the future as one of many soft drinks.

With this strategy in place, it remained for the company leaders to ensure their product a distinctive place in the arcana of common soda fountain options. One of their central problems remained how to inveigle children into becoming lifelong Coca-Cola drinkers while observing their pledge never to show a child under the age of twelve in an advertisement. While the advertising of Coca-Cola is an epic tale, no single feature stands out as clearly or has had such a broad impact on popular culture as Coca-Cola's most brilliant response to this apparent dilemma: the invention of the modern Santa Claus.

Sundblom Santa advertisement for Coca-Cola. This is one of many Sundblom paintings that created the American icon of Santa Claus. The fat, red-nosed, red-cloaked, jolly Coca-Cola-drinking version of Santa Clause became a defining image of American cultural life.

Santa Claus, as we all know, is a portly, white-haired gentleman with a snowy beard, broad smile, rosy cheeks, red nose, wearing a costume somewhat resembling bright red flannel underwear with a broad belt and big black boots, happily busy with the delivery of toys on snowy Christmas Eves. What many may not realize is that this image of Santa is an American, twentieth-century invention, created by Haddon Sundblom, a Swedish artist in the employ of Coca-Cola, and promoted relentlessly into the apotheosis of a folk hero. Before Sundblom's work, Santa Claus was represented in a variety of ways. In Europe he had traditionally been a serious, even severe, tall, thin man wearing any of the primary colors. In the popular recitation piece "A Visit from St. Nicholas," written by Clement Moore, a Columbia University professor, in the 1920s, Santa became a jolly elf only a few inches high.

In their book *Dream of Santa*, Charles and Taylor relate how in 1931, posing his friend Lou Prentice, a retired salesman, as his first model, Sundblom painted the first depiction of the Santa Claus we know in America today. After Prentice's death, Sundblom used himself as a model, refining his creation further. The Coca-Cola Company built a small advertising industry around Sundblom's Coke-guzzling saint, who was invariably aided in completing his eleemosynary labors by the lift provided by sugar and caffeine—an advertising effort aimed, obviously, primarily at young children who would, in the course of things, grow into succeeding generations of Coca-Cola consumers. New Sundblom productions were used on billboards and in magazine advertisements year after year, until his last two paintings were completed in 1964.

The Buzz Beyond: Supercolas and Other High-Dose Caffeinated Soft Drinks

In February 1996, Beverage Marketing Corporation, which offers consulting and information services to the global beverage industries, reported that Coca-Cola Classic was the best-selling soft drink in America, followed by Pepsi-Cola, Diet Coke,

Dr Pepper, Mountain Dew, Diet Pepsi, Sprite, 7-UP, Caffeine Free Diet Coke, and Caffeine Free Diet Pepsi.[10] Insiders in the soft drink industry and outsiders trying to get in have noticed that the top six brands have one thing in common: They all contain caffeine. Following the maxim "If a little is good, then a lot is better," a number of companies have offered or are preparing to offer some soft drinks containing more caffeine and others in which the presence of caffeine is a more emphatic component of their market identity.

The first of these high-caffeine soft drinks was Jolt Cola. In a brief company history posted on the Internet, called "Where did Jolt Come From?," Jolt represents its founder, C. J. Rapp, as a pioneer. In 1985, when Jolt Cola was introduced, their story runs, most beverage companies were pushing a "less is more" approach to new products: fewer calories, less sugar, and less caffeine. Rapp had the vision to buck this trend and put the slogan "Twice the Caffeine" on every bottle and can. What they don't mention in this article is that Jolt originally boasted "Twice the Sugar" as well. But even though more caffeine might seem to call for more sugar to counteract the increased bitterness, Jolt today has trimmed its sugar to standard levels, but kept the caffeine content as high as ever, which gives the drink a distinctive "bite" that some people find pleasant.

Rapp says that his product was inspired by college students who were "concocting elixirs to help them study for exams," perhaps a veiled reference to the use of methamphetamine, dexamphetamine, and caffeine pills. He sees a tie-in between Jolt's success and the renaissance in coffeehouse culture: "Just as coffee bars began showing up in every city from Boston to Seattle, Jolt, the espresso of colas, took the soft drink market by storm."

In the 1990s many new high-caffeine soft drinks are flooding the market worldwide. The triumph of Jolt is perhaps more apparent in Rapp's mind than in the marketplace, as evidenced by the fact that most comments about the product consist of people asking each other if it is still being made and if so where it can be found. Recently we found a grocer in Philadelphia who stocked it. But on returning several weeks later, it was gone, and the owner explained that the distributor was not expected for an indeterminate period.

Another way of looking at it, however, is that, difficult to find as Jolt may have become, people still remember it and seek it out. There can be no doubt that high-caffeine soft drinks can have a distinctive flavor. Jolt itself is a superior product and easily the best-tasting cola on the market. The extra caffeine gives it "point," a word used to designate piquant bitterness, such as that which is vital to fine coffee's appeal. Significantly, Jolt, unlike Coca-Cola or Pepsi, is still sweetened with cane sugar, and the clarity of cane sugar, which is far less cloying than cheap corn syrup substitutes, combines with the additional caffeine to create a bittersweet flavor that is hard to beat.

The cola nut is not the source of either the flavoring for or the caffeine content of cola soft drinks. However, other carbonated caffeinated beverages, such as some made from the guarana berry, actually depend for their flavor and stimulant power on the high caffeine content of the fruit or nut itself.

Brazilians consume more than six billion quarts of soft drinks a year, making

Brazil the third-largest soft drink market in the world, after Mexico and the United States, and guarana-based drinks make up 25 percent of this market. Antarctica, a local company, and Coca-Cola currently sell the brands that dominate guarana beverage sales, but PepsiCo has announced plans to take them on with a new line of drinks flavored with plain guarana and guarana mixed with peach, passion fruit, and acerola, a citrus-flavored Brazilian berry. Pepsi is also test marketing a guarana drink in the United States called "Josta," for which guarana is the primary flavor and source of caffeine.

In the late 1990s a new soft drink was created by Steve Gariepy to advance his ambition to market guarana, which he describes as a natural energy source. He hits every questionable note, from vulgarity, pandering to children's interest in drugs, false historical puffing, and scientific misinformation:

> Whatever your reaction may be to the name, you won't forget it, and you certainly won't forget the effect this drink will have on you!
> ... GUTS is geared toward consumers from ages 12 to 24, but it will appeal to anyone who is interested in tapping into a natural energy source. The main flavor of this amber-colored drink is the Paulina Cupana fruit, also known as Guarana, praised by the Andiraze aboriginals of Brazil for thousands of years as a stimulant on both mind and body. Today, Guarana is one of the most sought-after ingredients in "smart drinks," a new category of beverages consumed by youth at "Rave parties" (drug and alcohol free) all across North America. The Guarana berry has 2.5 times the caffeine per ounce as coffee, giving GUTS almost twice the jolt as a regular cola. Pepsi, for example, has 3.2 mg of caffeine per fluid ounce, compared to GUTS that has almost double that amount. The fruit extract is 100% organic, which places GUTS in the burgeoning category of "New Age" beverages.

Note that if GUTS has twice the correctly stated 3.2 mg per ounce caffeine content of Pepsi, it would have only about a third the caffeine per ounce of average coffee. The drink may be "New Age," but the snake oil sales tactics are as ancient as the imaginary Andiraze Indians are supposed to have been by the author of this release.[11]

An interesting phenomenon is the Austrian dominance in the production and consumption of European high-caffeine "energy drinks," including Red Bull, Blue Sow, Dark Dog, and Flying Horse, to name a few. Austrians, often stereotyped as slow moving and hypochondriacal, consume more than one-third of such beverages produced in Europe. Red Bull, for example, sold 150 million cans in 1996, more than a third in Austria alone.

The use of colas, especially trendy high-caffeine soft drinks such as Kick, Nitro Cola, Semtex, GUTS, Afri-Cola, and the old, original Jolt Cola, are enjoying a kind of cult upsurge among computer programmers. The reason was explained in a recent article by David Ramsey in *MacWEEK* responding to a reader's query, "Why do programmers drink so much cola?"[12] Some of the answers to this question are discussed in chapter 16, "Thinking Over Caffeine."

The biggest news in the area of highly caffeinated soft drinks is the entry of the giant Coca-Cola Company into the $4-billion-a-year "heavy citrus" soft drink market,

President and Mrs. Clinton gulping Coca-Cola straight from the bottle during a visit to the Moscow Coca-Cola plant, May 1995. (Reuters/Jim Bourg/Archive Photos)

80 percent of which currently belongs to Mountain Dew, with the brand Surge. The specter of Wiley's concerns about the propriety of selling caffeinated soft drinks to young consumers arises in connection with this highly spiked drink, because the company intends to market this high-caffeine, high-calorie beverage to twelve- to thirty-four-year-olds, especially boys and men. The first television advertisement for Surge was aired during the 1997 Super Bowl. The marketing of Surge marks the first time caffeine itself has been brought to center stage by the manufacturer of a comestible product with a large international market. To a certain extent, what constitutes a high-caffeine soft drink is in the mind of the regulator. Consider that while Mountain Dew is an ordinary soft drink in the United States, it is too supercharged with caffeine to be legally sold on the British market.

The Straight Dope: Vivarin, NoDoz, and Other Caffeine Pills

As the purveyors of caffeine indefatigably repeat, caffeine is the only alertness aid approved for sale by the FDA. This means that companies like SmithKline Beecham, the makers of Vivarin, the largest-selling caffeine pill, and Bristol-Myers Squibb, the makers of NoDoz, and their competitors are in the enviable yet problematic position of being the legal producers and sellers of one of the only over-the-counter psychoactive stimulant drugs outside the matrix of a food or beverage.

Vivarin, which dominates sales, boasts about two-thirds of an estimated $50 million to $60 million market for caffeine pills that are sold through food, drug, and mass merchandise outlets. Additional, hard-to-track sales not included in this market estimate are made through health food stores, convenience stores, rest stops, and college campuses.

Selling drugs, that is, "drugs" in the sense of compounds that can change your mood or even get you high or addicted, may seem like a great business in many ways. But because of increasing concerns about drug use in general and the health of children in particular, the manufacturers of caffeine pills and tablets face a delicate marketing problem: how to promote the responsible use of their products without ever seeming to promote their use by those under eighteen or the abuse of stimulants by adults.

One of the first things marketers do to solve their problems is to determine the profile of their potential consumers. The makers of Vivarin, after many years of experience, have isolated three distinct groups that are good prospects for their product: college students, truck drivers, and bodybuilders. Accordingly, Vivarin's marketing efforts primarily target them. Irrespective of which of these three groups to whom any given promotional material is addressed, all the claims made on behalf of Vivarin have this common thread: Caffeine can significantly improve mood, briefly deter fatigue, and improve performance as a consequence of these effects. Noticeably absent are any claims that caffeine can augment specific human physical or mental capacities, such as increasing endurance or improving learning skills. The maker's cautionary remarks to all three groups are also of a piece: that caffeine is no substitute for sleep and that individual responses vary widely, so each person must learn through experience how caffeine affects him.

Alertness aids containing at least 100 mg of caffeine must feature this FDA warning: "The recommended dose of this product contains about as much caffeine as a cup of coffee. Limit the use of caffeine-containing medications, food, or beverages while taking this product because too much caffeine may cause nervousness, irritability, sleeplessness and occasionally rapid heartbeat."

The college student staying up all night to complete a term paper or prepare for a final exam is one of the most obvious potential consumers of caffeine pills. Because such claims have not received the official imprimatur of the federal authorities, nowhere do the makers of Vivarin adduce the studies demonstrating that caffeine confers limited but significant improvements in the ability to solve math problems or memorize facts. Instead they say only that caffeine can improve moods, including feelings of confidence, and increase alertness, without serious significant mental or physical side effects, and that it is particularly useful in improving performance during "all-nighters." Vivarin has also tried to capitalize on the nexus of computers, college students, and caffeine by promoting its own home page on the Internet and offering contests and dating services through online channels.

Although many credible claims have been asserted for caffeine's ability to increase endurance or strength and also for its power to help the body burn fat faster, Vivarin limits its claims to the power of caffeine to help bodybuilders start their daily work-outs with an upbeat attitude. The company's claims for caffeine's bodybuilding benefits, again, are limited to "producing greater alertness, heightened concentration, and reduced mental fatigue."

Researchers also have found that caffeine benefits the third group targeted for Vivarin sales: truck drivers and, to a lesser extent, anyone who needs to be on the road for a long time. Caffeine has been repeatedly shown to improve driver safety by increasing alertness. For example, a 1996 study in the *Annals of Internal Medicine* that found coffee-drinking nurses to have dramatically lower suicide rate than non-coffee-drinking nurses also found a dramatically lower rate of driving accidents. Because falling asleep at the wheel causes about one hundred thousand accidents every year in the United States, causing about fifteen hundred deaths, Vivarin has made driving alertness a kind of mission. However, the company is careful to include in its promotional material admonitory remarks from the National Sleep Foundation and the AAA Foundation for Traffic Safety. They caution that highway hypnosis, the fatigue and drowsiness that frequently results from long hours on the road staring at ribbons of highway, is different from sleep deprivation, although the specific ways in which this should alter our understanding of how to use caffeine are omitted. Another admonition is that caffeine at best can create a temporary boost in alertness and deter fatigue for a short time. When a person becomes seriously sleep deprived, it is impossible to prevent the occurrence of so-called micro-sleeps, or brief naps that last about four or five seconds. At 55 miles an hour, this is the equivalent of 100 yards of unconscious and presumably hazardous progress on the road.

Even in this age of the coffeehouse renaissance, caffeine pills continue to be a significant source of caffeine for Americans. Physically and intellectually, caffeine does seem to be the energy booster of champions.

caffeine culture and le fin de millénaire

"Café Society" could be given a broader meaning today than it had in earlier times. It formerly designated the clique of fashionable or bohemian loungers who frequented coffeehouses. It could now be used as a name for our society at large, the "society of the café," where people meet, mingle, hang out, or rendezvous with a date. The leading situation comedies of the 1990s on network television support this view. In place of 1980s shows like *Cheers*, which was set in a Boston tavern, were mid-1990s shows such as *Friends*, *Frasier*, and *Seinfeld*, in which the characters regularly assembled over a cup of coffee in either a coffee shop or a café, and the show *Ellen*, in which a bookstore café was a stock setting for comic routines.

Behind the scenes and on the sets, caffeine is a vital source of energy for the production crew and actors. According to *Entertainment Weekly*, on *Frasier* the stars were served the expensive Starbucks Espresso Roast, while the extras and crew were offered assorted flavors from the Coffee Bean & Tea Leaf. On the set for *Ellen*, the caffeine supply was more democratic: Foodcraft's Finest Kona Island Blend was available to all. Some sitcom performers think caffeine may provide too much energy and have decided to avoid it while working. "Michael Richards, who bounced off the walls each week on *Seinfeld* as Kramer, abstains from coffee drinking. Imagine what he'd be like on espresso," an article in *Entertainment Weekly* says.

The idea that caffeine could replace alcohol and that the coffeehouse could replace the tavern is as old as the coffeehouse itself. Coffee earned the epithet "wine of Islam," and we have seen how in Islamic countries, forbidden alcohol, caffeine was a successful substitute for alcohol and the coffeehouse for the tavern. Although alcohol today is legal in every Western society, there can be little question that, at least in centers of urban sophistication, its regular use is falling into increasing disfavor. There seems to be a general drift away from intoxicants, especially strong ones. An attending phenomenon is the decline of singles bars and dance clubs, in the wake of a new squeamishness about sex. Coffeehouses seem to offer an alternative to the dissolution and dissipation associated with the barroom, while still affording an opportunity for people to meet and converse.

The American coffeehouse is sometimes modeled, with greater or lesser fidelity, on the typical Italian espresso bar. There are purportedly more than two thousand such bars in Italy, and they usually are long, narrow, functional spaces with metal countertops and shelves stacked with liquor bottles. They usually have no stools and few tables and chairs, and the use of the tables they have requires payment of a premium price. The patron steps up to the bar, orders an espresso that comes served in a plain white mug, gulps it down, and leaves. There are no coffeepots in most Italian offices, so these places have a following that their American counterparts can only envy.

One import from these Italian shops is the *barista*, a man who makes a career of running the espresso machines. Increasing numbers of tiny American establishments are opening in nooks all over the country, sometimes called "espresso windows." One in Washington, D.C., occupies the ninety-six-square-foot space vacated when an elevator was relocated. However, American "designer" espresso bars are more upscale and tend to rely for their atmosphere on such appurtenances as cherry wood paneling and ceramic tile floors. As one Starbucks proprietor said of his company's cafés, "We want our stores to be an extension of your home."

Who's Doing It: Caffeine Consumption Patterns

There have been few field studies of caffeine consumption patterns, that is, who uses it, how they use it, and how often they use it, especially outside of the United States. However, it is obvious that there is considerable variation in this consumption among individuals and populations.[1]

Some overall observations can be reliably made:

- Age: Caffeine consumption increases progressively with age until stabilizing in middle age and demonstrating a small reduction in old age. This increase of use with age is one of the most bedeviling confounders in long-term studies of the health effects of caffeine use.
- Gender: Most studies find either no difference in consumption levels between men and women, or they find a very small difference, with one or the other sex found to consume more. Of course many such studies beg the question of exposure levels to caffeine, because women on average weigh less than men, and exposure is a function of body weight. Another confounding factor is that, overall, women metabolize caffeine faster than men.
- Abstainers: At least 90 percent of people surveyed consistently acknowledge they use coffee or tea. The prevalence of caffeine use is even higher, if soft drinks and other dietary sources are considered. One Australian study conducted in 1983 found that only about 3 percent of the population were actual caffeine abstainers.[2] Another recent study found that 95 percent of Finns and Norwegians say they drink at least one cup of coffee a day. Although no one can say exactly, it is likely that 90 percent of people worldwide are regular, most often daily, caffeine users. Less than 5 percent are abstainers, in the respect that

This cartoon satirizes two aspects of the American coffeehouse craze, spearheaded by the Star-bucks outlets nationwide: These coffeehouses seek to provide a comfortable home away from home, and they are turning up everywhere, even where we might least have expected them. (David Sipress, 1995)

they never consume caffeine from any source. This leaves about 5 percent in the category of occasional users.

- Generations: Over the centuries attitudes toward different beverages have var-ied widely from one era to the next. David Musto, a Yale professor, has iden-tified a seventy-year cycle of oscillations in attitudes toward the consumption of alcohol, a cycle that has been especially apparent in the United States. Most people are myopically oblivious to this long-term pattern.[3] According to Musto, America in the late 1990s was about twenty years into its third era of temper-ance. Alcohol consumption, which peaked around 1980, has demonstrated more than a 15 percent decline, the biggest drop coming in distilled spirits and lesser decreases in wine and beer. Obviously, we should expect the cyclic use of the major temperance beverages, including caffeinated drinks, to be the inverse of the cyclic use of alcohol. And in fact, caffeine use has exploded in the last few decades, even though industry data indicate that there was a progres-sive decrease in coffee as a source between 1962 and 1982. However, more recently, especially in specialty coffee consumption, usage is once again increas-ing, while the decline in alcohol consumption continues.

the world of caffeine

Average Annual Alcohol Consumption in America

Year	per adult in gallons of ethanol
1700	5.7 (in England)
1790	5.8
1830	7.1
1840	3.1
1860	2.1
1890	2.1
1900	2.1
1920	0.9
1940	1.56
1980	2.76

Adapted from David Musto, "Alcohol and American History,"
Scientific American, April 1996.

Today in the United States more than 80 percent of adults consume caffeine on a daily basis. The average daily consumption among all adults is approximately 200 mg per day and among caffeine consumers is approximately 280 mg. Applying the standards and definitions discussed in our section on caffeine dependence, this would mean 75 million people fit the criteria for moderate caffeine dependence.

The average daily consumption of coffee in many other countries is considerably higher than in the United States. The highest coffee consuming-countries, in descending order, are: Finland, Sweden, Denmark, Norway, Belgium, the Netherlands, Germany, Austria, Switzerland, and France. All have higher levels than the United States, with Finland, Sweden, Denmark, and Norway boasting consumption levels from two to three times as great.[4]

The United States' consumption of coffee declined by nearly 40 percent between 1962, the year in which the highest levels were reached, and 1982, with most of the decline occurring in the first ten years of this period. Because the average number of cups per coffee drinker declined only 20 percent, we know that many people quit drinking coffee entirely. The decline of caffeine intake from coffee was even greater, for in the same period the consumption of decaffeinated coffee as a percentage of total coffee consumption increased from 3 percent to 20 percent. During these twenty years, however, consumption of soft drinks more than doubled, and because all five top-selling soft drinks contain caffeine, there seems to have been not so much a decline in total caffeine intake as a partial switch from coffee to soda as the vehicle of ingestion.

Baby Boomers and Caffeine

In 1996, a magazine called *New Choices* conducted a national survey of the first baby boomers, born in 1946, and just turning fifty. They found that about two-thirds are happy with their sex lives, and the same percentage are unhappy about their career choices. When speaking of drugs, of those expressing a preference, the largest number, 27 percent, cited exercise [*sic*], and the next largest, 25 percent, cited caffeine as their drug of choice.[5]

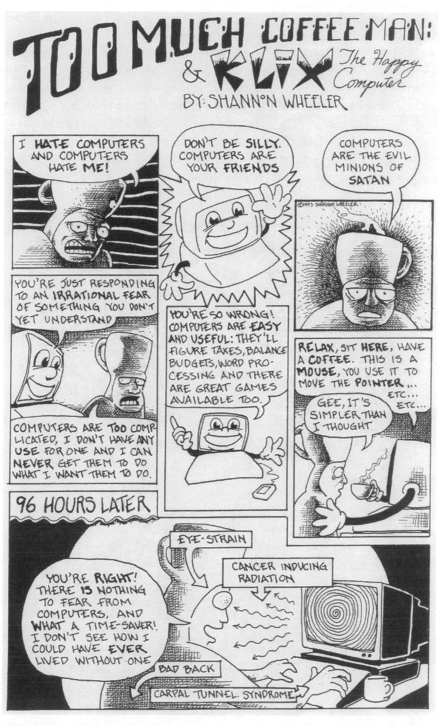

Too Much Coffee Man & Klix, the Happy Computer, cartoon strip by Shannon Wheeler, from a series dedicated to lampooning the effects produced by excessive coffee use. In this cartoon, the user gains confidence in using a computer after drinking one cup of coffee, but ends up suffering from the effects of working for four days straight, presumably as a result of the excessive use of caffeine. (By permission of the artist)

Why should caffeine have topped the long list of recreational drugs once popular with this group? For those of the "flower power" generation, now at the height of maturity, whose tastes were jaded by enveloping euphorics and timber-rattling stimulants, common caffeine has reemerged as the drug of choice. No doubt it was forgotten in the wild drug party that started in Haight-Ashbury in the mid-1960s and eventually made its way around the world and back. To those who binged on methamphetamine, cocaine, heroin, LSD, Quaaludes, or any of a long list of agents used for excitement in the wake of Timothy Leary and acid rock, caffeine did not even rise to the level of notice as a psychoactive substance. After all, it was not only legal and a fixture of the straight, business-driven world, but even the most timid grandmother would take it in her tea.

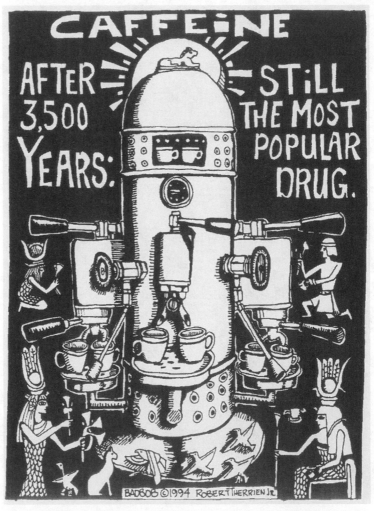

"Caffeine—After 3,500 Years: Still the Most Popular Drug," cartoon by Robert Therrien, Jr., a.k.a., BADBOB. In this fanciful version of caffeine history, hieroglyphs depict Egyptians attending an oversized espresso machine, even though, of course, there is no evidence that either the Egyptians or any other people knew of coffee or caffeine as early as 3,500 years ago. (By permission of the artist)

Thirty years later, the terrible hangover brought on by all that overindulgence has finally lifted. Now people are looking for a different high, one that is enjoyable but safe, one that not only does not destroy a productive life but can actually improve it. That's why all eyes have turned back to caffeine. As a drug, caffeine works: It wakes you up, improves your cognitive powers, increases your energy output—and yet it is, for all anybody can tell to date, remarkably safe for healthy adults to use in normal quantities.

Generations X, Y, and Z and Caffeine

Some of us still harbor a mental image of the coffeehouse as a den of idle adults, indulging in a relatively innocent form of recreation. Many also imagine that the taste for coffee is itself an acquired one that rarely sets in before age twenty-one. But in fact an increasing number of the nation's thirty-five hundred coffeehouses are becoming kiddy capitals, attracting unprecedented numbers of children in their early teens, who are, from all reports, consuming coffee in copious caffeine-charged gulps that would give many grown-ups the jitters.

Why the coffeehouse? It is a place that thirteen- to sixteen-year-olds can come to hang out, sometimes into the early-morning hours, talk, watch people, and do so in an "adult" environment that has, at least to their innocent sensibilities, an aura of sophistication. Unlike bars, coffeehouses are open to children because many do not serve alcohol. They offer an alternative to the video arcade, the local mall, or the street corner as a congenial spot to assemble. And where else can a kid go to get a legal high? Children generally are not permitted to drink alcohol, smoke cigarettes, or enjoy many of the other minor vices that make adult life tolerable. Is it any wonder that they flock to the centers of refreshment that make caffeine abundantly available in a variety of attractive and delicious presentations? Some people are questioning the possible deleterious effects of all that caffeine on their systems. No one really knows if caffeine use in children has any harmful effects, although so far none have been demonstrated. Meanwhile, we can assert with confidence that drinking coffee is better for a teenager than drinking alcohol or sniffing cocaine.

Brewings and Doings: Caffeine Mainstays and Curiosities

At the end of 1994 Celestial Seasonings, famous as the United States' largest man-ufacturer of herbal teas, which have no caffeine, began marketing six flavors of caf-feine-rich black teas, the market category which accounts for 90 percent of retail tea sales. The real innovation, demonstrating an increase in awareness of caffeine among consumers, was the simultaneous addition of "caffeine meters," displayed on the side of each box of black tea, showing shoppers the caffeine content of the tea in milligrams as compared with the caffeine in coffee, cola, and chocolate.

For the first time, we hear people saying, "I need some caffeine to wake up," instead of "I need some coffee." Courses in preparing coffee, tea, and chocolate, and about their history as comestibles have been offered for years. Today, courses at adult extension schools are being offered in "Caffeine Culture." There is little question that caffeine has finally caught the full attention of many of the people who have been using it so relentlessly. It is interesting to explore some of the signs of this new awareness of caffeine.

Spike Coffee—The Coffee for Caffeine Addicts

Some people may drink coffee for its taste, others for both taste and the caffeine lift, but the targeted consumers for Spike, a brand that touts itself as containing "50 percent more caffeine," are interested in the drug content only. The ads, which feature a graphic display of Spike's relatively greater caffeine content than other sources and a logo of a cup of coffee being injected by a syringe presumably filled with caffeine, fail to mention that the beans containing the most caffeine are of the *robusta* variety, inferior by every measure of taste to the justifiably more coveted and more expensive *arabica* beans.

Caffeine and, Well, Water

Perhaps one the most dramatic tributes to the rising interest in caffeine is the introduction of the drink Water Joe by Johnny Beverage Inc. in 1996. Touted as "the leading caffeine-enhanced water," Water Joe is a no-frills product for people who don't want any chlorine, calories, sugar, or artificial flavorings, but do want pure artesian well water laced with a generous dose of caffeine. Among Water Joe's promotional suggestions: Make your morning coffee with Water Joe for an extra boost. One large group of potential Water Joe drinkers comprises athletes or dieters who want the boost of caffeine but know they must be careful to compensate for the dehydration that it can induce. But perhaps Water Joe's biggest market is among those who don't like coffee but still crave the lift it provides. David Marcheschi, president of Chicago-based Johnny Beverage, was among their number. Explaining that he thought up the idea for caffeinated water while in college, he recalls, "I didn't like coffee or colas, but I still needed to study."

How much caffeine does a bottle of Water Joe contain? The advertising says as much as one cup of coffee. This specification doesn't really tell us very much, and the product label doesn't add any information. The dose claimed by some of the press coverage is 70 mg of caffeine added to a half-liter, 16.9-ounce, bottle. There is no question that Water Joe lives up to its claims not to contain any calories, sugars, or preservatives and not to stain teeth, but does it "taste just like water," as the company's promotional literature suggests? Johnny Beverage claims that it relies on a method developed by a flavor chemist to mask caffeine's usually bitter taste. However, company officials refused to discuss this claim with us in any way. Our informal taste test found people about evenly divided among those who tasted only pure spring water and those who detected a faint flavor, which we attribute to the presence of caffeine.

Mixing Your Drinks: Caffeine and Alcohol

In 1995 Starbucks Coffee Company, with more than 650 retail operations, joined forces with Redhook Ale Brewery to create Double Black Stout, dark roasted malt beer targeted at specialty coffee and beer drinkers alike. Redhook president and CEO Paul Shipman says that the idea for the new brew came up in an impromptu conversation over a cup of coffee. The final product is the result of diligent testing and blending of test brews. According to the companies' public relations people, the brewers and coffee specialists experienced an amazing synergy, because "the similarities of brewing fine beer and roasting fine coffee were an inspiration to the whole group and resulted in a brew that showcases the best of both products." After primary fermentation of the stout, Redhook adds brewed Starbucks coffee to the beer. The resulting mix is supposed to combine the full, roasted flavor of stout with the aroma and flavor of arabica coffee. Starbucks coffee specialists have chosen a blend of Central American coffees for the beer, which is said to deliver "remarkable rich, roasted coffee notes to Double Black Stout."

Carbonated Coffee

North American Coffee Partnership, the joint venture formed in August 1995 by Pepsi-Cola and Starbucks, test marketed a new product: Mazagran, a lightly carbonated beverage made with Starbucks coffee. Touted as a new version of a 150-year-old beverage supposedly once popular with the French Foreign Legion, it will be sold at Starbucks fountains and in bottles in grocery stores.

Another similar product, also by PepsiCo, hit U.S. grocers' shelves in mid-1996: Pepsi-Kona, a coffee-flavored carbonated cola drink, so soda and coffee lovers can finally have it both ways. A new mixed drink called a "Turbo Coke" seems in line with this product: a tall glass of Coke with ice and a shot of espresso.

The Coffee Shop Connection—Keeping Them off the Streets

Holland is one of the few European countries that never experienced a movement to ban coffee or tea. Carrying on this tradition of tolerance, today in the Netherlands, where the use and possession of small amounts of marijuana is not customarily subjected to legal sanctions, young and old flock to establishments euphemistically known as "coffee shops" to buy and smoke marijuana while they sit around sipping their favorite caffeinated drink. There are examples of small communities where the civic leaders have applied for and received funding from the national government to support the establishment of such coffee shops intended to provide teenagers with a salubrious place to hang out and get high.

Caffeine Currents: From Coffee to Tea?

In 1996, reports began circulating in the press about a new enthusiasm for specialty teas, following the success of the specialty coffee trend, although, in one reporter's words, it "hasn't taken off with the fervor of a caffeine buzz." In Seattle and Portland, two of the cities to initiate the coffeehouse revival in the United States, the use of tea is on the rise. Even the British tea garden and Japanese teahouse are undergoing new incarnations, as teahouses open for business in markets heavily saturated with more traditionally American cafés.

What is the motivation for the switch from coffee to tea? Partly it's the social connotations. The partisans of tea associate it with leisurely conversation and relaxation as opposed to their more frenetic associations with coffee. Partly it's a matter of the taste. Some people like caffeine but just don't like the taste of coffee. Steve Smith, founder of Tazo Teas, produces bottles of what he calls "microbrewed" teas.

He also runs several tea bars in specialty supermarkets and at universities such as Harvard and Portland State.

Is the tea trend here to stay? We can't say for sure, but one sign of the times is the fact that even Starbucks now sells a half-dozen varieties of tea.

Kopi Luak Coffee: Waste Not, Want Not

If you think that Jamaica Blue Mountain is the scarcest and costliest coffee, you are unfamiliar with Kopi Luak.

Coffee's propagation in Africa, India, and Indonesia and the harvesting of the world's rarest and most expensive beans are intimately linked with the dietary and excretory habits of a certain curious animal called the civet cat. In Krapf's nineteenth-century account of his missionary work in Africa, he states, without elaboration, that the civet cat may have been responsible for introducing the coffee plant into the Ethiopian highlands from central Africa:

> According to the Arabian tradition, the civet-cat brought the coffee-bean to the mountains of the Arusi and the Itta-Gallas, where it grew and was long cultivated, till an enterprising merchant carried the coffee-plant five hundred years ago, to Arabia, where it soon became acclimatized.[6]

Supposedly, the beans emerge still covered with their original mucilage or silver skin. In 1740 Spanish Jesuits brought coffee seedlings from Java to the Philippines, where the plant proliferated dramatically, largely as a result of the dietary preferences of the native civet cat, which, like the African civet cat spoken of by Krapf, enjoyed the fruit and spread the indigestible seeds in its droppings.[7]

The animal in question is one of the three species of palm civets in the genus *Paradoxurus*, the family Viverridae. Its relatives include mongooses, civets, and genets. Two of the three species are confined to India and Sri Lanka, while the third, *Paradoxurus hermaphroditus*, is found throughout Southeast Asia, the East Indies, the Philippines, and Africa. Other names for the animal include "musang," and "toddy cat."

Despite some of its many aliases, however, *Paradoxurus* is not a true cat. These cute animals, with catlike faces, have long gray-brown fur with dorsal stripes and lateral spots and a long tail. They live five or more years, are about one and a half to two and a half feet long, and weigh six or seven pounds. Although they feed on small animals they also eat bulbs, nuts, and fruits, which is how they enter the history of coffee.

Other animals play a part in spreading coffee as well. In 1922, William Ukers reported that in some regions of India, birds and monkeys enjoy eating the ripe coffee berries because of their tasty pulp. The beans, however, pass undigested through their alimentary canals. Gathered by the natives, these beans are recycled to make so-called monkey coffee.[8] In *Coffee Botany, Cultivation, and Utilization* (1961), Frederick L. Wellman offers an account of varied relationships between animals and the proliferation of the coffee plant, giving birds the credit of spreading coffee within Africa, from Ethiopia into the Sudan, and the civet cat for doing so in Hawaii.[9]

In 1994, after a thirteen-year search, Mark Montanous, while in Europe, finally found a Dutch coffee broker who had what he claimed were the raw, green Indonesian kopi luak beans. Montanous bought 70 pounds for $7,000 and now is retailing it virtually at cost at $105 a pound, making it easily the most expensive coffee in the world.

Is it worth it? We are told that this coffee is not to everyone's taste. Even though some people claim it has a delightful heavy, musty, caramel taste and aroma, others find it strong and repellent. So far, Montanous has sold about 45 pounds, with a few repeat (apparently satisfied) customers.

When Caffeine-Free Is Definitely Better for Your Health

The first detailed intensive study of water quality of the Mississippi River was released in 1996 by the U.S. Geological Survey, Department of the Interior. Thousands of samples were collected for this study from 1987 through 1992, during ten separate sampling trips that were timed to show the effects of high water, low water, rising water levels, and falling water levels. Several years of subsequent laboratory analysis produced the results. Geological Survey chief hydrologist Bob Hirsch commented on the significance of the study: "The contaminants we measure in the Mississippi represent a report card on our clean-up efforts on the streams and rivers that drain nearly half the country."

Not surprisingly, the scientists checked for levels of such contaminants as lead and detergents. They also checked for, and discovered, caffeine. Because in this region caffeine is found only in coffee, tea, chocolate, and soft drinks consumed only by humans, when it is found in domestic sewage it can be used to track the extent to which that sewage is diluted by the Mississippi River. Concentrations of caffeine in the river indicate that domestic sewage may be diluted as much as a thousandfold. Whether this is an acceptable level is a question best left to ecological experts, but it seems clear that caffeine-free river, lake, or spring water is definitely the least hazardous to your health.[10]

When Is Caffeine Not Caffeine?

Misinformation about caffeine abounds today, even as it did in the days of Simon Pauli and Buntekuh. Herbal remedy sales representatives take advantage of a generalized concern about caffeine to help push "alternative" products, for which they promise the same or greater benefits. Unfortunately for the unwary, the active ingredient in many of these nostrums is either caffeine or caffeine compounded, potentially dangerously, with ephedrine, which is sometime referred to as "ma-huang," the Chinese herb from which it is derived. The following ad on the Internet for EXTRA BOOST was particularly amusing because it touts a guarana-based supplement as a medicine to reduce "cravings for caffeine," a claim which is certainly true, because one of its active ingredients *is* caffeine.

For anyone imagining that EXTRA BOOST is a magical new remedy, the letdown comes quickly, as soon as the two active ingredients are described:

Guarana:

   This is a plant that grows in the northern and western portions of Brazil. Reportedly, its seeds have been used for centuries by the natives of the Amazon for added energy and mental alertness.

Mahuang:

   Imported from China, this plant, according to the Chinese, reduces the desire for food, metabolizes fat, increases energy and mental alertness.

Another ad, this time for guarana capsules, is more accurate, declaring, "Guarana is a caffeine-rich extract that, in addition to 2–3 times the caffeine found in coffee, also contains xanthine compounds such as theobromine and theophylline. Made into a popular Brazilian cola drink, guarana is consumed for energy and stimulation. Guarana has also been used traditionally as an anti-diuretic, a nerve tonic, to reduce hunger, and to relieve headaches, migraines and PMS symptoms."

From Cyberspace to Outerspace to a Pretty Face: Caffeine on the Internet and Beyond

   A cybercafé is a coffeehouse in cyberspace. That is, it is a coffeehouse without a house and without coffee. So in what sense is it a coffeehouse at all? In the sense that the coffeehouse serves as a universal symbol for a forum in which friendly strangers, often gathered from the fringes of society, can convene to discuss art, politics, science, or almost any other subject matter. That is what the coffeehouse was in the lands of its inception, the cities, villages, and travelers' inns of the Middle East in the sixteenth century. That is what it was in England in the seventeenth century, in Greenwich Village in the 1950s, in Seattle in the 1980s, and that is what it is in cyberspace as we enter the third millennium. At the traditional coffeehouse people sit at little tables, sip coffee, read the news, and meet and talk face to face. At the cybercafé, there are little monitors and keyboards, at which people sit, sip coffee, search the web and chat with people around the world. Thus the cybercafé carries forward the tradition of coffeehouse conversation into the twenty-first century.

   The notion of the "extended café" that the cybercafé embodies is not as unprecedented as it may appear at first. Since at least the nineteenth century, the word "café," which simply means "coffee" in French, has been used worldwide to designate establishments that serve alcohol or absinthe and light food, occasionally featuring musical performers, and only incidentally serving coffee. It also designates a small, plain or fancy, informal restaurant. For whatever reasons, the word "coffee" has come to signify public places for gathering to drink, talk, eat, or be entertained. Rather than diminishing our estimate of caffeine's importance, this linguistic generalization suggests that caffeine's social significance is both deep and broad.

   What do a design studio in Atlanta, a poetry magazine in San Francisco, a software module for Apple computers, and a new multiplayer Internet game have in common? They all go by the name "caffeine." Suddenly *caffeine*, not just its vehicles coffee and tea, is on everyone's tongue. A network magazine supporting proprietary online services recently issued a list of the Best of the Web. One category, including about a dozen sites, most of which feature high-tech products, was "Coffee and Caffeine." A Canadian food information bureau uses the acronym CAFFEINE for its home page. Another example of its acronymic use is Computer Aided Fast Fabrication Exploration in Engineering, an Internet site hailing from Berkeley.

Perhaps it is because of the profile of caffeine's cognitive effects, its power to increase alertness, speed, diligence, and retention, especially in repetitive tasks, that computer people are among the leading caffeine consumers in America. Or perhaps it's just that they get weary from long hours writing and using software. Whatever the reason, the link between computer work and caffeine is pretty much taken for granted as a fact of popular culture. For example, in a 1996 news article, "What computer users really want in a keyboard," Joe Fasbinder, a UPI reporter, describes a computer keyboard with a special feature aimed at caffeine users: "if you spill any 'computer-programmer' fluids (i.e., anything with caffeine in it), you can simply keep typing, or take the thing to the kitchen sink, run some water over it and let it dry out."

In the roiling seas of the Internet it's difficult for one person to make a big splash. One man who is trying is Shannon Wheeler. He has dedicated himself to creating and disseminating comic books, T-shirts, and other pop culture paraphernalia celebrating the culture of caffeine and the adventures of a character with a large coffee cup permanently affixed to the top of his head, called simply the "Too Much Coffee Man." Another Internet caffeine promoter, Robert Therrien, or BADBOB, as he calls himself, is a former student at Antioch, a caffeine aficionado, Internet maven, cartoonist, and something of a versifier. In his cartoons he cries out with existential angst over the cognitive, emotional, and social dissonances that ripple outward from the caffeine habitué.[11]

An effort to use caffeine to promote products is found in a 1995 *Working Woman* article on new skin creams.[12] The article features information on Clinique's Moisture On-Call, ($30/1.7 oz), a product that, according to Shirley Weinstein, Clinique's vice president of product development, "uses caffeine to catalyze the production of lipids, substances that keep the skin moist and unlined, at the basal-cell layer. Results begin to show in about a month, the amount of time it takes cells to move from the bottom of the epidermis to its surface." Weinstein referred our inquiries to the company's public relations department, which left us a message to the effect that Clinique did not "participate in books." And so we have no information about how caffeine gets the lipid-producing juices flowing.

A news story from China illustrates how caffeine there is placed in the same category as the West places dangerous narcotics. It was reported by the Heilongjiang *Daily*, dateline Beijing, March 29, 1995, that police in northern China arrested a ring of seventeen caffeine dealers who were attempting to close a deal to sell a large quantity of caffeine pills. Like opium and other psychoactive drugs, caffeine is a controlled substance in China. Police seized 85 pounds of caffeine and more than one million caffeine pills, with a reputed street value of several hundred thousand dollars. The ring had illegally diverted the caffeine from a pharmaceutical shipment en route from Beijing.[13]

Cartoons by Robert Thierrien, Jr., a.k.a. BADBOB. These energetic images, among a series by the artist celebrating caffeine's place in contemporary culture, have been widely reproduced on T-shirts and coffee mugs. (By permission of the artist)

In the 1960s, the days of acid rock, songs such as "Lucy in the Sky with Diamonds" and "Spoonful" celebrated drugs such as LSD and cocaine. In the more timid culture of the 1990s, caffeine has become a drug noticed and venerated by the young. There have been several recent songs about the mind- and body-altering power of caffeine in coffee. We have also noticed an increase in the word "caffeine" figuring into phrases, such as "he needs a shot of caffeine," that formerly referenced other drugs such as adrenaline.

An Internet thread in the alt.drugs.caffeine newsgroup began with a message to the effect that a handful of chocolate-covered coffee beans, which are "SO easy to just sit and munch," release as much caffeine when eaten as you get from drinking a cup of coffee, so it is wise to be careful and not eat the whole bag. In response a member of a rock band called Cathead reminisced about some uses of whole beans backstage before concerts:

> Before every show (back in the good old days) we would share a bag (i.e. You know the bags they offer in the bulk section of Safeway?) of espresso beans. I can only say that each show back then was really intense . . . every time.[14]

Is the coffee and tea party really nearly over? Some people, evidently disgusted with the caffeine craze sweeping the world at the turn of the millennium, have lined up to prophesy the end of the excitement. Several books have appeared in the last few years cautioning people about the supposed dangers of caffeine consumption. One of their number is *Caffeine Blues: Wake up to the Hidden Dangers of America's #1 Drug*, by Stephen A. Cherniske (Warner Books, 1998). The publisher states that this book, which presents a daunting panoply of dire warnings about caffeine reminiscent of Simon Pauli, "exposes the harmful side effects of caffeine and gives readers a step-by-step program to reduce intake, boost energy, create a new vibrant life and recognize the dangers." Another is *Danger: Caffeine*, by Patra M. Sevastiade (Rosen Publishing Group, 1998), a book intended for children five to nine that "explains how caffeine affects the body and the harm overuse of it can cause." Still another is *Addiction-Free—Naturally: Liberating Yourself from Tobacco, Caffeine, Sugar, Alcohol, Prescription Drugs, Cocaine, and Narcotics*, by Brigette Mars (Inner Traditions International, 2000), which, as the title makes obvious, puts caffeine in some pretty nasty company. A more unusual contribution to cautionary caffeine literature is *Brief Epidemiology of Crime: With Particular Reference to the Relationship between Caffeine and Alcohol Use and Crime*, by Peter D. Hay (Peter D. Hay, 1999).

Organizations have arisen to help people avoid what their members regard as the evils of caffeine. Among them are Caffeine Anonymous, a twelve-step program of caffeine addicts who gather weekly at a church to support each other's efforts to quit. More radical are the efforts of Caffeine Prevention Plus, a nonprofit organization "dedicated to caffeine and coffee prevention." A consultant for this redoubtable group recently wrote an article advocating that coffee be made an illegal substance because of the harm it poses for coffee drinkers and society. In his scientismic polemic to outlaw caffeine, he explains that the putative therapeutic benefits of caffeine are figments of the "coffee lobby" and that there are other compounds available to do anything caffeine can do and do it better. In addition, according to this group, caffeine is solely responsible for more than 25 percent of British bad business decisions, including the Barings bank disaster, and is believed to be involved in aggravating more than 50 percent of all marital disputes in the United States.

PART 4
the natural history of caffeine

Caffeine
USP/FCC   (Anhydrous)

WARNING: MAY BE HARMFUL IF INHALED OR SWALLOWED. HAS CAUSED MUTAGENIC AND REPRODUCTIVE EFFECTS IN LABORATORY ANIMALS. INHALATION CAUSES RAPID HEART RATE, EXCITEMENT, DIZZINESS, PAIN, COLLAPSE, HYPOTENSION, FEVER, SHORTNESS OF BREATH, HEADACHE, INSOMNIA, NAUSEA, VOMITING, STOMACH PAIN, COLLAPSE AND CONVULSIONS, MAY CAUSE DIGESTIVE DISTURBANCES, CONSTIPATION, CARDIAC DISORDERS AND DEPRESSED MENTAL STATES. SKIN CONTACT CAUSES SIMILAR SYMPTOMS AS IN THOSE OF INHALATION. MAY CAUSE EPIGASTRIC PAIN, CARDIAC AND RESPIRATORY DISORDERS AND DEPRESSED MENTAL STATES. EYE CONTACT MAY CAUSE IRRITATION, REDNESS AND CONJUNCTIVITIS. INGESTION MAY PRODUCE GASTROINTESTINAL IRRITATION, VOMITING, AND CONVULSIONS. FATALITIES HAVE BEEN KNOWN TO OCCUR.
TARGET ORGANS AFFECTED: Eyes, Skin, Central Nervous System, Respiratory and Gastrointestinal Tract. Provide general dilution ventilation or use recommended NIOSH respirator listed in Material Safety Data Sheet.
FIRST AID - INHALATION Remove from exposure area to fresh air immediately. If breathing has stopped, give artificial respiration. Keep person warm and at rest. Get medical attention immediately. SKIN Remove contaminated clothing and shoes. Wash affected area with soap or mild detergent and large amounts of water (approximately 15-20 minutes). Get medical attention immediately. EYES Wash eyes immediately with large amounts of water, occasionally lifting upper and lower lids until no evidence of chemical remains (approximately 15-20 minutes). Get medical attention. INGESTION If victim is conscious and not convulsing, immediately give 2 to 4 glasses of water. Induce vomiting by touching finger to back of throat. Get medical attention immediately.

REFER TO MATERIAL SAFETY DATA SHEET FOR ADDITIONAL INFORMATION

Fisher
ChemAlert
Guide

For laboratory and manufacturing use only. Not intended for household use.

500 gm
01728-500
Alkaloids, Solid, n.o.s.
UN1544

FisherChemical
Fisher Scientific

caffeine in the laboratory

After the fall of Rome, the sciences originated by the Greeks lay quiescent for more than a millennium, eventually falling under the spell of such alchemical adepts as Albertus Magnus (1193–1280) and Philippus Aureolus Paracelsus (1490–1541). These sciences were quickened in Restoration England by the members of one of the oldest and most important coffee klatches in history, the Royal Society. Still one of the leading scientific societies in the world, the Royal Society began in 1655 as the Oxford Coffee Club, an informal confraternity of scientists and students who, as we said earlier, convened in the house of Arthur Tillyard after prevailing upon him to prepare and serve the novel and exotic drink. To appreciate the audaciousness of the club members, we must remember that coffee was then regarded as a strange and powerful drug from a remote land, unlike anything that had ever been seen in England. It was not, at first, enjoyed for its taste, as it was brewed in a way that most found bitter, murky, and unpleasant, but was consumed exclusively for its stimulating and medicinal properties. The members of the Oxford Coffee Club took their coffee tippling to London sometime before 1662, the year they were granted a charter by Charles II as the Royal Society of London for the Improvement of Natural Knowledge.

Historical reflection on changing fashions in drug use might justify the saying, "By their drugs you shall know them." Members of the Sons of Hermes, the leading alchemical society of the Middle Ages, experimented with plants and herbs, almost certainly including the Solanaceæ family, commonly known as nightshades, which comprises thorn apple, belladonna, madragrora, and henbane.[1] These plants contain the hallucinogenics atropine, scopolamine, and hyoscyamine, which were used historically as intoxicants and poisons and more recently as "truth serums." These drugs often produce visions, characteristically inducing three-dimensional psychotic delusions, often populated with vividly real people, fabulous animals, or otherworldly beings. Because of atropine's ability to bring about a transporting delirium, witches rubbed an atropine-laced ointment into their skin to induce visions of flying.

Obviously, the Solanaceæ drugs are as well-suited to the fabulous, symbolic, magical, transformational doctrines of alchemy as caffeine is to the rational, verifiable, sensibly grounded, and literal endeavors of modern science.

It may therefore not be entirely adventitious that the thousand-year lapse of European science in the Middle Ages, during which naturalism commingled promiscuously with magic, ended at the same time that the first coffeehouses opened in England and that coffee, fresh from the Near East, became suddenly popular with the intellectual and social avant-garde in Oxford and London. The aristocratic Anglo-Irish Robert Boyle (1627–91), the father of modern chemistry, regarded in his time as the leading scientist in England, was a founding member of the original Oxford Coffee Club. Credited with drawing the first clear line between alchemy and chemistry, Boyle formulated the precursor to the modern theory of the elements, achieving the first significant advance in chemical theory in more than two thousand years.[2] Within a few years after the English craze for caffeine began, the modern revolutions, not only in chemistry, but in physics and mathematics as well, were well under way. Twentieth-century scientific studies suggest that caffeine can increase vigilance, improve performance, especially of repetitive or boring tasks such as laboratory research, and increase stamina for both mental and physical work. In consequence of its avid use by the most creative scientists of the second half of the seventeenth century, caffeine may well have expedited the inauguration of both modern chemistry and physics and, in this sense, have been the only drug in history with some responsibility for stimulating the formulation of the theoretical foundations of its own discovery.

Caffeine and Chemistry

Caffeine is a chemical compound built of four of the most common elements on earth: carbon, hydrogen, nitrogen, and oxygen. The pure chemical compound is collected as a residue of coffee decaffeination, recovered from waste tea leaves, produced by methylating the organic compounds theophylline or theobromine, or synthesized from dimethylurea and malonic acid. At room temperature, caffeine, odorless and slightly bitter, consists of a white, fleecy powder resembling cornstarch or of long, flexible, silky, prismatic crystals. It is moderately soluble in water at body temperature and freely soluble in hot water. Caffeine will not melt; like dry ice, it sublimes, passing directly from a solid to a gaseous state, at a temperature of 458 degrees Fahrenheit.[3]

The formula for caffeine is $C_8H_{10}N_4O_2$, which means that each caffeine molecule comprises eight atoms of carbon, ten atoms of hydrogen, four atoms of nitrogen, and two atoms of oxygen. However, to understand the structure and properties of caffeine, or of any chemical compound, it is necessary not only to identify its atomic constituents but also to describe the way in which these constituents fit together. A compound's chemical name articulates this chemical structure and serves to designate how its parts are arranged and connected. Caffeine has several chemical names, or alternative ways of representing its structure, the most common of which is 1,3,7-trimethylxanthine. The name revealing its structure most fully is 1H-Purine-2,6-dione, 3,7-dihydro-1,3,7-trimethyl. Other chemical designations for caffeine include:

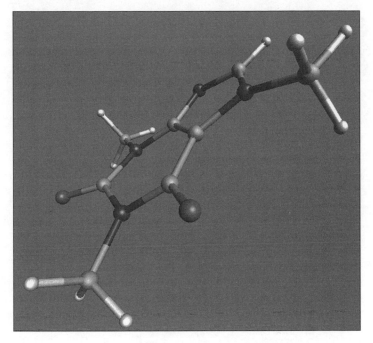

A computer-generated model of the caffeine molecule.

1,3,7-Trimethyl-2, 6-dioxopurine
7-Methyltheophylline
Methyltheobromine

To understand the way in which these names represent caffeine's structure, it is helpful to consider them in the context of the structural descriptions of caffeine's parent compound, purine, and of caffeine's isomers, or close relations.

Caffeine is one of a group of purine alkaloids, sometimes called methylated xanthines, or simply, xanthines. Other methylated xanthines include theophylline, theobromine, and paraxanthine. All three are isomers, or chemical variations, of caffeine, and all three are primary products of caffeine metabolism in human beings. Purine itself is an organic molecule composed entirely of hydrogen and nitrogen. All purine bases, including caffeine, are nitrogenous compounds with two rings in the molecules, five- and six-membered, each including two nitrogen atoms. The purine alkaloid xanthine is created when two oxygen atoms are added to purine.

The other purine alkaloids, in turn, are built out of xanthine by adding methyl groups, that is, groups of one carbon and three hydrogen atoms, in varying numbers and positions. For example, caffeine, a trimethylxanthine, the most common methylxanthine in nature, is xanthine with three added methyl groups, in the first, third, and seventh positions. Similarly, theophylline (1,3-dimethylxanthine) consists of xanthine with methyl groups in the first and third positions, theobromine (3,7-dimethylxanthine), consists of xanthine with methyl groups in the third and seventh positions, and paraxanthine (1,7-dimethylxanthine) consists of xanthine with methyl groups in the

Purine   Xanthine

Caffeine

Theophylline   Theobromine   Paraxanthine

The molecular structure of caffeine and related compounds.

Photomicrographs of caffeine crystals at a magnification of 28x. (Photograph taken by Paul Barrow at BioMedical Communications, University of Pennsylvania Medical Center, © 1999 Bennett Alan Weinberg and Bonnie K. Bealer.)

first and seventh positions. Because the body transforms caffeine into each of these isomers, they may well play a part in caffeine's health effects.

Although purine itself does not occur in the human body, chemicals in the purine family are widely present there as throughout nature. In fact, in addition to being the parent compound of caffeine and other methylxanthines, purine is the parent compound of adenine and guanine, two of the four basic constituents of the nucleotides that form RNA and DNA, the molecular chains within the cells of every living organism that determine its genetic identity. Some scientists have speculated that, because of this similarity to genetic material, caffeine and its metabolites may introduce errors into cell reproduction, causing cancer, tumors, and birth defects. As of this writing, there is no credible evidence to substantiate such fears.

The Metabolism of Caffeine:
From Cup to Bowl, or A Remembrance of Things Passed

Because caffeine is water soluble and passes easily through all cell membranes, it is quickly and completely absorbed from the stomach and intestines into the bloodstream, which carries it to all the organs. This means that, soon after you finish your cup of coffee or tea, caffeine will be present in virtually every cell of your body. Caffeine's permeability results in an evenness of distribution that is exceptional as compared with most other pharmacological agents; because the human body presents no significant physiological barrier to hinder its passage through tissue, the concentrations attained by caffeine are virtually the same in blood, saliva, and even breast milk and semen.

Caffeine's stimulating effects largely depend on its power to infiltrate the central nervous system. This infiltration can only be accomplished by crossing the blood-brain barrier, a defensive mechanism that protects the central nervous system from biological or chemical exposure by preventing large molecules, such as viruses, from entering the brain or its surrounding fluid. Even following intravenous injection, many drugs fail to penetrate this barrier to reach the central nervous system, while others enter it much less rapidly than they enter other tissues. One of the secrets of caffeine's power is that caffeine passes through this blood-brain barrier as if it did not exist.

The maximum concentrations of caffeine in the body, including in the blood circulating in the brain that is responsible for caffeine's major stimulating effects, is typically attained within an hour after consumption of a cup of coffee or tea. Absorption is somewhat slower for caffeine imbibed in soft drinks. It is important to remember that the concentration of caffeine in any person's body is a function not only of the amount of caffeine consumed but of the person's body weight. After drinking a cup of coffee with a typical 100 mg of caffeine, a 200-pound man would attain a concentration of about 1 mg per kilogram of body weight. A 100-pound woman would attain about 2 mg per kilogram and would therefore (all other metabolic factors being considered equal) experience double the effects experienced by the man.

What becomes of all this ambient caffeine permeating your cells?

Factors Affecting Rate of Caffeine Metabolism in Humans

Slows Metabolism	Speeds Metabolism
alcohol	cigarettes
Asian	Caucasian*
man	woman
newborn	child
oral contraceptives	
liver damage	
pregnancy	

Note: A Japanese non-smoking man who was drinking alcohol with his coffee would probably feel the effects of caffeine about five times longer than would an Englishwoman who smoked cigarettes but did not drink or use oral contraceptives. If the man had liver damage, the difference could be even more dramatic. Remember this variability the next time you hear apparently contradictory reports from your friends about what caffeine does to them.
*Richard M. Gilbert, *Caffeine: The Most Popular Stimulant*, p. 62.

Caffeine and most other chemical compounds you ingest ultimately make their way to the liver, the body's central blood purification factory. The bloodstream carries caffeine from the stomach and intestines, throughout the body, and, ultimately, by means of the hepatic portal vein, through the liver. There it is metabolized, or converted into secondary products, called "metabolites," which are finally excreted in the urine. More than 98 percent of the caffeine you consume is converted by the body in this way, leaving the remainder to pass through your system unchanged.

Caffeine's biotransformation is complex, producing more than a dozen different metabolites. The study of these transformations in human beings has been impeded by the fact that the metabolic routes for caffeine demonstrate a remarkable variety among different species. This means that experiments with rats, mice, monkeys, and rabbits, for example, are of limited value in advancing our knowledge of what happens to caffeine in human beings. However, over the past two decades, sophisticated techniques for identifying the components of the caffeine molecule, distinguishing them from very similar compounds, and tracing the fate of caffeine in the body have revealed the human metabolic tree in considerable detail.

These extensive studies disclose that the liver accomplishes the biotransformation of caffeine in two primary ways:

- Caffeine, a trimethylxanthine, may be "demethylated" into dimethylxanthines and monomethylxanthines by being stripped of either one or two of its three methyl groups.

- Caffeine may be oxidized and converted to uric acids. This means that an oxygen atom is added to the caffeine molecule.

The first of these mechanisms predominates, with the result that the principal metabolites of caffeine found in the bloodstream are the dimethylxanthines: paraxanthine, into which more than 70 percent of the caffeine is converted, theophylline, and theobromine. Paraxanthine is thus a sort of second incarnation of caffeine.

Although there are multiple alternative paths by which caffeine is metabolized in human beings, all of these pathways end in one or another uric acid derivative, which is then excreted in the urine. Complicating this picture is the fact that the profile of urinary metabolites, that is, the relative mix of the final metabolic products, exhibits marked variation among individuals, with differences observed as between children and adults, smokers and non-smokers, women who are taking oral contraceptives and those who are not.

An additional complicating factor is the fact that chemical metabolism can present cybernetic dynamics, which in this case means that the very process of metabolizing a methylxanthine can alter the speed at which additional amounts of methylxanthines will be metabolized. For example, it has been shown that the methylxanthine theobromine, a constituent of cacao and one of the primary metabolites of caffeine, is a metabolic inhibitor of theobromine itself, of theophylline, and possibly of caffeine as well. Studies reveal that daily intake of theobromine decreases the capacity to eliminate methylxanthines. This could mean, for example, that if you regularly eat chocolate, coffee or tea may keep you awake longer. Conversely, subjects on a methylxanthine-free diet for two weeks increased their capacity to eliminate theobromine. The fact that asthma patients being treated with theophylline need careful monitoring and frequent dosage adjustments is probably a result of these cybernetically governed variations in methylxanthine metabolism.

One of the challenges faced by researchers attempting to analyze any chemical compound's health effects is the fact that a drug's metabolites often have more significant effects than did the original drug itself. Scientists are still unsure as to what degree and in what respects caffeine's metabolites are responsible for its effects, although most would agree that its methylxanthine products contribute to the physical and mental stimulation that is a hallmark of caffeine consumption.

Caffeine gets in and out of your body quickly. The same high solubility in water that facilitates its distribution throughout the body also expedites its clearance from the body. Because caffeine passes through the tissues so completely, it does not accumulate in any body organs. Because it is not readily soluble in fat, it cannot accumulate in body fat, where it might otherwise have been retained for weeks or even months, as are certain other psychotropic drugs such as marijuana. Because caffeine also demonstrates a relatively low level of binding to plasma proteins, its metabolism is not prolonged by the sequential process by which, in chemicals that are highly bound, additional amounts dissociate from the protein as the unbound fraction is excreted or metabolized, extending the active life of the drug in the body.

The degree to which a drug lingers in the body, its kinetic profile, is quantified by what physiologists call its "half-life," the length of time needed for the body to eliminate one-half of any given amount of a chemical substance. For most animal species, including human beings, the mean elimination half-life of caffeine is from two to four hours, which means that more than 90 percent has been removed from the body in about twelve hours. However, the observed half-life can be influenced by several factors and therefore demonstrates considerable individual and group variation.

For example, women metabolize caffeine about 25 percent faster than men. But if women are using oral contraceptives, their rate of caffeine metabolism is dramatically slowed. In addition, pregnancy results in a considerable increase the half-life with a concomitant increase in exposure by the fetus.[4] Because caffeine is metabolized in the liver, hepatic impairment will also slow caffeine's metabolism. Newborn infants are dramatically less capable of metabolizing caffeine than are adults, probably because their livers are unable to produce the requisite enzymes, an incapacity that extends the drug's half-life in them to eighty-five hours. Some studies suggest that many other factors, including the use of other drugs, can raise or lower the metabolic rate from the mean value. For example, cigarette smoking doubles the rate at which caffeine is eliminated, which means that smokers can drink more coffee and feel it less than non-smokers. Drinking alcohol slows the elimination rate, which means that drinkers feel the caffeine in their coffee more than non-drinkers.[5] Research has even suggested that the rate of caffeine metabolism varies among the races, based on findings that Asians metabolize the drug more slowly than Caucasians.[6]

Relative Half-Life of Caffeine

Subject	Half-Life (in hours)
Healthy adults	3 to 7.5 (mean, 3.5)
Pregnant women	<18
Preterm infants	65 to 100
Term infants	82
3- to 4.5-month-olds	14.4

Adapted from *Drug Facts and Comparisons*, p. 928.

These metabolic findings help us to understand the strong social association between cigarettes and coffee. We picture the writer at his word processor, drinking big mugs of strong coffee as he puffs away at an endless sequence of smokes. We also imagine the typical coffeehouse habitué, gesticulating in a cloud of smoke as he converses with his fellow coffee drinkers. These images make sense. Heavy smokers, to achieve the same stimulating effects, would have to drink far more coffee than non-smokers. See part 5 of this book, "Caffeine and Health," for a full discussion of how heavy caffeine use may delay or prevent some of the serious lung complications that can result from smoking, which would constitute an additional strong bond between the two.

The metabolic profile of caffeine may also help to account for the common attempt to use caffeine to combat the effects of alcohol. It is true that the degree of alcohol intoxication is a function of the alcohol level in the blood, a level that cannot be altered by caffeine. However, caffeine, because it is felt more persistently by those who are drinking alcohol, may in fact have a more sustained stimulating effect and in this way help the drinker dissipate the grogginess that is associated with excess boozing.[7]

The French essayist Michel de Montaigne (1533–92) did not trust physicians because he thought that each person, knowing himself best, is the best judge of the conditions conducive to his own health. Today nearly everyone agrees that good medical doctors and their expert care are indispensable for well-being. Nevertheless, even our quick review of the variability and complexity of caffeine's metabolism suggests that, whatever the general profile of its behavioral and physical effects, each person must consider his own personal and medical history in order to understand how caffeine might affect him.

Mechanism of Action: Caffeine Kicks In

Most caffeine advocates and many caffeine opponents agree that caffeine helps to keep a person awake, increases energy, improves mood, and enhances the ability to think clearly. In an effort to discover how and to what degree caffeine does these and other things, scientists have investigated it more extensively than any other drug in history. Central to the long-standing debate over health concerns about the use of coffee and tea was the question of how these drinks do what they do, that is, what caffeine's mechanism of action in the human body is. The Russo-Swiss scientist Gustav von Bunge, a late-nineteenth-century professor at Basel University, who originated the concept of the hematogen in 1885, authored a precursor of contemporary theories. Bunge hypothesized that an unconscious longing of the body to increase its stores of xanthine, a substance present in small quantities in all tissues, was satisfied by caffeine, because of their chemical similarity.[8] Although this explanatory mechanism is fanciful by today's scientific standards, it does recognize caffeine's membership in the xanthine family and attempts to tie its action to the functions of related compounds naturally occurring in the body.

In approaching the question of how caffeine works, scientists today are confronted with the complex circumstance that the drug produces an effect, and in certain instances more than one effect, on the cardiovascular, respiratory, renal, and central and peripheral nervous systems. Partly as a consequence of this complexity, no one has identified caffeine's mechanism of action with any certainty. Particularly unclear are the sources of its psychostimulant and cardiovascular effects.

A good way to begin our inquiry into the possible mechanisms underlying caffeine's effects is to briefly consider the ways other stimulants, such as amphetamine and cocaine, have been understood to operate.

Stimulants seem to work in one of two ways, as agonists or antagonists. Agonists are substances that aid drug or bodily processes by increasing or decreasing the production or effectiveness of hormones or neurotransmitters that, through the modulation of neuromediators, cause nerve cells to fire more frequently and more energetically. Antagonists, or agents that work to reduce the action of drug or bodily processes, augment or diminish the uptake of neurotransmitters that, had they been allowed to reach their uptake sites, would have caused the nerve cells to fire more or less frequently or energetically. In rough laymen's terms, the stimulants in the first group help you generate or utilize a charge of energy, while those in the second group delay the dampening or dissipation of whatever energy is already circulating.

Amphetamine and methamphetamine work in the first of the ways described above. Amphetamines are essentially artificial adrenaline, and, when they circulate in the bloodstream, all the effects of increased adrenaline production are experienced. Amphetamine exerts most of its central nervous system (CNS) effects by releasing oxygen-containing organic compounds, or amines, from their storage sites in the nerve terminals. Its analeptic, or alerting, effect and a component of its muscle-stimulating action are thought to be mediated by the release of the hormone norepinephrine by the brain. Other components of motor stimulation and the stimulating effects of amphetamine are probably caused by the release of the neurotransmitter dopamine.

Cocaine works in the second way. Where amphetamine stimulates increased production of a neurotransmitter such as dopamine, cocaine achieves many reinforcing effects by inhibiting the uptake of dopamine by the neurons. Both mechanisms result in increased concentrations of dopamine at the synapses, or junctures connecting the neurons.

Although the use of stimulants in both categories can be self-reinforcing, only stimulants that depend for their effects on the first mechanism tend to produce tolerance and physical dependence, two major clinical manifestations of addiction. Stimulants that depend for their effects on the second mechanism tend to remain effective at or near the original dose, and, although they may produce psychical habituation, that is, a strong mental craving, they do not create a true physical dependence or metabolic tolerance characterized by somatic, or bodily, withdrawal symptoms.

Modern investigations into the pharmacology of caffeine are both intricate and inconclusive. Although techniques have become dramatically more sophisticated in the past few decades and researchers have applied tremendous energies and considerable resources to unraveling the tangled skein of caffeine's course of action in the human body, the results are not only difficult for a layman to understand but are ambiguous and tentative at best, even when considered by the experts. Three theories have successively enjoyed favor in the last two decades, and two of these three have already been discredited. The fate of the third remains undecided.

The three major theories that have been recently adduced to explain the mechanism of action of caffeine and the other methylxanthines are:

- Calcium mobility theory or the translocation of intracellular calcium;
- Phosphodiesterase inhibition theory, or the mediation by increased accumulation of cyclic adenosine monophosphate (cAMP) due to inhibition of phosphodiesterase; and
- Adenosine blockade theory, or the competitive blockade of adenosine receptors.

Calcium Mobility Theory

Inotropic agents are drugs that increase the force of cardiac muscle contraction, thereby tending to increase cardiac output. The most important group of inotropic agents includes digitalis, found in the foxglove plant, which has been used to stimulate the heart muscle in cardiac arrest for hundreds of years. There are several classes of inotropic agents with different mechanisms of action. One type of inotropic agent is caffeine and related methylxanthines, such as theophylline.

Inotropic agents can influence the body's response to neurotransmitters through affecting the output of neuromediators such as cyclic adenosine 3-, 5-monophosphate, which indirectly increases the influx of calcium ions into the cells, and thereby increases the force of contraction of the heart muscles. An increase in intracellular calcium increases the force of contraction, since intracellular calcium ions are responsible for initiating the shortening of muscle cells.

It now appears that caffeine achieves these effects only at toxic dose levels, from ten to a hundred times greater than those normally consumed in coffee, tea, or soft drinks. Consequently it is virtually impossible that calcium translocation is important in explaining the general effects of dietary caffeine.

Phosphodiesterase Inhibition: The cAMP Cycle of Energy Release

The human body stores energy in the muscles in the form of sugars called "glycogens." When you need a burst of energy, for example, when you are exercising or when you have delayed eating, glycogen is quickly released and burned as fuel. In the late 1950s, researchers discovered that a hormone called cyclic adenosine monophosphate, or "cAMP," which mediates the actions of many neurotransmitters and hormones in the nervous system, played a central role in the regulation of glycogen metabolism. It was demonstrated that, by increasing the persistence of cAMP, through a relatively complex process involving the inhibition of another hormone, phosphodiesterase, caffeine prolongs or intensifies the effect of adrenaline and thus enhances the ability of your body to burn glycogen. This mechanism was widely advanced as the mechanism of caffeine's stimulating action in the body.

However, the effect of caffeine on cAMP is modest, even at concentrations well above typical plasma concentrations in humans. In fact, in order to achieve blood levels of caffeine equal to those in the studies supporting this hypothesis, a 200-pound man would have to drink fifty cups of coffee in a few minutes. Thus, as with the intracellular calcium hypothesis, the mechanism of phosphodiasterase inhibition appears to be of limited importance in explaining the effects of caffeine observed at the levels attained by its ordinary consumption.

Adenosine Blockade: The Newest Theory on the Block

If a neurotransmitter or neuromodulator is to achieve any effect, it must reach the sites designed to accomplish its uptake into the human nervous system. Any substance that blocks this uptake prevents or reduces the effects of the neurotransmitter or neuromodulator it is blocking.

Adenosine is a neuromodulator with mood-depressing, hypnotic (sleep-inducing), and anticonvulsant properties and tends to induce hypotension (low blood pressure), bradycardia (slowed heartbeat), and vasodilatation. It also decreases urination and gastric secretion. Adenosine decreases the rate of spontaneous nerve cell firing and depresses evoked nerve cell potentials in the brain by inhibiting the release of other neurotransmitters that control the excitability, or responsiveness, of central neurons. The newest theory about caffeine's mechanism of action is that it acts as a competitive antagonist of adenosine; that is, it achieves most of its stimulant effects by blocking the uptake of, and thereby the actions of, adenosine.

To put matters simply, there are only so many receptors where adenosine can "plug itself in" to the nervous system, the way a key fits into a lock. Caffeine counterfeits the key. By doing so, caffeine blocks many of adenosine's points of entry, and thus prevents the body from being affected by adenosine's depressing and hypnotic effects. The result, according to this theory, which arose in the early 1970s, is that when we ingest caffeine we are unable to become tired or sleepy as we would otherwise have done. This theory holds that caffeine, by inhibiting the actions of adenosine, produces a whole slew of effects which are opposite adenosine's. Such a mechanism would account, for example, for caffeine's ability to increase respiration, urination, and gastric secretion.[9]

The ultimate evaluation of this theory of caffeine's mechanism of action is complicated by the variety of adenosine receptors and their differing roles in different tissues. However, because, with typical dietary doses of caffeine, blood levels of caffeine are believed to be too low to appreciably affect the non-adenosine mechanisms of action, adenosine antagonism appears to be the primary mechanism for caffeine's effects. It is not known if these other mechanisms may mediate some of the clinical effects produced when caffeine blood levels are unusually elevated, as may occur in cases of caffeine intoxication. A possible shortcoming of the adenosine blockade theory is that, even though it appears that the blockade of these receptors by caffeine has an important role in its pharmacology, caffeine's complex effects on behavior may not be fully explicable in terms of this blockade alone.[10] For example, alertness is informed by many neurotransmitter systems, only one of which is the noradrenalin system. Because chronic caffeine use effects changes in a number of other neurotransmitters, including norepinephrine, dopamine, serotonin, acetylcholine, GABA, and the glutamate systems in the brain, it remains for future researchers to determine what part if any these changes play in the behavioral effects associated with caffeine's use.

The very latest findings suggest that the adenosine story may actually tie caffeine's mechanism of action to that of other stimulants, such as amphetamines and cocaine, after all. In an unpublished study, Bridgette Garrett and Roland Griffiths maintain that caffeine enhances dopaminergic activity, "presumably by competitive antagonism of adenosine receptors that are co-localized and functionally interact with dopamine receptors. Thus caffeine, as a competitive antagonist at adenosine receptors, may produce its behavioral effects by removing the negative modulatory effects of adenosine from dopamine receptors, thus stimulating dopaminergic activity."[11] If true, this means that caffeine, like amphetamine or cocaine, *produces increased synaptic concentrations of dopamine*, an explanation consistent with findings that caffeine's behavioral effects are similar to those of these classic dopaminergically mediated stimulants.

Paradoxes and Problems and Unanswered Questions

A major paradox that arises when we attempt to understand caffeine's primary effects in terms of its role as an adenosine antagonist, or reuptake inhibitor, is that, were this its only operative mechanism, we would have trouble explaining the development of tolerance and physical dependence. Obviously tolerance, or increasing "resistance" to the drug, which requires caffeine users to progressively augment their dose in order to maintain its stimulant effects, is generally experienced by regular coffee drinkers; and dependence, as defined by the occurrence of withdrawal symptoms upon abrupt cessation of use, seems fairly common as well, and both tolerance and dependence have been well established in the literature.

However, the observation that caffeine produces increases of 10 to 20 percent in the number of brain adenosine receptors has prompted speculation that this increase may be the mechanism underlying withdrawal symptoms. The notion here is that the body is not completely fooled by the invasion of caffeine as an adenosine impostor and creates new receptor sites as compensation. When caffeine intake is reduced or eliminated, these extra sites combine with the original sites to uptake a greater amount of adenosine than is normal, with the result that adenosine's effects, including sleepiness and depression, are multiplied. Thus, this explanation would help account for many of the withdrawal symptoms produced by the abrupt reduction or cessation of caffeine use.

Unfortunately, there remain some inconsistencies that lead scientists to believe that this explanation is at best incomplete, for it cannot adequately serve to explain the development of tolerance. Tolerance to caffeine can increase to the point where it cannot be overcome by any dose, that is, where it becomes insurmountable, failing to duplicate its former effects in the user regardless of how high a dose is ingested, and there is no easy way to understand how the adenosine blockade theory could be consistent with insurmountable tolerances. In addition, as we have observed in our discussion of cocaine, there is no clear precedent of a competitive antagonist, such as caffeine, losing its potency after chronic administration. And, in fact, caffeine seems to retain its full potency as an adenosine antagonist, even in cases where an insurmountable tolerance to caffeine's stimulant effects has clearly been achieved. Finally, there seems to be no theoretical basis for expecting that an increase in the number of receptor sites should produce tolerance to the antagonist.

To put it simply, if caffeine's mechanism of action is explicable in terms of a competitive blockade of adenosine, we might expect withdrawal symptoms upon cessation of use, but we would still lack any explanation for the development of tolerance. Problems like these make it clear how far science still has to go if it is to reveal the secrets of caffeine. Exactly what it does and exactly how it does what it does are still largely unknown. Fortunately, it is possible to assess the effects of caffeine on human health by means of studies that are independent of a detailed knowledge of its underlying mechanisms.

Where the Caffeine Is

Few of us in Western countries today chew the leaves, bark, fruit, or nuts of caffeine-containing plants. We get our caffeine and other methylxanthines from drinks, foods, and pills. In the United States, about 70 percent of our caffeine is found in coffee beans, about 14 percent is found in tea leaves, more than 12 percent is in the form of the crystal caffeine, nearly 3 percent is found in cacao beans, and the remaining fraction from all other sources, including cola nut, maté, and guarana. Chocolate owes some of its stimulating power to the methylxanthine theobromine, and tea contains a small amount of theophylline. The caffeine in cola drinks is not derived from cola nuts, but is a superadded extract from coffee or tea. Caffeine is found in some over-the-counter medications, such as alertness aids and aspirin compounds, and in prescription medications, such as narcotic painkillers, as an adjuvant to their analgesic power.

In Appendix B are a number of charts listing various dietary and medicinal sources, with the amount of caffeine, theobromine, or theophylline found in each.

What Is a Cup?

A figure that is passed around, from one research paper or newspaper article to the next, is that a cup of coffee contains an average of 100 mg of caffeine. This sounds simple and straightforward and suggests that it is fairly easy to determine how much caffeine we are taking in when we have a cup of coffee. Unfortunately, when we scrutinize this figure, many uncertainties arise.

One problem is, exactly how much liquid is in a "cup of coffee"? A big mug or large paper cup, filled to the brim, may be 10 ounces or even 12 ounces or more. If not filled to the brim, a small cup may hold as little as 4 ounces. Amounts often quoted for cups are 5 ounces or 6 ounces, and the cup itself as a standard liquid measure is 8 ounces. So when we speak of a cup, we may be speaking of 4, 5, 6, 8, 10, 12 ounces or more. Another problem is, how much caffeine is in the coffee, ounce for ounce? This number will vary widely with such variables as method of preparation, type of coffee bean, method of roasting, and amount of coffee used.

The result of multiplying these two uncertainties produces a remarkably wide range for what might constitute the "correct" value for the amount of caffeine in a "cup" of coffee. A small cup of weak instant coffee might have as little as 50 mg. A large cup of infused coffee steeped for a long time with a lot of robusta beans might have 350 mg. Admittedly these are extreme values, but we believe that doses in the range of 100 to 250 mg are common. According to the Food and Drug Administration, a 5-ounce cup of coffee contains 40 to 180 mg of caffeine. Similar problems beset an evaluation of how much caffeine is found in a cup of tea.

Studies profiling the caffeine content of coffee and tea as actually served to restaurant customers or consumed at home are rare. One 1988 Canadian study, published in *Food and Chemical Toxicology*,[12] surveyed almost seventy "preparation sites," and found considerable differences from place to place and even between one day and the next at the same place. A review of the caffeine content of coffee brewed in almost sixty homes showed levels ranging from about 20 mg to nearly 150 mg per cup, more than a sevenfold variation. Coffee tested in eleven restaurants exhibited similar differences. Further, "decaf" served at restaurants sometimes had substantial amounts of caffeine. Finally, there were large variations in the caffeine content among the seventeen brands of instant coffee, even when prepared under controlled laboratory conditions.

The tests of tea showed a comparable variation in caffeine potency, although, of course, the average levels for tea were lower than those for coffee. According to the Republic of Tea Home Page, the following three factors determine how much caffeine is present in a cup of tea:

- The longer the leaves have been fermented, the greater their caffeine content. Green tea, which is unfermented, has the least caffeine; oolong, which is partially fermented, has about 50 percent more; and black tea, which is fully fermented, has three times as much.

- The longer tea is brewed, the more caffeine is present in the final drink. A cup of black tea infused for three minutes has 20 to 40 mg, while black tea infused for four minutes has 40 to 100 mg.[13]

- Finally, the caffeine in leaf powder, such as is found in tea bags, is more readily dissolved in water, and, all other factors being equal, it will have almost twice the caffeine as higher-quality full-leaf tea.[14]

It is almost impossible to guess, much less determine with any certainty, how much caffeine is in the coffee we order at restaurants, coffeehouses, and fast-food chains. Few field studies of caffeine content have been made. The following results are adapted from one such study, commissioned by New York City's WABC-TV Eyewitness News in December 1994, from Associated Analytical Laboratories. Note that a "medium" serving can be more than 13 ounces, and that the caffeine content per serving varies, even among these four samples of coffee, by nearly 100 percent.

Brand, Size	Net Serving Size	Total mg	mg/6oz
Dunkin' Donuts, regular	12.6 oz	275	147.6
Cooper's, medium	9.9 oz	146	99.6
West Side Deli, medium	13.5 oz	295	103.8
Dalton's Coffee, regular	8.9 oz	148	99.7

Similar discrepancies have been observed among the decaffeinated coffees served at leading chains across the country. In 1995, *Self* magazine submitted nine samples of decaffeinated coffee for analysis to Southern Testing & Research Laboratories in North Carolina. Most decaffeinated coffees had less than 10 mg per 6-ounce cup, but Starbucks had more than twice that much. As you review this chart, which also includes data from other similar studies, remember that most cups actually served contain at least 8 ounces of fluid. Results demonstrating such wide variability help to explain how even one cup of coffee sometimes seems to send you up like rocket, while other times a few cups won't even start your engines.

Caffeine Content in "Decaf"	
Brand	Mg/6-oz serving
Starbucks decaffeinated	25
Dunkin' Donuts decaffeinated	10
Au Bon Pain decaffeinated	7
Starbucks decaffeinated espresso	6
McDonald's decaffeinated	5
7-Eleven decaffeinated	4
Tetley decaffeinated tea	4
Cooper's decaffeinated	4
Dalton's decaffeinated	2
Sanka	1.5

Myths and misconceptions about caffeine content abound. The amount of caffeine that ends up in your cup of coffee is in part a function of the amount of caffeine contained in the beans you start with. In Appendix B is a list of the caffeine content of various beans as a percentage of total weight.[15] In general, the cheaper robusta beans contain almost double the caffeine found in the more expensive arabica beans. Although the two have an otherwise similar compositional profile of such components as minerals, proteins, and carbohydrates, arabica beans also contain significantly more lipids. Tea's variations in caffeine content depend primarily on the age of the leaves and on how the tea leaves have been cured. The caffeine content by percentage of weight of *sen-cha*, or green tea, is 2.8 percent; of *ma-cha*, or green powdered tea, is 4.6 percent; and of *ban-cha*, or coarse tea, is 2 percent.[16] Note that *ma-cha*, the tea most commonly used in the Japanese tea ceremony, which is green tea made from the smallest leaves of the just budding plant, has the highest concentrations of caffeine by weight of any tea, or of any plant source, for that matter. No caffeine is found in brews from herb and mint teas, as would be expected, since the plants from which they are made do not contain caffeine.

Maté also is an important source of caffeine, but it is even more difficult to estimate how much caffeine is in a cup of maté than it is to do so for a cup of coffee or tea. In addition to *Ilex paraguariensis*, as many as sixty varieties of plants are used in making the drink. To make matters even more confusing, the caffeine content of maté leaves varies widely according to their age at the time of harvesting. Young maté leaves have at least 2 percent caffeine of their dry weight, while adult leaves, those more than a year old, have about 1.5 percent, and old leaves, those more than two years old, have only about .7 percent.

Guarana is a major source of caffeine for millions of South Americans and is also widely sold in Europe and the United States in herbal elixirs and powders in health food stores. Typical of these products is "Magic Power," sold in two forms and which has the following ingredients (assuming 5 percent caffeine by weight in seeds as stated in their literature):

- 15 ml alcohol with 5 g guarana seeds, 250 mg caffeine per bottle
- Guarana capsules with 500 mg seeds, 25 mg caffeine per capsule

In Brazil, where guarana carbonated drinks are widely available, some consumers claim the effects are somewhat different from coffee's, because guarana doesn't produce jitters. This difference may be their imagination, or it may, as we have seen in other cases of natural drugs, be the result of the chemical complexity of guarana or the fact that it contains other active alkaloids in addition to caffeine.

The amount of caffeine found in chocolate and other cacao products is relatively small. A 1.58-ounce milk chocolate Hershey bar has 12 mg, and an average 6-ounce cup of chocolate prepared from a mix has 5 mg. Appendix B lists the caffeine content of other chocolate products.[17]

So how much caffeine *is* in a cup of coffee? Most cups of coffee of about 6 ounces probably contain between 60 and 180 mg of caffeine, which means that 100 mg, the value usually adduced, is as good as any. This is the value repeated throughout this book, and it is meant to be understood in the context of all the reservations and qualifications expressed in this section. The actual content in your cup can range from 40 mg to 400 mg.

Soft Drinks

Soft drinks are a major dietary source of caffeine. The amount in each varies widely. Jolt Cola, at or near the top of any list, has 70 mg in a 12-ounce can, Coca-Cola has 46 mg, and Canada Dry Diet Cola has 1 mg. Coca-Cola has 7.2 mg more caffeine in a 12-ounce serving than its nearest rival in market share, Pepsi, according to the FDA. The agency says the differences don't appear to have any health consequences. Even though caffeine is on the FDA's GRAS list, the list of food additives "generally recognized as safe," the agency has expressed reservations about excessive caffeine consumption by children and any consumption by pregnant women. But FDA spokesman Jim Greene said in reference to most of the soft drinks ranked, "the effect of the milligram differences among these products is basically nil in the long run."

Interestingly, 7-Up, one of the best-selling soft drinks in the United States, has made the absence of caffeine the basis for a recent advertising campaign.

Over-the-Counter and Prescription Medications

Caffeine is used as one ingredient in a variety of over-the-counter and prescription compounds. The FDA's National Center for Drugs and Biologics lists more than one thousand over-the-counter brands with caffeine as an ingredient. These fall into four categories: analgesics, cold remedies, appetite suppressants, and diuretics. Several of the most popular brands are listed in the appendix. In addition, caffeine is the only active ingredient in a number of so-called alertness aids, such as Vivarin, which contains 200 mg per pill, and NoDoz, which contains 100 mg per pill.

Where the Theobromine and Theophylline Are

Each of the methylxanthines considered here—caffeine, theobromine, and theophylline—acts as a physical and mental stimulant, but each has a somewhat different profile of somatic effects. For example, theobromine is a more potent diuretic than either caffeine or theophylline, while theophylline is more suitable for use as a bronchodilator. Cacao is the major source of theobromine, although it contains small amounts of caffeine as well, and its total methylxanthine content will vary with the variety of the plant and the fermentation process. Tea contains a small amount of theophylline in addition to its predominant methylxanthine, caffeine. Maté leaves are a small source of these methylxanthines, though the amounts are so small that some investigators have failed to detect them. The dried leaf has been reported to contain 0.3 percent theobromine and .004 percent theophylline by weight.[18] In addition to caffeine, theobromine, and theophylline, there are other, so-called minor, purine alkaloids, which are found in extremely tiny amounts in coffee.

Methylxanthine Content of Cacao Products

Chocolate Product	Percent Methylxanthine by Weight
Sweet chocolate	.36% to .63% theobromine .017% to .125% caffeine
Cocoa butter	1.9% theobromine .21% caffeine
Chocolate liquor or baking chocolate	1.2% theobromine .21% caffeine
Milk chocolate	.15% theobromine .02% caffeine

Product	Caffeine %	Theophylline %	Theobromine %
Coffee	1.34	trace	trace
Tea	3.23	.03	.17
Cacao	.20	trace	1.50
Maté, cola nut, guarana	2.0	——	.10

Extracting Caffeine: Industrial Processes and Mr. Wizard's Laboratory

The United States imports great quantities of caffeine for medical purposes and for spiking soft drinks, most of which is extracted from poor-quality coffee beans or waste tea leaves or collected as a by-product of the decaffeination of coffee and tea. Two techniques are used to produce decaffeinated coffee: bean decaffeination and extract decaffeination. Both are performed on the raw beans to minimize spoilage or loss of aroma.

Bean decaffeination is used when the bean moisture level is less than 40 percent. This process involves static or rotating drums with a water-saturated solvent, such as dichloromethane or supercritical carbon dioxide, selective for caffeine.

Extract decaffeination is used when the bean moisture content is more than 60 percent. In this process, raw coffee beans are usually soaked in nearly boiling water for a few minutes to a few hours, and the resulting liquid is decaffeinated either by liquid-liquid extraction with any of the solvents used in the first method or by selective absorption of caffeine on acid-treated active carbon. Alternative adsorption processes which do not rely on solvents to recover the caffeine from the extract are called "water decaffeination."[19]

Extracting caffeine crystals from tea or coffee is a standard first-year organic chemistry experiment. Many people, far removed from academic laboratories, have wondered if there was some easy way to do the same. An amateur chemist provided an approximation of a home extraction process, although with the availability of Vivarin at every corner pharmacy and supermarket, its hard to understand why anyone would risk trying it, something that we, in any case, strongly recommend against:

Mix 180 proof ethanol with very finely ground coffee and mash together. Filter off the solvent. Evaporate the paste and, when dry, dissolve in boiling vodka, until the volume is reduced by about 80 percent. Allow the liquid to sit and cool for two days. If you have done everything right, when you return you should find white caffeine crystals precipitating from the solution.[20]

Pure caffeine is extremely toxic, and must be handled with hooded ventilation systems, masks, and gloves. Largely for this reason, chemical supply companies are not permitted to sell it to individual purchasers.

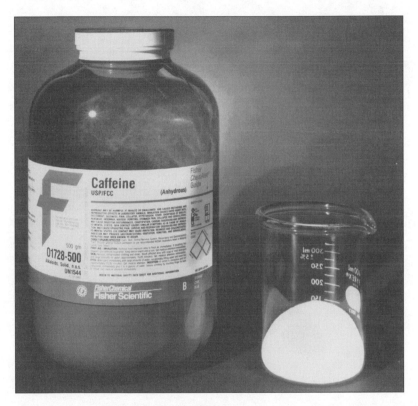

Jar containing pure pharmaceutical-grade caffeine, featuring a chilling warning label, which reads in part: "**WARNING! MAY BE HARMFUL IF INHALED OR SWALLOWED. HAS CAUSED MUTAGENIC AND REPRODUCTIVE EFFECTS IN LABORATORY ANIMALS. INHALATION CAUSES RAPID HEART RATE, EXCITEMENT, DIZZINESS, PAIN, COLLAPSE, HYPOTENSION, FEVER, SHORTNESS OF BREATH. MAY CAUSE HEADACHE, INSOMNIA, NAUSEA, VOMITING, STOMACH PAIN, COLLAPSE AND CONVULSIONS. MAY CAUSE DIGESTIVE DISTURBANCES, CONSTIPATION, CARDIAC DISORDERS, AND DEPRESSION. MAY CAUSE EPIGASTRIC PAIN, CARDIAC AND RESPIRATORY DISORDERS, AND DEPRESSED MENTAL STATES. EYE CONTACT MAY CAUSE IRRITATION, REDNESS, AND CONJUNCTIVITIS. INGESTION MAY PRODUCE GASTROINTESTINAL IRRITATION, VOMITING, AND CONVULSIONS. FATALITIES HAVE BEEN KNOWN TO OCCUR.** *Target Organs Affected*: Eyes, Skin, Central Nervous System, Repiratory and Gastrointestinal Tract." (Photograph by Paul Barrow, Biomedical Communications, University of Pennsylvania Medical Center, © 1999 Bennett Alan Weinberg and Bonnie K. Bealer.)

caffeine and the plant kingdom

"My Vegetable Love ..."

It is probably significant that the most widespread words in the world—borrowed into virtually every language—are the names of the four great caffeine plants: coffee, cacao, cola, and tea.

—E. N. Anderson, *The Food of China*, 1988

Caffeine, a chemical sometimes called "theine," "guaranine," or "matein," according to whether tea, guarana, or maté, rather than coffee, is regarded as its eponymous natural source, occurs in the nuts, berries, beans, seeds, pods, hulls, leaves, and barks of several dozen varieties of plants. Every year, more than 120,000 tons of caffeine are consumed worldwide, enough to spike 260 cups of coffee or tea per person per year, or about five cups a week for every man, woman, and child on earth. A little over half of this tonnage comes from coffee beans and a little less than half of it comes from tea leaves. The remaining tiny fraction comes mostly from cacao pods, and also from maté leaves, cola nuts, and a small residue from all other sources.[1] (Because very little caffeine is synthesized in laboratories, we examine the provenance of caffeine exclusively in terms of its vegetable sources.)

Why Plants Contain Caffeine

Caffeine supplies people with a physical and mental boost. But why did plants evolve the ability to produce it? The answer is that caffeine provides plants with protection by killing harmful bacteria and fungi and causing sterility in certain destructive insects. Because, over the passage of years, caffeine permeates the surrounding soil, it may also inhibit the growth of weeds that might otherwise have choked the plants. Caffeine's potent antibiotic, antifungal, pest-killing powers may explain why *Coffea robusta*, which produces a larger amount of the drug, is much hardier than its more delicate cousin, *Coffea arabica*.

Source	Plant Part	Approx. caffeine by percentage of weight	Major sites of cultivation today	Popular mode of consumption
Coffee bean (*Coffea arabica* and *Coffea robusta*)	Seed	1.1 (arabica)– 2.2 (robusta)	Brazil, Colombia	Coffee
Tea (*Camellia sinensis*)	Leaf, bud	3.5	India, China	Tea
Cacao (*Theobroma cacao*)	Seed	.03	West Africa, Brazil	Cocoa and chocolate products
Cola nut (*Cola acuminata*, *Cola nitida*)	Seed	1.5	West Africa	Chewing cola nuts and cola tree
Maté (*Ilex paraguariensis*)	Leaf	<.7	South America	Yerba maté
Yaupon (*Ilex cassine*, *Ilex vomitoria*)	Leaf, berry	(unknown)	(not cultivated)	Cassina
Guarana (*Paulinia capana*)	Seed	>4	Brazil	Soft drinks and guarana bars
Yoco (*Paulliniayoco*)	Bark	2.7	South America	Yoco tea

Adapted from Spiller, p. 187.

Caffeine Vincit Omnia

Worldwide, 120,000 tons of caffeine are consumed annually:

- Coffee is the source of 54%
- Tea is the source of 43%
- Cocoa pods, cola nuts, maté leaves, guarana, are the source of 3%

1 ton = 910,000 grams = 9.1 million cups of coffee at 100 mg/cup
13.65 million cups of tea at 66 mg/cup

54% of 120,000 = 64,800 tons of caffeine from coffee per year

43% of 120,000 = 51,600 tons of caffeine from tea per year

58,968,000,000 grams » 600 billion cups of coffee a year @ 100 mg per cup

70,434,000,000 » 700 billion cups of tea a year @ 65 mg per cup

This adds up to 1,300 billion or 1.3 trillion cups of coffee and tea per year.

Some of these data are adapted from Gilbert.

However, in using caffeine as a biochemical weapon, plants are indeed "hoisted by their own petard," because the very drug that helps them destroy their enemies ultimately kills them as well. Nature's intricacy is again instanced in the mechanisms that caffeine-containing plants use in a doomed attempt to limit damage to themselves from caffeine's poisonous effects. For example, coffee seedlings produce and store caffeine away from the site of cell division, which are very sensitive to toxins. Nevertheless, caffeine eventually devastates the plants that produced it, for as caffeine-bearing bushes or trees age and the soil around them becomes increasingly rich in caffeine absorbed from the accumulation of fallen leaves and berries, it eventually attains a level toxic not only to microbial enemies but to the plant itself as well. It is partially because of this toxicity that coffee plantations tend to degenerate after ten to twenty-five years. In a sense, these plants lose their lives as a result of steadily producing the drug that humanity loves best.

One of the first scientists to explore the theory that caffeine production evolved to protect plants from insects was Dr. James Nathanson, a neurologist at Harvard Medical School. In an article published in 1984 in *Science* magazine, Nathanson proposed that caffeine and related compounds could be used as the basis for a new class of insecticides.[2] His tests with powdered tea and coffee, as well as with chemically pure caffeine and other methylxanthines, found that these compounds interfered with the behavior and growth of many insects and insect larvae. Mosquito larvae drowned when they became so confused that they could not swim to the surface to breathe. Concentrated caffeine killed adult insects in hours or days after exposure. Caffeine also demonstrated a considerable synergistic killing power when combined with other natural insecticides, sometimes increasing the effectiveness of known agents by a factor of ten.

The neurotoxicity of caffeine as a natural chemical defense mechanism for plants against insects explains the discombobulation of the spiders enlisted for a recent NASA study of the ways exposure to various chemicals alters the ways they spin their webs.[3] Some scientists think that spider web testing can replace some much more expensive toxicity testing in humans or higher animals. The theory is that the changes in the spider webs are a function of the degree of toxicity of the chemical administered prior to spinning. The more deformed a web becomes, the more toxic the chemical is supposed to have been. Because of the web's structural similarities to crystal lattices, the degree of web deformation can be quantified with statistical crystallography techniques. Using an image data-analysis program, the NASA scientists analyzed the images of webs spun by spiders who were sober and intoxicated on various substances in terms of "numbers of cells and average areas, perimeters, and radii of cells."[4]

The results are fairly clear and, if they can be generalized in any way to human beings, are not very encouraging for caffeine aficionados. In a "Talk of the Town" feature, a *New Yorker* columnist says that although they may not realize it, "scientists at NASA labs . . . have identified the chemical agent responsible for human error," by which he means caffeine:

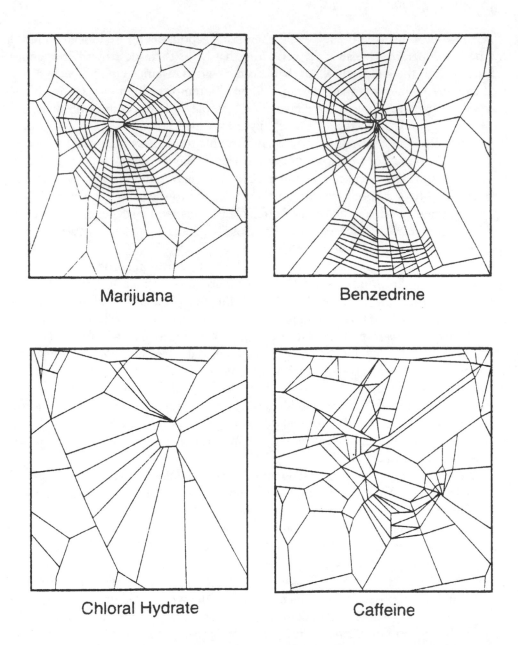

Drawing of spider webs spun under the influence of various psychoactive drugs. The web spun by *Araneus diadematus*, the common house spider, is altered when the spider is exposed to chemicals. When juxtaposed with the drawing of a normal web, four drawings of spider webs spun by spiders exposed to marijuana, benzedrine, chloral hydrate, and caffeine demonstrate varying degrees of malformation. The results are obvious, even without the use of a sophisticated graphic analyzer. Compared with the webs spun normally or under the influence of marijuana, benzedrine, or chloral hydrate, the one spun after the administration of caffeine is clearly the most deformed. Each of the other webs exhibits an evident "hub and spokes" pattern, presumably the most fundamental aspect of the web paradigm. The caffeine web has lost any trace of this design and is almost completely disrupted.

The structure of the web spun by the spider under the influence of marijuana is pretty close to the conventional one, but is unfinished. The benzedrine web is meticulous in places but has huge gaps. The chloral hydrate web is a stray collection of strands. The illuminating example is caffeine. Anyone who has ever had a tip from an excitable stockbroker go south, or had the rearview fall off his brand new car when he slammed the door and discovered it was made on the night shift, or examined the film of his baby's christening and found streaks of light in place of his child's beaming face will be struck by the slipshod, disorderly, ill-planned, chaotic, and slaphappy structure laid down by the spider intoxicated by caffeine.[5]

It should be remembered that if a range of doses has not been studied, comparisons as between different drugs are virtually meaningless. And, of course, in comparing the effects of caffeine with those of other chemicals, both the *New Yorker* and NASA seem to be forgetting that caffeine acts as a natural chemical defense mechanism for plants against insects, a fact that may go a long way in explaining the perplexity of the poor spider.[6]

Despite caffeine's neurotoxic effects on some harmful insects, one species of beneficial bugs seem to enjoy the caffeine rush, at least if we are to believe the account of John Klapac, an East Coast beekeeper who feeds his little buzzers with the dregs from 55-gallon commercial containers of soft drink syrup. Klapac explains, "The bees love it—they get hyper from all the caffeine." Evidently his bees don't have access to enough nectar to last through the winter, and the sugary syrup, which they transform into a honeylike substance, is a perfect nutritional supplement. "Strawberry syrup makes a red product with strawberry flavor," he adds, "and cola syrup produces an almost black substance with a cola-like taste."

The Coffee Shrub (genus *Coffea*)

Coffee is a tropical glossy-leafed evergreen shrub or bush belonging to the genus *Coffea* of the Rubiacæe, or madder, family that is the source of several powerful pharmaceutical agents in addition to caffeine, including ipecac and quinine. Most of the twenty-five-odd species of the coffee plant grow wild in the tropics of the eastern hemisphere. The branches of every species bear small, creamy white flowers with a sweet fragrance like jasmine blossoms. Although *Coffea* is divided botanically into four groups, the coffee we drink comes from plants that all belong to one of these groups, *Eucoffea*. Some wild members of the other three groups are used by African natives as decorative vegetation and others as stimulants, but their fruit is generally inedible, and they have no currency in commerce.

The earliest known and cultivated species is *Coffea arabica*, "the coffee shrub of Arabia," indigenous to the Ethiopian massif. Now grown mostly in Latin America, it accounts for 75 percent of all coffee consumption worldwide. The other commercially important species, *Coffea canephora*, the main variety of which is *robusta*, supposed to have originated in Uganda and the Congo, is widely cultivated in Africa and Madagascar. Both species are also cultivated in Asia.

Engraving from Dufour, *Traitez Nouveaux*. This engraving shows a branch from the coffee tree, a cylindrical instrument for roasting coffee, and a few roasted coffee beans themselves. (The Library Company of Philadelphia)

Component	Arabica (mg/kg)	Robusta (mg/kg)
Caffeine	9,000–14,000	15,000–26,000
Theobromine	35–40	25–80
Theophylline	7–23	86–344
Paraxanthine	3–4	8–9
Theacrine	0	11
Liberine	5	7–11
Methylliberine	0	3

Adapted from Garattini, "Composition of Coffee."

In addition to *Coffea arabica* and *Coffea robusta*, the species *Coffea liberica*, native to Liberia, is much larger and sturdier than either and is under commercial cultivation in Africa. It is reported to produce an inferior-tasting brew that is high in caffeine. An allied Liberian species, *Coffea excelsa*, a vigorous plant discovered in 1905, yields beans that are small, bright yellow, and, like *liberica*, high in caffeine.

By the beginning of the eighteenth century, the Dutch, French, Spanish, Portuguese, and English began introducing *Coffea arabica* into tropical colonies from Java to Jamaica. After obtaining the plant in 1725, Brazil quickly became and still remains the world's largest supplier of coffee.

The Tale of Gabriel d'Erchigny de Clieu and the Purloined Plant

One of the great romances in the history of caffeine is the saga of how, in 1723, the prolific progenitor of what was to become the great Latin American plantations made the journey to the New World in the exigent care of a young aristocratic French military officer. The story is rooted over a century earlier, at a time when the Dutch, foremost in international trade, became the first to cultivate the exotic coffee tree in Europe after successfully transporting a specimen from Mocha in 1616. Efforts to cultivate seedlings in France failed until 1714, when the French government negotiated the delivery of a healthy five-foot tree from the Amsterdam botanical gardens established by Willem Wissen, which was presented by the burgomaster to Louis XIV and ceremoniously planted by the famous botanist de Jussieu in the Jardin des Plantes in Paris. In a seminal historical position similar to that of three "Oriental" stallions, Darley Arabian, Godolphan Barb, and Byerly Turk, the acknowledged ancestors of all thoroughbred horses, this anonymous Arabian plant is known to have been the progenitor of most of the coffee trees of South America, Central America, and Mexico.

Gabriel d'Erchigny de Clieu, an enterprising naval officer, harbored a clandestine ambition when he temporarily returned to France from his post in colonial Martinique: He planned to secret a coffee plant from the royal gardens and introduce its cultivation to the West Indies. Getting his hands on one of the few rare bushes then under cultivation in Europe posed a daunting challenge. De Jussieu, conservator of the royal botanical gardens, guarded his precious charges with the jealousy of the dragon around the tree of golden apples. But, like Jason, de Clieu cannily circumvented the dreadful monitor that stood between him and the completion of his quest. We learn from his correspondence that, plunging into the intrigue of the court of Louis XIV, he employed the services of an aristocratic young lady to prevail on M. de Chirac, the royal physician, to purloin one of the exotic plants from the royal conservatory.

Embarking at Nantes in 1723, de Clieu, according to his published accounts, brought with him a single plant, which he installed in a glass-framed box intended to serve as a portable greenhouse. The crossing was a difficult one, and de Clieu heroically surmounted both human and natural adversities in order to triumphantly bring his charge to port in Martinique.

A fellow passenger, a young man who spoke French with a Dutch accent and was, perhaps, a Dutch espionage agent acting to protect his country's trade interests, played the villain of the story by trying, unsuccessfully, to spoil de Clieu's project. On one occasion de Clieu surprised the mysterious stranger when, after opening the framed glass enclosure, the interloper had reached in to snap off a twig. De Clieu writes:

> It is useless to recount in detail the infinite care that I was obliged to bestow upon this delicate plant during a long voyage, and the difficulties I had in saving it from the hand of a man who, basely jealous of the joy I was about to taste, through being of service to my country, and being unable to get this coffee-plant away from me, tore off a branch.[7]

In addition to being menaced by this spiteful nemesis, de Clieu shared with his fellow passengers a narrow escape from capture by Tunisian pirates and another from destruction in a heavy storm, which smashed the greenhouse but left the slip unscathed. However, the greatest threat to survival, both of the people and the plant, was a long calm that sustained itself until the supply of drinking water was nearly exhausted and what was left had to be rationed for the remaining weeks of the trip. De Clieu writes:

> Water was lacking to such an extent that for more than a month I was obliged to share the scanty ration of it assigned to me with my coffee plant, upon which my happiest hopes were founded and which was the source of my delight. It needed much succor, the more in that it was extremely backward, being no larger than the slip of a pink.[8]

De Clieu by no means relaxed his vigilant care when at last disembarking in Martinique, where he planted the precious slip on his estate at Precheur. He writes:

> Arriving at home my first care was to set out my plant with great attention in the part of my garden most favorable to its growth. Although keeping it in view, I feared many times that it would be taken from me; and I was at last obliged to surround it with thorn bushes and to establish a guard about it until it arrived at maturity. . . . This precious plant which had become still more dear to me for the dangers it had run and the cares it had cost me.

As a result of his ministrations, the tree "multiplied with extraordinary rapidity and success," and the first harvest was gathered in 1726. De Clieu describes the ensuing tropical storms, in the course of which Martinique's cacao plantations were apocalyptically destroyed, clearing the way for the progeny of his charge. He was so successful that he was "enabled to send plants to Santo Domingo, Guadeloupe and other adjacent islands," where they also flourished.

Even without the advantage of a flood to clear the ground, coffee plantations sprang up in other French colonies in the New World and, in fact, the first coffee bush planted in Brazil, destined to become the world's biggest coffee supplier, was a descendant of this French planting as well. By the end of the eighteenth century, coffee was under cultivation throughout the West Indies and in Mexico, Costa Rica, Venezuela, Guatemala, and Puerto Rico. In 1746, de Clieu, by then a ship's captain and honorary commander of the Royal and Military Order of Saint Louis, was presented by the secretary of the navy at the court of Louis XV. The king, who, unlike his father Louis XIV, had learned to appreciate the beverage, honored de Clieu for his cultivation of coffee by returning him to Martinique as governor of the island.

Oddly enough, the story of Lt. Colonel Francisco de Melo Palheta, the military man responsible for planting the first coffee tree in Brazil, which itself became the progenitor of that country's largest single crop to this day, is evocative of de Clieu's. Palheta was a Spanish officer sent from Brazil to French Guiana to arbitrate an international controversy. While there, he engaged in an affair with the governor's wife, who, in recognition of his erotic favors, gave him a bouquet at his departure in which was concealed a cutting of a coffee tree. Hitherto, the plant had been jealously and successfully kept from the Spanish colonies by the French and Dutch, but this smuggled lover's gift breached their security, and so the Brazilian coffee line began.

Coffee Cultivation

Coffea arabica flourishes in areas with moderate rainfall, about forty to sixty inches evenly distributed throughout the year, and at altitudes of between four thousand and five thousand feet above sea level (although in Ecuador it is cultivated as high as ninety-four hundred feet, while in subtropical Hawaii it is grown at sea level), and grows best where the temperature remains close to 68 degrees Fahrenheit. Unlike most tropical plants, *Coffea arabica* can withstand low temperatures, although it is killed by frost. While the wild coffee tree grows to a height of twenty-five to thirty-five feet, the commercially cultivated variety of *Coffea arabica* attains only about sixteen feet and, to facilitate harvesting, is frequently trimmed to the height of a man.

Coffea arabica produces abundant small, white, highly fragrant blossoms that develop in clusters, three or four years after planting. Flowers that open on a dry, sunny day produce more fruit than those opening on a wet day because of a greater opportunity for wind and insect pollination. The stunning beauty of a coffee estate in flower is transient: After two or three days, even gentle breezes will strip the flowers away, leaving behind only the dark green foliage and the berries. About six to eight months later, what are called the berries (or, more properly, the drupes), about one-half to three-quarters of an inch long, ripen, changing from dark green to yellow, then to red, and finally to deep crimson. Because of their size, color, and gloss at maturity, the ripe berries are called "cherries" by farmers and processors. Beneath the red skin of these cherries is a moist, sweet-tasting fleshy pulp, good for eating, that surrounds the green coffee bean. Most cherries contain two locules, each locule housing a seed, or bean. The seeds are each sheathed by two coverings: a thin, hard endocarp, called the "parchment," and a thin translucent membranous pellicle, called the "silver skin." Some cherries contain three beans, while others, generally those at the tips of the branches, contain only one round bean, known as a "peaberry." All parts of the fruit and the leaves contain caffeine.

The berries are picked by hand or shaken from the bush onto mats, producing a yield per acre that varies enormously, because a single tree, depending on its individual character and on climate and altitude, can produce between one and twelve pounds of dried beans a year. The best time for harvesting varies with the region in which the coffee is grown. Under ideal conditions, as in Java, planting is staggered throughout the year, blooming and fruiting are continuous, and therefore the coffee can be harvested almost continuously. Where conditions are less than perfect, as in parts of Brazil, coffee is harvested in the winter only.

Gourmet coffees are exclusively high-quality, mild varieties of *Coffea arabica* ("mild" in the coffee trade means lacking harsh, hard taste characteristics), principally from Latin America, excluding Brazil. Excellent varieties of *Coffea arabica* are also obtained from Kenya, Tanzania, Ethiopia, and Cameroon and the Yemen. Originally, all fine coffees came exclusively from the Yemen, from where they were shipped to the world through the port of Mocha. Soon after World War I, the wells of Mocha dried up, and coffee cultivation was largely abandoned. Today, the relatively small amount of coffee exported from the Yemen leaves through the port of Hodeida, but it still carries the traditional name of Mocha, which has never stopped being synonymous in the public's mind with the best beans. Most Brazilian coffees are also varieties of *Coffea arabica*, but they are characterized by less refined flavor and aroma than those of the mild group.

In Costa Rica, competitively cultivating the *Coffea arabica* plant is essential to the nation's livelihood. This means producing an abundant crop and processing it quickly and well. Traditionally, small coffee farmers tended their patches of plants. Today, they are being replaced by large plantation holders, who are increasingly planting an improved strain of *Coffea arabica* called "sun coffee." The name for this variety, developed in the early 1970s, derives from the fact that, unlike other strains of the coffee tree that require a mixture of sun and shade, these new plants need, and can stand up to, the unremitting tropical blaze. That means that they can be planted without the benefit of a surrounding shade species. This is good news for farmers who are trying to increase coffee yields, because the entire acreage under cultivation can be dedicated exclusively to coffee plants. As against this agrarian strategy, some environmentalists argue that creating an exclusive crop, or monocrop, of coffee results in catastrophic soil erosion, causing massive damage to the land within a few years.

In 1898 the French merchant Emil Laurent took advantage of the recent discovery, made in Uganda near Lake Victoria, of *canephora*, a new species of *Coffea*. After identifying a variety of *canephora*, which he called "*Coffea lauurentii*," he brought it for marketing to a Belgian horticultural firm. The firm decided that applying the name "robusta" to this variety would be conducive to sales of this harsher and more heavily caffeine-charged brew by suggesting both a robust flavor and a robust kick. The beans from *Coffea robusta*, although yielding coffee with a flatter and less aromatic flavor than *Coffea arabica* varieties, are nevertheless widely used, particularly in the form of soluble, or instant, coffees.

The hardiness of the plant is also suggested by its name, for *Coffea robusta* possesses greater strength and, because it contains nearly twice the caffeine (1.3 percent of the dry weight of *arabica* beans, as compared with 2.4 percent of the dry weight of *robusta* beans), greater resistance to disease and insects than *Coffea arabica*. It yields more fruit, grows at lower altitudes and in a wider variety of soil conditions, and adapts to warm humid climates to which *Coffea arabica* is not well suited. It also produces a full crop within four years, less than half the time needed for *Coffea arabica*. *Coffea robusta* berries take from two to three months longer to ripen than do *Coffea arabica* berries, though the plants typically yield larger harvests. Harvesting is easier because the *Coffea robusta* berries stay on the tree when they are fully ripe, instead of dropping off as do *Coffea arabica* berries, and so the picking can be delayed to suit the planter's convenience. These differences mean that it costs less to grow and harvest *Coffea robusta* than *Coffea arabica* coffee, which accounts for its increasing use as a source of cheap blenders and as the basis of instant coffees, despite its inferior taste. Many familiar commercial coffee products are mixtures that combine the characteristics of different species and varieties, blended to satisfy a wide range of consumer tastes.

Like *Coffea arabica*, *Coffea robusta* flourishes between the Tropics of Capricorn and Cancer. *Coffea robusta* prefers rainfall of about 75 inches a year and temperatures of 60 to 80 degrees Fahrenheit. The biggest difference between the conditions favored by *Coffea arabica* and those favored by *Coffea robusta* is that *Coffea robusta* demonstrates a tolerance to more extreme conditions. Most notable is its ability to withstand humidity without succumbing to the bane of *Coffea arabica*, leaf spot disease (*Hemileia vastatrix*).[9]

Despite Laurent's efforts on behalf of *Coffea robusta*, *Coffea arabica* remains the more widely grown, but many regions where temperature and humidity are high, especially those that have experienced the devastation of leaf spot disease, have been replanted with *Coffea robusta*. *Coffea robusta* coffees are now the major species grown in the less mountainous regions closest to the equator. African varieties of *Coffea robusta* today represent more than 25 percent of all coffee used in the United States and Europe.[10]

Coffee Oddities and Curiosities

Those embarked on an ongoing hunt for the best cup of coffee should find it tantalizing to discover that there is a species superior to *Coffea arabica*—declared by many to be the species of genus *Coffea* producing the most aromatic and flavorful coffee beans in the world—that is currently unavailable and likely to remain so for the indefinite future. *Coffea stenophylla*, by historical accounts, was considered superior to *Coffea arabica* in a number of important respects: It is a hardier plant, it produces a larger crop, and, most importantly for the coffee connoisseur, the brewed beans have a richer taste. In these respects *Coffea stenophylla* would seem to combine the advantages of both *Coffea arabica* and *Coffea robusta* and go them each one better. But bad timing doomed *Coffea stenophylla* to the limbo of uncultivated crops. The plant was discovered growing wild in Sierra Leone and introduced to various English colonies in 1895, at the same time that a massive epidemic of rust disease was eradicating many plantations. To recover from the blight, the farmers needed a plant that would turn out a crop as quickly as possible. This pointed them away from *Coffea stenophylla*, the main disadvantage of which is requiring nine years to reach maturity, two years longer than *Coffea arabica* and five years longer than *Coffea robusta*. As a result, even though it's hardier and it produces more beans once it gets started, *Coffea stenophylla* has never gained a foothold in the marketplace.[11]

It has been reliably determined by French and German investigators that several species of *Coffea*, including *Coffea gallienii*, *Coffea bonnieri*, *Coffea mogeneti*, which grow wild in the Comoro Islands and Madagascar, are absolutely caffeine free. However they contain a bitter substance, cafamarine, that makes their beans unfit for use.[12]

A tea was and still is prepared from the leaves of the coffee plant, most notably in Arabia, Sumatra, and the West Indies. It is infused from the roasted leaves of the coffee tree in the same manner as regular tea, and it is preferred, where consumed, to coffee brewed from the bean.[13] In Sumatra the bean crop was frequently ravaged by insects, and the growers, seeking a substitute that would contain caffeine, collected the leaves in their stead. The discovery that the leaves are high in caffeine was exploited during World War I by Dutch factories, who bought them by the ton in order to extract the stimulant for use by combat troops.

Another sort of coffee tea is a peninsular habit of Arabia and has been since at least the middle of the sixteenth century. In the land from which the coffee bean came, a beverage, commonly preferred in summer because of its "cooling" humoral properties, and exclusively consumed by the discriminating, was brewed from the husks of the bean. The decoction is said to resemble a sort of spicy, aromatic tea more than it does either modern Western or Turkish coffee.

The Kentucky Coffee Tree (*Gymnocladus dioica*) is a plant native to central and eastern North America and eastern China. Settlers ground the seeds to make a drink with some resemblance to coffee. Like guarana and yoco, these plants contain lather-producing saponin, but, unlike them, do not contain any caffeine.[14]

In sum, the primary botanical differences between the most popular and widely used coffee plants, *Coffea arabica* and *Coffea robusta*, are these: *Coffea robusta* will grow at relatively low altitudes, will tolerate higher temperatures and heavier rainfall, demands higher soil humus content, and is generally more resistant to disease. *Coffea arabica* beans are oval and green to yellowish green in color, while *Coffea robusta* beans are rounder and tend toward brownish shades. Of course the most important difference between the two species as far as coffee drinkers are concerned is that coffee made from *Coffea arabica* tastes and smells much better. Avicenna, the great Arab philosopher and physician, may have gotten it right a thousand years ago when he recommended beans "of a lemon color, light, and of a good smell."[15]

The Tea Bush: *E Pluribus Unum* (*Camellia sinensis*)

There are many ways of classifying the drinks called "teas" and a bewildering variety of names for dozens of different types: black, green, oolong, China, Assam, flavored, scented, decaffeinated, tonics, barks, decoctions, infusions, and ptisanes, and an entire lexicon of trade names, such as "English Breakfast tea." These rubrics codify differences in botanical varieties, growing conditions, admixtures, and methods of processing tea, but also include many drinks made exclusively from herbs and plants that are botanically unrelated to tea.

In simple fact, the tea leaves used in brewing tea grow on a single species, *Camellia sinensis*, a plant native to northern India, Tibet, and possibly China, regions where it is still chiefly cultivated. Yet because of ignorance about the differences produced by different processing methods and the fact that *Camellia sinensis* boasts a great number of varieties, or subspecies, for centuries there was considerable confusion as to whether there was one or more species of the plant. It was not until 1958 that botanists agreed internationally that there was one species with many varieties. Two of these varieties, Assam and China tea, have major commercial importance.

The two-hundred-year-old confusion over how to classify the tea bush began with the father of all botanical nomenclature, Carl von Linné (1707–78), or Carolus Linnæus, Swedish botanist and inventor of the twofold naming system for classifying plants (which supplanted the clumsy Latin phrases employed previously) that is still used today. In *Species Plantarium* (1753), Linnæus divided tea into two species: the *viridis*, which produced green teas, and the *bohea*, which produced black. However, as stated

Engraving from Dufour, *Traitez Nouveaux*. This French engraving shows two Chinese farm workers with their wicker baskets harvesting "Chinese tea on the bush" in the highlands, an exotic image for the seventeenth-century European audience for whom it was created. (The Library Company of Philadelphia)

above, it is now accepted that all tea, including both the prolific Assam (*assamica*) and the hardy China (*sinensis*) teas, are varieties of a single species, *Camellia sinensis*.

The bewilderment over the meaning of tea types has been exacerbated by the fact that there are three distinct methods of processing tea leaves, each resulting in a recognizably different product: black tea, green tea, or oolong tea. Black tea (called "red tea" in China, after the color of the beverage rather than the darker color of the dried leaves) is created when fresh green leaves are withered after plucking, spread out to dry, and then crushed by rollers to bring out the aromatic oils; the crushed leaves then oxidize, or ferment, and assume their characteristic brown color. Green tea is produced by firing or steaming the fresh leaves immediately after picking, a step which prevents the leaves from oxidizing and precludes the natural fermentation that would otherwise occur. Oolong tea is prepared like black tea, but its leaves are allowed to ferment for only a short time before drying and turn only partially brown, acquiring a flavor that shares something of both black and green teas.[16]

The divisions of black, green, and oolong tea are based entirely on these differences in processing. It is possible to make all three kinds from the same tea bushes, something which is often done. However, certain regions typically specialize in producing a certain type, and because of this people often mistakenly think the tea grown in each place is botanically distinct. For example, virtually all Japanese tea is green, almost all Indian tea is black, while China produces green, black, and oolong tea.

All types of tea, as they are commonly prepared, contain less caffeine than coffee. Black tea infused for five minutes contains about 40 to 100 mg of caffeine in each cup; if infused for only three minutes it contains about half this amount. Green tea has less caffeine than black. Tea bags, because they contain broken leaves, produce a drink that contains more caffeine. In addition to caffeine, tea contains polyphenols, commonly known as "tannins," and aromatic or essential oils. In China, medicines are made from the tannins to treat a variety of diseases including kidney and liver conditions. The essential oils are the source of tea's distinctive aroma and reputedly act as a digestive aid. Green tea contains more essential oils than black, which typically loses some of these in its longer processing, and therefore green tea has a stronger scent.[17]

Linnæus Brings Home the Tea: Osbek's Trek and Other Tea Adventures

In the first half of the eighteenth century, when Linnæus undertook his lifework of classifying flora in accordance with a twofold scheme of his own devising, the world was a much bigger place than it is today. The great scientist's acquaintance with the tea plant was limited by Chinese restrictions on foreign travelers and the unreliability of untutored observations of laymen who had somehow completed the difficult journey. Driven by scientific curiosity, Linnæus made a deal with the Swedish East India Company according to which one of his students would annually sail with the fleet for China and would so be able to return with specimens and accurate information about local conditions. Getting his hands on a tea plant, however, proved to be more difficult than he had originally thought.

Linnæus' initial hopes rested on the shoulders of a young student, Per Osbek, who, like most of Linnæus' mariner protégés, served as ship's chaplain to pay for his food during the voyage. Although Osbek returned with a profuse variety of plants and pages of detailed observations, his attempt to deliver a tea plant was defeated by misadventures. One plant was knocked into the sea when Osbek's crew fired the ship's cannons in the traditional salute on departure. On a second voyage, he managed to bring a plant within sight of the Cape of Good Hope, only to watch it blow overboard during a sudden storm that recalls the one that menaced de Clieu and his coffee plant on his return to Martinique.

Succeeding efforts fared no better. A contemporary of Linnæus, Magnus von Lagerstroem, a director of the Swedish trading company, was proud of the plant he carried from China to Uppsala, Sweden, where it was cultivated for two years before it was found to be not a tea plant at all, but another species of *Camellia*. A genuine tea plant was in fact delivered to Uppsala only a short time thereafter, but, because it was so valuable on arrival it was placed in the commandant's room for safekeeping, where it was promptly devoured by rats.

Success finally came in 1763. In that year a ship commanded by one Captain Eckburg returned to Sweden from China with potted seeds that germinated and sprouted during the trip home. Even here fate intervened, for when on arrival Eckburg sent half the plants to Linnæus in Uppsala, they were destroyed in transit. The remaining half, however, he carried to Uppsala himself, and on October 3, after years of trying, Linnæus became the first man in Europe to possess growing tea plants.[18]

The Cultivation of Tea

Camellia sinensis is an evergreen bush or treelike shrub that resembles a myrtle tree, partly because of the conical shape of its leaves. Every spring, it yields fragrant white blossoms, about an inch in diameter, similar in appearance to apple blossoms or wild roses. Each blossom becomes a fruit, about an inch in diameter, inside of which grows one to three seeds, a little smaller than apple seeds, in each of four cells.

Camellia sinensis can grow in climates ranging from Mediterranean to tropical and at altitudes from sea level to eight thousand feet, but flourishes at altitudes of between two thousand and sixty-five hundred feet and in areas receiving moderate rainfall. The most commonly cultivated variety, *Camellia sinensis assamica*, or Assam tea, has little resistance to cold and grows well only in tropical areas. The Assam tea plant, which is considered a tree, has large leaves, about ten inches long, and, left uncultivated, can grow to a height of fifty feet. These tough little trees are hard to kill, and in China they frequently live longer than one hundred years. China tea, or *Camellia sinensis sinensis*, which has been commercially cultivated for nearly two thousand years, offers lower yields than Assam tea but produces a more delicately flavored beverage. The China tea plant is considered a bush rather than a tree because it is multistemmed, even though it attains a natural height as great as twenty feet. It has stiff, serrated four-inch leaves. China tea can tolerate brief cold periods and thus higher altitudes than Assam tea. In the 1800s China tea was cultivated in South Carolina, but the plantations were abandoned because high labor costs made them unprofitable. However, many wild plants still survive in this area.

Because tea bushes grow luxuriantly in a climate that is hot and wet, preferably with at least one hundred inches of rainfall per year, tea is grown commercially in the humid regions surrounding the equator. Although in China it is often still grown on patches of wasteland, as recommended by the ancient sage of tea, Lu Yü, it flourishes best in rich soil. Like coffee trees, tea bushes usually grow best and produce better tea in the shade of trees planted nearby to protect them from the scorching tropical sun. In mountainous areas below six thousand feet, the leaves develop slowly, are more tender, and produce a higher concentration of caffeine.

Lu Yü's eighth-century *Classic of Tea* mentions a wild tea tree in Szechuan so large that two men with outstretched arms were required to encircle its trunk. In recent times many such wild trees, towering up to forty feet, have been found in southern and eastern Szechuan and in Yunnan and Guizhou provinces along the lower reaches of the Lancang, Nu, Qu, Pan, and Hongshui Rivers. A King Tea Tree, the largest ever discovered, was found growing wild in 1939. It is judged to be more than seventeen hundred years old and is still growing in the forested Xishuangbanna region of Yunnan near the Burma border. It is 108 feet tall, with a main trunk more than a yard in diameter.[19]

In nature, tea cross-pollinates, a gene-shuffling process subject to the inherent uncertainty of any sexual reproduction. The only way growers can reproduce a bush exactly is with a technique known as "layering," in which a branch still on a living bush is bent and buried until it roots. Although this method effectively clones superior plants, it is expensive, and most tea planters still take their chances with shrubs grown from seeds in nursery beds. After about six months, six-inch seedlings are transplanted to the tea garden. The young plants are set out in rows at three- to six-foot intervals and left to grow unimpeded for two years. A fairly level tea garden will be tenanted by three to four thousand bushes per acre.

Following three additional years of careful tending, the plants are fully developed and ready for their first plucking. Thereafter, each will be pruned to a height of three to five feet and plucked. Pruning is vital to the production of tea because it stimulates the growth of flush, the tender young leaves from which tea is made. If left to its natural course, the plant would stop yielding flush, the sap passages would gradually become occluded, the twigs would harden into wood, and the existing leaves would become larger and tougher until they became completely unsuitable for brewing. As James Norwood Pratt, in *A Tea Lover's Treasury*, explains with more melodrama, bathos, and empathy than is usual in botanical accounts:

> Constant pruning and plucking keeps the bush desperately striving for full tree-hood and perpetually producing new leaves and buds. . . . The poor tea bush is kept in this state of unrelieved anxiety from about age 2 to something over 50, when its yield begins to decrease, and, to avoid labor and sorrow, it's uprooted and replaced. It dies without once having been allowed to flower and seed.[20]

Even under such grimly unremitting cultivation, each tea bush produces at most only ten ounces of finished dry leaf a year.

Both Assam and China tea plants are trimmed to waist height, not only to stimulate the bush, but to make plucking the leaves easier. Ideally, only young leaf shoots and the unopened leaf bud, rich in caffeine and the organic compounds that give tea its aroma and flavor, are harvested. Plucking only the young leaves without destroying the health of the plant is a highly skilled job. Superior tea results when only the growth bud, or "pekoe," and the next youngest leaf are taken. Lower grades of tea are the products of "coarse" plucking, in which the bud, the first two leaves, and the old leaf below them are all taken, along with that much more of the twig. Unfortunately, to reduce costs, mechanical shearing, producing a coarse tea of uneven quality, is on the increase. For example, the Russians, who raise tea in Georgia north of the Caucasus, employ a self-propelled mechanical tea plucker of their own invention. However, the best teas are high-grown on terrain that precludes mechanization, and even industrialized countries like Japan and Taiwan still pluck their teas by hand. Because of improvements in cultivation and harvesting techniques, an acre in Assam that produced three hundred pounds of tea a hundred years ago may yield as much as fifteen hundred pounds today.

Despite all the efforts to bring tea planting to the West, only the Russian introduction became commercially important. In 1893, using the offspring of plants that had been planted in the botanical gardens of Sukahm, a Black Sea port, and which had been the subject of agricultural experimentation for almost fifty years, C. S. Popoff transported fifteen Chinese foremen and laborers to farm his estates and teach his Russian countrymen how to raise tea, thus instituting a crop that has been a valuable source of revenue for the region of Georgia ever since.

Like the cultivation of coffee, the cultivation of tea is fraught with many curiosities. In Sri Lanka, the Tamil-speaking Hindus who pluck tea leaves bury their dead between the tea rows.[21] It is said that in early China, tea pluckers were virgin girls under fourteen, who wore new gloves and a new dress daily.[22] They were required to abstain from eating fish and certain meats, so that their breath wouldn't taint the flavor of the leaves, and to bathe before going to the fields, for a similar reason.[23] Tea will not grow for some time where lightning has struck or on the site of former human habitation—or so the Chinese farmers' lore teaches.[24]

The Cacao Tree (*Theobroma cacao*)

Cacao is the bitter powder made from the ground, roasted beans of the cacao tree (*Theobroma cacao*), called cacao or cocoa beans, with most of their fat removed. The family Sterculiaceae, to which the genus *Theobroma* belongs, has one other member of major economic importance, *Cola*. "*Theobroma*" is scientific Latin (from Greek roots) for "drink of the gods," and the genus was so named by Linnæus in 1753[25] for the fact that the cacao tree was a sacred plant to the Aztecs, who cultivated it and used it in their religious rites. In 1502, when cacao seeds were brought back to Spain by Columbus, the cacao tree became the first caffeinated plant on record to reach Europe.

Twenty-two species of the genus *Theobroma* have been distinguished, but only *cacao* is raised commercially. Another species, *bicolor*, is grown in Latin American family gardens as a source of beans or of a sweet pulp used for confections, and in Mexico it is used to make a drink called *pataxte* or to adulterate more expensive chocolate. Genetic investigation of other species is being pursued in the hope of improving the cacao tree's yield and increasing its resistance to disease.

Engraving from Dufour, *Traitez Nouveaux*. This French engraving illustrates a branch from the cacao tree, two harvested cacao pods, and a vanilla pod. Vanilla was among the many ingredients added to flavor chocolate drinks. (The Library Company of Philadelphia)

According to the botanist José Cuatrecasas,[26] cacao originally grew wild from Mesoamerica to the Amazon basin. The trees in the intermediate areas died out, and, by the time human beings came to notice cacao, the northern and southern regions had evolved two distinct varieties. Both of these varieties of the species *cacao* are commercially cultivated: *criollo* ("native"), with long, pointed pods, which grows in Mexico and Central America, and *forastero* ("foreign"), with hard, round pods, which grows south of Panama. The Aztecs and Maya cultivated *criollo* exclusively, and its beans were the ones enjoyed by the seventeenth-century European aristocracy. The planting of *forastero* started with the Spanish conquerors. *Criollo* may have been the early favorite because its beans require little or no fermentation while *forastero* cacao must be fermented to make a palatable drink.[27] Like *Coffea arabica*, *criollo* has a distinctive, subtle flavor, but *forastero* has become the dominant variety worldwide, supplying more than 80 percent of the world's chocolate, because, like *Coffea robusta*, it is more vigorous and produces a greater yield. [28]

Though *Theobroma* is endemic to Central and South America, principally to the upper Amazon and Orinoco river basins, it is grown today around the world between the twentieth parallels, except in the central and eastern parts of Africa, where poor soil and dry climate make its cultivation impossible. West Africa, including Ghana, Nigeria, Cameroon, and the Ivory Coast, presents ideal conditions for cacao, and in consequence has become the largest regional exporter today, with a production of more than 750,000 tons of dried beans a year. Ghana was formerly the single top national producer in the world, with more than 400,000 tons a year, but because of political instabilities has yielded this rank to the Ivory Coast. In Latin America, Brazil is first, with 350,000 tons, followed by the Dominican Republic, Ecuador, Colombia, Venezuela, and Mexico. Cacao is also now grown widely in the Far East, in Indonesia, Malaysia, and New Guinea.

Theobroma cacao is an evergreen tree that, in the dense jungle habitat of the primary rainforest, is sparsely branched and can reach heights of fifty feet. However, when planted in unshaded plantations, it branches densely and rarely exceeds fifteen feet. Cacao trees begin to bear fruit after four or five years, attain full maturity in about ten years, and often continue bearing pods for more than sixty years. In periodic flushes throughout the year, cacao trees produce new leaves that quickly turn from a pinkish green to a deep green on the upper surface and a soft lighter green on the lower surface. The mature leaves, in two rows along the branches, are elliptical and may be as long as twenty inches.

After two or three years, each tree displays more than ten thousand small flowers, which grow on short stalks directly from the old wood of the trunk or main branches. These abundant unscented flowers, exhibiting a dazzling range of pastel colors, are pollinated by midge flies, although fewer than 5 percent produce mature pods, and fewer than twenty to fifty fully developed fruits appear at any one time. A fully grown pod is six to ten inches long and three to four inches thick and contains about thirty to fifty oval purple beans, each about one and one-half inches in diameter, surrounded by a pale pink pulp. As the fruit, or pod, ripens, it advances from green through a range of colors, including yellow, orange, red, and purple. Although the fresh beans are bitter, the sweet, pungent aroma and flavor of the whitish pulp that surrounds them attracts birds, monkeys, and other animals that split the pods, devour the pulp, and discard the seeds, scattering them widely throughout the jungle. Partly as a result of this foraging, cacao trees now grow wild in almost every corner of South America.[29]

The techniques of harvesting and drying the beans have remained fairly constant for centuries. Each pod is cut from the tree with a machete, the worker careful to avoid damaging the flower beneath it. Within a couple of days, the pods are split open, usually by hand. Once the husks have been discarded, the fresh beans and pulp are mixed with yeast and placed in wooden boxes. During the following week, the beans, fermenting at temperatures up to 120 degrees Fahrenheit, are thoroughly transformed, until finally attaining much of their characteristic flavor. Following fermentation the beans are spread out in the sun to dry and raked several times a day for three to five days. Although wood- or oil-burning rotary dryers are sometimes used to speed the process, sun-dried beans have the richest flavor. In the process of drying, the beans acquire their universally recognized "chocolate brown" color.

Theobroma cacao is cultivated below 1,000 feet altitude and grows exclusively between the latitudes of 20 north and 20 south. Other factors being equal, the productive yield of the tree increases toward the equator. The cacao tree requires a warm, humid climate and does best with sixty to eighty inches of rainfall a year. It thrives at shade temperatures of 65 to 95 degrees Fahrenheit but can do well in the 105 degrees Fahrenheit common in West Africa.[30]

At the time Cortés arrived in Latin America, cacao was being actively traded in the Aztec capital and, because the Indians had managed a wild crop and raised trees from seeds on their own plantations, probably among the Yucatan farmers as well. However, once the conquistadors had subdued the natives, Spanish colonial governments assumed control of Indian agriculture, attaining a monopoly on cacao's production and its trade in Europe. As a result, cacao sustained its position as Spain's top export crop until the early seventeenth century. Perhaps there is some unknown magic to members of the Sterculiaceæ family, for as cola nuts were in Africa, cacao beans were used as money in Central America as late as the eighteenth century.

Cacao Goes to Africa . . . and Beyond

Africa is the world leader in cacao production. In 1590, the Spanish exported Venezuelan seedlings to Fernando Po, a small equatorial island near the coast of western Africa with a warm, wet climate and rich, well-drained soil. It became the first site of cacao cultivation outside Latin America. Ghana, however, was the first country of mainland Africa to attempt large-scale cacao cultivation. Teteh Quashie, who became a folk hero as a result, is credited with the institution of Ghana's most valuable cash crop. A blacksmith who had worked as a migrant laborer on a cacao plantation in Fernando Po, Quashie brought pods back to his homeland. He started a cacao nursery in 1881 and began selling the pods to native farmers. The result was a cacao crop that today is the biggest in the world. Cacao from Ghana has set the standard for basic chocolate flavor, because her beans were fermented and cured with distinctive skill, and, in consequence, Ghana's cacao has dominated the British and European markets for much of the twentieth century. Quashie is honored by a number of public buildings and monuments bearing his name in recognition of his seminal accomplishments.[31]

The Spanish also took cacao west from the Americas. In 1663, Pedro de Laguna sailed on a galleon with cacao seeds from Acapulco to Manila. Ever since, chocolate has been a favorite food throughout the Philippines, and today many families grow a few cacao trees in their yards or in small orchards with other tree crops, such as mangos or bananas, and use the dried beans themselves or sell them in produce markets.

When cacao demand increased in the seventeenth century, the French contested the Spanish monopoly on the crop, instituting cacao production in Martinique and Saint Lucia around 1660. The Dutch also began cacao production in the Dutch East Indies, and, as a result, Indonesia still produces seventy-five thousand tons of beans every year.

Cacao and Caffeine

The well-known stimulating effects of cacao are the result of the additive or even synergistic effects of caffeine and one of caffeine's cousins, the methylxanthine theobromine. Cacao powder averages about 2 percent theobromine and .2 percent caffeine. Both the caffeine and theobromine levels of the beans varies with the varietal type and is also affected by the fermentation process. Theobromine, commercially extracted from seed wastes,[32] although much weaker milligram for milligram than caffeine, in sufficient quantities acts as a diuretic, smooth muscle relaxant, cardiac stimulant, and vasodilator. Which of these methylxanthines is predominant in producing cacao's effects?

In a 1994 Johns Hopkins University study, caffeine was discriminated or detected by different subjects in threshold doses ranging between about 2 mg to just more than 180 mg, while theobromine was detected in doses ranging between 100 mg to 1,000 mg.[33] According to this measure, milligram for milligram, among individuals in the same subject group, caffeine was from three to fifty times more potent than theobromine. However, because about ten times as much theobromine as caffeine can typically be present in chocolate (a 1.5-ounce of chocolate bar can contain between 100 and 240 mg theobromine and 10 to 30 mg of caffeine), it is unclear which of these chemicals predominates. A cup of hot chocolate or glass of chocolate milk, prepared from a typical commercial mix, supplies about 60 mg of theobromine and about 5 mg of caffeine. The dose in a 1.5-ounce chocolate bar exceeds the theobromine discrimination threshold in about 15 percent of the subjects, while that of caffeine exceeds this threshold in over 50 percent of the subjects, suggesting that caffeine may be the more powerful stimulating component in most people. While the overall pharmacological effects of these drugs are similar, recent studies show that caffeine has a quicker onset, a shorter duration of action, and a longer list of differentiable physical and mental effects than theobromine.

Maté (Yerba Maté, *Ilex paraguariensis*); Cassina (Yaupon holly, *Ilex vomitoria*)

After the coffee, tea, and cacao trees, yerba maté is the largest source of caffeine consumed in the world. The astringent beverage maté (*Gon gouha*), which has given its name to the plant from which it is infused, is the coffee and tea of a large group of people in Argentina, Brazil, Paraguay, Uruguay, Ecuador, and Chile, in that it is the main source of caffeine in their diet. Although a large amount of yerba maté is produced under cultivation, the best maté is reputed to come from wild trees. More than 250,000 tons of yerba maté leaves are harvested every year, containing about 3,000 tons of caffeine, or nearly 3 percent of the world's total, enough to enliven, very roughly, fifty billion cups of maté. Much of Brazilian and Paraguayan production is exported to Argentina, Chile, and Uruguay.[34]

Ilex paraguariensis is a species of holly native to Brazil, Paraguay, and Argentina, growing to a height of sixty to ninety feet in the wild, with oval dark green leaves six to eight inches long, and producing small white flowers. When cultivated it is trimmed to twelve to eighteen feet. The flowers form in the leaf axils and at the base of the small branches. Although harvesting begins three to five years after planting, full productivity is attained in ten years and continues for about another ten years. As with tea, a superior product is produced from very young, unopened leaflets. Harvesting is performed by Indians who climb the trees, clear them of vines, and cut off the smaller leafy branches, leaving the larger ones to maintain the health of the tree. The branches are bundled and briefly toasted by drawing over an open fire to dry, while stopping short of charring. After further drying at a processing factory, which takes about fifteen hours, during which the temperature is kept below 200 degrees Fahrenheit to avoid loss of caffeine potency, a threshing process is used to separate the leaf from the bark and twigs. The resulting leaf is sifted for grading and blending, then packed in 50- to 150-pound bags. It is aged for six months to a year and a half to produce a palatable beverage.

As is the case with *Camellia sinensis*, there has been a divergence of opinion about its botanical nomenclature. Today, however, it is generally acknowledged that *paraguariensis* is a single species with many varieties. The leaves are sold either green, producing a beverage with a disagreeable bitter astringency, or roasted, yielding a drink with a pleasant smoky flavor. Rich in vitamin C and tannins as well as caffeine, a 6-ounce cup of maté as it is usually prepared contains about the same amount of caffeine as a cup of tea. The Guarani Indians of Paraguay used yerba maté as a stimulant and to prevent scurvy. Today it is extensively cultivated in Argentina, where maté drinking is a social event that can continue for hours, and maté is the most popular caffeine-containing drink. It is also widely used in Paraguay, where it has been known as "Paraguay tea" for at least a century.[35]

A comparison of maté and ordinary tea was noted by two English writers toward the end of the nineteenth century. The first wrote that, as between coffee, tea, and chocolate:

> Of the three beverages . . . tea is the one which nearest resembles maté; but between tea and maté there is much difference in taste, and though I believe that maté deserves some degree of popularity here, it should by no means be put forward as resembling tea, but as a new drink for the English people.[36]

The second likened the effects of the maté's active principle to that of theine, the name given to caffeine as occurring in tea, and stated that some authorities claim maté is a species of tea. [37]

The methylxanthine content of maté, which is generally accepted as the basis for its use as a beverage, has been extensively investigated. Reported caffeine concentrations range from about 1 percent to 2 percent, the young leaves having the highest levels. However, because the beverage maté is brewed from as many as sixty different species of the *Ilex* genus, and, as noted below, because of the way it is prepared, a determination of the average caffeine levels occurring in the drink is problematic. Theobromine and theophylline may also occur in maté, although some investigators have failed to detect them. However, even if present, their concentrations in the dried leaf are pharmacologically insignificant.

Long before the Spanish explorers arrived in the early sixteenth century, the plant was infused by the indigenous population to make a beverage in those areas of South America to which it is native. Like the other caffeinated botanicals, maté was also employed as a means of exchange. "*Maté*" is a Spanish word derived from an Inca word meaning "calabash." In South America, the leaves of yerba maté are infused and drunk in a calabash through a six-inch reed or silver straw with a bulb-shaped strainer (*bombilla*) to screen out the sediment. The native word for the plant is "*caa*," but the Spanish called it "*Yerba*." Maté's use was eagerly adopted by the colonists, who found it so desirable that the governor of Paraguay gave settlers the right to impress the natives to collect the leaves for its preparation. Jesuit priests, who arrived in Paraguay around 1550, took control of the producing areas and began cultivation of selected varieties to ensure a good supply, and, in consequence, the drink has often been called "Jesuit tea." Paraguayan prisoners brought back to Brazil by Portuguese invaders helped spread the knowledge of the drink in Brazil. Almost all Argentinean and Brazilian maté is produced through cultivation, while much of the Paraguayan leaf has been harvested from jungle plants.

When the tealike beverage is prepared in the traditional South American manner, boiling water is poured over the dried leaves in a small silver-mounted calabash about the size of an apple; in family circles the gourd and *bombilla* are passed around like a pot pipe. However, today a teapot and cups are frequently used instead of a gourd and straw. About one-half to two ounces of leaves are used for each quart of water or heated milk, and sugar and lemon are often added when milk has not been used. Because several successive infusions are made from the same leaf by adding more boiling water, it is very difficult to approximate the caffeine content of the resulting beverage. The best estimates suggest a range from about 25 mg per 6-ounce serving, about as much as a very weak cup of tea, up to about 100 mg, or the same as a cup of instant coffee.

Maté leaves are sold in many health food stores, usually as ingredients in herbal tea mixtures, such as Celestial Seasonings "Morning Thunder." As is the case with other exotic caffeine-containing plant products, packages of maté sometimes misrepresent the product as a caffeine-free herbal tea.

In North America, the cured leaves of the yaupon holly, *Ilex vomitoria*, also called "cassina" or "Appalachian holly,"[38] have been similarly infused for centuries to make cassina, a hot, stimulating drink. In 1542, Narvaez and Cabeza de Vaca, Spanish explorers of North America, described how cassina was used to make a ceremonial black drink and medicinal potation by the coastal Indians of North Carolina. In 1562, Capatain Laudonnière, who had sailed with the blessing of King Charles IX of France to find a suitable place to relocate French Protestants, was presented with basketfuls of cassina and observed the plant was used for currency among the natives.

As recently as 1924, assemblies of Creek Indian men are described as taking concentrated infusions of cassina continually for two or three days running, in part to induce vomiting and receive its beneficial purgative effects.

Curing processes were developed early in this century by the Bureau of Chemistry of the United States Department of Agriculture for producing three types: green, black, and "cassina maté." The last most closely resembles yerba maté.[39] Even with the full backing of the federal government, none of these efforts resulted in a commercially viable drink.

Cola (*Cola acuminata; Cola nitida*)

Cola nuts are the caffeine-rich nuts of *Cola acuminata* and *Cola nitida*, evergreen forest trees native to tropical West Africa. The trees are members of the same botanical family as cacao and are widely cultivated in South America and have also been transported to India and China. Cola trees, which resemble chestnut trees, reach sixty feet in height. The brown, oblong nuts, about two inches long, are picked by hand and dried in the sun for use as ingredients in medicines and soft drinks.

Cola nuts, which have an acerbic, aromatic flavor, are commonly chewed by African laborers and other natives to reduce hunger and fatigue. In addition to a large dose of caffeine, cola nuts contain the glucoside kolanin, a fruit sugar that may contribute to their powerful revivifying effects.[40] In Nigeria, for example, office workers often rely on chewing cola nuts for the same purpose as American white-collar employees drink coffee, and, as a gesture of hospitality, visitors to private homes are frequently offered cola nuts to chew. A cola nut brew, called "Sudan coffee" by the Arabs and "African tea" by others, was long used by the nomadic tribes of Somalia, the Sudan, and other African countries. In Brazil and the West Indies, the nuts are used to help sober up drunks and as a hangover remedy, much as some people use coffee in America and Europe,[41] and with just as little success.

A sign of the importance of cola to the Africans is the story of its divine origin:

> One day when the Creator was on earth observing the sons of men and busy among them, he put aside a piece of the cola nut which he was chewing and forgot to take it with him when he went away again. A man saw this and seized the dainty morsel. His wife tried to prevent him from tasting the food of God. The man, however, placed it in his mouth and found that it tasted good. While he was still chewing, the Creator returned, sought the forgotten piece of cola, and saw how the man tried to swallow it. He quickly grasped at his throat and forced him to return the fruit. Since that time there can be seen in the throat of man the "Adam's apple," trace of the pressure of the fingers of God.[42]

The earliest mentions of the fruit may have occurred in the writings of El Ghafeky, a twelfth-century Spanish physician, and of the thirteenth-century Arab botanist Ebn El-Baithar. While their descriptions of a certain fruit sound as if cola is being referred to, their characterization of the seeds seems not to fit this identification. In any case, the word "cola" first occurs in the last half of the sixteenth century, in the works of Clusius and other writers who learned of the existence of the plant from returning European travelers and explorers.

Louis Lewin (1850–1929), a German pharmacologist, physician, and researcher, reports in his book *Phantastica* that, as late as 1920, cola nuts still played an important part

> in the social life and commercial relations of these peoples [the inhabitants of the Sudan between the Atlantic and the source of the Nile]. Much trouble is taken in order to obtain the drug. The Haussa, for instance, organize long caravan-journeys to the country of the Ashanti, and their arrival is an important event for the latter. Those who have no money to buy the drug beg. Rich people ingratiate themselves by distributing nuts or pieces of nuts. The inhabitant Kano in northern Nigeria does not hesitate to sell his horse or his best slave, his two most important possessions, in order to enjoy his favorite pastime. Indeed, it is not rare for a poor man to seize an already half-masticated piece of another person's nut and to continue chewing it.[43]

Lewin adds that, at this time, "These nuts, like every eagerly desired substance which modifies cerebral activity, are fairly expensive. Every thing, even slaves, can be bought with nuts."

In some African countries these caffeine-containing nuts are so valuable and widely coveted for their stimulating power that they continue to be used as local currency.

Like other caffeinated botanicals in Arabia, China, and South America, cola nuts are important fixtures of the ceremonies of everyday African life. In Nigeria, for example, a marriage proposal is accompanied by the white variety of cola nuts and a refusal is accompanied by red cola nuts. Cola is also a necessary part of every dowry. In addition, "Oaths are sworn on the kola nut, friendships or hostilities are symbolized by kola and some nuts are even buried with the dead."[44]

The sorcerers of the Konkomba, a tribe living in the Oti Plain, part of the former French and British territories of northern Togoland, are well known to specialize in administering fatal medicines to procure the death of their victims. Cola nuts havs a cleft down the middle that these magicians have used as a convenient repository for their poisons. Therefore, as a precaution, tribe members will not eat cola nuts given to them by strangers. The usual procedure is to "accept the nut, thank the giver, and, later, throw it away."[45]

Cola nuts have a strong taste and, compared with other natural sources, contain a strong concentration of caffeine. However, contrary to a common belief, the flavor of cola soft drinks does not come from these nuts and neither does their caffeine. While it is true that cola soft drinks contain significant doses of caffeine, their insignificant cola nut content contributes only about 5 percent of the total. The rest of the caffeine in colas and all of the caffeine found in other sodas is a by-product of coffee and tea decaffeination that has been added to the citrus, vanilla, cinnamon, and other flavoring components of these drinks.

A curiosity is gotu cola, also known as Indian pennywort, a traditional Chinese medicinal herb believed by some to prolong life. This swamp plant is native to China,

Sri Lanka, and South Africa and has been used as a folk remedy for leprosy, cancer, skin disorders, arthritis, hemorrhoids, and tuberculosis. It has also been used as an energy tonic, aphrodisiac, and treatment for mental disorders. In the United States it is an ingredient in many herbal "energy formulas." A common misconception is that gotu cola contains caffeine. Although it is true that gotu cola may well contain anti-inflammatory glycosides, agents that can heal skin ulcers, it contains no caffeine whatsoever.

Guarana (*Paullinia cupana*) and Yoco (*Paullinia yoco*)

Guarana (*Paullinia cupana*) is a woody climbing plant of the soapberry family (Sapindaceae), native to the Amazon basin. It has large leaves, clusters of short-stalked flowers, and yields a fruit about the size of a coffee berry, usually containing a single seed. The genus took its name from its discoverer, C. F. Paulini, a German botanist who died in 1712.[46] Guarana seeds, named for the Guaranis Indians,[47] are roasted and brewed to make a stimulating drink popular in South America. It has a bitter, astringent taste, and a faint coffeelike odor. The caffeine content of these seeds is about three times greater than that of an equivalent weight in coffee beans. Because guarana has such a high concentration of the drug, it was used in the nineteenth century as a source of the compound for medicinal purposes.[48] The bark of the yoco tree (*Paullinia yoco*), a sister species to guarana, is also used like guarana seeds to prepare a caffeinated drink.

To make the tea, guarana seeds are shelled and washed and pounded into a fine powder, which is kneaded with water into dough and shaped into cylinders. When these rods are dried in the sun or over a low fire, they become very hard and assume a russet color. About a half a teaspoonful is grated from these sticks, which are sometimes called "guarana bread" or "Brazilian cocoa," and dissolved, along with sugar, in hot water. As typically prepared, the resulting brew, which is known as "Brazilian tea," carries a bigger caffeine charge than coffee. Guarana's astringency, like tea's, is caused by tannin. In addition to containing caffeine, guarana and yoco each yield a chemical that produces soapy lather, saponin, which is used in tropical countries as a soap substitute. Saponin has the unusual property of stupefying fish when thrown into small streams.[49]

The habit of Brazilian miners, who believe that the beverage is not only refreshing but preventative of many diseases, is to carry a guarana stick, which is almost as hard as stone, together with the palate bone or scale of a big fish with which to grate it. The Orinoco Indians, who give their name to the valley to which cacao is indigenous, ferment the crushed seeds until nearly putrid and infuse the product with hot water.

Guarana is also commonly sweetened and bottled as a carbonated soft drink, similar in effect, if not in flavor, to our familiar cola sodas. In the United States, guarana is sometimes an ingredient in herbal teas, and capsules of guarana powder are sold in health food stores, under such brand names as ZING. These products are often misleadingly marketed as new organic stimulants from the Amazon rainforest, taking advantage of the fact that most people are unaware that caffeine is found in plants other than coffee or tea. Here is an excerpt from a French advertisement for guarana pills that supplies a fanciful history, while also trying to convince its readers that guarana is popular in the United States today:

The Amazon Indians used it for centuries to give them strength. In the Tupi language, "guarana" means "making war." Many who used it could enjoy up to six women at a time and achieved an advanced age. It was only in the seventeenth century that guarana was discovered by Father Felip Betendorf and was made known to western civilizations. The commercialization of guarana began in 1958, and soon after it became the tonic plant and fortifying agent most used and most popular in Brazil. It is equally widely used in the United States.

Caffeine's Competitors: Coca, Khat, Ephedra, Betel, and Yohimbé

Caffeine is not the only naturally occurring stimulating alkaloid that has been consumed as a beverage, food, or masticatory. Here is a brief description of some other botanical uppers and their sources.

Coca

The coca plant (*Erythroxylon coca*) is a small tree or shrub with tiny white flowers native to the region of the Andes Mountains. The natural source of the drug cocaine, the leaves have been mixed with powdered lime and chewed by natives as a stimulant and panacea since ancient times.

Usually planted from seeds, the seedlings are raised in a nursery for up to ten months. Once replanted, the amount of cultivation lavished on them varies with the size and location of the plantation. When the tree is about six feet tall, pickers, in the spring and again in the fall, gather the leaves, which are then cured and dried, before being powdered for local use or sold for extraction. When supplies from South America fell short of worldwide demand, coca was cultivated in the East Indies, with the result that much of the legal international trade originates in Java.[50]

In the regions to which it is native, powdered coca leaves are freely available in local markets. The chewing is a general practice among Andean laborers, who claim that, as a result of their use of the leaves, they can work for days with little food or rest. Distances in the region are sometimes reckoned in *cocadas*, the range that can be traversed on one chew. The admixture of lime is considered indispensable to producing any effect, and lime is similarly used in commercial processing to extract the alkaloid, cocaine.

Coca leaf use creates an apparently minimal detriment to the people who chew it and the society in which they live. In striking contrast are the detrimental effects of using extracted cocaine, a practice generally associated with personal instability, drug dependence, paranoia, violence, and eventual psychosis. The reasons for these marked differences are unclear. Scientists point to the slower rate of absorption from chewing as compared with smoking or injection, to a different set of social mores, and suggest that there may be other active alkaloids in the leaf that moderate the effects of cocaine in a way that is not achieved when the extracted chemical is consumed by itself. The fact is that science today has not solved the mystery of these disparate effects, and a similar uncertainty and confusion surrounds the differences between the effects created by each of the plants listed in this section when compared with the effects of the chemical extracts of each plant's "active principle." We like to think that our contemporary science has all the basic answers, but insofar as understanding the way these psychoactive plants do what they do, the answers still elude us.

Khat

In 1892, when James Walsh published his book on tea, he mentioned an "Arabian tea" that he called "Cathadules," which he said was prepared from the leaves of shrub "extensively cultivated there for that purpose, as much attention being bestowed upon it by the natives as on coffee. This preparation is sometimes also called 'Abyssinian tea.'" He observed, "The leaves are also chewed, when green, like those of the coca in South America, being highly intoxicating, particularly in the wild state."[51]

Khat (qat, kat, chat, *murmungu, mirra,* or *miraa*), or *Catha edulis,* is an evergreen shrubby tree whose fresh leaves and young twigs are chewed for their stimulating effect and is also the name for the popular beverage brewed from its leaves and used by millions in a wide area of East Africa and the Middle East. But it is in the Yemen, the traditional home of coffee, that khat's use has for centuries been a pervasive social institution that colors family, work, and recreational activities and associations. Although its consumption is general in the Yemen among men, women, and children, in neighboring countries its use is more limited. For example, it is reported that truck drivers are the primary regular users of this plant in Kenya.

Ever since khat came to European attention from its widespread use in the Middle East, it has been assumed to contain the same stimulant as coffee and tea. Therefore the active ingredient was, on analogy with "caffeine," given the name "cathine." Today it is known that khat contains no caffeine but does contain several active chemicals, some of which are alkaloid stimulants structurally similar to amphetamines. Cathinon is thought to cause the primary stimulant qualities of khat, while cathine and norephedrene are said to contribute to its other somatic effects, such as brachiodilation, or enlargement of the passages leading to the lungs. Based on an analysis of twenty-two khat samples of diverse origins, one group of researchers determined that, in 100 grams of fresh leaves, there are 120 mg of cathine, 36 mg of cathinone, and 8 mg of norephedrine. The leaves lose their potency when they dry out, which is one reason khat use has not spread beyond the areas of its cultivation. Unlike coca leaves, the leaves of khat, which have a bitter, astringent taste, are swallowed after they are chewed.

Yemen's extremes of altitude and variations in soil and climate make it suitable for the cultivation of a diverse variety of crops. Mediterranean fruits such as oranges and grapes are grown on the slopes, and bananas, cotton, dates, tobacco, and mangos are produced on the coastal plain. Coffee and khat are grown in the central highlands, and, together with cotton, constitute the biggest cash crops. Coffee had long been the most important export of the Yemen, famous for its superior mocha, so called because, in the sixteenth and seventeenth centuries, Mocha was its primary port of egress into the world market. Though the best Arabian coffee, among the most prized and expensive anywhere, is still grown in the Yemeni district of San'a, coffee cultivation is losing ground to the more profitable cultivation of khat, for Yemeni khat, like Yemeni coffee, is considered to be of superior quality. Strange to say, the Yemen, which all the world thinks of as the first home of fine coffee, has become intensely preoccupied with the use of a different psychoactive stimulant plant, to the extent that coffee there, in both use and cultivation, has been relegated to a distant second.

In 1996, Hamza Hendawi, in an Associated Press article datelined San'a, Yemen, described how "from the finest private homes to the dusty streets . . . almost every man in Yemen chews khat." He explains that government officials are concerned because a majority of the male population is stoned for at least part of every day. The bitter leaves are chewed slowly, forming a small ball that chewers roll around in their cheeks, as tobacco chewers do with snuff. In 2000, a bundle of six to ten branches sells for between fifty cents and fifty dollars, depending on its quality. A typical khat fix costs about three dollars, a staggering sum in a country with an average daily per capita income of about a dollar a day.

A common sight is men walking home from the market carrying bundles of khat. Khat chewing is often done at home during daily sessions that can bring together two dozen or more men from early afternoon until evening. However, taxi drivers, street vendors, and businessmen often chew it during the working day, and students chew it to keep awake at night while studying for exams. Ali Abdullah Saleh, the president of Yemen, a khat lover himself, still makes certain his troops receive their daily rations, as he did during their conflict with rebels in southern Yemen a few years ago.

In 2000, Donna Abu-nasr, in another Associated Press article datelined San'a, reports how increasing numbers of women are becoming regular khat users as well. After primping and scenting themselves for the occasion, they gather in their own version of afternoon tea, parties at which a light meal of sandwiches and desserts accompanies khat chewing and intoxication. Tea and soft drinks are frequently served to alleviate the dry mouth that is a side effect of Khat consumption.[52]

Khat nay-sayers include Mohammed Yehia al-Sharafi, a neuropsychiatry professor and head of Yemen's University of Applied Sciences, who says that although small doses can reduce anxiety, regular use—and it *is* used with uncanny regularity—causes gastritis, inflammation of the gums, depression, poor appetite, and loss of sexual potency. Sharafi believes that most of khat's attraction is the way it imbues its users with a sense of inspiration, a feeling of being full of important ideas that merit long, ebullient speeches. Khat's proponents, who in addition to the president include many prominent citizens, see in the drug the encouragement of some of the same desirable social effects that coffee's early proponents adduced. "Khat sessions remove all social divisions and bring together men from different walks of life," comments Wad'ai, one of Yemen's most respected judges and himself a devoted khat chewer. Besides, according to Wad'ai, "It is not addictive as people say. That is why we don't need it when we are traveling outside Yemen."

In a country in which khat cultivation consumes 75 percent of the irrigation water and occupies more than 80 percent of the arable land, an important goal of some factions in the government has been to decrease the production and use of khat. But an active trade has continued despite their attempts. Like the recurring efforts in many countries throughout the ages to ban caffeine-containing beverages, these measures enjoyed little success.

Ephedra

Ephedras are leafless desert bushes native to arid regions throughout the world. They are related to pine trees and bear tiny cones. Several species of genus *Ephedra* contain the drug ephedrine, a stimulant alkaloid that is used as a treatment for asthma. Since ancient times in China, the dry stems of *Ephedra vulgaris* have been boiled with water to make a pleasant-tasting, although some say bitter, stimulating tea. American ephedra, which grows throughout North America, is known as "Mormon tea," because early Mormon settlers used it instead of caffeinated beverages, which are prohibited by their religion. Ma-huang, made from the more potent Chinese species *Ephedra sinica*, *Ephedra equisetina*, and *Ephedra intermedia*, has been a traditional medicine in China since well before the introduction of tea in that country. Until the development of synthetic ephedrine, the alkaloid extracted from these species was used in the West as the basis for nasal and bronchial remedies for relieving congestion and to treat low blood pressure.[53] Today, extracts from these plants are common ingredients of herbal stimulants sold in health food stores. The FDA has recently warned about the dangers of the increasingly common use by the young of ephedra products as intoxicants and diet aids, especially when they are compounded with caffeine.

The plants are harvested in autumn, dried in the sun, and cut into pieces. When used as a powdered medicinal, the pieces are boiled in water, sometimes with honey, and then roasted until dry. It is still prescribed in China for typhoid, colds, coughing, and as a painkiller. Today, synthetic ephedrine and a closely related compound, pseudonorephedrine, are ingredients in dozens of prescription and over-the-counter allergy and cold medications.

Betel

"Betel" can refer to either of two unrelated plants, the areca palm, known as the "betel palm" (*Areca catechu*), or the betel pepper, known as the "pan plant" (*Piper betle*). The "betel nut," or seed of the areca palm, is wrapped in the so-called betel leaf of the betel pepper, and the two are chewed together as a stimulant throughout southern Asia and the East Indies. Many Western readers will be surprised to learn that chewing betel is a steady habit for about 10 percent of the world's population.[54]

The areca palm, first described by Theophrastus (374–287 B.C.) in about 340 B.C., is cultivated in India, Sri Lanka, Thailand, Malaysia, and the Philippines. Its unbranched trunk can reach fifty feet but is only about one and a half feet around, with a cluster of up to a dozen palm fronds sprouting from the top. The fruit, about the size of an egg, has a tough rind that contains a hard seed, or nut. The fruit is picked in the fall, before it is fully ripe, and is husked, boiled, and finally sun-dried until it turns dark brown or black.

The stimulating ingredient in betel nuts is the alkaloid arecoline, a drug used by veterinarians as a worming agent. (This is not the same as "black catechu," an extract for dyeing and tanning, which, confusingly enough, is taken from the wood of the areca palm.)

For more than two thousand years the natives of the regions where the "betel palm" grows have used this combination drug.[55] Betel chewing was recorded in China by the fourth century, where the nut, then as now, was known under its Malay name, *"pinang."* Travelers to the Far East have long noted the habit among the natives. Marco Polo in the thirteenth century and Ibn Batuta in the fourteenth century described how betel was consumed together with the areca nut and lime and noted its intoxicating effects. Polo tells us:

> You should know that these people, and indeed all the peoples of India, are addicted to the habit, which affords them some satisfaction, of carrying almost continually in their mouths a certain leaf called *tambur*. They go about chewing this leaf and spitting out the resulting spittle. This habit prevails especially among the nobles and magnates and kings. They mix the leaves with camphor and other spices and also with lime, and go about continually chewing them. And this habit is very beneficial to their health. [56]

As we have seen, Bacon mentions the drug in 1627 in *Sylva Sylvarum*, describing how it is chewed with lime, in a list of intoxicants that includes opium, tobacco, and coffee. In the first quarter of the twentieth century, Lewin, who did extensive field research into psychoactive botanicals, observed:

> The passion for the drug is common to all, both men and women, to every age and class: princes, priests, workmen, and slaves consume it. All religions participate. Christians, especially coloured missionaries, Mohammedans, Buddhists, Brahmans, Fetishists, and other sects. All races are addicted to the drug, Caucasians, Mongols, Malays, Papuans, Alfurus, etc.[57]

Those who enjoy betel prepare to chew the dried pieces of the nut of the areca palm by wrapping it in the fresh leaf of the betel pepper smeared with a lime paste and perhaps flavored with cloves, tamarind, or other spices. The use of the betel pepper leaf and lime increases salivation and helps to bring out the active alkaloids of the areca nut. When the betel nuts and leaves are chewed, a large amount of red saliva is produced, which temporarily colors the gums and lips. However, the practice does not stain the teeth black, as has sometimes been claimed, an error arising from the fact that some of the chewers deliberately stain their teeth black for cosmetic effect or have poor nutrition and dental hygiene.

Yohimbé

Yohimbé is the bark of an African tree (*Corynanthe yohimbe*) containing a crystalline alkaloid stimulant called "yohimbine." The bark has an acrid, spicy flavor and has been used for centuries in central Africa as an aphrodisiac. In the United States, yohimbé bark is occasionally available at herb stores and can be brewed into an invigorating tea for use as an aphrodisiac. Some say it causes tingling feelings up and down the spine.

Some scientists say that yohimbine stimulates sexual arousal by irritating the urinary tract, as do cantharides found in powdered blister beetles (a folk medicine administered to male livestock to encourage breeding that is sometimes called "Spanish fly" when used by people).[58] Others say that its aphrodisiac reputation is simply the result of the power of suggestion, because the stimulating powers of yohimbé are produced only when it is consumed in toxic doses. Still a third faction suggests that there must be other, unknown active constituents in yohimbé bark, because yohimbine alone does not seem to produce the same effects as the bark extract.

Yohimbine, perhaps the main active constituent in yohimbé bark, is an alpha-2 adrenergic antagonist. Alpha-2 autoreceptors act as a kind of thermostat to regulate adrenergic activity. Some of the noradrenaline released by a neuron returns to its alpha-2 autoreceptor, which then reduces the amount of noradrenaline it secretes. This cybernetic control mechanism is similar to a thermostat, which registers the temperature and reduces the amount of heat produced when the air warms up. Unlike simple agonists, which universally activate receptors, yohimbine, by blocking the alpha-2 autoreceptors, actually induces an amplification of noradrenergic activity.

Yohimbine is an ingredient in some folk medicines sold around the world to treat impotence, as increased adrenergic activity seems to help stimulate sexual function. Yohimbine is contraindicated in people with high blood pressure, heart problems, or problems with anxiety, all of which can be exacerbated by increased adrenergic activity. It should never be combined with any other stimulant or any monoamine oxidase (MAO) inhibitor.

CAFFEINE

AFTER ,500 EARS:

STILL THE MOST POPULAR DRUG.

PART 5

caffeine and health

BADBOB ©1994 ROBERT THERRIEN Jr

caffeine and the body
Health Effects, Reproductive Issues,
and Fitness

What is it in man's devious make-up that makes him round on the seemingly more wholesome and pleasurable aspects of his environment and suspect them of being causes of his misfortunes? Whatever it is, stimulants of all kinds (and especially coffee and caffeine) maintain a position high on the list of suspicion, despite a continuing lack of real evidence of any hazard to health.

—Editorial, *British Medical Journal*, 1976, I:1031

Coffee and caffeine have long been suspected of causing illnesses ranging from myocardial infarction, arrhythmias, hypertension, hyperlipidemia, gout, and anxiety, to fibrocystic breast disease, various cancers and birth defects, and osteoporosis. No other agent in the human environment has been as frequently associated with such a variety of chronic-degenerative, even malignant diseases.

—Siegfried Heyden, "Coffee and Cardiovascular Disease," 1993

Caffeine and, before caffeine was identified, coffee, tea, and chocolate, have been said to cause, exacerbate, palliate, or cure an enormous variety of diseases and have also been said to confer marvelous benefits, including increases in both intellectual and physical capacities. If, like the great majority of people in the world, you use caffeine regularly, you are faced with a complex, confusing, and often apparently contradictory cacophony of traditional and contemporary claims about its effects on human health. In former centuries, caffeine lovers had no guidance but the often fanciful discourses of the medical men of their time. We are fortunate that, in the last half of the twentieth century, a explosion of general medical knowledge and a large number of controlled experiments have shed scientific light on many of caffeine's effects. It has been often and truly said that caffeine is the most studied drug in history. Yet, because of its nearly universal use, the variety of its modes of consumption, its presence in and effects on nearly all bodily systems, and its occurrence in chemically complex foods and beverages, together with the complexity of the social and psychological factors that shape its use, caffeine may also be one of the least adequately understood. Despite tremendous scientific scrutiny, many central health questions about caffeine remain unanswered or even unaddressed.

Caffeine is like the air. You don't see it and usually hardly notice it, but it's there all the same, and it becomes part of you in a critical metabolic exchange that involves every cell in your body. Considering that the sensorium and biomass of the human race is virtually awash in caffeine, and has been besotted so for hundreds of years, and that an overwhelming majority of people in almost every nation, including young and old, healthy and infirm, rich and poor, has made the regular use of this psychoactive stimulant more popular than the habitual use of any other drug, what do we really know of caffeine? What do we know of what it is doing for us, doing to us, even doing to our unborn children? The answer, as should become clear after reviewing the very impressive record of studies presented in the following chapters and the appendices, and evaluating both the findings and limitations of this research, is, "not nearly as much as we need to know."

The lack of adequate information about caffeine's health effects is evident in the disagreements that exist among experts. For example, the FDA, as recently as the late 1980s, reaffirmed its earlier position that medical evidence demonstrated no adverse health consequences from caffeine in soft drinks, and the National Academy of Sciences' National Research Council and the U.S. Surgeon General's office agreed that no risk to health had been shown for moderate caffeine intake. In contrast, many researchers, adducing the complexity of caffeine's effects on the human body and the many aspects of these effects that have received limited research attention, argue that such a "clean bill of health" is not fully justified.

The *acute* administration of caffeine under experimental conditions in which the subject has no tolerance to caffeine has been correlated with certain unmistakable physiological responses, including temporary increases in blood pressure, catecholamine levels, rennin activity, cortisol, free fatty acid levels, urine output, and gastric secretions. In contrast, *regular* caffeine consumption does not continue producing elevation in any of these levels. Nor does chronic caffeine ingestion elevate cholesterol or glucose levels. Older people using caffeine regularly demonstrate no change in blood pressure or heart rate, and even continuous heavy use does not increase the risk of developing high blood pressure. The most recent studies contradict earlier findings of a positive correlation between caffeine and heart attacks, kidney and bladder cancers, pancreatic cancer, anxiety, fibrocystic breast disease, and hyperlipidemia. Less clear is the evidence concerning the link between maternal caffeine consumption and the health of the newborn.[1]

Many beneficial effects of caffeine are well established, and others may be coming to light. Caffeine is a powerful bronchodilator in asthma patients and provides possible protection against the adverse pulmonary effects of smoking.[2] It also increases the length of time that chronic, stable angina patients can walk without feeling pain. Some researchers think that caffeine is effective as a therapy for neonatal apnea and could be effective as a topical treatment of atopic dermatitis.[3] It has long been recognized as an analgesic adjuvant, or enhancer of pain medications. Caffeine is also useful in averting acute hypotension (a sudden drop in blood pressure), such as that which sometimes occurs after breakfast, especially in the elderly; people experiencing this problem are advised to consume about 200–250 mg of caffeine, or about two cups of coffee, each day.[4]

The difficulties of interpreting health care studies are suggested by a juxtaposition of two articles that were published in 1983 in the *New England Journal of Medicine*. One study asserted that arrhythmias are induced in susceptible patients with about two cups of coffee or the equivalent amount of caffeine. The other challenged the significance of this conclusion, stating, "What is not yet appreciated is that ventricular premature beats are innocuous in the overwhelming majority of persons. They no more augur sudden death than a sneeze portends pneumonia."[5,6]

Coffee and tea contain so many different pharmacologically active substances that there is no easy way to isolate the effects of caffeine from those of the other substances they contain. It has even been found that the method of preparation as well as the amount consumed alters the ultimate effects on human health, especially the effects on the cardiovascular system.

Additional confounding factors plaguing research into coffee's effects are well summarized by Silvio Garattini, researcher and editor of *Caffeine, Coffee, and Health*, who comments that although there are many epidemiological studies on the health effects of caffeine and coffee, their probative value is limited by the high correlation between smoking or alcohol consumption and coffee drinking. That is, it is often almost impossible to isolate the effects arising from coffee from those arising instead from smoking or alcohol. Garattini points out that it is also difficult to come up with a universal definition of coffee consumption, because of the differences between types of coffee beans, different methods of roasting, and the varying ways of preparing coffee even in the same population. To make the situation worse, nondrinkers of coffee may also differ from coffee drinkers in their other dietary habits or aspects of their lifestyle, and in the disposition to different diseases.[7]

Individual differences in sensitivity to caffeine, differences that are often traced to inherited variations in the rate of caffeine metabolism, are another source of confusion. Few studies have been done pertaining to these differences. Although it seems likely that caffeine sensitivity, like most other quantifiable natural variables, should follow a normal bell curve of distribution, and therefore exhibit a range of values, some investigators recognize in some people a qualitatively different response than is observed in the general population. Anecdotal accounts of these unusual reactions suggest a peculiar sensitivity that goes beyond the range of normal distribution. Drug discrimination studies provide evidence for wide individual differences in sensitivity to caffeine and document that some people can detect remarkably small amounts of the drug. As reported in the *Handbook of Experimental Pharmacology*, in a chapter by Griffiths and Mumford, the lowest dose detected by research subjects ranged from 1.8 to 178 mg, with about 70 percent of them detecting 56 mg or less and about 35 percent detecting 18 mg or less.[8] Other scientists have purportedly identified more unusual reactions. For example, researcher S. S. Hayreh, in a 1973 study, gives an account of his own extreme sensitivity to caffeine, which he describes as manifested in "dizziness, weakness, and tremors, lasting two hours, and my pulse-rate went very high,"[9] effects he claims are experienced by many others. The significance of such observations remains uncertain, as researcher Jack James explains: "It is not clear whether these reactions represent pronounced, normal responses to a large caffeine dose, or whether the subject's reactions denote a peculiar sensitivity to the drug."[10]

An example of the equivocal and uncertain effects of caffeine is the current debate over whether caffeine is implicated in stimulating the symptoms of attention deficit disorder (ADD) or whether it is a possible cure for ADD or both. In other words, no one yet knows if it causes, relieves, or does not effect a given set of symptoms, an uncertainty reminiscent of the humoral debates of the sixteenth and seventeenth centuries as to whether coffee was "wet" or "dry" or "hot" or "cold" or all of these things at once.

Despite the daunting array of cautionary and compromising considerations, it is difficult not to acknowledge the concordant and apparently probative conclusions of certain large-scale, well-designed studies. For example, a study of more than twelve thousand men and women with high blood pressure and high cholesterol levels, the first large-scale prospective study of caffeine and all causes of death, concluded that there was no "relationship between coronary heart disease events or total mortality and coffee consumption"[11] in this high-risk group. The same result—that is, an absence of any relation between caffeine consumption and all or any causes of death—was found by a 1990 study of forty-five thousand men, published in the *NEJM*,[12] and also by the Framingham study,[13] the Evans County study (1960–69),[14] and the Gothenburg, Sweden, study.[15]

When evaluating the probative significance of these studies and the others referenced in this section, consider that any study demonstrating that there is no link between coffee and a given disease entity probably excludes any link with caffeine as well; while a study that demonstrates a link with coffee leaves open the question of whether caffeine or some other agent in coffee is responsible for the outcome.

Caffeine and the Cardiovascular System

The inquiry into the cardiovascular effects of caffeine is more than a century old, and clinical studies in human subjects have proliferated since the 1970s. It is now well established that the administration of caffeine to people without a history of its use produces both a transient mild pressor effect, or increase in blood pressure, and a biphasic effect on heart rate—that is, lower doses slow, and higher doses quicken, the heartbeat. Yet, despite such acute effects on people who haven't used caffeine recently, virtually all studies reveal *no long-term effect on the heart of any kind from caffeine.*

How can this be? The development of a tolerance to caffeine, which is to say, a resistance to its effects, probably explains the disparity between the apparent acute, or immediate, effects of caffeine consumption on non–caffeine users and the absence of harmful consequences in long-term users. As the tolerance to the cardiovascular effects of caffeine develops, the impact initially observed quickly declines or even disappears. The one category of risk that has not been extensively considered is the long-term cardiovascular effects of occasional coffee drinking in people without a tolerance. This means that you may be safer drinking coffee every day than you would be doing so once or twice a week. Another area requiring investigation is the interaction between stress and caffeine consumption on long-term blood pressure levels. Extrapolating from the results of studies on caffeine and heart attacks, it appears, however, that even the combination of caffeine and stress will rarely have any clinical impact.[16]

Increased blood pressure is a cause of congestive heart failure and a major cause of death. An increase in either systolic pressure, which is the pressure associated with the contraction of the heart muscle, or diastolic pressure, which is associated with its relaxation, can be dangerous, but an elevated diastolic pressure, or lower number given in a blood pressure reading, is the more critical. Conversely, lowered blood pressure is associated with a lowered incidence of congestive heart failure and other cardiovascular diseases. It is therefore of significant interest to note that a 1989 Norwegian study of thirty thousand middle-aged men and women demonstrated that drinking more than one cup of coffee a day is positively correlated with a *reduction* in both systolic and diastolic blood pressure. In other words, people who drink a cup of coffee every day tend to have lower blood pressure than people who do not.[17]

The short-term effects of caffeine on blood pressure are just the opposite. People not used to caffeine experience an immediate increase in blood pressure, that is, a moderate pressor effect, and a related reduction in heart rate, or bradycardia, of brief duration, usually less than four hours. These effects apparently cease when caffeine is consumed regularly and a tolerance develops.[18,19]

These studies considered people with normal blood pressure. But what if your blood pressure is high to begin with? What will caffeine do to you then? In 1984 D. Robertson, a medical researcher, undertook a study of hypertensives and found that, as in the earlier study of people with normal pressure, acute responses of elevated blood pressure and slowed heart rate were observed to occur the first day and to disappear thereafter. Robertson concluded that the acute response to caffeine was actually less in hypertensives than in normal people, and that "tolerance developed rapidly and completely." Other researchers have concluded that there was no association between caffeine consumption and all or any causes of mortality among this large group of hypertensives.

An interesting aside is that, in days gone by, caffeine was sometimes used by anesthetists during surgery to increase dangerously low blood pressure. Its effect was transitory, and it would not be considered reliable enough to be the drug of choice today. Dr. Adriani, who was the anesthetist in chief at Charity Hospital New Orleans for many years, describes this procedure in a 1940 textbook he wrote. One of his students gave the following account in 1996: "I'm a 'vintage' nurse anesthetist. In my salad days, I used caffeine sodium benzoate as a stimulant to raise a patient's blood pressure, during surgery. It is no longer used, as there are better drugs available. The dose I used was .5 gram, given subcutaneously."

Caffeine and Cholesterol, Heart Attacks, and Coronary Heart Disease

Lipids comprise a group of organic compounds, including fatty acids, waxes, phospholipids, and steroids, that are stored in the body as fat and used as energy reserves. Lipids contain cholesterol, as do all animal fats, and elevated serum cholesterol levels are strongly correlated with heart attacks, strokes, and early death.

Since the phenomenon was first noticed in 1970, many studies have confirmed that the use of unfiltered (sometimes mislabeled "boiled") coffee can contribute significantly to an increase in serum cholesterol levels in both men and women, especially in those whose levels were elevated to begin with. A 1990 thesis published in the Netherlands reviewing twenty-four studies differentiated the effects of different brewing methods. In conclusions supported by subsequent European studies, the author found *filtered coffee produced little if any increase in cholesterol levels*, while in contrast unfiltered coffee was correlated with an increase amounting to as much as 15 percent. The fact that different brewing methods produce such a variation in effects on lipid levels may help explain why the cholesterol-raising effects of coffee have been shown to vary widely between different nationalities. A dramatic example of this effect is the substantial drop of cholesterol levels over the last fifteen years in Finland paralleling the change from infusion to filter-drip as the most popular method of brewing coffee.

Most researchers think that some strong, naturally occurring ingredient of coffee is responsible for these effects and that caffeine is in no way implicated. Roasting itself forms fatty acids such as cafestol, kahweol, and their derivatives. Most of these lipids remain in the spent grounds, but the amount that get into your coffee cup can vary from 1 to 40 mg, depending on the fineness of the grind and the method of preparation. Many researchers think that there is an as yet unknown substance, present in the oil of all coffees, that acts as a cholesterol-raising factor.[20] In any event, caffeine consumption levels seem to have no correlation with cholesterol levels.

More significantly for lay readers, the Framingham Heart Study also found that levels of coffee consumption had *"no influence on the rate of coronary heart disease,"*[21] and the study found no evidence to support the hypothesis that the level of caffeine consumption is related to the death rates from strokes in hypertensive patients.

Caffeine and Hemostasis and Fibrinolysis[22]

Hemostasis is any process which stops bleeding, notably including the body's coagulation process, or clotting. Fibrinolysis is the process by which the body breaks down clots, averting thrombosis, a pathological condition in which a thrombus, or blood clot, forms within a blood vessel. In an artery supplying the brain, these clots can result in a stroke, and in an artery supplying the heart, they can result in a heart attack.

No effect by either coffee or caffeine on the coagulation process has been observed.

However, very curious and interesting effects of caffeine on fibrinolysis have been suggested by recent research. In order to understand the importance of these effects, consider that reduced fibrinolysis is strongly associated with an increase in heart attacks. That is to say, when the process of breaking down clots is rendered less efficient, the resulting undissolved blockages can become dangerous and even life threatening. Conversely, an increase in the efficiency of fibrinolysis can help protect against heart attacks; drugs are now used to boost the body's ability in this respect, helping to dissolve blood clots that the body cannot handle. Because studies have found that clot-dissolving time is reduced by regular coffee drinking but remains unaffected by decaffeinated coffee drinking, many researchers think that caffeine is probably the agent responsible for this difference. If this is true, caffeine must operate in effectively the same way as certain pharmaceutical products designed to reduce the risks of heart attacks and strokes, thus counterbalancing the otherwise deleterious effects of coffee on clotting time.[23]

Caffeine and the Respiratory System

Asthma, a respiratory disorder marked by a reversible airway obstruction, with attending difficulty in breathing, wheezing, cough, and thick mucus production, is the most common breathing affliction. As many as 10 percent of children suffer from asthma to the extent that they require medical treatment.[24] Caffeine, at first administered in the vehicle of strong coffee, has been used to relieve the symptoms of asthma for hundreds of years. Its primary respiratory effect is an increase in the respiratory rate, which corresponds closely with plasma caffeine levels. In patients with asthma, caffeine functions as a relaxant of bronchial tissue or a bronchodilator. Today, theophylline, another methylxanthine, is also widely used for the same purpose, because it has almost twice the potency in this respect and is thought to be less toxic to the central nervous system than caffeine. Widespread experience in treating newborns with caffeine for neonatal apnea, or arrested breathing, which often occurs in premature infants, has presented an unusual opportunity to study its possible toxic effects. Although some agitation does occur at the levels used in treatment, there is an absence of toxicity in newborns. However, as with other potential detrimental effects of the methylxanthines, a definitive answer about its possible effects on growth and development awaits further research, for which reason the treatment of infants with caffeine is discontinued as soon as possible, usually after only a few weeks.

Everyone knows from common experience that cigarette smokers have a far higher likelihood of being caffeine fanciers as well. Perhaps, as in Walsh's words, "Under such a fact there may be more significance than science has yet elicited"—more significance than has been understood until recently, that is. Medical researcher D. R. Lima, in 1989, investigated the theory that *caffeine might help protect smokers against the development of chronic bronchitis and pulmonary edema.*[25] Both smokers and non-smokers were tested after smoking a cigarette with or without an accompanying cup of coffee. Coffee was found to provide protection against the adverse pulmonary effects of smoking. In researcher Jack James' words, "The investigators concluded that regular intake of coffee might be beneficial to smokers in delaying the development of chronic obstructive lung disease."[26] Obviously more research is needed to define these benefits more precisely. However, based on current results of studies of caffeine's effects on pulmonary function, we can responsibly assert that caffeine may have important therapeutic potential in this respect.

In the 1970s, the American Heart Association recommended that people who wanted to quit smoking should concurrently stop drinking coffee and eliminate all sources of caffeine. Subsequent studies have suggested that the American Heart Association's strategy only complicates matters. After all, sudden withdrawal from caffeine can have unpleasant consequences that certainly won't ameliorate the withdrawal effects of stopping cigarette smoking and may even make them more difficult to cope with.

However, one caveat for those attempting to quit smoking is in order. We now know that cigarettes increase the rate of caffeine metabolism and shorten or attenuate its effects in smokers. This means that smokers must consume more caffeine to achieve the same effects as non-smokers, which may be one reason smokers drink more coffee than non-smokers. Therefore, cigarette smokers who are cutting down or eliminating tobacco should *reduce* their caffeine intake, especially if it was high to begin with, because, in the absence of smoking, caffeine will have a much stronger and longer-lasting effect on them than they had been accustomed to experiencing. To put it simply, if a heavy smoker is used to drinking four cups of strong coffee to wake up, he might find that, after discontinuing his cigarette habit, two cups will accomplish the same purpose.[27]

Caffeine and Cancer and Tumor Activity

No disease inspires more dread than cancer, perhaps in part because, in our aging population, cancer's incidence is on the rise. Although more potent treatments are developed every year, we are still far from attaining a complete understanding of what cancer is and what its causes are, and people are reasonably afraid of anything that they think causes the disease. In recent decades caffeine has sometimes been called a carcinogen; for example, a 1981 study created a concern more than a link with pancreatic cancer. As it turned out, this fear was unfounded.

Since early studies indicated a positive correlation between caffeine in high concentrations and cancer in animals, this connection has been widely studied. Results, however, have been contradictory, even though doses so high that they are unlikely ever to be experienced by people have invariably been used: Depending on the dose, the timing of administration, and the experimental protocol, caffeine appears to raise or lower cancer incidence.[28]

Much of the information putatively pertaining to caffeine as a possible cause of cancer is compromised by the fact that most studies have been based on usage profiles of coffee, not of caffeine itself, and because coffee contains more than 100 active chemicals, it presents a particularly complex matrix, within which it is difficult to disentangle the singular role of caffeine. We must wonder, for example, if or to what extent the suggestions of a positive correlation between coffee and bladder cancer are related to its caffeine content. Certainly skepticism about the role of caffeine is aroused when we consider those studies of bladder cancer in which the results of the use of decaffeinated coffee were indistinguishable from the results of the use of regular coffee.[29] Coffee contains several other suspected carcinogens, including creosote, pymdine, and miscellaneous tars, all created by the heat of roasting,[30] and some claim that the polycyclic aromatic hydrocarbons that are responsible for coffee's taste and smell also cause cancer, although the fact that coffee contributes less that .1 percent of dietary intake of these substances makes that notion seem alarmist.[31] In addition, there are sticklers who admonish that carcinogenic dioxins in bleached coffee filters leach into the drink. To confuse matters even more, cafestol and kahweol, present in your cup of coffee in amounts proportional to the oil content, are non-mutagenic and in animal experiments have shown cancer-protective activity with relatively large doses.[32]

However, despite this confusion, because the possible relationship between coffee and cancer has been so extensively considered in the past thirty years, while there has been very little investigation of caffeine and cancer and tumor activity apart from the matrix of coffee, it is worth reviewing summaries of these results for whatever light they may shed on the question of caffeine.

Fibrocystic breast disease, a condition characterized by benign fibrous lumps in the breast, is not dangerous, but it can be very painful, and the cysts that it produces drive many women to their doctors for tests to rule out breast cancer. Since the late 1970s, some researchers have suspected a causal link between caffeine and this condition, and an early study suggested that caffeine abstinence might reduce symptoms of the disease. A 1986 National Cancer Institute (NCI) study of over three thousand women found no evidence of any correlation between caffeine use and benign tumors, fibrocystic breast disease, or breast tenderness.[33] However, a subsequent study by the institute of more than fifteen hundred women concluded that women consuming 250 mg of caffeine (about as much as in two cups of coffee) daily experienced a 50 percent increase in the condition, while those consuming 500 mg experienced nearly a 150 percent increase. Such results have led one researcher to claim that a caffeine-free regimen supplemented by 800 mg of vitamin E daily can provide substantial relief for two-thirds of women with fibrocystic breast disease.[34]

In a Norwegian cohort study on coffee use of more than fifteen thousand people, from 1967 to 1978, no significant positive correlation was found between coffee use and any disease, including all cancers.[35] In 1990 the International Agency for Research of Cancer, after performing an extensive review of research on digestive, bladder and urinary tract, breast, and other cancer sites, published a monograph summarizing findings on coffee and cancer. The results tended to confirm the Norwegian study's conclusions. They specifically excluded any link between caffeine use and the incidence of cancer of the oral cavity, esophagus, stomach, liver, breast, ovaries, kidney, or the lympho-recticular system, including Hodgkin's disease, non-Hodgkin's lymphomas, and lymphatic and myeloid leukemia.

Caffeine and Children and Young Adults

By all accounts exposure to caffeine begins early for most people, very early. More than 75 percent of infants tested exhibit detectable levels of caffeine in their blood at birth.[36] Even though small children and adolescents apparently ingest less caffeine than most adults, their exposure, measured in terms of serum levels, may be higher, because the concentration of caffeine in the body is a function of body weight. However, one 1991 study determined that children five to eighteen have an average intake of just under 40 mg, about half of a cup of coffee, and that this averages to the equivalent of 1 mg/kg,[37] much less than the adult mean intake of 3 mg/kg.[38] Unfortunately, such broad averaging of children from preschool age to college age, with widely varying body weights and patterns of caffeine usage, does little to reassure us about the more extreme components that are lost in taking the mean value.

The best overall estimates of caffeine consumption levels in infants and children are more than twenty years old. They were compiled by the National Academy of

Sciences GRAS Survey Committee in 1977.[39] So far, caffeine has made the GRAS list, being "generally recognized as safe," every year. The committee's results indicated that about 18 percent of infants under two years old consumed some caffeine in any given two-week interval. In the six- to eleven-month-old group, the mean intake of the entire group was 4.2 mg a day, but the mean intake of those who consumed caffeine was an incredible 77 mg a day. Although this is about as much as in a typical cup of coffee, it should be remembered the exposure of infants is much higher than it is for adults, because of the immaturity of the infant's metabolic pathways and its dramatically smaller body weight. In this age group, exposure occurred chiefly as a result of mothers administering cola to their children as a remedy for colic.

Perhaps you have always taken it for granted that a substance in general use by children must be safe for them. Unfortunately, this may not be true. A recent study of more than six hundred preschool children in Long Island found a positive correlation between high caffeine use and reports by parents of uncontrollable energy or hyperactivity, impulsiveness, headaches, restlessness, and other behavioral problems. Because these symptoms are all associated with attention deficit disorder (ADD), Dr. Mitchell Schare of Hofstra University, who conducted the study, suggests that many diagnoses of ADD may actually be misdiagnoses based on problems actually arising from caffeine use. On the other side of the question, other studies apparently demonstrate that children diagnosed as hyperactive are no more sensitive than adults to caffeine,[40] and a 1984 study concluded that caffeine was not a cause of ADD.[41]

In 1994, the *Journal of Child and Adolescent Psychiatry* published a study of children ages eight to twelve warning that, although caffeine may improve children's attention to detail and their manual dexterity, it also increases their anxiety. The researcher expressed concern over the findings, because caffeine is widely used, even among the youngest children, while its effects on them have not been extensively studied. Because caffeine, in addition to being found in coffee and hot tea, is also found in carbonated soft drinks, iced tea, and hot chocolate, which are favorite drinks of children, the paradox of the "unstudied most widely studied drug" emerges most critically in relation to the lack of knowledge about its health effect on the young. In children and teenagers the dietary sources of caffeine, in order of importance, were found to be tea, soft drinks, and coffee. Chocolate foods and beverages were the lowest of these dietary sources of caffeine, but they constitute the major source of dietary theobromine for children as well as adults. The statistical breakdown for preschooler caffeine consumption: iced tea (mostly bottled, e.g., Snapple, Arizona), 42 percent; colas (all brands), 35 percent; and all others (chocolate milk, hot tea, coffee, non-cola soft drinks), 23 percent.[42]

After decades of speculation, beginning with the Wiley debates early in the century, information is coming to light that gives new life to concerns about targeting children as consumers of caffeinated soft drinks. Studies in the last decade have shown that children respond to the caffeine in soft drinks the way we would expect them to respond to an addictive drug. One concluded that children eleven to fifteen are sensitive to the reinforcing effects of caffeine levels in soft drinks,[43] while another actually demonstrated caffeine withdrawal in children ten years old after they stopped drinking soda. Obviously parents should be mindful of the habit-forming potential of caffeine when considering what beverages to permit their children.

Because of the risks we have adumbrated and other fears, some consumer groups concerned with children's health issues have spoken out against advertising that they believe encourages children to use pills of any kind, including vitamins and caffeine. The Action for Children's Television (ACT) group succeeded in persuading the Federal Trade Commission to ban vitamin ads directed at children in 1972. In the early 1980s, the same group questioned the propriety of television ads for caffeine pills in shows directed primarily at young children. The ad to which they refer showed one child admonishing another child, who was nodding at his desk, "If you don't graduate, we're in trouble. Here, revive with Vivarin."[44] These ads have since been discontinued, and Vivarin and other producers of caffeine-based alertness aids are careful to target only an adult market.

Caffeine and Drug Combinations and Counterfeits

Caffeine is frequently added to amphetamines, amphetamine-based hallucinogens, LSD, cocaine, and even heroin to augment their psychoactive effects. For example, Reuters reported that French customs agents arrested a woman at a toll both north of Paris on December 26, 1994. In the rented car were her two children, twelve pounds of heroin, and enough paracetamol and caffeine to cut it into 150,000 doses worth nearly $3 million on the street.

In 1984 prosecutors secured the first Philadelphia conviction on record for intent to distribute a look-alike drug substance. In this case, the guilty party had been found with more than fifteen hundred caffeine capsules that resembled "black beauties," bathtub amphetamines that have been sold in the form of black capsules since the 1960s. Although he faced up to five years' imprisonment, he received three years' probation and a $300 fine. "You can buy them legitimately," an assistant district attorney said of the seized caffeine capsules. "You just can't sell them."[45]

In 1996 customs officers in Hong Kong searched a suspicious car parked at a garage and discovered a camera bag under the driver's seat containing a pound of relatively pure heroin and a pound of caffeine powder. In a follow-up bust, officers uncovered a heroin cutting operation at an apartment, including about five pounds of heroin, thirty pounds of caffeine, and equipment to mix the two. Adding caffeine gives a chemical boost to the drug, simulating a popular and extremely dangerous combination of heroin and cocaine called a "speedball."

Rave parties are usually large wild dance bashes in which many of the participants take potent psychedelic and stimulant drug combinations to help them stay awake to drink and dance all night. The most popular drug is the street drug ecstasy, a combination of several psychoactive drugs, most often including an amphetamine derivative, LSD, and caffeine. Recently a police raid in Perth, Australia, recovered a batch of ten off-white, imperfectly pressed tablets of ecstasy that contained, along with the usual ingredients, a dangerous addition: heroin. Caffeine has already been implicated in an incident at a Los Angeles New Year's Eve rave party in which dozens of partygoers were hospitalized with serious symptoms, including difficulty breathing and hallucinations. Police confiscated about ten thousand vials of Biolife FX, bottled by Biolife Bioproducts Ltd., based in San Diego. Tests showed that the key active ingredients were caffeine and kava kava, an extract of the African kava root that creates a mild depressant or hypnotic effect. All the partygoers recovered. The FDA is currently investigating whether to take action against the manufacturer for failing to adequately warn consumers about the high level of caffeine in the product.

The Other Methylxanthines: Theobromine and Theophylline

Theobromine is relatively weak, milligram for milligram, compared with its sister methylxanthines, caffeine or theophylline.[46] Nevertheless, because cacao contains eight times more theobromine than it does caffeine, theobromine is nearly as important to its stimulating effects as the smaller amount of caffeine.[47]

The clinical use of theophylline is more frequent than that of caffeine.[48] Unlike caffeine, which is readily available in effective doses from a variety of natural sources, theophylline, where it does occur, is present in such small amounts that its effects are negligible. Therefore, to reach effective doses, theophylline must be specially administered. Theophylline is used in several effective inhalers, such as Primatene Mist, for bronchodilation. However, the FDA, after receiving reports of life-threatening side effects and even death, recently declared over-the-counter *oral* combination drug preparations containing theophylline, such as Primatene tablets, to be neither safe nor effective.

There is particular concern over the increased danger posed by the combination of theophylline and ephedrine, which occurs in bronchodilator products as well as OTC cough and cold remedies. The FDA, which would like to remove them from the market, also cites the fact that these products are often sold as weight control or muscle building agents, for which purposes their effectiveness has not been proved.

Although all three are closely related chemically, caffeine, theophylline, and theobromine have different profiles of action. A brief summary of these effects, listed in order of their clinical significance, follows.

Sources and Clinical Effects of Methylxanthines
Effects are listed in order of clinical significance.

Caffeine
Sources: Coffee, tea, cola nuts, maté, guarana.
Effects: Stimulant of central nervous system, cardiac muscle, and respiratory system, diuretic. Delays fatigue.

Theophylline
Sources: Tea
Effects: Cardiac stimulant, smooth muscle relaxant, diuretic, vasodilator.

Theobromine:
Sources: Cacao, also present in traces in cola nuts and tea.
Effects: Diuretic, smooth muscle relaxant, cardiac stimulant, vasodilator.

Caffeine and Birth Defects

The nature of caffeine's effects on birth abnormalities and fertility is probably the most urgent unresolved question that remains to be addressed by future researchers. In this section we present what is known today about these effects and, in Appendix D, explain the formidable methodological confounders—that is, factors that confuse the interpretation of the data—that researchers in this area must surmount before these effects can be understood.

The consensus of the medical and scientific community is that, to avoid risk to the fetus, women ought to curtail caffeine use during pregnancy, although authorities differ about the nature or extent of the dangers of failing to do so. But the worrisome fact is that, despite this admonition, most women using caffeine continue throughout pregnancy, with an average intake among users of more than 200 mg a day. As a result, the great majority of babies begin life with detectable levels of the drug in their blood.[49,50] Because fetal exposure to caffeine is so pervasive, any unfavorable effect on the health of the newborn, even one with a very low incidence, could mean tens of thousands of defective births a year in the United States alone. It is therefore critical to investigate the effect of caffeine exposure on the outcomes of pregnancy as exhaustively as possible.

Two facts about caffeine metabolism increase concern over the harm that could be posed by maternal caffeine use.

First, caffeine metabolism dramatically slows during gestation. The metabolic rate drops progressively, falling to one-half normal during the second trimester, and to one-third normal during the third trimester,[51] before returning to normal within the week following delivery. This means that caffeine that is ingested by the woman in the last few months of pregnancy will remain in her system three times longer than usual, and, consequently, that the exposure of her unborn child to caffeine will last three times longer.[52]

Second, the livers of the fetus and newborn are unable to metabolize caffeine. Because of the incapacity of their hepatic enzyme systems, their livers cannot transform caffeine into its metabolites, so the drug lingers in their systems much longer than in either children or adults, until it is finally excreted, virtually unchanged, in the urine.[53] One researcher found the mean elimination time in infants being treated for apnea with caffeine was one hundred hours, fifteen times the adult average, and other scientists report a range up to about 350 hours in premature infants.[54] These dramatic metabolic decrements, however, are short-lived. The infant's capacity to metabolize caffeine progressively increases in the first months of life until it reaches the adult level of three to seven hours by the eighth month,[55] though full maturity of the metabolic pathways of caffeine may not be achieved until the end of the first year.[56]

Because the risk of gross morphological abnormalities is high only in the first trimester, one would not expect that a decrease in the mother's ability to metabolize caffeine occurring *later* in the pregancy could significantly increase the risk of these abnormalities. Happily, the latest studies convincingly exclude maternal caffeine use as a cause of such gross morphological abnormalities in human infants.

Caffeine and Morphological Abnormalities

Teratology, from the Greek roots meaning "the study of monsters," is the examination of congenital abnormalities and defects. Teratologies are often associated with maternal exposure to drugs or chemicals, because the fetus is much more vulnerable than either a child or an adult to their adverse effects, with different risks attaching to different stages of fetal development. As we have seen, the greatest risk for gross morphological defects, which is to say, for obvious deformations of the skeleton, face, or major organs, is associated with the first trimester. Although all drugs and chemicals come under scrutiny with regard to such dangers, there are special reasons caffeine has been singled out for concern.

The structural similarity between caffeine and some of the building blocks of DNA—that is, the DNA base pairs adenine and guanine[57]—sometimes called the "DNA purines," raised the ominous possibility that caffeine may interfere with the functioning or replication of genetic material. This threat spurred extensive laboratory investigations and epidemiological studies, for if caffeine does interfere with DNA, there is no limit to the severity or extent of the dangers it would pose. Nowhere would these dangers be more acute than in the first weeks following conception, when each cell is a repository of information needed for the development of a major bodily system, and when damage to the DNA of any one cell could result in a gross malformation. According to a 1992 review of the literature published by the Johns Hopkins University School of Hygiene and Public Health, scientists posit several mechanisms by which caffeine could inflict genetic damage:[58]

- Caffeine may be an intercalator; that is, it may interpose itself into the DNA sequence
- Caffeine may inhibit enzymes that catalyze DNA
- Caffeine may damage DNA
- Caffeine potentiates the toxic effects on cells of ionizing radiation, alkylators (drugs used in the chemotherapeutic treatment of cancer), and other mutagens on eucaryotic cells (cells with true nuclei)

Despite this menacing list of hypothetical mechanisms and a clear determination that caffeine is "mutagenic in bacteria, fungi, plants and human cell cultures,"[59] *no epidemiological association has been demonstrated between caffeine use and adverse outcomes of pregnancy, with particularly reassuring exclusionary findings with regard to major malformations.* Although gross morphological defects can consistently be induced in laboratory animals by administering toxic doses of caffeine, producing serum levels that would be fatal in people, no relationship between maternal caffeine consumption and congenital skeletal malformations or malformations of any organs has been found in human beings.[60] Studies suggesting caffeine's harmful effects on the fetus prompted the FDA, in 1980, to institute a recommendation that pregnant women should eliminate caffeine intake or keep it as low as possible. However, a shift in the scientific estimate of caffeine's reproductive dangers is represented by the reassessment of this warning made by the FDA in 1984. At that time, Dr. Sanford Miller, director of the

FDA's Bureau of Foods, said that caffeine during gestation is probably acceptable if limited to the amount in two or three cups of coffee daily, and that fears about its effects were based on animal studies in which enormous amounts were given to pregnant rats in a single dose. Today, although caffeine is no longer suspect in major teratologies, the original FDA warning remains in place, and has been recently reaffirmed, because of fears relating to less obvious injuries.[61]

Caffeine and Non-Morphological Abnormalities: From Low Birthweight to Behavioral Dysfunction

Much less attention has been paid to the effects of caffeine on premature births, spontaneous abortions, or the comparatively subtle processes of intrauterine development. Because the risks of low birthweight and other less obvious abnormalities increase throughout pregnancy, the progressively slowing metabolic passage of caffeine poses a greater threat of these dangers than of gross morphological defects. Unfortunately, there is still considerable uncertainty about caffeine's effect on such subtler defects. However, widespread experience treating newborns with caffeine for apnea, which provides an unusual opportunity to study its possible toxic effects, strongly suggests that "the fetus during the later states of pregnancy . . . should be fairly robust to the systemic levels associated with typical patterns of maternal caffeine consumption."[62]

Virtually all of the larger and better constructed studies demonstrate no correlation of prematurity with caffeine use.[63,64] However, the literature remains contradictory as to whether caffeine has any correlation with spontaneous abortions. A number of major studies[65,66] found no significant association. In contrast, a 1992 study of more than fifty thousand pregnant women[67] reported a small but significant dose-dependent increase in spontaneous abortions. Those who believe the increase in the miscarriage rate is real explain it by offering an unsubstantiated conjecture that caffeine enters the egg just before the opportunity for implantation and may interfere with implantation, so that the blastocyst, or fertilized egg, is lost or develops abnormally.[68]

Almost forty years ago, two scientists issued a warning about the potential dangers to fetal development resulting from paternal caffeine consumption immediately prior to conception. Noting that the concentration in sperm cells is virtually identical to the serum levels, they stated, "germ cells are bathed in a caffeine solution of fluctuating concentration."[69] The significance of this effect is still unknown today.

Since 1980, a few animal studies have apparently confirmed an association between behavioral abnormalities in the fetus and maternal use of caffeine, raising concerns that similar effects may obtain in people. However, there have been few studies of neurobehavioral effects in humans, and these have conflicting results. One prospective study, which followed children from before birth to age seven, showed caffeine had no effects on the neurodevelopment of infants or children.[70] In contrast, another showed "poor neuromuscular development and greater arousal and irritability in neonates."[71]

Dr. Leo Leader of the School of Obstetrics and Gynecology at the University of New South Wales has also investigated the effect coffee has on unborn babies. His early findings suggest that, within about twenty minutes after the mother drinks a cup of coffee, the caffeine stimulates fetal movement. Other studies have already shown that caffeine intensifies the contraction of the heart and that even moderate doses of caffeine (200 mg) decrease placental blood flow.[72]

In a more speculative vein, generalized prenatal learning ability has been purportedly measured by determining how long a fetus takes to stop reacting to the repeated buzzing of an electric toothbrush pressed to the outside of a mother's stomach. Initially, the fetal heart rate increases and the fetus demonstrates increased movement. Then, through a basic learning response called "habituation," normal babies stop reacting between ten and fifty buzzes. Leader has demonstrated that fetuses who were able to demonstrate habituation did significantly better in tests of movement, socialization, language, and behavior between a year and two years after birth than those who were not. Chemicals ingested by the mother can cause an immediate reaction in the fetus's ability to learn. For example, for about two hours after a mother smoked a cigarette, the fetal ability to respond to the buzzing was found to be absent or impaired. Dr. Leader intends to test if caffeine accelerates or slows the fetal response to the buzzing toothbrush.

Can a pregnant woman addict a fetus to caffeine? In other words, if a woman uses coffee, tea, or caffeinated soft drinks during pregnancy, can her baby be born with the symptoms of caffeine withdrawal? A 1988 study identified five babies who were born suffering from withdrawal syndrome; however, the levels of caffeine used by their mothers were remarkably large, averaging fifteen cups of coffee or two quarts of cola each day.[73] Another study, completed the same year, found that eight children of heavy-caffeine-using mothers demonstrated unusual levels of irritability, jitteriness, and vomiting, with an absence of any of the usual causes for such symptoms.[74] Some investigators have speculated that caffeine withdrawal could be implicated in neonatal apnea (an idea bolstered by the fact that caffeine is an effective treatment for apnea) and sudden infant death syndrome (SIDS), while others suggest the possibility that maternal caffeine use during pregnancy may be associated with childhood diabetes.[75]

If a woman continues drinking caffeinated beverages while nursing, the caffeine from her breast milk enters the infant's system at a time when the child metabolizes it imperfectly or not at all. Thus the effect on the infant is multiplied many times during a period in which its neurodevelopment can still be affected.[76] Despite the obvious possibility of a hazard, the Association of Women's Health, Obstetric & Neonatal Nurses published a pamphlet in cooperation with IFIC, the public relations arm of a food industry–sponsored scientific organization, advising:

> The American Academy of Pediatrics Committee on Drugs has reviewed the effects of caffeine on breast feeding and reported that moderate caffeine consumption has no effect on breast feeding.
>
> As with all foods, pregnant and lactating women should apply the principle of moderation. . . . A reasonable guideline is around 300mg daily.[77]

Caffeine and Fertility

Perhaps no area of concern over caffeine's effect on health has a longer history or has been the subject of more confusion than fertility. Long before caffeine had been isolated, coffee was charged with reducing fertility in both men and women and with reducing the sexual appetites of men. As we saw, the latter effect was the subject of heated broadsides against coffeehouses from the distaff side in seventeenth-century London.

Repeated studies have failed to find a dose-related correlation between caffeine consumption and the risk of either delayed conception or persistent infertility in women. A typical example is a retrospective study of more than two thousand post-delivery women that found no association with delayed conception.[78] It concluded that the average time to conception (four or five months) for women who consumed the equivalent of one cup of coffee a week was similar to the time to conception for those who consumed more than two cups a day. In addition, the study found that caffeine consumption was not a risk factor for primary infertility. However, because other studies suggest that caffeine intake *can* contribute to delaying conception, perhaps the best advice for women who are intending to become pregnant is to minimize or eliminate caffeine intake, at least until more proof of its consequences has been gathered. [79]

Because caffeine permeates every cell of the body with ease, the concentrations of caffeine in male gonadal tissue and seminal fluid are virtually identical to those that occur in the blood. Therefore it has been widely conjectured that caffeine has dose-related effects on the number and structure of spermatozoa. Its varying effects on sperm motility are well-documented.[80] When semen is exposed to high concentrations of caffeine immediately prior to artificial insemination, the increased motility is sufficient to double a woman's chances of getting pregnant. It is not known if there are deleterious effects on the sperm that may later increase the likelihood of miscarriage. Oddly enough, the profile of some of caffeine's effects on sperm observed both in vitro and in vivo closely resembles that predicted by the Yerkes-Dodson principle, enunciated in 1908, that the "relationship between arousal and performance efficiency takes the form of an inverted-U,"[81] which is to say that performance is best at intermediate arousal levels and drops off in states of low arousal, such as when a person is bored or tired, or in states of high arousal, as when a person is anxious or under stress. This means that the effects of caffeine on sperm cells increase with the dose until a certain level is reached, whereupon additional doses of the drug have less and less impact, and still higher doses progressively reverse its initial effects.

Researchers L. Dlugosz and M. B. Bracken comment on these findings:

> In several in vitro assays, human sperm motility and sperm progression increased with the addition of caffeine. However in other assays, more detrimental effects on spermatozoa ultrastructure and penetrating ability were observed at high concentrations than at low concentrations of caffeine. In a study of 446 men attending

an infertility clinic, men who drank 1–2 cups of coffee per day had *increased* sperm motility and density compared with subjects who drank no coffee. However, men who drank more than 2 cups per day had *decreased* sperm motility and density…. Current data are too sparse to draw conclusions about the effects of caffeine consumption on male infertility.[82]

Thus, although the effect of large doses on fertility in men is still undetermined, moderate doses of caffeine may even help a man to father a child, and the dynamics of caffeine's effects on sperm seem to resemble those ascribed to alcohol on sexual performance in the traditional aphorism, "A little stimulates; a lot depresses."

Caffeine and Weight Loss

Once upon a time, men who wished to set themselves on a thorny quest chose to pursue the Holy Grail, the cup used by Christ at the Last Supper, a draught from which would confer all earthly and heavenly benisons. Today the quest for the Grail has been replaced by the quest for a "fat pill," a safe, pharmacologically active chemical that a person can ingest to reduce and keep off excess fat. Presumably the scientist who discovers and the first company that markets such a wondrous medicament will eclipse Bill Gates and Microsoft as the greatest financial success story in modern times.

The key words here are "safe" and "reduce and keep off." Many stimulants, especially powerful ones such as amphetamines and cocaine, effectively suppress appetite and increase metabolic rates. In other words, they help burn fat at a faster rate than normal. The problem is that their use is not safe and that, irrespective of their dangers, the capacity, at least of cocaine, to reduce your appetite seems to wear off as usage continues. A full range of amphetamine derivatives have been legal prescription drugs for decades, but they are rarely prescribed today, as some of them once were, as treatments for obesity or aids for weight loss. To fill the void left by their removal, natural medicine enthusiasts have marketed a variety of quack nostrums promising to "burn fat" or "speed up metabolism."

Despite repeated claims of tabloid headlines touting these breakthroughs, few people believe that such a fat-burning substance actually exists or is even in the early stages of development. The amazing truth, however, is that common caffeine might be the fat-burning wonder drug everyone has been looking for all along.

Dr. John William Daly, one of the most respected researchers on the pharmacology of caffeine, states in his 1993 review paper "The Mechanism of Action of Caffeine"[83] that, in addition to its effects on the cardiovascular, respiratory, renal, and central nervous systems, caffeine affects adipose (fat) tissue by stimulating lipolysis, that is, by increasing the catabolism, or burning, of fat. Additionally, caffeine partially blocks the effect of adenosine and adenosine analogs, neurotransmitters that inhibit lipolysis. In other words, caffeine enables your body to burn fat faster and might help you to lose weight.

There is some clinical evidence of this effect. People undertaking exercise studies under controlled conditions demonstrate more weight loss if their exercise was preceded by a very hefty dose of caffeine. Caffeine increases the level of circulating fatty acids, so-called free fatty acids, or FFA, released from adipose tissue. Between one and two hours after consumption, or according to other studies, three to four hours or more after consumption, caffeine has been shown, under certain conditions, to increase the oxidation of these as fuel and hence to enhance fat oxidation. Caffeine has been used for years by runners and endurance athletes to improve performance, presumably by enhancing fatty acid metabolism. It seems effective in those who are not habitual users. Some studies suggest that this effect is most pronounced during long-duration low-intensity exercise, where lipids play a more important role in energy production, and that the effects are most noticeable in persons who are not highly trained athletes.

Caffeine may also work in other ways to help weight loss. It increases basal metabolic rate and resting metabolic rate, in both lean and obese subjects, by as much as 15 percent, and keeps these rates elevated for at least two hours after ingestion.[84] Additionally, there is ample anecdotal evidence that caffeine, like other stimulants, such as amphetamine and cocaine, is an appetite suppressant.

The practical question remains: Can caffeine be an effective aid to weight loss, and if so, under what conditions and to what degree will it augment the efforts of diet and exercise in shedding pounds? As with so many questions about caffeine and health, the answer seems to be a combination of "it depends" and "nobody knows." There have been many studies of the interaction of caffeine and exercise and of the effects of caffeine on levels of FFA and fat oxidation. The conclusions are apparently contradictory, providing support for just about any combination of conclusions you might choose to argue. The effects of caffeine on energy output, endurance, and fat metabolism vary widely on account of many factors: the complexity of the human system, the variations in how much caffeine is consumed, how long before the trial it is consumed, how long the exercise is continued, the physical condition of the subject, the tolerance of the subject to caffeine, and which muscles are being used in the exercise. Psychogenic effects may also be important: People may not perceive themselves as growing tired when they have ingested caffeine, and therefore they may continue their efforts longer. More carefully designed studies are needed to define the contributions of this slew of confounders. Meanwhile, there is good evidence that caffeine can help at least some people doing some exercises to do them longer and burn more fat while doing them.

Caffeine and Exercise and Athletic Performance: Is Caffeine an Ergogenic Aid?

There is a widespread conviction among many athletes and sportsmen that caffeine boosts performance in terms of endurance and energy output, and that, in short, using caffeine helps you to increase your speed and capacity to lift weights, and in general to excel in athletic pursuits. Many long-distance cyclists, runners, and cross-country skiers use caffeine during competition. Even racehorses are sometimes doped with and tested for caffeine.

The belief in the power of caffeine to augment athletic capacity is reflected in a 1962 decision by the International Olympic Committee (IOC) to restrict caffeine use by participants in the games to a urinary concentration of 15 mg/litre. The uncertainty about the effects of caffeine is reflected in the IOC's repeated flip-flops over whether to continue restricting it and, if so, how much to allow in the serum levels of participants. Subsequent to the initial ban, the IOC dropped caffeine from its list of restricted drugs, and then, in 1984, restored it. Athletes alleged that, because of wide variations in the metabolism of caffeine among individuals, consumption of as little as 350 mg had caused some participants to nearly flunk the test. Because readings above the allowable level are regarded as deliberate attempts to "dope" the athlete, a 1988 study by researcher van der Merwe attempted to determine how much caffeine would put a competitor out of action. He administered varying amounts of caffeine by serving coffee, tea, and soft drinks to nine healthy subjects, within a fifteen-minute period. Although the doses ranged up to 1,000 mg, as much as in ten cups of coffee, no urinary levels were found to exceed 14 mg/litre, as measured three hours after ingestion. Consistent with other researchers, van der Merwe found that about 75 to 90 percent of the ingested caffeine appeared in the urine and the observed concentrations were independent of the dietary source. He concluded that it was impossible to flunk the IOC test as a result of the ordinary consumption of caffeinated beverages and that any athlete who failed to pass should be presumed to have resorted to caffeine to enhance his performance.[85] Although a number of athletes have run into trouble over their urinary levels of caffeine, so far the IOC itself has disqualified only one participant on this account, an Australian pentathlon competitor in the Seoul Olympics in 1988.[86]

Interest in caffeine's benefits to exercise increased in the late 1970s after studies from the Human Performance Laboratory at Ball State University suggested that 200 mg of caffeine exerted a significant effect on an athlete's endurance. Other studies have failed to confirm this conclusion, and some have suggested that the observed improvements were a consequence of a placebo effect. Determining the answer comes down to evaluating whether caffeine has ergogenic effects—that is, whether it can improve aerobic performance or the capacity of the body for physical work.

The body gets the energy needed to power muscles in at least three different ways, depending on whether the energy expenditure is of short, moderate, or extended duration. Energy is also burned differently by muscles of different sizes. For example, the large muscles of the legs, used in treadmill walking, burn energy differently from the smaller leg muscles, primarily used in cycling, which may be more responsive to the benefits of lipid mobilization. In addition, people in excellent physical condition, such as athletes, burn energy differently from people in a more ordinary state of dilapidation. Other variables include caffeine dose, pre-exercise food consumption, and individual variations in response and tolerance. All of these factors confuse our attempts to make sense out of the apparently inconsistent research findings about the effects of caffeine on energy output, endurance, and weight loss.

The basic theory underlying claims that caffeine can improve athletic performance is based on three assertions. The first is its ability to increase the efficiency with which the body burns fat, already alluded to in the weight-loss discussion above. This is considered the primary source of caffeine's power to act as an ergogenic aid and to increase endurance for intense exercise, especially when duration approaches or exceeds one hour. Increased FFA mobilization delays the depletion of glycogen by encouraging the muscles to use fat as fuel, making the spared glycogen available to delay exhaustion, especially at high exercise intensities for which glycogen sparing is critical. This effect is minimized at exercise below the anaerobic threshold, that is, in low-intensity exercise, and experiments have shown that ingesting 400 mg of caffeine before such exercise did not affect either FFA or carbohydrate utilization.

The second claim is caffeine's ability to reduce the rate of glycogen consumption—that is, it increases the efficiency with which the body burns sugars. Because glycogen is a primary source of energy for exercise, exhaustion occurs and exercise intensity must generally be reduced once glycogen has been depleted. This glycogen-sparing effect is greatest in the first fifteen minutes of exercise, during which glycogen utilization declines as much as 50 percent. The saved glycogen remains available during the later stages of exercise with the result that the athlete can continue longer before exhaustion occurs.

The third assertion is caffeine's power to lower the rate of perceived exertion (RPE)—that is, to reduce our sense of fatigue. Some studies have shown that when athletes are asked to rate how hard they are working, some report significantly less exertion after consuming caffeine.

The popularity of sports snacks is increasing as athletes and exercisers search for anything that can give them an edge. When the National Academy of Sciences evaluated six purported performance boosters for the U.S. Army, the only ones they endorsed as effective were those that contained carbohydrates or caffeine. Although other ingredients might show promise, no claims can be supported without further research. These conclusions have been bolstered by studies, such as the one which demonstrated that the intake of sucrose, with or without caffeine, improved running time and distance from about forty minutes and six miles to about fifty-five minutes and nine miles.[87] Other studies showed that consumption of about 900 mg of caffeine, which produce urinary levels just within the limits of the IOC, increased endurance time from fifty to more than seventy minutes.

In their quest for a chemical means of improving performance, many turn to over-the-counter combination products that contain both caffeine and ephedrine. An example of such a product is Formula One, a nostrum touted by its manufacturers as the "world's first scientifically valid, gimmick free approach to weight management," which contains a combination of ma-huang and cola nut. This combination was recently banned by the FDA in a new ruling that outlawed all products containing a combination of caffeine and ephedrine, stating that they can cause "severe injury or death in some people who consume them."

We should be mindful of a range of possible impairments in performance that may counterbalance the possible improvements in output that may be obtained with caffeine. By increasing digestive secretions, caffeine may cause stomach discomfort and thereby impede performance. And perhaps more important, because caffeine is a diuretic, it may promote excess urination, which in turn could lead to dehydration, one of the primary problems for athletes, especially endurance athletes, because the fatigue experienced as a result of dehydration is indistinguishable from the normal fatigue of hard training. Excessive urination can also cause a loss of vitamins and minerals essential to peak athletic performance, although it must be noted that some studies have found no effect from caffeine on either fluid balance or thermoregulation during exercise. In light of such considerations, however, athletes should be mindful of the possibility that intestinal problems or dehydration might create an acute disadvantage in the middle of an athletic event which more than offsets any earlier advantage.

In summary, the effects of caffeine as an athletic performance booster are still uncertain. It remains for future researchers to satisfactorily evaluate caffeine's effect on an ordinary activity such as walking, by designing an experiment comparing the effect of a range of caffeine doses on well-hydrated, moderately trained subjects walking in controlled environments for an extended time. Such low-intensity exercise studies would help determine caffeine's part in FFA mobilization.[88]

16

thinking over caffeine
Cognition, Learning,
and Emotional Well-Being

BACON says, Coffee "comforts the head and heart, and helps digestion"; Dr. WILLIS says, "being daily drank, it wonderfully clears and enlightens each part of the soul, and disperses all the clouds of every function." The celebrated Doctor HARVEY used it often; VOLTAIRE lived almost on it; and the learned and sedentary of every country have recourse to it, to refresh the brain, oppressed by study and contemplation.
—Benjamin Moseley, M.D., *A Treatise Concerning the Properties and Effects of Coffee*, 1785

The saying goes, "You can't be too rich or too thin," to which perhaps could be added, "or too smart," because, even if each man is correct about how bright he conceives himself to be, he would find it still better to be even a bit sharper. How far would you go to acquire, for example, a drug that would enable you to perform better on an IQ test, an SAT test, or a Bar examination? Or one that would help you to prepare your taxes or balance your checkbook more accurately, solve chess problems or crossword puzzles more readily, make better investments, or program a computer with more acuity, or even drive home more safely? Surprisingly, you might not have to go very far, because caffeine, in many ways, is a "smart pill" that can do just those things.

As demonstrated by scientific evidence and common experience, caffeine is a rare and wonderful substance that safely improves many mental functions, including alertness, memory, learning, and cognition. As early as 1933, one researcher analyzed the effects of caffeine on solving more than 250 chess problems, comparing performance of test subjects with and without caffeine. He observed a consistently remarkable improvement in performance with caffeine.[1] Such improvements were reflected in a 1960s advertising campaign that dubbed coffee "The Think Drink."

However, as to what the nature of this improvement may be or how great its extent, there is little agreement anywhere. Some people are convinced that they can't think clearly or precisely without caffeine, while others say it makes them jittery and error prone. Naturally, behavioral scientists have been eager to discover the secret of caffeine's ability to improve the brain's information processing. Two complementary hypotheses explaining this remarkable power are supported by experimental data. The first hypothesis, sometimes called the "non-specific energetic" theory, attributes caffeine's enhancement of mental functions to a generalized energizing effect. The second hypothesis, sometimes called the "specific cognitive" theory, attributes these enhancements to specific effects on brain or neural activity. Finally, a "cognitive-energetic" theory, combining the two, has also been formulated and may offer the most complete and best-integrated elucidation of the phenomena.

J. E. Barmack, in a paper published in the *Journal of Experimental Psychology* in 1940, was one of the first to advance the non-specific energetic theory. Barmack recognized the possibility that caffeine's overall antihypnotic and antifatigue properties could be part of the story, but, observing that caffeine increased the rate at which people can add numbers, advanced the notion that caffeine acts non-specifically on "some central process or processes concerned with alertness" that "allay the development of a bored attitude to a task."[2] This idea is supported by many studies of continuous performance, over a period of a half-hour or more of what experimental psychologists call a "vigilance task," one that requires prolonged attention and responsiveness but little physical activity. In real life, caffeine improves long-term performance on vigilance tasks such as solving arithmetic problems, driving a car, or flying an airplane. Its effects are most apparent when people have been working at their tasks for some time and are minimal when tasks are just begun. When people are allowed to take breaks to alleviate boredom and fatigue, no significant benefit from using caffeine is observed. These findings, based solely on studies of vigilance tasks, apparently confirm Barmack's theory, that caffeine acts by "refreshing" a fatigued person, so that the enhancing effects of caffeine on long-term performance will obtain on any task that is performed repetitively, monotonously, and requires continuous attention.[3]

The specific cognitive theory, championed by H. Nash in his 1962 book *Alcohol and Caffeine*,[4] asserts that caffeine acts directly on "specific neural capacities" that are intrinsic to a given task and that it enhances performance on these tasks irrespective of whether a person is fatigued. This idea was suggested to Nash by his examination of performances of several different short-term tasks, some of which exhibited improvement after caffeine was ingested, while others remained unaffected. Nash argues that the benefits of caffeine on performance depend not on an improvement in general energy levels, as Barmack had asserted, but instead on specific benefits related to the nature of the task at hand. Abandoning the metaphor of the organism as an energy system, Nash relied on another metaphor, one that became and remains the most generally accepted in cognitive psychology today: that of the human organism as an information-processing system. He observed improvement in the performance of a number of tasks, such as adding numbers, immediate recall, and word fluency. These benefits were realized even on brief tests administered when the subjects were rested and alert, and neither fatigued nor bored. In contrast, he found no improvement in tests of abstract reasoning, using language, deduction, estimating time intervals, or spotting arithmetic mistakes. The overall conclusion from such studies has been that caffeine "facilitates the speed, but not the memory, component of the task."

If Barmack's non-specific energizing theory is correct, we should expect caffeine to improve cognitive performance only when a person has become bored or tired. If Nash's specific cognitive theory is correct, we should expect an improvement even when a person is rested and alert to start with, but this improvement would be observed only in some tasks and not others. However, because these theories are complementary rather than inconsistent, which is to say, they could both be true at the same time, we must also consider the syncretic hypothesis of A. F. Sanders, who argues that the improvements in mental capacity caused by caffeine are a function of *both* the energy level of the subject *and* the cognitive nature and demands of the task.[5] Aiming to unite the energetic and cognitive models of human information processing, Sanders published his idea in 1983 that caffeine's effect on performance is best understood as a function of both the energetic state of the person and the cognitive requirements of the task.

Unfortunately, even with the advancement of Sanders' cognitive-energetic theory, the scientific community remains far from a complete and consistent explanation of caffeine's sometimes apparently paradoxical effects on human performance. For example, an adverse effect has been observed on the attempt to repeat numbers backward, while a beneficial effect has been observed on the attempt to repeat them in their original order. In addition, caffeine impaired some factors of cognitive intelligence, while improving those related to speed. In other cases, caffeine had a deleterious effect on a given task until that task was practiced, whereupon the use of caffeine resulted in an improvement.[6] Another troubling inconsistency is the low level of test-retest reliability. That is, the results of studies of caffeine's effects, particularly on the performance of complex tasks, vary widely, forcing us to wonder which conclusions are the correct ones.[7]

Nevertheless, overall, scientific studies have confirmed some specific effects on cognition and learning: Caffeine improves the performance of simple, familiar, routine tasks, and it impairs or fails to affect the accomplishment of complex, novel, unpracticed tasks. Perhaps the reason for this difference is that, by conferring extra energy, caffeine causes a person to work more quickly but possibly less carefully.[8]

This explanation is in line with experiments that show that caffeine can stimulate fast and strong but incorrect reactions. For example, an experienced computer programmer may report that using caffeine makes well-practiced programming assignments easier to complete, while it appears to sometimes interfere with the successful solution of new and very difficult programming problems. Because real-life problems frequently present both sorts of challenges, and the nature and distribution of these challenges will vary as among different subjects performing the same tasks, caffeine should be expected to produce a complex array of sometimes contrary effects. In other words, although in some ways caffeine may give us a beneficial boost in our capacity to perform certain tasks, in others it may induce us to make precipitous, overeager choices, or to "jump the gun," interfering with the circumspection necessary for accurate decisions. Perhaps a quick trigger finger is good for the artist's hand, if the testimony of artists, musicians, and writers such as Balzac, Voltaire, Samuel Johnson, Beethoven, and Goethe about caffeine's importance in their creative lives is to be accepted. However, psychology, which has yet to attain a coherent understanding of creativity, cannot shed much light on caffeine's effects on the creative process.

In the laboratory it is easy to create experimental tasks, such as one requiring subjects to identify or remember numbers or colors flashing across a screen, in which few if any of the study's participants will have been previously practiced. In life, however, most significant tasks are repeated and even systematically studied and practiced with the intent of improving performance. In addition, in many work situations, because people choose the jobs they pursue, they will often be performing those tasks for which they have the greatest innate abilities. For these reasons, it is essential, in predicting the effect caffeine will have on a person's performance of a given task, to take into account not only the features of the task itself, but also to reckon with the competency of the person performing it.

Is programming a computer difficult or easy? Many people would find even basic programming tasks challenging, complex, novel, and creative. Experienced, well-practiced, and talented programmers might find many of these same programming tasks easy, simple, familiar, and routine. Caffeine might therefore affect performances on a simple programming test in opposite ways: The performance of the person who had little competency with programming, either because of lack of specific experience or specific ability, might well be impaired by caffeine. The performance of the person who was eminently competent in programming, either because of extensive experience or specific ability, might well be given a significant boost.

The effects of caffeine on task performance in real life are complicated still further by the fact that life's tasks are compound in nature, and, even for the same person, certain elements of a task may be challenging and other elements easy, so that caffeine would exert a variable effect on different stages and parts of the task. We can reasonably speculate that, overall, the more competent you are in performing a task, the more caffeine will help you do even better, while the less able you are in coping with a task, the more likely it is that caffeine will fail to affect or even impair your efforts. If this notion turns out to be true, the use of sufficiently large doses of caffeine, by tending to push lower scores lower and higher scores higher, should serve to flatten the bell curve of an IQ test into a sort of flying saucer.

A curious twist to this question is the possibility that caffeine may affect introverted people differently from the way it affects extroverted people. One study concluded that, when posed with challenging mental tasks, such as proofreading or solving mathematical problems, impulsive, extroverted people get a boost in performance from caffeine, while those who describe themselves as less impulsive and more introverted often suffer marked detriments after caffeine ingestion. Another study of caffeine's differing effects on extroverts and introverts performing both simple and complex tasks came to similar conclusions. The routine or simple task was to pick out a letter each time it occurred on a page of type. The challenging or complex task was to answer word analogies and sentence completion questions from the Graduate Record Examination. This study seemed to confirm that everybody tends to do better the higher the dose, if the task is extremely simple. However, on the complex task, the extroverts' performance improved in a dose-dependent correlation with caffeine, while the introverts' performance worsened.

One additional possibility pertaining to competency comes to mind: If caffeine's impairment of challenging tasks is a result of prompting us to "jump the gun," perhaps a person can learn to compensate for this sort of overeager "coupling" even when riding high on caffeine, learning to pause in order to perform the necessary evaluation for a correct choice. If this can be done, then a savvy caffeine consumer might find that he can multiply the number of tasks in which caffeine is helpful and the degree to which it is helpful, and reduce the number and degree to which it causes impairment.

Caffeine and Memory

In recent years, in addition to continuing studies of caffeine's effects on complex mental activities such as reasoning and learning, researchers have paid increasing attention to its effects on short-term memory. Overall, the results show that caffeine improves performance on tasks that require remembering small amounts of information and impairs or leaves unaffected performance on tasks requiring remembering a great deal. An example of a more demanding sort of memory task is a test in which subjects listen to or read long lists of words and are then asked to remember as many as possible. The experimenters note either no effect from caffeine or perhaps even a small impairment. Another way of conceptualizing these effects is provided by the Humphreys-Revelle[9] model, according to which tasks that are primarily dependent on information processing, such as vigilance, simple arithmetic, or reaction time, are improved, because they make relatively small demands on short-term memory, while tasks with a high short-term memory component may be unaffected or adversely affected. Unfortunately, there is much ambiguity in the data that do exist about these effects. When weighing the conclusions of existing research, we would do well to remember a well-designed 1974 memory experiment by researcher V. E. Mitchell and his colleagues, the cautionary results of which were reminiscent of the title of Luigi Pirandello's play *Right You Are, If You Think You Are*, because they seem to demonstrate that performance was improved by caffeine when and only when the participants were told that they had ingested the drug.[10]

Nevertheless, millions of students use caffeine to fuel "all-nighters." Based on the available scientific evidence, how does this use of caffeine affect studying and test taking? Caffeine helps people to feel less drowsy and less fatigued, be better able to perform some manual or perfunctory tasks, such as typing or calculating, and, under certain circumstances, to be more capable of sustaining rapid thought and to remember more. However, some studies have found that caffeine does not significantly alter numerical reasoning, short-term memory of complex data, or verbal fluency. In other words, caffeine may help you to stay awake, but it won't necessarily improve your intellectual skills.

Students depending on caffeine to extend their study time should also be aware of its possible adverse effects when taken in large quantities and be prepared for the crash after its stimulating powers subside. As Socrates suggested, the best guide for students is to know themselves: From a couple of Vivarin tablets, the sensitive may experience restlessness, anxiety, nausea, headache, tense muscles, and sleep disturbances, or a subsequent letdown, while others, from a much higher dose, might feel fine.

A recent startling discovery by Menachem Segal, professor of neurosciences at the Weizmann Institute in Rehovot, Israel, and an expert on neuromodulators in the brain, suggests that caffeine causes changes to brain cells that are likely to have profoundly beneficial effects on *long-term memory*.[11] In earlier research, Segal discovered that increasing the amount of calcium absorbed by brain cells is one way of improving long-term memory. Because caffeine augments the ability of these cells to metabolize calcium, Segal studied the effects of adding caffeine directly to the hippocampus, an area of the brain that is critical to learning and long-term memory, to test the hypothesis that the calcium levels inside the cells would rise as a result. The outcome of his experiment confirmed this conjecture, proving that caffeine increased the calcium levels in brain cells. But Segal also observed a more astonishing phenomenon: *Caffeine caused existing dendritic spines, the branching extensions at the ends of nerve cells that allow them to make synaptic connections with each other, to grow longer and even caused new spines and branches to develop as well.* Although no direct experimental data are available on the actual effects, if any, of caffeine on long-term memory,[12] neuroscientists have long believed that an improvement in "wiring" does in fact improve both long-term memory and learning. If this connection is demonstrated in future studies, caffeine would be confirmed as *the only known substance that can augment brain functions by altering the physical structure of the brain.*

Caffeine and Alertness

Few people would ever question that caffeine helps to keep you awake and alert during the day. In 1990 this phenomenon was first systematically investigated under laboratory conditions and quantified using sophisticated measuring techniques: Researcher Zwyghuizen-Doorenbos led a group of scientists who orally administered 250 mg of caffeine at 9 A.M. and 1 P.M. on two successive days. Checking repeatedly for objective parameters of wakefulness and alertness, they determined that caffeine does in fact help keep people awake and alert. More surprisingly, the subjects who had been previously given caffeine continued to demonstrate increased alertness over the placebo group, even on the third day of the experiment, on which a placebo containing no caffeine was administered to all participants. In discussing this study, researcher Jack James concludes that this extended effect is psychological rather than pharmacological, asserting the "development of conditioned alerting responses to certain contextual stimuli that had been associated with caffeine (e.g., the coffee beverage vehicle used to administer the drug) during the previous two days."[13] In ordinary parlance, this means that if you think you are drinking a caffeinated beverage, you may wake up just as if you had actually drunk it simply because you expect that you will.

A broad range of studies from the 1930s through the 1990s have produced conflicting findings about caffeine's effect on reaction time.[14] Some of the apparently contradictory results may be explained in terms of the 1987 findings of researcher J. D. Roache and R. R. Griffiths, who found that reaction times were improved more by a dose of 400 mg of caffeine than by doses of 200 mg or 600 mg.[15,16] In other words, there is no simple, linear relationship between dosage and improvement in reaction time of which we could state, "If some is good, more is better." Other studies have confirmed that varying amounts of caffeine produced similarly differing effects on reaction time, finding, for example, that in young adults 300 mg of caffeine significantly improved scores, while doses of 600 mg left them unaffected.

As in the debate over the nature and extent of improvements in *cognitive performance*, there has been some controversy over whether caffeine can improve *psychomotor performance* only if you are fatigued to begin with or whether it improves such performance even in a well-rested person. Most researchers agree that it is now well established that the beneficial effects of caffeine are found both before and after decrements in performance owing to fatigue. For example, it has been demonstrated that real-life and simulated automobile driving performance levels are improved by caffeine, irrespective of whether the person was tired or well rested to start.[17]

Alertness, the complex of mental capacities that suffer during sleep loss, was studied by Michael H. Bonnet and colleagues in 1994 when he compared the value of caffeine and naps in helping to sustain performance during two days and nights of sleep loss.[18] Previous studies had shown that performance during sleep loss is, not surprisingly, "improved by prophylactic naps as a function of varying nap length." Bonnet compared the improvement conferred by naps with that realizable with either repeated or single-dose administration of caffeine. As would be expected, the results showed that an eight-hour "nap," which is to say, a good night's sleep, did more to improve performance, mood, and alertness than any sort of caffeine regimen and that the benefits lasted longer than the effects of caffeine, which peak and lose effect within six hours. The study also found that naps could be combined effectively with small repetitive doses of caffeine to maintain alertness. Nothing lasts forever, though. Bonnet concludes that neither a nap nor repeated doses of caffeine could preserve performance, mood, and alertness past twenty-four hours. Beyond that, caffeine's effects in these respects approached those of a placebo.

Is It All an Illusion? The Caffeine Chippie or the Hidden Need for Caffeine

One of the definitions of drugs that produce a physical dependence is that the abrupt cessation of their use will cause people to perform tests poorly and feel listless and generally "blue." Leading caffeine researcher Jack James advances a theory that *a nearly universal yet unacknowledged physical dependence on caffeine may have confounded the results of many studies that purported to show the psychomotor advantages conferred by the drug.*[19] His argument is plausible: If nearly everyone uses caffeine nearly every day, then when a scientist takes a pool of subjects and administers caffeine to one part of the group and withholds it from the others, those not receiving caffeine will enter varying stages of caffeine withdrawal and therefore will perform more poorly than those who are not suffering from withdrawal. In effect, James is asserting that most people have what among heroin users is called a "chippie," a low-grade habit, of which the habituated person is sometimes unaware, that renders them mildly dysphoric and uncomfortable when deprived of the drug. Such heroin users would probably demonstrate better performance if given a small amount of heroin, simply because the heroin would restore them to a normal metabolic balance and remove the impediment of the mild withdrawal syndrome. If James is correct, all the "improvements" worked by caffeine in psychomotor or cognitive performance may simply be artifacts of an unknown caffeine chippie or a hidden need for caffeine that impairs the habitué when he stops using it. The only way to determine if a nearly universal addiction is distorting experimental findings is to make sure that all the subjects in a given study have been weaned off of caffeine for at least a week or two, so that they begin without any taint of addiction.

Java Jitters or Caffeine Conniptions: Caffeine and Anxiety

It may be nothing to worry about, but anxiety, including such symptoms as unwarranted trepidation, apprehension, agitation, turmoil, and uneasiness, is the most common psychological disorder in the United States. In severe cases, it erupts into recurring panic attacks, the symptoms of which include increased heart rate, palpitations, jitters, irritability, perspiration, and rapid breathing. Caffeine is generally recognized by researchers as an anxiogenic substance—that is, one that is productive of anxiety. The pharmacological basis of this effect remains uncertain. One possible contributory mechanism is the process by which caffeine binds to adenosine receptors, interfering with the systems that would otherwise have reduced anxiety. (Binding to benzodiazepine and endorphin receptors have been cited as well, but at ordinary levels of consumption this activity appears too small to be of significance.) Another is that caffeine interferes with the noradrenergic system so as to increase the release of adrenaline.[20] Adrenaline, the hormone the adrenal glands excrete in response to excitement, stress, or fear, produces a more rapid and stronger heartbeat and more rapid and deeper breathing, and it can also produce anxiety. Some claim that caffeine in combination with emotional distress causes the release of more adrenaline than emotional distress alone, suggesting that even if it cannot cause anxiety, caffeine may exacerbate it.

In 1971 R. Lynn, a leading British researcher, conducted a monumental study of personal traits and practices and physical and psychological disorders, including psychiatric disorders, cigarette smoking, suicide, coronary heart disease, and anxiety. Observing that the peoples of different nations suffered from different levels of anxiety, Lynn hypothesized that, in those countries in which anxiety levels were high, people would tend to consume less caffeine in order to avoid exacerbating their problems with it. His theory was confirmed by the data. In those countries in which caffeine consumption is low, anxiety is relatively higher, and in those in which it is high, anxiety is lower. Several studies have supported Lynn's conclusion.[21] It has been shown that patients with panic disorder have lower caffeine consumption and that panic attacks can be induced even in normal people challenged with high doses of caffeine.[22]

People with high caffeine consumption have higher usage rates of anxiety-reducing drugs such as benzodiazepine or meprobamate, when compared to those with moderate to low caffeine use. No one is sure if they consume higher levels of caffeine in order to shake off the sedative effects of the minor tranquilizers, or if they take minor tranquilizers to counteract the anxiety resulting from high doses of caffeine, or even if there is simply a certain population that enjoys using mild psychoactive substances of both the stimulating and sedating varieties.

In any case, the studies dispel one illusion: the image of the nervous, edgy caffeine user. Only excessive caffeine use is correlated with anxiety. If a correlation with normal use can be stated, it is that the people who do not consume caffeine are more likely to have problems with their nerves than those who do. The members of the population who consume caffeine are dispositionally more relaxed than the general population, and, conversely, those who do not consume caffeine are more jittery than most.

As reflected in a new specific and separate diagnosis category in the American Psychiatric Association's *Diagnostic and Statistical Manual IV (DSM-IV)*, psychiatrists now believe that caffeine can produce a distinct anxiety disorder, over and above the symptom of anxiety that appears as a component of caffeine intoxication and caffeine withdrawal. The *DSM-IV* states that, as with the anxiety induced by other psychoactive substances such as cocaine, caffeine-induced anxiety disorder can resemble panic disorder, generalized anxiety disorder, social phobia, or even obsessive-compulsive disorder. There have been no studies on the prevalence or incidence of caffeine intoxication anxiety or applying the *DSM-IV* set of diagnostic criteria.

Caffeine and Depression and Aggression

Just as it is conjectured that Nervous Nellies spontaneously adjust their caffeine intake downward to avoid its anxiolytic effects,[23] it is also supposed that some depressives increase their consumption in order to multiply the benefit from caffeine's euphoric and stimulating powers.[24] In other words, they effectively self-medicate with caffeine to dissipate the dark clouds of lassitude, lethargy, and despair that hover around them. The studies remain inconclusive. An example of the ambiguity that still lingers is found in the Tromsø Heart Study, conducted in 1983, of almost 150,000 people, which found significant correlations between high coffee consumption and depression in women (but not in men). However, because this correlation disappears when the results are adjusted for cigarette smoking, it is difficult to draw any conclusions.

A number of studies have found that people who drink at least two portions of caffeinated beverages a day report improved moods, a better social disposition, and more self-confidence and energy. Two large-scale studies, apparently demonstrating lower rates of suicide among coffee drinkers, strongly suggest that caffeine can significantly ameliorate long-term depression and even make life worth living for some people. A 1993 Kaiser Permanente Medical Care Program study of more than one hundred thousand men and women, reported in the *Annals of Epidemiology*, examined the effects of coffee and tea on mortality and found a lower risk of suicide among people who ingested more caffeine. Under the direction of Arthur Klatsky, M.D., a cardiologist, the study tracked nearly 130,000 Northern California residents, including the records of 4,500 who died during the research, and demonstrated a statistically significant lower rate of suicide among coffee drinkers than coffee abstainers. Klatsky asserted that this was not a fluke finding, because the study was very large, involved a multiracial population of men and women, and examined closely many factors related to mortality such as alcohol consumption and smoking. Another large-scale study, of more than 85,000 female nurses, conducted by Dr. Ichiro Kawachi of Harvard Medical School and Brigham and Women's Hospital in Boston, funded by the National Institutes of Health and published by the *Archives of Internal Medicine* in 1996, concluded that women who drink coffee are less likely to commit suicide than those who do not. Even though coffee drinkers appear to engage in the sort of behavior that would increase their risk of depression and suicide (for example, they tend to smoke more and drink more alcohol than non–coffee drinkers and have higher levels of perceived stress), they seem to be highly protected. This study also found that only 100 mg of caffeine a day, about one cup of coffee, could produce increased feelings of well-being, energy, and motivation for work. However, specialists in depression argue that Kawachi failed to control for several factors, including the effects of antidepressants, high-blood-pressure medication, and whether depressed subjects had been told not to drink coffee by their doctors.

There are few studies of the effects of caffeine on human emotional states other than anxiety and depression. However, some researchers have hypothesized that caffeine may operate to decrease aggression, arguing that an increase in benzodiazepine activity increases aggression, and, as we have seen, caffeine inhibits benzodiazepine activity. Studies in 1983 and 1984 by D. R. Cherek[25] examining the effects of caffeine administration on aggressive behavior seem to confirm these findings in humans. Mindful of the aggressive response normally elicited when someone has money taken from him, Cherek designed an experiment in which subjects were promised certain immediate rewards for their performance. He then pretended to renege on his promises, giving the participants, who had received either caffeine tablets, coffee, decaffeinated coffee, or a placebo, the impression that they had been "ripped off." He found that those who had ingested either coffee or caffeine were more tolerant of being cheated. However, the specter of dubiety that haunts many other caffeine-related inquiries appears in connection with the issue of mood effects as well. For, in contrast with Cherek's work, the 1987 study by Roache and Griffiths mentioned earlier, in which subjects consumed between 200 and 600 mg of caffeine, produced small increases in scores on the Profile of Mood States Questionnaire (POMS) for hostility and anger, while also demonstrating an increase in friendliness.[26]

Caffeine and Sleep

J. A. Brillat-Savarin, perhaps the most celebrated chef in history, wrote, in *The Physiology of Taste* (1805), "It is beyond doubt that coffee greatly excites the cerebral powers; also any man who drinks it for the first time is bound to be kept from a share of his natural sleep." In fact, everywhere caffeine-containing beverages have been consumed, people have recognized that, just as they can help you to stay awake, they can also interfere with a good night's sleep. The most common sleep disturbance associated with caffeine is insomnia, although there is, oddly enough, a complaint called "hypersomnia," or too much sleep, also sometimes consequent to its use. Among researchers, it is generally accepted that caffeine is a common cause of sleep disturbances. In fact, according to P. B. Dews, a leading caffeine researcher, the disturbance of nighttime sleep is much more pronounced and dose dependent than caffeine's daytime effects.[27]

Despite great variation in the amount of sleep that people need, ranging from as few as three to as many as twelve hours, with an average of seven to nine, certain general observations are possible. For example, scientists divide sleep into dreamless sleep and the sleep during which we dream. REM is an acronym for "rapid eye movement," and dreaming sleep is called REM sleep because during our dreams we follow the action, as it were, by shifting our "gaze" back and forth. Non-REM sleep usually lasts about an hour or more and then shifts to REM sleep for about thirty minutes, in a pattern called the "ultradian rhythm" that is repeated four to six times throughout the night. Non-REM sleep, which itself comprises four states of progressively deeper dreamless sleep, constitutes about 75 percent of our sleep, and is characterized by lowered heart and respiration rates, while REM sleep is marked by deep muscular relaxation accompanied by increased or irregular heart and respiration rates and vivid dreaming.[28] At the beginning of the night's sleep, deeper non-REM sleep is a greater proportion of the ultradian cycle than toward the end of the night's sleep, during which the proportion of lighter REM sleep increases. Interrupting or interfering with either REM or non-REM sleep causes a sleep deficit that the body seeks to restore over succeeding nights. A mounting sleep deficit can impair concentration, diminish energy and performance during the day, and increase anxiety and depression. Extreme sleep deprivation can cause paranoia and hallucinations. One in three adults regularly suffers from sleep problems, and medications are resorted to as a remedy by millions.

Caffeine's effects on sleep depend on a variety of factors, such as dosage, tolerance to caffeine, individual sensitivity to caffeine, the time between caffeine ingestion and the attempt to sleep, and the ingestion of other psychoactive substances. There are studies confirming the common experience that acute doses of caffeine in the evening delay falling asleep and result in poorer sleep quality. For example, a Japanese study showed that it takes four times longer than normal to get to sleep after drinking a strong cup of coffee. But caffeine can do more than interfere with falling asleep: It can also produce alterations in the onset of REM sleep, total sleep time, and certain characteristics of non-REM sleep, such as shortening the deeper phases of non-REM sleep and lengthening the lighter phases. It does not appear that caffeine affects the length of the REM phase of sleep.[29] Heavy caffeine users toss and turn more in bed, perhaps because caffeine increases muscle tension and restlessness. Such movements can also cause frequent awakening.[30] In addition, people who consume caffeine before bedtime are more easily awakened by sudden noises. Brain-wave studies show that caffeine disturbs sleep during the first three to four hours. A study of subjects over age fifty found sleep was reduced by as much as two hours when caffeine was taken in the evening. Because older people sleep less than younger people anyway, this diminution represents a proportionately greater loss than it would for younger people.[31]

Just as people vary in the amount of sleep they need, they vary in the effect caffeine has on their sleep. You have almost certainly met people who claim to be able to sleep well after drinking a couple strong cups of coffee immediately before retiring. Even stranger is the fact that some people are not only capable of sleeping well after consuming caffeine but actually sleep too much, experiencing a condition of pathologic sleepiness called "hypersomnia," as a result of consuming it. As "Pathologic Sleepiness Induced by Caffeine," a paper published by Quentin R. Regestein in 1989 in the *American Journal of Medicine*, states:

The aforementioned patients had severe sleepiness that decreased or remitted after they discontinued caffeine. In some individuals, therefore, heavy use of caffeine apparently provokes sleepiness. This is difficult to explain since caffeine is a stimulant. . . . The unusual magnitude of the sleepiness and the rarity of this apparent association between caffeine and excessive sleepiness, even in sleep clinic patients, suggest an idiosyncratic phenomenon.[32]

Another strange effect, which might be called the "reverse placebo" effect, was observed by A. Goldstein in a 1964 study. Participants in his experiment were all given caffeine. Those who knew they had taken the drug were less likely to complain of wakefulness than those who were not informed whether they had taken caffeine or a placebo.[33] Perhaps this could also be called the "bravado effect," whereby people are reluctant to confess a disturbance from what is ordinarily considered a mild agent, such as caffeine. Surveys based on *subjective* responses clearly indicate that how much caffeine people say they use is not related to how much difficulty they say they have sleeping, and insomniacs do not report high caffeine use, defined as three or more cups of coffee a day. In any case, most studies confirm that the closer to bedtime you consume caffeine, the more likely it is to interfere with sleep. However, as we have observed in our discussion of metabolic variation, some people metabolize caffeine much more slowly than others, and their sleep may be disturbed even by caffeine consumed twelve hours or more earlier.

Other studies of delayed sleep onset and poorer sleep quality, as evaluated on *objective* criteria such as EEG measurements, confirmed the well-recognized large variation among subjects in terms of caffeine's effect on sleep (intersubject variation) and also documented a similar large variation in the effect on the same subject on different nights (intrasubject variation). These studies have also demonstrated that sleep disturbances due to caffeine are more likely to occur in people who are not regular caffeine consumers and that the regular use of caffeine and a concomitant caffeine tolerance tends to diminish the disruptive effect of caffeine on sleep.

Overall, the leading research projects based on objective criteria demonstrate that caffeine intake near bedtime increases tossing and turning, reduces deep sleep and increases light sleep, has no effect on REM sleep, increases the time it takes to fall asleep up to threefold, decreases total sleep time by nearly two hours, and increases spontaneous awakenings. People who have not consumed caffeine before bedtime will fall back to sleep after being awakened early in the night more slowly than they will after being awakened later on. However, caffeine consumed shortly before bedtime reverses this pattern, creating the shortest delay in falling back to sleep in the first part of the night. Because the average plasma half-life for caffeine, a measure of how long it remains in the bloodstream, is between three and seven hours, a large enough dose would tend to sustain this effect throughout half the night. Although differing rates at which caffeine is metabolized by different people are generally thought to be the basis of the differences of effects among them, another school of thought attributes the variations in caffeine's effect on sleep among individuals to differences in neural response sensitivity.[34]

17

caffeine dependence, intoxication, and toxicity

The recognition of syndromes of intoxication, withdrawal, and dependence suggests that caffeine is like other psychoactive drugs.

—Roland R. Griffiths, *JAMA*, 1994

A typical lethal dose of caffeine is 10 grams. A shot of espresso has 100 mg. So it ought to take a nice round 100 shots, or say 50 double cappucinos, to get to that big café in the sky.

—Excerpt from posting in alt.drugs.caffeine, February 1996

Progress in understanding drug dependence has been impeded by a host of non-scientific moral, emotional, and legal factors. Fear of lethal drugs of abuse, such as heroin and cocaine, has clouded what might otherwise have been a neutral and relatively straightforward evaluation of the nature and extent of the habit-forming properties of less dangerous agencies, such as marijuana and caffeine, engendering confusion and doing little to encourage much-needed studies.

The word "dependence" is used in scientific literature in at least two distinct ways. "Physical dependence" is defined by the occurrence of a withdrawal syndrome after cessation of the use of a substance. Opium, cigarettes, and coffee each contain a psychoactive drug producing physical dependence: morphine, nicotine, and caffeine, respectively. "Clinical dependence syndrome" usually includes physical dependence, but also involves a pattern of pathologic behavior. Drugs that can support a clinical dependence syndrome are usually considered drugs of abuse. A heroin addict, whose behavior is deleteriously conditioned by his need to acquire the drug, exhibits clinical dependence syndrome. In contrast, a cancer patient under extended treatment with opioids will demonstrate physical dependence, but would probably not display any other symptoms of clinical dependence.

Caffeine unquestionably supports a physical dependence, as proved by the withdrawal symptoms associated with its abrupt discontinuation. It also has several additional characteristics in common with drugs that support a clinical dependence syndrome. These characteristics include both caffeine's ability to improve people's moods, self-confidence, and energy and what researchers call its ability to act as a reinforcer, or what in laymen's terms might be phrased as "the more you get, the more you want" factor. Yet despite the reasonableness of the hypothesis and considerable anecdotal evidence, it has been demonstrated only recently that there actually are users whose pattern of caffeine consumption merits a diagnosis of clinical dependence syndrome. In the American Psychiatric Association's *DSM-IV*, caffeine was the only psychoactive substance listed as supporting a physical dependence but not a clinical dependence syndrome. If research in this area continues, caffeine will probably lose this distinction by the time of the publication of the *DSM-V*.

Physical Dependence and Withdrawal

As early as 1893, a researcher, N. Bridge, reported on a series of patients presenting a variety of symptoms he attributed to the use of coffee or tea, concluding that eliminating caffeine from their diets could be beneficial.[1] However, he warned that patients who terminated their caffeine use abruptly were at risk for developing a severe headache. In consequence he recommended a regimen similar to the one favored by physicians today, reducing coffee consumption gradually over a week or more.

Headaches associated with the abrupt cessation of caffeine use have been experienced by millions in their daily lives and constitute the most typical feature of caffeine withdrawal and the most immediate evidence that caffeine supports a physical dependence. Other common symptoms of caffeine withdrawal, some of which the reader may have experienced when unable to enjoy his accustomed morning brew, can include:

- Sleepiness: drowsiness, yawning
- Work difficulty: impaired concentration, lassitude, decreased motivation for work
- Irritability: decreased contentedness, well-being, and self-confidence
- Decreased sociability: reduced friendliness and talkativeness
- Flulike symptoms: muscle aches and stiffness, hot or cold spells, nausea or vomiting, and blurred vision

Additional reported symptoms are increased depression or anxiety or impaired psychomotor performance.

In a detailed, carefully controlled study in 1986, Roland Griffiths provided a more detailed schedule of caffeine withdrawal symptoms than had been available previously. He found that caffeine withdrawal generally begins within twelve to twenty-four hours after discontinuing caffeine use. It generally peaks within twenty-four to forty-eight hours, and it lasts from about two days to a week.[2] As with many of the manifestations of caffeine use, there is considerable variability both between people and within the same person in the effects, duration, and severity of caffeine withdrawal.

The single best estimate of the incidence of caffeine withdrawal symptoms in a clinical setting was provided in a 1992 study[3] of more than sixty normal adults with low to moderate daily caffeine consumption, an average of 235 mg a day, or the equivalent of about two cups of coffee. This was a double-blind study, that is, one in which neither the researcher nor the subject knows who is receiving caffeine and, if so, in what quantities. More than 50 percent of the participants who did not receive caffeine had moderate to severe headaches, about 10 percent had symptoms associated with anxiety and depression, and about another 10 percent had significantly high ratings of fatigue. Nearly 15 percent used analgesics for aches and pains occasioned by withdrawal.

What is it about the cessation or relative decrease in the intake of caffeine that generates the range of physical and psychological problems listed above? Caffeine withdrawal is probably caused by the cessation of adenosine antagonism, which is caffeine's chief pharmacological mechanism of action. When caffeine use ceases, caffeine's supression of adenosine ceases, and it is natural that the abstainer should experience sluggishness, torpor, difficulty in concentrating, and depression. In addition, the prior use of caffeine may have resulted in a compensatory increase in the number of adenosine receptor sites, intended by the body to help restore the level of adenosine to that which existed before regular caffeine use.[4] Specifically, caffeine withdrawal symptoms may be partially explained by the decrease in central nervous system activity and the increase in cerebral blood flow associated with increased adenosine activity. The results of an EEG study which demonstrated increased alpha and beta voltage in the frontal-central cortex during caffeine withdrawal has been interpreted as being consistent with the hypothesis that caffeine withdrawal may be due to cerebral blood flow changes.[5]

The most common and notorious feature of caffeine withdrawal is the headache, which, consistently with the above analysis, has been described as a feeling of cerebral fullness. Typically it is a generalized throbbing headache that can, in extreme cases, be accompanied by flulike symptoms such as nausea and vomiting. The caffeine withdrawal headache is worsened with physical exercise and, not surprisingly, is relieved by caffeine. The withdrawal headaches usually abate within two to four days, although some subjects continue reporting sporadic headaches for ten days or more after cessation of caffeine use. It should be noted that several reports have concluded that sudden extreme increases in caffeine or coffee consumption can also produce headaches.

The caffeine withdrawal headache has frequently been observed in a hospital setting. One registered nurse at a hospital reports what turns out a common pre- and post-operative observation of caffeine withdrawal: "When I worked in an ambulatory surgery setting, many patients who were NPO [not to eat or drink anything] and therefore [had gone] without their usual cup of caffeine since the night before would experience quite severe headaches if they were still NPO by 11 A.M. or so. For most routine caffeine users, the *first* thing they said in the recovery area was 'Can I get some coffee?! I have a headache!' The phenomenon occurred often enough that even nurses new to the area caught on pretty quickly, and widespread enough for it to be a topic of informal conversation during nationwide nurses' conventions!"[6] Recently some surgical teams have given patients caffeine intravenously to avoid headaches and other withdrawal symptoms during the operation and recovery periods.

This complex of caffeine withdrawal symptoms is compellingly reminiscent of what might be termed the "addict's flu," the generalized withdrawal symptoms common to many addictive drugs, notably including heroin and other opiates and barbiturates. The symptoms of withdrawal from these drugs are typically much more severe than those exhibited in the flulike symptoms of caffeine withdrawal, but the pattern of symptoms, including fatigue, aches and pains, irritability, running nose, perspiration, and cravings for the drug, are otherwise identical.

Several studies have found that both the likelihood of caffeine withdrawal and its severity increase as the daily dose attained before cessation is increased. However, it has been shown that caffeine withdrawal can occur after discontinuation of surprisingly low regular doses of caffeine, as little as 100 mg per day, which is the equivalent of about one cup of coffee or two cans of cola.

There is one report of eight infants with suspected caffeine withdrawal born to mothers who had moderate to heavy caffeine consumption during their pregnancies (200–1,800 mg a day). The infants' symptoms, including irritability, jitteriness, and vomiting, began an average of about twenty hours after birth and then abated completely.[7]

The possible onset of caffeine withdrawal makes it advantageous for caffeine users to plan ahead as they approach circumstances where it may be necessary or desirable to eliminate caffeine. Because many general medical conditions can have signs and symptoms that are similar to caffeine withdrawal, it is necessary to systematically exclude other explanations for the symptoms. An adequate differential diagnosis should encompass conditions as diverse as viral illnesses, sinus conditions, migraine or tension headaches, other drug withdrawal states, such as amphetamine or cocaine withdrawal, and idiopathic drug reactions.

Clinical Dependence Syndrome

Opinions vary among psychologists and psychiatrists about whether caffeine should be branded, along with heroin, cocaine, and nicotine, as a drug of abuse, that is, as an agent supporting a clinical dependence syndrome. The majority opinion, supported in studies by Strain, Griffiths, and others at the Department of Psychiatry and Behavioral Sciences, the Johns Hopkins University School of Medicine, and reported in *JAMA* in 1994,[8] provides clinical evidence supporting a caffeine clinical dependence syndrome similar to the dependence syndromes of heroin and cocaine but milder.[9] A minority of professionals, citing the modest and transient discomforts of caffeine withdrawal, assert that caffeine has little in common with dangerous psychoactive drugs of abuse and should not be described as supporting a clinical dependence syndrome.[10]

The best opinion seems to be an amalgam of the two. On the one hand, there is no doubt that caffeine, like cocaine, has all the hallmarks of a drug that supports a clinical dependence syndrome: It produces the subjective effects of euphoria, energy, and self-confidence; it demonstrates a "reinforcing effect," that is, the capacity of a pharmacological agent to encourage sustained use; and, finally, as we have noted, it supports a physical dependence, including a developed tolerance and withdrawal symptoms on cessation.[11] On the other hand, it is clear that caffeine's subjective effects, reinforcing effects, and withdrawal symptoms are far less pronounced than the recognized drugs of abuse, such as cocaine, dextroamphetamine, or pentobarbital, and therefore, caffeine's clinical dependence syndrome, if it indeed exists, cannot be uncritically equated with the clinical dependence syndromes of these other drugs.[12]

Extrapolating from a telephone survey of two hundred Vermont residents conducted by a group of researchers in 1992[13] (the only study using standardized psychiatric criteria to evaluate the prevalence of caffeine clinical dependence), and applying the estimate that more than 80 percent of all American adults consume caffeine daily, with an average consumption among users of nearly 300 mg a day, we could venture that, in the United States alone, 75 million people would fit the criteria for moderate caffeine clinical dependence syndrome. The average daily consumption and, therefore, the estimate of the levels of this dependence syndrome in other countries may be considerably higher.

So the question remains: Does caffeine, like cocaine, support compulsive use, that is, an habitual pattern of self-administration persisting despite untoward personal, health, economic, or social consequences and repeated attempts to discontinue taking it? It is very difficult to determine the extent to which the nearly universal use of caffeine, in some surveys reaching 92 to 98 percent of North American adults, is, in one researcher's words, "due to its centrally mediated stimulus functions, rather than liking the taste of hot coffee, or the fact that drinking coffee is such a socially acceptable behavior."[14] Although anecdotal reports of the regular patterns of consumption engaged in by most caffeine users satisfy the criterion of habitual use, there is little evidence to help us decide whether the strength of the desire to persist in these patterns would satisfy the definition of compulsive behavior. Nevertheless, it remains a credible speculation that a minority of caffeine users consume caffeine compulsively, to the extent that they would find it difficult to reduce or eliminate it from their diet. Whatever the outcome of current studies, it is safe to assert that caffeine dependence, like other drug dependence syndromes, in all likelihood represents the interaction of social and cultural forces, of individual histories and predispositions operating at the same time as a psychoactive substance that produces pleasant mood-altering and reinforcing effects.

Is Caffeine a Drug of Abuse?

If asked to explain the nature of a drug of abuse, many people might answer, "I may not be able to define a drug of abuse, but I know one when I see one." Consideration of patterns of drug use in other societies, however, may disturb such comforting smugness. As we saw in the Yemen, for example, the plant khat, which contains a very powerful stimulating, habituating, and intoxicating drug, is brewed into tea, much in the way we use caffeine, and is used by the great majority of both children and adults. Outside observers have frequently assumed that khat is a drug of abuse and that the Yemeni population suffers from an addiction problem, similar to Western problems with heroin and cocaine, that should be addressed by every available educational, social, and legal countermeasure. Most people who live in the Yemen, however, do not share this opinion. The same question arises for us in relation to caffeine: If an entire society accepts a pattern of drug use, is that use, by definition, a normal one?

Researchers attempting to determine whether caffeine should be branded a drug of abuse have suggested that the word "addiction" be restricted to those conditions in which physical dependence and clinical dependence syndrome both obtain. Hirsh asserted that an addictive drug was one that engenders a "compulsion" or "an overwhelming involvement that pervades the total life activity . . . to the exclusion of all other interests,"[15] and concluded that caffeine, like other methylxanthines, was not addictive. R. R. Griffiths and colleagues have argued that to qualify as a drug of abuse a substance must have *both* reinforcing effects *and* produce harmful effects on the user and the society. Caffeine's reinforcing effects make it a candidate to be considered as a drug of abuse, but, Griffiths cautions, its classification as such must await a fuller appraisal of its possible deleterious effects.[16]

Looking at the question from a different angle, we note that the remorseless metabolic and psychical demand for certain intoxicants combines with their portability to enable them to function as money in a black market. In fact, one hallmark of a psychoactive drug of abuse, therefore, is a history of its use as a medium of exchange. Opium, for example, is as good as money among black-market traders in Southeast Asia. Cocaine is like gold bullion to the cartel managers of South America. Similarly, caffeine-rich seeds, beans, and processed leaves have frequently served as mediums of exchange throughout the world. In some African countries, cola nuts are still used as money, the way the Maya, and other South Americans until the eighteenth century, used cacao beans. In China and Russia, dried tea leaves were pressed into bricks and

Photograph of Russian brick tea money. (Courtesy of Chase Manhattan Archives)

Photograph of Russian brick tea money. (Courtesy of Chase Manhattan Archives)

used as currency. In Egypt and elsewhere among the Moslems, coffee was used as tender in the marketplace from the beginning of the sixteenth century.

Caffeine Intoxication: Too Much of a Good Thing

Many consumers of coffee, tea, and cola, never having entertained an association between caffeine and drug use, may be surprised to learn that the massive modern catalogue of psychiatric problems, the *Diagnostic and Statistical Manual of Mental Disorders (DSM-IV)*, includes an entry for "Caffeine Intoxication," which it describes either as an acute drug overdose condition, occurring after the ingestion of a large amount of caffeine, or as a chronic condition, otherwise known as "caffeinism" or "caffeism," associated with the regular consumption of large amounts of caffeine.

There is nothing new about the awareness of caffeine intoxication, for it has been well described as a psychiatric disorder for more than a hundred years. Yet despite long-standing recognition, which perhaps began with the coining of the Arabic word *"marqaha,"* or "caffeine high," in the sixteenth century, there is, even today, little information available about its prevalence or incidence.

In 1896 J. T. Rugh[17] reported the case of a traveling salesman who had resorted to excessive coffee consumption to maintain an intense pace of work and was troubled by nervousness, involuntary contractions in the arms and legs, a sense of impending danger, and sleep disturbance. Similar reports of caffeine intoxication first appear in medical literature from the middle of the 1800s, and the profile of common symptoms remains unchanged today. The most common are anxiety or nervousness, insomnia, gastrointestinal disturbances, irregular heartbeat, tremors, and psychomotor agitation. Other reported symptoms include excessive urination, headaches, diarrhea, and irregular breathing.

An interesting and unusual case was reported to *JAMA* early in 1914 by Otis Orendorff, M.D., of Canon City, Colorado. "A young miss, 18, an office clerk, of a slight, frail physique, had ordinary symptoms of asthenopia [eyestrain] for four years," Orendorff wrote. She grew worse over a period of several months. Although tests were administered and full correction for her vision was provided, she experienced no relief. The patient was alternately exhilarated and depressed. She had memory lapses and maintained a "deportment with an indifference to the usual conventionalities and proprieties." She had intermittent headaches, apparently not caused by work, but that increased when she attempted to read. She had insomnia at night but fell asleep at work. Her condition was getting serious. The physician was at his wits' end, when the patient asked him "if there could be any danger in an overindulgence of Coca-Cola? stating that she drank from three to six glasses a day. In addition, she had two or three cups of strong coffee at mealtime, sometimes taking but little other nourishment." He reports prompt improvement on curtailing her daily caffeine ingestion, concluding, "I feel that such a case is of interest from an ophthalmologic point of view and also because it indicates that the profession should be more alive to the pernicious influence in habit formation of some of the popular beverages served to young persons at public 'slop' fountains."[18]

Unknown to the typical coffee or tea drinker, there exists a subterranean culture of undetermined extent in which caffeine is consumed with the fixed intention of inducing intoxication. That is, many people across the country and around the world regularly use large doses of caffeine to get high. In doing so, they frequently encounter many of the symptoms of toxicity, somatic and psychological, that we discuss in this chapter.

Internet news groups are electronic confraternities in which people who have generally never met each other post public messages, photographs, and even sound files pertaining to a common interest. If you access such newsgroups as "alt.drugs.caffeine" or "alt.coffee" on any given day, you are certain to find questions, comments, confessions, misgivings, and boasts regarding the use of large amounts of caffeine. Here are quotations from Internet postings, which are rife with misinformation and misspellings:

Q: What are some of the affects you've experienced when you suck down too much caffeine?

A: I actually seem to get less alert. Well, actually the only effect I get from overdosing on caffeine is severe nausea and vomiting. Man, I just go numb in my hands and feet and start shaking all over, as my mind and body go hyper. I can't focus, can't think straight. I go through oscillating emotional states, and I experience cold sweats, shaking, and sometimes tachycardia. I usually have oscillations from paranoid to psychotically calm and back again, along with racing thoughts, while getting slight muscle cramps.

   A friend of mine snorted pharmaceutical grade caffeine once; he said it was extremely harsh on the nasal lining and not worth the buzz.

Q: I know a guy who once smoked a teabag and he claims that it gave him a buzz. Does anybody know if what he said is true?

A: Yes it works, i did it in england with the cheap tea they give you in a generic (low end) hotel, you just unfold the tea bag, you roll it up into something resembling a joint, and you light it, it is next to impossible to keep it lit though. oh it is the caffeine in it that gets you buzzed, the problem is that it goes away after about an hour and it leaves you with a bitch of a headache and some really bad cotton mouth.

• • •

I have used both caffeine and ephedrine together. It was related to one of my experiments, how to stay awake and keep going one whole week. I had to use quite a lot. I would say round 1500–2000mg caffeine per day and around 200–300mg ephedrine. Finally me and my head were quite mixed up. I was sleeping two hours a day and I kept this up for 19 days. I didn't just think that I saw God, I thought I was God. . . . I only drink coffee now. Be careful.

(See Appendix B, table 5, for the diagnostic criteria for caffeine intoxication from the *Diagnostic and Statistical Manual of Mental Disorders*.)

It is clear that scientists have little hard data on which to base conclusions about the prevalence of caffeine intoxication. The uncertainty is exacerbated by the failure of some researchers to distinguish between chronic high caffeine consumption and caffeine intoxication, or similarly, the failure to distinguish between an isolated episode of caffeine intoxication and chronic intoxication. Because caffeine is the most widely used drug on earth, we can be sure that, sooner or later, both the prevalence and incidence of caffeine intoxication will be better characterized by applying the rigorous criteria for diagnosis, standardized assessments, and representative sampling techniques that have been applied to intoxicants such as alcohol, cocaine, and morphine.

Really heavy caffeine consumption has often been observed among institutionalized schizophrenics, as this curious letter, captioned "Coffee Eating in Chronic Schizophrenics," from two psychiatrists to the *American Journal of Psychiatry* (July 1986) vividly attests:

Caffeinism, a psychophysiologic syndrome in DSM-III, is a clinically important syndrome per se, and as a co-diagnosis it may complicate the course of affective, anxiety, and thought disorders. The methylxanthines are the major pharmacoactive ingredient in many readily available caffeinated foods, beverages, and over-the-counter medications. To highlight a possibly important pattern of pathological consumption behavior that may produce caffeinism, we report three observations of coffee eating that occurred among chronic schizophrenic inpatients of a large state psychiatric hospital.

Mr. A, age 27, was frequently seen carrying around nearly empty jars of instant coffee, at which times he had an observable brown "mustache." When asked, he volunteered that he and another patient pooled their money on Friday "paydays" to buy instant coffee, usually 6–10 oz. jars. Then, over several hours they would consume the coffee "for kicks" using plastic spoons. Nurses stated that they could tell when these patients had eaten coffee because they were more irritable and prone to "act up"; they also required more medications.

Ms. B, age 53, presented her physician with an obviously heart-felt and generous gift: a paper cup filled with instant coffee and plastic spoon "to help eat it." She stated that she ate instant coffee when she could afford it and that she shared it with fellow patients. She said she "enjoyed the feeling" it gave her.

A third observation was of an incident in the breezeway between wards. A patient dropped a large jar of instant coffee. Despite the broken glass and the objections of staff, patients immediately crowded around and knelt down to scoop up the apparently precious powder, eating it directly off the floor.

These cases are not unique. Patients attest to the wide popularity of coffee eating in the hospital, where it seemed to be a shared social activity. Coffee eating is one of several examples of psychopharmacologically potent consumption behaviors that alter the clinical management of the psychotic patient. Such aberrant behaviors include excess coffee and tea ingestions, tobacco and marijuana abuse, and ethanol and self-induced water intoxication.[19] Patients have co-abused coffee and trihexylphenidyl, a combination that produces hallucinations and euphoria.

These incidents are of clinical concern because caffeine is reported to exacerbate the clinical course of schizophrenia. Caffeine products may alter psychopharmacologic management by several mechanisms. First, the methylxanthines induce hepatic microsomal enzymes, which results in faster neuroleptic degradation. Second, patients may use caffeine to reverse the sedative side effects of antipsychotic drugs. Third, coffee (as a complex compound) forms insoluble precipitates with some antipsychotic medications, thus reducing their absorption. Fourth, the methylxanthines are adenosine antagonists that modulate CNS norepinephrine, serotonin, dopamine, and other neurotransmitters. Caffeine may thereby alter antipsychotic action at the neurotransmitter level. Coffee eating may represent a potentially malignant cause of caffeinism. Four ounces of instant coffee typically contain 5 g of caffeine, which in toxicological terms is about one-half the median lethal dose. The more general problem is that caffeinism among chronic hospitalized patients may be a widespread and clinically important problem.

Given the potent opiate receptor binding activity of coffee, we wonder whether naloxone might be worth investigation as a blocker of this aberrant consumption behavior.

John I. Benson, M.D., Augusta, GA
Joseph J. David, M.D., Charlottesville, VA

Another psychiatric problem associated with excessive caffeine consumption is delirium, which is sometimes present in cases of extreme caffeine intoxication. For example, caffeine-induced delirium has been reported in a man who chugged down large amounts of coffee, cola, and 800 mg of caffeine tablets while competing in the Iditarod sled dog race held between Anchorage and Nome, Alaska. He experienced tremor and alteration in his level of consciousness, anxiety, visual illusions and hallucinations, vertigo, and impaired memory consistent with an episode of delirium. While in this case and others delirium has been attributed to excessive caffeine use, the degree to which factors such as fatigue and sleep deprivation may have contributed to the delirium is not readily determinable. However, even though the redoubtable *DSM-IV*, the bible of psychiatric diagnosis, does not yet officially recognize caffeine as one of the agents that can produce a "substance intoxication delirium," it seems probable that caffeine, like other psychoactive substances, should produce delirium if taken in sufficiently high doses.

Can Caffeine Kill?

If you take enough caffeine, it can kill you. The value generally accepted for a fatal overdose, and one given by pharmacology texts for fifty years, is about 10 grams for the average adult, about as much as in one hundred cups of coffee. In more precise clinical terms, the LD-50 of caffeine, that is, the lethal dosage for 50 percent of the population, is estimated at 10 grams for oral administration. However, the lethal dosage for any individual varies directly with body weight, and about 150 mg/kg to 200 mg/kg of caffeine is the usual estimate for the LD-50 for adult human beings. That is, those who weigh 150 pounds will have an LD-50 of at least 10 grams. However, because fatalities are very rare, and deaths have occurred at 5 to 50 grams, it is impossible to have confidence in this exact figure.

Acute toxic symptoms occur at levels as low as 50 mg/kg, equivalent to about 3.5 grams for a 150-pound person, about as much as in 35 cups of coffee. Even these levels are not usually attainable from dietary sources.[20] Milder caffeine intoxication symptoms, including anxiety, insomnia, and gastrointestinal disturbances, can occur after a 150-pound man ingests as little as 250 mg, or about 3 mg/kg.

Researcher Jack James cites what may be the first account of caffeine poisoning, dating from 1883. In this description, a sixty-three-year-old man "survived an oral overdose of caffeine after developing various cardiovascular, CNS, and gastrointestinal symptoms."[21] Others have not been so fortunate. An account published in 1959 of a thirty-five-year-old woman who, after arriving at the hospital in a state of insulin shock, was accidentally injected with a caffeine solution instead of glucose,[22] died after experiencing convulsions and respiratory arrest. Subsequent investigation determined that she had received 3.2 grams, raising her serum concentration of caffeine to 57 mg/kg.

Most of the cases where caffeine was the cause of death were the result of the accidental administration of caffeine by hospital staff. Typical examples are those of a fifteen-month-old boy and a sixty-one-year-old man, each given about 18 grams of caffeine orally. Another is a forty-five-year-old woman who was given 50 grams of caffeine instead of 50 grams of glucose.

In "A Fatal Ingestion of Caffeine," a 1977 article in *Clinical Toxicology*, written by J. E. Turner and R. H. Cravey, of the Office of the Sheriff–Coroner, Toxicology Laboratory, Santa Ana, presents one of the rare caffeine-associated deaths. According to the authors, the thirty-four-year-old woman who was to die from a massive overdose of caffeine

> complained of weakness and experienced episodes of vomiting. Upon retiring, her breathing became progressively labored, and she began to suffer convulsions. A rescue unit found her in coma. Upon arrival at the hospital, there was no audible heart beat, pulse, or breath sounds. She was in a state of acidosis (pH 6.8, arterial blood)

with cyanosis about the neck and mouth. She had assumed an opisthotonic posture [a severe muscle spasm, in which the back arches and head and heels bend back, such as occurs in the final stages of tetanus]. Resuscitative efforts lasted one hour. . . .

Autopsy revealed general congestion, particularly of the lungs, liver, and brain stem. Direct cause of death was attributed to pulmonary edema.[23]

Toxicological Findings after a Fatal Caffeine Overdose

Specimen	Caffeine Content
Blood	10.6 mg/100 ml
Liver	11.6 mg/100 g
Kidney	12.4 mg/100 g
Brain	10.8 mg/100 g
Gastric	43 mg total, plus three partially undissolved tablets

Turner and Cravey, "A Fatal Ingestion of Caffeine," *Clinical Toxicology* 10 (3): 341–44 (1977).

To comprehend the blood values of the deceased, consider that a 300 mg dose of caffeine, about as much as in two strong cups of coffee, result in a maximum blood concentration of about .5 mg/100 ml in a 200-pound adult, or less than 5 percent of the level found in this autopsy.

The survivor of what is probably the largest dose of caffeine on record is a twenty-one-year-old woman, estimated to have ingested a total of 106 grams, taken in the form of more than four hundred tablets, each containing 250 mg of caffeine. Despite an astonishing serum caffeine concentration of nearly 300 mg/ml, the patient was said to have shown "no residual neurological deficit" when discharged from the hospital four days later.[24]

Although people who consume caffeine are less likely to commit suicide than non-consumers, there are outstandingly rare suicide attempts utilizing high doses of the drug, which, under extreme circumstances, may in fact prove fatal, and there have been at least two reports of suicides by caffeine overdose.[25] Caffeine may be used to commit suicide so infrequently partially because few people know if it could kill them or how much it would take to kill them. The infrequency of accidental death may be a result of the emetic (purgative) effect of the drug. If there is evidence that a patient has significantly overdosed on caffeine, it should be treated as a medical emergency requiring intensive monitoring, symptomatic treatment for rapid or irregular heartbeat and seizures, aspiration of the stomach, and assessment of the serum caffeine level. Serum readings of more than 1 milligram per milliliter are generally considered toxic. Caffeine overdose has also been treated successfully with hemoperfusion, or flushing the blood supply clean with fluids.

Because infants and young children are much more vulnerable to the toxic effects of caffeine than adults, even when the discrepancies in their body weights have been factored out, researchers say that in infants 40 mg/ml is probably toxic.[26] There is a case of a child who died from orally ingesting less than 5.5 grams, or the equivalent of about five cups of coffee.[27]

Finally, the habit of smoking cigarettes must be mentioned again in relation to caffeine toxicity. There is an unholy bond between the habits of smoking cigarettes and drinking coffee. Although the precise figures vary, every survey indicates that a higher percentage of smokers drink coffee regularly than do non-smokers and that of regular coffee drinkers, smokers drink more of it than do non-smokers. We have noted repeatedly how variable the kinetic profile, or speed of metabolic passage, of caffeine can be among different people or in the same person at different times. Most people do not realize, however, that giving up cigarettes causes a profound slowing of caffeine's half-life, creating a toxic hazard for people who continue their previous levels of caffeine intake, unaware that, if they are no longer smoking, their coffee or tea will have a greater and more sustained effect on them than they had become accustomed to.

epilogue
A Toast to the Future

In the course of its relatively brief history, caffeine has become the world's most popular drug. Its most common sources, coffee, tea, and chocolate, have been celebrated and promoted as productive of health, stamina, and creativity and have been condemned and banned as the corrupters of the body and mind and subverters of social propriety and civil order. Through coffee and the coffeehouse, caffeine has altered society and culture from the Middle East to Europe, America, and beyond, justifying the fears of Islamic clerics and sultans and Western kings and police chiefs that the institutions purveying caffeine would undermine the stability and insularity of social and political order and religious practice. Through tea, teaism, and the afternoon tea, caffeine has subtly shaped the spiritual and aesthetic ideals of the Orient and given the British Empire, the most extensive imperial realm the world has ever seen, a universal symbol of civility, restraint, refinement, and social order. Through caffeinated soft drinks, caffeine has perfected its conquest of humanity, extending its community of users to children.

What powers or properties of caffeine have enabled it to exert such a broad influence on human history?

For one thing, caffeine is an intoxicant. As Freud observes in *Civilization and Its Discontents* (1930), man averts suffering by means of the enjoyment of four things: the enjoyment of illusions, or what Coleridge called "the willing suspension of disbelief"; the enjoyment of beauty, which beauty, we have been told by Keats, is "a joy forever"; the enjoyment of what we can have instead of the pursuit of the unattainable, which is called "displacement"; and, lastly, the enjoyment of intoxicants, or chemical intoxication. Freud might therefore have responded to the question "Why do people take drugs?" with the reply "Why not?" For it should come as no surprise that if caffeine, as an intoxicant, answers essentially to man's quest for happiness, it should be among the general pleasures of mankind.

What this observation leaves unaddressed is why caffeine should have emerged so recently from the large, diverse collection of available intoxicants to become both the most popular drug on earth, used regularly by more than 90 percent of everyone alive, and the most inconspicuous as well. For caffeine is as unnoticed as it is ubiquitous, suffusing our systems unremarked, despite its presence in our bodies from birth (and even before birth) through childhood, adulthood, and old age.[1]

Because the nature and extent of caffeine's effects are widely variable among different people and in the same person at different times, different people use caffeine for different reasons, and the same person uses caffeine for different reasons at different times. This diversity of effects and purposes may be one reason caffeine is the most popular drug on earth. But this same diversity also suggests that a complete understanding of caffeine will elude us until we have fully disentangled the complexities of human life itself.

Of course, caffeine comes to us accompanied by delights beyond its power to intoxicate: the sensual appeal of its most commonly enjoyed vehicles, coffee, tea, and chocolate. And caffeine itself should not be overlooked as an important component of their taste. The taste threshold for caffeine, that is, the minimum concentration at which it can be detected by the tongue (about .02mM/L [millimole per liter]), is the same order of magnitude as actually found in a cup of coffee. However, caffeine's contribution to the taste of coffee and other beverages is greater than this number suggests, because, at levels far below the threshold of perception, caffeine affects the taste of sweet, bitter, and salty foods or drinks, and therefore affects the overall taste mix of coffee's and tea's many flavoring components. In this book we have not discussed the art of beverage preparation, except as an aside, preferring to follow the disclaimer found in *A Compleat History of DRUGGS*, in which the early-eighteenth-century author, speaking of recipes for chocolate, explains:

> I did not think it proper to give you the Composition here, since there are so many Books that treat of it, and the Compositions are so various, that every one is for pleasing his own Fancy.[2]

We have discussed what we think constitutes the most important reason for caffeine's prominence in the modern world: It gives men the power to regulate their biological systems so as to make them more conformable with the demands of exacting and highly integrated schedules. Perhaps another reason for caffeine's enduring appeal is that, as compared with many other intoxicants, it is mild and benign. Although it can produce undesirable effects, from jitteriness and insomnia to withdrawal headaches and sleepiness, few people, as far as we know, find their health broken by caffeine use, and few lose their jobs, families, or fortunes because of excessive caffeine consumption. Of course part of the difference between caffeine and stronger, more dangerous drugs is simply a legal artifact. No one really knows to what extent caffeine use would follow the patterns of the abuse of other drugs if it were to join them as a controlled or illegal substance, or, conversely, to what extent the patterns of abuse of other drugs would abate if they, like caffeine, were obtainable legally.

What is the future of the coffeehouse? All we can be certain of is that it has one and will continue to have one. We recently read of two high school alumnae from

Philadelphia's Main Line who met, for the first time in a decade, by chance in the Pumpernickel Café in Kathmandu, Nepal. Can there be any doubt that, if and when there are settlements on Mars, coffeehouses will be among the first amenities available to the émigrés? The coffeehouse, which changes, adapts, and diversifies, merits recognition as the most protean institution in history. In coffeehouses, men met and plotted the American, French, Russian, and Chinese revolutions, dissected dolphins, invented and wrote newspapers, underwrote international commerce, conducted love affairs, and bandied and exchanged every sort of idea. In seventeenth- and eighteenth-century London, quack doctors treated patients and sold patent medicines at the coffeehouses. In Los Angeles at the end of the millennium a young lawyer has opened a coffeehouse in hope of practicing law there. To the concept of the *tabula rasa*, the blank slate of the mind on which experience writes, an idea of Locke's so favored by the generation of Addison and Steele, who worked and played in the coffeehouses, might be added the *mensa rasa*, the cleared table of the coffeehouse, across which every sort of opinion might be sounded and every sort of person faced.

Chemical intoxicants have been widely enjoyed since the remotest prehistoric times. We know that the production and consumption of alcohol from fermented plant matter are universal practices and have either arisen independently or been adopted into every place where human beings have lived. Yet the use of caffeine began to assert itself only within historical times, emerging as a relatively localized practice, first documented as coffee drinking in the Yemen, or as tea drinking in China and Japan, before suddenly exploding over the entire surface of the globe within the last few hundred years. Most cultivars, such as wheat, have been raised as long as they have been known, generally long before the time of written records. Yet the caffeinated plants, which are by far the largest cash crops on earth today, were still unknown within historical times, even in the regions in which they are today often mistakenly imagined to have originated.

Whether, like coffee, which was brought by Gabriel as a medicinal gift for Solomon or Mohammed, like tea, which was discovered by Shen Nung or carried by the missionary Bodhidharma, or, like chocolate, which was brought by Quetzalcoatl from heaven for the enjoyment of his people, the great caffeine-bearing plants were described as gifts from the gods in the earliest cultures into which they are known to have been introduced. The religious of many faiths have been repeatedly associated with the early uses of caffeine and the cultivation and propagation of the plants in which it occurs, as illustrated in examples such as the Sufis with coffee, the Buddhist monks with tea, the Aztec god-king with chocolate, and the Jesuits with all three and maté as well.

The seeds or leaves of the caffeine-bearing plants have been recurringly used as money, as cacao beans were by the Maya and Aztecs, cassine leaves by the North American Indians, cola nuts by the Africans, coffee beans by the Arabs, and bricks of tea by the Chinese and the Russians, a use that places them in the very small class of negotiable substances such as gold, silver, and precious jewels.

Today, more than any time before, caffeine is the dominant, nearly universal drug of the human race. It was in the steaming cups of coffee or tea that sat alongside the men who created the first newspapers. It is in the steaming cups of coffee or tea or, nearly as often, in the cold colas or other carbonated soft drinks that sit by those who design and use the Internet software and websites that are taking us into the third millennium.

Other drugs have had their days, for the use of many intoxicants is cyclic, rising and falling over the decades and centuries. Certainly caffeine use has not remained constant, nor can it be absolutely asserted that its use has demonstrated an unbroken increase in every nation in every decade. Yet, during the five centuries since word of the caffeinated beverages reached Europe, the coffee bean alone has come to account for a greater share of international trade than any other agricultural commodity, and these beverages have reached every quarter of every country on the earth. We can be fairly certain that this ubiety is unlikely to be compromised in the new millennium. Indeed, if our observations about the attractions of caffeine as a benign intoxicant and conversational stimulant and its uses to help us conform to our schedules, increase our physical and mental endurance, even spark our creative imaginations are correct, then this strange crystal, which may have evolved as a natural insecticide, has a shining future in the centuries ahead.

Selling the caffeinated beverages is and is likely to remain a great business. The cost of the imported green beans in a cup of coffee, sold retail at between seventy-five cents and five dollars, depending on where you buy it, is about seven cents. The cost of the roasted, ground coffee in a cup is less than twenty cents.[3] Few people, however, are ever likely to shun the café because of the big markup in price.

Is caffeine safe? The answers given in part 5—"Nobody knows" or "It depends"— are still the most accurate. As of this writing, caffeine appears to be remarkably non-toxic and to have been associated with few, if any, large-scale health problems. Unfortunately, in proportion to the extent of our exposure to caffeine, too little is yet known about its health effects for smugness. For example, questions have recently arisen again about whether caffeine increases the risk for developing high blood pressure. And there is no question that more work must be done to determine its effects on the fetus, in light of the fact that more than 75 percent of infants are born with detectable amounts of caffeine in their blood.

Caffeine has played a part in medicine, religion, painting, poetry, learning, love, life, and death. It figures prominently in the accords and enmities and the exchanges of trade and intelligence that constitute the history and intercourse of nations; and it is also a vitalizing and nearly indispensable agent in the singular lives of the over-whelming majority of the world's six billion people. Caffeine propels both idleness and industry. In the coffeehouse, it feeds idleness, whether it is the productive idleness of talk of politics, art, or social engagement, or the useless or even inimical idleness of gaming and gossip; in the workplace, it fuels the mental and physical stimulation that make possible long hours, punctuality, alertness, and alacrity; and in the studio, it stirs the artist's imagination and creative energies. And it does these things with little or no harm to the prudent user. Of no other drug, nor any other agency known to man, can we say the same.

The London Coffeehouse during the Commonwealth and Restoration

This broadside, distributed by Pasqua Rosée, proprietor of London's first coffee-house, was the first printed advertisement for coffee in England. After informing the reader that coffee hails from the "deserts of Arabia," Rosée recommends that half a pint of the water in which the ground beans had been boiled should be downed on an empty stomach, a manner of consumption intended to maximize the bewilderingly wide range of pharmacological benefits specified in the remainder of the text. It is interesting to note that coffee is presented as a drug only and no notice is taken of its possible enjoyment as a comestible. Note especially the reference to its humoral properties, "cold and dry," and how it readies a person for work and interferes with sleep:

THE VERTUE OF THE COFFEE DRINK
First made and publickly sold in England by Pasqua Rosee.

The grain or berry called coffee, groweth upon little trees only in the deserts of Arabia. It is brought from thence, and drunk generally throughout all the Grand Seignour's dominions. It is a simple, innocent thing, composed into a drink by being dried in an oven, and ground to powder, and boiled up with spring water, and about half a pint of it to be drunk fasting an hour before, and not eating an hour after, and to be taken as hot as possibly can be endured; the which will never fetch the skin oft the mouth, or raise any blisters by reason of that heat.

The Turks' drink at meals and other times is usually water, and their diet consists much of fruit; the crudities whereof are very much corrected by this drink.

The quality of this drink is cold and dry; and though it be a drier, yet it neither heats nor inflames more than hot posset. It so incloseth the orifice of the stomach, and fortifies the heat within, that it is very good to help digestion; and therefore of great use to be taken about three or four o'clock afternoon, as well as in the morning. It much quickens the spirits, and makes the heart lightsome; it is good against sore eyes, and the better if you hold your head over it and take in the steam that way. It suppresseth fumes exceedingly, and therefore is good against the head-ache, and will very much stop any defluxion of rheums that distil from the head upon the stomach, and so prevent and help consumptions and the cough of the lungs.

It is excellent to prevent and cure the dropsy, gout, and scurvy. It is known by experience to be better than any other drying drink for people in years, or children that have any running humours upon them, as the king's evil, &tc. It is a most excellent remedy against the spleen, hypochondriac winds, and the like. It will prevent drowsiness, and make one fit for business, if one have occasion to watch, and therefore you are not to drink of it after supper, unless you intend to be watchful, for it will hinder sleep for three or four hours.

It is observed that in Turkey, where this is generally drunk, that they are not troubled with the stone, gout, dropsy, or scurvy, and that their skins are exceeding clear and white. It is neither laxative nor restringent.

> *Made and sold in St. Michael's-alley, in Cornhill,*
> *by Pasqua Rosee, at the sign of his own head.*

During the Commonwealth and throughout the Restoration, coffeehouses were an ebullient forum for a heterogeneous assembly, including rich and poor, aristocrats and merchants, academics and the unlettered. To introduce restraints that might prevent disharmony and disorder and encourage conviviality, proprietors printed the following bill of regulations on large sheets, which they posted conspicuously on coffeehouse walls. The list, which encompasses rules of governing foul language, blasphemy, breaches of etiquette, gambling, paying for your fare, and treating others to a "dish" of the beverage that brought such a mixed group together, gives us a vivid picture of life in the coffeehouses in their first decades in England. It is addressed to men only, since women were barred from the English coffeehouses of the day:

> *Enter, Sirs, freely, but first, if you please,*
> *Peruse our civil orders, which are these.*
> First, gentry, tradesmen, all are welcome hither,
> And may without affront sit down together:
> Pre-eminence of place none here should mind,
> But take the next fit seat that he can find:
> Nor need any, if finer persons come,
> Rise up for to assign to them his room;
> To limit men's expense, we think not fair,
> But let him forfeit twelve-pence that shall swear[.]
> He that shall any quarrel here begin,
> Shall give each man a dish t' atone the sin;
> And so shall he, whose compliments extend
> So far to drink in coffee to his friend;
> Let noise of loud disputes be quite forborne,
> Nor maudlin lovers here in corners mourn,
> But all be brisk and talk, but not too much;

On sacred things, let none presume to touch,
Nor profane Scripture, nor saucily wrong
Affairs of state with an irreverent tongue:
Let mirth be innocent, and each man see
That all his jests without reflection be;
To keep the house more quiet and from blame,
We banish hence cards, dice, and every game;
Nor can allow of wagers, that exceed
Five shillings, which ofttimes do troubles breed;
Let all that's lost or forfeited be spent
In such good liquor as the house doth vent.
And customers endeavour, to their powers,
For to observe still, seasonable hours.
Lastly, let each man what he calls for pay,
And so you're welcome to come every day.

The "Triumphs of London, 1675," by Thomas Jordan (1612–85), English poet and pamphleteer, was a poem celebrating the marvels of coffeehouse society, particularly as the center of news, rumors, controversies, and the exchange of information. The lines "So great an university, / I think there n'er was any; / In which you may a scholar be, / For spending of a penny" were the origin of the famous coffeehouse epithet, "penny university."

Triumphs of London, 1675

You that delight in wit and mirth,
   And love to hear such news
That come from all parts of the earth,
   Turks, Dutch, and Danes, and Jews:

I'll send ye to the rendezvous,
   Where it is smoaking new;
Go hear it at a coffee-house,
   It cannot but be true.

There battails and sea-fights are fought,
   And bloudy plots displaid;
They know more things than e'er was thought,
   Or ever was bewray'd:

No money in the minting-house
   Is half so bright and new;
And coming from the Coffee-House,
   It cannot but be true.

Before the navies fell to work,
   They knew who should be winner;
They there can tell ye what the Turk
   Last Sunday had to dinner.
Who last did cut Du Ruiter's corns,
   Amongst his jovial crew;
Or who first gave the devil horns,
   Which cannot but be true.

A fisherman did boldly tell,
   And strongly did avouch,
He caught a shole of mackerell,
   They parley'd all in Dutch;
And cry'd out, Yaw, yaw, yaw, mine hare,
   And as the draught theyh drew,
They stunk for fear that Monk was there:
   This sounds as if 'twere true.

There's nothing done in all the world,
   From monarch to the mouse;
But every day or night 'tis hurl'd
   Into the coffee-house:

What Lilly or what Booker cou'd
   By art not bring about,
At Coffee-house you'll find a brood,
   Can quickly find it out.

They know who shall in times to come,
   Be either made or undone,
From great St. Peter's-street in Rome,
   To Turnbal-street in London.

        •   •   •

They know all that is good or hurt,
   To damn ye or to save ye;
There is the college and the court,
   The country, camp, and navy.
So great an university,
   I think there ne'er was any;
In which you may a scholar be,
   For spending of a penny.

Here men do talk of everything,
   With large and liberal lungs,
Like woman at a gossiping,
   With double tire of tongues,
They'll give a broadside presently,

'Soon as you are in view:
With stories that you'll wonder at,
 Which they will swear are true.

You shall know there what fashions are,
 How periwigs are curl'd;
And for a penny you shall hear
 All novels in the world;
Both old and young, and great and small,
 And rich and poor you'll see;
Therefore let's to the Coffee all,
 Come all away with me.

In June 1667, after Charles II had spent the money allotted by Parliament for the English navy on debauchery, Du Ruiter, a Dutch admiral, took advantage of the vulnerability of the English position, blockading the Medway and Thames and destroying fortifications as far as Chatham and Gravesend. General Monk and Prince Rupert were then commanders of the English fleet. William Lilly (1602–1681), the celebrated English astrologer during the Commonwealth, predicted a victory over Charles I, which was regarded as fulfilled in the battle at Naseby. Jonathan Booker (1603–1667), another English astrologer, was a fishing-tackle maker on Tower Street during the reign of Charles I, before becoming a Cromwell partisan and winning popular acclaim by foretelling "the downfall of King and Popery." Turnbal, now called Turnbull Street, had been a red-light district since Elizabethan times.

In his essay "London Coffee Houses in 1685," Lord Thomas Babington Macaulay (1800–1859), English historian, essayist, and statesman, celebrates the coffeehouses of the Restoration, particularly Will's, where the patrons converged from all quarters of English society, and where intellectual conversations, such as discussions of Aristotle's requirement that the tragic drama be limited by the famous unities of place and time, were common fare. Will's was especially renowned as the favorite haunt of John Dryden, the poet laureate, whose regular chair was moved from its place nearest the fire in winter to the cool air of the balcony in summer:

Nobody was excluded from these places who laid down his penny at the bar. Yet every rank and profession, and every shade of religious and political opinion had its own headquarters.

There were houses near St. James' Park, where fops congregated, their heads and shoulders covered with black or flaxen wigs, not less ample than those which are now worn by the Chancellor and by the Speaker of the House of Commons. The atmosphere was like that of a perfumer's shop. Tobacco in other form than that of richly scented snuff was held in abomination. If any clown, ignorant of the usages of the house, called for a pipe, the sneers of the whole assembly and the short answers of the waiters soon convinced him that he had better go somewhere else.

Nor, indeed, would he have far to go. For, in general, the coffee-houses reeked with tobacco like a guard room. Nowhere was the smoking more constant than at Will's. That celebrated house, situated between Covent Garden and Bow Street, was sacred to polite letters. There the talk was about poetical justice and the unities of place and time. Under no roof was a greater variety of figures to be seen. There were earls in stars and garters, clergymen in cossacks and bands, pert Templars, sheepish lads from universities, translators and index makers in ragged coats of frieze. The great press was to get near the chair where John Dryden sate. In winter that chair was always in the warmest nook by the fire; in summer it stood in the balcony. To bow to the Laureate, and to hear his opinion of Racine's last tragedy, or of Bossu's treatise on epic poetry, was thought a privilege. A pinch from his snuff-box was an honor sufficient to turn the head of a young enthusiast.

There were coffee-houses where the first medical men might be consulted. Dr. John Radcliffe, who, in the year 1685, rose to the largest practice in London, came daily, at the hour when the Exchange was full, from his house in Bow street, then a fashionable part of the capital, to Garraway's, and was to be found, surrounded by surgeons and apothecaries, at a particular table.

There were Puritan coffee-houses where no oath was heard, and where lank-haired men discussed election and reprobation through their noses; Jew coffee-houses, where dark-eyed money changers from Venice and Amsterdam greeted each other; and Popish coffee-houses, where, as good Protestants believed, Jesuits planned over their cups another great fire, and cast silver bullets to shoot the king.

appendix 6
Supplementary Tables

Table 1. Caffeine Content of Foods and Beverages

Food or Beverage	Mg of Caffeine
COFFEE (6-oz cup)	
Drip	130–180
Percolated	75–150
Espresso (1.5 to 2 oz)	100
Instant	50–130
Decaffeinated	2–6
TEA (6-oz cup)	
1 minute brew	10–40
3 minute brew	20–55
5 minute brew	25–100
Instant	15–35
Canned iced tea (12 oz)	55–90
CHOCOLATE PRODUCT	
Hot chocolate, from mix (6 oz)	10
Chocolate milk (6 oz)	4
Milk chocolate (1 oz)	6
Dark chocolate (1 oz)	20
Baking chocolate (1 oz)	35
M&M's (1.75 oz)	15
Hershey's Candy Bar (1.58 oz)	12
Hershey's Special Dark Bar (1.3 oz)	36
MISCELLANEOUS FOODS	
Dannon Coffee Yogurt (100 ml)	25
Cocoa Puffs breakfast cereal (100 g)	2
Häagen Dazs Coffee Ice Cream ($^{1}/_{2}$ cup)	32

Table 2. Caffeine Percentage by Weight: Natural Sources

Source	Range of Percentage of Caffeine by Weight
Roasted coffee beans	0.8 to 1.8
Tea leaves	2.0 to 4.1
Cocoa beans	.97 to 1.7
Cola nuts	1.0 to 2.2

Table 3. Caffeine Content of Soft Drinks

Drink (12 oz)	Mg of Caffeine
Jolt Cola	70
Mr. Pibb	59
Mountain Dew	54
Diet Mountain Dew	55
Mello Yellow	53
Tab	47
Coca-Cola	46
Diet Coke	46
Shasta Cola	45
Shasta Cherry Cola	45
Shasta Diet Cola	45
Dr Pepper	40
Diet Dr Pepper	40
Pepsi-Cola	38
Diet Pepsi	36
Aspen	36
RC Cola	36
Diet RC	36
Diet Rite	36
Canada Dry Cola	30
Canada Dry Diet Cola	1
7-Up	0

Adapted from FDA statistics, 1984, published in *FDA Consumer*

Table 4. Caffeine Content of Medications

Type of Medication	Caffeine Content (mg per pill or capsule)
ANALGESICS	
Vanquish	33
Anacin	32
Excedrin	65
Midol	32
COLD REMEDIES	
Coryban-D	30
Dristan	0
Triaminicin	30
APPETITE SUPPRESSANTS	
Dexatrim	200
Prolamine	140
DIURETICS	
Aqua Ban	100
PRESCRIPTION MEDICATIONS	
Cafergot	100
Darvon Compound	32
Fiorinal	40
Migralam	100
Percodan	32
ALERTNESS AIDS	
Vivarin	200
NoDoz	100

Table 5. Diagnostic Criteria for Caffeine Intoxication

A. Recent consumption of caffeine, usually in excess of 250 mg (e.g., more than 2–3 cups of brewed coffee).

B. Five (or more) of the following signs, developing during, or shortly after, caffeine use:

    (1)   restlessness
    (2)   nervousness
    (3)   excitement
    (4)   insomnia
    (5)   flushed face
    (6)   diuresis
    (7)   gastrointestinal disturbance
    (8)   muscle twitching
    (9)   rambling flow of thought and speech
    (10) tachycardia or cardiac arrhythmia
    (11) periods of inexhaustibility
    (12) psychomotor agitation

C. The symptoms in Criterion B cause clinically significant distress or impairment in social, occupational, or other important areas of functioning.

D. The symptoms are not due to a general medical condition and are not better accounted for by another mental disorder (e.g., an anxiety disorder).

From *Diagnostic and Statistical Manual of Mental Disorders (DSM-IV)*, American Psychiatric Association, 1994, p. 213.

Table 6. Caffeine in Arabica Coffees of the World

Type of Coffee	Caffeine Content as a percentage of weight
VARIETALS/STRAIGHTS	
Brazil Bourbons	1.20
Celebes Kalossi	1.22
Colombia Excelso	1.37
Colombia Supremo	1.37
Costa Rica Tarrazu	1.35
Ethiopian Harrar-Moka	1.13
Guatemala Antigua	1.32
Indian Mysore	1.37
Jamaican Blue Mountain/ Wallensford Estate	1.24
Java Estate Kuyumas	1.20
Kenya AA	1.36
Kona Extra Prime	1.32
Mexico Pluma Altura	1.17
Mocha Mattari (Yemen)	1.01
New Guinea	1.30
Panama Organic	1.34
Sumatra Mandheling-Lintong	1.30
Tanzania Peaberry	1.42
Zimbabwe	1.10
BLENDS AND DARK ROASTS	
Colombia Supremo Dark	1.37
Espresso Roast	1.32
French Roast	1.22
Vienna Roast	1.27
Mocha-Java	1.17
DECAFS (Swiss Water Process) All approximately .02	

appendix c

Additional Studies
of Caffeine's Physical Effects

Caffeine and the Cardiovascular System

At least one study, published in 1996 by Dr. Lucy Mead and Dr. Michael Klag, both of Johns Hopkins University, has found a dose-related correlation between coffee consumption and the development of high blood pressure. This long-term study of more than one thousand male former Johns Hopkins medical students began in 1947, when the study's founder, Dr. Carolyn Thomas, sought to identify the risk factors for developing high blood pressure. This is the only major study that, after excluding confounders such as family history, elevated blood pressure at the beginning of the study, smoking, and obesity, identified a strong link between coffee and hypertension. If the results are borne out by future research, coffee and caffeine intake may be considered an important factor in the causes of hypertension. However, even Mead and Klag say that such a conclusion is premature.

An additional important study minimizing caffeine's effect on pre-existing high blood pressure is the Hypertension Detection and Follow-up Program, "a community-based five-year (1974–79) collaborative trial of antihypertensive treatment."[1] The study considered more than ten thousand people between ages thirty and sixty-nine, from fourteen different population groups throughout the United States, who had a diastolic blood pressure of 90 Hg (high-normal) or above when the study began. After studying the subjects' caffeine consumption from coffee, tea, and cola, researchers concluded there was no exacerbation of their condition owing to caffeine.

However, despite these results, the preponderance of studies suggests that *caution among hypertensives may still be indicated*. For example, a 1995 study by researcher B. H. Sung, "Caffeine Elevates Blood Pressure Response to Exercise in Mild Hypertensive Men," published in the *American Journal of Hypertension*, found an increase in blood pressure, heart rate, and work load on the heart after taking caffeine, even in some non-hypertensive men. Sung tested thirty men, twelve of whom had normal blood pressure (under 130/80) and eighteen of whom suffered from mild hypertension (levels between

140/90 and 160/95), who were given about 300 mg of caffeine mixed with grapefruit juice. Although only one non-hypertensive subject experienced any adverse effects with caffeine ingestion, four of the hypertensive subjects exhibited readings above 230/120, and seven showed increases in blood pressure that the experimenters called "excessive." The normotensive subjects demonstrated no increase in heart rate, while the hypertensive group exhibited significantly greater heart rates on the days they consumed caffeine. The authors concluded that caffeine may cause a constriction of small arteries throughout the body and that the effects were great enough that people with high blood pressure should avoid using caffeine before and during their exercise.[2] Because fifty million Americans suffer from high blood pressure, if the effect is confirmed, this may be the most important danger caffeine offers to human health, apart from a still unevaluated threat posed by fetal or neonatal exposure.

Caffeine and Exercise: Good or Bad for Your Cardiovascular System?

Several studies have suggested that, in a healthy person, caffeine can actually improve the way the heart responds to exercise. For example, a 1995 study of caffeine conducted by Bruce Hardy, a pediatric cardiology fellow at Oregon Health Sciences University in Portland, and his colleagues at this institution found that, in patients with normal blood pressure, a dose of caffeine can *help* the heart handle exercise by slowing the heart rate, reducing blood pressure, and thus easing the work load on the heart. If these results seem surprising or even paradoxical to you, you are not alone. Hardy himself commented that "The outcomes of the study were a surprise to me. We would have thought the opposite would be true." Although his conclusions were based on observations of lowered blood pressure and increased heart output in six healthy young men, Hardy asserted that it was plausible to imagine that people with heart disease (but without arrhythmia) could also benefit from an amount of caffeine equivalent to two cups of coffee. If this is so, it contradicts the conventional medical wisdom that has prompted doctors to routinely advise patients with heart problems to stop drinking coffee.

Another exercise benefit for some heart patients was asserted in a 1984 study[3] that claimed caffeine was a "booster of pain-free walking time for patients with chronic stable angina."[4] This study found that drinking a couple cups of coffee increased the time such patients could exercise by as much as 12 percent, while decaffeinated coffee had no effect.

Caffeine and the Digestive System: Ulcers and Upset Stomach

In our effort to disentangle the gastrointestinal effects of caffeine from those of coffee, we quickly encounter the peculiar fact that, while caffeine will stimulate the release of water and sodium from the small intestine, coffee will not do so, suggesting that some agent in coffee may neutralize caffeine's effect in this regard. As most of us have experienced, coffee stimulates motility in the distal colon, that is, it promotes defecation; however, because this effect also occurs with decaffeinated coffee, it may have nothing to do with caffeine itself.

In a 1975 study by Cohen and Booth at the University of Pennsylvania,[5] the investigators found that coffee, whether caffeinated or decaffeinated, produced statistically significantly higher peak levels of gastric acid than caffeine alone. Parallel differences were found in their effects on esophageal-sphincter tone. As of this writing, the ingredient in coffee responsible for these effects on gastric acid and esophageal-sphincter tone has not been determined.[6]

Several studies subsequent to the work of Cohen and Booth have failed to find any causal relationship between caffeine and the incidence or exacerbation of peptic ulcers, although most of these considered caffeine's effects only tangentially, and interfering variables were not well excluded. In any case, it is clear that drinking decaffeinated coffee is not a recommended alternative to regular coffee for patients with either a peptic ulcer or gastroesophageal reflux, a condition that commonly produces the symptoms of heartburn.

Caffeine and PMS

Premenstrual syndrome (PMS), striking between four and fourteen days before the menstrual period, may affect half of all women, and it encompasses a broader variety of symptoms than Gulf War syndrome. Some of the more than one hundred symptoms that have been blamed on this condition are: irritability, tiredness, breast swelling and tenderness, headache, anxiety, depression, cravings for sweet or salty foods, acne, and changes in sleep patterns. It may last for a couple of days into the period and generally gets worse with age. The reasons for it are not known, but some relief, for the women it afflicts and the men who keep company with them, is ardently sought.

Since the mid-1980s, some researchers have suggested that caffeine use throughout the cycle may aggravate PMS. One of the first studies to provide solid evidence for this idea was conducted by Heinke Bonnlander, with results published in 1990 in the *American Journal of Public Health*. The study considered almost nine hundred women to find connections between diet and PMS, including an assessment of caffeine intake from all sources.[7] Women who drank eight to ten cups a day of coffee, tea, or cola were seven times more likely to have PMS than women who had no caffeine. Those who drank even one eight-ounce glass of a beverage containing caffeine were 50 percent more likely to suffer from PMS than women who drank none. Bonnlander concluded that there was a dose-related correlation between caffeine intake and the severity of PMS. As she puts it, "The more caffeine you have, the more severe PMS appears to be. Some people appear to be quite sensitive to caffeine," although she advises that more studies are needed to confirm her findings.

A pamphlet issued jointly by *Medical Economics* and Organon Inc., makers of a popular oral contraceptive, Desogen, quotes an excerpt from *The PDR Family Guide to Women's Health and Prescription Drugs* summarizing caffeine's purported effect on PMS:

> Caffeine is a major culprit of PMS symptoms.... Caffeine can exaggerate PMS-related problems such as anxiety, insomnia, nervousness, and irritability, and it can interfere with carbohydrate metabolism by depleting your body of vitamin B.

Reducing your caffeine intake . . . can provide almost instant relief. In fact, some doctors routinely advise eliminating caffeine from the diet before every menstrual period as a first step in coping with PMS.[8]

Caffeine may make PMS worse, but, because PMS is known to be linked to low calcium intake, depletion of the vitamin B complex, drops in serotonin levels, inadequate exercise, and many other factors, simply abstaining from caffeine is unlikely to allieviate all of its symptoms.

Caffeine and Osteoporosis

Osteoporosis, or abnormal loss of bony tissue, is a common bane of post-menopausal women, frequently resulting in fractures, pain, especially in the back of the neck, and a stooping posture. Because bone mass is primarily calcium, any factor that decreases the amount or absorption of calcium, such as long-term steroid therapy or immobilization, is a risk factor for this condition. A study by Heaney and Recker asserted a borderline association between caffeine consumption and increased levels of calcium excretion, but not with decreases in calcium absorption efficiency. A later study by Burger-Lux, Heaney, and Stegman, conducted in 1990, examined the effects of a moderate dose of caffeine (400 mg a day) on the calcium economy in healthy premenopausal women. Although the results showed a slight decrease in bone accretion, accelerated bone loss, and calcium pool turnover, the authors concluded that their findings supported the view that "moderate caffeine intake does not belong among factors that increase osteoporosis risk, at least for those women with higher calcium intakes."[9]

The Framingham Study, in evaluating the effects of long-term caffeine use over a twelve-year period, found that even one cup of coffee a day increased the risk of hip fracture, an injury commonly associated with osteoporosis, by almost 70 percent.[10] This dramatic increase of fracture rates is commonly confirmed by practicing orthopedic specialists.

The best recent study of the association of lifetime intake of coffee to bone mineral density of the hip and spine, which considered nearly one thousand post-menopausal women, was conducted by Barett-Connor and reported in *JAMA* in 1994. The bone density of the subjects at the hip and spine was measured by the degree to which they absorbed X-rays. Her study concluded that lifetime caffeinated coffee intake is positively correlated with reduced bone mineral density at both the hip and the spine, and that this correlation was observed independently of age, obesity, years since menopause, or the use of tobacco, estrogen, alcohol, thiazides, and calcium supplements.[11] The same study also found, though, "Bone density did not vary by lifetime coffee intake in women who reported drinking at least one glass of milk per day during most of their adult lives."[12] The authors caution that this includes women who drank considerably more milk than one glass a day. The research also suggests that only milk does the trick: Calcium supplements provided no protection against caffeine-induced bone shrinkage.[13]

Caffeine and the Elderly

Whatever effect caffeine has on you when you are young, you should be alert to changes that may occur in these effects as you grow older. In addition, because coffee consumption generally increases between adolescence and middle age, at which time it usually levels off, the effects of caffeine over time may increase accordingly.

Several studies have compared the differences in response to caffeine between older and younger people.

In 1988 Swift and Tiplady examined how the effects of caffeine on psychomotor performance changes with age.[14] A series of tests were administered to twelve subjects; six were eighteen to thirty-seven, and the other six were sixty-five to seventy-five. Both age groups demonstrated clear improvements in performance with caffeine use, but the profiles of these improvements were different in older and younger subjects. In results consistent with other studies of centrally acting drugs, the younger group was improved more on tasks depending on motor speed, while the old folks exhibited more improvement in attention and choice reaction time. Although not statistically dispositive, the data suggested that the elderly, overall, show a greater response to caffeine than the young.

Because the sleep time of people over fifty may be as much as two hours less than that of younger people, additional loss of sleep time, such as can be occasioned by caffeine, can represent a proportionally greater loss.[15] Many older people who have difficulty falling asleep are unaware that their medicines may contain caffeine. For example, Anacin and Excedrin, over-the-counter painkillers, and Darvon, a prescription painkiller, contain doses of caffeine that might keep many people awake. The Iowa 65+ Rural Health Study of three thousand people over sixty-five found that 5 percent were using medicines that contained caffeine, and that the ones who were doing so were twice as likely as the others to report problems falling asleep. The same study failed to discover any such correlation between sleep problems and coffee drinking. Perhaps this was because, in contrast with their spotty knowledge about their medications, people are universally aware that coffee contains caffeine, and therefore avoid drinking it in the evening.

Caffeine is useful in averting hypotension after eating among the elderly, especially that which occurs after eating breakfast. Patients with hypotension related to autonomic failure are advised to consume 200–250 mg of caffeine, or about two cups of coffee, with their breakfast.[16]

Older people often complain of cold hands and feet. Frequently, the cause is often undetermined and their condition may not be serious. Possible causes include poor circulation owing to diseased arteries, a side effect of certain medications, stress, or Raynaud's disease (a disorder that affects the flow of blood to the fingers and sometimes the toes). For people suffering from cold hands and feet, it may be important to avoid caffeine, which constricts blood vessels and could exacerbate the underlying condition.

One happy note: A recent University of Michigan study suggested that, for older people, caffeine may have aphrodisiac powers, because its researchers found that the elderly were more likely to have remained sexually active if they were coffee drinkers.

Caffeine and the Eyes

Caffeine may affect your eyes by constricting blood vessels, thereby increasing intraocular pressure and, with it, increasing your risk of developing glaucoma. Although no one has suggested that caffeine can in and of itself be regarded as a cause of glaucoma, one study indicated that in people genetically predisposed to developing the disease, coffee can increase their risk. Another study found that glaucoma patients who drink two cups of coffee a day show an increase in intraocular pressure, while normal patients who consumed two cups of coffee show no such increase. The greatest increases in intraocular pressure were found to occur in those who drink their coffee very quickly, consuming four cups an hour.

Caffeine also temporarily dilates the eyes, like other stimulants such as cocaine or amphetamine or adrenaline, and can therefore make it difficult to do close work, because dilated eyes cannot focus easily at short range.

Caffeine and Nutrition

Caffeine has been found to alter nutritional homeostasis—that is, the body's ability to maintain the proper levels of various nutrients, such as calcium, magnesium, and zinc—in experiments on pregnant rats. Theoretically caffeine may have similar effects in humans, although this has not been confirmed.

Caffeine consumed within one hour of eating may interfere with the absorption of dietary iron.[17] One study of maternal hemoglobin in non-smoking, teetotaler Costa Rican women found that iron deficiency occurred almost twice as frequently in coffee drinkers and that iron levels were also lower in their breast milk.

Grapefruit juice, which has been implicated in significantly altering the effects of several medicines, is known to raise the blood levels of caffeine.

Summary of the Medical Applications of Caffeine

> In recent years there has been a resurgence of interest in the therapeutic use of the natural methylxanthines and synthetic derivatives thereof, principally as a result of increased knowledge of their cellular basis of action and their pharmacokinetic properties.
>
> —Theodore W. Rall, "Drugs Used in the Treatment of Asthma," 1990[18]

Studies performed in the first half of the twentieth century in the pharmacology of caffeine and other methylxanthines confirmed traditional beliefs about their mood-elevating and analeptic powers and revealed other significant pharmacolgical properties that were subsequently put into therapeutic use. Although more effective treatments have displaced many of these early applications, new uses have more recently come to light. The methylxanthines share many pharmacological properties, but they can be distinguished in terms of the degree of some of their primary effects. The therapeutic uses of each is, obviously, determined in relation to these effects.[19] Most of caffeine's applications depend on its effect as a diuretic, cardiac muscle stimulant, central nervous system stimulant, smooth muscle relaxant, or elevator of plasma levels of FFA (free fatty acids).

Caffeine and Relieving and Preventing Pulmonary Problems

As we have repeatedly noted, caffeine and the other methylxanthines have long been used to help alleviate the symptoms of asthma. Less well known are studies demonstrating a protective effect of coffee drinking on the pulmonary complications of cigarette smoking. We have seen that smokers metabolize caffeine more rapidly than non-smokers, so that the caffeine exposure of a smoker who drank a cup of coffee would be lower than the exposure of the non-smoker, a fact that may account for the obviously increased rate of coffee consumption among smokers. Perhaps the occult destiny adduced by Walsh for caffeine is present here as well: For, strange to say, the increase in caffeine metabolism caused by smoking seems to result in an increase in use of caffeine, which in turn protects the smoker from the hazards of lung damage.

Methylxanthines have proved valuable in relieving apnea, or arrested breathing, in premature infants. Traditionally, theophylline has been chosen for this purpose, because a 1921 study demonstrated its greater potency in this respect, but more recently caffeine has been preferred by many physicians because the regimes for dosing (in part resulting from the longer half-life of caffeine in infants) are more easily managed and also because, paradoxically, administering theophylline to infants results in a greater buildup of caffeine in their systems than does the administration of caffeine.

Caffeine and Headaches and Pain Control

Because of its purported value as an analgesic adjuvant, caffeine has been used for decades in both non-narcotic and narcotic painkillers. Are these benefits genuine? Doctors disagree. One study demonstrated that the potency of analgesics compounded with caffeine was 40 percent greater than the same analgesics without caffeine. This means that, if you add caffeine to aspirin, for example, you will only need about two-thirds as much aspirin to achieve the same result as with aspirin alone. However, this does not mean that caffeine together with aspirin can relieve more intense pain than aspirin alone.[20]

Caffeine has been especially credited with the relief of headache pain, an effect that has been associated with its action as an adenosine antagonist. Caffeine has demonstrated vasoconstrictor effects on cerebral blood vessels, and it is believed that this action may augment its value in treating headaches, such as migraines, in which vasodilatation is a contributing factor. In addition, caffeine has a specific effect that can help migraine sufferers: It enhances the action of ergotamine, used in the treatment of migraine. This discovery was made by migraine patients who noted that strong coffee provided symptomatic relief, especially when combined with ergot alkaloids. The benefit is believed to result from the fact that caffeine increases ergotamine's oral and rectal absorption.

In at least one instance, caffeine was the cause of a major headache for one of the leading pharmaceutical companies. Excedrin, an over-the-counter Bristol-Myers Squibb analgesic, contains acetaminophen and caffeine. Recently, however, two 1,000-bottle lots of Excedrin caplets were accidentally filled with 200 mg of pure caffeine, as much as in a NoDoz caffeine caplet, another Bristol-Myers Squibb product.

Evidently the Excedrin gel tabs were being filled on the same processing line as NoDoz, and, despite all the computerized tracking, someone made a mistake. Bristol-Myers Squibb set up an 800 number to answer consumer questions and recalled the pills in question. Although the company feared an avalanche of bad publicity, the story received little news coverage. A company spokeswoman told us, "One adverse event was documented": a woman who, after taking the pills, was "treated and released," although what she was treated for was not specified. The company maintains that "untoward reactions to caffeine are not usually observed" at doses of less than 1,000 milligrams, but acknowledged that sensitivity to caffeine varies widely and that some people might have problems at lower doses.

Caffeine and Setting the Circadian Clock

A study by Dr. Margaret Moline of the New York Hospital–Cornell Medical Center, presented to the Boston Sleep Research Society in 1994, suggested that jet lag can be averted with judicious use of caffeine.[21] Moline isolated five middle-aged men from clocks, televisions, windows, or any other external indicia of the passage of time. All the men followed their natural sleep schedules and received only a placebo for the first five days. After this, they were allowed to go to sleep at their normal time, but were awakened six hours earlier than usual and given either a pill containing 200 mg of caffeine or a placebo. This sleep displacement simulated the displacement experienced by travelers from New York to London. The results strongly suggested that a subject who took caffeine helped to reset his body's clock with less intense disturbances and of a shorter duration than a subject who was given the placebo.

Books on jet lag often advise abstaining from caffeine for a week or two before a flight and then drinking several strong cups of coffee or tea at the correct hour to reset your biological clock to daytime after arriving at your destination. We have tried this and found that it works remarkably well.

Caffeine and Weight Control

We do not know enough to say if, or under what conditions, or for which subjects, or in what doses, caffeine can contribute to efforts to lose weight. Because it is evident that it can do so sometimes, for some people, anyone with a weight problem may be well advised to give caffeine a careful try, if he has no problems using caffeine to begin with.

Caffeine and Low Blood Pressure

Caffeine's therapeutic effects on low blood pressure caused by failure of the autonomic regulatory system, a condition afflicting about fifty thousand Americans, was investigated by researchers at Vanderbilt University Medical School in 1985. They administered two and one-half cups of coffee a day to patients with low blood pressure caused by autonomic failure, a disorder of the blood pressure regulatory mechanism that results in pressure so low that victims often faint when they stand up, especially after eating a meal. The autonomic nervous system controls the motor functions of the heart, lungs, intestines, and other internal organs. When experiencing autonomic failure, the body does not respond properly to conditions in which it needs to raise the blood pressure, such as while standing up or eating.

Caffeine has been shown to raise blood pressure in normal subjects, but only if they have not had any coffee in several days. Usually this effect wears off when coffee is consumed regularly. Nevertheless, as a result of his study, David Robertson, in a report in the *New England Journal of Medicine*, concluded, "We now advise our patients with autonomic failure to drink two cups of coffee with breakfast and to abstain for the rest of the day."[22]

Caffeine and Athletic Performance

The International Olympic Committee, convinced that caffeine has positive ergogenic effects—that is, that an athlete can increase output or endurance by using caffeine—has restricted the urine levels of caffeine that competing athletes may exhibit after a competition. Laboratory studies, however, are not so clear if or when or to what degree these beneficial effects occur, whether they are more or less likely to be observed in trained athletes than in people in average condition, whether they are observed more in relation to certain muscle groups, whether they are observed only when the activity in question is sustained at a very high level for a very long time, and other similar questions.

Caffeine and Skin Problems

Atopic dermatitis may be treatable with topical use of caffeine. Topical treatment with 30 percent caffeine in a hydrophilic base or in a hydrocortisone cream produces improvement in various forms of this skin condition, including pruritus, erythema, scaling, lichenification, oozing, and dermatitis. The improvement may be related to caffeine's ability to liberate water from epidermal and subcutaneous tissues.[23]

Caffeine and Parkinson's Disease

A high intake of caffeine may be associated with a lower incidence and slower progression of Parkinson's disease. A study reported in the *Journal of the American Medical Association* (May 24, 2000), led by G. Webster Ross, M.D., staff neurologist at the Department of Veterans Affairs in Honolulu, analyzed thirty years of data from the Honolulu Heart Program, which has followed more than 8,000 Japanese-American men since 1965. Age-adjusted incidence of Parkinson disease dropped dramatically, from *10.4 per 10,000* man-years in men who drank no coffee to *1.9 per 10,000* man-years in men who drank over 28 ounces, or about five 6-ounce cups, a day. A similar decline was observed for caffeine intake from sources other than coffee. Ross concluded that "caffeine has a medicinal effect. It could be treating motor symptoms."

As reported in an interview in *HealthScout* (May 23, 2000), Abraham Lieberman, M.D., professor of neurology at the University of Miami and medical director of the National Parkinson Foundation, attributes the possible role of caffeine in preventing Parkinson's Disease to its ability to block adenosine receptors and increase the levels of dopamine, which are low in people suffering from the disease. However, Lieberman maintains, further long-term studies of the progression of the disease are needed to establish the treatment potential of caffeine in Parkinson's disease more definitively.

Clinical Actions of the Methylxanthines

Desired Action	Preferred Agent
Cerebral Stimulation	Caffeine (Coffee)
Coronary Dilation	Theophylline (Tea)
Diuresis	Theobromine (Chocolate)
Respiratory Stimulant for Premature Infants	Caffeine or Theophylline

appendix d
Methodological Pitfalls

Everyone knows that scientists investigate the world by systematically testing hypotheses using carefully designed experiments. The results of their studies are presumably replicable and therefore their conclusions represent objective advances in scientific understanding. Unfortunately, in the area of human health, the complexity of the human body and mind and the inability of investigators to conduct potentially dangerous experiments on human beings as part of their research often make it difficult to make reliable judgments. There are three potential weaknesses of medical studies that pose problems for those seeking to understand caffeine's health effects: biased sample selection, inaccurately measured exposure, and failure to exclude confounding variables. Because these limitations can be seen most clearly in studies of caffeine's effects on the outcomes of pregnancy, it is valuable to examine in detail some of the methodological problems that bedevil scientists working on these questions. While reading this section, however, the reader should keep in mind that similar or identical problems attend investigations of every area of caffeine and human health discussed in this book.[1]

Sample Selection

Studies of the effects of caffeine consumption on reproductive hazards, including the risk of delayed conception, spontaneous abortion, prematurity, low birthweight, and major congenital malformations, multiplied like rabbits throughout the 1980s and 1990s. Although poor design has limited the value of many of them, the larger, more probative studies generally demonstrate no correlation between caffeine use and reproductive hazards of all kinds.[2] Yet, as is true for the results of any epidemiological studies, the value and weight of their conclusions depend on whether the people studied were selected in a way that did not prejudice or distort the outcomes.

Unfortunately, defective sample selection is endemic to studies of caffeine and human reproduction, in part because few researchers into reproductive hazards undertake studies with caffeine or coffee as their primary initial interest. Many even inquire about caffeine use only to divert attention from questions about other risk factors such as cigarettes and alcohol. Such casual treatment of caffeine is possible—and especially distressing—only because caffeine is so much a part of life that it is little noticed and then often only as an afterthought.

Exposure

It is evident that an accurate assessment of exposure, that is, the amount of caffeine consumed, is fundamental to any evaluation of a link between caffeine consumption and health. In fact, precision in measuring exposure is essential, because a dose-response relationship—that is, the tendency of increasing doses to elicit increasing responses—strongly suggests a causal relationship and cannot be evaluated without it. If a low exposure is correlated with low risk, moderate exposure with moderate risk, and high exposure with high risk, scientists are more inclined to posit a corresponding cause-and-effect connection. In the matter of adverse effects on pregnancy, such a relationship would exist if those pregnant women who consume more caffeine were at a higher risk for adverse effects than pregnant women who consume less, and it would lead us to think that caffeine exposure is the cause for these untoward outcomes.

Laboratory control studies rely on a number of stratagems, such as using decaffeinated coffee to which varying doses of caffeine have been added, to enable the researchers to record the exact amount of caffeine consumed. For epidemiologists, scientists who study the occurrence and causes of diseases in the field, however, it is rarely a simple matter to determine how much caffeine subjects have used. Tea and coffee cups commonly range from four to sixteen ounces.[3] So long as estimates of caffeine consumption are tied to coffee drinking, the wide variability of caffeine content in the beans and of roasting and brewing methods, which reflect regional variations and personal preferences, will limit the ability of epidemiologists to determine the actual levels of caffeine consumption. An additional problem is the unreliability of questionnaire answers, which may underestimate or overestimate intake. For example, in a recent breast cancer study in which records of caffeine consumption were kept and compared with later recollections of that consumption, it was found that the women studied reported an average of 75 mg a day less caffeine than they had actually ingested, while the women serving as controls underreported their consumption by only 40 mg a day.[4] In another study, pregnant controls were more likely to underreport consumption than women who had miscarried.[5] In any case, serum concentrations of caffeine's primary metabolites, such as paraxanthine, do not closely correspond with questionnaire answers about caffeine consumption. Discrepancies may reflect errors in recollection, varying methods of preparation, or differences in metabolic degradation rates. It is evident that, to accurately gauge caffeine exposure, future researchers must utilize not only questionnaires and cup counts, but biomarkers—that is, objective measures of caffeine and its metabolites in the body—as well.

Measuring exposure to the fetus is especially difficult because the amount of caffeine consumed and the speed at which it is metabolized vary throughout pregnancy. For example, because of the nausea associated with the first six months of pregnancy, consumption may be lower than usual during that period. Another confusing factor is that it takes longer for the body to get rid of caffeine's metabolites near the end of pregnancy.[6] Therefore, to avoid the unpleasant feelings associated with elevated blood levels of caffeine's metabolites, some women appear to reduce their consumption of caffeinated drinks during pregnancy.

A different sort of problem arises when exposure to caffeine is measured but effects of exposure to other drugs that may have been consumed along with it are overlooked. Yet another confounding exposure may arise from neglect of non-dietary sources of caffeine, such as over-the-counter and prescription medicines that people may not realize contain caffeinated and so fail to report.

Confounding Variables

We have already noted ways in which hidden variables can baffle attempts to understand the relationship between the use of caffeine and any given health outcome. Epidemiologists call such variables "confounders" that, according to one researcher, "plague the literature" about the link between caffeine and problems in human reproduction. An example is the confounding variable of maternal age. Coffee consumption tends to increase with age throughout the childbearing years and, at the same time, the risk of many reproductive hazards also increases with age past 25 or 30.[7]

People who drink coffee differ in significant ways—over and beyond their use of coffee—from those who do not, and those who drink a great deal of coffee differ from those who drink less. Comparisons of health effects are particularly problematic between members of these groups and people who do not use caffeine with respect to any health-related variable.[8] An example of material confusion results from the fact that people who drink little or no coffee tend to use less tobacco and alcohol than those who are heavy coffee drinkers. This kind of insidious confounder can easily engender false claims of a causal connection between coffee or caffeine and health problems.[9]

notes

OVERVIEW

1. Henry Watts, ed., *Dictionary of Chemistry*, vol. I, p. 707.
2. John Evelyn, *Works*, note, p. 11.
3. Sir Richard Steele, *Tatler*, April 12, 1709.

PROLOGUE

1. Johann Wolfgang von Goethe, *Versuch die Metamorphose der Pflanzen zu erklären (Attempts to Illustrate the Metamorphosis of Plants)*. In this book Goethe takes his place as a pioneer in the theory of evolution.
2. As P. Walden, in his essay "Goethe and Chemistry," states, "At Weimar the time had come for Goethe to reexamine his chemical knowledge and concepts, to transfer them into the realm of practice and reality, simultaneously, however, to give them a more solid theoretical foundation" (George Urdang, *Goethe and Pharmacy*, p. 15).
3. Fielding H. Garrison, *History of Medicine*, p. 262.
4. The singular distinction of Goethe's fame is that the paradigm of the widely celebrated writer began with him. Before Goethe, the authors of important books had enjoyed respect, but they had never become personal heroes to a large public. Although their works were honored, the authors themselves were uninteresting to the popular imagination. But from the time his early novel *The Sorrows of Young Werther* instigated suicides among teenagers across Europe, people everywhere became what we would today call Goethe's "fans."
5. Wolfgang von Goethe, *The Sorrows of Young Werther*, p. ix.
6. Berthold Anft, "Friedlieb Ferdinand Runge," p. 574.
7. It is the use of "sleepy substance" as an explanatory mechanism for morphine that Molière makes fun of in the *Imaginary Invalid* and that Nietzsche cites as typifying the silliness of the empiricists' arbitrary reifications.
8. We regret our inability to determine the first names of some of the scientists mentioned in our book.

CHAPTER 1

1. Dr. William Adams, professor at the University of Kentucky and author of *Nubia*, told us in an interview in 1997, "There is absolutely no evidence, textual or archaelogical, of any use of coffee in Nubia or Abyssinia before modern times."
2. For example, we have no accounts from the Crusaders (c. 1100–1300) that mention encounters with coffee.
3. Reverend Doctor J. Lewis Krapf, *Travels, Researches and Missionary Labours During Eighteen Years Residence in Eastern Africa*, p. 47.
4. James Bruce, *Travels to Discover the Source of the Nile*.

5. Perhaps, in addition to knowledge of the plant, the prerequisite for the spread of coffee is the discovery of the methods of roasting and infusing the bean. People seem to have entertained a limited inclination to chew the fruit, even when it had been kneaded with lard or butter, and, although swilling heavily reboiled raw coffee and swallowing the grounds gained a little more acceptance, roasting and infusion were the watershed inventions that transformed coffee from a rank medicinal powder or murky sedimented syrup into a beverage coveted for its flavor as well as its stimulating effects. Yet, in the end, even this answer does not completely resolve the mystery, because the flesh of the coffee berry is fragrant and good tasting and fully charged with caffeine. In fact, its apparent appeal adds a puzzle: Why did the use of the bean spread, despite the dislike expressed by so many for its taste, while the eating of the pleasant fruit remained a localized curiosity?

6. William Ukers, *All about Coffee*, p. 8, quoting from Dufour's translation.

7. Lenn E. Goodman, *Avicenna*, p. 36.

8. Ulla Heise, *Coffee and Coffee-Houses*, p. 11, quoting Liber canonis, Tractatus secundus, 1608, chapter 90.

9. Ukers, *All about Coffee*, p. 8.

10. William Gohlman, *The Life of Ibn Sina*, p. 36. Also see Goodman, *Avicenna*, p. 45, n. 13. The value of this resource, afterward destroyed by Suni zealots opposed to the Sultan's Shiite sympathies, should not be underestimated. In later life, Avicenna recalls rooms full of books dedicated to each subject, ancient or modern, where he saw "books whose titles are unknown to many, and which I never saw before or since."

11. That a leading thinker such as Avicenna should have mentioned the coffee bean and described some of its properties only deepens the mystery of the absence of any further references for several hundred years.

12. Ukers, *All about Coffee*, p. 8, quoting Leonhard Rauwolf, *Aigentliche beschreibung der Raisis so er vor diser zeit gegen auffgang inn die morgenlaender vilbracht*, Lauingen, 1582–83.

13. Giovanni Battista Montanus (1488–1551), Italian physician and classicist, tells us in his *Commentary* that Avicenna wrote the *Canon* "because he saw that neither the Greeks nor the Arabs had any book that would teach the art of medicine as an integrated subject." See Nancy Siraisi, *Avicenna in Renaissance Italy*, p. 20. See also, Goodman, *Avicenna*, p. 47, n. 38.

14. Anonymous editor, *Canon of Medicine*, "Introduction," no page, found in the library of the University of Pennsylvania.

15. Francis Ross Carpenter, in *The Classic of Tea*, p. 35, referencing Reinaud, *Relations des Voyage fait par les Arabes et les Persans dans l'Inde et . . . la Chine*, I, 1845, p. 40.

16. *The Odyssey*, translated by Samuel Butler, Book IV, lines 219–34. Pæon was a celebrated physician, mentioned also by Virgil and Ovid, with a truly upscale practice. He treated the wounds which the gods received during the Trojan War. On his account, physicians were sometimes called *Pæeonii* and medicinal herbs *Pæeonæ herbæ*.

17. Robert Fitzgerald aptly translates the phrase as "an anodyne."

18. Heinrich Eduard Jacob, *Coffee: The Epic of a Commodity*, p. 74, quoting Simon André Tissot, *Von der Gesundheit de Gelehrten*, Leipzig, 1769.

19. Sir Henry Blount, *A Voyage into the Levant*, pp. 20–21.

20. See John DeMers, *The Community Kitchen's Complete Guide to Gourmet Coffee*.

21. Jacob, *Epic of a Commodity*, p. 44.

22. The Arab legends of the first encounter with coffee, invariably set in Ethiopia or the Yemen, are often stocked with the full range of fabulous Oriental devices that are the mark of Islamic legends. One of these, an entry in the Omar cycle, is, in particular, worth our attention, and so begins

The Tale of Amorous Acolyte:
A Giant Ghost, Swirling Water, a Beautiful Princess, and the Coffee Tree

In the year 656 A.H. the mollah Schadheli, making his holy pilgrimage to Mecca in the company of Omar, his disciple, came as far as the wilderness of Ousab, to the Emerald Mountain. At once, he knew he would go no further.

"It is the will of Allah, blessed be his Name, that this very night I should die on this mountain," he told Omar. "When I am gone, a veiled personage will appear to you. Take care to obey his commands!" So saying, Schadheli entered the cave, lay upon a spread of cloth, and waited.

True to his word, as a religious man of honor, Schadheli died that night. Soon after, Omar, leaving the side of the body to refresh himself with the night air, was startled by a flash of light which, when his bedazzled eyes could again see, had left behind a giant spectre draped in a white veil. Summoning his courage, Omar demanded that the figure reveal his name. The phantom said nothing, but when he removed the veil, Omar recognized his late master, grown to height of thirty feet.

The giant visage stamped his foot on the rocky ground, splitting it, and a fountain of pure water burst from within the earth.

"Fill your bowl with water from this fountain," the spirit told Omar, his ghostly form already fading against the black desert sky and the jewel-like stars. Then, just before vanishing, he added, "Carry the bowl towards Mocha while the water yet swirls!"

Omar turned southward and set out toward the famous port. After journeying for three days and nights without food or sleep, holding the bowl before him and glancing continually to see if the water still turned within, suddenly he noticed it had stopped moving. When he looked up he saw that he had arrived in Mocha, where he soon discovered the people were suffering greatly from a terrible plague. Omar's prayers cured all who came before him. His reputation for healing spread quickly among the wise, reaching the ear of the vizier, a clever counselor to the Sultan. The Sultan, a trusting man, had a beautiful daughter whom he loved above all things and who lay as if dead within her chambers. He heeded his advisor by sending for the holy physician. Omar cured the girl and, entranced by her loveliness, made love to her as soon as she awoke.

With forbearance compelled by his gratitude for the city's rescue, and with the encouragement of his vizier, to whom Omar had given an amatory talisman (which made him irresistible in love), the Sultan spared Omar's life but exiled him back to the wilds of Ousab, where, as before, the holy man was left with only herbs for food and a cave for shelter.

Wearying of solitude and the barren waste, Omar cried out to his dead master, "Why have you sent me on this circular and ill-fated journey?" As if in response, a small green bird alighted in a nearby tree. When Omar came near, he saw the tree was covered with green leaves, small white flowers, and bright red fruit. He filled a basket with the berries, and later that night, when preparing to boil his dinner of herbs, he thought to break open the fruit and toss the seeds into the pot in their stead. The result, to his amazement and delight, was the aromatic and fortifying beverage we know today as coffee.

Others say that Omar's master gave him a small wooden ball which rolled of its own as if alive, instructing him to scrabble after until it stopped moving. The ball led him to a village where he effected cures by dispensing the boiled red berries of a stand of wild coffee trees growing nearby.

23. Ralph S. Hattox, *Coffee and Coffeehouses*, p. 15.
24. *Ibid.*, p. 14.
25. *Ibid.*, p. 74.
26. The time of caffeine's early proliferation was a turbulent one in the Yemen. The Pashas of San'a, who ruled the tiny domain, were appointed by either the sultan of Constantinople or the Ottoman Pasha in Cairo, depending on which of them had the upper hand that particular year. Until 1547, control of the Yemeni port city of Aden was contested between the Ottomans and the Portuguese, who had established bases on the Abyssinian side of the Red Sea. Although the Ottomans briefly succeeded in closing off trade from the area, within decades spices, especially pepper, were again reaching Egypt by way of the Yemen and the ports of the Hijaz. The imams, or local chiefs, enriched by trade and encouraged by ambitious Europeans, successfully contested Ottoman authority in San'a, so the spice traffic flourished again. This traffic was decisively and permanently redirected only when the Dutch and English developed the Cape route to the East in the seventeenth century. Fortunately for the Yemen's economic health, by that time coffee was already replacing spices as its most important item of trade. See Kamal S. Salibi, *A History of Arabia*, p. 150.
27. Hattox, *Coffee and Coffeehouses*, p. 61.
28. The *Bacchæ* is a play which, as William Arrowsmith comments in his introduction to his translation, is dimly reminiscent of the unsettling invasion of Hellas by the cult of Dionysus, an occurrence with obvious parallels to the advent of the coffeehouse culture in Islam.
29. One interesting detail of the testimony was a physician's assertion that Bengiazlah, a famous

contemporary of Avicenna, had taught that, according to humoral theory, coffee must be regarded as "hot and dry," not as unwholesomely "cold and dry," as Beg's witnesses claimed. Even at this early time, however, uncertainty prevailed about the meaning of the reference, and coffee's opponents answered that Bengiazlah had not been speaking of coffee at all, but of a drink also known as "kahwe" but made from a different plant.

30. Hattox, *Coffee and Coffeehouses*, p. 77.

31. Such references are scattered throughout *Reis' in die Morgenländer (Rauwolf's Travels)*, published at Frankfurt and Lauingen in 1582–83.

32. Joseph Walsh, *Coffee: Its History, Classification, and Description*, p. 7.

33. *Ibid.*, p. 6.

34. Robert Nicol, *A Treatise on Coffee: its properties and the best mode of keeping and preparing it*, pp. 11–12.

35. Maguelonne Toussaint-Samat, *History of Food*, p. 581.

36. Walsh, *Coffee: Its History*, p. 7.

37. Hattox, *Coffee and Coffeehouses*, p. 106, quoting Jaziri.

38. *Ibid.*, p. 111, quoting Jaziri.

39. *Ibid.*, p. 110, quoting Celibi.

40. Ukers, *All about Coffee*, p. 30, quoting Jean La Roque, *Voyage de L'Arabie Heureuse*, Paris, 1716.

41. Between 600 B.C. and A.D. 1900 the population of the Yemen remained almost constant at about 2.5 million. It was called, together with Oman, *Arabia Felix*, or "Fortunate Arabia" by the classical geographer Ptolemy. The Yemen's moderate climate contrasts with that of the barren interior of the Arabian peninsula, which Ptolemy called *Arabia Deserta*, or "Desert Arabia," and that of the Hijaz, which he called *Arabia Petræa*, or "Stony Arabia." Although only 10 percent of the total area of the peninsula, the Yemen has consistently sustained about 50 percent of Arabia's population since the introduction of agriculture in the third millennium B.C. These circumstances have both isolated the Yemen and helped define its identity, making it a kind of oasis of activity, surrounded by the ocean on one side and desert on the other, relatively remote from the major capitals of the world.

42. We can even surmise something about the date before which coffee could not have come into great prominence in Islam from the absence of any mention of coffee or coffeehouses by Antonio Menavino, who, in 1548, did not include coffee in a list of drinks drunk by the Turks. Nor did Pierre Belon mention the plant in 1558 in his list of Arabia's plants.

43. Philippe Sylvestre Dufour, *Traitez Nouveux & curieux Du Café, Du Thé et Du Chocolate*, p. 37.

44. Hattox, *Coffee and Coffeehouses*, pp. 81–82, quoting Pedro Teixeira, *The Travels of Pedro Teixeira*.

45. *Ibid.*, p. 81, quoting Jean de Thévenot, *Suite de Voyage du Levant*, Amsterdam, 1727.

46. Ukers, *All about Coffee*, p. 82, quoting George Sandys.

47. Hattox, *Coffee and Coffeehouses*, p. 99, quoting Thévenot.

48. Carston Niebuhr, *Travels through Arabia and other countries in the East*, vol. I, p. 126.

49. *Ibid.*, p. 73.

50. W. B. Seabrook, *Adventures in Arabia*, p. 72.

51. *Ibid.*, pp. 34–35.

52. *Ibid.*, p. 108.

53. *Ibid.*, pp. 172–73.

54. Alain Borer, *Rimbaud in Abyssinia*, p. 180.

55. *Ibid.*, pp. 183–84.

56. *Ibid.*, p. 186, quoting Arthur Rimbaud, letter to M. de Gaspary, Aden, November 9, 1887.

57. Edward Bramah, *Tea & Coffee*, p. 106.

58. Hattox, *Coffee and Coffeehouses*, p. 18.

59. This symbolic use of wine and intoxication is brilliantly exemplified in the original Persian of the *Rubaiyyat* of Omar Khayaam. Although the poem was hypnotically, musically, and sensually rendered into English by Fitzgerald, this familiar version, steeped in the celebration of sexual and alcoholic dissipation, is a reflection more of the hedonistic dream world of late Victorian repression in which the translator lived than it is of the spiritual life of the tenth-century Sufi author. For a version that purports to be truer to the original, see *The*

Original Rubaiyyat of Omar Khayaam, translated by Robert Graves and Omar Ali-Shah, Garden City, N.Y.: Doubleday, 1968.

60. *Encyclopædia Britannica*, "Arabia" (Yemen: Arab Republic), vol. 10, p. 906.
61. *Harper's Weekly*, New York, January 21, 1911.
62. Schapira et al., *Book of Coffee and Tea*, map, p. 79.
63. Krapf, *Travels, Researches*, p. 46.

CHAPTER 2 *tea*

1. Toussaint-Samat, *History of Food*, p. 605.
2. Quoted in Ukers, *All about Tea*, vol. I, p. 1.
3. Kit Chow and Ione Kramer, *All the Tea in China*, p. 2.
4. Quoted in Ukers, *All about Tea*, vol. I, p. 3.
5. Chow and Kramer, *All the Tea in China*, p. 3.
6. According to legend, Bodhidharma carried meditation too far, and his legs atrophied from disuse and dropped off. For this reason, images of him are generally legless and are sometimes called "snowmen."
7. Lü Yu, *Classic of Tea*, p. 12.
8. Adapted from Carpenter, *ibid.*, p. 15.
9. Schapira et al., *Book of Coffee and Tea*, p. 149.
10. Toussaint-Samat, *History of Food*, p. 596.
11. Schapira et al., *Book of Coffee and Tea*, p. 149.
12. Chow and Kramer, *All the Tea in China*, p. 3.
13. Schapira et al., *Book of Coffee and Tea*, p. 149.
14. Jennifer Anderson, *Introduction to Japanese Tea Ritual*, p. 21.
15. Lu Yü, *Classic of Tea*, p. 50.
16. This reference appears in Chang Yu-hsin's book, *A Record of Waters for Boiling Teas*.
17. Schapira et al., *Book of Coffee and Tea*, p. 150.
18. Lu Yü, *Classic of Tea*, p. 72.
19. *Ibid.*, pp. 105–7.
20. *Ibid.*, pp. 107–9.
21. *Ibid.*, p. 116.
22. Kakuzo Okakura, *The Book of Tea*, p. 12.
23. Lu Yü, *Classic of Tea*, p. 17.
24. Rand Castile, *The Way of Tea*, p. 49.
25. *Ibid.*, p. 30.
26. Okakura, *The Book of Tea*, p. 11.
27. Schapira et al., *Book of Coffee and Tea*, p. 148.
28. J. Anderson, *Japanese Tea Ritual*, p. 14.
29. Lu Yü, *Classic of Tea*, notes to p. 61, pp. 158–59.
30. J. Anderson, *Japanese Tea Ritual*, p. 17.
31. *Ibid.*, p. 18.
32. Castile, *The Way of Tea*, p. 49.
33. J. Anderson, *Japanese Tea Ritual*, p. 21.
34. Toussaint-Samat, *History of Food*, p. 597.

CHAPTER 3 *cacao*

1. Marcia Morton and Frederic Morton, *Chocolate: An Illustrated History*, pp. 3–4.
2. Sophie Coe and Michael Coe, *The True History of Chocolate*, p. 73.
3. Morton and Morton, *Chocolate*, pp. 3–4.
4. Coe and Coe, *True History*, p. 78.
5. *Ibid.*, p. 97.
6. Other explorers had the same experience. In *The Conquest of New Spain*, the seventeenth-

century explorer Bernal Diaz describes how the Aztecs "brought him in cups of pure gold a drink made from the cocoa plant, which they said he took before visiting his wives."

7. Morton and Morton, *Chocolate*, p. 4.
8. Nelson Foster and Linda Cordell, ed., *Chilies to Chocolate*, p. 105.
9. *Ibid.* Yet there is the Spanish painting of the gifts of the Magi, done about 1501, in which an American Indian is shown proffering a bowl of what looks like cacao.
10. Coe and Coe, *True History*, pp. 37–39. See also "Maya Writing," David Stuart and Stephen D. Houston, *Scientific American*, August 1989, pp. 82–89.
11. Foster and Cordell, *Chilies to Chocolate*, pp. 105–8.
12. Coe and Coe, *True History*, pp. 48–49. Also see David Stuart, "The Rio Azul Cacao Pot: Epigraphic Observations on the Function of a Maya Ceramic Vessel," *Antiquity* 62 (1988): 153–157.
13. Which we assume were all *criollo*.
14. Coe and Coe, *True History*, p. 51.
15. *Ibid.*, p. 87.
16. *Ibid.*, p. 12, quoting Gage.
17. *Ibid.*, pp. 11–12, quoting Gage.

CHAPTER 4 *monks and men-at-arms*

1. Coe and Coe, *True History*, p. 107. The Coes point out that the money reference was an interpolation found in the Italian edition but not in the lost original. The Coes' quotation is adapted from Samuel Morison, *Journals and Other Documents on the Life and Voyages of Christopher Columbus*, New York: Heritage Press, 1963, p. 327.
2. Barbara Grunes and Phyllis Magida, *Chocolate Classics*, p. 3.
3. Benjamin Moseley, *A Treatise Concerning the Properties and Effect of Coffee*, p. 40. We note that a different answer to a similar question about coffee's permissibility during a time of fasting was reached in Turkey. According to Moseley, "The Turks who frequently subsist a considerable time upon Coffee only, look on it as an aliment that affords great nourishment to the body:—for which reason, during the rigid fast of the *Ramadam*, or Turkish Lent, it is not only forbid, but any person is deemed to have violated the injunctions of his Prophet, that has had even the smell of Coffee."
4. Grunes and Magida, *Chocolate Classics*, p. 3.
5. Morton and Morton, *Chocolate*, p. 15.
6. Coe and Coe, *True History*, p. 156.
7. Henry Phillips, *The Companion for the Orchard*, p. 67.
8. *OED*, "cacao," quoting Blundevil, *Exerc. V. Ed.* 7, p. 568.
9. Jill Norman, *Coffee*, pp. 10–11.
10. Quoted in Ukers, *All about Coffee*, p. 53.
11. Wolfgang Schivelbusch, *Tastes of Paradise*, p. 92.
12. Norman, *Coffee*, pp. 11–12.
13. *Ibid.*, p. 14.

CHAPTER 5 *the caffeine trade supplants the spice trade*

1. Quoted in Ukers, *All about Tea*, vol. I, p. 24. This account is found in Samuel Purchas, *Purchas His Pilgrimes*, London, 1625.
2. Quoted in Ukers, *All about Coffee*, p. 31. Linschoten's book may have been the source for a common European belief that tea tenderizes meat, which became prevalent over a century later.
3. Nicol, *A Treatise on Coffee*, p. 121. Also see Jacob, *Epic of a Commodity*, p. 43
4. Denys Forrest, *Tea for the British*, pp. 19–21.
5. Vieussens, the first physician to perform chemical examination of the blood, the only Parisian follower of Sylvius, the great Dutch champion of Harvey and caffeine, also suffered condemnation by the Paris Faculty.

6. Ukers, *All about Tea*, vol. I, p. 33.
7. *Ibid.*, vol. II, p. 487.
8. *Ibid.*, vol. I, p. 72.
9. Jacob, *Epic of a Commodity*, p. 43.
10. Jardin Édelestan, *Le Caféier et le Café*, p. 16.
11. Ukers, *All about Coffee*, p. 87, who also mentions an admittedly unconfirmed account that, under the reign of Louis XIII, coffee was sold by a Levantine in the Petit Chatelet, as *cohove* or *cahoue*.
12. Disraeli explains, "It appears . . . that Thévenot, in 1658, gave coffee after dinner; but it was considered as the whim of a traveller; neither the thing itself, nor its appearance, was inviting: It was probably attributed by the gay to the humour of a vain, philosophical traveller. But ten years afterwards, a Turkish ambassador at Paris made the beverage highly fashionable. The elegance of the equipage recommended to the eye, and charmed the women: the brilliant porcelain cups in which it was poured; the napkins fringed with gold, and the Turkish slaves on their knees presenting it to the ladies, seated on the ground on cushions, turned the heads of the Parisian dames" (Isaac Disraeli, *Curiosities of Literature*, vol. II, p. 321).
13. In 1692, Damame Francois, a Parisian merchant, became the man to see about caffeine after receiving a royal patent to sell coffee and tea in France, which was to be exclusive throughout the nation for ten years.
14. He continues, "Members of good society in Paris did not then visit houses of public entertainment." Jacobs, *Epic of a Commodity*, p. 83.
15. Quoted in Ukers, *All about Coffee*, p. 95.
16. Quoted in Jacobs, *Epic of a Commodity*, p. 136.
17. Alfred Franklin, "Le café, le thé, et le chocolat," in *Arts et métiers de Parisiens du XII au XVIII siecle*, Paris, 1893.
18. In 1664, because of the astonishing arrival of four thousand French troops, when Louis XIV had sent in support of his fellow Christians despite his treaty with Mohammed IV, the Turks withdrew from Vienna's walls. Although the Turks had suffered defeat in battle, the terms of their retreat, according to which they assumed control of Hungary, were extremely favorable. What Suleiman Aga learned in Paris served to deter any further reliance on the Sun King. In 1683, the Turkish Janissaries were joined at the walls of Vienna by no French troops, whose arrival, had it suited Louis's whim to have sent them, would most certainly have reversed the defeat generally acknowledged to have marked the beginning of the decline of the Ottoman Empire. Louis XIV continued his remarkable flip-flopping, in 1684 signing a treaty with Leopold I of Austria and in 1688 sending troops against him just as he had done against the Turks.
19. Heise, *Coffee and Coffee-Houses*, p. 16.
20. Harold B. Segel, *The Vienna Coffeehouse Wits: 1890–1938*, pp. 8–9, citing Karl Teply, *Die Einfuhrung des Kaffees in Wien: Georg Franz Kolschitzky, Johannes Diodato, Isaak de Luca* (Vienna, Kommissionsverlag Jugend und Volk Wien-Munchen, 1980).
21. Heise, *Coffee and Coffee-Houses*, pp. 103–5
22. Manfred Hamm, *Coffee Houses of Europe*, p. 9.
23. Harry Rolnick, *The Complete Book of Coffee*, p. 142.
24. Quoted in Ukers, *All about Tea*, vol. I, pp. 31–32.
25. Casper David Friedrich, *Briefen und Bekenntnissen*, ed. Sigrid Hinz, Berlin, 1974, p. 35.

CHAPTER 6 *the late adopters*

1. Heise, *Coffee and Coffee-Houses*, p. 58, quoting Aton Schindler, *Biographic von Ludwig van Beethoven*, Leipzig, 1970, p. 436.
2. Germany has a well-deserved reputation for lagging behind in the European cultural, intellectual, artistic, and social movements that, eventually, are adopted by her as surely as they already have been by the rest of Europe, and she made no exception in her tardiness in taking up caffeine. Gilbert Highet in his brilliant tome *The Classical Tradition* (Oxford, 1949) theorized that the power of Luther's faith forestalled the development of reasoned natural-

istic inquiry in Germany. In consequence, Germany never experienced what in other European nations was called the Renaissance, or at least did not do so until long after the others, so that in that country the Renaissance overlapped the Romantic period. Goethe, for example, is only properly understood as both a Renaissance and a Romantic figure.

3. Jacob, *Epic of a Commodity*, p. 55.
4. *Ibid.*, p. 61.
5. *Ibid.*, p. 60.
6. Quoted in Ukers, *All about Coffee*, p. 41.
7. Heise, *Coffee and Coffee-Houses*, p. 9, quoting Adam Olearius, *Vermehrte newe Beschreibung der Muscowitisch und Persischen Reyse* (Schleswig, 1656).
8. *Ibid.*, p. 15.
9. *Ibid.*, p. 17, quoting *Journal*, number 25, 1686, Frankfurt.
10. Quoted in Ukers, *All about Coffee*, p. 42.
11. Quoted in Jacob, *Epic of a Commodity*, p. 151.
12. *Ibid.*, p. 150.
13. Schivelbusch, *Paradise*, p. 92.
14. Hamm, *Coffee Houses of Europe*, pp. 131–32.
15. Quoted in Morton, *Chocolate*, p. 67. The war against beer was still being waged. Goethe was a partisan of the temperance beverages. He wrote to Karl Ludwig von Knebel (1744–1844), a poet, translator, philologist, and tutor to the princes at the Weimar court, "If our people continue swilling beer and smoking as they now do for another three generations, woe to Germany! The effect will first become noticeable in the stupidity and poverty of our literature, at which our descendants will declare themselves greatly astonished!" (Adapted from quotation in Jacob, *Coffee: The Epic of a Commodity*, p. 59.)
16. Ukers, *All about Tea*, vol. I, p. 31.
17. *Ibid.*, p. 32.
18. Chow and Kramer, *All the Tea in China*, p. 16.
19. Ukers, *All about Tea*, vol. II, p. 96.

CHAPTER 7 *judgments of history*

1. Even chocolate was first offered for sale in North America by a Boston pharmacist in 1712, and its trade remained in the hands of apothecaries for many years. Norman, *Coffee*, p. 14.
2. In fact, inebriation is a function of blood-alcohol levels that can be reduced only by metabolization of alcohol by the liver. Drinking coffee cannot make you less drunk; it can only make you more wide awake, while you remain as drunk as before.
3. Norman, *Coffee*, p. 22.
4. *Ibid.*, p. 23.
5. Quoted in Schivelbusch, *Paradise*, p. 23.
6. *Ibid.*, p. 35.
7. Ukers, *All about Coffee*, p. 21, quoting *Reis' in die Morgenländer (Rauwolf's Travels in the Orient)*, published at Frankfort and Lauingen in 1582–83. Another translation of parts of the same passage reads:

> Among others there is an excellent drink which they greatly esteem. They call it "Chauve." It is almost as black as ink, and is a valuable remedy in disorders of the stomach. The custom is to drink it early in the morning, in public places, quite openly, out of earthenware or porcelain cups. They do not drink much at a time, and, having drunk, walk up and down for a little, before sitting down together in a circle. The beverage is made by adding to boiling water the fruit which they call "bunnu," which in size and color resembles laurel berries, the kernel being hidden away between two thin lobes of fruit. . . . The use of the drink is so general that there are many houses which make a practice of supplying it ready prepared; and also, in the bazaars, merchants who sell the fruit are plentiful. (Jacob, *Epic of a Commodity*, p. 42)

It is interesting that Rauwolf mentions both the Arabic word for the beverage as well as the Ethiopian name for the fruit, if we assume, with him, that *bunnu* is a variant of *bunc*.

8. Quoted in Ukers, *All about Coffee*, p. 8.
9. Simon Pauli, *Commentarius de Abusu Tabaci et Herbae Thee, etc.*, pp. 166–67.

10. *Ibid.*, pp. 112–13.
11. He asserts that betony "cures no les that forty-seven Disorders. . . . The *Asiatic Tea* is therefore far inferior to the *European Betony*." "He has as many virtues as betony" is still a common proverb in Spain. It was commonly supposed that, like the caffeinated beverages, betony could also induce intoxication, and, when dried and powdered as snuff, immoderate sneezing.

    Turner in his *British Physician* (1687) wrote of betony:

    > It would seem a miracle to tell what experience I had of it. This herb is hot and dry, almost to the second degree, a plant of Jupiter in Aries, and is appropriated to the head and eyes, for the infirmities whereof it is excellent, as also for the breast and lungs; being boiled in milk, and drunk, it takes away pains in the head and eyes. Some write it will cure those that are possessed with devils, or frantic, being stamped and applied to the forehead. (Quoted in Pamela Todd, *Forget-Me-Not*, p. 157.)

12. Quoted in Ukers, *All about Tea*, vol. I, p. 30, *Commentarius de Abusu Tabaci et Herbae Thee*, Rostock, Germany, 1635.
13. Pauli, *Commentarius*, pp. 169–70
14. Quoted in Ukers, *All about Tea*, vol. I, pp. 31–32. This physician is immortalized in Rembrandt's painting *Anatomy Lesson of Dr. Nicolaes Tulp*.
15. Garrison, *History of Medicine*, p. 262.
16. Ukers, *All about Tea*, vol. I, p. 32, citing Buntekuh, *Tractat van het Excellente Cruyt Thee*, The Hague, 1679.
17. Will and Ariel Durant, *The Age of Louis XIV*, p. 412.
18. Descartes' mechanistic model of the universe, one of the most celebrated ideas of the day, was, to its scientifically minded proponents, well exemplified on a small scale by Harvey's biometric demonstration of the circulation of the blood.
19. Ukers, *All about Coffee*, p. 28, quoting Jean La Roque, *Voyage de L'Arabie Heureuse*, Paris, 1716.
20. *Ibid.*, p. 28.
21. Quoted in Jacob, *Epic of a Commodity*, pp. 71–72.
22. The need for this book is demonstrated by another title that came out the same year in Lyon, *The Most Excellent Virtues of the Mulberry, Called Coffee*.
23. Nicol, *Treatise on Coffee*, pp. 21–22.
24. Octave Guelliot, *Treatise Du Caféisme Chronique*, p. 33.
25. Daniel Duncan, *Wholesome Advise against the Abuse of Hot Liquors*, p. 1.
26. *Ibid.*, p. 5.
27. *Ibid.*, pp. 11–12.
28. The truly revolutionary aspect of Harvey's discovery was not, however, the observation that the blood circulated. It was his demonstration of this fact by using quantitative or mathematical measures. Garrison, *History of Medicine*, p. 247.
29. Sherwin Nuland, *Doctors: The Biography of Medicine*, p. 126.
30. Heise, *Coffee and Coffee-Houses*, pp. 15–16.
31. Harvey apparently picked up one other cultural influence from his Islamic schoolmates. As Aubrey tells us: "He would say that we Europeans knew not how to order or governe our Woemen, and that the Turks were the only people used them wisely. I remember he kept a pretty young wench to wayte on him, which I guesse he made use of for warmeth-sake as King David did, and tooke care of here in his Will, as also of his man servant." Aubrey, *Brief Lives*, p. 131.
32. Quoted in John Ovington, *Essays upon the Nature and Qualities of Tea*, pp. 31–32.
33. *Ibid.*, pp. 20–22.
34. *Ibid.*, p. 31.
35. *Ibid.*, pp. 38–39. Frederick Slare (1647–1727), an English physician and chemist, was one of those rare unfortunates, like the twentieth-century researcher Hayreh, with whom coffee violently disagreed. Moseley asserts that Slare's problems with coffee were only the result of his excessive consumption, a point with which Slare might not have entirely disagreed:

    > Nor do I decry and condemn Coffee, though it proved very prejudicial to my own health, and brought paralytic affections upon me. I confess, in my younger days, I ignorantly used it in too great excess; as many daily do make use of this, and other

Indian drinks; though I have quite abandoned it for above thirty years, and soon recovered the good tone of my nerves, which continue steady to this day; yet I must own, Coffee to some people is of good use, when taken "in just proportion, &c." It is true that they (Indian drinks) do not agree with all constitutions, with some, only one of these entertaining liquids, as Green Tea; and with others, all of them disagree. (Quoted in Moseley, *Effects of Coffee*, footnote, pp. 59–60.)

36. Unfortunately coffeehouses themselves had become waiting and examination rooms for quack practitioners.

37. Pierre Pomet, Lemery, and Tournefort, *A Compleat History of DRUGGS*, pp. 87–89.

38. *Ibid.*, p. 130.

39. *Ibid.*, p. 131.

40. Walter Baker and Company, *Chocolate Plant*, p. 12, quoting Thomas Gage, *New Survey of the West Indies* (1648).

41. Anonymous, *Essay on the Nature, Use, and Abuse of Tea: In a letter to a lady: with an account of its mechanical operation*, pp. 14–15.

42. Phillips, *Orchard*, p. 68.

43. "The Spanish ladies make use of the oil drawn from the cacao-nut, as a good cosmetic to soften and smooth the skin, as it does not render it greasy or shiny, being a quicker drier and without smell" (*Ibid.*). Most people might assume that the cosmetic benefits of cacao oil, such as they might be, have nothing to do with caffeine, but certain recent studies suggest that caffeine may be effective as a topical treatment of atopic dermatitis, so perhaps the Spanish ladies knew something that it has taken medical science two hundred years to discover.

44. Quoted in Jacob, *Epic of a Commodity*, p. 73.

45. *Ibid.*, p. 74.

46. Quoted in Schivelbusch, *Paradise*, p. 48.

47. *Ibid.*, p. 48.

48. Moseley, *Effects of Coffee*, pp. 53–54.

49. *Ibid.*, pp. 27–29.

50. The most obvious beneficial effects of caffeine are clearly being designated, however unwittingly, in the following passage:

    Long watching and intense study are wonderfully supported by it, and without the ill consequences that succeed the suspension of rest and sleep, when the nervous influence has nothing to sustain it.
    We are told that travellers in Eastern Countries and Messengers who are sent with dispatches, perform their tedious journeys by the alternate effects of Opium and Coffee;—and that the dervies and religious zealots, in their abstemious devotions, support their vigils, through their nocturnal ceremonies, by this exhilarating liquor. (*Ibid.*)

51. *Ibid.*, pp. 41–47.

52. *Ibid.*, pp. 68–69.

53. Martin Gardener, *Fads and Fallacies in the Name of Science*, pp. 187–90.

54. Schivelbusch, *Paradise*, p. 43.

55. Samuel Hahnemann, *Der Kaffee in seinen Wirkungen*, Leipzig, 1803, quoted in Schivelbusch, *ibid*.

56. John Cole, Esq., "On the Deleterious Effects Produced by Drinking Tea and Coffee in Excessive Quantities," *Lancet* 2 (1833): 274–78.

57. *OED*, "Caffeine."

58. Cole, *Deleterious Effects*, p. 278. Notice the use of the diasthenic notion of disease and the mechanism by which caffeine produces illness in the organism. In 1905, Starling coined the term *hormone*, from the Greek "*hormon*," or "impelling," and originated the conception of hormones as chemical messengers, carried by the bloodstream to sites where they control bodily processes. In consequence of Starling's idea, dynamic metabolic theories progressively supplanted earlier diasthentic theories of pathology, which had referred illness to permanent structural or constitutional predispositions or tendencies of the body, either hereditary or acquired, that rendered it liable to certain special diseases.

59. Honoré de Balzac, *Traité des Excitants Modernes*, unpublished translation by Robert Onopa.

60. Arnaud Baschet, *Honore de Balzac: Essai sur l'Homme et sur l'Oeuvre*, Paris: Giraud et Dagneau, 1852; Geneva: Slatkin, 1973. Quoted in Graham Robb, *Balzac: A Biography*, p. 401.

CHAPTER 8 *postscript*

1. We know that, in the context of religious devotions, the Buddhists of China and the Sufis of Arabia had each relied on their own caffeinated beverage to help them conform to the discipline of prayer and meditation. Perhaps Europe encountered the need for a corresponding discipline in a civil context, with the advent of machines and the industrial age.

   In the fifteenth century people still usually judged the time by the height of the sun or the positions of the stars. But as the seventeenth century wore on, the entire continent ran increasingly by the clock, and caffeine is the indispensable analeptic that allowed men to live by the clock, to knit their working lives together and engage each other as cogs engage in a machine.

2. The Egyptians used sundials and clepsydrae, or water clocks, from about 1500 B.C., and the same rude instruments, or refinements of them, were relied on by every subsequent civilization until the invention of the accurate mechanical clock. This invention occurred in the eighth century in China and in a different form and not until the sixteenth century in Europe.

   The hours themselves varied in length by design in the ancient world. Their hour was not $1/24$ of the astronomical day, as it is for us, but $1/12$ of the actual time from sundown to sunrise. The length of the ancient hour changed with the season, equally between $3/4$ and $5/4$ of a modern hour. Among the Greeks, the sun during the day and the stars during the night were used to estimate these hours. Thus time, in the millennia before the invention of accurate mechanical clocks, was reckoned by rough estimates, so that "The length of a man's shadow indicated the progress of the day."

3. Hugh Tait, *Clocks and Watches*, p. 18.

4. Perhaps a coincidence? Consider that, as noted above, the sophisticated mechanical clock was first invented and used in China in the Han dynasty in the eighth century, exactly the time at which Lu Yü wrote *The Classic of Tea* and tea became a dominant force in Chinese culture. And, although not even the practical wheel, much less the mechanical clock, were known to the Maya in pre-Columbian days, these American methylxanthine pioneers are famous for their complex calendric calculations and have been often and justly called the people "obsessed with time."

5. In 1657, Saloman Coster, a clockmaker in the employ of Christian Huygens (1629–95), the Dutch polymath and celebrated rival of Newton, was the first to use the revolutionary pendulum mechanism to regulate a clock. The next year Huygens, whose attainments encompassed music, mechanics, astronomy, mathematics, and physics, published the first rigorous treatment of the pendulum mechanism and included detailed plans for constructing the pendulum clock. The reason the advent of this mechanism constituted such a critical advance is well explained in Tait's meticulously researched and abundantly illustrated *Clocks and Watches:*

   > The pendulum has inherent timekeeping properties because it is restored by gravity. Whereas the foliot and balance will remain in whatever position they may be in when they come to rest, the pendulum will always come to rest in the one position, the point in the arc where the pendulum bob is at its lowest, because of the force of gravity. By successfully applying a clock mechanism to keep the pendulum swinging, to count its swings, and translate them into hours and minutes on the dial, Christian Huygens made possible the production of clocks that were far more consistent timekeepers. Because the pendulum is subject to the physical law of gravity, it, unlike the foliot and balance, is less dependent on variations of force within the clockwork. (p. 51)

6. Caffeine and the Machine

   > I sing the body electric. . .
   > Walt Whitman

   Perhaps the profile of caffeine's cognitive effects is one reason that its use has expanded so dramatically since the advent of the scientific and industrial age. Caffeine seems to help biological systems, like people, to functionally conform with mechanical or electronic systems, such as industrial machines or computers. Some have a dour view of the resulting congruity. A more balanced view might encompass not only the indignities and inconveniences of finely regulated and cooperative economic lives, but also recognize the tremendous wealth, an abundance unimaginable in preindustrial, preurban centuries, that has been made possible only by a general ability of people to, in certain limited ways, function together like parts of a great machine. Without caffeine, many of the complex and far-reaching achievements of modern civilization could not have been realized. To those who malign the rigors and exigencies of contemporary work life, we commend this comment by Freud: "I find it a constant surprise, that, little as people are capable of existing in isolation, they nonetheless resent and feel as a heavy burden the cooperation and compromises that civilization demands of them."

7. Brian Harrison, *Drink and the Victorians*, p. 40.

8. Phillips, *Orchard*, p. 67, writes that chocolate "is esteemed the most restorative of all aliments, insomuch that one ounce of it is said to nourish as much as a pound of beef," and tells of a friend who, "during the retreat of Napoleon's army from the North, he fortunately had a small quantity of little chocolate cakes in his pockets, which preserved the life of himself and a friend for several days, when they could procure no other food whatever, and many of their brother officers perished for want."

9. Philip Morrison, review of *The Little Ice Age*, by Jean M. Grove, Methuen & Co. Ltd., *Scientific American*, May 1989, p. 142.

10. *Ibid*. Records demonstrate that, on either side of the North Atlantic, there was no climatic summer in 1816, resulting in the general destruction of corn and low yields of other crops, and subjecting the populations of Europe to what has been termed "the last great subsistence crisis in the Western world."

PART III *introduction*

1. Although informality and strenuous work are generally associated with coffee, just as ceremony and leisure are generally associated with tea, the Arabs of Cairo, at least, have reversed this pattern. In that city, much after the fashion of the Bedouins, coffee drinking is a complicated social affair, its forms reflecting the status of the host, his guests, political affiliations, offering a formal setting for exchanging information, telling stories, and resolving arguments. However, tea drinking is a much more casual undertaking and, in addition, tea, not coffee, is the stimulant preferred by laborers. As Louis Vaczek and Gail Buckland tell us, speaking of nineteenth-century practices in their book *Travellers in Ancient Lands*: "This beverage too was brewed so strong that the caffeine and tannin in a thimble-sized glass were enough to jolt one's system heartily. Boiled black tea, in fact, became the standard drug for heavy laborers, who stopped regularly to ease their exhaustion and hunger with gulps of syrupy, revitalizing black tea" (p. 162).

CHAPTER 9 *islands of coffee (1)*

1. Ukers, *All about Tea*, vol. I, p. 8.

2. *Ibid.*, p. 9.

3. Daisetz T. Suzuki, *Zen and Japanese Culture*, p. 293.

4. The tea ceremony itself can be illuminated for Western readers by comparing it with the dialectical method of Socrates. In the dialectic of Socrates, the goal was similar: to treat of the ordinary aspects of life with the hope of achieving an understanding beyond imagination (*eikasia*), sense perception (*pistis*), and even reason (*dianoia*), to reach an intuitive understanding of the Forms, the illumination of the soul that Plato called *noesis*. Like the Bodhisattva of Buddhist tradition, who after his enlightenment returns from the Void to lead his fellow creatures on the Path away from suffering, the philosopher of Plato's Allegory of the Cave, after escaping to see the world illuminated by the light of the Good, returns to teach the way of liberation to his still ignorant compatriots. (Plato does not use these four words for the degrees of knowing consistently throughout the *Republic*. However, this is the scheme he sets up to accompany the Allegory of the Cave.)

5. Suzuki, *Zen and Japanese Culture*, pp. 272–73.

6. *Ibid.*, p. 302.

7. Adapted from translation quoted in Okakura, *The Book of Tea*, p. 65. Rikyu's valediction was actually two poems, one Japanese and one Chinese, which Okakura has blended together.
8. Horst Hammitzsch, *Zen in the Art of the Tea Ceremony*, p. 31.
9. *Ibid.*, p. 31
10. Alan Watts, *The Way of Zen*, p. 190.
11. *Ibid.*, p. 194.
12. Okakura, *Book of Tea*, p. xi.
13. *Ibid.*, p. 2.
14. *Ibid.*, p. 7.
15. *Ibid.*, p. 5.
16. *Ibid.*, p. 7.
17. *Ibid.*
18. A. Watts, *Way of Zen*, p. 190.
19. Although several Europeans have prior claims, around 1900 Dr. Sartori Kato, a Japanese-American dentist, is credited with developing an early form of soluble, or instant, coffee.
20. Boye De Mente, *The Whole Japan Book*, p. 300.
21. Harry Rolnick, *The Complete Book of Coffee*, p. 37.
22. David Landau, "Specialty Coffee and Japan," *Coffee Talk Magazine*, September 1995.

CHAPTER 10 *islands of coffee (2)*

1. Quoted in Ukers, *All about Coffee*, p. 31.
2. *Ibid.*, p. 33.
3. *Ibid.*, p. 35, quoting Francis Bacon, *Sylva Sylvarum*, vol. 5, p. 26, London, 1627.
4. Quoted in Jacob, *Epic of a Commodity*, p. 44.
5. An example of this judgment is found in Bacon's *Advancement of Learning*, in which the author describes doctors as men who, frustrated by their incapacity to succeed in any other field of study, took up medicine as a last resort.
6. Ukers, *All about Coffee*, p. 53.
7. John Evelyn, *Works*, note, p. 11. More frequently quoted are Evelyn's words from an earlier edition: "He was the first I ever saw drink Coffe, which custome came not into England til 30 years after." Most commentators, following Ukers, explain that Evelyn must have meant "thirteen years" and not "thirty," because the first coffeehouse in England opened in 1650. However, it is more plausible that Evelyn was referring not to the opening of a single coffeehouse when he speaks of the "custom" of drinking coffee, but instead the time when coffee drinking became a common enjoyment throughout the country.
8. Ukers, *All about Coffee*, p. 36, quoting Anthony Wood, *Athenae Oxiensus*, vol. 2, col. 658, London, 1692.
9. Oliver Lawson Dick, *Aubrey's Brief Lives*, p. l, note viii.
10. Aytoun Ellis, *The Penny Universities: A History of the Coffee-Houses*, p. 18.
11. *Ibid.*, p. 24.
12. "The Trade of News also was scarce set up; for they had only the publick Gazette, till Kirk got a written news letter circulated by one Muddiman. But now the case is much altered; for it is become a custom, after Chapel, to repair to one or other of the Coffee Houses (for there are diverse) where Hours are spent in talking, and less profitable reading of News Papers, of which swarms are continually supplied from London. And the Scholars are so Greedy after News (which is none of their business) that they neglect all for it . . . a vast loss of Time grown out of a pure Novelty; for who can apply close to a subject with his Head full of the Din of a Coffee House?" (*Ibid.*, p. 27).
    Muddiman was an ex-schoolmaster turned journalist, a man with an unsavory reputation. In Cambridge, in 1659, he started *Newsbook*, a sixteen-page newspaper that was distributed at Kirk's coffeehouse, and he was also employed by the Commonwealth to help regulate the coffeehouse keepers, for whom the Puritans had little affection. In fact, Cromwell had overcome his scruples against the intoxicating power of caffeine and the unwholesome dens of the coffeehouses and refrained from banning coffee only on account of its medicinal value.

13. *Ibid.*, p. 28.
14. Aubrey gives a slightly different account of the origins of the Royal Society, which, however, comes to the same ending. In his biography of John Wilkins (1614–72), private chaplain to Charles I's nephew, and first secretary of the officially constituted Royal Society, he says,

> He was the principall Reviver of Experimentall Philosphy at Oxford, where he had weekely an experimentall philosophicall Clubbe, which began 1649, and was the *Incunabula* of the Royall Society. When he came to London, they mett at Bullhead taverne in Cheapside (e.g. 1658, 1659, and after) till it grew to big for a Clubb. The first beginning of the Royal Society (where they putt discourse in paper and brought it to use) was in the Chamber of William Ball, Esqr., eldest son of Sir Peter Ball of Deven, in the Middle Temple. They had meetings at Taverns before, but 'twas here where it formally and in good earnest sett up: and so they came to Gresham Colledge parlour.

15. John Timbs, *Clubs and Club Life in London*, pp. 269–70.
16. Bryant Lillywhite, *London Coffee Houses*, p. 467.
17. Aubrey, *Brief Lives*, p. 26.
18. Lillywhite, *London Coffee Houses*, p. 467.
19. The list was published by Thomas Dangerfield (1650–85), himself a perjurer and conspirator.
20. Bramah, *Tea & Coffee*, p. 107
21. Ellis, *Penny Universities*, p. 38.
22. Ukers, *All about Coffee*, p. 55.
23. Jacob, *Epic of a Commodity*, p. 95
24. *Ibid.*
25. Colin McEvedy and Richard Jones, *Atlas of World Population History*, p. 44.
26. The population had expanded rapidly in the thirteenth century, until it reached about five million and roughly stabilized. Great landlords prospered, but the median size of peasant farms fell, with no compensating productivity increase.
27. Nicol, *Treatise on Coffee*, p. 15.
28. Moseley, *Effects of Coffee*, p.20.
29. This year also marks the first mention of coffee in the statute books of England, for in 1660 a duty of fourpence a gallon was imposed on the prepared drink.
30. Disraeli, *Curiosities of Literature*, pp. 379–80.
31. In the introduction to his edition of *Curiosities of Literature*, Benjamin Disraeli, Isaac's famous son, relates how his father liked come to town to "read the newspapers at the St. James' Coffee-house," finding their "columns filled with extracts from the fortunate effusion of the hour," and that it was in this place that he first heard his own fame as a writer manifested in animated conversations. *Ibid.*, pp. xvi–xvii.
32. Evelyn, *Works*, note, p. 11.
33. Forrest, *Tea for the British*, p. 25.
34. Agnes Strickland, *Lives of the Queens of England*, vol. 5, p. 521.
35. Waller's poetic celebration of taking tea continued through the eighteenth century, for example, in the works of John Cooper (1723–69), called "the Laureate of the tea-table." Quoted in Walsh, *Tea*, p. 234.
36. Forrest, *Tea for the British*, p. 28.
37. Thomas Brown, *The Works of Thomas Brown*, vol. 3, p. 86.
38. *Tatler*, no. 148, Tuesday, March 21, 1710.
39. Certainly the dialogue was nothing new in the history of prose, for it had been a vital literary form from Plato's *Symposium* (fourth century B.C.) to Galileo's vernacular *Dialogue of Two World Systems* (1632), which, even though the scientist had obtained permission to write it, incurred his condemnation by the Inquisition.
40. Of course not everyone welcomed the new style. John, Baron Hervey of Ickworth (1696–1743), in his masterpiece, *Memoirs of the Reign of King George II*, depicts the life at court from George II's accession in 1727 to Queen Caroline's death in 1827. Written in a largely discursive and occasionally epigrammatical style, his prose conveys vivid, intimate images of royal lives. Speaking of himself in the third person, he writes that, as he entered the queen's bedroom at breakfast, "Lord Hervey found her [the ailing queen] and Princess Caroline together, drinking chocolate, drowned in tears."

Hervey's style is brilliantly realistic, and its sustained reportorial restraint is moving in the manner of Stendhal, but as third-person narrative it is at the antipode from dialogue. Neither did Hervey find any use for dialogue in polemics, complaining that an argument posed in dialogue was "stiff, forced, and unfair." Bonamy Dobrée, *English Literature in the Early Eighteenth Century*, p. 352.

41. As Socrates had said that the dialectic was an image of the activity of philosophy.
42. Quoted in Jacob, *Epic of a Commodity*, p. 97.
43. Dobrée in his outstanding *English Literature in the Early Eighteenth Century* (1959), while acknowledging the social impact of the coffeehouse, asserts that, as literary forums, they hosted insular cliques that could have had little influence on the development of ideas or letters. Dobrée cites Swift's quip, spoken of the clergy but which could have been applied with equal justice to other groups of coffeehouse attendees of the day, "They have their particular Clubs, and particular Coffee-Houses, where they generally appear in Clusters." We reply that, even if only in regard of their having been the places where the first newspapers were written and published, it is difficult to entertain an image of coffeehouse insularity. Further, London was small, and the critical influence of the judgments rendered in coffeehouses, from the redoubtable Rota to the Literary Club a century later, were enough to make or break a new book throughout the city. And, after all, many of the literary stars of the coffeehouses took their place alternately in one coffeehouse constellation or another, as their fancies of an evening inclined them in their courses.
44. *Ibid.*, p. 566.
45. Drabble, *The Oxford Companion to English Literature*, p. 227.
46. Quoted in Stella Margetson, *Leisure and Pleasure in the Eighteenth Century*, p. 39.
47. Although most of what we know of this illustrious society appears in Boswell's work, Macaulay tells us that the maligned follower of Johnson "was regarded with little respect by his brethren, and had not without difficulty obtained a seat among them." Thomas Macaulay, *Life of Johnson*, pp. 43–44.
48. *Ibid.*, p. 45.
49. *Ibid.*, pp. 44–45.
50. For example, *Great Britain's Postmaster*, a political and commercial publication, devoted an entire issue in 1707 to a dreadful poem called "The British Court," about the sublimities of the entourage of Queen Ann. As Dobrée, who describes Addison as "the first Victorian," explains in *English Literature in the Eighteenth Century*: "It was possibly in this way that a mass of new readers, intent in the first instance upon the actual, practical, the useful, came to regard verse as natural medium, would read at first, perhaps, Defoe's 'True Born Englishman,' . . . and finally [progress] to better things . . . even Pope's 'Windsor Forest.' (Dobrée, p. 8)
51. Dobrée, *English Literature*, p. 8.
52. Timbs, *Clubs and Club Life in London*, p. 323.
53. Macaulay, *Life of Johnson*, p. 51.
54. Kathleen Coburn, ed., *The Notebooks of Samuel Taylor Coleridge*, 1300, 8.49.
55. Tea also figured into the lives of the Romantic poets, as this snippet from 1802, written after a cross-country walk of many miles during the years Coleridge and Wordsworth were still collaborating on the *Lyrical Ballad*s, demonstrates:

> The Rocks, by which we passed, under the brow of one of which I sate, beside an old blasted Tree, seemed the very link by which Nature connected Wood & Stone. . .
> Here too I heard with a deep feeling the swelling unequal noise of mountain Water from the streams in the Ravines
> We now found that our Expedition to the Trossacks was rashly undertaken
> we were at least 9 miles from the Trossacks, no Public House there or here
> it was almost too late to return, and if we did, the Loch Lomond Ferry Boat uncertain. We proceeded to the first House in the first Reach, & threw ourselves upon the Hospitality of the Gentleman, who after some Demur with Wordsworth did offer us a Bed
> & his Wife, a sweet and matronly Woman, made Tea for us most hospitably. Best possible Butter, white Cheese, Tea, & Barley Bannocks.

56. Walsh, *Tea*, p. 234.
57. Coburn, *Coleridge*, 1490, 7.40.
58. The gentrification of the once socially catholic coffeehouse is evident in an account by an

Italian traveler, written in the same year (1724), of the pastimes available to the café society. *Ibid.*, p. 74.

59. Derek Jarrett, *England in the Age of Hogarth*, p. 202.
60. Quoted in Ukers, *All about Coffee*, p. 74.
61. Quoted in Okakura, *The Book of Tea*, p. 7.
62. Ukers, *All About Tea*, vol. II, p. 494.
63. *Ibid.*, vol. I, p. 48, quoting Sir John Hawkins, *The Life of Samuel Johnson, LL.D.*, London, 1787.
64. *The Literary Magazine*, no. 7, October 15–November 15, 1756; and no. 13, April 15–May 15, 1757.
65. R. O. Mennell, *Tea: An Historical Sketch*, p. 29.
66. *Ibid.*
67. *Ibid.* Even worse than the practices noticed in the statute, tea traders blended tea with ash leaves boiled in iron sulphate and sheep dung. See Helen Simpson, *The London Ritz Book of Afternoon Tea*, p. 13.
68. Simpson, *London Ritz*, p. 15.
69. The author is anonymous.
70. A contemporary doctor who was known for investigating adulterations.
71. Pepper dust.
72. *Oxford Book of English Traditional Verse*, no. 288, "London Adulterations," p. 335.
73. Daniel Pool, *What Jane Austen Ate, What Charles Dickens Knew*, p. 209.
74. *Oxford Book of English Traditional Verse*, no. 289, "How Five and Twenty Shillings Were Expended in a Week," p. 337.
75. Adapted from M. A. Spiller, *The Methylxanthine Beverages and Foods*, p. 204.

CHAPTER 11 *the endless simmer*

1. Quoted in Ukers, *All about Coffee*, p. 122.
2. *Ibid.*, p. 106.
3. Mark Twain, *Autobiography*, 1924, reprinted in Helen Morrison, *The Golden Age of Travel*.
4. Timbs, *Club Life in London*, p. 286.
5. Wiley's story is told in elaborate detail in Mark Pendergrast's book *For God, Country, and Coca-Cola* (1993).
6. Quoted in Pendergrast, *ibid.*, p. 112.
7. *Ibid.*, pp. 119–20.
8. Harry Hollingworth and L. Hollingworth, "The Influence of Caffeine on Mental and Motor Efficiency," *Archives of Psychology* 20 (1912): 1–166.
9. Pendergrast, *For God*, p. 121.
10. "Beverage Marketing," *Dow Jones News*, February 6, 1996.
11. Another high-caffeine soft drink advertisment, which was withdrawn from at least one Akron suburb in response to public displeasure, read, "Gotta problem with the taste of Kick soda? Call 1-800-BITE-ME." Billboards with that piquant message on behalf of Kick were posted in three Ohio communities. A spokesman for the company explained that its intent had been to be tasteless and tacky to attract the soda's targets market of high school and college men. The telephone number, by the way, isn't real: It lacks the requisite eleventh digit.
12. David Ramsey, "Caffeine Can Be Your Friend," *MacWEEK*, 7.16 (April 19): 62.

CHAPTER 12 *caffeine culture and le fin de millénaire*

1. Laboratory studies to date, in which subjects are challenged with larger single doses, shed little light on the ways in which most people actually use caffeine, that is, ingesting it in small amounts throughout the day and taking relatively little after dinner.
2. M. J. Shirlow, "Patterns of Caffeine Consumption," *Human Nutrition: Applied Nutrition* 37a (1983): 307–13.

3. David Musto, "Alcohol in American History," *Scientific American*, April 1996, p. 78.
4. In terms of dollars, coffee, cacao, and tea are each important agricultural products. In terms of dollar value, coffee is the largest agricultural commodity in the world, and it is second only to oil among all commodities. In 1985 the world value of trade in coffee every year was more than $15 trillion, that of cacao exceeded $7 trillion, and that of tea topped $2.5 trillion, with a total world value of these three caffeine crops of near $25 trillion annually.
5. Mark Schogol, "Personal Briefing," *Philadelphia Inquirer*, January 10, 1996.
6. Krapf, *Travels, Researches*, p. 47. Krapf, who wrote in the middle of the nineteenth century, reports that already by his time, African coffee from the Kaffa region was being exported to Arabia and sold as genuine Mocha. This practice persists today.
7. Heise, *Coffee and Coffee-Houses*, pp. 20–21.
8. Ukers, *All about Coffee*, p. 275.
9. Frederick L. Wellman, *Coffee Botany, Cultivation, and Utilization*.
10. More information about these studies of drinking water is available from Ed Swibas, USGS Colorado District, Box 25046, MS 415, Denver, CO 80225.
11. His poem "The Caffeine" is widely posted in newsgroups and found in several web pages.
12. *Working Woman*, November 1995, p. 100.
13. International trade in caffeine has become a contentious issue at least in India, where in 1995 the Chemicals and Fertilizers Ministry officials in New Delhi, responding to petitions from Indian pharmaceutical firms, announced duties on imports of both caffeine and theophylline.
14. The Cathead homepage is http://www.efn.org/~garl_p_s/Cathead/CatheadPage.html.

CHAPTER 13 caffeine in the laboratory

1. Johannes Fabricius, *Alchemy*, p. 11.
2. Before Boyle, the Greek philosopher Empedocles had taught that four underived and indestructible substances, fire, water, earth, and air, were the constituents from which all other things are compounded, and this theory had reigned unchallenged since ancient times.
3. Manufacturer's Standard Data Sheet (excerpt):

   MSDS FOR CAFFEINE
   1—PRODUCT IDENTIFICATION
   PRODUCT NAME: CAFFEINE
   FORMULA: $C_8H_{10}N_4O_2$
   FORMULA WT: 194.19
   CAS NO.:   00058–08–2
   NIOSH/RTECS NO.:   EV6475000
   COMMON SYNONYMS: 1,3,7-TRIMETHYLXANTHINE
   PRODUCT CODES: E268
   EFFECTIVE: 10/25/85

4. Silvio Garattini, *Caffeine, Coffee, and Health*, p. 400.
5. Jack E. James, *Caffeine and Health*, p. 81. On caffeine's slowing of the metabolization of alcohol, James cites J. George et al., "Influence of Alcohol on Caffeine Consumption and Caffeine Elimination," *Clinical and Experimental Pharmacology and Physiology* 13 (1986): 731–36; M. C. Mitchell et al., "Inhibition of Caffeine Elimination by Short Term Ethanol Administration," *Journal of Laboratory and Clinical Medicine* 101 (1983): 826–34. James also notes that Nash's speculative antagonistic effect between caffeine and alcohol may occur, but if it does, is probably clinically insignificant, citing R. Fudin and R. Nicastro, "Can Caffeine Antagonize Alcohol-Induced Performance Decrements in Humans?" *Perceptual and Motor Skills* 67 (1988): 375–91.
6. Richard Gilbert, *Caffeine: The Most Popular Stimulant*, p. 62. Gilbert states, "Some of the variability in the rates of caffeine metabolism is inherited. Asians, for example, appear to metabolism caffeine differently and more slowly than Caucasians. Some of the variability, however, may be the result of experience with caffeine. Regular caffeine users may metabolize caffeine more quickly, though this has not yet been proven."
7. Jack James, *Caffeine and Health*, p. 81. Caffeine's ability to antagonize alcohol-induced drowsiness is the one antagonism which he finds the most credible.

8. Jacob, *Epic of a Commodity*, p. 22.
9. Another related theory, of questionable probative value, is that caffeine achieves its effects by benzodiazepine receptors that regulate the activity of GABA (gamma-amino butyric acid), an amino acid highly concentrated in the central nervous system that has a very powerful depressant effect on neuronal discharge. An antagonistic effect on these receptors, by inhibiting the action of GABA, could account for caffeine's stimulant effect. However, although the antagonism between caffeine and benzodiazepines in vitro and in vivo is clearly established, the concentrations of caffeine reached after coffee consumption leave doubts about the significance of this effect in dietary doses of caffeine. (Garattini, *Caffeine, Coffee, and Health*, p. 401)
10. Garattini, *Caffeine, Coffee, and Health*, p. 97.
11. Bridgette E. Garrett and Roland R. Griffiths, "The Role of Dopamine in the Behavioral Effects of Caffeine in Animals and Humans," unpublished monograph, July 30, 1996.
12. Bozidar Stavric et al., *Food and Chemical Toxicology*, Canada's Health Protection Branch, March 1988, as reported in article by Boyce Rensberger, *Washington Post*, April 25, 1996.
13. For the median values for tea prepared from tea bags of black tea, averages among all brands, see the 1979 study by Bunker and McWilliams, published in the *Journal of the American Dietetic Association*. The same study found that the amount of caffeine in tea increases with brewing time and that the finer the particles of tea leaves, the more caffeine is extracted into the cup. The mean caffeine contents for all brews of regular black bag tea per cup were 28 mg for one-minute brews, 44 mg for three-minute brews, and 47 mg for five-minute brews. Black tea contained more caffeine than green teas.
14. The Republic of Tea Home Page, "Caffeine and Tea: Five Considerations."
15. *Newsletter*, Mountain Bros. Coffee Co., San Francisco.
16. Shoku-hin 80 calorie seibun-hyo (*The Ingredient List of 80-Calorie Foods*, ed. Aya Kagawa and Jyoshi Eiyo Daigaku, Women's Nutrition College, 1980).
17. *Bowes and Church's Food Values of Portions Commonly Used*, by Anna De Planter Bowes. Philadelphia: Lippincott, 1989, pp. 261–62.
18. Spiller, *Methylxanthine Beverages*, p. 181.
19. Garattini, *Caffeine, Coffee, and Health*, p. 37.
20. Private correspondence from George Stiper, Ph.D.

CHAPTER 14 *caffeine and the plant kingdom*

1. Gilbert, *Most Popular Stimulant*, p. 27.
2. J. Nathanson, *Science*, October 5, 1984.
3. Warren E. Leary, "Caffeine in plants seen as insecticide," *Philadelphia Inquirer*, October 5, 1984.
4. NASA's Marshall Space Flight Center researchers reported varying results when they gave various mind-altering substances to household spiders, then observed their webs. The spiders exposed to marijuana did the best spinning. Dr. David Noever, head of the research team, stated that the worst web was spun by a spider dosed with caffeine. "Using Spider-Web Patterns to Determine Toxicity," *NASA Technical Briefs* MFS-28921, April 1995, study at Marshall Space Flight Center, Alabama, by David A. Noever et al.
5. *New Yorker*, June 5, 1995, p. 34.
6. Leary (see note 3).
7. *Année Littéraire*, Paris, 1774, vol. VI, p. 217.
8. *Ibid*. De Clieu's heroic husbandry has been glorified in prose and poetry by his admiring countrymen. Joseph Alphonse Esménard (1769–1811), a Creole poet of indifferent gifts who delighted in maritime themes, describes his devotion through the dreadful calm, writing that the officer, though parched by the broiling sun,

> Yet does not slake his own consuming thirst,
> But drop by drop revives the sapling first,
> His suffering eased by what his visions show,
> Who from this shoot sees great plantations grow.
> (Our translation)

9. Spiller, *Methylxanthine Beverages*, p. 77.
10. *Ibid.*
11. Timothy James Castle, *The Perfect Cup*, p. 10.
12. Ukers, *All about Coffee*, p. 284.
13. Joseph Walsh, *Tea: Its History and Mystery*, p. 49
14. Bayard Hora, ed., *Oxford Encyclopaedia of Trees of the World*, p. 210.
15. Ukers, *All about Coffee*, p. 8.
16. McCoy and Walker, *Coffee and Tea*, pp. 163–64.
17. Chow and Kramer, *All the Tea in China*, p. 92.
18. Lu Yü, *Classic of Tea*, pp. 39–40.
19. Chow and Kramer, *All the Tea in China*, p. 77.
20. *Ibid.*, p. 214. Perhaps there is something in the water that makes people in the tea trade wax emotional, producing their own versions of "Tea and Sympathy" when discoursing on this subject. For example, when boiling water is poured over the curling leaves in a pot, and they release their caffeine and tannin, this is luridly called the "agony of the leaves" by those in the tea business.
21. James Norwood Pratt, *Tea Lover's Treasury*, p. 212.
22. Toussaint-Samat, *History of Food*, p. 305.
23. Lu Yü, *Classic of Tea*, p. 21.
24. Pratt, *Tea Lover's Treasury*, p. 212.
25. Coe and Coe, *True History*, p. 18.
26. José Cuatrecasas, "Cacao and Its Allies: A Taxonomic Revision of the Genus Theobroma," *Contributions from the United States National Herbarium* 35, part 6. Washington, D.C., 1964.
27. Spiller, *Methylxanthine Beverages*, p. 152.
28. Robert Schery, *Plants for Man*, p.594.
29. Phillips reports an unusual use for the wood: "It is from the wood of this tree that our most esteemed German flutes have for some years past been made, as they are not so subject to swell by using as those made from Box-wood; which swelling often causes a variation of half a note, as after being played on for short time the tone become sharper. The cacao flutes have also an objectionable quality, *viz.*, as they are subject to crack by use, and will not stand the breath of different persons. A respectable professor of this instrument, among other instances, informed us of a gentleman who after having played on a cacao flute for seven years without accident, sold it to a friend, by whose breath alone three joints were split, in the course of a few months practice." (Phillips, *Orchard*, p. 71)
30. *Ibid.*, p. 152.
31. Foster and Cordell, *Chilies to Chocolate*, pp. 105–8.
32. Schery, *Plants for Man*, p. 316.
33. G. K. Mumford et al., "Discriminative Stimulus and Subjective Effects of Theobromine and Caffeine in Humans," *Psychopharmacology* 115 (1994): 1–8.
34. Spiller, *Methylxanthine Beverages*, p. 179.
35. J. Alfred Wanklyn, *Tea, Coffee, and Cocoa*, p. 58.
36. *Ibid.*
37. Joseph Walsh, *Tea: Its History and Mystery*, p. 46.
38. Maud Grieve, *A Modern Herbal*, p. 609.
39. Ukers, *All about Tea*, vol. I, p. 503.
40. *Encyclopædia Britannica*, "Angiosperms," vol. 13, p. 722 (1990).
41. *Encyclopædia Britannica*, "Kola nut," vol. 6, p. 937 (1990).
42. Louis Lewin, *Phantastica: A Classic Survey on the Use and Abuse of Mind-Altering Plants*, p. 224.
43. *Ibid.*, p. 223.
44. *Ibid.*, p. 226.
45. David Tait, "Konkomba Sorcery," appearing in John Middleton, ed., *Magic, Witchcraft, and Curing*, p. 157.
46. Grieve, *Modern Herbal*, p. 381.
47. According to one source, *guarana* means "to make war" in the indigenous tongue, so named because it was thought to confer strength and valor.
48. Joseph Walsh, *Tea: Its History and Mystery*, p. 47.

49. *Encyclopædia Britannica*, "Angiosperms," vol. 13, p. 753.
50. Schery, *Plants for Man*, p. 309.
51. Joseph Walsh, *Tea: Its History and Mystery*, p. 47.
52. Donna Abu-nasr, "Yemen's Costly Habit: Chewing Khat Leaves," *Philadelphia Inquirer*, March 26, 2000.
53. Schery, *Plants for Man*, p. 317.
54. *Encyclopaedia Britannica*, "Betel," vol. 2, p. 172 (1990).
55. John G. Kennedy, *The Flower of Paradise*, p. 239.
56. Marco Polo, *The Travels*, p. 186.
57. E. N. Anderson, *The Food of China*, p. 138.
58. *Encyclopaedia Britannica*, "Aphrodisiac," vol. 1, p. 480 (1990).

CHAPTER 15 *caffeine and the body*

1. Garattini, *Caffeine, Coffee, and Health*, p. 177.
2. *Ibid.*, p. 178
3. James, *Caffeine and Health*, p. 339.
4. D. Robertson et al., "The Health Consequences of Caffeine," *Annals of Internal Medicine* 98 (1983): 641–53.
5. J. Onrot et al., "Hemodynamic and Humoral Effects of Caffeine in Autonomic Failure, Therapeutic Implications for Post-Prandial Hypotension," *NEJM* 313 (1985): 549–54.
6. T. B. Graboys et al., "Coffee, Arrhythmias, and Common Sense," *NEJM* 308 (1983): 835–36.
7. Garattini, *Caffeine, Coffee, and Health*, p. 401.
8. Charles R. Schuster and Michael J. Kuhar, ed., *Handbook of Experimental Pharmacology*, Heidelberg, pp. 315–41.
9. S. S. Hayreh, letter to *Lancet* I (1973): 45.
10. James, *Caffeine and Health*, p. 293.
11. A. W. Caggiula et al. (for the MR FIT group), "Coffee Drinking, Coronary Heart Disease, and Total Mortality." Presented at Tenth World Congress of Cardiology, September 14–19, 1986, Washington, D.C.
12. D. E. Grobbee et al., "Coffee, Caffeine, and Cardiovascular Disease in Men," *NEJM* 323 (1990): 1026–32.
13. P. W. F. Wilson et al., "Is Coffee Consumption a Contributor to Cardiovascular Disease? Insights from the Framingham Study," *Archives of Internal Medicine* 149 (1989): 1169–72.
14. Siegfried Heydens et al., "Coffee Consumption and Mortality: Total Mortality, Stroke Mortality, and Coronary Heart Disease Mortality," *Archives of Internal Medicine* 138 (1978): 1472–75.
15. L. Wilhelmsen et al., "Coffee Consumption and Coronary Heart Disease in Middle Aged Swedish Men," *Acta Med Scand* 201 (1977): 547–52.
16. Garattini, *Caffeine, Coffee, and Health*, p. 174.
17. This effect was so pronounced that it was thought by the researchers to at least partially counterbalance the potentially dangerous cholesterol-raising effects that the study also correlated with drinking non-filtered coffee. Many other studies have confirmed these observations.
18. Garattini, *Caffeine, Coffee, and Health*, p. 161.
19. *Ibid.*, p. 163. Studies in the 1980s by David Robertson profiled the tolerance to caffeine's hemodynamic and neurohumoral (of or pertaining to a chemical transmitted by a neuron, such as acetylcholine, serotonin, dopomine, or epinephrine) effects among people with normal and high blood pressure. He concluded that, while his study confirmed the moderate pressor effect of caffeine, it "demonstrated rapid and essentially complete tolerance to the hemodynamic and neurohumoral effects over as short a period as three to four days."
20. Garattini, *Caffeine, Coffee, and Health*, p. 25.
21. *Ibid.*, p. 184.
22. *Ibid.*
23. In fact, an important study, conducted in the United States in 1990 and published in *The*

New England Journal of Medicine, found an increase in heart attacks correlated with the consumption of decaffeinated coffee, while observing no such effect for regular coffee. Some scientists explain this difference by adducing the possible role of caffeine in counteracting some of the harmful physiological effects of the coffee in which it is found.

24. Alfred Gilman, *Goodman and Gilman's The Pharmacological Basis of Therapeutics*, p. 618.

25. D. R. Lima, "Cigarettes and Caffeine," *Chest* 95 (1989): 255–56.

26. James, *Caffeine and Health*, p. 339.

27. *Ibid.*, p. 22.

28. Garattini, *Caffeine, Coffee, and Health*, p. 402.

29. *Ibid.*, p. 382.

30. Bonnie Edwards, *America's Favorite Drug*, p. 24.

31. Garattini, *Caffeine, Coffee, and Health*, p. 34.

32. *Ibid.*, p. 25.

33. A. D. McDonald et al., "Cigarette, alcohol, and coffee consumption and congenital defects," *American Journal of Public Health* 82 (1986): 91–93.

34. Marilyn Elias, "Low-Cost Help For Breast-Cyst Pain," *USA Today*, April 28, 1992, p. 1D, reporting on a paper presented by Dr. Bruce Drukker, Michigan State University Medical School, East Lansing, addressing the American College of Obstetricians and Gynecologists meeting in Las Vegas in April 1992.

35. Garattini, *Caffeine, Coffee, and Health*, p. 348.

36. J. L. Brazier and B. Salle, "Conversion of Theophylline to Caffeine by the Human Fetus," *Seminars in Perinatology* 5 (1981): 315–20.

37. H. Roberts, "Caffeine Consumption," paper presented at American Academy of Pediatrics Clinical Pharmacology Session, New Orleans, October 1991.

38. See P. B. Dews, ed., *Caffeine*, chapter by J. J. Barone and H. Roberts, "Human Consumption of Caffeine."

39. Committee on GRAS List Survey, Phase III: Estimating Distribution of Daily Intakes of Caffeine, National Academy of Sciences, Washington, D.C.

40. P. B. Dews, "Caffeine Research: An International Overview," presented at ISLA meeting, Sydney, 1986. See also J. Hathcock, ed., *Nutritional Toxicology*, chapter by J. Bergman and P. B. Dews, "Dietary Caffeine and Its Toxicity."

41. Rappoport et al., "Behavioral Effects of Caffeine in Children," *Archives of General Psychology* 41 (1984): 1073–79.

42. "Iced Tea and Crazy Kids," Lidia Wasowicz, UPI Science Writer.

43. Kelly L. Hale and John R. Hughes et al., "Caffeine Self-Administration and Subjective Effects in Adolescents," *Experimental and Clinical Psychopharmacology* 3, no. 4 (1995): 364–70.

44. "Vivarin Ad Is Attacked in Philadelphia Inquirer," United Press International Edition, August 27, 1984, E6.

45. Henry Goldman, "Caffeine Pills Put Man On 3 Years' Probation," *Philadelphia Inquirer*, December 14, 1984.

46. Because cacao contains eight times more theobromine than it does caffeine, theobromine is nearly as important a contributor to its stimulating effects as the smaller amount of caffeine.

47. Theobromine is also highly toxic to dogs, and accidental chocolate poisoning kills quite a few each year. See Clarence M. Fraser, ed., *The Merck Veterinary Manual*, pp. 1643–44.

48. Garattini, *Caffeine, Coffee, and Health*, p. 214.

49. "Of all women giving birth in Yale–New Haven Hospital in a four-month period in 1990–1991, only 26% reported no caffeine intake in the first month of pregnancy." L. Dlugosz and M. B. Bracken, "Reproductive Effects of Caffeine: A Review and Theoretical Analysis," *Epidemological Reviews* 14 (1992): 83–98.

50. J. L. Brazier and B. Salle, "Conversion of Theophylline to Caffeine by the Human Fetus," *Seminars in Perinatology* 5 (1981): 315–20. See also M. Dumas et al., "Systematic Determination of Caffeine Plasma Concentrations at Birth in Preterm and Fullterm Infants," *Developmental Pharmacology and Therapeutics* 4 (1982): 182–86.

51. A. Aldridge et al., "The Disposition of Caffeine during and after Pregnancy," *Seminars in Perinatology* 5 (1981): 310–314.

52. "In pregnancy there is a considerable increase in the half-life of caffeine and therefore an increase in exposure," Garattini, p. 400.

53. S. A. Pearlman et al., "Caffeine Pharmokinetics in Pre-Term Infants Older than Two Weeks," *Developmental Pharmacology and Therapeutics* 12 (1989): 65–69.

54. A. Wakamatsu et al., "Change of Plasma Half-Life of Caffeine during Caffeine Therapy for Apnea in Premature Infants," *Acta Paediatrica Japonica* 29 (1987): 595–99.

55. *Ibid.*

56. O. Carrier et al., "Maturation of Caffeine Metabolic Pathways in Infancy," *Clinical Pharmacology and Therapeutics* 44 (1988): 145–51.

57. Ghazi M. Al-Hachim, "The Teratogenicity of Caffeine: A Review," *European Journal of Obstetrics and Gynecology and Reproductive Biology* 31 (1988): 237.

58. L. Dlugosz and M. B. Bracken, "Reproductive Effects of Caffeine: A Review and Theoretical Analysis," *Epidemiological Reviews* 14 (1992): 83–98.

59. Dlugosz states, "In animal studies, caffeine is teratogenic at doses that are almost impossible to reach in humans, the peak level being more important than the total exposure over time." Garattini, *Caffeine, Coffee, and Health*, p. 95.

60. *Ibid.*, p. 353.

61. Victor Cohn, "Caffeine Warning Is Reassessed," *Philadelphia Inquirer*, March 2, 1984, p. A3.

62. Jack James, *Caffeine and Health*, p. 223.

63. J. Olsen et al., "Coffee Consumption, Birthweight, and Reproductive Failures," *Epidemiology* 2 (1991): 370–74. See also S. Linn et al., "No Association between Coffee Consumption and Adverse Outcomes of Pregnancy," *NEJM* 306 (1982): 141–45.

64. Brenda Eskenazi, "Caffeine During Pregnancy: Grounds for Concern?" *JAMA* 270, no. 24 (1993): 2973–74. Perhaps surprisingly, the evidence *against* a positive correlation with prematurity is regarded as evidence *in favor* of a positive correlation with low birthweight, because it means that increasing rates of prematurity can be ruled out as a contributing factor where low birthweights seem to occur. One researcher cites more than fifteen studies that have examined the relationship between caffeine consumption and low birthweight, claiming that all of the larger and better constructed studies demonstrate no correlation. (See Olsen et al., and Linn et al., note 63). In contrast, citing a 1989 study of caffeine and low birthweight by B. J. Caan and M. K. Goldhaber ("Caffeinated Beverages and Low Birthweight: A Case Controlled Study," *American Journal of Public Health* 79 [1989]: 1299–1300), in which caffeine users had three times the likelihood of non-users of delivering a low birthweight baby, Jack James asserts that, although no correlation has been proved, there are serious reasons for concern. A commentary on the literature appearing in *JAMA* in 1993 agrees with James, asserting that most studies find consumption of more than 300 mg a day increases the risk for low birthweight, while stating that the results for lower consumption levels are ambiguous or conflicting.

65. Linn et al. (see note 63).

66. B. Watkinson and P. A. Fried, "Maternal Caffeine Use before, during, and after Pregnancy and Effects upon Offspring," *Neurobehavioral Toxicology and Teratology* 7 (1985): 9–17.

67. B. G. Armstrong et al., "Cigarette, Alcohol, and Coffee Consumption and Congenital Defects," *American Journal of Public Health* 82 (1993): 91–93.

68. Until recently, no study had been undertaken to exclude the possible confounding effects of nausea on the relationship between spontaneous abortion and caffeine consumption, known as the Stein-Susser hypothesis (Z. Stein and M. Susser, "Miscarriage, Caffeine, and the Epiphenomena of Pregnancy: Specifying the Analytic Model," *Epidemiology* 2 [1991]: 163–67). Because nausea is more common in pregnancies that come to term, aversion for alcohol, food, and caffeine is possible, and such aversion would skew the results of epidemiological studies to falsely suggest that the use of caffeine was correlated with miscarriage. However, one study, by Kline in 1991, found that an adjustment for nausea and vomiting did not affect the results.

69. A. Goldstein and R. Warren, "Passage of Caffeine into Human Gonadal and Fetal Tissue" *Biochemical Pharmacology* 11 (1962): 168.

70. Dlugosz and Bracken, p. 90 (see note 58).

71. S. W. Jacobson et al., "Neonatal Correlates of Prenatal Exposure to Smoking, Caffeine, and Alcohol," *Infantile Behavioral Development* 7 (1984): 253–65.
72. Eskenazi (see note 64).
73. D. B. Thomas, "Neonatal Abstinence Syndrome," *Medical Journal of Australia* 148 (1988): 598.
74. J. D. McGowan et al., "Neonatal Withdrawal Symptoms after Chronic Ingestion of Caffeine," *Southern Medical Journal* 81 (1988): 1092–94.
75. J. Tuomilehto et al., "Coffee Consumption as a Trigger for Insulin Dependent Diabetes Milletus in Childhood," *BMJ* 300 (1990): 623–42.
76. Eskenazi (see note 64).
77. "Caffeine and Women's Health," pamphlet published by the Association of Women's Health, Obstetric & Neonatal Nurses in conjunction with IFIC, May 1994.
78. M. R. Joesoef et al., "Are Caffeinated Beverages Risk Factors for Delayed Conception?" *Lancet* (January 20, 1990): 136–37.
79. The credibility of these studies is undermined by confounders. For example, a Danish study of more than ten thousand pregnant women conducted by Olsen in 1991 found a drop in fertility in women who had regularly consumed more than eight cups of coffee or tea a day, but as these women were also smokers, no conclusions about caffeine can be drawn.

    A controversial study from Johns Hopkins University of more than fifteen hundred women, conducted by Cynthia Stanton and published in 1995 in the *American Journal of Epidemiology* found that, of women who neither smoked nor consumed large amounts of caffeine, less than 10 percent took a year or more to conceive, while of women who consumed more than 300 milligrams of caffeine a day, 20 percent took a year or more to conceive. One finding that may at first seem peculiar was that though smokers were about 15 to 20 percent less likely than non-smokers to become pregnant in any given month, their rate of conception was not affected by caffeine intake. A possible explanation is that, because smoking greatly increases the rate of caffeine metabolism, the exposure of smokers is much lower than it otherwise appears.

    The merits of the study's conclusions have been challenged by some fertility specialists. Dr. Mona Shangold, professor of obstetrics and gynecology at the Medical College of Pennsylvania and Hahnemann University, said the study's protocol was seriously flawed because the investigators made no attempt to control for co-variables such as the frequency of intercourse, or the health and habits of the men involved in the pregnancy attempts. Dr. Shangold concludes women who are trying to become pregnant should not be advised to avoid caffeine on the basis of this article. The National Coffee Association, not surprisingly, agrees that the study should not cause concern.
80. J. V. Ruzich et al., "Objective Assessment of the Effect of Caffeine on Sperm Motility and Velocity," *Fertility and Sterility* 48 (1987): 891–93.
81. Jack James, *Caffeine and Health*, p. 250.
82. Dlugosz and Bracken, p. 90 (see note 58).
83. Garattini, *Caffeine, Coffee, and Health*, pp. 97–150.
84. Jack James, *Caffeine and Health*, p. 30.
85. For comparison, consider that Wilcox has determined that two to three hours after consumption, two cups of coffee or a Vivarin would produce urinary levels of only about 3 mg/litre.
86. International Intrigue and Virtue Rewarded as Innocent Britisher Triumphs Over German Attempts to Frame Him as Caffeine Hound:

    In 1994 Simon Wigg, a former captain of the England speedway team, before a crowd of 22,000 and on his Czech-made Jawa bike won a record fifth world long-track cycling title in a competition staged in Mariensky-Lasne, in the Czech Republic. According to *Speedway Times*, a London magazine:

    > Just a year ago, the British rider won the world title only to be accused of testing positive for excessive caffeine, disqualified and then reinstated when the tests, carried out by the respected Koln Institute in Germany, were discredited.
    > Wigg's caffeine level, initially below the minimum limit, was arbitrarily multiplied by a factor of three by the institute, and it was not until the Auto Cycle Union, the governing body in Britain, supported by drug-testing centres in Canada and

Australia, strongly objected to the decision, that Wigg's test was nullified. To add to the suspicions, Karl Maier, a German, would have become the world champion had Wigg's ban been upheld. . . .

[Despite vindication,] Wigg, twice the British speedway champion and six times the grass-track champion, still lost an estimated £30,000 in sponsorship because of the accusations.

According to the newspaper story, the villain of the tale was the head of the Koln Institute and a member of the medical commission of the International Olympic Committee. Wigg said that if he ever met the man face to face, he would, "punch him on the nose."

87. Barry Steven Cohen, "Does Caffeine Have An Ergogenic Benefit On Low Intensity Exercise Performance in a Warm Environment?" unpublished manuscript, p. 56, note 110.
88. *Ibid.*, p. 58.

CHAPTER 16 *thinking over caffeine*

1. H . O. G. Holck, "Effect of Caffeine on Chess Problem Solving," *Journal of Comparative Psychology* (1933): 301–11.
2. J. E. Barmack, "The Time of Administration and Some Effects of 2 grams of Alkaloid Caffeine," *Journal of Experimental Psychology* 27 (1940): 690–98.
3. Garattini, *Caffeine, Coffee, and Health*, p. 296.
4. The information-processing approach consists of studying the flow of information through the system, monitoring the sequence of processing and transformations between input and output. In its various forms, the information-processing metaphor has guided research on quite complex behavior and has allowed the generation of extensive theories concerning the nature of such phenomena as perception, memory, attention, problem solving, language, and decision making. Garattini, *Caffeine, Coffee, and Health*, p. 301.
5. A. F. Sanders, "Towards a Model of Stress and Human Performance," *Act Psychology* 1, no. 53 (1983): 61–97.
6. In a visual-search task, caffeine hurt performance when the target was six letters but helped when it was only two. In a recent study, the ability to solve a maze was unaffected by caffeine, while caffeine promoted the regularity and fluency of letter cancellation task performance.
7. A. C. Bittner et al., "Performance Evaluation Tests for Environmental Research (PETER): Evaluation of 114 measures," *Precept. Mot. Skills* 63 (1986): 683–708.
8. This analysis is apparently is in accord with the Yerkes-Dodson principle. See Jack James, *Caffeine and Health*, p. 250.
9. M. S. Humphreys and W. Revelle, "Personality, Motivation, and Performance: A Theory of the Relationship between Individual Differences and Information Processing," *Psychological Review* 91 (1984): 153–84.
10. V. E. Mitchell et al., "Drugs and Placebos: Effects of Caffeine on Cognitive Performance," *Psychological Reports*, 35 (1974): 875–83.
11. Segal's findings were presented in a proceeding of the National Academy of Sciences, October 1999.
12. "In the context of learning and memory, it is interesting to note that xanthines, such as theophylline, enhanced long-term potentiation, an elector-physiological model of memory" in guinea pigs. Y. Tank et al., "Effect of Xanthine Derivatives on Hippocampal Long-term Potentiation," *Brain Research* 522 (1990): 63–68.
13. Jack James, *Caffeine and Health*, p. 305.
14. *Ibid.*, p. 248.
15. J. D. Roache and R. R. Griffiths, "Interactions of Diazepam and Caffeine: Behavioral and Subjective Dose Effects in Humans," *Pharmacology, Biochemistry and Behavior* 26 (1987): 801–12.
16. B. H. Jacobson and B. M. Edgley, "Effects of Caffeine on Simple Reaction Time and Movement Time," *Aviation, Space, and Environmental Medicine* 58 (1987): 1153–56.
17. W. J. Baker and G. C. Theologus, "Effects of Caffeine on Visual Monitoring," *Journal of*

Applied Psychology 56 (1972): 422–27. E. G. Regina et al., "Effects of Caffeine on Alertness in Simulated Automobile Driving," *Journal of Applied Psychology* 59 (1974): 483–89.

A 1993 study of ten coffee drinkers at Wake Forest University, Winston-Salem, North Carolina, found that caffeine does improve certain reflex brain functions. Subjects drank one or two cups of coffee twenty minutes before beginning "eyeblink startle reflex" tests, consisting of short bursts of "white noise" images. Schiacato, lead researcher, said that the blink reflexes, the sort of involuntary responses that occur too fast for voluntary control, of the coffee drinkers sustained a performance better than the non-drinkers. When exposed to redundant or repeated stimuli, involuntary responses taper off as a result of fatigue. In effect, the brain learns to ignore the stimulus. If caffeine can slow this "ignoring" response, as these experiments suggest, it may increase performance of repetitive tasks, such as driving late at night and seeing the same highway lights, white lines, and road surface, over and over. ("Cup Of Coffee Really Does Perk Up Brain," *USA Today*)

18. Michael H. Bonnet et al.,"The Use of Caffeine Versus Prophylactic Naps in Sustained Performance," *Sleep* 18(2): 97–104. (The American Sleep Disorders Association and Sleep Research Society)

19. Jack James, "Does Caffeine Enhance or Merely Restore Degraded Psychomotor Performance?" *Neuropsychobiology* 30 (1994): 124–25.

20. James, *Caffeine and Health*, p. 290.

21. W. H. Loke et al.,"Caffeine and Diazepam: Separate and Combined Effects on Mood, Memory, and Psychomotor Performance," *Psychopharmacology* 87 (1985): 344–50. See also Loke, "Effects of Caffeine on Mood and Memory," *Physiology and Behavior* 44 (1988): 367–72.

22. James, *Caffeine and Health*, p. 294.

23. M. A. Lee, "Anxiety and Caffeine Consumption in People with Anxiety Disorders," *Psychiatry Research* 15 (1985): 211–17.

24. J. F. Neil, "Caffeinism Complicating Hypersomnic Depressive Syndromes," *Comprehensive Psychiatry* 19 (1978): 377–85.

25. D. R. Cherek, "Effects of Caffeine on Human Aggressive Behavior," *Psychiatry Research*, 8 (1983): 137–45, and "Regular or Decaffeinated Coffee and Subsequent Human Aggressive Behavior," *Psychiatry Research* 11 (1984): 251–58.

26. Roache and Griffiths (see note 15).

27. Sleep and wakefulness occur as phases of a cycle called the "circadian rhythm," with a natural length of about twenty-five hours, a peak in the late afternoon, and a trough between three and four in the morning. Though the pattern of the circadian rhythm is determined primarily from within, external factors, such as the alternation of light and dark and habits of work and leisure, conjoin to "squash" it into twenty-four hours.

28. These characteristic regular patterns in the sleep state, as measured by the EEG, are termed the "sleep structure" and are taken to represent the quality and depth of sleep.

29. Edwards, *America's Favorite Drug*, p. 71.

30. As Jan Snel suggests in his paper "Coffee and Caffeine: Sleep and Wakefulness," the "effects of caffeine on the sleep-wake cycle depend both on the level of arousal, determined by more or less constant 'trait' factors, such as age and personality, and by short-term 'state' factors, such as time of day, fatigue, or nutritional items" (Garattini, *Caffeine, Coffee, and Health*, p. 256).

31. Edwards, *America's Favorite Drug*, p. 71.

32. Quentin R. Regestein, "Pathologic Sleepiness Induced by Caffeine," *American Journal of Medicine* 87 (1989): 587–88.

33. A. Goldstein, "Wakefulness Caused by Caffeine," *Archiv fur Experimentelle Pathologie und Pharmakologie* 248 (1964): 269–78.

34. A recent fad in the United States, using the hormone melatonin to sleep better, as well as to stay young and cure most of humanity's ills, is interesting for our subject, because caffeine may be a potent suppressor of it. Melatonin is thought to be the natural hormone that some say regulates our internal time clock and sleep patterns. Twenty-five subjects who were given 200 mg of caffeine tablets experienced a significant reduction in melatonin levels in their blood that persisted for eight hours. The peak serum levels of melatonin averaged 25 mg/ml without caffeine but only 14 mg/ml when caffeine had been ingested.

According to Jo Robinson, the co-author of a recent authoritative book on melatonin, "If you drink coffee and are under bright lights, you will get an even greater reduction in melatonin levels. Taking supplemental melatonin will offset this effect." V. K. P. Wright, "Effects of Caffeine, Bright Lights, and Their Combination on Nighttime Melatonin," *Sleep Research* 24 (1995): 458.

CHAPTER 17 *caffeine dependence, intoxication and toxicity*

1. N. Bridge, "Coffee-drinking as a Frequent Cause of Disease," *Trans Assoc Am Physicians* 8 (1893): 281–88.
2. R. R. Griffiths et al., "Human Coffee Drinking: Manipulation of Concentration and Caffeine Dose," *Journal of the Experimental Analysis of Behavior* 45 (1986): 133–48.
3. K. Silverman et al., "Withdrawal Syndrome after the Double-Blind Cessation of Caffeine Consumption," *NEJM* 327 (1992): 1109–14.
4. See Spiller, *Methylxanthine Beverages*, and Jack James, *Caffeine and Health*, p. 33.
5. R. Reeves et al., "Quantitative Changes During Caffeine Withdrawal," presented at the annual meeting of the College of Problems on Drug Dependence, Palm Beach, Florida, June 1994.
6. Conversation with an anonymous registered nurse. She suggested that clinics performing ambulatory or outpatient surgeries and the American Society of Post Anesthesia Nurses might be able to provide more information about this effect.
7. J. D. McGowan et al., "Neonatal Withdrawal Symptoms after Chronic Ingestion of Caffeine," *Southern Medical Journal* 81 (1988): 1092–94.
8. Eric Strain et al., "Caffeine Dependence Syndrome: Evidence from Case Histories and Experimental Evaluations," *JAMA* 272 (1994): 1043–48.
9. For an expansion of this viewpoint, see Griffiths et al., "Caffeine Dependence," *JAMA*, October 1994.
10. Garattini, *Caffeine, Coffee, and Health*, p. 213.
11. R. R. Griffiths et al., "Relative Abuse Liability of Triazolam: Experimental Assessment in Animals and Humans," *Neuroscience and Biobehavioral Reviews* 9 (1985): 133–51.
12. R. R. Griffiths and P. P. Woodson, "Reinforcing Properties of Caffeine: Studies in Humans and Laboratory Animals," *Pharmacology, Biochemistry, and Behavior* 29 (1988): 419–27.
13. J. R. Hughes et al., "Indications of Caffeine Dependence in a Population-Based Sample." In *Problems of Drug Dependence*, ed. L. S. Harris. Washington, D.C.: U.S. Government Printing Office, NIDA Research Monograph #132 (NIH Publication No. 93–3505), pp. 19–28, 1993.
14. Stephen J. Heishman et al., "Stimulus Functions of Caffeine in Humans: Relation to Dependence Potential," *Neuroscience and Biobehavioral Reviews* 16 (1992): 281.
15. Spiller, *Methylxanthine Beverages*, p. 287.
16. R. R. Griffiths et al., "Human Coffee Drinking: Reinforcing and Physical Dependence Producing Effects of Caffeine," *Journal of Pharmacology and Experimental Therapeutics* 239 (1986): 416–25.
17. J. T. Rugh, "Profound Toxic Effects from the Drinking of Large Amounts of Strong Coffee," *Medical and Surgical Reporter* 75 (1896): 549–50.
18. "A Letter to the Editor of *JAMA*," 62 (1914): 1828–29, by Otis Orendorff, M.D., Canon City, Colorado.
19. Water intoxication is a result of lowering the sodium balance in the blood, creating sensations similar to drunkenness, and can be achieved only by gulping at least twenty-four quarts of water a day. It's a transient pleasure at best, vanishing when, as quickly occurs with urination, the body adjusts this level to normal. According to one neuropharmacologist's report, a man actually died from drinking too much water while high on the drug ecstasy at a rave party.

    By the way, someone must have been eating tea as well, at least in the nineteenth century, to judge by Alcott's comments in 1839 "that the eaters of tea grounds are especially noted for this leathery complexion . . . as a considerable part of the tanning properties remains in the tea leaves after it has been infused in the usual manner." William Alcott, *Tea and Coffee*, Boston 1839, p. 22.

20. Jack James, *Caffeine and Health*, p. 69.
21. *Ibid.*, p. 68.
22. S. Jokela and A. Vartiainen, "Caffeine Poisoning," *Acta Pharmacologica et Toxicologica* 15: (1959): 331–34.
23. J. E. Turner and R. H. Cravey, "A Fatal Ingestion of Caffeine," *Clinical Toxicology* 10, no. 3 (1977): 341–44.
24. R. V. Nagesh and K. A. Murphy, "Caffeine Poisoning Treated by Hemoperfusion," *American Journal of Kidney Diseases* 12 (1988): 316–18. See also Jack James, *Caffeine and Health*, p. 68.
25. R. L. Alsott et al., "Report of a Human Fatality Due to Caffeine," *Journal of Forensic Sciences* 14 (1972): 135–37. See also J. Bryant, "Suicide by Ingestion of Caffeine—Letter," *Archives of Pathology and Laboratory Medicine* 105 (1981): 685–86.
26. P. B. Kulkarni and R. D. Dorand, "Caffeine Toxicity in the Neonate," *Pediatrics* 64 (1979): 254–55.
27. V. J. M. Dimaio and J. C. Garriott, "Lethal Caffeine Poisoning in a Child," *Forensic Science* 3 (1974): 275–78.

EPILOGUE *a toast to the future*

1. We don't know if any autopsy data is available, but probably there is caffeine in most corpses.
2. Pomet, Lemery, and Tournefort, *A Compleat History of DRUGGS*, "Of FRUITS," Of Chocolate, p. 132.
3. Spiller, *Methylxanthine Beverages*, p. 188.

APPENDIX C *additional studies of caffeine's physical effects*

1. Hypertension Detection and Follow-up Program Cooperative Group, "Five-Year Findings of the Hypertension Detection and Follow-up Program," *JAMA* 242 (1979): 2562–71.
2. B. H. Sung, "Caffeine Elevates Blood Pressure Response to Exercise in Mild Hypertensive Men," *American Journal of Hypertension*, December 1995.
3. K. M. Piters, "Coffee Boosts Pain-Free Walking Time for Patients with Chronic Stable Angina" (presented to the Western Section of the American Association for Clinical Research, Carmel, California), *Medical World News*, March 12, 1984, p. 137.
4. Garattini, *Caffeine, Coffee, and Health*, p. 178.
5. S. Cohen and J. H. J. Booth, "Gastric Acid Secretion and Lower-Esophagaeal-Sphincter Pressure in Response to Coffee and Caffeine," *NEJM* 293 (1975): 897–99.
6. Contradictory data abound. Later studies have suggested that caffeine is capable of stimulating gastric acid secretion and that its effects in this respect are additive to the same effects produced by other ingredients of coffee. Other studies have found that caffeine may be the only agent that stimulates gastric acid secretion without increasing lower esophageal-sphincter pressure.
7. Bruce Goldfarb, "Caffeine Increases Severity of PMS," *USA Today*, September 24, 1990, p. 1D, citing Heinke Bonnlander, *American Journal of Public Health*, September 1990.
8. From a pamphlet issued jointly by Organon Inc., makers the most popular oral contraceptive, Desogen, and *Medical Economics*, an excerpt from *The PDR Family Guide to Women's Health and Prescription Drugs*, pp. 6–7.
9. R. P. Heaney and R. R. Recker, "Effects of Nitrogen, Phosphorus, and Caffeine on Calcium Balance in Women," *Journal of Laboratory Clinical Medicine* 99 (1982): 46–55. M. J. Burger-Lux, R. P. Heaney, and M. R. Stegman, "Effect of Moderate Caffeine Intake on the Calcium Economy of Premenopausal Women," *American Journal of Clinical Nutrition* 52 (1990): 722–25.

10. D. P. Kiel et al., "Caffeine and the Risk of Hip Fracture: Framingham Study," *American Journal of Epidemiology* 132 (1990): 675–84.
11. E. Barett-Connor et al., "Coffee-Associated Osteoporosis Offset by Daily Milk Consumption," *JAMA* 271, no. 4 (1994): 280–83.
12. *Ibid.*
13. *Ibid.*
14. C. G. Swift and B. Tiplady, "The Effects of Age on the Response to Caffeine," *Psychopharmacology* 94 (1988): 24–31.
15. Edwards, *America's Favorite Drug*, p. 71.
16. J. Onrot et al., "Hemodynamic and Humoral Effects of Caffeine in Autonomic Failure, Therapeutic Implications for Post-Prandial Hypotension," *NEJM* 313 (1985): 549–54.
17. C. Sue Sewester, ed., *Drug Facts and Comparisons*, p. 929.
18. Alfred Gilman, ed., *Goodman and Gilman's The Pharmacological Basis of Therapeutics*, p. 619.
19. Adapted from D. M. Graham, *Nutrition Reviews* 36, April 4, 1976, p. 101.
20. Jack James, *Caffeine and Health*, p. 336.
21. Her talk at the Sleep Research Society meeting in Boston, reported in Marilyn Elias et al., "Coffee and a Wake-Up Call May Help Ground Jet Lag," *USA Today*, June 9, 1994, p. 5D.
22. David Robertson et al., "Hemodynamic and Humoral Effects of Caffeine in Autonomic Failure," *NEJM* 313 (1985): 549–55.
23. Sewester, *Drug Facts*, p. 928.

APPENDIX D *methodological pitfalls*

1. Garattini, *Caffeine, Coffee, and Health*, p. 344. Our discussion relies on the work of Alan Leviton, who in his 1992 article "Coffee, Caffeine, and Reproductive Hazards in Humans" provides a clear, well-reasoned exposé of a range of protocol defects and the ways in which they can undermine the putative value of a study's conclusions.
2. *Ibid.*, p. 343.
3. *Ibid.*, p. 347.
4. C. M. Friedenreich et al., "An Investigation of Recall Bias in the Reporting of Past Food Intake Among Breast Cancer Cases and Controls," *Annals of Epidemiology* 1 (1991): 439–53.
5. L. Fenster et al., "Assessment of Reporting Consistency in a Case Control Study of Spontaneous Abortions," *American Journal of Epidemiology* 133 (1991): 477–88.
6. A. Aldridge et al., "The Disposition of Caffeine during and after Pregnancy," *Seminars in Prenatal Care* 5 (1981): 310–14. See also R. Knutti et al., "The Effect of Pregnancy on the Pharmacokinetics of Caffeine," *Archives of Toxicology* (supplement) 5 (1982): 187–92.
7. Garattini, *Caffeine, Coffee, and Health*, p. 348.
8. J. Istvan and J. D. Matarazzo, "Tobacco, Alcohol, and Caffeine Use: A Review of their Interrelationships," *Psychological Bulletins* 95 (1984): 301–26.
9. An example of possible confounding within the area of reproductive hazards is an apparent relationship between coffee consumption and spontaneous abortions. Because nausea is more common in pregnancies that come to term, and nausea decreases the use of coffee, the supposed correlation between coffee and abortions is probably an artifact, because both relatively higher coffee consumption and spontaneous abortions are each co-variables of an unseen underlying factor, in this case, probably suboptimal implantation of the egg in the uterine wall, rather than coffee being a cause of fetal loss. To complicate the question still further, a new supposition has recently arisen that caffeine or coffee interferes with optimal implantation, and may thus be a cause of spontaneous abortions after all.

references

Alcott, William A. *Tea and Coffee*, Boston: George W. Light, 1839.

Anderson, E. N. *The Food of China*. New Haven: Yale University Press, 1988.

Anderson, Jennifer. *Introduction to Japanese Tea Ritual*. Albany: State University of New York Press, 1991.

Anft, Berthold. "Friedlieb Ferdinand Runge: A Forgotten Chemist of the Nineteenth Century." *Journal of Chemical Education* (November 1955): 566–74.

Aubrey's Brief Lives. Ed. Oliver Lawson Dick. London: Secker and Warburg, 1950.

Balzac, Honoré de. *Traite des Excitants Modernes*. 1839. Ed. Pierre Alechinsksy and Michel Butor, Arles, 1994.

Bickerman, E. J. *Chronology of the Ancient World*. Ithaca: Cornell University Press, 1980.

Blount, Sir Henry. *A Voyage into the Levant*. London, 1671.

Borer, Alain. *Rimbaud in Abyssinia*. Trans. Rosmarie Waldrop. New York: William Morrow and Company, 1984.

Boxer, C. R. *The Dutch Seaborne Empire: 1600–1800.* London: Penguin, 1990.

Bramah, Edward. *Tea & Coffee*. London: Hutchinson of London, 1972.

Braudel, Fernand. *Capitalism and Material Life: 1400–1800*. Trans. Miriam Kochan. New York: Harper & Row, 1973.

Brill, E. J., ed. *The Encyclopedia of Islam*. Leyden, The Netherlands, 1978.

Brillat-Savarin, Jean Anthelme. *The Physiology of Taste*. Paris, 1825. Reprint, trans. M. F. K. Fisher. Washington, D.C.: Counterpoint, 1995.

Brown, Thomas. *The Works of Thomas Brown*. London, 1719.

Bruce, James. *Travels to Discover the Source of the Nile*. Edinburgh: G.G.J. and J. Robinson, 1790.

Burton, Harry E. *The Discovery of the Ancient World*. 1932. Reprint, Freeport, N.Y.: Books for Libraries Press, 1969.

Burton, Sir Richard. *Lake Regions of Central Africa*. London: Longman, Green, Longman, and Roberts, 1860.

———. *Tales from the Arabian Nights, Selected from The Book of the Thousand Nights and a Night, translated and annotated by Richard F. Burton*. Ed. David Shumaker. New York: Gramercy Books, 1977.

Burton, Robert. *The Anatomy of Melancholy*. 1632. Reprint, ed. Floyd Dell and Paul Jordan Smith. New York: Tudor Publishing Company, 1927.

Canon of Medicine. Np, 1987. University of Pennsylvania Library, R135.8/A95.

Castile, Rand. *The Way of Tea*. New York: John Weatherhill, 1971.

Castle, Timothy James. *The Perfect Cup: A Coffee Lover's Guide to Buying, Brewing and Tasting*. New York: Aris Books, Addison Wesley, 1991.

Charles, Barbara Fahs, and J. R. Taylor. *Dream of Santa*. New York: Gramercy Books, 1992.

Cuatrecasas, José."Cacao and Its Allies: A Taxonomic Revision of the Genus Theobroma." *Contributions from the United States National Herbarium* 35, part 6. Washington, D.C., 1964.

Chow, Kit, and Ione Kramer. *All the Tea in China*. San Francisco: China Books and Periodicals, 1990.

Clark, Wesley, D.C. Brater, and A. R. Johnson. *Goth's Medical Pharmacology*. St. Louis: C. V. Mosby Company, 1988.

Coburn, Kathleen, ed. *The Notebooks of Samuel Taylor Coleridge, Vol. I, 1794–1804*. New York: Pantheon, 1957.

Coe, Sophie D., and Michael D. Coe. *The True History of Chocolate*. London: Thames and Hudson, 1996.

Cole, John, Esq. "On the Deleterious Effects Produced by Drinking Tea and Coffee in Excessive Quantities." *Lancet* 2 (1833): 274–78.

Crone, Patricia. *Meccan Trade and the Rise of Islam*. Princeton, N.J.: Princeton University Press, 1987.

Curtis, John. *Ancient Persia*. London: British Museum Publications, 1989.

Davids, Kenneth. *Coffee: A Guide to Buying, Brewing, & Enjoying*. Santa Rosa, Calif.: Cole Group, 1991.

De Mente, Boye. *The Whole Japan Book*. Phoenix: Phoenix Books, 1983.

DeMers, John. *The Community Kitchen's Complete Guide to Gourmet Coffee*. New York: Simon and Schuster, 1986.

DeSomogyi, Joseph. *A Short History of Oriental Trade*. Hildensheim, 1968.

Dews, P. B. *Caffeine*. New York: Springer-Verlag, 1984.

Diagnostic and Statistical Manual of Mental Disorders: DSM-IV. 4th ed. Washington, D.C.: American Psychiatric Association, 1994.

Dick, Oliver Lawson, ed. *Aubrey's Brief Lives*. London: Secker and Warburg, 1950.

Disraeli, Isaac. *Curiosities of Literature, edited with notes and memoire by his son, Benjamin Disraeli*. London: Frederick Warne and Company, 1848.

Dobrée, Bonamy. *English Literature in the Early Eighteenth Century: 1700–1740*. London: Oxford University Press, 1964.

Drabble, Margaret. *The Oxford Companion to English Literature*. 5th ed. Oxford: Oxford University Press, 1985.

Duffy, John. *From Humours to Medical Science: A History of American Medicine*. 2nd ed. Urbana: University of Illinois Press, 1993.

Dufour, Philippe Sylvestre. *Traitez Nouveux & curieux Du Café, Du Thé et Du Chocolate*. Lyons: Chez Jean Girin, & B. Riviere, 1685.

Duncan, Daniel. *Wholesome Advise against the Abuse of Hot Liquors, Particularly of Coffee, Chocolate, Tea, Brandy, and Strong-Waters, with directions*. Printed for H. Rhodes at the Star, the Corner of Bride Lane in Fleet Street, and A. Bell at the Cross-Keys and Bible in Cornhill, near the Royal-Exchange. London, 1706.

Dunkling, Leslie, and Gordon Wright. *The Wordsworth Dictionary of Pub Names*. Hertfordshire, U.K.: Wordsworth Editions, 1994.

Durant, Will, and Ariel Durant. *The Story of Civilization*. Vols. 7 and 8. New York: Simon and Schuster, 1961, 1963.

Édelestan, Jardin. *Le Caféier et le Café*. Paris, 1895.

Edwards, Bonnie. *America's Favorite Drug: Coffee and Your Health*. Berkeley: Odonian Press, 1992.

Eissler, Kurt Robert. *Goethe: A Psychological Study*. Detroit: Wayne State University Press, 1963.

Ellis, Aytoun. *The Penny Universities: A History of the Coffee-Houses*. London: Martin Secker and Warburg, 1956.

Essay on the Nature, Use, and Abuse of Tea: In a letter to a lady: with an account of its mechanical operation. James Bettenham for James Lacy at the Ship between the two Temple Gates, Fleet Street. London, 1722; 2nd. ed., 1725.

Evelyn, John. *Works*. Ed. E. S. DeBeer. London: Oxford University Press, 1959.

Fabricius, Johannes. *Alchemy*. London: Diamond Books, 1994.

Forrest, Denys. *Tea for the British: The Social and Economic History of a Famous Trade*. London: Chatto and Windus, 1973.

Foster, Nelson, and Linda Cordell, eds. *From Chilies to Chocolate: Food the Americas Gave the World*. Tucson: University of Arizona Press, 1992.

Fraser, Clarence M. *The Merck Veterinary Manual*. 7th ed. Rahway, N.J.: Merck & Co., 1991.

Galilco. *Discoveries and Opinions*. Trans. Stillman Drake. New York: Anchor, 1957.

Garattini, Silvio, ed. *Caffeine, Coffee, and Health*. New York: Raven Press, 1993.

Gardener, Martin. *Fads and Fallacies in the Name of Science*. New York: Dover Publications, 1957.

Garrison, Fielding H. *History of Medicine*. 4th ed. Philadelphia: W. B. Saunders, 1929.

Gilbert, Gustav. *The Constitutional Antiquities of Sparta and Athens*. London, 1895.

Gilbert, Richard M. *Caffeine: The Most Popular Stimulant*. New York: Chelsea House, 1992.

Gillespie, Charles C., ed. *Dictionary of Scientific Biography*. New York: Charles Scribners' Sons, 1975.

Gilman, Alfred, ed. *Goodman and Gilman's The Pharmacological Basis of Therapeutics*. 8th ed. New York: Pergamon Press, 1990.

Goethe, Wolfgang. *The Sorrows of Young Werther*. Trans. Elizabeth Mayer and Louise Bogan. New York: Vintage Books, 1973.

———. *Versuch die Metamorphose der Pflanzen zu erklären (Attempts to Illustrate the Metamorphosis of Plants)*. Gotha, Germany: Carl Wilhelm Ettinger, 1790.

Gohlman, William, ed. *Autobiography: The Life of Ibn Sina*. New York, 1974.

Goodman, Lenn E. *Avicenna*. London: Routledge, 1992.

Grieve, Maud. *A Modern Herbal*. 1931. Reprint, New York: Hafner Press, 1974.

Grove, Jean M. *The Little Ice Age*. New York: Methuen & Co. Ltd., 1989.

Grunes, Barbara, and Phyllis Magida. *Chocolate Classics*. Chicago: Contemporary Books, 1993.

Guelliot, Octave. *Treatise Du Caféisme Chronique*. Rheims, 1895.

Hale, William Harlan. *The Horizon Cookbook: An Illustrated History of Eating and Drinking Through the Ages*. American Heritage, 1968.

Hammitzsch, Horst. *Zen in the Art of the Tea Ceremony*. Trans. Peter Lemesurier, 1958. New York: Penguin Books, 1979.

Harrison, Brian. *Drink and the Victorians*. Pittsburgh: University of Pittsburgh Press, 1971.

Hathcock, J., ed. *Nutritional Toxicology*. New York: Academic Press, 1987.

Hattox, Ralph S. *Coffee and Coffeehouses: The Origins of a Social Beverage in the Medieval Near East*. Seattle: University of Washington Press, 1991.

Hedrick, U. P., ed. *Sturtevant's Notes on Edible Plants*. Albany, N.Y.: J. B. Lyons, State Printers, 1919.

Heise, Ulla. *Coffee and Coffee-Houses*. West Chester, Pa.: Schiffer Publishing, 1987.

Hobhouse, Henry. *Seeds of Change*. New York: Harper & Row, 1986.

Hofmann, Paul. *The Viennese: Splendor, Twilight, and Exile*. New York: Anchor Books, Doubleday, 1988.

Hora, Bayard, ed. *Oxford Encyclopaedia of Trees of the World*. London: Oxford University Press, 1981.

Huddleston, Sisley. *Paris Salons, Cafés, Studios*. Philadelphia, Pa.: J. B. Lippincott Company, 1928.

Hyamson, Albert M. *A Dictionary of Universal Biography*. London: Routledge and Kegan Paul, 1976.

Jacob, Heinrich Eduard. *Coffee: The Epic of a Commodity*. Trans. Eden Paul and Cedar Paul. New York: Viking Press, 1935.

James, Jack E. *Caffeine and Health*. London: Harcourt Brace Jovanovich, 1991.

Jarrett, Derek. *England in the Age of Hogarth*. New York: Viking Press, 1974.

Kamal, Hassan. *Encyclopaedia of Islamic Medicine*. General Egyptian Book Organization, University of Pennsylvania Library, R143K33.

Keay, John. *The Honourable Company: A History of the English East India Company*. New York: Macmillan, 1991.

Kennedy, John G. *The Flower of Paradise*. Dordrecht: D. Reidel, 1987.

Krapf, J. Lewis. *Travels, Researches and Missionary Labours During Eighteen Years Residence in Eastern Africa*. Boston: Ticknor and Fields, n.d.

Kummer, Corby. *The Joy of Coffee*. Shelburne, Vt.: Chapters, 1995.

La Roque, Jean. *Voyage de L'Arabie Heureuse*. Paris, 1716.

Latham, Robert, ed. *The Shorter Pepys*. Berkeley: University of California Press, 1985.

Leggett, Trevor. *A First Zen Reader*. Rutland, Vt.: Charles E. Tuttle, 1966.

Lewin, Louis, M.D. *Phantastica: A Classic Survey on the Use and Abuse of Mind-Altering Plants*. 1st English edition, 1931. Reprint, Rochester, Vt.: Park Street Press, 1998.

Lillywhite, Bryant. *London Coffee Houses*. London: George Allen and Unwin, 1963.

Lu Yü. *The Classic of Tea*. Trans. Francis Ross Carpenter. Boston: Little, Brown, 1974.

Margetson, Stella. *Leisure and Pleasure in the Eighteenth Century*. London: Cassell and Company, 1970.

Massengill, Samuel, M.D. *A Sketch of Medicine and Pharmacy, and a View of its Progress by the Masengill Family from the Fifteenth to the Twentieth Century*. Bristol, Tenn.: S. E. Messengill Company, 1943.

McCoy, Elin, and John Frederick Walker. *Coffee and Tea*. New York: Theron Raines, 1991.

McEvedy, Colin, and Richard Jones. *Atlas of World Population History*. Middlesex, U.K.: Penguin Books, 1978, reprint 1985.

McEvedy, Colin. *The New Penguin Atlas of Medieval History*. London: Viking Penguin, 1992.

———. *The Penguin Atlas of Ancient History*. London: Penguin, 1967.

Mennell, Robert O. *Tea: An Historical Sketch*. London: Effingham Wilson, 1926.

Middleton, John. *Magic, Witchcraft, and Curing*. New York: The Natural History Press, Doubleday, 1967.

Morison, Samuel. *Journals and Other Documents on the Life and Voyages of Christopher Columbus*. New York: Heritage Press, 1963.

Morosini, Gianfrancesco. *Le Relazioni degli Ambasciatori Veneti al Senato durantes il Secolo Decimosesto*. Ed. Eugenio Albèri. Series 3, vol. 3. Florence, 1855.

Morrison, Helen Barber, ed. *The Golden Age of Travel*. New York: Twayne Publishers, 1951.

Morton, Marcia, and Frederic Morton. *Chocolate: An Illustrated History*. New York: Crown, 1986.

Moseley, Benjamin, M.D. *A Treatise Concerning the Properties and Effects of Coffee*. London, 1785.

Nash, H. *Alcohol and Caffeine*. Springfield, Mass.: Thomas, 1962.

Neugebauer, O. *The Exact Sciences in Antiquity*. 2nd ed. Reprint, New York: Barnes & Noble Books, 1993.

Nicol, Robert. *A Treatise on Coffee: its properties and the best mode of keeping and preparing it*. 2nd ed. London: Baldwin & Cradock, 1831.

Niebuhr, Carston. *Travels through Arabia and other countries in the East*. Trans. Robert Heron. Edinburgh, 1792.

Norman, Jill. *Coffee*. London: Bantam Books, Dorling Kindersley Edition, 1992.

Nuland, Sherwin B. *Doctors: The Biography of Medicine*. New York: Random House, Vintage Books, 1988, 1995.

Okakura, Kakuzo. *The Book of Tea*. 1906. New York: Dover Publications, 1964.

Ovington, John, M. A. *Essay upon the Nature and Qualities of Tea*. London: R. Roberts, 1699.

Pauli, Simon. *Commentarius de Abusu Tabaci et Herbae Thee, etc*. Rostock, 1635.

Pendergrast, Mark. *For God, Country and Coca-Cola*. New York: Macmillan, 1993.

Phillips, Henry. *The Companion for the Orchard: An Historical and Botanical Account of Fruits Known in Great Britain*. London: Henry Colburn and Richard Bentley, 1831.

Polo, Marco. *The Travels*. London: Penguin, 1958.

Pomet, Pierre, Lemery, and Tournefort. *A Compleat History of DRUGGS*. Trans. from the French. London: R. Bonwicke et al., 1712; 4th edition, 1748.

Pool, Daniel. *What Jane Austen Ate, What Charles Dickens Knew*. New York: Simon and Schuster, 1993.

Pratt, James Norwood. *Tea Lover's Treasury*. Santa Rosa, Calif.: Cole Group, 1982.

Priestley, J. B. *Man and Time*. London: Bloomsbury Books, 1989.

Pryor, Felix, ed. *The Faber Book of Letters*. London: Faber and Faber, 1988.

Read, Anthony, and David Fisher. *Berlin Rising: Biography of a City*. New York: W. W. Norton, 1994.

Reade, Arthur. *Tea and Tea Drinking*. London: Samson Low, 1884.

Republic of Tea Inc. *The Book of Tea and Herbs*. Santa Rosa, Calif.: Cole Group, 1993.

Riemer, Andrew. *The Habsburg Café*. New York: HarperCollins, 1993.

Robb, Graham. *Balzac: A Biography*. New York: W. W. Norton & Company, 1994.

Roden, Claudia. *Coffee*. London: Penguin Group, 1981.

Rolnick, Harry. *The Complete Book of Coffee*. Printed for Melitta by Rolf Stacker Associates Advertising. Hong Kong, 1982.

Roseberry, William, Lowell Gudmundson, Mario Samper Kutschbach. *Coffee, Society, and Power in Latin America*. Baltimore: Johns Hopkins University Press, 1995.

Roth, Rodris. *Tea Drinking in 18th-Century America: Its Etiquette and Equipage*. United States National Museum Bulletin 225, Contributions from the Museum of History and Technology, Paper 14: 61–91, Washington D.C.: Smithsonian Institution, 1961.

Rothenberg, Mikel A., M.D., and Charles F. Chapman. *Dictionary of Medical Terms*. Hauppauge, N.Y.: Barron's Educational Series, 1989.

Rowe, J. W. F. *The World's Coffee*. London: Her Majesty's Stationery Office, 1963.

Rudorff, Raymond. *The Belle Epoque: Paris in the Nineties*. New York: Saturday Review Press, 1972.

Rush, R. *The Lady & Gentleman's Tea-Table and Useful Companion*. Houndsditch, London: J. C. Kelley, 1818.

Saintsbury, George. *A History of English Prose Rhythm*. London: Macmillan, 1922.

Salibi, Kamal S. *A History of Arabia*. Beirut: Caravan Books, 1980.

Schapira, Joel, David Schapira, and Karl Schapira. *The Book of Coffee & Tea*. New York: St. Martin's Press, 1982.

Schery, Robert. *Plants for Man*. Englewood Cliffs, N.J.: Prentice-Hall, 1972.

Scheurleer, D. F. Lunsingh. *Chinese Export Porcelain*. New York: Pitman Publishing Corporation, 1974.

Schivelbusch, Wolfgang. *Tastes of Paradise*. New York: Vintage Books, Random House, 1993.

Schuster, Charles R., and Michael J. Kuhar, eds. *Handbook of Experimental Pharmacology*. Heidelberg: Springer-Verlag, 1996.

Schuyler, William, ed. *Macaulay's Life of Samuel Johnson*. New York: Macmillan, 1917.

Seabrook, W. B. *Adventures in Arabia*. New York: Blue Ribbon Books, Harcourt, Brace, 1927.

Segel, Harold B. *The Vienna Coffeehouse Wits: 1890–1938*. West Lafayette, Ind.: Purdue University Press, 1993.

Seigel, Jerrold. *Bohemian Paris*. New York: Viking Penguin, 1986.

Sewester, C. Sue, ed. *Drug Facts and Comparisons*. St. Louis: Facts and Comparisons Division, J. B. Lippincott Company, 1990.

Sibree, James. *The Great African Island, Chapters on Madagascar*. London: Trubner and Company, 1880.

Simpson, Helen. *The London Ritz Book of Afternoon Tea*. New York: Arbor House, 1986.

Siraisi, Nancy. *Avicenna in Renaissance Italy*. Princeton, N.J.: Princeton University Press, 1987.

Spiel, Hilde. *Vienna's Golden Autumn: 1866–1938*. New York: Weidenfeld and Nicolson, 1987.

Spiller, M. A. T*he Methylxanthine Beverages and Foods: Chemistry, Consumption, and Health Effects*. New York: Alan R. Liss, 1984.

Stanley-Baker, Joan. *Japanese Art*. London: Thames & Hudson, 2000.

Stavric, Bozidar. Canada's Health Protection Branch, *Food and Chemical Toxicology*, March 1988.

Stevens, Wallace. *Poems*. Ed. Samuel French Morse, 1947. Reprint, New York: Vintage Books, 1959.

Strickland, Agnes. *Lives of the Queens of England*. London, 1882.

Stuart, David. "The Rio Azul Cacao Pot: Epigraphic Observations on the Function of a Maya Ceramic Vessel." *Antiquity* 62 (1988): 153–57.

Stuart, David, and Stephen D. Houston. "Maya Writing." *Scientific American*, August 1989, 82–89.

Sutherland, James. *The Oxford Book of English Talk*. Oxford: Oxford University Press, 1953.

Suzuki, Daisetz T. *Zen and Japanese Culture*. Bollingen Series LXIV. Princeton: Princeton University Press, 1959.

Tait, Hugh. *Clocks and Watches*. London: British Museum Publications, 1983.

Taylor, John. *Egypt and Nubia*. Cambridge, Mass.: Harvard University Press, 1991.

Taylor, Norman. *Plant Drugs That Changed the World*. New York: Dodd, Mead, 1965.

Teply, Karl. *Die Einfuhrung des Kaffees in Wien: Georg Franz Kolschitzky, Johannes Diodato, Isaak de Luca*. Vienna: Kommissionsverlag Jugend und Volk Wien-Munchen, 1980.

Thomas, Gertrude. *Richer than Spices*. New York: Alfred A. Knopf, 1965.

Timbs, John. *Clubs and Club Life in London with Anecdotes of its Famous Coffee Houses, Hostelries, and Taverns, from the Seventeenth Century to the Present*. London: John Camden Hotten, 1872.

Todd, Pamela. *Forget-Me-Not: A Floral Treasury*. Boston: Little, Brown, 1993.

Toussaint-Samat, Maguelonne. *History of Food*. Trans. Anthea Bell. Cambridge: Blackwell, 1994.

Tracy, James D. *The Rise of Merchant Empires*. Cambridge: Cambridge University Press, 1990.

Ukers, William. *All about Coffee*. New York: The Tea and Coffee Trade Journal, 1922.

———. *All about Tea*. New York: The Tea and Coffee Trade Journal, 1935.

Urdang, George. *Goethe and Pharmacy*. Madison: American Institute of the History of Pharmacy, 1949.

Vaczek, Louis, and Gail Buckland. *Travellers in Ancient Lands: A Portrait of the Middle East, 1839–1919*. Boston: New York Graphic Society, Little, Brown, 1981.

Vafi, H. and Pamela Vafi. *How to Get a Good Night's Sleep*. Holbrook, Mass.: Bob Adams, 1994.

Von Eckardt, Wolf, and Sander L. Gilman. *Bertolt Brecht's Berlin: A Scrapbook of the Twenties*. New York: Anchor Press, Doubleday, 1975.

Walker, Ernest P. *Mammals of the World*. Baltimore: Johns Hopkins University Press, 3rd ed., 1975.

Walsh, Joseph M. *Coffee: Its History, Classification, and Description*. Philadelphia: Henry T. Coates & Company, 1894.

———. *Tea: Its History and Mystery*. Philadelphia: Henry T. Coates & Company, 1892.

Walsh, Reverend R. *Narrative of a Journey from Constantinople to England*. Philadelphia: Carey, Lea, and Carey, 1828.

Walter Baker and Company. *The Chocolate Plant and Its Products*. Cambridge, U.K.: John Wilson and Son, 1896.

Wanklyn, J. Alfred. *Tea, Coffee and Cocoa*. London: Treubner and Company, 1874.

Watts, Alan W. *The Way of Zen*. New York: Vintage Books, Alfred A. Knopf, 1957.

Watts, Henry, ed. *Dictionary of Chemistry*, Vol. I. London: Longmans, 1863.

Weil, Andrew. *Natural Health, Natural Medicine*. Boston: Houghton Mifflin, 1990.

Weil, Andrew, and Winifred Rosen. *From Chocolate to Morphine*. Boston: Houghton Mifflin, 1983.

Wellman, Frederick L. *Coffee Botany, Cultivation, and Utilization*. New York: Interscience Publishers, 1961.

Wells, H. G. *The Outline of History*. 1920. Garden City, N.Y.: Doubleday, 1961.

Wilhelm, Richard. *The I Ching*. Trans. Cary F. Baynes. Princeton, N.J.: Bollingen Series, Princeton University Press, 1968.

Young, Isabel. *The Story of Coffee*. New York: Bureau of Coffee Information, 1936.

index